The Heath Reader

The Heath Reader

Boyd Litzinger
Saint Bonaventure University

D. C. Heath and Company
Lexington, Massachusetts / Toronto

International Standard Book Number: 0-669-05416-X

Library of Congress Catalog Card Number: 82-81618

ACKNOWLEDGEMENTS

John Quincy Adams, "Inauguration Day" excerpted from *The Diary of John Quincy Adams, 1794–1845*, edited by Allan Nevins. Reprinted with permission of The Trustees of Columbia University in the City of New York. All rights reserved.

Isaac Asimov, "The Nightmare of Life Without Fuel" from *Time*, April 25, 1977. Copyright 1977 Time Inc. All rights reserved. Reprinted by permission from *Time*.

Wambly Bald, "Tea with Gertrude Stein" from the *Chicago Tribune*, Paris edition, April 7, 1931. Copyrighted, 1931, Chicago Tribune. Used with permission.

Richard A. Blake, "Simply Super: A Review of *Superman*" from *America*, January 13, 1979. Reprinted with permission of America Press, Inc., 106 West 56th Street, New York, N. Y. 10019. Copyright © 1979. All rights reserved.

Harold O. J. Brown, "Superman on the Screen: Counterfeit Myth?" from *Christianity Today*, April 20, 1979. Copyright 1979 by *Christianity Today*. Reprinted by permission.

Marshall J. Brown, "Tighter Controls on Pistols Won't Deter Attacks, Murder." Copyright © 1981 Buffalo Courier-Express Inc.

James L. Buckley, "Three Cheers for the Snail Darter" from *National Review*, September 14, 1979. Copyright © 1979 by National Review, Inc., 150 East 35th Street, New York, N. Y. 10016.

William F. Buckley, Jr., "Capital Punishment." Reprinted by permission of G. P. Putnam's Sons from *Execution Eve and Other Contemporary Ballads* by William F. Buckley, Jr. Copyright © 1972–75 by William F. Buckley, Jr.

James D. Burke, "Observation and Exploration." Reprinted with permission of the *Encyclopedia Americana*, Copyright 1977, The Americana Corporation.

Rachel Carson, "The Birth and Death of Islands" from *The Sea Around Us* by Rachel L. Carson. Copyright © 1950, 1951, 1961 by Rachel L. Carson; renewed 1979 by Roger Christie. Reprinted by permission of Oxford University Press, Inc.

John Ciardi, "Is Everybody Happy?" from *Saturday Review*. Copyright © 1964 by *Saturday Review*. All rights reserved. Reprinted with permission.

Merrel D. Clubb, Jr., "And God Created Person." Reprinted by permission of the Modern Language Association of America from *MLA Newsletter*, March 1974.

Alistair Cooke, "Letter to an Intending Immigrant" from *One Man's America* (1952), by Alistair Cooke. Reprinted by permission of Alfred A. Knopf, Inc. This material was first presented as a talk in the BBC series "Letter from America."

Earl Daniels, "Upon Julia's Clothes" from *The Explicator*, I, No. 5 (March 1943) a publication of the Helen Dwight Reid Educational Foundation. Reprinted by permission.

Wayne H. Davis, "Overpopulated America." Reprinted with permission from *The New Republic*, January 19, 1970. Copyright © Wayne H. Davis.

Joan Didion, "The Santa Ana" from "Los Angeles Notebook" from *Slouching Towards Bethlehem* by Joan Didion. Copyright © 1967, 1968 by Joan Didion. Reprinted by permission of Farrar, Straus and Giroux, Inc.

Annie Dillard, "Untying the Knot" from pp. 72–74 in *Pilgrim at Tinker's Creek* by Annie Dillard. Copyright © 1974 by Annie Dillard. Reprinted by permission of Harper & Row Publishers, Inc.

Edith Efron, "The Soaps—Anything But 99⁴⁴/₁₀₀ Percent Pure." Reprinted with permission from *TV Guide* magazine. Copyright © 1965 by Triangle Publications, Inc., Radnor, Pennsylvania.

Jean Bethke Elshtain, "Family Reconstruction" from *Commonweal*, August 1, 1980. Reprinted by permission of Commonweal Publishing Co., Inc.

Anne Frank, "D-Day" excerpted from *Anne Frank: The Diary of a Young Girl*. Copyright 1952 by Otto H. Frank. Reprinted by permission of Doubleday & Company, Inc.

Nikki Giovanni, "I Fell Off the Roof One Day (A View of the Black University)." Copyright by Nikki Giovanni. Reprinted by permission of the author.

Robert A. Goldwin, "Is It Enough to Roll with the Times?" from *Change* magazine, vol. 7, no. 4, (May, 1975). Copyright by the Council on Learning, 271 North Avenue, New Rochelle, N. Y. 10801.

Robert Graves, "No-Man's Land" excerpted from *Goodbye to All That* by Robert Graves. Reprinted by permission of the author.

Florence R. Greenberg, "The Cantor Carved" excerpted from "Father Was a Rabbi" from *Lives and Voices* by Florence R. Greenberg. Copyright © 1972 by The Jewish Publication Society of America. Reprinted by permission.

Graham Greene, "The First Acceptance" excerpted from *A Sort of Life* by Graham Greene. Copyright

© 1971 by Graham Greene. Reprinted by permission of Simon & Schuster, a Division of Gulf & Western Corporation.

J. B. S. Haldane, "On Being the Right Size" from *Possible Worlds* by J. B. S. Haldane. Reprinted by permission of the publisher.

Edmund Hillary, "Everest Conquered" excerpted from *High Adventure* by Edmund Hillary. Reprinted by permission of Hodder and Stoughton Limited.

David Hoekema, "Capital Punishment: The Question of Justification." Copyright 1979 Christian Century Foundation. Reprinted by permission from the March 28, 1979 issue of *The Christian Century*.

Langston Hughes, "I, Too." Copyright 1926 by Alfred A. Knopf, Inc. and renewed 1954 by Langston Hughes. Reprinted from *Selected Poems*, by Langston Hughes, by permission of Alfred A. Knopf, Inc.

James Jeans, "Why the Sky Looks Blue" from *The Stars in Their Courses* by James Jeans, Cambridge University Press. Reprinted by permission.

B. R. Jerman, "Browning's Witless Duke." Reprinted by permission of the Modern Language Association of America from *PMLA*, 72 (1957), 488–93.

Stanley Kauffmann, "A Review of *Superman*," published in *The New Republic*. Copyright © 1979 by Stanley Kauffmann. Reprinted by permission of Brandt & Brandt Literary Agents, Inc.

Helen Keller, "Everything Has a Name" from *The Story of My Life* by Helen Keller. Reprinted by permission of Doubleday & Company, Inc.

Grace King, excerpt from *Memories of a Southern Woman of Letters*. Copyright © 1932 by Macmillan Publishing Co., Inc. Reprinted by permission.

Maxine Hong Kingston, "Parents" ["Mother"] excerpted from *The Woman Warrior: Memoirs of a Girlhood among Ghosts* by Maxine Hong Kingston. Copyright © 1975, 1976 by Maxine Hong Kingston. Reprinted by permission of Alfred A. Knopf, Inc.

Joseph Wood Krutch, "What Are Flowers For?" from *The Best Nature Writing of Joseph Wood Krutch* (1969). Copyright © 1964 by Joseph Wood Krutch. Reprinted by permission of William Morrow & Company.

Pat Mainardi, "Politics of Housework" from *Ms.* magazine. Reprinted by permission.

Mary Manning, "A Visit to Belfast." Copyright © 1972, by The Atlantic Monthly Company, Boston, MA 02116. Reprinted by permission.

Mary McCarthy, excerpt from "The Vassar Girl" from *On the Contrary* by Mary McCarthy. Copyright © 1946, 1947, 1949, 1950, 1951, 1952, 1953, 1954, 1955, 1958, 1959, 1960, 1961 by Mary McCarthy. Copyright © 1951 by The Curtis Publishing Company. Reprinted by permission of Farrar, Straus and Giroux, Inc.

Margaret Mead, "The Egalitarian Error" from *A Way of Seeing* (1970) by Margaret Mead and Rhoda Metraux. Copyright © by Margaret Mead and Rhoda Metraux. By permission of William Morrow & Company.

Thomas Merton, "The Decision" excerpted from *The Seven Storey Mountain* by Thomas Merton, copyright 1948 by Harcourt Brace Jovanovich, Inc.; copyright renewed 1976 by The Trustees of the Merton Legacy Trust. Reprinted by permission of the publishers.

James Michener, "Portugal and Spain" excerpted from *Iberia* by James A. Michener. Copyright © 1968 by Random House, Inc. Reprinted by permission of Random House, Inc.

N. Scott Momaday, "The Way to Rainy Mountain." Reprinted by permission from *The Way to Rainy Mountain* by Scott Momaday © 1969 by the University of New Mexico Press. First published in *The Reporter*, January 26, 1967.

Alleen Nilsen, "Sexism in English: A Feminist View" from the book *Female Studies VI: Closer to the Ground*, editors Nancy Hoffman, Cynthia Secor, and Adrian Tinsley. Reprinted with permission of The Feminist Press, Box 334, Old Westbury, New York 11568. All rights reserved under international and Pan-American Copyright conventions.

Michael Novak, "Further Reflections on Ethnicity." Reprinted with permission of *The Novak Report*, 918 F Street, N.W., Washington, DC; from Michael Novak, *Further Reflections on Ethnicity* © 1977.

Pliny the Younger, "Vesuvius Erupts" from *Letters and Panegyrics*, translated by Betty Radice for *The Heath Reader*. Copyright © 1969 by the President and Fellows of Harvard College. Reprinted by permission of Harvard University Press and The Loeb Classical Library.

Laurence Perrine, "Browning's Shrewd Duke." Reprinted by permission of the Modern Language Association of America from *PMLA*, 74 (1959), 157–59.

Katherine Anne Porter, "The Witness." Copyright by Katherine Anne Porter. Reprinted from her volume *The Leaning Tower and Other Stories* by permission of Harcourt Brace Jovanovich, Inc.

Richard J. Roth, "Despite Evidence and Reason, Pro-Gun Talk Won't Go Away." Copyright © 1981 Buffalo Courier-Express Inc.

Elisabeth Schneider, "Upon Julia's Clothes" from *The Explicator*, XIII, No. 5 (March 1956). Reprinted by permission of the author.

Dorothy Z. Seymour, "Black Children, Black Speech" from *Commonweal*, November 19, 1971. Reprinted by permission of Commonweal Publishing Co., Inc.

Edith Sitwell, "John Mytton" reprinted from *English Eccentrics* by Edith Sitwell by permission of the publisher, Vanguard Press, Inc. Copyright © 1957 by Edith Sitwell.

C. P. Snow, "Einstein" from *A Variety of Men*, by C. P. Snow (New York: Charles Scribner's Sons).

Freya Stark, excerpt from *The Freya Stark Story*. This material originally appeared in *Traveller's Prelude* published by John Murray, Ltd. Reprinted by permission.

Judy Syfers, "I Want a Wife" from *Ms.* magazine. Reprinted by permission of the author.

Deems Taylor, "The Monster" from *Of Men and Music* by Deems Taylor. Reprinted by permission of Simon & Schuster, a Division of Gulf and Western Corporation, and Joan Kennedy Taylor and her agent, Curtis Brown Associates, Ltd.

James Thurber, "The Secret Life of Walter Mitty." Copyright © 1942 James Thurber. Copyright © 1970 Helen W. Thurber. From *My World and Welcome to It*, published by Harcourt Brace Jovanovich.

Time, "Zip Out." Copyright 1946 Time Inc. All rights reserved. Reprinted by permission from *Time* magazine.

Evelyn Waugh, "England Enters World War II" excerpted from *The Diaries of Evelyn Waugh*, edited by Michael Davie. Copyright © 1976 by The Estate of Evelyn Waugh. Reprinted by permission of Literistic, Ltd. and Little, Brown and Company.

Gideon Welles, "Lincoln Is Assassinated" excerpted from *The Diary of Gideon Welles*, Volume II. Copyright 1909, 1910 by Edgar T. Welles. Copyright 1911 by Edgar T. Welles and Houghton Mifflin Company. Reprinted by permission of Houghton Mifflin Company.

Eudora Welty, "Why I Live at the P.O." Copyright 1941, 1969 by Eudora Welty. Reprinted from her volume *A Curtain of Green and Other Stories* by permission of Harcourt Brace Jovanovich, Inc.

A. B. C. Whipple, "An Ugly Footprint in the Sand." *Life* © 1970, Time, Inc. Reprinted with permission.

Richard Wright, "The Library Card," chapter XIII (pp. 214–222) from *Black Boy* by Richard Wright. Copyright 1937, 1942, 1944, 1945 by Richard Wright. Reprinted by permission of Harper & Row Publishers, Inc.

Preface

Teaching freshmen to write is a challenging and satisfying job. The mechanical work—marking, grading, and the like—is more demanding and time-consuming than many nonteachers dream. But the satisfactions are also great. Young people are particularly open to new ideas when they start college, and there are few subjects in which their growth can be seen so clearly as in the first composition course they take. Entering freshmen are predisposed to learn, and correct writing is a skill that can be taught. This book is meant to make their job of learning, and yours of teaching, a little easier.

Three principles, tested in nearly thirty years of teaching freshmen, went into the making of this book. The first is that students in an English composition course need regularly assigned readings to supplement their work in grammar or rhetoric textbooks. I have found that the week-in, week-out assignment and class discussion of grammar or rhetorical modes unsupported by a good reader can become an exercise worthy of Mr. Gradgrind. Not that students should not be taught the principles of induction or proper use of analogies; certainly, students need these tools of good thinking and good writing. But they are *tools*, and the student must learn their use. "Write a persuasive paper using inductive logic," the students are told. "On what?" they ask—and very properly. *The Heath Reader* is meant to help provide the "what." It is, first of all, designed to be a source of ideas for students—a means of stimulating their minds and memories, of unlocking their own imaginations.

For this reason, I have chosen a great many readings, some quite short, rather than twenty or thirty very long essays. The variety of sources is deliberately wide, intentionally eclectic, in style as well as content, so as to increase the opportunities for catching the student's interest. Victor Hugo's bombast may work upon the imagination that Graham Greene's calmness or Joan Didion's quiet grace failed to move. A well-selected book of readings also supplies models of form as well as ideas for writing. To talk about comparison and contrast is one thing, to illustrate effectively in the lecture room another; but to give examples of the principles in action is an excellent reinforcement.

A second principle has been to set before the student a high proportion of selections from writers of permanent interest. This does not mean that only the classics of *belles lettres* are here included. I have ranged through many disciplines for examples of articulate men and women expressing significant ideas in good language. Ours is a living language, and I subscribe to Bertrand Russell's definition of correct English as "the habits of speech of educated people." Evelyn Waugh, Joseph Wood Krutch, and Mary McCarthy, yes; but also James Jeans, Mark Twain, and Annie Dillard. The scientists, the journalists, and the historians help to provide a rich and varied fare.

The third principle has been to appeal frankly to the interests of those who will teach this material. No one wants to turn the course in prose composition into an exercise in literary explication, but I think that teachers will work more effectively with material they can respect and admire than with the quotidian results of yesterday's irrelevancies. A textbook ought not to be deliberately dull. I must also add, considering the current make-up of college curricula, that the freshman reader may offer one of the very few chances some college students will have to meet the classics in a formal course and to discover that there is much to be gained from reading writers like Booker T. Washington and James Fenimore Cooper. Surely, no one could be the worse for having been exposed to ideas in the form of a poem by John Keats or a short story by Kate Chopin.

As to organization, this reader is divided into four sections—Exposition, Description, Narration, and Persuasion. Composing these larger sections are the several chapters, *each one centered on a single "idea" and each illustrating a single rhetorical mode.* Within a given chapter, I have followed, but not slavishly, a pattern: the first selections are usually brief and provide a relatively uncluttered example of the rhetorical method; subsequent selections tend to be longer and to illustrate the rhetorical method as it is ordinarily used, that is, combined with other devices authors employ to make a point. For example, Chapter 3, "The Eye of the Traveler," centers on comparison and contrast. The chapter opens with James A. Michener's brief comparison of Spain with Portugal, but the final entry shows Mark Twain using comparison and contrast as one of a number of techniques in "Rome and St. Peter's Overwhelm Us." Enough examples are given so that an instructor has considerable freedom of choice.

I have tried to keep the editorial apparatus to a useful minimum. There are introductions to each large section and to each chapter, but these are necessarily general: this book is not meant to replace, but to supplement, the basic text for a composition course. Brief headnotes identify the author and, where necessary, establish a context for the reading. Individual selections are ordinarily followed by a list of key or difficult words the student may need to look up, questions meant to shed light on form and content (usually in that order), and topics for writing. Starting from the premise that students must take an active part in their own education, I have provided this apparatus to help them, not to do their thinking for them, to overwhelm them with information, or to supply them with facts that they can get from the context of the selection or from a dictionary. An appendix offers some elementary instruction in writing the 500-word essay, with suggestions students may find helpful in handling other assignments in writing.

And improved student writing is, after all, the goal of English instructors everywhere. I hope that you will find this book to be of some help towards that goal, a source of ideas and examples upon which your students can draw.

In "The Two Races of Men," Charles Lamb divided the entire human race into two parts, borrowers and lenders. Editors of freshman readers are more closely allied to the former than to the latter. As a result, they owe much to many, a fact I am happy to admit. I have sought advice and ideas in many quarters and have drawn upon the experience of my own teachers and students; I have profited even when particular suggestions have had to be forgone. Those who have helped include my colleagues here at Saint Bonaventure University and elsewhere, most of them experienced teachers of composition but others specialists in areas as diverse as biology and business, chemistry and children's literature; teaching assistants and graduate students; authors, editors, publishers, business executives, and family members—all of them, I trust, friends.

Particular thanks are due to Daniel Barnes (Ohio State University), Santi Buscemi (Middlesex Community College), Larry Carver (University of Texas at Austin), Carol Cavallo (Suffolk County Community College), Lynn Garrett (Louisiana State University), Daniel Brislane, Anthony Farrow, Stephen Gray-Lewis, Leo Keenan, James Martine, John Mulryan, Patrick Panzarella, Mary Anne Schofield, Richard Simpson, Joseph Tedesco, and William Wehmeyer (Saint Bonaventure University); Lois Bragg, Diane DeLyser, Eileen Goble, Mary Harding, Claire Parrella, Lauren Pringle, Clare Smith, and Linda Vecchi; Jeanne Domeracki, Annemarie Mark, Laura McGovern, and William Miori; Nicholas Amato, John Apczynski, Peter Barrecchia, John Biter, Steven Brown, Stephen Eaton, Philip Eberl, Edward Eckert, Alfred Finocchio, Alfred Fix, Richard Gates, Cosmas Girard, Joseph Greer, Fred Handler, Russell Jandoli, Paul Joliet, Erick Laine, Marianne Laine, Richard Lipka, Francis Letro, Elizabeth Mayer, Cheryl Moore, Anthony Murphy, Michael O'Hear, Timothy Quinn, Joseph Rue, Paul Schafer, Carl Wagner, John Watson, James White, and Jeffrey White.

George Gath encouraged me to do this book. Lori Fowler and Meg Flanders helped me in the early editorial stages. Gordon Lester-Massman has been my editor at D. C. Heath and Company and has been a source of encouragement at every turn. Carol Ryan and Jackie Unch have helped keep my errors to a minimum.

Finally, I must acknowledge family obligations. My wife, Toni, has provided the patience which made work on *The Heath Reader* possible. By attending college simultaneously, my children, Michael and Gretchen, have made it almost necessary. I dedicate this book to the three of them.

Boyd Litzinger
Saint Bonaventure University

Contents

2

Attempting Definitions / The Nature of Education

3

Comparing and Contrasting / The Eye of the Traveler

4

Classifying and Distinguishing / The Melting Pot

7

Analyzing Processes / The World of Science and Technology

PART II · *Description*

8

Describing Persons / Eccentric Lives

9

Describing Places / Where Are You Going; Where Have You Been?

10

Describing Events / Breakthrough!

PART III · *Narration*   261

11

Diaries, Journals, and Notebooks / Private Reactions to Public Events   263

12

Autobiography / Crossroads

13

The Short Story / The Best-Laid Plans   317

PART IV · *Persuasion*   365

14

The Use of Logic / Democratic Government   367

15

The Tricks and Tools of Argument / Divided Opinions   400

16

Interpretation / What Did They Mean?

To the Student

In reading this book, as in entering college, you will make a number of new acquaintances. Some will reassure you, a few may disturb you, and others will challenge you. Nearly all of them you will find at least interesting.

Many of the authors represented in this book are alive today; others died centuries ago. Whatever their dates, their words are full of vitality—able to persuade, to entertain, to challenge, and to stimulate both by what they say and by how they say it.

I hope that you will enjoy the readings and find in them a source of ideas for class discussion and for related writing assignments. The word lists and questions that follow the selections will help by providing points to consider as you think through and perhaps reread parts of a particular work. The glossary at the back of the book explains terms that will be useful in discussion of the various selections.

The introductions to the four major sections of the book and to each chapter and selection provide commentaries on the aims of particular kinds of writing and the techniques that writers employ to reach their aims. This material, along with the Appendix, which offers specific advice on writing the 500-word essay, is meant to help you in planning, organizing, and expressing your own ideas in writing.

The best help, of course, comes from your own desire to educate yourself. With that in mind, try to approach each assignment carefully and with an open mind. Don't be afraid to disagree with the author or to question his methods or his conclusions. Enjoy what the author has achieved, but measure his ideas against your own. You will find yourself growing intellectually and, when the time for writing comes, you will find yourself equipped with plenty of ideas and a growing confidence in your ability to express them effectively.

PART I

Exposition

Although the lines between them are sometimes blurred, we usually distinguish among four kinds of writing: *exposition, description, narration,* and *persuasion.* Exposition, the focus of this section of *The Heath Reader,* is the most common kind of writing we use. It includes all of the modes of composition demonstrated in Chapters 1 through 7, and writers whose primary aim is persuasion, narration, or description often find exposition helpful or necessary.

In literal terms, *exposition* is the act of explaining or setting forth: expository writing informs readers about a subject, sets something before them, and explains it by means of an appeal to their understanding.

Many skills are involved in expository writing, but the starting point is always clear thinking about the subject at hand. What is it you want to explain to your readers? What information must you give them about the subject? In what order should you present the information? As you can see, you must have the readers as well as the subject clearly in mind. After all, it is they whom you are trying to enlighten.

Suppose you are the secretary of the freshman class and have been asked by the president to notify the members of a forthcoming meeting. It is up to you now to compose a suitable notice. Your task is simple exposition.

If you ask yourself the classic questions What? Who? Where? When? and Why?, you will see exactly what information the class requires and what, therefore, your notice must convey. *What* is the subject? A meeting. *Who* is invited? The members of the freshman class. *Where* will the meeting take place? In the small auditorium in the Student Center. *When* will it begin? At noon Friday, December 15. *Why* is it being held? To decide whether to support a proposal for a major reallocation of the class budget. You will still have to decide on the order that will best convey the information, and you must be careful to avoid ambiguous or misleading directions, but you can see that your notice has all but written itself: "There will be a meeting of the freshman class at noon Friday, December 15, in the small auditorium in the Student Center. We will discuss Bill Bradley's proposal to make certain changes in the approved class budget. You can get an advance copy of this proposal from any of the class officers or from the Dean of Students."

Sometimes, of course, expository writing is much more complex—as when writers try to explain a complicated matter like, let us say, the relationship between vocational and liberal education or the steps which led Japan to attack Pearl Harbor in 1941. In such cases writers will state their aims in a carefully phrased thesis sentence that serves them as a helpful guide to what they must do. The "five W's" will be answered, but the structure (beginning, middle, and end), supporting evidence, and methods of development will naturally be more complex than those required by our secretarial notice. The result will be an expository essay.

1

Using Examples and Illustrations / The Good Life

"Give me an instance," you are told when you assure a friend that jogging will help him in practical ways. "First, you'll sleep better at nights. Next, you'll find that jogging gives you a good excuse to be alone for a little while each day. Finally, you'll look more attractive once you get rid of that potbelly." You have given three examples of how jogging will help him.

Using examples and illustrations is a common and effective way to explain ideas. Their use is the most basic technique of expository writing because examples make the abstract concrete, the vague clear, the general specific.

The more carefully the writer selects examples, the more lucid the explanation becomes—and the better able the reader is to understand. The writers in this chapter are concerned with "the good life." But it isn't enough to say, "Thoreau and Judy Syfers desire the good life." Of course they do. The "good life" Thoreau pursued, however, differs considerably from the one Ms. Syfers posits. The examples, the details of day-to-day life—its activities, routines, annoyances and aspirations—illustrate what otherwise would have been an uninformative generality.

The entire chapter is a study in diversity, even though most of the authors range themselves with the "simple livers." In Holmes's poem, the speaker begins with a few simple wishes but seems to end up wanting quite a lot to nurture his contentment. Freya Stark seems to show that contentment is within easy reach, but Judy Syfers argues that wives may have to fight for it. To John Ciardi the pursuit of happiness may be a wild-goose chase for us modern materialists. In this set of vivid examples we may find some help in revising our own ideas of living well.

Is Everybody Happy?

JOHN CIARDI (1916–), a contemporary poet, teacher, editor, and critic, wrote a regular column for the *Saturday Review* in which he mused on the American scene.

1   The right to pursue happiness is issued to Americans with their birth certificates, but no one seems quite sure which way it ran. It may be we are issued a hunting license but offered no game. Jonathan Swift seemed to think so when he attacked the idea of happiness as "the possession of being well-deceived," the felicity of being "a fool among knaves." For Swift saw society as Vanity Fair, the land of false goals.

2   It is, of course, un-American to think in terms of fools and knaves. We do, however, seem to be dedicated to the idea of buying our way to happiness. We shall all have made it to Heaven when we possess enough.

3   And at the same time the forces of American commercialism are hugely dedicated to making us deliberately unhappy. Advertising is one of our major industries, and advertising exists not to satisfy desires but to create them—and to create them faster than any man's budget can satisfy them. For that matter, our whole economy is based on a dedicated insatiability. We are taught that to possess is to be happy, and then we are made to want. We are even told it is our duty to want. It was only a few years ago, to cite a single example, that car dealers across the country were flying banners that read "You Auto Buy Now." They were calling upon Americans, as an act approaching patriotism, to buy at once, with money they did not have, automobiles they did not really need, and which they would be required to grow tired of by the time the next year's models were released.

4   Or look at any of the women's magazines. There, as Bernard DeVoto once pointed out, advertising begins as poetry in the front pages and ends as pharmacopoeia and therapy in the back pages. The poetry of the front matter is the dream of perfect beauty. This is the baby skin that must be hers. These, the flawless teeth. This, the perfumed breath she must exhale. This, the sixteen-year-old figure she must display at forty, at fifty, at sixty, and forever.

5   Once past the vaguely uplifting fiction and feature articles, the reader finds the other face of the dream in the back matter. This is the harness into which Mother must strap herself in order to display that perfect figure. These, the chin straps she must sleep in. This is the salve that restores all, this is her laxative, these are the tablets that melt away fat, these are the hormones of perpetual youth, these are the stockings that hide varicose veins.

6   Obviously no half-sane person can be completely persuaded either by such poetry or by such pharmacopoeia and orthopedics. Yet someone is obviously trying

to buy the dream as offered and spending billions every year in the attempt. Clearly the happiness-market is not running out of customers, but what is it trying to buy?

The idea "happiness," to be sure, will not sit still for easy definition: the best one can do is try to set some extremes to the idea and then work in toward the middle. To think of happiness as acquisitive and competitive will do to set the materialistic extreme. To think of it as the idea one senses in, say, a holy man of India will do to set the spiritual extreme. That holy man's idea of happiness is in needing nothing from outside himself. In wanting nothing, he lacks nothing. He sits immobile, rapt in contemplation, free even of his own body. Or nearly free of it. If devout admirers bring him food he eats it; if not, he starves indifferently. Why be concerned? What is physical is an illusion to him. Contemplation is his joy and he achieves it through a fantastically demanding discipline, the accomplishment of which is itself a joy within him. 7

Is he a happy man? Perhaps his happiness is only another sort of illusion. But who can take it from him? And who will dare say it is more illusory than happiness on the installment plan. 8

But, perhaps because I am Western, I doubt such catatonic happiness, as I doubt the dreams of the happiness-market. What is certain is that his way of happiness would be torture to almost any Western man. Yet these extremes will still serve to frame the area within which all of us must find some sort of balance. Thoreau—a creature of both Eastern and Western thought—had his own firm sense of that balance. His aim was to save on the low levels in order to spend on the high. 9

Possession for its own sake or in competition with the rest of the neighborhood would have been Thoreau's idea of the low levels. The active discipline of heightening one's perception of what is enduring in nature would have been his idea of the high. What he saved from the low was time and effort he could spend on the high. Thoreau certainly disapproved of starvation, but he would put into feeding himself only as much effort as would keep him functioning for more important efforts. 10

Effort is the gist of it. There is no happiness except as we take on life-engaging difficulties. Short of the impossible, as Yeats put it, the satisfactions we get from a lifetime depend on how high we choose our difficulties. Robert Frost was thinking in something like the same terms when he spoke of "The pleasure of taking pains." The mortal flaw in the advertised version of happiness is in the fact that it purports to be effortless. 11

We demand difficulty even in our games. We demand it because without difficulty there can be no game. A game is a way of making something hard for the fun of it. The rules of the game are an arbitrary imposition of difficulty. When the spoilsport ruins the fun, he always does so by refusing to play by the rules. It is easier to win at chess if you are free, at your pleasure, to change the wholly arbitrary rules, but the fun is in winning within the rules. No difficulty, no fun. 12

The buyers and sellers at the happiness-market seem too often to have lost their sense of the pleasure of difficulty. Heaven knows what they are playing, but it seems 13 a dull game. And the Indian holy man seems dull to us, I suppose, because he seems to be refusing to play anything at all. The Western weakness may be in the illusion that happiness can be bought. Perhaps the Eastern weakness is in the idea that there is such a thing as perfect (and therefore static) happiness.

14   Happiness is never more than partial. There are no pure states of mankind. Whatever else happiness may be, it is neither in having nor in being, but in becoming. What the Founding Fathers declared for us as an inherent right, we should do well to remember, was not happiness but the *pursuit* of happiness. What they might have underlined, could they have foreseen the happiness-market, is the cardinal fact that happiness is in the pursuit itself, in the meaningful pursuit of what is life-engaging and life-revealing, which is to say, in the idea of *becoming*. A nation is not measured by what it possesses or wants to possess, but by what it wants to become.

15   By all means let the happiness-market sell us minor satisfactions and even minor follies so long as we keep them in scale and buy them out of spiritual change. I am no customer for either puritanism or asceticism. But drop any real spiritual capital at those bazaars, and what you come home to will be your own poorhouse.

Vocabulary

insatiability, pharmacopoeia, orthopedics, rapt, catatonic, arbitrary, cardinal, puritanism, asceticism

Questions

1. Are Ciardi's examples of the pursuit of happiness apt?
2. Do you agree that advertising exists to create desire?
3. Look at the advertisements in the next popular magazine you see. Does the character of the ads change from the front of the publication to the back? How?
4. What extremes of "happiness" does Ciardi propose?
5. Is there a pleasure in "taking pains," in making large efforts?
6. Are the rules essential to the fun of games?
7. "Happiness is . . . in becoming." Do you agree?

Topics for Writing

No Rules, No Fun

Happiness Is . . .

Advertising: Who Needs It?

from The Freya Stark Story

FREYA STARK   (1893–), born in France and having lived for most of her life in Italy, is an adventurous Englishwoman who has won recognition as an authority on the Middle East, mountaineering, and embroidery.

It is wise to discover what our happiness is made of. Of the ingredients of 1
which mine is made I think the presence of goodness comes first, and the affection
of a few people I can understand and care about is second. The third is sunshine.
After these, and close upon them, comes some sort of daily beauty, preferably a
spacious view; and after that and side by side—expressions perhaps of the same
desire—domestic servants of an old-fashioned friendly sort, and an atmosphere of
sequence in time, a regular procession and not a disorderly scramble towards
eternity. I like to have as much as possible of the background of this procession in
sight, and could never live happily for long in a country where no winding footpaths
have been made by the steps of my predecessors. That is why I care little for deserts,
unless a caravan route, crossing them, makes the long human endeavour, the slow
repeated victory, more plainly visible by the nearness and constant obvious possibility of defeat. United to this feeling for time as it passes, so that I will not even
separate it, is a delight in learning as much of the world as I can before I leave it. I
think that these pleasures—all receptive—are more essential to me than my own
work. They mean more than any applause or esteem, for the voice of other people
only touches if it carries affection; and I can imagine nothing more barren than to
be admired and not loved.

Though human loves come second on the list, coupled with the sun, I have 2
also had, ever since childhood and no doubt in my very bones, a curiosity due to
detachment. It is not really detachment but rather a *wideness* that makes me feel
intimately about a number of things that to many people are remote and strange.
Every view, to appeal to me, must have a distance; every friendship, a depth below
the surface; every work of art, some quality brought out from the unknown. The
absence of this quality makes me generally dislike newspapers, debates, or the
knick-knacks made for tourists: it makes me like things like telegraph wires (especially when they hum in the wind) or corners that turn *outward*, all skylines, all
mirrors of water great or small, an orchestra tuning in, or the funny snatches of
random voices that the wireless picks up as you turn it about—so different from its
set orations; the sudden remarks of unexpected people, and the little involuntary
gestures that move, as a leaf moves, and reveal what is so much greater than
themselves.

In this intimacy I long ago discovered a refuge from loneliness, and I suppose it 3
gives me a certain independence, for I know that, if my own sort of life fails me, I

can still take a genuine delight in the mere passing of the world along its way. This is a lucky capacity, if one does not use it to escape, but faces closer relationships with their ecstasies and sorrows and welcomes them when they come, knowing only (through what heartfelt experience) that there is a sanctuary in case of need. And I have often wondered whether this sort of detachment is not a humble workaday relative of the undeserved and unexpected grace by which the contemplative are visited, which brings with it a security of union not only with human, but with intangible things as well.

Vocabulary

domestic, predecessors, caravan, receptive, detachment, wireless, orations, involuntary, refuge, capacity, ecstasies, sanctuary, workaday, grace, contemplative, intangible

Questions

1. Single out the ingredients of the author's recipe for happiness.
2. What makes these pleasures "receptive"?
3. Does it surprise you that she places "the presence of goodness" first? Which of her pleasures would rank first with you?
4. Freya Stark prizes her spirit of detachment, but she recognizes a potential danger in it. What is that danger?
5. Freya Stark has spent much of her life traveling to exotic places—Arabia and Turkey, for example—at a time when few Western women adventured so far. Her ideas of happiness seem, not surprisingly, nicely fitted to the traveler of her time. But times have changed. Women are far more independent today, the means of travel have changed, our sense of the exotic has been affected (by television, for example). How would these changes affect a modern traveler?

Topics for Writing

The Modern Adventurer: New Challenges

The Modern Adventurer: New Pleasures

Lighting and Paving

BENJAMIN FRANKLIN (1706–1790) achieved fame in many areas of human activity. But whether as statesman or inventor, amateur scientist or public benefactor, Franklin believed that innocent happiness was a good pursuit and that serving others was the best way of pleasing God. The following paragraphs are from his *Autobiography*.

. . . Our city, tho' laid out with a beautiful regularity, the streets large, straight, and crossing each other at right angles, had the disgrace of suffering those streets to remain long unpaved; and in wet weather the wheels of heavy carriages ploughed them into a quagmire so that it was difficult to cross them. And in dry weather the dust was offensive. I had lived near what was called the Jersey Market and saw with pain the inhabitants wading in mud while purchasing their provisions. A strip of ground down the middle of that market was at length paved with brick so that being once in the market they had firm footing, but were often over shoes in dirt to get there. By talking and writing on the subject, I was at length instrumental in getting the street paved with stone between the market and the bricked foot pavement that was on each side next the houses. This for some time gave an easy access to the market, dry-shod. But the rest of the street not being paved, whenever a carriage came out of the mud upon this pavement, it shook off and left its dirt upon it, and it was soon covered with mire, which was not removed, the city as yet having no scavengers. After some enquiry I found a poor, industrious man who was willing to undertake keeping the pavement clean by sweeping it twice a week and carrying off the dirt from before all the neighbours' doors, for the sum of sixpence per month, to be paid by each house. I then wrote and printed a paper, setting forth the advantages to the neighborhood that might be obtained by this small expence: the greater ease in keeping our houses clean, so much dirt not being brought in by people's feet; the benefit to the shops by more custom, as buyers could more easily get at them; and by not having in windy weather the dust blown in upon their goods, etc., etc. I sent one of these papers to each house and in a day or two went round to see who would subscribe an agreement to pay these sixpences. It was unanimously signed and for a time well executed. All the inhabitants of the city were delighted with the cleanliness of the pavement that surrounded the market, it being a convenience to all; and this raised a general desire to have all the streets paved, and made the people more willing to submit to a tax for that purpose. After some time I drew a bill for paving the city and brought it into the Assembly. It was just before I went to England in 1757 and did not pass till I was gone, and then with an alteration in the mode of assessment, which I thought not for the better, but with an additional provision for lighting as well as paving the streets, which was a great improvement.

It was by a private person, the late Mr. John Clifton, giving a sample of the utility of lamps by placing one at his door that the people were first impressed with the idea of lighting all the city. The honour of this public benefit has also been ascribed to me, but it belongs truly to that gentleman. I did but follow his example and have only some merit to claim respecting the form of our lamps differing from the globe lamps we at first were supplied with from London. Those we found inconvenient in these respects: They admitted no air below; the smoke therefore did not readily go out above, but circulated in the globe, lodged on its inside, and soon obstructed the light they were intended to afford, giving, besides, the daily trouble of wiping them clean; and an accidental stroke on one of them would demolish it and render it totally useless. I therefore suggested the composing them of four flat panes, with a long funnel above, to draw up the smoke, and crevices admitting air below, to facilitate the ascent of the smoke. By this means they were kept clean, and did not grow dark in a few hours as the London lamps do, but continued bright till morning; and an accidental stroke would generally break but a single pane, easily repaired. I have sometimes wondered that the Londoners did not, from the effect holes in the bottom of the globe lamps used at Vauxhall have in keeping them clean, learn to have such holes in their street lamps. But those holes being made for another purpose, viz., to communicate flame more suddenly to the wick by a little flax hanging down thro' them, the other use of letting in airs seems not to have been thought of. And therefore, after the lamps have been lit a few hours, the streets of London are very poorly illuminated.

2   . . . Some may think these trifling matters not worth minding or relating. But when they consider that tho' dust blown into the eyes of a single person or into a single shop on a windy day is but of small importance, yet the great number of the instances in a populous city and its frequent repetitions give it weight and consequence; perhaps they will not censure very severely those who bestow some attention to affairs of this seemingly low nature. Human felicity is produced not so much by great pieces of good fortune that seldom happen as by little advantages that occur every day. Thus, if you teach a poor young man to shave himself and keep his razor in order, you may contribute more to the happiness of his life than in giving him a thousand guineas. The money may be soon spent, the regret only remaining of having foolishly consumed it. But in the other case he escapes the frequent vexation of waiting for barbers and of their sometimes dirty fingers, offensive breaths, and dull razors. He shaves when most convenient to him and enjoys daily the pleasure of its being done with a good instrument. With these sentiments I have hazarded the few preceding pages, hoping they may afford hints which sometime or other may be useful to a city I love, having lived many years in it very happily—and perhaps to some of our towns in America.

Vocabulary

quagmire, scavengers, felicity, guinea, vexation, hazarded

Questions

1. Modern readers (and writers) are unused to long paragraphs. Is Franklin's first paragraph hard to follow?
2. Can you detect an organizing principle in this paragraph?
3. Does it surprise you that an unquestionably great man should devote thought and work to such common matters as paving and street lights?
4. Is Franklin right when he claims that "human felicity is produced not so much by great pieces of good fortune . . . as by little advantages that occur every day"?

Topics for Writing

The "Little Advantages" in Life

Great Happiness vs. Small

A Convenience I Couldn't Do Without

Economy

HENRY DAVID THOREAU   (1817–1862), author and gentle rebel, traveled (as he said) "a great deal in Concord." Living simply, observing nature, philosophizing with wry humor on the human condition, he challenged (and challenges) the values adopted by the acquisitive society. This selection is from *Walden, or Life in the Woods.*

1   When I wrote the following pages, or rather the bulk of them, I lived alone, in the woods, a mile from any neighbor, in a house which I had built myself, on the shore of Walden Pond, in Concord, Massachusetts, and earned my living by the labor of my hands only. I lived there two years and two months. At present I am a sojourner in civilized life again.

2   I should not obtrude my affairs so much on the notice of my readers if very particular inquiries had not been made by my townsmen concerning my mode of life, which some would call impertinent, though they do not appear to me at all impertinent, but, considering the circumstances, very natural and pertinent. Some have asked what I got to eat; if I did not feel lonesome; if I was not afraid; and the like. Others have been curious to learn what portion of my income I devoted to charitable purposes; and some, who have large families, how many poor children I maintained. I will therefore ask those of my readers who feel no particular interest in me to pardon me if I undertake to answer some of these questions in this book. In most books, the *I,* or first person, is omitted; in this it will be retained; that, in respect to egotism, is the main difference. We commonly do not remember that it is, after all, always the first person that is speaking. I should not talk so much about myself if there were anybody else whom I knew as well. Unfortunately, I am confined to this theme by the narrowness of my experience. Moreover, I, on my side, require of every writer, first or last, a simple and sincere account of his own life, and not merely what he has heard of other men's lives; some such account as he would send to his kindred from a distant land; for if he has lived sincerely, it must have been in a distant land to me. Perhaps these pages are more particularly addressed to poor students. As for the rest of my readers, they will accept such portions as apply to them. I trust that none will stretch the seams in putting on the coat, for it may do good service to him whom it fits.

3   I would fain say something, not so much concerning the Chinese and Sandwich Islanders as you who read these pages, who are said to live in New England; something about your condition, especially your outward condition or circumstances in this world, in this town, what it is, whether it is necessary that it be as bad as it is, whether it cannot be improved as well as not. I have travelled a good deal in Concord; and everywhere, in shops, and offices, and fields, the inhabitants have appeared to me to be doing penance in a thousand remarkable ways. What I have

heard of Bramins sitting exposed to four fires and looking in the face of the sun; or hanging suspended, with their heads downward, over flames; or looking at the heavens over their shoulders "until it becomes impossible for them to resume their natural position, while from the twist of the neck nothing but liquids can pass into the stomach"; or dwelling, chained for life, at the foot of a tree; or measuring with their bodies, like caterpillars, the breadth of vast empires; or standing on one leg on the tops of pillars,—even these forms of conscious penance are hardly more incredible and astonishing than the scenes which I daily witness. The twelve labors of Hercules were trifling in comparison with those which my neighbors have undertaken; for they were only twelve, and had an end; but I could never see that these men slew or captured any monster or finished any labor. They have no friend Iolaus to burn with a hot iron the root of the hydra's head, but as soon as one head is crushed, two spring up.

I see young men, my townsmen, whose misfortune it is to have inherited **4** farms, houses, barns, cattle, and farming tools; for these are more easily acquired than got rid of. Better if they had been born in the open pasture and suckled by a wolf, that they might have seen with clearer eyes what field they were called to labor in. Who made them serfs of the soil? Why should they eat their sixty acres, when man is condemned to eat only his peck of dirt? Why should they begin digging their graves as soon as they are born? They have got to live a man's life, pushing all these things before them, and get on as well as they can. How many a poor immortal soul have I met well-nigh crushed and smothered under its load, creeping down the road of life, pushing before it a barn seventy-five feet by forty, its Augean stables never cleansed, and one hundred acres of land, tillage, mowing, pasture, and wood-lot! The portionless who struggle with no such unnecessary inherited encumbrances, find it labor enough to subdue and cultivate a few cubic feet of flesh.

But men labor under a mistake. The better part of the man is soon plowed into **5** the soil for compost. By a seeming fate, commonly called necessity, they are employed, as it says in an old book, laying up treasures which moth and rust will corrupt and thieves break through and steal. It is a fool's life, as they will find when they get to the end of it, if not before. It is said that Deucalion and Pyrrha created men by throwing stones over their heads behind them:—

Inde genus durum sumus, experiensque laborum,
Et documenta damus quâ simus origine nati.

Or, as Raleigh rhymes it in his sonorous way,—

From thence our kind hard-hearted is, enduring pain and care,
Approving that our bodies of a stony nature are.

So much for a blind obedience to a blundering oracle, throwing the stones over their heads behind them, and not seeing where they fell.

Most men, even in this comparatively free country, through mere ignorance **6** and mistake, are so occupied with the factitious cares and superfluously coarse labors of life that its finer fruits cannot be plucked by them. Their fingers, from excessive toil, are too clumsy and tremble too much for that. Actually, the laboring man has not leisure for a true integrity day by day; he cannot afford to sustain the manliest relations to men; his labor would be depreciated in the market. He has no time to be anything but a machine. How can he remember well his ignorance—which his growth requires—who has so often to use his knowledge? We should feed and clothe him gratuitously sometimes, and recruit him with our cordials, before we judge of him. The finest qualities of our nature, like the bloom on fruits, can be preserved only by the most delicate handling. Yet we do not treat ourselves nor one another thus tenderly.

7   Some of you, we all know, are poor, find it hard to live, are sometimes, as it were, gasping for breath. I have no doubt that some of you who read this book are unable to pay for all the dinners which you have actually eaten, or for the coats and shoes which are fast wearing or are already worn out, and have come to this page to spend borrowed or stolen time, robbing your creditors of an hour. It is very evident what mean and sneaking lives many of you live, for my sight has been whetted by experience; always on the limits, trying to get into business and trying to get out of debt, a very ancient slough, called by the Latins *aes alienum*, another's brass, for some of their coins were made of brass; still living, and dying, and buried by this other's brass; always promising to pay, promising to pay, to-morrow, and dying to-day, insolvent; seeking to curry favor, to get custom, by how many modes, only not state-prison offences; lying, flattering, voting, contracting yourselves into a nutshell of civility, or dilating into an atmosphere of thin and vaporous generosity, that you may persuade your neighbor to let you make his shoes, or his hat, or his coat, or his carriage, or import his groceries for him; making yourselves sick, that you may lay up something against a sick day, something to be tucked away in an old chest, or in a stocking behind the plastering, or, more safely, in the brick bank; no matter where, no matter how much or how little.

8   I sometimes wonder that we can be so frivolous, I may almost say, as to attend to the gross but somewhat foreign form of servitude called Negro Slavery, there are so many keen and subtle masters that enslave both North and South. It is hard to have a Southern overseer; it is worse to have a Northern one; but worst of all when you are the slave-driver of yourself. Talk of a divinity in man! Look at the teamster on the highway, wending to market by day or night; does any divinity stir within him? His highest duty to fodder and water his horses! What is his destiny to him compared with the shipping interests? Does not he drive for Squire Make-a-stir? How godlike, how immortal, is he? See how he cowers and sneaks, how vaguely all the day he fears, not being immortal nor divine, but the slave and prisoner of his own opinion of himself, a fame won by his own deeds. Public opinion is a weak tyrant compared with our own private opinion. What a man thinks of himself, that it is which determines, or rather indicates, his fate. Self-emancipation even in the West Indian provinces of the fancy and imagination,—what Wilberforce is there to bring that about? Think, also, of the ladies of the land weaving toilet cushions against the last day, not to betray too green an interest in their fates! As if you could kill time without injuring eternity.

9   The mass of men lead lives of quiet desperation. What is called resignation is confirmed desperation. From the desperate city you go into the desperate country,

and have to console yourself with the bravery of minks and muskrats. A stereotyped by unconscious despair is concealed even under what are called the games and amusements of mankind. There is no play in them, for this comes after work. But it is a characteristic of wisdom not to do desperate things.

When we consider what, to use the words of the catechism, is the chief end of   10
man, and what are the true necessaries and means of life, it appears as if men had deliberately chosen the common mode of living because they preferred it to any other. Yet they honestly think there is no choice left. But alert and healthy natures remember that the sun rose clear. It is never too late to give up our prejudices. No way of thinking or doing, however ancient, can be trusted without proof. What everybody echoes or in silence passes by as true to-day may turn out to be falsehood to-morrow, mere smoke of opinion, which some had trusted for a cloud that would sprinkle fertilizing rain on their fields. What old people say you cannot do, you try and find that you can. Old deeds for old people, and new deeds for new. Old people did not know enough once, perchance, to fetch fresh fuel to keep the fire a-going; new people put a little dry wood under a pot, and are whirled round the globe with the speed of birds, in a way to kill old people, as the phrase is. Age is no better, hardly so well, qualified for an instructor as youth, for it has not profited so much as it has lost. One may almost doubt if the wisest man has learned anything of absolute value by living. Practically, the old have no very important advice to give the young, their own experience has been so partial, and their lives have been such miserable failures, for private reasons, as they must believe; and it may be that they have some faith left which belies that experience, and they are only less young than they were. I have lived some thirty years on this planet, and I have yet to hear the first syllable of valuable or even earnest advice from my seniors. They have told me nothing, and probably cannot tell me anything to the purpose. Here is life, an experiment to a great extent untried by me; but it does not avail me that they have tried it. If I have any experience which I think valuable, I am sure to reflect that this my Mentors said nothing about.

One farmer says to me, "You cannot live on vegetable food solely, for it   11
furnishes nothing to make bones with"; and so he religiously devotes a part of his day to supplying his system with the raw material of bones; walking all the while he talks behind his oxen, which, with vegetable-made bones, jerk him and his lumber-ing plow along in spite of every obstacle. Some things are really necessaries of life in some circles, the most helpless and diseased, which in others are luxuries merely, and in others still are entirely unknown.

The whole round of human life seems to some to have been gone over by their   12
predecessors, both the heights and the valleys, and all things to have been cared for. According to Evelyn, "the wise Solomon prescribed ordinances for the very dis-tances of trees; and the Roman praetors have decided how often you may go into your neighbor's land to gather the acorns which fall on it without trespass, and what share belongs to that neighbor." Hippocrates has even left directions how we should cut our nails; that is, even with the ends of the fingers, neither shorter nor longer. Undoubtedly the very tedium and ennui which presume to have exhausted the variety and the joys of life are as old as Adam. But man's capacities have never been

measured; nor are we to judge of what he can do by any precedents, so little has been tried. Whatever have been thy failures hitherto, "be not afflicted, my child, for who shall assign to thee what thou hast left undone?"

13   We might try our lives by a thousand simple tests; as, for instance, that the same sun which ripens my beans illumines at once a system of earths like ours. If I had remembered this it would have prevented some mistakes. This was not the light in which I hoed them. The stars are the apexes of what wonderful triangles! What distant and different beings in the various mansions of the universe are contemplating the same one at the same moment! Nature and human life are as various as our several constitutions. Who shall say what prospect life offers to another? Could a greater miracle take place than for us to look through each other's eyes for an instant? We should live in all the ages of the world in an hour; ay, in all the worlds of the ages. History, Poetry, Mythology!—I know no reading of another's experience so startling and informing as this would be.

14   The greater part of what my neighbors call good I believe in my soul to be bad, and if I repent of anything, it is very likely to be my good behavior. What demon possessed me that I behaved so well? You may say the wisest thing you can, old man,—you who have lived seventy years, not without honor of a kind,—I hear an irresistible voice which invites me away from all that. One generation abandons the enterprises of another like stranded vessels.

15   I think that we may safely trust a good deal more than we do. We may waive just so much care of ourselves as we honestly bestow elsewhere. Nature is as well adapted to our weakness as to our strength. The incessant anxiety and strain of some is a well-nigh incurable form of disease. We are made to exaggerate the importance of what work we do; and yet how much is not done by us! or, what if we had been taken sick? How vigilant we are! determined not to live by faith if we can avoid it; all the day long on the alert, at night we unwillingly say our prayers and commit ourselves to uncertainties. So thoroughly and sincerely are we compelled to live, reverencing our life, and denying the possibility of change. This is the only way, we say; but there are as many ways as there can be drawn radii from one centre. All change is a miracle to contemplate; but it is a miracle which is taking place every instant. Confucius said, "To know that we know what we know, and that we do not know what we do not know, that is true knowledge." When one man has reduced a fact of the imagination to be a fact to his understanding, I foresee that all men will at length establish their lives on that basis.

16   Let us consider for a moment what most of the trouble and anxiety which I have referred to is about, and how much it is necessary that we be troubled, or at least careful. It would be some advantage to live a primitive and frontier life, though in the midst of an outward civilization, if only to learn what are the gross necessaries of life and what methods have been taken to obtain them; or even to look over the old day-books of the merchants, to see what it was that men most commonly bought at the stores, what they stored, that is, what are the grossest groceries. For the improvements of ages have had but little influence on the essential laws of man's existence: as our skeletons, probably, are not to be distinguished from those of our ancestors.

By the words, *necessary of life*, I mean whatever, of all that man obtains by his
own exertions, has been from the first, or from long use has become, so important
to human life that few, if any, whether from savageness, or poverty, or philosophy,
ever attempt to do without it. To many creatures there is in this sense but one
necessary of life, Food. To the bison of the prairie it is a few inches of palatable
grass, with water to drink; unless he seeks the Shelter of the forest or the mountain's
shadow. None of the brute creation requires more than Food and Shelter. The
necessaries of life for man in this climate may, accurately enough, be distributed
under the several heads of Food, Shelter, Clothing, and Fuel; for not till we have
secured these are we prepared to entertain the true problems of life with freedom
and a prospect of success. Man has invented, not only houses, but clothes and
cooked food; and possibly from the accidental discovery of the warmth of fire, and
the consequent use of it, at first a luxury, arose the present necessity to sit by it. We
observe cats and dogs acquiring the same second nature. By proper Shelter and
Clothing we legitimately retain our own internal heat; but with an excess of these,
or of Fuel, that is, with an external heat greater than our own internal, may not
cookery properly be said to begin? Darwin, the naturalist, says of the inhabitants of
Tierra del Fuego, that while his own party, who were well clothed and sitting close
to a fire, were far from too warm, these naked savages, who were farther off, were
observed, to his great surprise, "to be steaming with perspiration at undergoing such
a roasting." So, we are told, the New Hollander goes naked with impunity, while
the European shivers in his clothes. Is it impossible to combine the hardiness of
these savages with the intellectualness of the civilized man? According to Liebig,
man's body is a stove, and food the fuel which keeps up the internal combustion in
the lungs. In cold weather we eat more, in warm less. The animal heat is the result
of a slow combustion, and disease and death take place when this is too rapid; or for
want of fuel, or from some defect in the draught, the fire goes out. Of course the
vital heat is not to be confounded with fire; but so much for analogy. It appears,
therefore, from the above list, that the expression, *animal life*, is nearly synonymous with the expression, *animal heat*; for while Food may be regarded as the Fuel
which keeps up the fire within us,—and Fuel serves only to prepare that Food or to
increase the warmth of our bodies by addition from without,—Shelter and Clothing also serve only to retain the *heat* thus generated and absorbed.

The grand necessity, then, for our bodies, is to keep warm, to keep the vital
heat in us. What pains we accordingly take, not only with our Food, and Clothing,
and Shelter, but with our beds, which are our nightclothes, robbing the nests and
breasts of birds to prepare this shelter within a shelter, as the mole has its bed of grass
and leaves at the end of its burrow! The poor man is wont to complain that this is a
cold world; and to cold, no less physical than social, we refer directly a great part of
our ails. The summer, in some climates, makes possible to man a sort of Elysian
life. Fuel, except to cook his Food, is then unnecessary; the sun is his fire, and
many of the fruits are sufficiently cooked by its rays; while Food generally is more
various, and more easily obtained, and Clothing and Shelter are wholly or half
unnecessary. At the present day, and in this country, as I find by my own experience, a few implements, a knife, an axe, a spade, a wheelbarrow, etc., and for the

studious, lamplight, stationery, and access to a few books, rank next to necessaries, and can all be obtained at a trifling cost. Yet some, not wise, go to the other side of the globe, to barbarous and unhealthy regions, and devote themselves to trade for ten or twenty years, in order that they may live,—that is, keep comfortably warm,—and die in New England at last. The luxuriously rich are not simply kept comfortably warm, but unnaturally hot; as I implied before, they are cooked, of course *à la mode.*

19   Most of the luxuries, and many of the so-called comforts of life, are not only not indispensable, but positive hindrances to the elevation of mankind. With respect to luxuries and comforts, the wisest have ever lived a more simple and meagre life than the poor. The ancient philosophers, Chinese, Hindoo, Persian, and Greek, were a class than which none has been poorer in outward riches, none so rich in inward. We know not much about them. It is remarkable that *we* know so much of them as we do. The same is true of the more modern reformers and benefactors of their race. None can be an impartial or wise observer of human life but from the vantage ground of what *we* should call voluntary poverty. Of a life of luxury the fruit is luxury, whether in agriculture, or commerce, or literature, or art. There are nowadays professors of philosophy, but not philosophers. Yet it is admirable to profess because it was once admirable to live. To be a philosopher is not merely to have subtle thoughts, nor even to found a school, but so to love wisdom as to live according to its dictates, a life of simplicity, independence, magnanimity, and trust. It is to solve some of the problems of life, not only theoretically, but practically. The success of great scholars and thinkers is commonly a courtier-like success, not kingly, not manly. They make shift to live merely by conformity, practically as their fathers did, and are in no sense the progenitors of a nobler race of men. But why do men degenerate ever? What makes families run out? What is the nature of the luxury which enervates and destroys nations? Are we sure that there is none of it in our own lives? The philosopher is in advance of his age even in the outward form of his life. He is not fed, sheltered, clothed, warmed, like his contemporaries. How can a man be a philosopher and not maintain his vital heat by better methods than other men?

20   When a man is warmed by the several modes which I have described, what does he want next? Surely not more warmth of the same kind, as more and richer food, larger and more splendid houses, finer and more abundant clothing, more numerous, incessant, and hotter fires, and the like. When he has obtained those things which are necessary to life, there is another alternative than to obtain the superfluities; and that is, to adventure on life now, his vacation from humbler toil having commenced. The soil, it appears, is suited to the seed, for it has sent its radicle downward, and it may now send its shoot upward also with confidence. Why has man rooted himself thus firmly in the earth, but that he may rise in the same proportion into the heavens above?—for the nobler plants are valued for the fruit they bear at last in the air and light, far from the ground, and are not treated like the humbler esculents, which, though they may be biennials, are cultivated only till they have perfected their root, and often cut down at top for this purpose, so that most would not know them in their flowering season.

I do not mean to prescribe rules to strong and valiant natures, who will mind their own affairs whether in heaven or hell, and perchance build more magnificently and spend more lavishly than the richest, without ever impoverishing themselves, not knowing how they live,—if, indeed, there are any such, as has been dreamed; nor to those who find their encouragement and inspiration in precisely the present condition of things, and cherish it with the fondness and enthusiasm of lovers,—and, to some extent, I reckon myself in this number; I do not speak to those who are well employed, in whatever circumstances, and they know whether they are well employed or not;—but mainly to the mass of men who are discontented, and idly complaining of the hardness of their lot or of the times, when they might improve them. There are some who complain most energetically and inconsolably of any, because they are, as they say, doing their duty. I also have in my mind that seemingly wealthy, but most terribly impoverished class of all, who have accumulated dross, but know not how to use it, or get rid of it, and thus have forged their own golden or silver fetters.

Vocabulary

sojourner, impertinent, Bramins (Brahmins), slough, dilating, palatable, Elysian, radicle, dross

Questions

1. Thoreau praises the simple life. Is such a life too simple for us today?
2. Do most people "lead lives of quiet desperation"? Do you know examples from your own experience?
3. Why is it a misfortune to have inherited a house, a barn, or a farm?
4. Do you think Thoreau is trying to shirk responsibility?
5. Thoreau accuses his contemporaries of living beyond their means, running into debt, living on credit. What would he think about our modern credit-card economy?
6. Could you live the "good life" as Thoreau illustrates it? Could society follow his example?

Topics for Writing

Life in the Slow Lane

The Weight of Ownership

The "Gross Necessaries" in the Eighties

I Want a Wife

JUDY SYFERS This article appeared, appropriately enough, in the first issue of *Ms.*, an avowedly feminist magazine.

1   I belong to that classification of people known as wives. I am A Wife. And, not altogether incidentally, I am a mother.

2   Not too long ago a male friend of mine appeared on the scene from the Midwest fresh from a recent divorce. He had one child, who is, of course, with his ex-wife. He is obviously looking for another wife. As I thought about him while I was ironing one evening, it suddenly occurred to me that I, too, would like to have a wife. Why do I want a wife?

3   I would like to go back to school so that I can become economically independent, support myself, and, if need be, support those dependent upon me. I want a wife who will work and send me to school. And while I am going to school I want a wife to take care of my children. I want a wife to keep track of the children's doctor and dentist appointments. And to keep track of mine, too. I want a wife to make sure my children eat properly and are kept clean. I want a wife who will wash the children's clothes and keep them mended. I want a wife who is a good nurturant attendant to my children, arranges for their schooling, makes sure that they have an adequate social life with their peers, takes them to the park, the zoo, etc. I want a wife who takes care of the children when they are sick, a wife who arranges to be around when the children need special care, because, of course, I cannot miss classes at school. My wife must arrange to lose time at work and not lose the job. It may mean a small cut in my wife's income from time to time, but I guess I can tolerate that. Needless to say, my wife will arrange and pay for the care of the children while my wife is working.

4   I want a wife who will take care of *my* physical needs. I want a wife who will keep my house clean. A wife who will pick up after my children, a wife who will pick up after me. I want a wife who will keep my clothes clean, ironed, mended, replaced when need be, and who will see to it that my personal things are kept in their proper place so that I can find what I need the minute I need it. I want a wife who cooks the meals, a wife who is a *good* cook. I want a wife who will plan the menus, do the necessary grocery shopping, prepare the meals, serve them pleasantly, and then do the cleaning up while I do my studying. I want a wife who will care for me when I am sick and sympathize with my pain and loss of time from school. I want a wife to go along when our family takes a vacation so that someone can continue to care for me and my children when I need a rest and a change of scene.

5   I want a wife who will not bother me with rambling complaints about a wife's duties. But I want a wife who will listen to me when I feel the need to explain a

rather difficult point I have come across in my course of studies. And I want a wife who will type my papers for me when I have written them.

I want a wife who will take care of the details of my social life. When my wife   6
and I are invited out by my friends, I want a wife who will take care of the babysitting arrangements. When I meet people at school that I like and want to entertain, I want a wife who will have the house clean, will prepare a special meal, serve it to me and my friends, and not interrupt when I talk about the things that interest me and my friends. I want a wife who will have arranged that the children are fed and ready for bed before my guests arrive so that the children do not bother us. I want a wife who takes care of the needs of my guests so that they feel comfortable, who makes sure that they have an ashtray, that they are passed the hors d'oeuvres, that they are offered a second helping of the food, that their wine glasses are replenished when necessary, that their coffee is served to them as they like it. And I want a wife who knows that sometimes I need a night out by myself.

I want a wife who is sensitive to my sexual needs, a wife who makes love   7
passionately and eagerly when I feel like it, a wife who makes sure that I am satisfied. And, of course, I want a wife who will not demand sexual attention when I am not in the mood for it. I want a wife who assumes the complete responsibility for birth control, because I do not want more children. I want a wife who will remain sexually faithful to me so that I do not have to clutter up my intellectual life with jealousies. And I want a wife who understands that *my* sexual needs may entail more than strict adherence to monogamy. I must, after all, be able to relate to people as fully as possible.

If, by chance, I find another person more suitable as a wife than the wife I   8
already have, I want the liberty to replace my present wife with another one. Naturally, I will expect a fresh, new life; my wife will take the children and be solely responsible for them so that I am left free.

When I am through with school and have acquired a job, I want my wife to   9
quit working and remain at home so that my wife can more fully and completely take care of a wife's duties.

My God, who *wouldn't* want a wife?   10

Vocabulary

incidentally, nurturant, hors d'oeuvres, replenished, monogamy

Questions

1. Point out three examples of "wifely" behavior.
2. Do you sometimes get the feeling that the husband is looking for a mother instead of a wife? What are some instances of "motherly" behavior here?

3. Judging from your own family, what elements of truth do you find most striking in "I Want a Wife"?
4. Is Judy Syfers condemning marriage or the double standard?

Topics for Writing

I Want a Husband

I Want My Mother!

Contentment

OLIVER WENDELL HOLMES (1809–1894), poet and physician—for a time he was dean of Harvard Medical School—took a light-hearted look at most things. In poems and in a series of essays called *The Autocrat of the Breakfast-Table,* he held forth on various subjects in the pages of the *Atlantic Monthly,* which he helped found in 1857. His son, who bore the same name, became a justice of the United States Supreme Court.

"Man wants but little here below."

Little I ask; my wants are few;
   I only wish a hut of stone,
(A *very plain* brown stone will do,)
    That I may call my own;—
And close at hand is such a one,   5
In yonder street that fronts the sun.

Plain food is quite enough for me;
   Three courses are as good as ten;—
If Nature can subsist on three,
    Thank Heaven for three. Amen!   10
I always thought cold victual nice;—
My *choice* would be vanilla-ice.

I care not much for gold or land;—
   Give me a mortgage here and there,—
Some good bank-stock,—some note of hand,   15
    Or trifling railroad share;—
I only ask that Fortune send
A *little* more than I shall spend.

Honors are silly toys, I know,
   And titles are but empty names;—   20
I would, *perhaps*, be Plenipo,—
    But only near St. James;—
I'm very sure I should not care
To fill our Gubernator's chair.

Jewels are baubles; 't is a sin   25
    To care for such unfruitful things;—
One good-sized diamond in a pin,—

Some, *not so large*, in rings,—
A ruby and a pearl, or so,
Will do for me;—I laugh at show.

My dame should dress in cheap attire;
(Good, heavy silks are never dear;)—
I own perhaps I *might* desire
Some shawls of true cashmere,—
Some marrowy crapes of China silk,
Like wrinkled skins on scalded milk.

I would not have the horse I drive
So fast that folks must stop and stare:
An easy gait—two, forty-five—
Suits me; I do not care;—
Perhaps, for just a *single spurt*,
Some seconds less would do no hurt.

Of pictures, I should like to own
Titians and Raphaels three or four,—
I love so much their style and tone,—
One Turner, and no more,—
(A landscape,—foreground golden dirt,—
The sunshine painted with a squirt.)—

Of books but few,—some fifty score
For daily use, and bound for wear;
The rest upon an upper floor;—
Some *little* luxury *there*
Of red morocco's gilded gleam,
And vellum rich as country cream.

Busts, cameos, gems,—such things as these,
Which others often show for pride,
I value for their power to please,
And selfish churls deride;—
One Stradivarius, I confess,
Two Meerschaums, I would fain possess.

Wealth's wasteful tricks I will not learn,
Nor ape the glittering upstart fool;—
Shall not carved tables serve my turn,
But *all* must be of buhl?
Give grasping pomp its double share,—
I ask but *one* recumbent chair.

Thus humble let me live and die,
   Nor long for Midas' golden touch,
If Heaven more generous gifts deny,
   I shall not miss them *much*,—   70
Too grateful for the blessing lent
Of simple tastes and mind content!

Vocabulary

victual, plenipo(tentiary), gubernator, crapes, vellum, fain, buhl, recumbent

Questions

1. Holmes draws his examples from nineteenth-century life. What substitutions would you suggest to update the poem?
2. Do we all have false notions of what it would take to make us happy?

Topics for Writing

The More We Have, the More We Want

I Could Do with Less

2

Attempting Definitions /
The Nature of Education

"Truth? What is truth?" said Pilate. He was asking for a definition (but he seems to have believed there was no satisfactory one, for he "would not stay for answer"). A definition states the meaning of a term; it explains the essential quality or the nature of a word, an idea, or a thing.

Good definitions are often simple, but they must be complete. Sometimes a synonym will do: *slumber* can be defined as *sleep*. But to define *hat* as "a covering for the head" or *dog* as "a domesticated four-legged animal" will not do because those descriptions could fit a babushka as well as a fedora, a cat as well as Fido.

Definitions can also be complex. Indeed, they must be when they attempt to explain abstractions or difficult concepts. *Liberty, love,* and *truth,* for instance, call for extended definitions. Still, if we are to make ourselves understood to others, if we want our discourse to be fruitful, we must define our terms. Two people cannot have a useful discussion of "Alcoholism on the College Campus" if one defines *alcoholic* as "one who ingests alcohol" and the other as "one who gets drunk twice a week."

The authors in this chapter use definitions to explain the nature of education. John Henry Newman gives us detailed designs for an education, whereas Francis Bacon concentrates upon the uses of various kinds of study—none of them actually requiring a faculty or a classroom. This last is a point upon which Walt Whitman and Robert Louis Stevenson might agree, even though neither would probably be happy to think that education is a way of correcting one's weaknesses and disciplining one's mind. That discipline leads in the setting of a modern women's college, according to Mary McCarthy, to a "respect for the unorthodox"—and Nikki Giovanni outlines an education that is unorthodox in a way many Vassar women may not have conceived. As a result, you have an opportunity to measure your own idea of an education against some classic and challenging standards.

from The Vassar Girl

MARY MCCARTHY (1912–), essayist, novelist, and short story writer, is a sharp observer of the social scene. This selection is from her book *On the Contrary.*

A wistful respect for the unorthodox is ingrained in the Vassar mentality. The Vassar freshman still comes through Taylor Gate as I did, with the hope of being made over, redirected, vivified. The daughter of a conservative lawyer, doctor, banker, or businessman, she will have chosen Vassar in all probability with the idea of transcending her background. And if she does not have such plans for herself, her teachers have them for her. If she is, say, a Vassar daughter or a girl from a preparatory school like Chapin or Madeira who chose Vassar because her friends did, her teachers, starting freshman year, will seek to "shake her up," "emancipate" her, make her "think for herself." This dynamic conception of education is Vassar's hallmark.

The progressive colleges have something similar, but there the tendency is to orient the student in some preconceived direction—toward the modern dance or toward "progressive" political thinking, while at Vassar, by and large, the student is almost forbidden to take her direction from the teacher. "What do *you* think?" is the question that ricochets on the student if she asks the teacher's opinion; and the difference between Vassar and the traditional liberal college (where the teacher is also supposed to keep his own ideas in the background) is that at Vassar the student is obliged, every day, to proffer hers.

Thus at a freshman English class I recently visited, the students were discussing Richard Hughes' *The Innocent Voyage,* a book whose thesis is that children are monsters, without moral feeling in the adult sense, insane, irresponsible, incapable of conventional grief or remorse. This idea was very shocking to perhaps half the class, well-brought-up little girls who protested that children were not "like that," indignant hands waved in the air, anguished faces grimaced, while a more detached student in braids testified that her own experience as a baby-sitter bore Mr. Hughes out. The teacher took no sides but merely smiled and encouraged one side and then the other, raising a hand for quiet when the whole class began shouting at once, and interrupting only to ask, "Do you really know children? Are you speaking from what you have seen or remember, or from what you think *ought* to be so?" This book plainly was chosen not because it was a favorite with the professor or even because of its literary merits but because it challenged preconceptions and disturbed set ideas.

The effect of this training is to make the Vassar student, by the time she has reached her junior year, look back upon her freshman self with pity and amazement. When you talk to her about her life in college, you will find that she sees it as

27

a series of before-and-after snapshots: "When I came to Vassar, I thought like Mother and Daddy . . . I was conservative in my politics . . . I had race prejudice . . . I liked academic painting." With few exceptions, among those who are articulate and who feel that the college has "done something" for them, the trend is from the conservative to the liberal, from the orthodox to the heterodox, with stress on the opportunities Vassar has provided for getting to know "different" people, of opposite opinions and from different backgrounds.

5   Yet the statistical fate of the Vassar girl, thanks to Mother and Dad and the charge account, is already decreed. And the result is that the Vassar alumna, uniquely among American college women, is two persons—the housewife or matron, and the yearner and regretter. The Vassar graduate who has failed to make a name for herself, to "keep up," extend her interests, is, because of her training, more poignantly conscious of backsliding than her contemporary at Barnard or Holyoke. And unlike the progressive-college graduate, on the other hand, who has been catered to and conciliated by her instructors, the Vassar girl who drifts into matronhood or office work is more inclined to blame herself than society for what has happened, and to feel that she has let the college down by not becoming famous or "interesting." The alumnae records are full of housewives, doctors, teachers, educators, social workers, child-welfare specialists, public-health consultants. But the Vassar dream obdurately prefers such figures as Inez Milholland, '09, who rode a white horse down Fifth Avenue campaigning for woman suffrage; Edna St. Vincent Millay, '17, the *révoltée* girl-poet who made herself a byword of sexual love and disenchanted lyricism; Elizabeth Hawes, '25, iconoclastic dress designer, and author of *Fashion Is Spinach*. The Vassar romanticism will pass over a college president in favor of an author or journalist—Constance Rourke, '07, pioneer folklorist and author of *American Humor*; Muriel Rukeyser, ex-'34, Eleanor Clark, Elizabeth Bishop, '34, poets and writers, Jean Poletti, '25, Lois ("Lipstick" of *The New Yorker*) Long, '22, Beatrice Berle, '23, noted for her opinions on marriage and for the twin bathtubs she and her husband, Adolf A. Berle, Jr., shared in their Washington house—and it will recognize as its own even such antipodal curiosities as Elizabeth Bentley, '30, the ex-Communist spy queen, and Major Julia Hamblet, '37, the first woman to enlist in the Marines.

6   The incongruities on this list are suggestive. An *arresting performance* in politics, fashion, or art is often taken by the Vassar mind to be synonymous with true accomplishment. The Vassar dynamism drives toward money and success and the limelight in a truly Roman fashion, when it is not yoked to their opposite— service. With its alertness, its eagerness to *do* things, it tends, once the academic restraints are removed, to succumb to a rather journalistic notion of what constitutes value.

7   In the arts, after the first few intransigent gestures, Vassar talent streams into commercial side lines—advertising, fashion writing, publicity, promotion—and here assurance and energy case the Vassar success woman in an elephant-hide of certainties—a sort of proud flesh. This older Vassar career woman is nearly as familiar to American folklore as the intrepid young Portia or Rosalind she may at one time have passed for. Conscious of being set apart by a superior education,

confident of her powers in her own field of enterprise, she is impervious to the universe, which she dominates, both mentally and materially. On the campus, she is found at vocational conferences, panel discussions, committee meetings—she is one of those women who are always dominating, in an advisory capacity. In the world, she is met in political-action groups, consumers' leagues, on school boards and in charitable drives, at forums and roundtables. Married, almost professionally so, the mother of children, she is regarded as a force in her community or business, is respected and not always liked. Vassar, of course, has no patent on this model of the American woman, but there is a challenge in the Vassar atmosphere that makes her graduates feel that they owe it as a positive duty to the college and to the human community to be outstanding, aggressive, and secure.

Vocabulary

unorthodox, vivified, transcending, emancipate, dynamic, ricochets, proffer, conventional, grimaced, preconceptions, academic, heterodox, statistical, decreed, uniquely, poignantly, catered, conciliated, obdurately, *révoltée*, disenchanted, lyricism, iconoclastic, antipodal, incongruities, arresting, synonymous, succumb, intransigent, assurance, "proud flesh," intrepid, impervious, forums, patents

Questions

1. Why is the Vassar woman's "respect for the unorthodox" called "wistful"?
2. What distinguishes Vassar from the "progressive" colleges?
3. The teacher in the English class McCarthy visited was less active, probably, than some of the teachers you have known. Is her style appropriate to the Vassar idea of education?
4. Why is it the fate of the Vassar woman to be a "yearner and regretter"?
5. Does your college seem to impart a distinctive character to its graduates? If so, how would you describe that character? If not, why do you think it does not?

Topics for Writing

You Can Always Tell a —— Grad!

My Most Effective Professor

Of Studies

FRANCIS BACON (1561–1626), statesman and politician of Shakespeare's England, wrote utopian literature *(The New Atlantis)* and philosophical work *(Novum Organum)* as well as those compact explorations called the *Essays.*

1   Studies serve for delight, for ornament, and for ability. Their chief use for delight is in privateness and retiring; for ornament, is in discourse; and for ability, is in the judgment and disposition of business; for expert men can execute, and perhaps judge of particulars, one by one; but the general counsels, and the plots and marshalling of affairs come best from those that are learned. To spend too much time in studies is sloth; to use them too much for ornament is affectation; to make judgment wholly by their rules is the humour of a scholar. They perfect nature, and are perfected by experience; for natural abilities are like natural plants, that need pruning by study; and studies themselves do give forth directions too much at large, except they be bounded in by experience. Crafty men contemn studies, simple men admire them, and wise men use them; for they teach not their own use; but that is a wisdom without them and above them, won by observation. Read not to contradict and confute, nor to believe and take for granted, nor to find talk and discourse, but to weigh and consider. Some books are to be tasted, others to be swallowed, and some few to be chewed and digested; that is, some books are to be read only in parts; others to be read but not curiously; and some few to be read wholly, and with diligence and attention. Some books also may be read by deputy, and extracts made of them by others; but that would be only in the less important arguments and the meaner sort of books; else distilled books are, like common distilled waters, flashy things. Reading maketh a full man; conference a ready man; and writing an exact man. And, therefore, if a man write little, he had need have a great memory; if he confer little, he had need have a present wit; and if he read little, he had need have much cunning, to seem to know that he doth not. Histories make men wise; poets, witty; the mathematics, subtile; natural philosophy, deep; moral, grave; logic and rhetoric, able to contend: *Abeunt studia in mores!* [Studies develop into habits.] Nay, there is no stand or impediment in the wit but may be wrought out by fit studies; like as diseases of the body may have appropriate exercises. Bowling is good for the stone and reins [gonads and kidneys], shooting for the lungs and breast, gentle walking for the stomach, riding for the head, and the like. So if a man's wit be wandering, let him study the mathematics; for in demonstrations, if his wit be called away never so little, he must begin again. If his wit be not apt to distinguish or find differences, let him study the school-men; for they are *cymini sectores* [hairsplitters]! If he be not apt to beat over matters, and to call up one thing to prove and illustrate another, let him study the lawyers' cases. So every defect of the mind may have a special receipt.

Vocabulary

sloth, contemn, confute, subtile, receipt

Questions

1. Is this essay unified tightly enough to justify its single-paragraph form?
2. Does Bacon define *studies* or the *uses* of studies? Pick out illustrations.
3. *Delight, ornament, ability*—are these marks of the educated man today?
4. Why does writing make a man "exact"? Doesn't talking serve as well?
5. Natural philosophy in Bacon's time would include the sciences in our day. Does the study of science make one "deep"?
6. Bacon seems to think that education is a cure for moral and intellectual imbalances. Do you agree?
7. What does Bacon mean by "To spend too much time in studies is sloth"?
8. If you had to choose, would you select college courses that repair your weaknesses or build your present strengths? Why?

Topics for Writing

Writing Maketh a Tired Man

Sloth on Our Campus

My Greatest Educational Deficiency, Its Cause and Cure

What Is a University?

JOHN HENRY NEWMAN (1801–1890), an English scholar who converted to Roman Catholicism and eventually became a cardinal, wrote *The Idea of a University*, a complete philosophical outline for the Catholic university later established (on somewhat different lines) in Dublin. This selection from *The Rise and Progress of Universities* is a good example of the lucid style for which he was famous in his own time. It is still a model of clarity.

1   If I were asked to describe as briefly and popularly as I could, what a University was, I should draw my answer from its ancient designation of a *Studium Generale* or "School of Universal Learning." This description implies the assemblage of strangers from all parts in one spot;—*from all parts*; else, how will you find professors and students for every department of knowledge? and *in one spot*; else, how can there be any school at all? Accordingly, in its simple and rudimental form, it is a school of knowledge of every kind, consisting of teachers and learners from every quarter. Many things are requisite to complete and satisfy the idea embodied in this description; but such as this a University seems to be in its essence, a place for the communication and circulation of thought, by means of personal intercourse, through a wide extent of country.

2   There is nothing far-fetched or unreasonable in the idea thus presented to us; and if this be a University, then a University does but contemplate a necessity of our nature, and is but one specimen in a particular medium, out of many which might be adduced in others, of a provision for that necessity. Mutual education, in a large sense of the word, is one of the great and incessant occupations of human society, carried on partly with set purpose, and partly not. One generation forms another; and the existing generation is ever acting and reacting upon itself in the persons of its individual members. Now, in this process, books, I need scarcely say, that is, the *litera scripta*, are one special instrument. It is true; and emphatically so in this age. Considering the prodigious powers of the press, and how they are developed at this time in the never-intermitting issue of periodicals, tracts, pamphlets, works in series, and light literature, we must allow there never was a time which promised fairer for dispensing with every other means of information and instruction. What can we want more, you will say, for the intellectual education of the whole man, and for every man, than so exuberant and diversified and persistent a promulgation of all kinds of knowlege? Why, you will ask, need we go up to knowledge, when knowledge comes down to us? The Sibyl wrote her prophecies upon the leaves of the forest, and wasted them; but here such careless profusion might be prudently indulged, for it can be afforded without loss, in consequence of the almost fabulous fecundity of the instrument which these latter ages have invented. We have sermons in stones, and books in the running brooks; works larger and more com-

prehensive than those which have gained for ancients an immortality, issue forth every morning, and are projected onwards to the ends of the earth at the rate of hundreds of miles a day. Our seats are strewed, our pavements are powdered, with swarms of little tracts; and the very bricks of our city walls preach wisdom, by informing us by their placards where we can at once cheaply purchase it.

I allow all this, and much more; such certainly is our popular education, and   3
its effects are remarkable. Nevertheless, after all, even in this age, whenever men are really serious about getting what, in the language of trade, is called "a good article," when they aim at something precise, something refined, something really luminous, something really large, something choice, they go to another market; they avail themselves, in some shape or other, of the rival method, the ancient method, of oral instruction, of present communication between man and man, of teachers instead of learning, of the personal influence of a master, and the humble initiation of a disciple, and, in consequence, of great centres of pilgrimage and throng, which such a method of education necessarily involves. This, I think, will be found to hold good in all those departments or aspects of society, which possess an interest sufficient to bind men together, or to constitute what is called "a world." It holds in the political world, and in the high world, and in the religious world; and it holds also in the literary and scientific world.

If the actions of men may be taken as any test of their convictions, then we   4
have reason for saying this, viz.:—that the province and the inestimable benefit of the *litera scripta* is that of being a record of truth, and an authority of appeal, and an instrument of teaching in the hands of a teacher; but that, if we wish to become exact and fully furnished in any branch of knowledge which is diversified and complicated, we must consult the living man and listen to his living voice. I am not bound to investigate the cause of this, and anything I may say will, I am conscious, be short of its full analysis;—perhaps we may suggest, that no books can get through the number of minute questions which it is possible to ask on any extended subject, or can hit upon the very difficulties which are severally felt by each reader in succession. Or again, that no book can convey the special spirit and delicate peculiarities of its subject with that rapidity and certainty which attend on the sympathy of mind with mind, through the eyes, the look, the accent, and the manner, in casual expressions thrown off at the moment, and the unstudied turns of familiar conversation. But I am already dwelling too long on what is but an incidental portion of my main subject. Whatever be the cause, the fact is undeniable. The general principles of any study you may learn by books at home; but the detail, the colour, the tone, the air, the life which makes it live in us, you must catch all these from those in whom it lives already. You must imitate the student in French or German, who is not content with his grammar, but goes to Paris or Dresden: you must take example from the young artist, who aspires to visit the great Masters in Florence and in Rome. Till we have discovered some intellectual daguerreotype, which takes off the course of thought, and the form, lineaments, and features of truth, as completely and minutely, as the optical instrument reproduces the sensible object, we must come to the teachers of wisdom to learn wisdom, we must repair to the fountain, and drink there. Portions of it may go from thence to the ends of the

earth by means of books; but the fulness is in one place alone. It is in such assemblages and congregations of intellect that books themselves, the masterpieces of human genius, are written, or at least originated.

5   The principle on which I have been insisting is so obvious, and instances in point are so ready, that I should think it tiresome to proceed with the subject, except that one or two illustrations may serve to explain my own language about it, which may not have done justice to the doctrine which it has been intended to enforce.

6   For instance, the polished manners and high-bred bearing which are so difficult of attainment, and so strictly personal when attained,—which are so much admired in society, from society are acquired. All that goes to constitute a gentleman,—the carriage, gait, address, gestures, voice; the ease, the self-possession, the courtesy, the power of conversing, the talent of not offending; the lofty principle, the delicacy of thought, the happiness of expression, the taste and propriety, the generosity and forbearance, the candour and consideration, the openness of hand;—these qualities, some of them come by nature, some of them may be found in any rank, some of them are a direct precept of Christianity; but the full assemblage of them, bound up in the unity of an individual character, do we expect they can be learned from books? are they not necessarily acquired, where they are to be found, in high society? The very nature of the case leads us to say so; you cannot fence without an antagonist, nor challenge all comers in disputation before you have supported a thesis; and in like manner, it stands to reason, you cannot learn to converse till you have the world to converse with; you cannot unlearn your natural bashfulness, or awkwardness, or stiffness, or other besetting deformity, till you serve your time in some school of manners. Well, and is it not so in matter of fact? The metropolis, the court, the great houses of the land, are the centres to which at stated times the country comes up, as to shrines of refinement and good taste; and then in due time the country goes back again home, enriched with a portion of the social accomplishments, which those very visits serve to call out and heighten in the gracious dispensers of them. We are unable to conceive how the "gentlemanlike" can otherwise be maintained; and maintained in this way it is.

7   And now a second instance: and here too I am going to speak without personal experience of the subject I am introducing. I admit I have not been in Parliament, any more than I have figured in the *beau monde*; yet I cannot but think that statesmanship, as well as high breeding, is learned, not by books, but in certain centres of education. If it be not presumption to say so, Parliament puts a clever man *au courant* with politics and affairs of state in a way surprising to himself. A member of the Legislature, if tolerably observant, begins to see things with new eyes, even though his views undergo no change. Words have a meaning now, and ideas a reality, such as they had not before. He hears a vast deal in public speeches and private conversation, which is never put into print. The bearings of measures and events, the action of parties, and the persons of friends and enemies, are brought out to the man who is in the midst of them with a distinctness, which the most diligent perusal of newspapers will fail to impart to them. It is access to the fountain-heads of political wisdom and experience, it is daily intercourse, of one kind or another, with the multitude who go up to them, it is familiarity with

business, it is access to the contributions of fact and opinion thrown together by many witnesses from many quarters, which does this for him. However, I need not account for a fact, to which it is sufficient to appeal; that the Houses of Parliament and the atmosphere around them are a sort of University of politics.

As regards the world of science, we find a remarkable instance of the principle which I am illustrating, in the periodical meetings for its advance, which have arisen in the course of the last twenty years, such as the British Association. Such gatherings would to many persons appear at first sight simply preposterous. Above all subjects of study, Science is conveyed, is propagated, by books, or by private teaching; experiments and investigations are conducted in silence; discoveries are made in solitude. What have philosophers to do with festive celebrities, and panegyrical solemnities with mathematical and physical truth? Yet on a closer attention to the subject, it is found that not even scientific thought can dispense with the suggestions, the instruction, the stimulus, the sympathy, the intercourse with mankind on a large scale, which such meetings secure. A fine time of year is chosen, when days are long, skies are bright, the earth smiles, and all nature rejoices; a city or town is taken by turns, of ancient name or modern opulence, where buildings are spacious and hospitality hearty. The novelty of place and circumstance, the excitement of strange, or the refreshment of well-known faces, the majesty of rank or of genius, the amiable charities of men pleased both with themselves and with each other; the elevated spirits, the circulation of thought, the curiosity; the morning sections, the outdoor exercise, the well-furnished, well-earned board, the not ungraceful hilarity, the evening circle; the brilliant lecture, the discussions or collisions or guesses of great men one with another, the narratives of scientific processes, of hopes, disappointments, conflicts, and successes, the splendid eulogistic orations; these and the like constituents of the annual celebration, are considered to do something real and substantial for the advance of knowledge which can be done in no other way. Of course they can but be occasional; they answer to the annual Act, or Commencement, or Commemoration of a University, not to its ordinary condition; but they are of a University nature; and I can well believe in their utility. They issue in the promotion of a certain living and, as it were, bodily communication of knowledge from one to another, of a general interchange of ideas, and a comparison and adjustment of science with science, of an enlargement of mind, intellectual and social, of an ardent love of the particular study, which may be chosen by each individual, and a noble devotion to its interests.

Such meetings, I repeat, are but periodical, and only partially represent the idea of a University. The bustle and whirl which are their usual concomitants, are in ill keeping with the order and gravity of earnest intellectual education. We desiderate means of instruction which involve no interruption of our ordinary habits; nor need we seek it long, for the natural course of things brings it about, while we debate over it. In every great country, the metropolis itself becomes a sort of necessary University, whether we will or no. As the chief city is the seat of the court, of high society, of politics, and of law, so as a matter of course is it the seat of letters also; and at this time, for a long term of years, London and Paris are in fact and in operation Universities, though in Paris its famous University is no more, and in London a University scarcely exists except as a board of administration. The newspapers, magazines, reviews, journals, and periodicals of all kinds, the publishing trade, the libraries, museums, and academies there found, the learned and scientific societies, necessarily invest it with the functions of a University; and that atmosphere of intellect, which in a former age hung over Oxford or Bologna or Salamanca, has, with the change of times, moved away to the centre of civil government. Thither come up youths from all parts of the country, the students of law, medicine, and the fine arts, and the *employés* and *attachés* of literature. There they live, as chance determines; and they are satisfied with their temporary home, for they find in it all that was promised to them there. They have not come in vain, as far as their own object in coming is concerned. They have not learned any particular religion, but they have learned their own particular profession well. They have, moreover, become acquainted with the habits, manners, and opinions of their place of sojourn, and done their part in maintaining the tradition of them. We cannot then be without virtual Universities; a metropolis is such: the simple question is, whether the education sought and given should be based on principle, formed upon rule, directed to the highest ends, or left to the random succession of masters and schools, one after another, with a melancholy waste of thought and an extreme hazard of truth.

10   Religious teaching itself affords us an illustration of our subject to a certain point. It does not indeed seat itself merely in centres of the world; this is impossible from the nature of the case. It is intended for the many not the few; its subject matter is truth necessary for us, not truth recondite and rare; but it concurs in the principle of a University so far as this, that its great instrument, or rather organ, has ever been that which nature prescribes in all education, the personal presence of a teacher, or, in theological language, Oral Tradition. It is the living voice, the breathing form, the expressive countenance, which preaches, which catechises. Truth, a subtle, invisible, manifold spirit, is poured into the mind of the scholar by his eyes and ears, through his affections, imagination, and reason; it is poured into his mind and is sealed up there in perpetuity, by propounding and repeating it, by questioning and requestioning, by correcting and explaining, by progressing and then recurring to first principles, by all those ways which are implied in the word "catechising." In the first ages, it was a work of long time; months, sometimes years, were devoted to the arduous task of disabusing the mind of the incipient Christian of its pagan errors, and of moulding it upon the Christian faith. The Scriptures indeed were at hand for the study of those who could avail themselves of them; but St. Irenaeus does not hesitate to speak of whole races, who had been converted to Christianity, without being able to read them. To be unable to read or write was in those times no evidence of want of learning: the hermits of the desert were, in this sense of the word, illiterate; yet the great St. Anthony, though he knew not letters, was a match in disputation for the learned philosophers who came to try him. Didymus again, the great Alexandrian theologian, was blind. The ancient discipline, called the *Disciplina Arcani,* involved the same principle. The more sacred

doctrines of Revelation were not committed to books but passed on by successive tradition. The teaching on the Blessed Trinity and the Eucharist appears to have been so handed down for some hundred years; and when at length reduced to writing, it has filled many folios, yet has not been exhausted.

But I have said more than enough in illustration; I end as I began;—a University is a place of concourse, whither students come from every quarter for every kind of knowledge. You cannot have the best of every kind everywhere; you must go to some great city or emporium for it. There you have all the choicest productions of nature and art all together, which you find each in its own separate place elsewhere. All the riches of the land, and of the earth, are carried up thither; there are the best markets, and there the best workmen. It is the centre of trade, the supreme court of fashion, the umpire of rival talents, and the standard of things rare and precious. It is the place for seeing galleries of first-rate pictures, and for hearing wonderful voices and performers of transcendent skill. It is the place for great preachers, great orators, great nobles, great statesmen. In the nature of things, greatness and unity go together; excellence implies a centre. And such, for the third or fourth time, is a University; I hope I do not weary out the reader by repeating it. It is the place to which a thousand schools make contributions; in which the intellect may safely range and speculate, sure to find its equal in some antagonist activity, and its judge in the tribunal of truth. It is a place where inquiry is pushed forward, and discoveries verified and perfected, and rashness rendered innocuous, and error exposed, by the collision of mind with mind, and knowledge with knowledge. It is the place where the professor becomes eloquent, and is a missionary and a preacher, displaying his science in its most complete and most winning form, pouring it forth with the zeal of enthusiasm, and lighting up his own love of it in the breasts of his hearers. It is the place where the catechist makes good his ground as he goes, treading in the truth day by day into the ready memory, and wedging and tightening it into the expanding reason. It is a place which wins the admiration of the young by its celebrity, kindles the affections of the middle-aged by its beauty, and rivets the fidelity of the old by its associations. It is a seat of wisdom, a light of the world, a minister of the faith, an Alma Mater of the rising generation. It is this and a great deal more, and demands a somewhat better head and hand than mine to describe it well.

Such is a University in its idea and in its purpose; such in good measure has it before now been in fact. Shall it ever be again? We are going forward in the strength of the Cross, under the patronage of the Blessed Virgin, in the name of St. Patrick, to attempt it.

Vocabulary

rudimental, promulgation, Sibyl, fecundity, placards, luminous, disputation, *beau monde,* panegyrical, eulogistic, periodical, desiderate, transcendent

Questions

1. Is the entire first paragraph a definition of *university*?
2. In his next-to-last paragraph, Newman defines *university* in different words. Which definition do you prefer? Why?
3. The middle of Newman's essay proceeds by analogies to manners, statesmanship, and science. Are these analogies effective or needlessly repetitive?
4. Although he prizes the written word, Newman argues that oral teaching, "present communication between man and man," is necessary. Can televised instruction supply that need? Is television, perhaps, the "intellectual daguerreotype" to replace person-to-person learning?
5. Does the college lecture supply that need?
6. "In every great country, the metropolis itself becomes a sort of necessary University . . . . " Do you agree?
7. Have America's largest universities, those that enroll 25,000 or more students, become the intellectual metropolises of today?
8. How much of your education is due to association with "students come from every quarter for every kind of knowledge"?

Topics for Writing

The Collision of Mind with Mind: Education or Confusion?

Why I Came to Dear Old Alma Mater

I Fell Off the Roof One Day
(A View of the Black University)

NIKKI GIOVANNI   (1943–) is an educator as well as a poet and short-story writer.

It's obvious that we need a Black university. Someone asked a Cornell student   1
why the Black women wanted to live apart from the white girls. She answered that
one night a sister was straightening her hair and a white girl reported the sister for
smoking pot. The straightening comb is a drug but not marijuana. We need to get
away from them. It would appear to some that a Black university is already in
existence. Wherever Black people gather, feeling and information are being transmitted. That's all a school does. What some are asking for is a way to certify that
feeling and knowledge. It's for us to follow our traditions. Ever try to organize in a
Black neighborhood? The first thing that must be done is that you must live there,
as the residents live there. You must know the language and life style of the people.
You must, if you are to be successful, be the people. Walking into a strange
neighborhood is like applying for a job. The first thing the residents want to know is
how long you been here; how long you gonna stay? That's asking you for
certification. When you want to join church they ask, when did you find Jesus?
They ask you to certify yourself. When you join the Nation you must learn lessons
which if successfully completed will certify you to become a member. No one asks
the mayor, the governor, or the local presiding Mafia official for permission to take
care of this level of business. Yet we somehow assume that we aren't qualified to run
our schools, own and operate our own apartment buildings, run our health and
educational programs. It is for us to certify ourselves. Course it's no big thing.
Logically speaking we are the only people who want it done correctly for us anyway.
It's bound to be better if it's Black. Maybe we'll put a big poster up in Harlem and
train lights on it a thousand times brighter than those advertising *Hair* saying IT'S
BOUND TO BE BETTER—IF IT'S BLACK. That should be the first lesson taught at any
Black institute.

The questions raised about the Black university center around things like   2
should we try to build buildings or should we function in any way we can. In
Harlem, I'm told there are five hundred churches and three hundred bars. To me
that makes eight hundred school buildings—to be used as we see fit. It would be a
beautiful sight to see a sign hanging from Small's Paradise Lounge, AFRO-AMERICAN
HISTORY FROM 1664 TO 1886. 8 A.M. TO 4 P.M. DAILY. PROFESSOR LERONE BENNET
GUEST LECTURER THIS WEEK. Or to pass Abbyssinia Baptist Church's sign: 11:50-
3:35 DR. MATTHEW WALKER LECTURING ON THE ALIMENTARY CANAL AS IT RESPONDS
TO THE LIVER DURING EMOTIONAL CRISIS. Or Andre's, where we learn that FRIDAY
AND SATURDAY ONLY LEWIS ALCINDOR WILL GIVE DEMONSTRATIONS OF DEFENSIVE

PLAYING DURING THE LAST THREE MINUTES OF A TIGHT GAME. Or at the Apollo, REVEREND JAMES CLEVELAND IN DEMONSTRATION LECTURE OF WHAT MUSIC HAS MEANT TO HIM. There will be three classes daily. Register now. Yeah, that's the Black University, and we ought to be putting it in motion. We can do it all over the nation; we can move people around that need to be moved around and have the people in local positions who can function. We can set our standards and give our own degrees—if we want to deal with that kind of thing. A piece of sheepskin is no more and quite a lot less than lambswool. A few words written in a dead language, either English or Latin, never said that you know only what someone tried to teach you. Qualification is based on action and functioning—nothing else. We need and will continue to need a strong apprentice program. We will have to take our pupils with us teaching as well as learning. The people will always decide the relevancy of what we're doing. When we hear complaints we will listen and update. Where there is no response we will replace. And we will have our university. Which will be a total involvement with a total community—wherever these communities are found. There's no need to worry that we haven't invented a bomb; we will learn that we must control the mentalities that do. It doesn't matter that we aren't transplanting hearts; our medicine will bring babies into the world, keep them well, and let the sick and dying die in dignity. It certainly doesn't matter that we don't own IBM or something that inane; our computations will come back to earth for earth people and earth people will be able to compute. The Black University already exists; it's for us to recognize it, not create it. And this is good. Our work is crystal-clear. The question is, are we teachers ready to learn—are we leaders ready to follow?

Vocabulary

certification, alimentary, apprentice, relevancy, inane, computations

Questions

1. Is Ms. Giovanni's definition of a university stated or implied? Can you express it in a single sentence?
2. Why should the first lesson taught at a Black institution be "It's Bound to Be Better—If It's Black"? Do you agree?
3. In what sense does her Black University already exist?
4. Do you agree that all a school does is transmit "feeling and information"? If you do not agree, explain why you think the statement false.
5. She asserts that teachers should learn from students, leaders from followers. Is this mere rhetoric, or do you see some truth in what she says?

Topics for Writing

What Teachers Can Learn from Students

It Won't Work, Ms. Giovanni

The Common Sense Beneath the Rage

An Apology for Idlers

ROBERT LOUIS STEVENSON (1850–1894) wrote everything from lovely poems for children, *A Child's Garden of Verses*, to classic adventures like *Kidnapped*, to the tingling ghost story, "Markheim." The easygoing attitude expressed so artfully here is typical of the English personal essay, of which he was a master.

The greatest difficulty with most subjects is to do them well; therefore, please 1
to remember this is an apology. It is certain that much may be judiciously argued in favour of diligence; only there is something to be said against it, and that is what, on the present occasion, I have to say. To state one argument is not necessarily to be deaf to all others, and that a man has written a book of travels in Montenegro, is no reason why he should never have been to Richmond.

It is surely beyond a doubt that people should be a good deal idle in youth. For 2
though here and there a Lord Macaulay may escape from school honors with all his wits about him, most boys pay so dear for their medals that they never afterwards have a shot in their locker, and begin the world bankrupt. And the same holds true during all the time a lad is educating himself, or suffering others to educate him. It must have been a very foolish old gentleman who addressed Johnson at Oxford in these words: "Young man, ply your book diligently now, and acquire a stock of knowledge; for when years come upon you, you will find that poring upon books will be but an irksome task." The old gentleman seems to have been unaware that many other things besides reading grow irksome, and not a few become impossible, by the time a man has to use spectacles and cannot walk without a stick. Books are good enough in their own way, but they are a mighty bloodless substitute for life. It seems a pity to sit, like the Lady of Shalott, peering into a mirror, with your back turned on all the bustle and glamour of reality. And if a man reads very hard, as the old anecdote reminds us, he will have little time for thoughts.

If you look back on your own education, I am sure it will not be the full, vivid, 3
instructive hours of truantry that you regret; you would rather cancel some lacklustre periods between sleep and waking in the class. For my own part, I have attended a good many lectures in my time. I still remember that the spinning of a top is a case of Kinetic Stability. I still remember that Emphyteusis is not a disease, nor Stillicide a crime. But though I would not willingly part with such scraps of science, I do not set the same store by them as by certain other odds and ends that I came by in the open street while I was playing truant. This is not the moment to dilate on that mighty place of education, which was the favourite school of Dickens and Balzac, and turns out yearly many inglorious masters in the Science of the Aspects of Life. Suffice it to say this: if a lad does not learn in the streets, it is because he has no faculty of learning. Nor is the truant always in the streets, for if he prefers, he may go out by the gardened suburbs into the country. He may pitch on some tuft

of lilacs over a burn, and some innumerable pipes to the tune of the water on the stones. A bird will sing in the thicket. And there he may fall into a vein of kindly thought, and see things in a new perspective. Why, if this be not education, what is? We may conceive Mr. Worldly Wiseman accosting such an one, and the conversation that should thereupon ensue:—

"How now, young fellow, what dost thou here?"

"Truly, sir, I take mine ease."

"Is not this the hour of the class? and should'st thou not be plying thy Book with diligence, to the end thou mayest obtain knowledge?"

"Nay, but thus also I follow after Learning, by your leave."

"Learning, quotha! After what fashion, I pray thee? Is it mathematics?"

"No, to be sure."

"Is it metaphysics?"

"Nor that."

"Is it some language?"

"Nay, it is no language."

"Is it a trade?"

"Nor a trade neither."

"Why, then, what is't?"

4   "Indeed, sir, as a time may soon come for me to go upon Pilgrimage, I am desirous to note what is commonly done by persons in my case, and where are the ugliest Sloughs and Thickets on the Road; as also, what manner of Staff is of the best service. Moreover, I lie here, by this water, to learn by root-of-heart a lesson which my master teaches me to call Peace, or Contentment."

5   Hereupon Mr. Worldly Wiseman was much commoved with passion, and shaking his cane with a very threatful countenance, broke forth upon this wise: "Learning, quotha!" said he; "I would have all such rogues scourged by the Hangman!"

6   And so he would go his way, ruffling out his cravat with a crackle of starch, like a turkey when it spread its feathers.

7   Now this, of Mr. Wiseman's, is the common opinion. A fact is not called a fact, but a piece of gossip, if it does not fall into one of your scholastic categories. An inquiry must be in some acknowledged direction, with a name to go by; or else you are not inquiring at all, only lounging; and the work-house is too good for you. It is supposed that all knowledge is at the bottom of a well, or the far end of a telescope. Sainte-Beuve, as he grew older, came to regard all experience as a single great book, in which to study for a few years ere we go hence; and it seemed all one to him whether you should read in Chapter xx., which is the differential calculus, or in Chapter xxxix., which is hearing the band play in the gardens. As a matter of fact, an intelligent person, looking out of his eyes and hearkening in his ears, with a smile on his face all the time, will get more true education than many another in a life of heroic vigils. There is certainly some chill and arid knowledge to be found upon the summits of formal and laborious science; but it is all round about you, and for the trouble of looking, that you will acquire the warm and palpitating facts of

life. While others are filling their memory with a lumber of words, one-half of which they will forget before the week be out, your truant may learn some really useful art: to play the fiddle, to know a good cigar, or to speak with ease and opportunity to all varieties of men. Many who have "plied their book diligently," and know all about some one branch or another of accepted lore, come out of the study with an ancient and owl-like demeanour, and prove dry, stockish, and dyspeptic in all the better and brighter parts of life. Many make a large fortune, who remain underbred and pathetically stupid to the last. And meantime there goes the idler, who began life along with them—by your leave, a different picture. He has had time to take care of his health and his spirits; he has been a good deal in the open air, which is the most salutary of all things for both body and mind; and if he has never read the great Book in very recondite places, he has dipped into it and skimmed it over to excellent purpose. Might not the student afford some Hebrew roots, and the business man some of his half-crowns, for a share of the idler's knowledge of life at large, and Art of Living? Nay, and the idler has another and more important quality than these. I mean his wisdom. He who has much looked on at the childish satisfaction of other people in their hobbies, will regard his own with only a very ironical indulgence. He will not be heard among the dogmatists. He will have a great and cool allowance for all sorts of people and opinions. If he finds no out-of-the-way truths, he will identify himself with no very burning falsehood. His way takes him along a by-road, not much frequented, but very even and pleasant, which is called Commonplace Lane, and leads to the Belvedere of Commonsense. Thence he shall command an agreeable, if no very noble prospect; and while others behold the East and West, the Devil and the Sunrise, he will be contentedly aware of a sort of morning hour upon all sublunary things, with an army of shadows running speedily and in many different directions into the great daylight of Eternity. The shadows and the generations, the shrill doctors and the plangent wars, go by into ultimate silence and emptiness; but underneath all this, a man may see, out of the Belvedere windows, much green and peaceful landscape; many firelit parlours; good people laughing, drinking, and making love as they did before the Flood or the French Revolution; and the old shepherd telling his tale under the hawthorn.

Vocabulary

kinetic, emphyteusis, stillicide, quotha, metaphysics, sloughs, work-house, dyspeptic, recondite, indulgence, plangent, belvedere

Questions

1. Would *loafing* be an adequate substitute for *idling* here?
2. Stevenson sets up straw men to knock down in an effort to persuade the reader

that "idling" is a legitimate mode of education. Pick out two examples. What makes them easy to knock over?

3. This informal essay ends on a poetic note, "the old shepherd telling his tale under the hawthorn." It is a calculated effect. Try to analyze it.
4. Do you see a difference between knowledge and learning? Can you give examples of the difference?
5. What skills would the Idler be able to offer a prospective employer?

Topics for Writing

The Idler vs. the Workaholic

Education through Idling: A Personal Experience

The Idler Applies to Corporation XYZ

When I Heard the Learn'd Astronomer

WALT WHITMAN (1819–1892), journalist and revolutionary free-verse poet, was self-taught in most things. *Leaves of Grass* (1855) shocked Americans both by its free form and by its "vulgar" inclusiveness. In rejecting the astronomer's lecture for a first-hand look at the stars, Whitman is only following the advice of his intellectual father, Ralph Waldo Emerson.

When I heard the learn'd astronomer,
When the proofs, the figures, were ranged in columns before me,
When I was shown the charts and diagrams, to add, divide, and
    measure them,
When I sitting heard the astronomer where he lectured with much   5
    applause in the lecture-room,
How soon unaccountable I became tired and sick,
Till rising and gliding out I wander'd off by myself,
In the mystical moist night-air, and from time to time,
Look'd up in perfect silence at the stars.   10

Vocabulary

unaccountable, mystical

Questions

1. When Whitman says "unaccountable," does he mean it? If not, why does he say it?
2. What is the effect of Whitman's repeated pattern of "when" clauses?
3. Is this poem an attack on a dull lecturer or on the process of formal education?

Topics for Writing

What Whitman Was Rebelling Against

If Whitman Were a Freshman Today

Is It Enough to Roll with the Times?

ROBERT A. GOLDWIN (1922–) shows a concern over the rush toward education tailored to the latest trends that is shared by many. The question is classic and, for young people naturally concerned about their future, serious: education for living or to make a living?

1   Many private institutions of higher education around the country are in danger. Not all will be saved, and perhaps not all deserve to be saved. There are low-quality schools just as there are low-quality businesses. We have no obligation to save them simply because they exist.

2   But many thriving institutions that deserve to continue are threatened. They are doing a fine job educationally, but they are caught in a financial squeeze, with no way to reduce rising costs or increase revenues significantly. Raising tuition doesn't bring in more revenue, for each time tuition goes up, the enrollment goes down, or the amount that must be given away in student aid goes up. Schools are bad businesses, whether public or private, not usually because of mismanagement but because of the nature of the enterprise. They lose money on every customer, and they can go bankrupt either from too few students or too many students. Even a very good college is a very bad business. That has always been true.

3   It is such colleges, thriving but threatened, I worry about. Low enrollment is not their chief problem. Even with full enrollments, they may go under. Efforts to save them, and preferably to keep them private, are a national necessity. There is no basis for arguing that private schools are inherently better than public schools. Examples to the contrary abound. Anyone can name state universities and colleges that rank as the finest in the nation and the world. It is now inevitable that public institutions will be dominant, and therefore diversity is a national necessity. Diversity in the way we support schools tends to give us a healthy diversity in the forms of education. In an imperfect society such as ours, uniformity of education throughout the nation could be dangerous. In an imperfect society, diversity is a positive good. Ardent supporters of public higher education know the importance of sustaining private higher education.

4   Diversity is a familiar argument, and a sound one, for sustaining a mixture of private and public educational institutions. But let me suggest another, perhaps less familiar argument: There are public elements and private elements in different kinds of education, striving toward different educational goals. Vocational or career education programs are designed to give the student salable skills and enable him to find a useful job. The public has an interest because skills are needed to keep our economy going, and so there is a public reason to provide such training. But the student's new skills are his exclusively, to sell as he chooses. This private aspect gives him a private reason to pay for the training. We get the benefit of his skills; he gets the income for himself.

Another element of education might be called civic education. One important function of schools is development of an understanding of government and of the rights and duties of citizens. Especially in a democratic republic such as ours, citizens must be skilled in understanding the powers of government, and how those powers must be limited if our fundamental rights are to be secured. We are in danger if our many governments do too much or too little, and the only way to find the moderate middle ground is through education.

The public has a very great stake in this task of civic education. If one is skilled in good citizenship, fellow citizens benefit at least as much. Is it the business of colleges to train good citizens? I think it is, at a higher and more discerning level than in grade schools, which means a more questioning and challenging level. Undergraduates should inquire into the nature of the American government, its past, its present, its future—not as in graduate programs, from the detached viewpoint of the political scientist or the professional historian, but from the viewpoint of the concerned citizen who is part of a living community facing problems.

There is a third element of education that is harder to name and that cannot easily be classified in terms of the benefits—who gets them or what they are. Some call these studies valueless. I call them invaluable. I mean those skills called the liberal arts. We don't often think of liberal studies as connected with skills, but in fact the liberal skills are the highest and hardest skills.

There is a story that Euclid was giving a first geometry lesson to a young man, demonstrating the first theorem of geometry, the construction of an equilateral triangle. When he finished, the young man asked, "But Euclid, what shall I gain by learning such things?"

Now consider how Euclid might have answered. He might have said, "Learn this and the theorems that follow, and when you get to the end of the first book of only forty-seven theorems, you will learn the Pythagorean theorem, which depends on this first theorem. And with that Pythagorean theorem you will have the basis of physics, and vectors of forces, and be able to design a bridge that will not fall down when the chariots cross. And with that theorem you will have the basis of trigonometry, which you can use to survey your next real estate purchase. That theorem also starts you on an understanding of irrational numbers, a great advance in number theory." Euclid might have said all of that—and more—to explain the practical benefits that could flow, and have flowed, from studying his first theorem.

Instead, Euclid turned to another in the group and said, "Give this man a coin since he must show a profit for everything he learns."

Why should he have given such a scornful response to that question? My guess is that Euclid was greatly disappointed in the young man because he did not see at once that mathematics is a liberal skill, in addition to being a powerful practical skill. Euclid hoped that the young man's heart would be gladdened, his spirit enlivened, his soul lifted, his mind expanded at the first experience of geometrical proof.

We call such studies "the humanities," because when we engage in them we discover something extraordinary about ourselves. We discover how exciting being human can be. We find we can develop very special skills that imitate the Creator himself, for we too can make new worlds, not out of nothing, but with nothing more than a pencil, a straight edge, and a mind. Such humanistic skills are also called liberal because they free us from the restraint of our material existence and let us soar as free men and women in the realm of the mind.

13   In a recent speech, Terrel H. Bell, U.S. Commissioner of Education, gave some advice to the leaders of small private colleges, from a different point of view than mine. He very properly said first that as U.S. Education Commissioner he had no right to tell anyone how to run his college. In fact, he said, there is a law against it. But he did feel that he had a personal responsibility to speak out candidly and exercise some leadership. I, of course, write on the same basis, expressing my own opinion, seeking to contribute to thinking on this vital question.

14   His message was that private colleges must "roll with the times" if they are to survive. The college that devotes itself "totally and unequivocally to the liberal arts today is just kidding itself." There is a "duty to provide our students also with salable skills. We are facing the worst economic situation that this country has seen since the end of World War II, with an unemployment rate of over eight percent. To send young men and women into today's world armed only with Aristotle, Freud, and Hemingway is like sending a lamb into the lion's den. It is to delude them as well as ourselves. But if we give young men and women a useful skill, we give them not only the means to earn a good living, but also the opportunity to do something constructive and useful for society. Moreover, these graduates will experience some of those valuable qualities that come with meaningful work—self-respect, self-confidence, independence."

15   At first glance it would seem that Commissioner Bell means that the study of liberal arts is a useless luxury we cannot afford in hard times. But I don't think that is his meaning. I think he is criticizing those who send students into the world of work without skills. There are, unfortunately, schools in which students do not develop useful skills, especially skills of analytical thinking and experimenting and calculating. I agree that it is unfair to students, and to all of us, just as Commissioner Bell says, to leave them to seek jobs in such an unprepared state.

16   But there is a problem in speaking of "salable skills." What skills are salable? Right now, skills for making automobiles are not highly salable, but they have been for decades and might be again. Skills in teaching are not now as salable as they were during the past twenty years, and the population charts indicate they may not be soon again. Home construction skills are another example of varying salability, as the job market fluctuates.

17   The first difficulty, then, is that if one wants to build a curriculum exclusively on what is salable, one will have to make the courses very short and change them very often, in order to keep up with the rapid changes in the job market. But will not the effort be in vain? In very few things can we be sure of future salability, and in a society where people are free to study what they want, and work where they want, and invest as they want, there is no way to keep supply and demand in labor in perfect accord.

18   A school that devotes itself totally and unequivocally to salable skills, especially in a time of high unemployment, sending young men and women into the world

armed with only a narrow range of skills, is also sending lambs into the lion's den. If those people gain nothing more from their studies than supposedly salable skills, and can't make the sale because of changes in the job market, they have been cheated. But if those skills were more than salable, if study made them better citizens and made them happier to be human beings, they have not been cheated. They will find some kind of job soon enough. It might even turn out that those humanizing and liberating skills are salable. Flexibility, an ability to change and learn new things, is a valuable skill. People who have learned how to learn can learn outside of school. That is where most of us have learned to do what we do, not in school. Learning to learn is one of the highest liberal skills.

There is more to living than earning a living, but many earn good livings by   19
the liberal skills of analyzing, experimenting, discussing, reading, and writing. Skills that are always in demand are those of a mind trained to think and imagine and express itself.

When the confidence of some is shaken, and many are confused about the   20
direction the nation ought to follow in a new world situation, then civic education is more important than ever. And when the foundations of Western civilization are being challenged, and resolution seems to falter because many people are not sure what we are defending and how we ought to defend it, then it seems to me we ought not to abandon liberal studies, but rather the reverse: We ought to redouble our commitment to that study, as if our lives depended on it.

Any college worthy of itself must set its sights higher than to "roll with the   21
times." It must strive to make the times roll our way. And only if we understand our time and try to shape it and make it conform to what is right and best, are we doing what we are capable of doing. Perhaps that is the right way to deal with the times— with daring and class and style—as befits a truly great people.

We have always known that America made no sense as just another nation, as   22
just one more power in the long historical parade. We have always known that we must stand for something special, or we don't stand at all. Without such a special commitment to liberty and justice for all, can America survive except perhaps under the most severe sort of dictatorship? What else can hold together such a vast and diverse territory and people? Liberal studies of human nature and the nature of things in general are not luxuries for us, but matters of life and death, and certainly a matter of our political liberty, which should be as dear to us as our lives.

Vocabulary

inherently, diversity

Questions

1. This is an argument in defense of liberal education. Does Goldwin define *liberal education*, or does he assume that you know its nature?

2. What definition of the college is implied in the sixth paragraph? Is it a partial definition or the clue to a complete one? Does it include the idea of "a liberal skill"?
3. What is the use of his story about Euclid and the "practical" student? Do you agree that "schools are bad businesses"?
4. Is "liberal skill" a contradiction in terms?
5. Compare Goldwin's notion of liberal with Newman's.
6. Is anyone sent into postgraduation life "armed only with Aristotle, Freud, and Hemingway"? Does this imply that you are "armed with" only the courses you take?
7. To what degree are your personal academic choices influenced by your eventual entry into the job market?

Topics for Writing

Liberal Skill: A Contradiction

Liberal Skill: No Contradiction

Education for Life or for Making a Living?

Goldwin and Newman on "Liberal"

3

Comparing and Contrasting /
The Eye of the Traveler

Comparing and contrasting are such natural habits of mind that we sometimes forget how important they are in our lives. From infancy we notice similarities (the dog is like the cat—both are warm, have tails, run) and differences (the dog is different from the cat—one barks, one meows; one wags its tail in pleasure, the other in anger). When we notice the similarities between things, we are comparing them; when we notice the differences, we are contrasting.

We learn by comparing and contrasting the new and unfamiliar with the old and familiar. We see a citron for the first time. What is it like? Well, we notice that it bears some similarity to a lemon: it is pale yellow and it has a rind. On the other hand, we notice that the citron is larger and more acrid than the lemon.

Observation is the key. The more careful and detailed the observations, the more effectively can the reader see similarities and differences in the subject under discussion.

Writers employ two basic techniques when they compare or contrast. Sometimes they will deal with, say, two people point by point: their heights first, then their ages, their occupations, and so on. But at other times, the writer may find it better to describe the first person completely, then move on to the second, and finally emphasize similarities and differences in a summary. The choice of technique is just another of the decisions writers habitually make.

Travel presents rich opportunities for comparison and contrast. James Michener gives a balanced view of two countries he knows well, but many of the authors in this chapter are seeing places for the first time and are writing for people who haven't seen them at all. In these cases, they often shed light on the unfamiliar by setting it against the familiar. Frances Trollope depends largely, and Hippolyte Taine somewhat, upon this method, whereas Charles Dickens leans much less upon this technique. Mary Manning uses the theatre to highlight the contrast between Belfast and her ordinary world, and Mark Twain develops his contrast by creating an imaginary traveler returned to Rome from a visit to the New World. We see something of the world through the eyes of seasoned travel writers, and in this way, wistfully or otherwise, we can compare strange places with our own.

Portugal and Spain

JAMES A. MICHENER (1907–), the author of panoramic novels like *Chesapeake, Hawaii,* and *Centennial,* is a wide traveler and careful observer. This selection is from *Iberia,* published in 1968.

1   I am often asked to compare Portugal and Spain, and the simple truth seems to be that whichever of these two countries one visits first continues as his preference. No one can be more energetic in defense of a new-found land than the Englishman, Frenchman or American who has visited Portugal first and then moved on to Spain: he loves the first and is never easy in the second. I discovered this when I traveled westward across Spain with an American couple who had worked for some years at our embassy in Lisboa, for it was touching to watch how apprehensive they were of all things Spanish and how their spirits revived the closer they got to their beloved Portugal. "We wouldn't feel safe drinking Spanish water, thank you. We've been all through Portugal and we've never seen villages as dirty as those in Spain. Doesn't anyone have paint in this country? The fact is, we feel safe in Portugal but in Spain you never know. Our police are so much better." As we approached the western border of Spain it became a question of whether we should take our lunch in Spanish Badajoz, which I preferred because of the great seafood zarzuela I knew was waiting, or press on to Portuguese Elvas, which lay just across the border. "Oh," my embassy friends said, "we'd never want to eat in a Spanish restaurant if a clean Portuguese one were nearby."

2   Well, the first of the two countries that I saw was Spain and my affection has always rested there. It was not until my trip with the Lisboa couple that I saw the peninsula through Portuguese eyes, and when I did this I had to admit that of the two countries Portugal was the cleaner, the better organized, the better controlled; it was not illogical that the knowing English had elected this small country as their choice of Europe. But I also found that it lacked the culture of Spain; there was no Portuguese Velázquez, no Victoria, no García Lorca, no Santa Teresa, and of course no Seneca. The genius of the Iberian peninsula seemed to have resided principally in the more easterly regions, and it was for this reason that I preferred Spain.

3   On two different occasions after long stays in Portugal, I crossed into Spain and each time those of us in the automobile felt a surge of joy, an expansion of the spirit and a sense of growing nobility as we entered Spain. Once the driver of our car dismounted, rubbed his hands in Spanish soil and exulted in being home again. My joining him irritated my wife, who like many women preferred Portugal. "You're being silly and unfair," she protested. "Portugal is much finer than you admit it to be." The driver, who had been disappointed in Portuguese girls, replied, "There's one thing I'll admit. It's the only country in the world where a man's mistress is apt to be uglier than his wife."

Vocabulary

apprehensive, zarzuela, genius, Iberian, peninsula

Questions

1. Michener's first and last paragraphs deal with typical reactions to the two countries, prejudices perhaps. Why at first did Michener prefer Spain to Portugal?
2. Does his opinion change when he sees Portugal with an American couple? Why does he still prefer Spain?
3. His middle paragraph contrasts the virtues of the two countries. Does this contrast tell you anything about the writer?

Topics for Writing

My Two Favorite Places: A Comparison

Our Campus Today and As I First Saw It: A Contrast

A Visit to Belfast

MARY MANNING Although Mary Manning's article was published in *The Atlantic* for May 1972, it has a terrible currency even now.

> It has been reserved for the twentieth century
> to show the spectacle of inquisitors who persecute
> without faith and martyrs who expire without
> hope.
>
> AARLAND USSHER

1   It is a dying city, a broken city, a city almost without hope, for where do we go from here? The heart still beats faintly in the University, in beautiful outlying suburbs, in the brave little Lyric Theater, in the few discothèques where the students, girls and boys, line up for hours in the wintry nights just to get in—to have a drink, to listen to the music of the outside world. The few visitors must stay in guesthouses. Hotels, because of the bombings, are increasingly dangerous. But the heart is still beating faintly. Like a patient in intensive care, Belfast, having survived several heart attacks, may survive, for Belfast has a tough Northern heart; it may just make it.

2   I traveled up to this beleaguered city the weekend of what is now known as Bloody Sunday to review a Lyric Theater production for the fortnightly paper *Hibernia*, which carries all the news unfit to print—in England that is—for the British public has been kept diplomatically uninformed, as indeed has the United States. Dickens, of course, would have sensed that it was an ominous day. He would have marked the leaden skies, the feeling of snow; or was it, could it have been, fear in the air? Nature is a strangely canny barometer. He would have felt the menace in the lashing cruel seas spilling over the coastline between Dublin and Dundalk. The seabirds—sure sign of storm—had flown inland, had covered the fields with the vivid whiteness of their wings. Cattle and sheep huddled forlornly under the bare trees and hedges or near the sheds, for the grazing land was stiff with a hard, cruel frost. So we sat, my companion Catherine and I, in the virtually empty "excursion" train Dublin to Belfast, known in happier times as "the Contraceptive Special," and stared out upon the sad landscape flying past us. The little restaurant car which serves late breakfasts and snack lunches and in which one usually had to stand in line for a table was occupied only by a mother with two children, all three with hacking coughs. A few journalists and cameramen were in the bar drinking stout. Even the dreadful canned music which was blaring out waltzes from old Vienna faltered and came to a dead stop as we reached the Border. Only those who have heard it recognize the voice of doom when a Northern voice drones out, or rather groans out, over the loudspeaker, "NEWRY," for this is the fatal

border town which is one of the principal customs barriers between the North and the rest of Ireland.

"God's sake!" Catherine nudged me. "Look below on the road." We caught   3
our first glimpse of the Saracen tanks and the British soldiers in battle dress searching cars, trucks, civilians, rifles slung over their shoulders. "Milk cans!" Catherine giggled. "The biggest bomb ever was found in a milk can." And now we were in Ulster, that godforsaken province; we were in the war zone. Just before the train drew into Victoria Station, a dismal structure from which even John Betjeman could hardly draw inspiration, printed in enormous white-washed lettering on a bombed-out factory wall was PREPARE TO MEET THY GOD. It was our welcome to Belfast.

"Incidents"

One associates a station, especially a terminus, with excitement, with loving   4
reunions. Not here anymore. Only H. M. Customs greets you, a few hagridden taxi drivers, and a quorum of disillusioned porters. And there is a mean acrid smoky smell, and a pall of smoke hangs low from the arched ironwork of the roof. But thanks be to God, my good friend Dr. Blank (one must not name names) was there waiting in the outer entrance, from which one could glimpse the light of day. He is a psychiatrist with a private practice and is also attached to one of the major city hospitals.

We followed him out onto the street where his car was parked; we were to   5
lunch with his family in a suburb, just east of the city center. "I'm very sorry," he murmured apologetically, "there's just been an incident—couple of cars bombed out, down to our right." As we climbed into the car we did hear the fire engines, and as we moved slowly forward in a long line of cars and buses, suddenly again the tanks were there, this time in front of us, and we were surrounded by Royal Ulster Constabulary men and again the British soldiers. "Ladies, if the shooting starts, just lie down on the floor of the car and hope for the best!" said he with the utmost aplomb. However, the shooting did not start; it was a minor "incident," and about fifteen minutes later we moved along. "We'll have to make a detour. We'll be passing now by the Falls Road, where the action is." He pointed toward one of those endless, gray, mean streets which make up the real Belfast. Ardoyne housing estate is boxes; the Falls Road is like those mining and mill towns in England, sprawling miles of them all exactly alike, all gray, all hopeless. No wonder people come out of those human warrens raging! That flatness, that gray uniformity, must sink into the soul and rot there. There were barbed-wire barricades across the entrance to the Falls Road, and around them scurried a few housewives with shopping bags. Everyone now scurries or scuttles in Belfast.

We drove slowly; one had to because of "incidents." "You must have come up   6
against a lot of mental damage?" I asked him. "Ah, yes, I'll tell you one story—the story of Willie John McDaid. He was a Protestant; not a member of the Orange Order, mind you. No bigot. He kept a small grocery shop. A nice gentle wee man meaning no harm to anybody. Well, six months ago when the Troubles were bad,

Willie John began getting calls warning him to shut up shop and get out with his Papist wife. Yes, his wife was a Catholic and as nice and gentle a woman as you could meet. But how could he get out? The wee shop was his living. So one night he was set upon and beaten across the face and head with an iron bar. When they brought him into the hospital he had no face left. We just saved his life, but we couldn't save his face or his sight. And I'm in there now, trying to save his mind, trying to pump hope back into him. His wife sits there, poor soul, day after day, holding his hand. That was Protestant bigots. But then I have a patient who lost her four-year-old girl in a bombing downtown while she was shopping. That was the IRA. I'm a Catholic myself, and I've never run into any trouble, and my sympathies naturally are basically with the minority; but killing and maiming of the innocents by indiscriminate bombing I cannot stomach. We're breeding a maimed generation up North, and we'll have in the next ten years a city of conditioned killers who have grown up in hate and violence and will never be psychically well again."

7   The graffiti on the buildings were like this (it reminded me of the Mouse's Tale in Alice):

> God is Love
> Come to Jesus
> To Hell with the Pope!
> Shit the IRA!
> Paisley put the kettle on
> And we'll all have a pee!
> Death to all traitors
> Jesus is Love
> They shall come to judgment
> Faulkner, Get Off Your Arse!
> Burn, Bernadette, burn
> Judgement!

Watching our startled faces, the doctor observed bitterly, "One may be certain that Cain liquidated Abel in the name of *Fraternité*." He said not another word, as we drove past boarded-up shops, cinemas, and of course innumerable churches. Outside one of these holy edifices I noticed a delicate white dappled winter cherry tree—a delicate *parapluie*, overhanging the gray wall. It seemed like a little message of hope. Our friend's house was situated in a prosperous suburb, in a tree-lined road with gentlemen's residences standing in their own grounds. As Thackeray once wrote, "Where the devil else would they stand?" Looking around the quiet roads, one could hardly believe in the scarred city below us. Behind our friend's house, above his garden, stretched a meadow in which an old white horse was nonchalantly grazing. "The peace!" I cried. "It's unbelievable!" My hostess laughed. "They blew up the transformer there behind the trees a few months ago. We were blacked out for ages. I never go down into the city to shop anymore. I've been in two bombings and that's enough." "I can't believe it," I said again, "your lovely garden there and a gardener!" There was indeed an ancient character mooching around the flower beds. And that silly old horse. "The only difference between man and brutes is that man knows he's one." "You're in a very bitter mood, dear," remarked his wife. He continued, "For instance, dogs, they're the most human of animals. Like man they hunt and kill in packs." "You obviously need your lunch," said his wife, but her eyes were sad.

After lunch we were driven back to the guesthouse in which we were to spend our night. Serried ranks, this time of red-brick respectability, at least four stories high, and faceless. "Lace curtain Protestants," grinned the doctor as he bade us good-bye and good luck. The house was specklessly, aridly clean; the temperature was polar and reminded me of boarding school, and the emptiness of the house was deafening. Our landlady was a little fresh-colored lady with dead blue eyes. She looked virginal, but was a widow. Our hearts sank as our feet ascended to the fourth floor. We passed the only bath and lav on the third floor. There was obviously no central heating, and each bedroom had a small one-bar electric heater. "Ladies," said she in her rather genteel middle-class Belfast patois, "you'll like a hot-water bag in your beds?" We almost shouted thank you, and very nearly added, at least three, please. When she had gone we looked at each other shiveringly. "We'll have to sleep in our clothes," said Catherine, "possibly even in our boots. This isn't a house, it's an igloo. What are you going to do now?" "Sleep," said I, flinging myself on the bed in my fur coat and my boots and drawing the eiderdown over me. "Well, I'm not going to stay here and get frostbitten. I'm going down to the shops." "You're mad, you'll get shot. You heard what the doctor's wife said." "To hell with that," said she, "I'll get things half price down there!" So off she went, and slumber overtook me, as they say, and an hour later Catherine woke me. "I waited half an hour for the effing bus," she exclaimed breathlessly; she was laden, I observed, with contraband. "I was frozen to the soul, and when one did come there wasn't an effing soul in it, and the conductor looked at me as if I was mad when I asked for city center. Jesus, Mary! Saturday afternoon and the city was empty. I was searched and frisked before I went into Robinson and Cleaver. The girls behind the counters were picking their noses and polishing their nails. Then I went into Marks and Spencer's. There was only a couple of British soldiers in there buying underclothes for their girl friends. Where are we going to eat? I'm starving." So was I. The landlady directed us to a respectable hotel just down the road to the left. So off we went.

The doors of the hotel were locked, and we were scrutinized through them by an old porter who allowed us in and locked up again after us. The manager, who was deathly pale and jaded-looking, wearing a sort of undertaker's suit, was wandering around jangling keys. There did not appear to be any real guests, but there was in the TV room, drinking and wolfing sandwiches, a group of journalists and cameramen. "On their way to Derry tomorrow," explained the manager. "You'll no be going up to Derry for march?" "No, thank God," said I heartily. We ate sandwiches and drank coffee and then tried to get a taxi to bring us to the theater. We had been warned not to walk. Haphazard snipers! If you want a taxi in Belfast on a Saturday, in this moment in history, forget it. "We'll have to start crying," said Catherine, trying to squeeze out a few tears. "Somebody might take pity on us." While we sat there waiting and trembling, the porter kept up a rumbling Shakespearean soliloquy with us: "I sit here, keepin' guard. I look outa this wee window

8

9

here, and when I see a car drive up with four of them bastards (we didn't dare ask which bastards) in it and one stays in the car with the engine running and then I knows there's trouble and I rings the alarm. We've had two bombings out there already. Seen the hedges all blackened?" At that moment, a tough-looking taxi driver who had been hanging around the hall stepped forward and said he'd run us to the theater; he was taking some of the journalists up to Derry, but they hadn't finished eating yet. His taxi service was suitably named Jetset, and I recommend it to anyone who cares to visit Belfast. The last thing I heard as our Jet driver hustled us out was one of the journalists shouting drunkenly, "Facts are seldom true and never conclusive!" And the low moaning of the porter.

Escape

10   We were fifteen minutes late arriving at the theater, and me reviewing the play. It is a beautiful little modern building in Stranmillis area, near the quays, overlooking the Lagan River, and the theater is there owing to the courage and persistence of an extraordinary woman, Mary O'Malley, and a group of devoted associates. Ironically the production was a new play by a Dublin author, Joe O'Donnell (it had been turned down in Dublin), called *The Lads*, and it was splendidly played and presented by a group of top-notch actors. The theater was packed with young and old enjoying every minute, escaping of course from the horrible realities outside. We drank coffee on the balcony during intermission with Mary O'Malley, John Boyd the dramatist, and Tomas McAnna, one of the Abbey directors who was up from Dublin to see *The Lads*, and several others.

11   We talked theater and avoided politics. "It's been hell," said Mary O'Malley, "but we're surviving. The theater is nearly always full. I'm free under English equity to hire English actors, and they come, they come. But there's not much laughter left in Belfast," she added sadly. Someone said, "Civilized human beings laugh most when they're sad and talk most when they're bored." "I don't see much civilization around here," someone else said. "Talking of religion . . ." "Don't," said another listener. "The only quite harmless and admirable mechanical invention is the prayer wheel of Tibet." "But I feel life in this theater," said I. "More than in Dublin, except perhaps the Peacock, which does keep one window half open on the outside world, and it's owing to McAnna, who's leaving us for America." "The Abbey has turned out some fine actors," said Boyd (his play *The Flats* was a smashing success at the Lyric). "Turned out is the right word," said I recklessly. "They're all in New York or London. And as for the Abbey, I wish *Riders to the Sea* had ridden into the sea and stayed there." The discreet silence could have been heard in Dublin!

12   We returned to our cold nest. Before taking off our coats, we leaned out of the window and looked out over the rooftops. There were no lights in the windows, no sounds of human revelry by night. It was not a sleeping silence; it was a mute, speechless, suffering silence, wholly unnatural. Suddenly it was broken. A Saracen tank patrol was rumbling toward our street. We quickly closed the windows and crept into our refrigerators. Our little landlady tapped on our door at eight precisely, for we had to catch the nine-thirty train back to Dublin. "I was afraid to turn in the

night," said Catherine piteously. "A sort of East wind blew in on me shoulders from somewhere." However, there was a sumptuous breakfast waiting for us in the dining room and the usual one-bar electric heater. With that blessed Northern efficiency she had called a taxi for us the night before. "You'll sign the guest book before you go?" and she stood beside us, as we signed, chafing her poor red hands. I looked at the last signature above mine. It was dated August, 1971.

Sensing my unspoken pity, she said, "It's been hard. I used to get the visitors from Dublin, but they don't come anymore. Mrs. O'Malley does send me actors, but they like to be near the theater and in a group."   13

We drove down the familiar route to the station, and I craned my neck to have a last look at the winter cherry tree. Alas and alas, a car had been bombed beside it during the night, and the white *parapluie* was now a dirty black umbrella. The streets were empty, but bells were already tolling, calling all good Christians to prayer. The skies were gray and somber, and already a few flakes of snow were falling. All I could think of as I sat in the train on the way to Dublin was the shortest verse in the Bible: "Jesus wept." And I didn't know then that thirteen people were to die in Derry that day.   14

Vocabulary

beleaguered, fortnightly, diplomatically, ominous, canny, barometer, virtually, stout, terminus, hagridden, quorum, disillusioned, acrid, pall, constabulary, aplomb, warrens, scurries, scuttles, papist, bigots, indiscriminate, maimed, psychically, graffiti, *fraternité*, edifices, *parapluie,* nonchalantly, serried, aridly, genteel, patois, eiderdown, contraband, scrutinized, haphazard, soliloquy, conclusive, quays, equity, discreet, revelry, sumptuous

Questions

1. Manning uses implied contrasts to make her point. For example, she tells us that a railway station is ordinarily a place of "excitement, loving reunions"— and then describes the Belfast station in somber terms. Can you find other instances of the implied contrast?
2. Do you find the Cain-and-Abel allusion apt?
3. Is it only the killers who will be psychologically twisted for life?
4. Why does Mary Manning wish that *Riders to the Sea* had never been written?
5. Why is the date she finds in the guest book significant?
6. In this instance, the people of the theater carried on in the face of real danger, exhibiting an extreme case of "The show must go on!" But some would argue that the arts—drama, music, poetry—are frivolous diversions in time of crisis. What is your opinion?

Topics for Writing

The Irish Question—Why Jesus Wept

Should Theaters Be Closed in Times of Crisis?

Peasants

FRANCES TROLLOPE (1780–1863), intrepid English traveler and prolific novelist, supported her family—Anthony Trollope (see Chapter 5) was her son—by means of her pen. Her attempt to establish a retail business in America helped confirm her poor opinion of our country. This selection is from her bitter *Domestic Manners of Americans* (1832).

1   Mohawk, as our little village was called, gave us an excellent opportunity of comparing the peasants of the United States with those of England, and of judging the average degree of comfort enjoyed by each. I believe Ohio gives as fair a specimen as any part of the Union; if they have the roughness and inconveniences of a new state to contend with, they have higher wages and cheaper provisions; if I err in supposing it a mean state in point of comfort, it certainly is not in taking too low a standard.

2   Mechanics, if good workmen, are certain of employment, and good wages, rather higher than with us; the average wages of a labourer throughout the Union is ten dollars a month, with lodging, boarding, washing, and mending; if he lives at his own expense he has a dollar a day. It appears to me that the necessaries of life, that is to say, meat, bread, butter, tea, and coffee, (not to mention whiskey), are within the reach of every sober, industrious, and healthy man who chooses to have them; and yet I think that an English peasant, with the same qualifications, would, in coming to the United States, change for the worse. He would find wages somewhat higher, and provisions in Western America considerably lower; but this statement, true as it is, can lead to nothing but delusion if taken apart from other facts, fully as certain, and not less important, but which require more detail in describing, and which perhaps cannot be fully comprehended, except by an eye-witness. The American poor are accustomed to eat meat three times a day; I never enquired into the habits of any cottagers in Western America, where this was not the case. I found afterwards in Maryland, Pennsylvania, and other parts of the country, where the price of meat was higher, that it was used with more economy; yet still a much larger portion of the weekly income is thus expended than with us. Ardent spirits, though lamentably cheap,[1] still cost something, and the use of them among the men, with more or less of discretion, according to the character, is universal. Tobacco also grows at their doors, and is not taxed; yet this too costs something, and the air of heaven is not in more general use among the men at America, than chewing tobacco. I am not now pointing out the evils of dram-drinking, but it is evident, that where this practice prevails universally, and often to the most frightful

---

[1]About a shilling a gallon is the retail price of good whiskey. If bought wholesale, or of inferior quality, it is much cheaper.

excess, the consequence must be, that the money spent to obtain the dram is less than the money lost by the time consumed in drinking it. Long, disabling, and expensive fits of sickness are incontestably more frequent in every part of America, than in England, and the sufferers have no aid to look to, but what they have saved, or what they may be enabled to sell. I have never seen misery exceed what I have witnessed in an American cottage where disease has entered.

But if the condition of the labourer be not superior to that of the English 3 peasant, that of his wife and daughters is incomparably worse. It is they who are indeed the slaves of the soil. One has but to look at the wife of an American cottager, and ask her age, to be convinced that the life she leads is one of hardship, privation, and labour. It is rare to see a woman in this station who has reached the age of thirty, without losing every trace of youth and beauty. You continually see women with infants on their knee, that you feel sure are their grand-children, till some convincing proof of the contrary is displayed. Even the young girls, though often with lovely features, look pale, thin, and haggard. I do not remember to have seen in any single instance among the poor, a specimen of the plump, rosy, laughing physiognomy so common among our cottage girls. The horror of domestic service, which the reality of slavery, and the fable of equality, have generated, excludes the young women from that sure and most comfortable resource of decent English girls; and the consequence is, that with a most irreverend freedom of manner to the parents, the daughters are, to the full extent of the word, domestic slaves. This condition, which no periodical merry-making, no village *fête*, ever occurs to cheer, is only changed for the still sadder burdens of a teeming wife. They marry very young; in fact, in no rank of life do you meet with young women in that delightful period of existence between childhood and marriage, wherein, if only tolerably well spent, so much useful information is gained, and the character takes a sufficient degree of firmness to support with dignity the more important parts of wife and mother. The slender, childish thing, without vigour of mind or body, is made to stem a sea of troubles that dims her young eye and makes her cheek grow pale, even before nature has given it the last beautiful finish of the full-grown woman.

"We shall get along," is the answer in full, for all that can be said in way of 4 advice to a boy and girl who take it into their heads to go before a magistrate and "get married." And they do get along, till sickness overtakes them, by means perhaps of borrowing a kettle from one and a tea-pot from another; but intemperance, idleness, or sickness will, in one week, plunge those who are even getting along well, into utter destitution; and where this happens, they are completely without resource.

The absence of poor-laws is, without doubt, a blessing to the country, but they 5 have not that natural and reasonable dependence on the richer classes which, in countries differently constituted, may so well supply their place. I suppose there is less alms-giving in America than in any other Christian country on the face of the globe. It is not in the temper of the people either to give or to receive.

I extract the following pompous passage from a Washington paper of Feb. 6 1829, (a season of uncommon severity and distress,) which, I think, justifies my observation.

7   "Among the liberal evidences of sympathy for the suffering poor of this city, two have come to our knowledge which deserve to be especially noticed: the one a donation by the President of the United States to the committee of the ward in which he resides of fifty dollars; the other the donation by a few of the officers of the war department to the Howard and Dorcas Societies, of seventy-two dollars." When such mention is made of a gift of about nine pounds sterling from the sovereign magistrate of the United States, and of thirteen pounds sterling as a contribution from one of the state departments, the inference is pretty obvious, that the sufferings of the destitute in America are not liberally relieved by individual charity.

8   I had not been three days at Mohawk-cottage before a pair of ragged children came to ask for medicine for a sick mother; and when it was given to them, the eldest produced a handful of cents, and desired to know what he was to pay. The superfluous milk of our cow was sought after eagerly, but every new comer always proposed to pay for it. When they found out that "the English old woman" did not sell any thing, I am persuaded they by no means liked her the better for it; but they seemed to think, that if she were a fool it was no reason they should be so too, and accordingly the borrowing, as they called it, became very constant, but always in a form that shewed their dignity and freedom. One woman sent to borrow a pound of cheese; another half a pound of coffee; and more than once an intimation accompanied the milk-jug, that the milk must be fresh, and unskimmed: on one occasion the messenger refused milk, and said, "Mother only wanted a little cream for her coffee."

9   I could never teach them to believe, during above a year that I lived at this house, that I would not sell the old clothes of the family; and so pertinacious were they in bargain-making, that often, when I had given them the articles which they wanted to purchase, they would say, "Well, I expect I shall have to do a turn of work for this; you may send for me when you want me." But as I never did ask for the turn of work, and as this formula was constantly repeated, I began to suspect that it was spoken solely to avoid uttering that most un-American phrase "I thank you."

Vocabulary

cottager, ardent (as in *ardent spirits*), physiognomy, irreverend, *fête*, teeming, destitution, poor-laws, pertinacious

Questions

1. According to Mrs. Trollope, why would English peasants be worse off if they came to America?
2. Why were American women worse off than men?
3. What were some of the effects upon girls who married young? Are these still true today?
4. "It is not in the temper of the people either to give or receive." Give examples.

5. Do you agree with Mrs. Trollope that the repeated offer to pay for generous treatment is the American's way of avoiding a single "thank you"?

Topics for Writing

The Perils of Early Marriage
American "Peasants"?
The Polite American
Mrs. Trollope's Manners

On the Train to Lowell

CHARLES DICKENS (1812–1870) hardly needs introducing. But he is more famous for *Pickwick Papers, A Christmas Carol,* and *Great Expectations* than for the accounts of his travels, which were widely read in his day and from which this section comes.

1   Before leaving Boston, I devoted one day to an excursion to Lowell. I assign a separate chapter to this visit; not because I am about to describe it at any length, but because I remember it as a thing by itself, and am desirous that my readers should do the same.

2   I made acquaintance with an American railroad, on this occasion, for the first time. As these works are pretty much alike all through the States, their general characteristics are easily described.

3   There are no first and second class carriages as with us; but there is a gentlemen's car and a ladies' car; the main distinction between which is that in the first, everybody smokes; and in the second, nobody does. As a black man never travels with a white one, there is also a negro car; which is a great blundering clumsy chest, such as Gulliver put to sea in, from the kingdom of Brobdignag. There is a great deal of jolting, a great deal of noise, a great deal of wall, not much window, a locomotive engine, a shriek, and a bell.

4   The cars are like shabby omnibuses, but larger; holding thirty, forty, fifty, people. The seats, instead of stretching from end to end, are placed crosswise. Each seat holds two persons. There is a long row of them on each side of the caravan, a narrow passage up the middle, and a door at both ends. In the centre of the carriage there is usually a stove, fed with charcoal or anthracite coal; which is for the most part red-hot. It is insufferably close; and you see the hot air fluttering between yourself and any other object you may happen to look at, like the ghost of smoke.

5   In the ladies' car, there are a great many gentlemen who have ladies with them. There are also a great many ladies who have nobody with them; for any lady may travel alone, from one end of the United States to the other, and be certain of the most courteous and considerate treatment everywhere. The conductor or check-taker, or guard, or whatever he may be, wears no uniform. He walks up and down the car, and in and out of it, as his fancy dictates; leans against the door with his hands in his pockets and stares at you, if you chance to be a stranger; or enters into conversation with the passengers about him. A great many newspapers are pulled out, and a few of them are read. Everybody talks to you, or to anybody else who hits his fancy. If you are an Englishman, he expects that that railroad is pretty much like an English railroad. If you say "No," he says "Yes?" (interrogatively,) and asks in what respect they differ. You enumerate the heads of difference, one by one, and he says "Yes?" (still interrogatively) to each. Then he guesses that you don't travel faster

in England; and on your replying that you do, says "Yes?" again (still interroga-tively), and, it is quite evident, don't believe it. After a long pause he remarks, partly to you, and partly to the knob on the top of his stick, that "Yankees are reckoned to be considerable of a go-ahead people too;" upon which *you* say "Yes," and then *he* says "Yes" again (affirmatively this time); and upon your looking out of window, tells you that behind that hill, and some three miles from the next station, there is a clever town in a smart lo-ca-tion, where he expects you have concluded to stop. Your answer in the negative naturally leads to more questions in reference to your intended route (always pronounced rout); and wherever you are going, you invari-ably learn that you can't get there without immense difficulty and danger, and that all the great sights are somewhere else.

If a lady take a fancy to any male passenger's seat, the gentleman who accom-panies her gives him notice of the fact, and he immediately vacates it with great politeness. Politics are much discussed, so are banks, so is cotton. Quiet people avoid the question of the Presidency, for there will be a new election in three years and a half, and party feeling runs very high: the great constitutional feature of this institution being, that directly the acrimony of the last election is over, the ac-rimony of the next one begins; which is an unspeakable comfort to all strong politicians and true lovers of their country: that is to say, to ninety-nine men and boys out of every ninety-nine and a quarter.

Except when a branch road joins the main one, there is seldom more than one track of rails; so that the road is very narrow, and the view, where there is a deep cutting, by no means extensive. When there is not, the character of the scenery is always the same. Mile after mile of stunted trees; some hewn down by the axe, some blown down by the wind, some half fallen and resting on their neighbours, many mere logs half hidden in the swamp, others mouldered away to spongy chips. The very soil of the earth is made up of minute fragments such as these; each pool of stagnant water has its crust of vegetable rottenness; on every side there are the boughs, and trunks, and stumps of trees, in every possible stage of decay, decompo-sition, and neglect. Now you emerge for a few brief minutes on an open country, glittering with some bright lake or pool, broad as many an English river, but so small here that it scarcely has a name; now catch hasty glimpses of a distant town, with its clean white houses and their cool piazzas, its prim New-England church and schoolhouse; when whir-r-r-r! almost before you have seen them, comes the same dark screen: the stunted trees, the stumps, the logs, the stagnant water—all so like the last that you seem to have been transported back again by magic.

The train calls at stations in the woods, where the wild impossibility of any-body having the smallest reason to get out, is only to be equalled by the apparently desperate hopelessness of there being anybody to get in. It rushes across the turnpike road, where there is no gate, no policeman, no signal: nothing but a rough wooden arch, on which is painted *"When the bell rings, look out for the Locomotive."* On it whirls headlong, dives through the woods again, emerges in the light, clatters over frail arches, rumbles upon the heavy ground, shoots beneath a wooden bridge which intercepts the light for a second like a wink, suddenly awakens all the slumbering echoes in the main street of a large town, and dashes on hap-hazard, pell-mell, neck or nothing, down the middle of the road. There—with mechanics working at their trades, and people leaning from their doors and windows, and boys flying kites and playing marbles, and men smoking, and women talking, and children crawling, and pigs burrowing, and unaccustomed horses plunging and rearing, close to the very rails—there—on, on, on—tears the mad dragon of an engine with its train of cars; scattering in all directions a shower of burning sparks from its wood fire; screeching, hissing, yelling, panting: until at last the thirsty monster stops beneath a covered way to drink, the people cluster round, and you have time to breathe again.

Vocabulary

Brobdignag, omnibus, anthracite, interrogatively, acrimony, pell-mell

Questions

1. According to Dickens, what are the points of similarity and difference between American and English railroads?
2. What words does Dickens use to portray peculiarities of American speech? How would Englishmen (presumably) pronounce *route*?
3. Is "mad dragon" an apt image for a speeding train?
4. Does Dickens make the train ride come alive for you? Has he tried to make you *feel* as well as *see* the ride? How has he done so?

Topics for Writing

My First Flight

Contrasting Accents: Mine and My Friend's

Sunday in London

HIPPOLYTE TAINE   (1828–1893), French literary critic and historian, had a keen insight into English literature and customs. This is from his *Notes on England* (1872).

Sunday in London in the rain: the shops are shut, the streets almost deserted; the aspect is that of an immense and a well-ordered cemetery. The few passers-by under their umbellas, in the desert of squares and streets, have the look of uneasy spirits who have risen from their graves; it is appalling.   1

I had no conception of such a spectacle, which is said to be frequent in London. The rain is small, compact, pitiless; looking at it one can see no reason why it should not continue to the end of all things; one's feet churn water, there is water everywhere, filthy water impregnated with an odour of soot. A yellow, dense fog fills the air, sweeps down to the ground; at thirty paces a house, a steam-boat appear as spots upon blotting-paper. After an hour's walk in the Strand especially, and in the rest of the City, one has the spleen, one meditates suicide. The lofty lines of fronts are of sombre brick, the exudations being encrusted with fog and soot. Monotony and silence; yet the inscriptions on metal or marble speak and tell of the absent master, as in a large manufactory of bone-black closed on account of a death.   2

A frightful thing is the huge palace in the Strand, which is called Somerset House. Massive and heavy piece of architecture, of which the hollows are inked, the porticoes blackened with soot, where, in the cavity of the empty court, is a sham fountain without water, pools of water on the pavement, long rows of closed windows—what can they possibly do in these catacombs? It seems as if the livid and sooty fog had even befouled the verdure of the parks. But what most offends the eyes are the colonnades, peristyles, Grecian ornaments, mouldings, and wreaths of the houses, all bathed in soot; poor antique architecture—what is it doing in such a climate? The flutings and columns in front of the British Museum are begrimed as if liquid mud had been poured over them. St. Paul's, a kind of Pantheon, has two ranges of columns, the lower range is entirely black, the upper range, recently scraped, is still white, but the white is offensive, coal smoke has already plastered it with its leprosy.   3

These spots are melancholy, being the decay of the stone. And these nude statues in memory of Greece! Wellington as a fighting hero, naked under the dripping trees of the park! That hideous Nelson, stuck on his column with a coil of rope in the form of a pig-tail, like a rat impaled on the top of a pole! Every form, every classical idea is contrary to nature here. A swamp like this is a place of exile for the arts of antiquity. When the Romans disembarked here they must have thought themselves in Homer's hell, in the land of the Cimmerians. The vast space which, in the south, stretches between the earth and the sky, cannot be discovered   4 by the eye; there is no air; there is nothing but liquid fog; in this pale smoke objects are but fading phantoms, Nature has the look of a bad drawing in charcoal which some one has rubbed with his sleeve. . . .

5   The population numbers three millions and a quarter; that makes twelve cities like Marseilles, ten cities like Lyons, two cities like Paris put together; but words upon paper are no substitutes for the sensation of the eyes. It is necessary to take a cab several days in succession, and proceed straight on towards the south, the north, the east, and the west, during a whole morning, as far as the uncertain limits where houses grow scanty and the country begins.

6   Enormous, enormous—this is the word which always recurs. Moreover, all is rich and well ordered; consequently, they must think us neglected and poor. Paris is mediocre compared with these squares, these crescents, these circles and rows of monumental buildings of massive stone, with porticoes, with sculptured fronts, these spacious streets; there are sixty of them as vast as the Rue de la Paix; assuredly Napoleon III demolished and rebuilt Paris only because he had lived in London. In the Strand, in Piccadilly, in Regent Street, in the neighbourhood of London Bridge, in twenty places, there is a bustling crowd, a surging traffic, an amount of obstruction which our busiest and most frequented boulevard cannot parallel. Everything is on a large scale here; the clubs are palaces, the hotels are monuments; the river is an arm of the sea; the cabs go twice as fast; the boatmen and the omnibus-conductors condense a sentence into a word; words and gestures are economised; actions and time are turned to the utmost possible account; the human being produces and expends twice as much as among us.

7   From London Bridge to Hampton Court are eight miles, that is, nearly three leagues of buildings. After the streets and quarters erected together, as one piece, by wholesale, like a hive after a model, come the countless pleasure retreats, cottages surrounded with verdure and trees in all styles—Gothic, Grecian, Byzantine, Italian, of the Middle Age, or the Revival, with every mixture and every shade of style, generally in lines or clusters of five, ten, twenty of the same sort, apparently the handiwork of the same builder, like so many specimens of the same vase or the same bronze. They deal in houses as we deal in Parisian articles. What a multitude of well-to-do, comfortable, and rich existences! One divines accumulated gains, a wealthy and spending middle-class quite different from ours, so pinched, so straitened. The most humble, in brown brick, are pretty by dint of tidiness; the window panes sparkle like mirrors; there is nearly always a green and flowery patch; the front is covered with ivy, honeysuckle, and nasturtiums.

8   The entire circumference of Hyde Park is covered with houses of this sort, but finer, and these in the midst of London retain a country look; each stands detached in its square of turf and shrubs, has two stories in the most perfect order and condition, a portico, a bell for the tradespeople, a bell for the visitors, a basement for the kitchen and the servants, with a flight of steps for the service; very few mouldings and ornaments; no outside sun-shutters; large, clear windows, which let in plenty of light; flowers on the sills and at the portico; stables in a mews apart, in order that their odours and sight may be kept at a distance; all the external surface covered with white, shining, and varnished stucco; not a speck of mud or dust; the

trees, the turf, the flowers, the servants prepared as if for an exhibition of prize products. How well one can picture the inhabitant after seeing his shell! In the first place, it is the Teuton who loves Nature, and who needs a reminder of the country; next, it is the Englishman who wishes to be by himself in his staircase as in his room, who could not endure the promiscuous existence of our huge Parisian cages, and who, even in London, plans his house as a small castle, independent and enclosed. Besides, he is simple, and does not desire external display; on the other hand, he is exacting in the matter of condition and comfort, and separates his life from that of his inferiors. The number of such houses at the West-end is astonishing! The rent is nearly £500; from five to seven servants are kept; the master expends from twelve to twenty-four hundred pounds a year. There are ten of these fortunes and these lives in England to every one in France.

Vocabulary

exudations, portico, catacombs, verdure, Cimmerian, divines, straitened, mews

Questions

1. In what ways is a deserted city like "a well-ordered cemetery"?
2. What other death images does Taine use?
3. What comparisons does Taine use to give you the idea of London's size? London's wealth? London's housing?

Topics for Writing

Sunday at Home
If Taine Visited Los Angeles (or another American city)

Rome and St. Peter's Overwhelm Us

MARK TWAIN   (1835–1910), born Samuel Langhorne Clemens, could be critical of the United States. But, as this piece from *Innocents Abroad* shows, he had a chauvinistic side as well.

1   What is is that confers the noblest delight? What is that which swells a man's breast with pride above that which any other experience can bring to him? Discovery! To know that you are walking where none others have walked; that you are beholding what human eye has not seen before; that you are breathing a virgin atmosphere. To give birth to an idea—to discover a great thought—an intellectual nugget, right under the dust of a field that many a brain-plow had gone over before. To find a new planet, to invent a new hinge, to find the way to make the lightnings carry your messages. To be the *first*—that is the idea. To do something, say something, see something, before *anybody* else—these are the things that confer a pleasure compared with which other pleasures are tame and commonplace, other ecstasies cheap and trivial. Morse, with his first message, brought by his servant, the lightning; Fulton, in that long-drawn century of suspense, when he placed his hand upon the throttle-valve, and lo, the steamboat moved; Jenner, when his patient with the cow's virus in his blood walked through the smallpox hospitals unscathed; Howe, when the idea shot through his brain that for a hundred and twenty generations the eye had been bored through the wrong end of the needle; the nameless lord of art who laid down his chisel in some old age that is forgotten now, and gloated upon the finished Laocoön; Daguerre, when he commanded the sun, riding in the zenith, to print the landscape upon his insignificant silvered plate, and he obeyed; Columbus, in the *Pinta's* shrouds, when he swung his hat above a fabled sea and gazed abroad upon an unknown world! These are the men who have really *lived*—who have actually comprehended what pleasure is—who have crowded long lifetimes of ecstasy into a single moment.

2   What is there in Rome for me to see that others have not seen before me? What is there for me to touch that others have not touched? What is there for me to feel, to learn, to hear, to know, that shall thrill me before it pass to others? What can I discover? Nothing. Nothing whatsoever. One charm of travel dies here. But if I were only a Roman! If, added to my own I could be gifted with modern Roman sloth, modern Roman superstition, and modern Roman boundlessness of ignorance, what bewildering worlds of unsuspected wonder I would discover! Ah, if I were only a habitant of the Campagna five and twenty miles from Rome! *Then* I would travel.

3   I would go to America, and see, and learn, and return to the Campagna and stand before my countrymen an illustrious discoverer. I would say:

4   "I saw there a country which has no overshadowing Mother Church, and yet

the people survive. I saw a government which never was protected by foreign soldiers at a cost greater than that required to carry on the government itself. I saw common men and common women who could read; I even saw small children of common country-people reading from books; if I dared think you would believe it, I would say they could write, also. In the cities I saw people drinking a delicious beverage made of chalk and water, but never once saw goats driven through their Broadway or their Pennsylvania Avenue or their Montgomery Street and milked at the doors of the houses. I saw real glass windows in the houses of even the common-est people. Some of the houses are not of stone, nor yet of bricks; I solemnly swear they are made of wood. Houses there will take fire and burn, sometimes—actually burn entirely down, and not leave a single vestige behind. I could state that for a truth, upon my death-bed. And as a proof that the circumstance is not rare, I aver that they have a thing which they call a fire-engine, which vomits forth great streams of water, and is kept always in readiness, by night and by day, to rush to houses that are burning. You would think one engine would be sufficient, but some great cities have a hundred; they keep men hired, and pay them by the month to do nothing but put out fires. For a certain sum of money other men will insure that your house shall not burn down; and if it burns they will pay you for it. There are hundreds and thousands of schools, and anybody may go and learn to be wise, like a priest. In that singular country, if a rich man dies a sinner, he is damned; he cannot buy salvation with money for masses. There is really not much use in being rich, there. Not much use as far as the other world is concerned, but much, very much use, as concerns this; because there, if a man be rich, he is very greatly honored, and can become a legislator, a governor, a general, a senator, no matter how ignorant an ass he is—just as in our beloved Italy the nobles hold all the great places, even though sometimes they are born noble idiots. There, if a man be rich, they give him costly presents, they ask him to feasts, they invite him to drink complicated beverages; but if he be poor and in debt, they require him to do that which they term to 'settle.' The women put on a different dress almost every day; the dress is usually fine, but absurd in shape; the very shape and fashion of it changes twice in a hundred years; and did I but covet to be called an extravagant falsifier, I would say it changed even oftener. Hair does not grow upon the American women's heads; it is made for them by cunning workmen in the shops, and is curled and frizzled into scandalous and ungodly forms. Some persons wear eyes of glass which they see through with facility perhaps, else they would not use them; and in the mouths of some are teeth made by the sacrilegious hand of man. The dress of the men is laughably grotesque. They carry no musket in ordinary life, nor no long-pointed pole; they wear no wide green-lined cloak; they wear no peaked black felt hat, no leathern gaiters reaching to the knee, no goatskin breeches with the hair side out, no hob-nailed shoes, no prodigious spurs. They wear a conical hat termed a 'nail-kag'; a coat of saddest black; a shirt which shows dirt so easily that it has to be changed every month, and is very troublesome; things called pantaloons, which are held up by shoulder-straps, and on their feet they wear boots which are ridiculous in pattern and can stand no wear. Yet dressed in this fantastic garb, these people laughed at *my* costume. In that country, books are so common that it is really no curiosity to see one. Newspapers also. They have a great machine which prints such things by thousands every hour.

5   "I saw common men there—men who were neither priests nor princes—who yet absolutely owned the land they tilled. It was not rented from the church, nor from the nobles. I am ready to take my oath of this. In that country you might fall from a third-story window three several times, and not mash either a soldier or a priest. The scarcity of such people is astonishing. In the cities you will see a dozen civilians for every soldier, and as many for every priest or preacher. Jews, there, are treated just like human beings, instead of dogs. They can work at any business they please; they can sell brand-new goods if they want to; they can keep drug stores; they can practise medicine among Christians; they can even shake hands with Christians if they choose; they can associate with them, just the same as one human being does with another human being; they don't have to stay shut up in one corner of the towns; they can live in any part of a town they like best; it is said they even have the privilege of buying land and houses, and owning them themselves, though I doubt that myself; they never have had to run races naked through the public streets, against jackasses, to please the people in carnival time; there they never have been driven by soldiers into a church every Sunday for hundreds of years to hear themselves and their religion especially and particularly cursed; at this very day, in that curious country, a Jew is allowed to vote, hold office, yea, get up on a rostrum in the public street and express his opinion of the government if the government don't suit him! Ah, it is wonderful. The common people there know a great deal; they even have the effrontery to complain if they are not properly governed, and to take hold and help conduct the government themselves; if they had laws like ours, which give one dollar of every three a crop produces to the government for taxes, they would have that law altered; instead of paying thirty-three dollars in taxes, out of every one hundred they receive, they complain if they have to pay seven. They are curious people. They do not know when they are well off. Mendicant priests do not prowl among them with baskets begging for the church and eating up their substance. One hardly ever sees a minister of the Gospel going around there in his bare feet, with a basket, begging for subsistence. In that country the preachers are not like our mendicant order of friars—they have two or three suits of clothing, and they wash sometimes. In that land are mountains far higher than the Alban Mountains; the vast Roman Campagna, a hundred miles long and fully forty broad, is really small compared to the United States of America; the Tiber, that celebrated river of ours, which stretches its mighty course almost two hundred miles, and which a lad can scarcely throw a stone across at Rome, is not so long, nor yet so wide, as the American Mississippi—nor yet the Ohio, nor even the Hudson. In America the people are absolutely wiser and know much more than their grandfathers did. *They* do not plow with a sharpened stick, nor yet with a three-cornered block of wood that merely scratches the top of the ground. We do that because our fathers did, three thousand years ago, I suppose. But those people have no holy reverence for their ancestors. They plow with a plow that is a sharp, curved blade of iron, and it cuts into the earth full five inches. And this is not all. They cut their

grain with a horrid machine that mows down whole fields in a day. If I dared, I would say that sometimes they use a blasphemous plow that works by fire and vapor and tears up an acre of ground in a single hour—but—but—I see by your looks that you do not believe the things I am telling you. Alas, my character is ruined, and I am a branded speaker of untruths."

Vocabulary

covet, sacrilegious, gaiters, mendicant, subsistence, friars

Questions

1. Twain contrasts himself with the great discoverers in science and the arts and travel. Does he prepare you adequately for the flat reply, "Nothing"?
2. By imagining himself a Roman returned from America filled with wonders to tell his fellow Romans, Twain manages to contrast the New World with the Old. Does this charade make his comments less offensive? Funnier?
3. Is Twain an "ugly American," a typical tourist who dislikes anything foreign?
4. What is this delicious "chalk and water" beverage? What does that tell you about America?
5. What does Twain seem to dislike about religion in Rome?
6. What other forces keep the Romans down? Is tradition one of these forces? If so, is Twain arguing against tradition?

Topics for Writing

There's No Place Like Home

The Ugly American, Mark Twain

Tradition: Killer or Nourisher?

4

Classifying and Distinguishing / The Melting Pot

A couple preparing for a garage sale go through attic, closets, basement, and spare room to assess their potential "stock." They end up making some decisions. A good many things, they find, they don't want to sell. The baby's first booties go into that category. Other things, like the lamp that no longer suits the redecorated living room, ought to bring a couple of dollars. Still other possessions—the Monopoly set with half the cards missing, the doll with the smashed head—are not worth keeping or selling. The couple have been classifying their possessions into three categories: keepers, sellers, throwaways.

Any time we deal with conglomerations of facts, people, or ideas, we tend to classify them—to impose a logical order on what otherwise might be chaos. Take a typical body of students. We can classify them by sex, by class, by cumulative index, by major, by height, by ethnic background, and so forth. Such classifications can help us to answer questions: How many sections of Accounting 100 should be offered next September? Should the college build another women's dormitory?

The writer looks for the distinguishing characteristics of the items in a group; those observations enable him to place individual items in categories with others that share similar characteristics. Logical order is thus made out of potential chaos, which helps us to understand both the subject and the class to which it belongs.

America, the Land of Immigrants, has fascinated writers since its beginnings. Country of origin, language, skin color, religion, and a dozen other characteristics have set Americans off one from another, and observers have struggled with problems of classification and distinction in efforts to define this new creature, the American, and to see how successfully we have, or have not, managed to absorb the diverse elements into unity.

Crèvecoeur sets the pace: his admiration for the new country shines in every line, and his image of the melting pot dominates the national consciousness and is reflected somehow in all the other writers. Maxine Hong Kingston, studying photographs of her parents, sees that adaptation is easier for some than for others, and Langston Hughes insists that the ignored black will share in the dream, though temporarily rejected. Although Florence Greenberg describes how a rabbi's family made a fairly confident adjustment with the support of a rich Jewish heritage, Alistair Cooke warns that the melting process takes more adjustment than Crèvecoeur had supposed. Finally, Michael Novak and Dorothy Seymour in different ways argue for the preservation of diversity in the face of pressures to melt into a dull sameness. We have a chance to see whether we fit into categories, either as persons or in the way we think about ourselves, and to ask if the image of the melting pot enriches or limits the way we think about the national ideal.

What Is an American?

MICHEL GUILLAUME DE CREVECOEUR (1735–1813), who wrote under the pen name Hector St. John, was a French writer and traveler, lover of nature, and interpreter of the "new" man, the American. His *Letters from an American Farmer*, from which this selection comes, was published in 1780.

1   What then is the American, this new man? He is either an European, or the descendant of an European, hence that strange mixture of blood, which you will find in no other country. I could point out to you a family whose grandfather was an Englishman, whose wife was Dutch, whose son married a French woman, and whose present four sons have now four wives of different nations. *He* is an American, who, leaving behind him all his ancient prejudices and manners, receives new ones from the new mode of life he has embraced, the new government he obeys, and the new rank he holds. He becomes an American by being received in the broad lap of our great *Alma Mater*. Here individuals of all nations are melted into a new race of men, whose labours and posterity will one day cause great changes in the world. Americans are the western pilgrims, who are carrying along with them that great mass of arts, sciences, vigour, and industry which began long since in the east; they will finish the great circle. The Americans were once scattered all over Europe; here they are incorporated into one of the finest systems of population which has ever appeared, and which will hereafter become distinct by the power of the different climates they inhabit. The American ought therefore to love this country much better than that wherein either he or his forefathers were born. Here the rewards of his industry follow with equal steps the progress of his labour; his labour is founded on the basis of nature, *self-interest*, can it want a stronger allurement? Wives and children, who before in vain demanded of him a morsel of bread, now, fat and frolicsome, gladly help their father to clear those fields whence exuberant crops are to arise to feed and to clothe them all; without any part being claimed, either by a despotic prince, a rich abbot, or a mighty lord. Here religion demands but little of him; a small voluntary salary to the minister, and gratitude to God; can he refuse these? The American is a new man, who acts upon new principles; he must therefore entertain new ideas, and form new opinions. From involuntary idleness, servile dependence, penury, and useless labour, he has passed to toils of a very different nature, rewarded by ample subsistence.—This is an American.

Vocabulary

alma mater, pilgrim, exuberant, despotic

76

Questions

1. The question-and-answer technique is an old one; here the question suggests its answer when Crèvecoeur classifies the American as "this new man." Single out some of the qualities that differentiate "this new man" from his predecessors.
2. Notice the distinctions Crèvecoeur emphasizes: "individuals" vs. "new race"; "once scattered" vs. "here incorporated." These help distinguish the American from his European contemporaries. Point out other elements of classification and division.
3. The idea of the "melting pot" fascinated Crèvecoeur. Do you know families like the one he describes in his third sentence? Have these elements "melted into a new race"?

Topics for Writing

Self-Interest vs. Selfishness

Is the Melting Pot Still Doing the Job?

An American: My Definition

Letter to an Intending Immigrant

ALISTAIR COOKE (1908–), writer, journalist, and television personality, was born in England. Many Americans know him as the host of *Masterpiece Theater*.

1   I was going downtown in the the subway and was flattened up against the door reading the morning paper of a man breathing into my ear. If anybody in this train had had room to ram his elbow into my lungs, chances are I wouldn't have noticed it. That would have been just an occupational hazard of traveling in New York during the Christmas shopping season. But what I became aware of after a mile or so was a gentle nudge somewhere down there in the direction of my floating rib. This was such a friendly gesture that I tried to swivel my eyeballs in the direction it was coming from. I saw the upturned face of a man who might have been about five feet three or, then again, might have been a six-footer simply frozen at that altitude. He grinned and asked me if my name was Cooke. I said it was and he said his name was Schofield and he'd been in school with me in England twenty . . . well, several years ago. Before we lurched to a stop, his stop, he had time to tell me that he was working in a big department store downtown and had been over here for just about two years. I asked him if he was here for good. He gave a little laugh and said he certainly was. "I just upped and left," he said, and the train stopped and he vanished into the gasping school of New Yorkers peering at us through the aquarium windows.

2   This whole episode didn't last longer than thirty seconds, but it made me glad for him and set me contrasting his obvious good spirits with the fate and the faces of other English people I've run into in the past few years who also "upped and left." There was, for instance, an English girl who decided when the war was over that instead of having her children come back home to her from Canada, she would join them over here and start a new life in a new land. Her boy, it turned out, developed one of those boy soprano voices of remarkable purity. She began to fret—in the little Canadian town she'd settled in—and think back longingly to the church schools in England where this voice might be trained. Of course, she was homesick for more things than an English boys' choir. It was a useful and sensible excuse to give to friends on this side. She is back in London now, very contented in austerity, and her boy is proudly singing his head off.

3   I think also of a young man in his middle twenties who came here, hit on a good job, and quickly acquired the usual admirations: the bright tension of New York, the vigor and irony of its people, the autumn weather, the food, the women, the motor parkways, the theater. For a time he didn't seem to notice that this was costing him twice or more what these good things would have cost him at home if he'd been able to get them. He didn't need to notice, because he was a bachelor and such things as insurance and social security seemed like an old man's babble. This young and strapping Englishman was undoubtedly by now uprooted. His en-

thusiasm for many American customs was really a surprised contempt for his own previous ignorance of them. This is not a good basis for permanent admiration and he began to lose some of them, as he came to take them for granted. His job didn't pan out, and he found in the short and ruthless space of one month that New York is a bad town, and America a bad country maybe, to be poor in. With what he had left he went to Jamaica. Restlessness of course is a personal thing, but there was a conflict in it that I've noticed in other Britons who've sailed in here with shining eyes and left after a time in a mixed mood that is not pleasant to admit, for it is a mixture of disappointment and defeat. There is surely nothing to be ashamed of in disappointment. But many of these intending settlers can hardly fail to feel that American life is a far more severe challenge than they had figured on, and it has beaten them.

A century ago the whole adventure was, I think, materially harder on the people who made it, but psychologically not so tough. They knew before they ever left home that they were coming to a land with many less material comforts than Europe had to offer. They knew that the essential qualifications were physical hardihood, self-reliance, cheerfulness in the face of the adversity that was bound to come sometime, an indifference to social niceties, and a shrugging acceptance of dirt, bad luck, violence, and bankruptcy. The visitors who didn't prepare themselves for these hazards had nowhere to turn for sympathy. Their criticisms sounded niggling and effeminate. Thus in 1820, Washington Irving described such Englishmen: "They miss some of the snug conveniences and petty comforts which belong to an old, highly-finished and over-populous state of society; where the ranks of useful labour are crowded, and many earn a painful and servile subsistence by studying the very caprices of appetite and self-indulgence. These minor comforts, however, are all-important in the estimation of narrow minds." 4

It sounds just like a British criticism of the traveling American today. Only the other day a young American film star (who was born on a small farm) caused a commotion in an "old, highly finished" hotel in Paris by demanding an air-conditioned room. 5

Nowadays an Englishman's complaints would not be likely to turn on such things. Now the material scales are weighted in America's favor. Today you can cross the three thousand miles of the American continent and never want for a private bathroom, a cement highway, a night baseball game, an airplane connection, a pair of nylon stockings, or a gallon of ice cream in six different flavors. 6

But the catch is that America is no more willing than it has ever been to give these things away for free. They are not in this country the luxuries that a secure upper class once exacted from a swarming and servile lower class. They are the minimum demands of comfort made by a population as fertile as its resources, in a country where comfort has accordingly turned into big business. A share of that comfort, a bigger share of satisfying and ingenious comfort than any other nation has ever known, can be bought by any worker with a steady wage. But the measure of that steady wage is the energy he can maintain. Visiting teams of British factory managers have remarked on the tenacity with which American workers compete through incentive schemes. You have only to lean out of any midtown window in 7

New York, or in a score of other cities, to notice the furious concentration and energy of construction workers while they are on the job. At four-thirty they will quit like an exploding light bulb, but up to that moment they haul and hammer and drill and bulldoze with fearful zest.

8   A little time ago I left my office, as I usually do, about seven in the evening (not having the instinctive zest of the natives) and saw that the whole lobby of the skyscraper office-building—which spans something like the floor-space of Piccadilly Circus—was covered with tarpaulin from which arose a network of ladders and scaffolding, a whole series of wooden platforms running about seven or eight feet from the ceiling. This scaffolding alone looked as if it might take a day or two to put up. But none of it was there at five o'clock when the offices of this building disgorged their three or four thousand employees. However, this was only the preparation for the job in hand. The job in hand was the painting of the whole of this great ceiling, which is about thirty feet from the ground. Sixteen men at various intervals were already up on the platforms and beginning to wave a kind of big flat brush, which from my angle looked about as wide as the tail of a whale. I had to come back that night to my office to catch the midnight news. There was not a man in sight, nor a paint brush, nor any tarpaulin or scaffolding. The night cleaners were already busy with their monster vacuum cleaners. And the ceiling was gleaming with its new paint.

9   This kind of shock greets the stranger wherever he goes. You have your house painted, or a wall knocked down, or new lighting sockets put in. And I should warn any incurable English perfectionist that half the time you will get a finished job something less than what would satisfy a first-rate craftsman. But this is neither their aim nor their interest. They do what they contract to do with remarkable speed and skill. Then they clean up your disordered home in a final cheerful burst and are on their way back to their wives, their shower-bath, their steak and television sets. These men get paid better than any working-men have ever been paid, allowing for the exchange, the higher cost of living, and all that. The painters I just told you about were earning a hundred and thirty dollars a week—forty-six pounds ten— which will take care of quite a lot of high cost of living. (I ought to add, though, that they pay just about the same, forty-six pounds ten, one week's wages, for the monthly rent of a small house.) If they work this way, they will keep their job. If they don't, they won't: that is the simple, brutal rule of life in America in prosperous times.

10   You can see how hard it is to start from scratch in this country, which already has a labor force of over sixty millions, and the fiercest kind of competition at all levels, from the laborer to the managing director. It sounds like a nightmare, and it may well be so to gentle, sensitive people who have no sympathy with the fight for life and merely want to earn enough money to give them leisure in their evenings, some fields to walk across, a little light and air. In the big cities of America these things too come at a high price. I sometimes feel that the house agents and real-estate men in all the big cities have measured every building and gauged exactly how many cubic inches of every little room are touched by sunlight for a few hours of the day. That room, once the real-estate agents discover its secret, will have its rent doubled. Several million middle-class families in the cities of England have a

little back garden which they could reproduce in New York for a mere five thousand pounds.

It is hard for the romantic Englishman or woman to talk to Americans about these anxieties. Apart from seeming a chronic complainer, you will also tend to sound to Americans like a kind of immigrant they were long ago warned about. Washington Irving was on to this type too and wrote of them: ". . . they may have pictured America to themselves an El Dorado, where gold and silver abounded, and the natives were lacking in sagacity; and where they were to become strangely and suddenly rich in some unforeseen, but easy manner."   11

Well, that sort of character will be around for quite a time yet, but he grows increasingly peevish. It may be that present-day America, or rather the movie and magazine myths about it, attracts a semi-playboy type that is too soft to take the known risks of a hundred years ago. Unfortunately, the austerity and anxiety of Europe produce, too, many unassuming and honest people who are looking for nothing more than a competence and a little peace and quiet. To the newcomer there is no easy guarantee of it. Sons of wealth can have it without any effort, for this country now has the biggest class of hereditary rich of any nation on earth. But for the newcomer there will be little concern about how he lived or what he was used to, or the kind of people he moved among. If he wants the same society in America, he must buy his way into it. Not what you seem to be, but what you prove you can do: that is still, for the stranger, the persistent pioneer requirement. You have been warned.   12

Vocabulary

austerity, niceties, niggling, sagacity

Questions

1. Cooke distinguishes among several reasons that immigrant Englishmen leave America. List them.
2. Cooke implies that American workers differ from English workers in several respects. What are those differences? Does Cooke admire the American worker uncritically?
3. The economic scene has changed somewhat since Cooke wrote this essay. Has the American working class changed in the meantime? How so?
4. Are Americans fairly classified as fierce competitors? What examples support this view? Are there examples to support the classification of the English as "romantic"?

Topics for Writing

A Letter to an Intending Immigrant Today

The American Worker, Eighties Style

Parents

MAXINE HONG KINGSTON (1940–) Now a teacher at the University of Hawaii, Maxine Hong Kingston has explored her roots in *China Men* and *The Woman Warrior: Memoirs of a Girlhood among Ghosts.*

1   Once in a long while, four times so far for me, my mother brings out the metal tube that holds her medical diploma. On the tube are gold circles crossed with seven red lines each—"joy" ideographs in abstract. There are also little flowers that look like gears for a gold machine. According to the scraps of labels with Chinese and American addresses, stamps, and postmarks, the family airmailed the can from Hong Kong in 1950. It got crushed in the middle, and whoever tried to peel the labels off stopped because the red and gold paint came off too, leaving silver scratches that rust. Somebody tried to pry the end off before discovering that the tube pulls apart. When I open it, the smell of China flies out, a thousand-year-old bat flying heavy-headed out of the Chinese caverns where bats are as white as dust, a smell that comes from long ago, far back in the brain. Crates from Canton, Hong Kong, Singapore, and Taiwan have that smell too, only stronger because they are more recently come from the Chinese.

2   Inside the can are three scrolls, one inside another. The largest says that in the twenty-third year of the National Republic, the To Keung School of Midwifery, where she has had two years of instruction and Hospital Practice, awards its Diploma to my mother, who has shown through oral and written examination her Proficiency in Midwifery, Pediatrics, Gynecology, "Medecine," "Surgary," Therapeutics, Ophthalmology, Bacteriology, Dermatology, Nursing, and Bandage. . . .

3   The school seal has been pressed over a photograph of my mother at the age of thirty-seven. The diploma gives her age as twenty-seven. She looks younger than I do, her eyebrows are thicker, her lips fuller. Her naturally curly hair is parted on the left, one wavy wisp tendrilling off to the right. She wears a scholar's white gown, and she is not thinking about her appearance. She stares straight ahead as if she could see me and past me to her grandchildren and grandchildren's grandchildren. She has spacy eyes, as all people recently from Asia have. Her eyes do not focus on the camera. My mother is not smiling; Chinese do not smile for photographs. Their faces command relatives in foreign lands—"Send money"—and posterity forever— "Put food in front of this picture." My mother does not understand Chinese-American snapshots. "What are you laughing at?" she asks.

4   The second scroll is a long narrow photograph of the graduating class with the school officials seated in front. I picked out my mother immediately. Her face is exactly her own, though forty years younger. She is so familiar, I can only tell whether or not she is pretty or happy or smart by comparing her to the other women. For this formal group picture she straightened her hair with oil to make a chin-length bob like the others'. On the other women, strangers, I can recognize a

curled lip, a sidelong glance, pinched shoulders. My mother is not soft; the girl with the small nose and dimpled underlip is soft. My mother is not humorous, not like the girl at the end who lifts her mocking chin to pose like Girl Graduate. My mother does not have smiling eyes; the old woman teacher (Dean Woo?) in front crinkles happily, and the one faculty member in the western suit smiles westernly. Most of the graduates are girls whose faces have not yet formed; my mother's face will not change anymore, except to age. She is intelligent, alert, pretty. I can't tell if she's happy.

The graduates seem to have been looking elsewhere when they pinned the   5
rose, zinnia, or chrysanthemum on their precise black dresses. One thin girl wears hers in the middle of her chest. A few have a flower over a left or a right nipple. My mother put hers, a chrysanthemum, below her left breast. Chinese dresses at that time were dartless, cut as if women did not have breasts; these young doctors, unaccustomed to decorations, may have seen their chests as black expanses with no reference points for flowers. Perhaps they couldn't shorten that far gaze that lasts only a few years after a Chinese emigrates. In this picture too my mother's eyes are big with what they held—reaches of oceans beyond China, land beyond oceans. Most emigrants learn the barbarians' directness—how to gather themselves and stare rudely into talking faces as if trying to catch lies. In America my mother has eyes as strong as boulders, never once skittering off a face, but she has not learned to place decorations and phonograph needles, nor has she stopped seeing land on the other side of the oceans. Now her eyes include the relatives in China, as they once included my father smiling and smiling in his many western outfits, a different one for each photograph that he sent from America.

He and his friends took pictures of one another in bathing suits at Coney Island   6
beach, the salt wind from the Atlantic blowing their hair. He's the one in the middle with his arms about the necks of his buddies. They pose in the cockpit of a biplane, on a motorcycle, and on a lawn beside the "Keep Off the Grass" sign. They are always laughing. My father, white shirt sleeves rolled up, smiles in front of a wall of clean laundry. In the spring he wears a new straw hat, cocked at a Fred Astaire angle. He steps out, dancing down the stairs, one foot forward, one back, a hand in his pocket. He wrote to her about the American custom of stomping on straw hats come fall. "If you want to save your hat for next year," he said, "you have to put it away early, or else when you're riding the subway or walking along Fifth Avenue, any stranger can snatch it off your head and put his foot through it. That's the way they celebrate the change of seasons here." In the winter he wears a gray felt hat with his gray overcoat. He is sitting on a rock in Central Park. In one snapshot he is not smiling; someone took it when he was studying, blurred in the glare of the desk lamp.

Vocabulary

ideographs, abstract, midwifery, pediatrics, therapeutics, gynecology, ophthalmology, bacteriology, dermatology, tendrilling, spacy, posterity, sidelong, precise, dartless, reaches, emigrants, barbarians, skittering

Questions

1. Point out two instances in which Mrs. Kingston distinguishes Chinese characteristics from American ones.
2. Do you find the "joy" ideographs appropriate?
3. Are there relics in your family that speak of another country or another culture?
4. Do you think the author is reading too much into the picture of her mother?
5. Do the playful photos of her father prove that he is becoming westernized, or are there other possible explanations for these poses?

Topics for Writing

What Mr. Hong Was Probably Thinking

A Family Relic

I, Too

LANGSTON HUGHES (1902–1967), a leading figure of the Harlem Renaissance, was born in Mississippi but traveled widely in this country and in
Europe. He published in magazines and wrote books—fiction, children's
books, and autobiography as well as poetry.

I, too, sing America.

I am the darker brother.
They send me to eat in the kitchen
When company comes,
But I laugh,   5
And eat well,
And grow strong.

Tomorrow,
I'll be at the table
When company comes.   10

Nobody'll dare
Say to me,
"Eat in the kitchen,"
Then.

Besides,   15
They'll see how beautiful I am
And be ashamed—

I, too, am America.

Questions

1. Why can the speaker laugh when he is sent to the kitchen? Is it because he
   sees the futility of attempts to shut him out?
2. Can you find signs of sadness as well as defiance in this poem?
3. Why will "they" be ashamed?
4. Who makes the classification of people into "kitchen people" and "dining-
   room people"? Do such classifications hold when one party refuses to accept
   them?

5. Do you classify people on the basis of qualities, skills, shared interests, or what? Whom do you include in your version of "dining-room people"?

Topics for Writing

Kitchen People

The Dining Room Today: Open or Closed?

Black Children, Black Speech

DOROTHY Z. SEYMOUR (1928–) In this article, which first appeared in *Commonweal,* Dorothy Seymour draws upon her long experience of teaching children to read. She has also written for children and has been an editor and an educational consultant.

"Cmon, man, les get goin'!" called the boy to his companion. "Dat bell ringin'. It say, 'Git in rat now!' " He dashed into the school yard.

"Aw, f'get you," replied the other. "Whe' Richuh? Whe' da' muvvuh? He be goin' to schoo'."

"He in de' now, man!" was the answer as they went through the door.

In the classroom they made for their desks and opened their books. The name of the story they tried to read was "Come." It went:

> Come, Bill, come.
> Come with me.
> Come and see this.
> See what is here.

The first boy poked the second. "Wha' da' wor'?"

"Da' wor' *is*, you dope."

"*Is?* Ain't no wor' *is*. You jivin' me? Wha' da' wor' mean?"

"Ah dunno. Jus' *is*."

To a speaker of Standard English, this exchange is only vaguely comprehensible. But it's normal speech for thousands of American children. In addition it demonstrates one of our biggest educational problems: children whose speech style is so different from the writing style of their books that they have difficulty learning to read. These children speak Black English, a dialect characteristic of many inner-city Negroes. Their books are, of course, written in Standard English. To complicate matters, the speech they use is also socially stigmatized. Middle-class whites and Negroes alike scorn it as low-class poor people's talk.

Teachers sometimes make the situation worse with their attitudes toward Black English. Typically, they view the children's speech as "bad English" characterized by "lazy pronunciation," "poor grammar," and "short, jagged words." One result of this attitude is poor mental health on the part of the pupils. A child is quick to grasp the feeling that while school speech is "good," his own speech is "bad," and that by extension he himself is somehow inadequate and without value. Some children react to this feeling by withdrawing; they stop talking entirely. Others develop the attitude of "F'get you, honky." In either case, the psychological results are devastating and lead straight to the dropout route.

It is hard for most teachers and middle-class Negro parents to accept the idea that Black English is not just "sloppy talk" but a dialect with a form and structure of its own. Even some eminent black educators think of it as "bad English grammar" with "slurred consonants" (Professor Nick Aaron Ford of Morgan State College in Baltimore) and "ghettoese" (Dr. Kenneth B. Clark, the prominent educational psychologist).

4   Parents of Negro school children generally agree. Two researchers at Columbia University report that the adults they worked with in Harlem almost unanimously preferred that their children be taught Standard English in school.

5   But there is another point of view, one held in common by black militants and some white liberals. They urge that middle-class Negroes stop thinking of the inner-city dialect as something to be ashamed of and repudiated. Black author Claude Brown, for example, pushes this view.

6   Some modern linguists take a similar stance. They begin with the premise that no dialect is intrinsically "bad" or "good," and that a non-standard speech style is not defective speech but different speech. More important, they have been able to show that Black English is far from being a careless way of speaking the Standard; instead, it is a rather rigidly-constructed set of speech patterns, with the same sort of specialization in sounds, structure, and vocabulary as any other dialect.

The Sounds of Black English

7   Middle-class listeners who hear black inner-city speakers say "dis" and "tin" for "this" and "thin" assume that the black speakers are just being careless. Not at all; these differences are characteristic aspects of the dialect. The original cause of such substitutions is generally a carry-over from one's original language or that of his immigrant parents. The interference from that carryover probably caused the substitution of /d/ for the voiced *th* sound in *this*, and /t/ for the unvoiced *th* sound in *thin*. (Linguists represent language sounds by putting letters within slashes or brackets.) Most speakers of English don't realize that the two *th* sounds of English are lacking in many other languages and are difficult for most foreigners trying to learn English. Germans who study English, for example, are surprised and confused about these sounds because the only Germans who use them are the ones who lisp. These two sounds are almost nonexistent in the West African languages which most black immigrants brought with them to America.

8   Similar substitutions used in Black English are /f/, a sound similar to the unvoiced *th*, in medial word-position, as in *birfday* for *birthday*, and in final word-position, as in *roof* for *Ruth* as well as /v/ for the voiced *th* in medial position, as in *bruvver* for *brother*. These sound substitutions are also typical of Gullah, the language of black speakers in the Carolina Sea Islands. Some of them are also heard in Caribbean Creole.

9   Another characteristic of the sounds of Black English is the lack of /l/ at the end of words, sometimes replaced by the sound /w/. This makes a word like *tool* sound like *too*. If /l/ occurs in the middle of a Standard English word, in Black English it may be omitted entirely: "I can hep you." This difference is probably caused by the instability and sometimes interchangeability of /l/ and /r/ in West African languages.

One difference that is startling to middle-class speakers is the fact that Black   10
English words appear to leave off some consonant sounds at the end of words. Like
Italian, Japanese and West African words, they are more likely to end in vowel
sounds. Standard English *boot* is pronounced *boo* in Black English. *What* is *wha*.
Sure is *sho*. *Your* is *yo*. This kind of difference can make for confusion in the
classroom. Dr. Kenneth Goodman, a psycholinguist, tells of a black child whose
white teacher asked him to use *so* in a sentence—not "sew a dress" but "the other
so." The sentence the child used was "I got a *so* on my leg."

A related feature of Black English is the tendency in many cases not to use   11
sequences of more than one final consonant sound. For example, *just* is pronounced *jus'*, *past* is *pass*, *mend* sounds like *men* and *hold* like *hole*. *Six* and *box* are
pronounced *sick* and *bock*. Why should this be? Perhaps because West African
languages, like Japanese, have almost no clusters of consonants in their speech. The
Japanese, when importing a foreign word, handle a similar problem by inserting
vowel sounds between every consonant, making *baseball* sound like *besuboru*. West
Africans probably made a simpler change, merely cutting a series of two consonant
sounds down to one. Speakers of Gullah, one linguist found, have made the same
kind of adaptation of Standard English.

Teachers of black children seldom understand the reason for these differences   12
in final sounds. They are apt to think that careless speech is the cause. Actually,
black speakers aren't "leaving off" any sounds; how can you leave off something you
never had in the first place?

Differences in vowel sounds are also characteristic of the non-standard lan-   13
guage. Dr. Goodman reports that a black child asked his teacher how to spell rat.
"R-a-t," she replied. But the boy responded "No ma'am, I don't mean rat mouse, I
mean rat now." In Black English, *right* sounds like *rat*. A likely reason is that in
West African languages, there are very few vowel sounds of the type heard in the
word *right*. This type is common in English. It is called a glided or dipthongized
vowel sound. A glided vowel sound is actually a close combination of two vowels; in
the word *right* the two parts of the sound "eye" are actually "ah-ee." West African
languages have no such long, two-part, changing vowel sounds; their vowels are
generally shorter and more stable. This may be why in Black English, *time* sounds
like *Tom*, *oil* like *all*, and *my* like *ma*.

Language Structure

Black English differs from Standard English not only in its sounds but also in   14
its structure. The way the words are put together does not always fit the description
in English grammar books. The method of expressing time, or tense, for example,
differs in significant ways.

The verb *to be* is an important one in Standard English. It's used as an   15
auxiliary verb to indicate different tenses. But Black English speakers use it quite
differently. Sometimes an inner-city Negro says "He coming"; other times he says
"He be coming." These two sentences mean different things. To understand why,

let's look at the tenses of West African languages; they correspond with those of Black English.

16   Many West African languages have a tense which is called the habitual. This tense is used to express action which is always occurring and it is formed with a verb that is translated as *be*. "He be coming" means something like "He's always coming," "He usually comes," or "He's been coming."

17   In Standard English there is no regular grammatical construction for such a tense. Black English speakers, in order to form the habitual tense in English, use the word *be* as an auxiliary: *He be doing it. My Momma be working. He be running.* The habitual tense is not the same as the present tense, which is constructed in Black English without any form of the verb *to be: He do it. My Momma working. He running.* (This means the action is occurring right now.)

18   There are other tense differences between Black English and Standard English. For example, the non-standard speech does not use changes in grammar to indicate the past tense. A white person will ask, "What did your brother say?" and the black person will answer, "He say he coming." (The verb *say* is not changed to *said*.) "How did you get here?" "I walk." This style of talking about the past is paralleled in the Yoruba, Fante, Hausa, and Ewe languages of West Africa.

19   Expression of plurality is another difference. The way a black child will talk of "them boy" or "two dog" makes some white listeners think Negroes don't know how to turn a singular word into a plural word. As a matter of fact, it isn't necessary to use an *s* to express plurality. In Chinese and Japanese, singular and plural are not generally distinguished by such inflections; plurality is conveyed in other ways. For example, in Chinese it's correct to say "There are three book on the table." This sentence already has two signals of plural, *three* and *are*; why require a third? This same logic is the basis of plurals in most West African languages, where nouns are often identical in the plural and the singular. For example, in Ibo, one correctly says *those man*, and in both Ewe and Yoruba one says *they house*. American speakers of Gullah retain this style; it is correct in Gullah to say *five dog*.

20   Gender is another aspect of language structure where differences can be found. Speakers of Standard English are often confused to find that the non-standard vernacular often uses just one gender of pronoun, the masculine, and refers to women as well as men as *he* or *him*. "He a nice girl," even "Him a nice girl" are common. This usage probably stems from West African origins, too, as does the use of multiple negatives, such as "Nobody don't know it."

21   Vocabulary is the third aspect of a person's native speech that could affect his learning of a new language. The strikingly different vocabulary often used in Negro Non-standard English is probably the most obvious aspect of it to a casual white observer. But its vocabulary differences don't obscure its meaning the way different sounds and different structure often do.

22   Recently there has been much interest in the African origins of words like *goober* (peanut), *cooter* (turtle), and *tote* (carry), as well as others that are less certainly African, such as *to dig* (possibly from the Wolof *degan*, "to understand"). Such expressions seem colorful rather than low-class to many whites; they become

assimilated faster than their black originators do. English professors now use *dig* in their scholarly articles, and current advertising has enthusiastically adopted *rap*.

Is it really possible for old differences in sound, structure, and vocabulary to persist from the West African languages of slave days into present-day inner city Black English? Easily. Nothing else really explains such regularity of language habits, most of which persist among black people in various parts of the Western Hemisphere. For a long time scholars believed that certain speech forms used by Negroes were merely leftovers from archaic English preserved in the speech of early English settlers in America and copied by their slaves. But this theory has been greatly weakened, largely as the result of the work of a black linguist, Dr. Lorenzo Dow Turner of the University of Chicago. Dr. Turner studied the speech of Gullah Negroes in the Sea Islands off the Carolina coast and found so many traces of West African languages that he thoroughly discredited the archaic-English theory.   23

When anyone learns a new language, it's usual to try speaking the new language with the sounds and structure of the old. If a person's first language does not happen to have a particular sound needed in the language he is learning, he will tend to substitute a similar or related sound from his native language and use it to speak the new one. When Frenchman Charles Boyer said "Zees ees my heart," and when Latin American Carmen Miranda sang "Souse American way," they were simply using sounds of their native languages in trying to pronounce sounds of English. West Africans must have done the same thing when they first attempted English words. The tendency to retain the structure of the native language is a strong one, too. That's why a German learning English is likely to put his verb at the end: "May I a glass beer have?" The vocabulary of one's original language may also furnish some holdovers. Jewish immigrants did not stop using the word *bagel* when they came to America; nor did Germans stop saying *sauerkraut*.   24

Social and geographical isolation reinforces the tendencies to retain old language habits. When one group is considered inferior, the other group avoids it. For many years it was illegal to give any sort of instruction to Negroes, and for slaves to try to speak like their masters would have been unthinkable. Conflict of value systems doubtless retards changes, too. As Frantz Fanon observed in *Black Skin, White Masks*, those who take on white speech habits are suspect in the ghetto, because others believe they are trying to "act white." Dr. Kenneth Johnson, a black linguist, put it this way: "As long as disadvantaged black children live in segregated communities and most of their relationships are confined to those within their own subculture, they will not replace their functional nonstandard dialect with the nonfunctional standard dialect."   25

Linguists have made it clear that language systems that are different are not necessarily deficient. A judgment of deficiency can be made only in comparison with another language system. Let's turn the tables on Standard English for a moment and look at it from the West African point of view. From this angle, Standard English: (1) is lacking in certain language sounds, (2) has a couple of unnecessary language sounds for which others may serve as good substitutes, (3) doubles and drawls some of its vowel sounds in sequences that are unusual and   26 difficult to imitate, (4) lacks a method of forming an important tense, (5) requires an unnecessary number of ways to indicate tense, plurality and gender, and (6) doesn't mark negatives sufficiently for the result to be a good strong negative statement.

27   Now whose language is deficient?

28   How would the adoption of this point of view help us? Say we accept the evidence that Black English is not just a sloppy Standard but an organized language style which probably has developed many of its features on the basis of its West African heritage. What would we gain?

29   The psychological climate of the classroom might improve if teachers understood why many black students speak as they do. But we still have not reached a solution of the main problem. Does the discovery that Black English has pattern and structure mean that it should not be tampered with? Should children who speak Black English be excused from learning the Standard in school? Should they perhaps be given books in Black English to learn from?

30   Any such accommodation would surely result in a hardening of the new separatism being urged by some black militants. It would probably be applauded by such people as Roy Innis, Director of CORE, who is currently recommending dual autonomous education systems for white and black. And it might facilitate learning to read, since some experiments have indicated that materials written in Black English syntax aid problem readers from the inner city.

31   But determined resistance to the introduction of such printed materials into schools can be expected. To those who view inner-city speech as bad English, the appearance in print of sentences like "My mama, he work" can be as shocking and repellent as a four-letter word. Middle-class Negro parents would probably mobilize against the move. Any stratagem that does not take into account such practicalities of the matter is probably doomed to failure. And besides, where would such a permissive policy on language get these children in the larger society, and in the long run? If they want to enter an integrated America they must be able to deal with it on its own terms. Even Professor Toni Cade of Rutgers, who doesn't want "ghetto accents" tampered with, advocates mastery of Standard English because, as she puts it, "if you want to get ahead in this country, you must master the language of the ruling class." This has always been true, wherever there has been a minority group.

32   The problem then appears to be one of giving these children the ability to speak (and read) Standard English without denigrating the vernacular and those who use it, or even affecting the ability to use it. The only way to do this is to officially espouse bi-dialectism. The result would be the ability to use either dialect equally well—as Dr. Martin Luther King did—depending on the time, place, and circumstances. Pupils would have to learn enough about Standard English to use it when necessary, and teachers would have to learn enough about the inner-city dialect to understand and accept it for what it is—not just a "careless" version of Standard English but a different form of English that's appropriate in certain times and places.

33   Can we accomplish this? If we can't, the result will be continued alienation of a large section of the population, continued dropout trouble with consequent loss of earning power and economic contribution to the nation, but most of all, loss of

faith in America as a place where a minority people can at times continue to use those habits that remind them of their link with each other and with their past.

Vocabulary

comprehensible, dialect, stigmatized, inadequate, consonants, militants, liberals, repudiated, premise, intrinsically, defective, voiced, unvoiced, linguists, medial, Creole, instability, psycholinguist, tendency, sequences, glided, dipthongized, significant, auxiliary, tenses, correspond, plurality, inflections, gender, vernacular, casual, assimilated, archaic, discredited, isolation, retards, ghetto, subculture, functional, deficient, accommodation, separatism, autonomous, facilitate, syntax, repellent, mobilize, stratagem, permissive, denigrating, vernacular, espouse, appropriate, alienation, consequent

Questions

1. What distinguishes Black English from "sloppy talk"?
2. Has the author convinced you that Black English is a true dialect, with a structure and form?
3. Is she asking us to accept Black English as an alternate Standard English? Do you think we should?
4. Is the situation of inner-city Blacks different, linguistically, from that of other immigrant groups—say, the Italians or the Germans—who came to America without knowing how to speak Standard English?
5. Do you tend to classify people by their use of English? Why?
6. Most people use at least two levels of language, depending on circumstances. In informal settings, among close friends, you probably use slangier, racier, grammatically looser speech than you do when speaking formally or among strangers. Do you think one of these levels is superior to the other? Which one better reflects the "real you"?

Topics for Writing

All Languages Are Created Equal

We Must Adhere to a Standard

The Cantor Carved

FLORENCE R. GREENBERG's (1898–?) piece comes from her longer reminiscence, "Father Was a Rabbi," published in a larger collection of immigrant memoirs printed by the Jewish Publication Society of America.

1   Father always delivered two sermons each week. Friday night he spoke in English, Saturday morning in German. It was a strenuous task, and finally the services of a cantor or assistant were procured for him. The young man was a foreigner, a young German with a very pleasing voice—and an obnoxious personality. He used to stand in front of the mirror and say: "I like myself—I am very pretty"—but he was one of the people (and there was quite a long list) whom Mother insisted we had to be nice to.

2   With this admonition in mind I consulted the boys during our parents' absence, and we decided to invite the cantor to dinner on Saturday after services. Friday morning I called the butcher and told him to send the usual order, forgetting to mention that Mother was away. My Mother liked to "draw" her own chickens, so the butcher sent one with all its innards—only the feathers had been removed.

3   Irving was in the house when the chicken was delivered. Together we gazed at it. What a fine bird! The feet were still on and so was the head. "I can cook it, I'm sure," I said. "I've watched Mother often enough, but what am I supposed to do with the head and feet?" "Oh," Irving replied, "there's nothing to that!"—and he took the hatchet and quickly removed the offending appendages. "All right, now go ahead and cook it." I took the chicken to the sink, carefully washed it, picked off the few little pin feathers, and feeling very proud of myself placed the bird in the soup kettle, added celery, onions, and carrots, as I'd seen Mother do, filled the pot with water, and went about my other household tasks. Soon the delicious aroma of chicken broth filled the air. It whetted our appetites and made us all conscious of the approaching Sabbath. Hours later, the chicken tender, I removed it from the broth and put it in the oven, from which it emerged brown, crisp, and tender. I strained the broth, and all was in readiness for the morrow.

4   Saturday dawned, and three little Reicherts went to temple. I had gotten up very early to set the table, so that when we returned from services, dinner could be served almost immediately. Services over, I ran home ahead of the others. Victor and Irv followed with our guest. All was ready. We sat down to the table, and I brought in the steaming soup, to which noodles had been added.

5   "What a smart little girl you are, Florence!" the cantor beamed at me approvingly. "You'll make some man a fine wife some day," and he leaned over and playfully pinched me on the arm, leaving a mark which turned black and blue later in the day. "Yeah," said Victor, "it is pretty good soup at that." Irving, too, seemed to approve, and I ate every drop.

"And now the chicken—ah, I suppose you have chicken," the cantor observed   6
hopefully. "Of course there's chicken," I replied, "and I'm going to ask you to carve
it for me." "A pleasure, a pleasure," he beamed, rubbing his hands together in
anticipation.

I went to the kitchen and brought back the chicken. What a fine bird it was, to   7
be sure! Never had I been so proud of myself. My brothers, too, beamed in
approval; the cantor licked his lips and then, knife in hand, began to carve. A quick
slash down the breast, a peculiar plop like exploding gas—and a stench that slowly
filled the air. I had forgotten to "draw" the chicken and cooked it with all its
entrails. For a sickening moment the cantor regarded the fowl in front of him. Then
turning green, beads of perspiration forming on his forehead, he made a beeline for
the bathroom.

Victor, Irving, and I looked at the chicken, then at one another—and then   8
had hysterics at the table. We laughed until we cried, and then we laughed all over
again. Had we planned it, it could not have been more perfect. Fortunately, the
three of us had eaten the soup also, or I'm sure the cantor would have thought that
we'd planned to poison him. It would be many months before he ate in our home
again.

Vocabulary

cantor, appendages, entrails

Questions

1. Why didn't Florence carve the chicken? Does this say anything about her
   upbringing? Who carves in your family?
2. The Jewish mother appears frequently as a character in fiction and in television comedies—loving, but sometimes overbearing in her desire to be helpful.
   What elements in this narrative support the usual view?
3. Are the parents likely to be angry when they learn how the dinner turned out?
4. The mother is strong, the father hardworking and, as a rabbi, a figure of considerable authority. Have the children been overwhelmed by their parents'
   strength? What evidence supports your view?

Topics for Writing

The Case of the Embarrassed Guest—A True Story

The Carver in Our Family

My Most Memorable Meal

Further Reflections on Ethnicity

MICHAEL NOVAK (1933–), a contemporary theologian, political analyst, and social critic, grew up in the soft-coal region of western Pennsylvania. He has written novels, taught in universities, and counseled government officials, as well as commenting at large in a syndicated feature, *The Novak Report*.

1   During the presidential election of 1972, virtually every national magazine and television news show carried stories on "the ethnic vote." They usually, but not always, meant (as I had in *The Rise of the Unmeltable Ethnics*) "white Catholic ethnic." For they carried a host of *other* stories specifically on the Jewish vote, the black vote, the Latino vote. In a larger and more accurate sense, of course, all these groups are equally ethnic. Technically and accurately speaking, each of us is ethnic: each human being participates in a particular cultural history (or histories). The fundamental question "Who am I?" includes the question, "Who are we?" This "we" is particular as well as universal, ethnic as well as humanistic. So much is pretty obvious and straightforward.

2   But practice is not always so obvious and straightforward. Quite commonly, Americans hopelessly misunderstand one another because each fails to note how the contours of his own language and experience differ from those of the other, and neither can find keys to a relevant common culture. We are not skilled in identifying the many senses of reality, styles of exposition, families of symbols, loaded words, and other culturally freighted materials that thrive among us. Some people, of course, observe such cultural cues with great intuitive skill, even without being able to articulate how they do so. The rest of us constantly try—and err. For to catch cues accurately, one must understand both the cultural background and the person. Stereotypes won't suffice.

3   There are several theses about white ethnics that are conventional but wrong. Let me state them and argue against them.

4   1. *Ethnic consciousness is regressive.* In every generation, ethnic consciouness is different. The second generation after immigration is not like the first, the third is not like the second. The native language begins to disappear; family and residential patterns alter; prosperity and education create new possibilities. The new ethnicity does not try to hold back the clock. There is no possibility of returning to the stage of our grandparents.

5   Nevertheless, emotional patterns that have been operative for a thousand years do not, for all that, cease to function. Those of white ethnic background do not usually react to persons, issues, or events like blacks, or like Jews, or like Unitarians. In a host of different ways, their instincts, judgments, and sense of reality are heirs to cultural experiences that are now largely unconscious. These intuitive leads, these echoes of yet another language, yet another rhythm, yet another vision of reality, are resources which they are able to recover, if they should so choose.

Jimmy Breslin, for example, has lamented the loss of language suffered by the 6
American Irish. He urges Irish Americans to read Brendan Behan: "For a style is
there to examine, and here and there you get these wonderful displays of the
complete lock the Irish have on the art of using words to make people smile."
Breslin loves "the motion and lilt that goes into words when they are written on
paper by somebody who is Irish." He compares Behan's tongue to the language of
the 100,000 Irishmen marching down Fifth Avenue on March 17: "You can take all
of them and stand them on their heads to get some blood into the skull of thinking,
and when you put them back on their feet you will not be able to get an original
phrase out of the lot of them. They are Irish and they get the use of words while they
take milk from their mothers, and they are residing in the word capital of the world
and we find that listed below are the two fine passages representing some of the most
important Irish writing being done in the City of New York today." He then lists
business notices from Brady the Lawyer and Walsh the Insurance Man.

Jewish writers are strong by virtue of their closeness to the Jewish experience in 7
America—e.g., their sense of story, and irony, and dissent. Mike Royko writes with
a hard realism and a blend of humor that is distinctively Slavic; like *Good Soldier
Schweik*. Phil Berrigan refers to Liz MacAlister as "Irish," and shares a traditionally
tough Irish priest's suspicion of liberal intellectuals.

Authenticity requires that one write and act out of one's own experience, 8
images, subconscious. Such materials are not merely personal (although they *are*
personal) but also social. We did not choose our grandfathers.

2. *Ethnic consciousness is only for the old; it is not shared by the young.* It is 9
true that hardly anyone in America encourages ethnic consciousness. The church,
the schools, the government, the media encourage "Americanization." So it is true
that the young are less "conscious" of their ethnicity. This does not mean that they
do not have it. It does not mean that they do not feel joy and release upon
discovering it. Often, all one has to do is begin to speak of it and shortly they begin
recollecting, begin raising questions, begin exploring—and begin recovering.

Consider the enormous psychic repression accepted by countless families—the 10
repression required for learning a new language, a new style of life, new values and
new emotional patterns, during a scant three or four generations of Americanization. Many descendants of the immigrants who do not think of themselves as
"ethnic" experience a certain alienation from public discourse in America, from
the schools, from literature, from the media, and even from themselves. Nowhere
do they see representations of their precise feelings about sex, authority, realism,
anger, irony, family, integrity, and the like. They try to follow traditional American
models, of course: the classic Protestant idealism of George McGovern, for example. They see a touch of their experience in *Portnoy's Complaint*. But nowhere at
all, perhaps, will they see artistic or political models expressing exactly their state of
soul. Nowhere do they find artists or political leaders putting into words what
remains hidden in their hearts.

The young are more ripe for the new ethnicity than the old, for the new 11
ethnicity is an attempt to express the experience of *their* generation, not of an earlier
generation. It treats past history only as a means of illuminating the present, not as

an ideal to which they must return. The new ethnicity is oriented toward the future, not the past.

12   3. *Ethnic consciousness is illiberal and divisive, and breeds hostility.* The truth is the reverse. What is illiberal is homogenization enforced in the name of liberalism. What is divisive is an enforced and premature unity, especially a unity in which some groups are granted cultural superiority as models for the others. What breeds hostility is the quiet repression of diversity, the refusal to allow others to be culturally different, the enforcement of a single style of Americanism. Our nation suffers from enormous emotional repression. Our failure to legitimate a genuine cultural pluralism is one of the roots of this repression. Our rationalization is fear of disunity; and in the name of unity, uniformity is benignly enforced. (The weapon of enforcement is ordinarily shame and contempt.)

13   Countless young Italians were given lessons in school on how *not* to talk with their hands; Latin girls were induced to shave their lips and legs; Irish girls to hide their freckles; Poles to feel apologetic about their difficult names; Italians to dread association with criminal activity; Scandinavians and Poles to hate misinterpretations of their taciturnity and impassive facial expression; Catholics to harden themselves against the anti-Catholicism both of intellectual culture and of nativist America.

14   The assumption that ethnic consciousness breeds prejudice and hostility suggests that Americanization frees one from them. The truth is that *every* ethnic culture—including mainstream America, and, yes, even intellectual America—has within it resources of compassion and vision as well as capacities for evil. Homogenized America is built on a foundation of psychic repression; it has not shown itself to be exempt from bitter prejudices and awful hostilities.

15   America announces itself as a nation of cultural pluralism. Let it become so, openly and with mutual trust.

16   4. *Ethnic consciousness will disappear.* The world will end, too. The question is how to make the most fruitful, humanistic progress in the meantime. The preservation of ethnicity is a barrier against alienation and anomie, a resource of compassion and creativity and intergroup learning. If it *might* disappear in the future, it has *not* disappeared in the present. And there are reasons to work so that it never does. Who would want to live on a thoroughly homogenized planet?

17   5. *Intermarriage hopelessly confuses ethnicity.* Intermarriage gives children multiple ethnic models. The transmission of a cultural heritage is not a process clearly understood. But for any child a "significant other" on one side of the family or another may unlock secrets of the psyche as no other does. The rhythm and intensity of emotional patterns in families are various, but significant links to particular cultural traditions almost always occur. One discovers these links best by full contact with ethnic materials. It is amazing how persons who insist that they have a "very mixed" ethnic background, and "no particular" ethnic consciousness, exhibit patterns of taste and appreciation that are very ethnic indeed: a delight in the self-restraint of Scotsmen, discomfort with the effusiveness of Sicilians—or, by contrast, a sense of release in encountering Sicilian emotions, a constriction of nervousness faced with the puzzling cues of the culture of the Scots.

Cues for interpreting emotion and meaning are subtly learned, in almost   18
wholly unconscious, informal ways. These cues persist through intermarriage for an
indeterminate period. Cues to pain, anger, intimacy and humor are involved.
(Some passages of *The Rise of the Unmeltable Ethnics* were intended ironically and
written in laughter; some reviewers took them seriously.)

6. *Intelligent, sensitive ethnics, proud of their heritage, do not go around*   19
thumping their chests in ethnic chauvinism. Who would want chest-thumping or
chauvinism? But be careful of the definition of "good" ethnics, "well-behaved"
ethnics. Many successful businessmen, artists, and scholars of white ethnic background carry two sets of scars. On the one hand, they had to break from their
families, neighborhoods, perhaps ghettoes, and they became painfully aware of the
lack of education and experience among those less fortunate than they. On the
other hand, they had to learn the new styles, new images, and new values of the
larger culture of "enlightenment." The most talented succeed rather easily; those of
lesser rank have quietly repressed many all-too-painful memories of the period of
their transition. As surely as their grandparents emigrated from their homeland,
each generation has had to carry the emigration farther. Americanization is a
process of bittersweet memory, and it lasts longer than a hundred years.

7. *The new ethnicity will divide group against group.* The most remarkable fact   20
about the new ethnic consciousness is that it is cross-cultural. We do not speak only
of "Polish" consciousness or "Italian" consciousness, but of "white ethnic" consciousness. The new ethnicity is not particularistic. It stresses the general contours
of *all* ethnicity and notes analogies between the cultural histories of the many
groups. The stress is not only on what differentiates each group but also upon the
similarities of *structure* and *process* in which all are involved. In coming to recognize the contours of his or her own unique cultural history, a person is better able to
understand and to sympathize with the uniqueness of others'.

8. *Emphasis on white ethnics detracts from the first priority to be given blacks.*   21
On the contrary, blindness to white ethnics is an almost guaranteed way of boxing
blacks into a hopeless corner. A group lowest on the ladder cannot advance *solely* at
the expense of the next group. Any skillful statesman could discern that in an
instant. The classic device of the affluent and the privileged is to pretend to a higher
morality, while setting the lower classes in conflict with one another.

The most divisive force in America today is, ironically, precisely the "new   22
class" of liberal and radical academics, media personnel, and social service profes-
sionals that thinks itself so moral. Perhaps out of guilt feelings—or for whatever
reason—they have projected all guilt for "white racism" onto others. And, without
undergoing any of the costs themselves, they take sides or plainly appear to take
sides in the very sharp competition between lower-class people, white and black, for
scarce jobs, scarce housing, scarce openings in colleges, scarce scholarship funds.
They take sides not only with blacks against whites but also with militant blacks
against other blacks. For almost a decade they have made "white racism" the central
motif of social analysis, and have clearly given the impression that vast resources
were going for blacks, nothing for others.

It is easy for blacks, at least militant blacks, to voice their grievances on   23 television and in the papers. It is extremely difficult to get coverage of white ethnic grievances. They are not supposed to *have* grievances, it seems, only prejudices. All problems are defined as black-white problems, even when there are obviously real economic issues for real families in straitened circumstances. With all good intentions, therefore, the desire of liberals to give blacks highest priority has become exclusionary and divisive.

24   One can still give blacks highest priority, but in an inclusionary way that aims at coalitions of whites and blacks on the grievances they have in common. Newark is divided almost wholly between blacks and Italians; Detroit between Poles and blacks. Inadequate schools, the dangers of drugs, insufficient housing, the lack of support for families and neighborhoods—these grievances afflict white ethnics and blacks alike. If these problems are, by definition, problems of race, what sort of practical coalition can possibly grow? If they are perceived as problems of *class* (with ethnic variables) there is at least a practical ground for effective coalition.

25   In order for a political coalition to work well, people do not have to love one another; they do not have to share the same life style or cherish the same values. They have to be realistic enough to pursue limited goals in line with their own self-interest. Lower-middle-class blacks and white ethnics share more self-interests in common than either group does with any other. It is on the basis of shared self-interests that lasting political coalitions are built, and on no other.

26   9. *Ethnicity is all right for minorities, but not for the mainstream.* In America, every group is a minority. Even among white Anglo-Saxon Protestants there are many traditions. What is often called "mainline Protestantism," centered in the Northeast—Episcopal, Congregational, Presbyterian—is only one tradition within a far larger and more complex Protestant reality. The father of Senator George McGovern experienced prejudice in South Dakota because the kind of Methodist fundamentalism he represented was closer in style to the lower classes, not fashionable either among "mainline" Methodists nor among Germans and Scandinavians, who were mostly Lutheran. Each of these traditions affects the imagination in a different way. British Americans from small towns in New England live and work in quite different emotional and imaginative worlds from British Americans who are Brahmins in Boston and New York. Anglo-Saxon Protestants who are dirt-farmers in Georgia, Alabama, or East Tennessee feel just as much prejudice from Northeastern-style settlers as Polish or Italian Catholics; stereotypes of the Southern sheriff and the redneck function like those of the Irish cop and the dumb hard-hat. The Scotch Irish and the Scots have a vivid ethnic consciousness, as a conversation with John Kenneth Galbraith and Carey McWilliams, Jr., would make plain.

27   There is no good reason why we do not all drop our pretensions of being *like* everyone else, and attempt instead to enlarge the range of our sympathies, so as to delight in every observed cultural difference and to understand each cultural cue correctly and in its own historical context. Styles of wit and understatement vary. Each culture has its own traditions of emotional repression and expressiveness. Our major politicians are often misunderstood, systematically, by one cultural group or another; the cues they depend on are absent, or mean something else.

28   "The new ethnicity" has at least three components. First, there is a new

interest in cultural pluralism in our midst. It calls for a new sensitivity toward others in their differences. It means looking at America alert to nuances of difference, more cautious about generalizations about "Americans." Second, there is the personal, conscious self-appropriation of *one's own* cultural history—a making conscious of what perhaps one before had not even noticed about oneself. This component is a form of "consciousness raising." It is useful because ways of perceiving are usually transmitted informally, without conscious design or articulation. As one makes progress in appropriating one's own complexity, one finds it necessary to give others, too, more attentive regard. Thirdly, there is a willingness to share in the social and political needs and struggles of groups to which one is culturally tied, as a way of bringing about a greater harmony, justice and unity in American (and world) society. Rather than pretend to speak for all, or to understand all, we can each make a contribution toward what we can do best.

Vocabulary

regressive, psychic, alienation, premature, benignly, nativist, pluralism, humanistic, chauvinism, motif, straitened, Brahmins, stereotypes

Questions

1. What method does Novak use to organize the central portion of this selection?
2. In what way is the new ethnicity "oriented towards the future"?
3. Do you (or your parents) bear either of the "two sets of scars" Novak describes in section 6?
4. Do you agree that we should "delight in . . . cultural difference"? Do you delight in or are you irritated by accents and mannerisms unlike your own? For example, how do you react to "Y'all come back!" or the boisterous greetings of South Boston or the taciturnity of rural Vermont?
5. Does your family hug and kiss frequently? Does it make you uncomfortable to be among those who show family affection differently?

Topics for Writing

How My Family Shows Affection

The One Accent I Can't Stand

A Scar to Be Proud Of

5

Using Analogies/Love and Marriage

An analogy is an attempt to explain one thing by showing its similarity to a very different class of things. Put another way, it is a specialized form of comparison in which the writer uses something easily grasped to explain an idea or concept that might otherwise remain vague or abstract.

"All the world's a stage," wrote Shakespeare in *As You Like It,* "And all the men and women merely players." He then went on to explain "the world" in theater terms: men and women have entrances and exits; one man plays many roles—the infant, the schoolboy, the soldier, and, in his last scene, the dotard. If, as Shakespeare supposed, we are playgoers, his analogy will throw a distinctive light upon the vague phrase "the world."

Love and marriage are complex, sometimes vexing and mysterious, matters. James Thurber's Walter Mitty rules his roost only in his imagination. Pat Mainardi describes one aspect of marriage in terms of political struggle, and Edith Efron deplores the vicious image of love reflected in daytime television drama, whereas John Donne lets his loving couple part comforted by images so elaborate that we call them *metaphysical.*

Among these writers—hopeful, romantic, cynical, and comical—you will probably find one or more who express your own opinions and reflect what you have seen so far of love and marriage. One of their analogies may shed new light on an old mystery or set you to working out a more descriptive comparison of your own.

Politics of Housework

PAT MAINARDI   (1942–) has written for *Ms.* and is a frequent contributor to *Art News.*

Though women do not complain of the power of husbands, each complains of her own husband, or of the husbands of her friends. It is the same in all other cases of servitude; at least in the commencement of the emancipatory movement. The serfs did not at first complain of the power of the lords, but only of their tyranny.

JOHN STUART MILL
On the Subjection of Women

Liberated women—very different from Women's Liberation! The first signals   1
all kinds of goodies, to warm the hearts (not to mention other parts) of the most radical men. The other signals—HOUSEWORK. The first brings sex without marriage, sex before marriage, cozy housekeeping arrangements ("I'm living with this chick") and the self-content of knowing that you're not the kind of man who wants a doormat instead of a woman. That will come later. After all, who wants that old commodity anymore, the Standard American Housewife, all husband, home and kids? The New Commodity, the Liberated Woman, has sex a lot and has a Career, preferably something that can be fitted in with the household chores—like dancing, pottery, or painting.

On the other hand is Women's Liberation—and housework. What? You say   2
this is all trivial? Wonderful! That's what I thought. It seemed perfectly reasonable. We both had careers, both had to work a couple of days a week to earn enough to live on, so why shouldn't we share the housework? So I suggested it to my mate and he agreed—most men are too hip to turn you down flat. You're right, he said. It's only fair.

Then an interesting thing happened. I can only explain it by stating that we   3
women have been brainwashed more than even we can imagine. Probably too many years of seeing television women in ecstasy over their shiny waxed floors or breaking down over their dirty shirt collars. Men have no such conditioning. They recognize the essential fact of housework right from the very beginning. Which is that it stinks.

Here's my list of dirty chores: buying groceries, carting them home and putting   4
them away; cooking meals and washing dishes and pots; doing the laundry, digging out the place when things get out of control; washing floors. The list could go on but the sheer necessities are bad enough. All of us have to do these things, or get someone else to do them for us. The longer my husband contemplated these chores, the more repulsed he became, and so proceeded the change from the normally sweet, considerate Dr. Jekyll into the crafty Mr. Hyde who would stop at nothing to avoid the horrors of—housework. As he felt himself backed into a corner

laden with dirty dishes, brooms, mops and reeking garbage, his front teeth grew longer and pointier, his fingernails haggled and his eyes grew wild. Housework trivial? Not on your life! Just try to share the burden.

5   So ensued a dialogue that's been going on for several years. Here are some of the high points:

6   "I don't mind sharing the housework, but I don't do it very well. We should each do the things we're best at." MEANING: Unfortunately I'm no good at things like washing dishes or cooking. What I do best is a little light carpentry, changing light bulbs, moving furniture (how often do *you* move furniture?). ALSO MEANING: Historically the lower classes (black men and us) have had hundreds of years experience doing menial jobs. It would be a waste of manpower to train someone else to do them now. ALSO MEANING: I don't like the dull, stupid, boring jobs, so you should do them.

7   "I don't mind sharing the work, but you'll have to show me how to do it." MEANING: I ask a lot of questions and you'll have to show me everything every time I do it because I don't remember so good. Also don't try to sit down and read while I'M doing my jobs because I'm going to annoy hell out of you until it's easier to do them yourself.

8   "We used to be so happy!" (Said whenever it was his turn to do something.) MEANING: I used to be so happy. MEANING: Life without housework is bliss. No quarrel here. Perfect Agreement.

9   "We have different standards, and why should I have to work to your standards? That's unfair." MEANING: If I begin to get bugged by the dirt and crap I will say, "This place sure is a sty" or "How can anyone live like this?" and wait for your reaction. I know that all women have a sore called "Guilt over a messy house" or "Household work is ultimately my responsibility." I know that men have caused that sore—if anyone visits and the place *is* a sty, they're not going to leave and say, "He sure is a lousy housekeeper." You'll take the rap in any case. I can outwait you. ALSO MEANING: I can provoke innumerable scenes over the housework issue. Eventually doing all the housework yourself will be less painful to you than trying to get me to do half. Or I'll suggest we get a maid. She will do my share of the work. You will do yours. It's women's work.

10   "I've got nothing against sharing the housework, but you can't make me do it on your schedule." MEANING: Passive resistance. I'll do it when I damned well please, if at all. If my job is doing dishes, it's easier to do them once a week. If taking out laundry, once a month. If washing the floors, once a year. If you don't like it, do it yourself oftener, and then I won't do it at all.

11   "I hate it more than you. You don't mind it so much." MEANING: Housework is garbage work. It's the worst crap I've ever done. It's degrading and humiliating for someone of *my* intelligence to do it. But for someone of *your* intelligence . . .

12   "Housework is too trivial to even talk about." MEANING: It's even more trivial to do. Housework is beneath my status. My purpose in life is to deal with matters of significance. Yours is to deal with matters of insignificance. You should do the housework.

"This problem of housework is not a man-woman problem. In any relation- 13
ship between two people one is going to have a stronger personality and dominate."
MEANING: That stronger personality had better be *me*.

"In animal societies, wolves, for example, the top animal is usually a male 14
even where he is not chosen for brute strength but on the basis of cunning and
intelligence. Isn't that interesting?" MEANING: I have historical, psychological, anthropological and biological justification for keeping you down. How can you ask
the top wolf to be equal?

"Women's liberation isn't really a political movement." MEANING: The revolu- 15
tion is coming too close to home. ALSO MEANING: I am only interested in how I am
oppressed, not how I oppress others. Therefore the war, the draft and the university
are political. Women's liberation is not.

"Man's accomplishments have always depended on getting help from other 16
people, mostly women. What great man would have accomplished what he did if
he had to do his own housework?" MEANING: Oppression is built into the system and
I, as the white American male, receive the benefits of this system. I don't want to
give them up.

Participatory democracy begins at home. If you are planning to implement 17
your politics, there are certain things to remember:

1. He *is* feeling it more than you. He's losing some leisure and you're gaining 18
it. The measure of your oppression is his resistance.

2. A great many American men are not accustomed to doing monotonous, 19
repetitive work which never issues in any lasting, let alone important, achievement.
This is why they would rather repair a cabinet than wash dishes. If human en-
deavors are like a pyramid with man's highest achievements at the top, then keeping
oneself alive is at the bottom. Men have always had servants (us) to take care of this
bottom stratum of life while they have confined their efforts to the rarefied upper
regions. It is thus ironic when they ask of women—Where are your great painters,
statesmen, etc.? Mme. Matisse ran a millinery shop so he could paint. Mrs. Martin
Luther King kept his house and raised his babies.

3. It is a traumatizing experience for someone who has always thought of 20
himself as being against any oppression or exploitation of one human being by
another to realize that in his daily life he has been accepting and implementing (and
benefiting from) this exploitation; that his rationalization is little different from that
of the racist who says, "Black people don't feel pain" (women don't mind doing the
shitwork); and that the oldest form of oppression in history has been the oppression
of fifty percent of the population by the other fifty percent.

4. Arm yourself with some knowledge of the psychology of oppressed peoples 21
everywhere, and a few facts about the animal kingdom. I admit playing top wolf or
who runs the gorillas is silly but as a last resort men bring it up all the time. Talk
about bees. If you feel really hostile bring up the sex life of spiders. They have sex.
She bites off his head.

The psychology of oppressed peoples is not silly. Jews, immigrants, black men 22
and all women have employed the same psychological mechanisms to survive:

admiring the oppressor, glorifying the oppressor, wanting to be like the oppressor, wanting the oppressor to like them, mostly because the oppressor held all the power.

23   5. In a sense, all men everywhere are slightly schizoid—divorced from the reality of maintaining life. This makes it easier for them to play games with it. It is almost a cliché that women feel greater grief at sending a son off to a war or losing him to that war because they bore him, suckled him, and raised him. The men who foment those wars did none of those things and have a more superficial estimate of the worth of human life. One hour a day is a low estimate of the amount of time one has to spend "keeping" oneself. By foisting this off on others, man has seven hours a week—one working day more to play with his mind and not his human needs. Over the course of generations it is easy to see whence evolved the horrifying abstractions of modern life.

24   6. With the death of each form of oppression, life changes and new forms evolve. English aristocrats at the turn of the century were horrified at the idea of enfranchising working men—were sure that it signaled the death of civilization and a return to barbarism. Some working men were even deceived by this line. Similarly with the minimum wage, abolition of slavery, and female suffrage. Life changes but it goes on. Don't fall for any line about the death of everything if men take a turn at the dishes. They will imply that you are holding back the revolution (their revolution). But you are advancing it (your revolution).

25   7. Keep checking up. Periodically consider who's actually *doing* the jobs. These things have a way of backsliding so that a year later once again the woman is doing everything. After a year make a list of jobs the man has rarely if ever done. You will find cleaning pots, toilets, refrigerators and ovens high on the list. Use time sheets if necessary. He will accuse you of being petty. He is above that sort of thing (housework). Bear in mind that the worst jobs are, namely the ones that have to be done every day or several times a day. Also the ones that are dirty—it's more pleasant to pick up books, newspapers, etc., than to wash dishes. Alternate the bad jobs. It's the daily grind that gets you down. Also make sure that you don't have the responsibility for the housework with occasional help from him. "I'll cook dinner for you tonight" implies it's really your job and isn't he a nice guy to do some of it for you.

26   8. Most men had a rich and rewarding bachelor life during which they did not starve or become encrusted with crud or buried under the litter. There is a taboo that says women mustn't strain themselves in the presence of men—we haul around 50 pounds of groceries if we have to but aren't allowed to open a jar if there is someone around to do it for us. The reverse side of the coin is that men aren't supposed to be able to take care of themselves without a woman. Both are excuses for making women do the housework.

27   9. Beware of the double whammy. He won't do the little things he always did because you're now a "Liberated Woman," right? Of course he won't do anything else either . . .

28   I was just finishing this when my husband came in and asked what I was doing. Writing a paper on housework. Housework? he said. *Housework?* Oh my god how trivial can you get? A paper on housework.

Vocabulary

servitude, emancipatory, serfs, commodity, menial, significance, anthropological, participatory, rarefied, traumatizing, exploitation, rationalization, schizoid, cliché, foment, foisting, enfranchising, barbarism, suffrage, taboo, "double whammy"

Questions

1. The author of this article sees an analogy between politics and marriage as it relates to necessary household chores. What are some of the similarities that make the analogy valid?
2. Do you agree with the distinction drawn between Women's Liberation and liberated women? Why does she prefer the former?
3. Do you find her political tactics for the "housework revolution" effective?
4. In your experience, is it the housework or the repetitive nature of housework that people find repellent?

Topics for Writing

An Ideal Division of Chores

The Home: A Democracy or a Monarchy?

The Soaps—Anything But 99 44/100 Percent Pure

EDITH EFRON (1922–) This analysis of soap operas seems as pertinent today as it did in 1965, when it first appeared in *T.V. Guide.*

1   Some months ago, the sleepy, Victorian world of daytime drama made news. The news was that it had ceased to be sleepy and Victorian. In fact, said the reports, the soap operas were doing something no one could quite believe: "peddling sex."

2   Announced one astounded critic: "Folks squawking about cheap nighttime sex should harken to the sickly sexuality of daytime soap opera. *Love of Life* details frank affairs between married women and men; *Search for Tomorrow* has a single girl in an affair with a married man, result: pregnancy; *The Secret Storm* has another single girl expecting a married man's child."

3   And under the headlines "Era of Souped-Up Soapers" and "Torrid Days on TV Serial Front," *Variety*, the weekly newspaper of the entertainment industry, reported that there was a daytime "race to dredge up the most lurid incidents in sex-based human wretchedness," and cited "a torrid couch scene involving a housewife with gown cleaved to the navel who was sloshed to the gills on martinis, working her wiles on a husband (not hers). The fade to detergent blurb left little doubt as to the ensuing action."

4   Even a superficial investigation of events in the soap-opera world confirms that these reports are true.

5   To understand this phenomenon, one must enter the total universe of the soap operas. And if one does, one soon discovers that the central source of drama is not what it used to be in the old days, when the brave housewife, with husband in wheel chair, struggled helplessly against adversity. The soaps have shifted drastically on their axes; the fundamental theme today is, as Roy Winsor, producer of *Secret Storm*, puts it: "the male-female relationship."

6   More specifically, the theme of nine of the ten daytime shows on the air when this study was launched is the mating-marital-reproductive cycle set against a domestic background. The outer world is certainly present—one catches glimpses of hospitals, offices, courtrooms, business establishments—but the external events tend to be a foil for the more fundamental drama, which is rooted in the biological life cycle. Almost all dramatic tension and moral conflict emerge from three basic sources: mating, marriage and babies.

7   The mating process is the cornerstone of this trivalue system. The act of searching for a partner goes on constantly in the world of soap opera. Vacuous teenage girls have no thought whatever in their heads except hunting for a man. Older women wander about, projecting their intense longing to link themselves to unattached males. Heavily made-up villainous "career women" prowl, relentlessly seek-

ing and nabbing their prey: the married man. Sad, lonely divorcées hunt for new mates.

This all-consuming, single-minded search for a mate is an absolute good in the   8
soap-opera syndrome. Morality—and dramatic conflict—emerge from how the search is conducted. Accordingly, there is sex as approached by "good" people, and sex as it is approached by villains.

"Good" people's sex is a somewhat extraordinary phenomenon, which can best   9
be described as "icky." In *The Doctors*, Dr. Maggie confides, coyly, to her sister: "He kissed me." Her sister asks, even more coyly: "Did you want him to kiss you?" Maggie wriggles, and says: "He says I did." Then archly adds: "You know? I did." Maggie has already been married; her sister has had at least one lover. Coyness, not chastity, is the sign of their virtue.

"Good" people's sex is also passive, diffident and apologetic. In *The Doctors*,   10
Sam, after an unendurably long buildup, finally takes Dr. Althea, a troubled divorcée, in his arms, and kisses her once, gently, on the lips. He then looks rueful, says, "I'm sorry," and moves to look mournfully out the window. "I'm not," murmurs Althea softly, and floats out of the room.

The "good" people act like saddened goldfish; the villains, on the other hand,   11
are merely grotesque. One gets the impression that villains, both male and female, have read a lot of Ian Fleming, through several layers of cheesecloth.

To wit: a dinner between villainess Valerie Shaw and Dr. Matt in *The Doctors*   12
in which Valerie leers, ogles and hints ("A smart woman judges a man by his mouth. . . . Yours is strong and sensual. I'm glad I came to dinner"), announces she will be his "playmate" and boasts throatily, "I play hard and seriously—but not necessarily for keeps."

And in *Love of Life* a sinister chap named Ace drinks in a bar with a teen-age   13
girl who used to be his mistress. "We used to ignite," he breathes insinuatingly. They exchange a kiss—presumably so inflammable that the camera nervously cuts the picture off beneath their chins. "Not bad, baby," he gasps heavily.

This endless mating game, of course, has a purpose: It leads to marriage, the   14
second arch-value in the soap-opera universe. And the dominant view of marriage in the soaps is also worthy of mention. According to the "good" women, it consists of two ingredients: "love" and homemaking.

"Love," in the soaps, tends to be a kind of hospitalization insurance, usually   15
provided by females to male emotional cripples. In these plays, a woman rarely pledges herself to "honor and obey" her husband. She pledges to cure him of his alcoholism, to forgive his criminal record, paranoia, pathological lying, premarital affairs—and, generally, to give him a shoulder to cry on.

An expression of love, or a marriage proposal, in the daytime shows, often   16
sounds like a sobbing confession to a psychiatrist. In *Search for Tomorrow* Patti's father, a reformed drinker, took time out from brooding over his daughter's illegitimate pregnancy to express his "love" for his wife. It consisted of a thorough—and convincing—rehash of his general worthlessness and former drinking habits. "I need you," he moaned. "That's all I want," she said.

In *General Hospital* Connie's neurotic helplessness proved irresistible some   17 weeks ago; Dr. Doug declared his love. They engaged in a weird verbal competition as to who was more helpless than whom, who was more scared than whom, who "needed" whom more than whom. Doug won. Connie would be his pillar of strength.

18   Homemaking, the second ingredient of a "good" woman's marriage, is actually a symbolic expression of "love." There is a fantastic amount of discussion of food on these shows, and it is all strangely full of marital meaning. On *The Guiding Light* the audience sat through a detailed preview of the plans for roasting a turkey (the stuffing has raisins in it), which somehow would help get separated Julie and Michael together again. On *The Doctors* one ham was cooked, eaten and remorselessly discussed for three days; it played a critical role in the romance of Sam and Dr. Althea.

19   If domesticity is a marital "good," aversion to it is a serious evil. On *Secret Storm* a husband's arrival from work was greeted by a violent outburst by his wife, who handed him a list of jobs he had not done around the house. His neglect of the curtain rod was a sure sign that he was in love with a temptress who works in his office. Conversely, if a wife neglects her house, the marriage is rocky.

20   After mating and marriage, the third crucial value in the soap-opera universe is reproduction. The perpetuation of the species is the ultimate goal toward which almost all "good" people strive. And "The Baby" is the household god.

21   "Good" people discuss pregnancy endlessly. Young wives are either longing to be pregnant, worried because they are not pregnant, getting pregnant or fighting heroically "not to lose the baby." And at whatever stage of this process they happen to be, it justifies their being inept, irritable, hysterical and irrational.

22   "Good" men, needless to say, are unfailingly sympathetic to the reproductive process and are apparently fascinated by every detail of it. In *The Doctors* you knew one chap was a "good" husband because he referred to himself as "an expectant father" and earnestly discussed his wife's "whoopsing" with his friends.

23   The superlative value of "The Baby" is best revealed when he makes his appearance without benefit of a marriage license. He is usually brought into the world by a blank-faced little girl who has been taught to believe that the only valid goal in life is to mate, marry and reproduce, and who has jumped the gun. The social problem caused by this error in timing is solved in different ways. The girl has an abortion (Patricia, *Another World*); she loses the baby in an accident (Patti, *Search for Tomorrow*); she gives the baby up for adoption (Ellen, *As the World Turns*); she has the baby and marries its father (Julie, *Guiding Light*); she has the baby and marries someone else (Amy, *Secret Storm*).

24   The attitude of the baby-worshiping "good" people to this omnipresent social catastrophe is strangely mixed. The girl is viewed as a helpless victim of male villainy: "She loved the fellow too much," said Angie's father sadly in *General Hospital*. Of course, she has acquired the baby "the wrong way" and must—and does—suffer endlessly because of it. Nonetheless, she is having "The Baby." Thus she receives an enormous amount of sympathy, guidance and help from "good" people.

25   It seems almost unnecessary to say that only "bad" people in soap operas are

anti-baby. The fastest bit of characterization ever accomplished in the history of drama was achieved on *Secret Storm*, when Kip's father recently arrived on the scene. He said: "I can't stand all this talk about babies." This instantly established him as a black-hearted villain.

The worst people of all, in the soaps, however, are the "career women," unnatural creatures who actually enjoy some activity other than reproducing the species. With the single exception of *The Doctors*, which features two "good" career women, Drs. Maggie and Althea, even the feeblest flicker of a desire for a career is a symptom of villainy in a woman who has a man to support her. Some weeks ago, we could predict that Ann Reynolds, in *The Young Marrieds*, was heading for dire trouble. She was miserable over her lost career, she had no babies, and she said those most evil of words: "I want a purpose in life."   26

It is hardly surprising to discover that even when the female characters achieve their stated ideal, they are almost invariably miserable. A man to support them, an empty house to sit in, no mentally demanding work to do and an endless vista of future pregnancies do not seem to satisfy the younger soap-opera ladies. They are chronically bored and hysterical.   27

They also live in dread of the ever-present threat of adultery, because their husbands go outside every day and meet wicked career women. They also agonize frequently over the clash between their "needs as a woman" and their "needs as a mother."   28

The male denizens of this universe are equally miserable for parallel reasons. They suffer quite a bit from unrequited love. They are often sick with jealousy, tortured by their wives' jealousy of their careers and outer-world existence. They, too, have a remarkable amount of trouble reconciling their "needs as men" with their "needs as fathers."   29

So we find, amid all the gloom in Sudsville, a lot of drinking, epidemic infidelity, and countless cases of acute neurosis, criminality, psychotic breakdowns and postmaternal psychosis.   30

And this, dear reader, is the "sex" that the soap operas are "peddling" these days. It is a soggy, dreary spectacle of human misery, and is unworthy of all those "torrid" headlines. In fact, if one wants to be soured forever on the male-female relationship, the fastest way to achieve this state is to watch daytime drama.   31

The real question is not "where did all the sex come from?" but where did this depressing view of the male-female relationship come from? Hardened observers of TV's manners and mores have claimed that sex is being stressed in the soaps because it "sells." But the producers of soaps retort hotly that this has nothing to do with it. Their story lines, they insist, simply reflect social reality.   32

Says Frank Dodge, producer of *Search for Tomorrow*: "We always try to do shows that are identifiable to the public. These shows are a recognition of existing emotions and problems. It's not collusion, but a logical coincidence that adultery, illegitimate children and abortions are appearing on many shows. If you read the papers about what's going on in the suburbs—well, it's more startling than what's shown on the air."   33

"The moral fiber has been shattered in this Nation, and nothing has replaced   34 it," says Roy Winsor, producer of *Secret Storm.* "There's a clammy cynicism about life in general. It deeply infects the young. It leads to a generation that sits, passively, and watches the world go by. The major interest is the male-female relationship. That's the direction the daytime shows are going in. Some of the contemporary sickness has rubbed off onto TV."

35   A consultation with some authorities on feminine and family psychology seems to support these gentlemen's contentions about the soap operas. "They're realistic," says Dr. Harold Greenwald, training analyst of the National Psychological Association for Psychoanalysis and supervising psychologist of the Community Guidance Service in New York. "I think they're more realistic than many of the evening shows. They're reflecting the changes taking place in our society. There are fewer taboos. The age of sexual activity in the middle classes had dropped and it has increased in frequency. There is more infidelity. These plays reflect these problems."

36   Dr. William Menaker, professor of clinical psychology at New York University, says: "The theater, the novel, and the film have always reflected people's concern with the sexual life; and in this sense, what's on the air reflects these realities of life. Increasing frankness in dealing with these problems isn't a symptom of moral decay but rather reflects the confused values of a transitional period of sociosexual change.

37   "Unfortunately, the vision of sex that seems to emerge on these shows is mechanical and adolescent, immature. The 'love' seems equally childish; it is interacting dependency, rather than a mutual relating between two autonomous adults. As for anti-intellectualism of these shows, it is actually antifeminine. It shows the resistance of both writers and audience to the development of the total feminine personality. There is no doubt that these shows are a partial reflection of some existing trends in our society; it is not a healthy picture."

38   Finally, Betty Friedan, author of *The Feminine Mystique*, says: "The image of woman that emerges in these soap operas is precisely what I've called 'The Feminine Mystique.' The women are childish and dependent; the men are degraded because they relate to women who are childish and dependent; and the view of sex that emerges is sick. These plays reflect an image built up out of the sickest, most dependent, most immature women in our society. They do not reflect all women. In reality there are many who are independent, mature, and who possess identity. The soaps are reflecting the sickest aspect of women."

39   On the basis of these comments, one can certainly conclude that all this "sex-based human wretchedness" is on the air because it exists in society. And the producers' claims that this is dramatic "realism" appear to have some validity.

40   But does the fact that a phenomenon exists justify its incessant exploration by the daytime dramas? Two of the three experts consulted actively refrain from making moral judgments. Betty Friedan, however, does not hesitate to condemn the soap operas. "The fact that immature, sick, dependent women exist in our society is no justification for these plays," she says. "The soap operas are playing to this sickness. They are feeding it. They are helping to keep women in this helpless, dependent state."

Vocabulary

Victorian, harken, dredge, torrid, gills, wiles, superficial, adversity, axes, domestic, vacuous, syndrome, archly, diffident, apologetic, rueful, grotesque, cheesecloth, leers, ogles, sinister, insinuatingly, inflammable, paranoia, pathological, neurotic, remorselessly, domesticity, aversion, conversely, crucial, perpetuation, irrational, superlative, valid, omnipresent, catastrophe, vista, chronically, agonize, denizens, unrequited, reconciling, epidemic, psychotic, psychosis, collusion, coincidence, cynicism, contentions, taboos, clinical, transitional, mechanical, adolescent, dependency, autonomous, validity, phenomenon, incessant

Questions

1. Why are these afternoon dramas called "soap operas"?
2. Is the author exaggerating the morbid content of these programs?
3. If the soaps present such a gloomy picture of life, how do you account for their popularity?
4. Do you agree with Betty Friedan that these shows "are helping to keep women in this helpless, dependent state"?

Topics for Writing

Why the Soaps Succeed

Soap Operas: Reflections or Perversions of Reality?

Right On, Betty Friedan!

The Secret Life of Walter Mitty

JAMES THURBER (1894–1961) charmed generations of Americans with his fables, stories, plays, and cartoons. In Walter Mitty, he created one of the few modern characters destined to remain forever famous, like Rip van Winkle and a handful of other members of the hen-pecked tribe.

1   "We're going through!" The Commander's voice was like thin ice breaking. He wore his full-dress uniform, with the heavily braided white cap pulled down rakishly over one cold gray eye. "We can't make it, sir. It's spoiling for a hurricane, if you ask me." "I'm not asking you, Lieutenant Berg," said the Commander. "Throw on the power light! Rev her up to 8,500! We're going through!" The pounding of the cylinders increased: ta-pocketa-pocketa-pocketa-*pocketa-pocketa*. The Commander stared at the ice forming on the pilot window. He walked over and twisted a row of complicated dials. "Switch on No. 8 auxiliary!" he shouted. "Switch on No. 8 auxiliary!" repeated Lieutenant Berg. "Full strength in No. 3 turret!" shouted the Commander. "Full strength in No. 3 turret!" The crew, bending to their various tasks in the huge, hurtling eight-engined Navy hydroplane, looked at each other and grinned. "The Old Man'll get us through," they said to one another. "The Old Man ain't afraid of Hell!" . . .

2   "Not so fast! You're driving too fast!" said Mrs. Mitty. "What are you driving so fast for?"

3   "Hmm?" said Walter Mitty. He looked at his wife, in the seat beside him, with shocked astonishment. She seemed grossly unfamiliar, like a strange woman who had yelled at him in a crowd. "You were up to fifty-five," she said. "You know I don't like to go more than forty. You were up to fifty-five." Walter Mitty drove on toward Waterbury in silence, the roaring of the SN202 through the worst storm in twenty years of Navy flying fading in the remote, intimate airways of his mind. "You're tensed up again," said Mrs. Mitty. "It's one of your days. I wish you'd let Dr. Renshaw look you over."

4   Walter Mitty stopped the car in front of the building where his wife went to have her hair done. "Remember to get those overshoes while I'm having my hair done," she said. "I don't need overshoes," said Mitty. She put her mirror back into her bag. "We've been all through that," she said, getting out of the car. "You're not a young man any longer." He raced the engine a little. "Why don't you wear your gloves? Have you lost your gloves?" Walter Mitty reached in a pocket and brought out the gloves. He put them on, but after she had turned and gone into the building and he had driven on to a red light, he took them off again. "Pick it up, brother!" snapped a cop as the light changed, and Mitty hastily pulled on his gloves and lurched ahead. He drove around the streets aimlessly for a time, and then he drove past the hospital on his way to the parking lot.

5   . . . "It's the millionaire banker, Wellington McMillan," said the pretty nurse.

"Yes?" said Walter Mitty, removing his gloves slowly. "Who has the case?" "Dr. Renshaw and Dr. Benbow, but there are two specialists here, Dr. Remington from New York and Mr. Pritchard-Mitford from London. He flew over." A door opened down a long, cool corridor and Dr. Renshaw came out. He looked distraught and haggard. "Hello, Mitty," he said. "We're having the devil's own time with McMillan, the millionaire banker and close personal friend of Roosevelt. Obstreosis of the ductal tract. Tertiary. Wish you'd take a look at him." "Glad to," said Mitty.

In the operating room there were whispered introductions: "Dr. Remington,   6
Dr. Mitty. Mr. Pritchard-Mitford, Dr. Mitty." "I've read your book on strepto-thricosis," said Pritchard-Mitford, shaking hands. "A brilliant performance, sir." "Thank you," said Walter Mitty. "Didn't know you were in the States, Mitty," grumbled Remington. "Coals to Newcastle, bringing Mitford and me up here for a tertiary." "You are very kind," said Mitty. A huge, complicated machine, con-nected to the operating table, with many tubes and wires, began at this moment to go pocketa-pocketa-pocketa. "The new anesthetizer is giving way!" shouted an intern. "There is no one in the East who knows how to fix it!" "Quiet, man!" said Mitty, in a low, cool voice. He sprang to the machine, which was now going pocketa-pocketa-queep-pocketa-queep. He began fingering delicately a row of glistening dials. "Give me a fountain pen!" he snapped. Someone handed him a fountain pen. He pulled a faulty piston out of the machine and inserted the pen in its place. "That will hold for ten minutes," he said. "Get on with the operation." A nurse hurried over and whispered to Renshaw, and Mitty saw the man turn pale. "Coreopsis has set in," said Renshaw nervously. "If you would take over, Mitty?" Mitty looked at him and at the craven figure of Benbow, who drank, and at the grave, uncertain faces of the two great specialists. "If you wish," he said. They slipped a white gown on him; he adjusted a mask and drew on thin gloves; nurses handed him shining . . .

"Back it up, Mac! Look out for that Buick!" Walter Mitty jammed on the   7
brakes. "Wrong lane, Mac," said the parking-lot attendant, looking at Mitty closely. "Gee, Yeh," muttered Mitty. He began cautiously to back out of the lane marked "Exit Only." "Leave her sit there," said the attendant. "I'll put her away." Mitty got out of the car. "Hey, better leave the key." "Oh," said Mitty, handing the man the ignition key. The attendant vaulted into the car, backed it up with insolent skill, and put it where it belonged.

They're so damn cocky, thought Walter Mitty, walking along Main Street; they   8
think they know everything. Once he had tried to take his chains off, outside New Milford, and he had got them wound around the axles. A man had had to come out in a wrecking car and unwind them, a young, grinning garageman. Since then Mrs. Mitty always made him drive to a garage to have the chains taken off. The next time, he thought, I'll wear my right arm in a sling; they won't grin at me then. I'll have my right arm in a sling and they'll see I couldn't possibly take the chains off myself. He kicked at the slush on the sidewalk. "Overshoes," he said to himself, and he began looking for a shoe store.

When he came out into the street again, with the overshoes in a box under his   9
arm, Walter Mitty began to wonder what the other thing was his wife had told him

to get. She had told him twice, before they set out from their house for Waterbury. In a way he hated these weekly trips to town—he was always getting something wrong. Kleenex, he thought, Squibb's, razor blades? No. Toothpaste, toothbrush, bicarbonate, carborundum, initiative and referendum? He gave it up. But she would remember it. "Where's the what's-its-name?" she would ask. "Don't tell me you forgot the what's-its-name." A newsboy went by shouting something about the Waterbury trial.

10   . . . "Perhaps this will refresh your memory." The District Attorney suddenly thrust a heavy automatic at the quiet figure on the witness stand. "Have you ever seen this before?" Walter Mitty took the gun and examined it expertly. "This is my Webley-Vickers 50.80," he said calmly. An excited buzz ran around the courtroom. The judge rapped for order. "You are a crack shot with any sort of firearms, I believe?" said the District Attorney, insinuatingly. "Objection!" shouted Mitty's attorney. "We have shown that the defendant could not have fired the shot. We have shown that he wore his right arm in a sling on the night of the fourteenth of July." Walter Mitty raised his hand briefly and the bickering attorneys were stilled. "With any known make of gun," he said evenly, "I could have killed Gregory Fitzhurst at three hundred feet *with my left hand*." Pandemonium broke loose in the courtroom. A woman's scream rose above the bedlam and suddenly a lovely, dark-haired girl was in Walter Mitty's arms. The District Attorney struck at her savagely. Without rising from his chair, Mitty let the man have it on the point of the chin. "You miserable cur!" . . .

11   "Puppy biscuit," said Walter Mitty. He stopped walking and the buildings of Waterbury rose up out of the misty courtroom and surrounded him again. A woman who was passing laughed. "He said 'Puppy biscuit,'" she said to her companion. "That man said 'Puppy biscuit' to himself." Walter Mitty hurried on. He went into an A. & P., not the first one he came to but a smaller one farther up the street. "I want some biscuit for small, young dogs," he said to the clerk. "Any special brand, sir?" The greatest pistol shot in the world thought a moment. "It says 'Puppies Bark for It' on the box," said Walter Mitty.

12   His wife would be through at the hairdresser's in fifteen minutes, Mitty saw in looking at his watch, unless they had trouble drying it; sometimes they had trouble drying it. She didn't like to get to the hotel first; she would want him to be there waiting for her as usual. He found a big leather chair in the lobby, facing a window, and he put the overshoes and the puppy biscuit on the floor beside it. He picked up an old copy of *Liberty* and sank down into the chair. "Can Germany Conquer the World Through the Air?" Walter Mitty looked at the pictures of bombing planes and of ruined streets.

13   . . . "The cannonading has got the wind up in young Raleigh, sir," said the sergeant. Captain Mitty looked up at him through tousled hair. "Get him to bed," he said wearily. "With the others. I'll fly alone." "But you can't, sir," said the sergeant anxiously. "It takes two men to handle that bomber and the Archies are pounding hell out of the air. Von Richtman's circus is between here and Saulier." 'Somebody's got to get that ammunition dump," said Mitty. "I'm going over. Spot of brandy?" He poured a drink for the sergeant and one for himself. War thundered

and whined around the dugout and battered at the door. There was a rending of wood and splinters flew through the room. "A bit of a near thing," said Captain Mitty carelessly. "The box barrage is closing in," said the sergeant. "We only live once, Sergeant," said Mitty, with his faint, fleeting smile. "Or do we?" He poured another brandy and tossed it off. "I never see a man could hold his brandy like you, sir," said the sergeant. "Begging your pardon, sir." Captain Mitty stood up and strapped on his huge Webley-Vickers automatic. "It's forty kilometers through hell, sir," said the sergeant. Mitty finished one last brandy. "After all," he said softly, "what isn't?" The pounding of the cannon increased; there was the rat-tat-tatting of machine guns, and from somewhere came the menacing pocketa-pocketa-pocketa of the new flame throwers. Walter Mitty walked to the door of the dugout humming "Auprès de Ma Blonde." He turned and waved to the sergeant. "Cheerio!" he said. . . .

Something struck his shoulder. "I've been looking all over this hotel for you," said Mrs. Mitty. "Why do you have to hide in this old chair? How did you expect me to find you?" "Things close in," said Walter Mitty vaguely. "What?" Mrs. Mitty said. "Did you get the what's-its-name? The puppy biscuit? What's in that box?" "Overshoes," said Mitty. "Couldn't you have put them on in the store?" "I was thinking," said Walter Mitty. "Does it ever occur to you that I am sometimes thinking?" She looked at him. "I'm going to take your temperature when I get you home," she said.

They went out through the revolving doors that made a faintly derisive whistling sound when you pushed them. It was two blocks to the parking lot. At the drugstore on the corner she said, "Wait here for me. I forgot something. I won't be a minute." She was more than a minute. Walter Mitty lighted a cigarette. It began to rain, rain with sleet in it. He stood up against the wall of the drugstore, smoking. . . . He put his shoulders back and his heels together. "To hell with the handkerchief," said Walter Mitty scornfully. He took one last drag on his cigarette and snapped it away. Then, with that faint, fleeting smile playing about his lips, he faced the firing squad; erect and motionless, proud and disdainful, Walter Mitty the Undefeated, inscrutable to the last.

14

15

Vocabulary

distraught, craven, insinuatingly, bickering, pandemonium, inscrutable

Questions

1. Notice the change of tone between the dream sequences and Mitty's returns to reality. For example, he gives orders in his daydreams, but he takes them from rude people in life.
2. Obstreosis, streptothricosis, and some other "medical problems" don't exist. Why did Thurber invent them, when he could have used some perfectly legitimate, rare diseases in their place?

3. Find the logical links between Mitty's fantasies and realities. Can you some-times connect your dreams to something that has recently happened or is on your mind?
4. Why will Mitty wear his right arm in a sling?
5. What is wrong with his shopping list?
6. Does Mrs. Mitty know her husband or not?
7. In what way is Thurber's story true to life? Is it only the incompetent who engage in heroic daydreams?
8. What analogies can you make between the actual and the dream events of Mitty's day?

Topics for Writing

A Defense of Mrs. Mitty

The Mitty in Us All

Family Reconstruction

JEAN BETHKE ELSHTAIN (1941–) teaches political science at the University of Massachusetts, Amherst, and writes often on feminism and family matters. This essay appeared in *Commonweal*.

It has become a truism of our time that the contemporary family or, more accurately, contemporary families are under enormous social, economic, and ideological pressures. The family has frequently been singled out by certain segments within the feminist movement as *the* institution most deeply implicated in the oppression of women. Christopher Lasch, on the other hand, laments the breakdown of traditional modes of family authority and cites that breakdown as a key factor in the emergence of the "new narcissism in America." The Carnegie Council on Children criticizes, and calls for reform of, those institutions which sap the self-esteem and power of parents. Specifically, they, and French social theorist Jacques Donzelot in his recent book, *The Policing of Families*, are concerned with moves by the state and bureaucracies to further rationalize all dimensions of social life, including the family, in accordance with the imperatives of a capitalist or state socialist political economy. Inflationary pressures bear heavily on families and are the single factor which most fully accounts for that dramatic upheaval represented by the rise of the numbers of working women: most women work because they have no choice and at low-paying, dead-end jobs. The Carnegie Council estimates that one-fourth to one-third of all American children are born into families with financial strains so great children suffer basic deprivation, with 12 to 15 percent of these families falling below the United States government's official poverty line.

External pressures on the family and inner changes in family life—the "sexual revolution," alterations in intimacy, in the very touchstone of male-female relations—have increased tension between men and women even as they have opened up new possibilities for authentic reciprocity. Men and women alike are experiencing identity shifts and lacunae that are profoundly disorienting. On the question of the family—"love it or leave it"—women have been, and are, bitterly divided along class, ethnic, religious, and ideological lines. All of this adds up to what social theorist Jurgen Habermas has called a "legitimate crisis," the widespread draining of our social institutions, public and private, of their previous normative meaning and significance.

How do we, as social critics devoted to some ideal of family life, respond to these various and relentless pressures from all sides as well as "inside"? I see three basic responses to the pressures I have sketched briefly. The first is *family retrenchment*, a kind of family chauvinist movement, an attempt to reproduce a very traditional notion of the patriarchal family. One can envisage this response as a reactive-passive vector. Those caught up in familial retrenchment seek, often rather desperately, sometimes merely wistfully, to "turn back the clock" to some imagined good old days when men were men, women knew their place, children kept their place, and all was well. Individuals in the grips of family retrenchment react to events swirling about them by withdrawing into a militant reaffirmation that is indistinguishable in practice from a form of passive resignation. It's as if such persons were saying: "This is too much for me. I shall pretend I can make all these 'evils' go away by retreating within my four walls and embracing the bygone days of order, authority, and paternalism."

4   The second response, *family deconstruction*, is also a troubling one. It involves the notion that "progress" of some sort or another demands that we replace the family with other kinds of more efficient or less "destructive" ways of raising children, perhaps by turning them over to beneficent people trained for that very purpose. This response sometimes calls itself radical but it is in a deep sense nihilistic. One example of dangerous "deconstruction" in the absence of viable functional alternatives to the family may be found in Shulamith Firestone's radical feminist "classic," *The Dialectic of Sex*. Firestone depicts a social world of stark lovelessness in which pervasive force, coercion, manipulation and crude power roam undifferentiatedly over the landscape, suffusing society unto its innermost parts. The family, she argues, is in its essence a political institution, pervaded by the domination of the "female sex-class" by the "male-sex class" and serves as the key linchpin in a larger world order seen as a "total male power structure." Women must either destroy this world utterly or, according to another radical feminist, Susan Brownmiller, occupy the power structure in sufficient numbers to achieve a stalemate in the next war. In either case, the family collapses or is smashed. In Firestone's scenario for the future, test-tube babies will replace biological reproduction and every aspect of life will rest in the beneficent hands of a "new elite of engineers, cybernetricians." Although most statements of the family deconstruction option are not so extreme, they all share the presumption that the contemporary family is a thoroughly debased and hopeless institution and must be utterly eradicated or entirely transcended.

5   The deconstruction mode, a reactive-active stance, winds up covertly buttressing that mode with which it might be seen to be in implacable opposition, the family retrenchment mode. Let me explain. Each of these approaches to the crisis of contemporary family life ultimately fails to make contact with the deepest evolving needs of those human subjects who comprise the heart of the family's existence. The retrenchment approach, for example, seeks to negate the changes of heart, mind, and social arrangements brought about by the women's movement. But these changes cannot be denied: one can only attempt to repress them. In so doing, one creates a false veneer of certainty based on denial that can only worsen the tensions and strains upon family members, for it fails to respond creatively to the challenges (for crises are also challenges) of the day. The deconstruction mode also fails to treat its human subjects with the respect due reflective agents. It treats the human body, particularly the woman's body and its role in the reproductive cycle, with contempt. Worst of all, children become either a pity or a predicament—some "thing" to be efficiently managed, kept out of sight, under the guise of non-authoritarianism, to grow at their own "groovy" rate unbothered by nasty adults. The child's need for a

foundation of love and learning in an environment that favors and provides long-term particular attachments is denied. In other words, the child's developmental needs and requirements are never taken into account; thus, the retrenchment group and the deconstruction group, each in its own way, distorts the future by denying real human beings in the present.

There is, however, an alternative. I call it *family reconstruction*. This mode   6 involves an active, morally engaged and theoretically reflective approach to the crises and changes affecting family life. The family reconstruction position involves a commitment to a particular ideal of family existence that does not repeat earlier terms of female oppression or exploitation. It begins with an affirmation: some form of familial ties and mode of child-rearing is essential to attain the minimal bedrock of human social existence. What we call human capacities could not exist without a familial mode; for human beings to flourish a particular ideal of the family is necessary.

To state a presumptive case for familial ties, to argue that they are required to   7 make us minimally human, is *not* to detail the specific familial forms within which the creation and nourishment of humanity take place. That is a future task which demands our best and most worthy efforts. The point I wish to make now is that children incur an assault to their humanness, an affront they will know in the very tissue of their bio-psychic beings, if they suffer the diseases of neglect and non-attachment. A being without a presumptive need for attachments of a specific kind—concrete, particular and continuing—*would not suffer distortion and damage if such relations were absent*. Just as Marx's theory of alienation presupposes an ideal of human existence that would hold in the absence of damage done by exploitative and oppressive social structures, so the picture we now have of what happens to children in the absence of strong, early attachments to specific adult others, allows us to assert that we are dealing with an axiomatic of authentic human existence.

Children, if they are to be both morally and socially responsible and poten-   8 tially self-reflective adults, must be reared in a highly charged emotional setting in which they are loved in a manner that establishes basic trust. This requires the continuing presence of specific beloved others, for it is only through powerful, eroticized relations with such specific others, parents or their permanent, not temporary, surrogates that the child will be nurtured and protected in a way that allows his or her creation of self and others to be structured and mediated by parental care and concern. It is only through the child's internalization of specific others that he or she can later identify with non-familial human beings. These ties cannot emerge in abstract, diffuse, non-familialized settings. This is the moral imperative which animates the family reconstruction mode.

There is, of course, an irritant in the image, and that is that in order to provide   9 such trust and security for their children parents, in turn, must experience trust and security themselves in their relations with one another and with the "outside world." As Erik Erikson argued years ago, parents who are frustrated and de-meaned, rendered helpless in worklife and citizenship, will have great difficulty instilling such bedrock beliefs, ways of being, inside the family. Conflicts that emerge from "outside" get displaced "inside," into the very heart of the family's emotional existence. That is all too often our current reality. What this means is that those of us devoted to the family reconstructive mode cannot carry out our supremely important effort unless or until there are real structural changes in American life. This is where the heart of "politics and the family" truly lies—not in overpoliticizing our most intimate relations and turning the family into the war of all against all but in fighting the pressures at work from the outside which threaten to erode, impoverish, or preclude the flourishing of our most basic human ties.

Vocabulary

narcissism, imperatives, reciprocity, lacunae, nihilistic, cyberneticians, axiomatic, surrogates

Questions

1. Is the analogy of *family* and *political institution* in the fourth paragraph accurate? Where would the children fit into this political structure?
2. Elshtain uses a specialized vocabulary common among certain kinds of social scientists. Do you find such terms as *deconstruction, active-reactive stance,* and *authentic human existence* helpful? Could you find a simpler way to say *inflationary pressures*?
3. Do you agree that most working women work "because they have no choice"? Would you work if you had the choice not to work?
4. What is Elshtain's best argument against "family retrenchment"?
5. What do you think is her best argument for preserving the traditional family structure?

Topics for Writing

The Real Need to Work
The Family of the Future

A Valediction Forbidding Mourning

JOHN DONNE (1573–1631), English clergyman, writer and preacher of powerful meditations, is here seen in his role of metaphysical poet, relying on the development of involved images to convey an idea of confident love.

As virtuous men passe mildly away,
    And whisper to their soules, to goe,
Whilst some of their sad friends doe say,
    The breath goes now, and some say, no.

So let us melt, and make no noise, 5
    No teare-floods, nor sigh-tempests move,
T'were prophanation of our joyes
    To tell the layetie our love.

Moving of th'earth brings harmes and feares,
    Men reckon what it did and meant, 10
But trepidation of the spheares,
    Though greater farre, is innocent.

Dull sublunary lovers love
    (Whose soule is sense) cannot admit
Absence, because it doth remove 15
    Those things which elemented it.

But we by a love, so much refin'd,
    That our selves know not what it is,
Inter-assured of the mind,
    Care lesse, eyes, lips, and hands to misse. 20

Our two soules therefore, which are one,
    Though I must goe, endure not yet
A breach, but an expansion,
    Like gold to ayery thinnesse beate.

If they be two, they are two so 25
    As stiffe twin compasses are two,
Thy soule the fixt foot, makes no show
    To move, but doth, if the other doe.

And though it in the center sit,
    Yet when the other far doth rome,
It leanes, and hearkens after it,
    And growes erect, as that comes home.

Such wilt thou be to mee, who must
    Like th'other foot, obliquely runne.
Thy firmnes makes my circle just,
    And makes me end, where I begunne.

30 *(line 30)*
35 *(line 35)*

Vocabulary

valediction, profanation, laity, trepidation, sublunary

Questions

1. If ordinary folk are the laity, then the speaker and his lover are priests. What is the religion?
2. The first half of the poem advises a calm, tearless parting for these extraordinary lovers. The second half of the poem asserts that they will not really be parted. Which of the two images—gold expanded or the compass legs stretched—provides the better analogy?
3. How does her "firmness" make his circle "just"? (Check several meanings of *just*).

Topics for Writing

Parting Is Such Sweet Sorrow
Out of Sight, Out of Mind
Absence Makes the Heart Grow Fonder

6

Showing Cause and Effect/ Our Fragile World

Cause and effect are two sides of the same logical coin. For example, the careless carpenter tells us his thumb hurts. When we seek to explain *why*, we are seeking the cause. In this case, we find an answer: he missed the nail and hit his thumb with the hammer. The cause of his pain is the hammer blow. When we write a causal analysis, we try to identify and explain the *whys* of things, the causes of occurrences, experiences, or actions. Of course, consequences concern us too. Viewed in this perspective, the consequence (effect) of the hammer blow was a painful thumb.

Seeking causes and effects is not always so straightforward and simple a matter. For example, a particular effect may prove to be the result of a series of causes, a kind of chain reaction in which we must distinguish between immediate, or proximate, causes and final, or ultimate, causes. We know, for instance, that in Panama the incidence of malaria declined (the effect) when the mosquito population was decreased (the immediate cause) because the swamps, their breeding place, were drained (the ultimate cause). We can, if we wish, invert the order to distinguish immediate from ultimate effects: draining swamps > fewer mosquitos > less malaria.

The relationship between human beings and their environment makes for fascinating cause-and-effect observations and arguments. Isaac Asimov describes a future world dominated by an extreme fuel shortage, and Wayne Davis another sort of nightmare he sees at the moment: a disproportionate use of resources by Americans. A. B. C. Whipple reports on certain effects of oil spillage, and Joseph Wood Krutch suggests that a need for beauty, not utility only, may lie behind certain natural phenomena. One of our earliest American novelists, James Fenimore Cooper, portrays a true scene of destruction that we today can hardly believe. James Buckley celebrates the survival of one small creature as a result of man's intervention.

All of these writers would agree that man's actions in the world about him can have incalculable effects. *Incalculable* is the key word here, and it may cut both ways. These readings will inevitably stimulate you to ask a pair of fundamental questions: Does the world exist for man's use? What follows from my answer?

The Nightmare of Life Without Fuel

ISAAC ASIMOV (1920–) has done as much to popularize scientific knowledge as any other American of our time. He has published more than 200 books, fiction and nonfiction, and many more articles. This one appeared in *Time*.

1   So it's 1997, and it's raining, and you'll have to walk to work again. The subways are crowded, and any given train breaks down one morning out of five. The buses are gone, and on a day like today the bicycles slosh and slide. Besides, you have only a mile and a half to go, and you have boots, raincoat and rain hat. And it's not a very cold rain, so why not?

2   Lucky you have a job in demolition too. It's steady work. Slow and dirty, but steady. The fading structures of a decaying city are the great mineral mines and hardware shops of the nation. Break them down and re-use the parts. Coal is too difficult to dig up and transport to give us energy in the amounts we need, nuclear fission is judged to be too dangerous, the technical breakthrough toward nuclear fusion that we hoped for never took place, and solar batteries are too expensive to maintain on the earth's surface in sufficient quantity.

3   Anyone older than ten can remember automobiles. They dwindled. At first the price of gasoline climbed—way up. Finally only the well-to-do drove, and that was too clear an indication that they were filthy rich, so any automobile that dared show itself on a city street was overturned and burned. Rationing was introduced to "equalize sacrifice," but every three months the ration was reduced. The cars just vanished and became part of the metal resource.

4   There are many advantages, if you want to look for them. Our 1997 newspapers continually point them out. The air is cleaner and there seem to be fewer colds. Against most predictions, the crime rate has dropped. With the police car too expensive (and too easy a target), policemen are back on their beats. More important, the streets are full. Legs are king in the cities of 1997, and people walk everywhere far into the night. Even the parks are full, and there is mutual protection in crowds.

5   If the weather isn't too cold, people sit out front. If it is hot, the open air is the only air conditioning they get. And at least the street lights still burn. Indoors, electricity is scarce, and few people can afford to keep lights burning after supper.

6   As for the winter—well, it is inconvenient to be cold, with most of what furnace fuel is allowed hoarded for the dawn; but sweaters are popular indoor wear and showers are not an everyday luxury. Lukewarm sponge baths will do, and if the air is not always very fragrant in the human vicinity, the automobile fumes are gone.

7   There is some consolation in the city that it is worse in the suburbs. The suburbs were born with the auto, lived with the auto, and are dying with the auto.

One way out for the suburbanites is to form associations that assign turns to the procurement and distribution of food. Pushcarts creak from house to house along the posh suburban roads, and every bad snowstorm is a disaster. It isn't easy to hoard enough food to last till the roads are open. There is not much in the way of refrigeration except for the snowbanks, and then the dogs must be fought off.

What energy is left cannot be directed into personal comfort. The nation must survive until new energy sources are found, so it is the railroads and subways that are receiving major attention. The railroads must move the coal that is the immediate hope, and the subways can best move the people.   8

And then, of course, energy must be conserved for agriculture. The great car factories make trucks and farm machinery almost exclusively. We can huddle together when there is a lack of warmth, fan ourselves should there be no cooling breezes, sleep or make love at such times as there is a lack of light—but nothing will for long ameliorate a lack of food. The American population isn't going up much any more, but the food supply must be kept high even though the prices and difficulty of distribution force each American to eat less. Food is needed for export so that we can pay for some trickle of oil and for other resources.   9

The rest of the world, of course, is not as lucky as we are. Some cynics say that it is the knowledge of this that helps keep America from despair. They're starving out there, because earth's population has continued to go up. The population on earth is 5.5 billion, and outside the United States and Europe, not more than one in five has enough to eat at any given time.   10

All the statistics point to a rapidly declining rate of population increase, but that is coming about chiefly through a high infant mortality; the first and most helpless victims of starvation are babies, after their mothers have gone dry. A strong current of American opinion, as reflected in the newspapers (some of which still produce their daily eight pages of bad news), holds that it is just as well. It serves to reduce the population, doesn't it?   11

Others point out that it's more than just starvation. There are those who manage to survive on barely enough to keep the body working, and that proves to be not enough for the brain. It is estimated that there are now nearly 2 billion people in the world who are alive but who are permanently brain-damaged by undernutrition, and the number is growing year by year. It has already occurred to some that it would be "realistic" to wipe them out quietly and rid the earth of an encumbering menace. The American newspapers of 1997 do not report that this is actually being done anywhere, but some travelers bring back horror tales.   12

At least the armies are gone—no one can afford to keep those expensive, energy-gobbling monstrosities. Some soldiers in uniform and with rifles are present in almost every still functioning nation, but only the United States and the Soviet Union can maintain a few tanks, planes and ships—which they dare not move for fear of biting into limited fuel reserves.   13

Energy continues to decline, and machines must be replaced by human muscle and beasts of burden. People are working longer hours and there is less leisure; but then, with electric lighting restricted, television for only three hours a night, movies three evenings a week, new books few and printed in small editions, what is   14 there to do with leisure? Work, sleep and eating are the great trinity of 1997, and only the first two are guaranteed.

15   Where will it end? It must end in a return to the days before 1800, to the days before the fossil fuels powered a vast machine industry and technology. It must end in subsistence farming and in a world population reduced by starvation, disease and violence to less than a billion.

16   And what can we do to prevent all this now?

17   Now? Almost nothing.

18   If we had started twenty years ago, that might have been another matter. If we had only started fifty years ago, it would have been easy.

Vocabulary

ameliorate, subsistence

Questions

1. We usually think of demolition as destructive. Asimov believes that in 1997 we will think differently. Why?
2. Was it only the high price of gasoline that doomed the automobile to extinction?
3. What positive effects come from the disappearance of cars?
4. Will the subways make a comeback? Where? In your hometown?
5. How will suburbs be affected by the fuel shortage?
6. Why will we be forced to produce more food if our population is stable?
7. What dangers arise as a result of widespread undernutrition?
8. Asimov claims that by 1997 it will be impossible to do anything about the "nightmare." Do you agree? If you do, what steps would you recommend now to bring about a change?

Topics for Writing

Preparing for 1997

Looking Forward: A Day in the Year 2000

An Ugly New Footprint in the Sand

A. B. C. WHIPPLE's (1918–) article is a good example of the popular journalism by which we Americans are kept apprised almost daily of threats to the environment. The original publication of this article in *Life* was accompanied by a series of illustrations.

There were strangers on our beach yesterday, for the first time in a month. A new footprint on our sand is nearly as rare as in *Robinson Crusoe*. We are at the very edge of the Atlantic; half a mile out in front of us is a coral reef, and then nothing but 3,000 miles of ocean to West Africa. It is a wild and lonely beach, with the same surf beating on it as when Columbus came by. And yet the beach is polluted. 1

Oil tankers over the horizon have fouled it more than legions of picnickers could. The oil comes ashore in floating patches that stain the coral black and gray. It has blighted the rock crabs and the crayfish and has coated the delicate whorls of the conch shells with black goo. And it has congealed upon itself, littering the beach with globes of tar that resemble the cannonballs of a deserted battlefield. The islanders, as they go beachcombing for the treasures the sea has washed up for centuries, now wear old shoes to protect their feet from the oil that washes up too. 2

You have to try to get away from pollution to realize how bad it really is. We have known for the last few years how bad our cities are. Now there is no longer an escape. If there is oil on this island far out in the Atlantic, there is oil on nearly every other island. 3

It is still early here. The air is still clear over the island, but it won't be when they build the airstrip they are talking about. The water out over the reef is still blue and green, but it is dirtier than it was a few years ago. And if the land is not despoiled, it is only because there are not yet enough people here to despoil it. There will be. And so for the moment on this island we are witnesses to the beginning, as it were, of the pollution of our environment. 4

When you watch a bird over the beach or a fish along the reef you realize how ill-adapted man is to this environment anyway. Physically there is nothing he can do that some other creature cannot do better. Only his neocortex, the "thinking cap" on top of his brain, has enabled him to invent and construct artificial aids to accomplish what he could not do by himself. He cannot fly, so he has developed airplanes that can go faster than birds. He is slower than the horse, so he invented the wheel and the internal combustion engine. Even in his ancestral element, the sea, he is clumsy and short of breath. Without his brain, his artificial aids, his technology, he would have been unable to cope with, even survive in, his environment. But only after so many centuries is his brain dimly realizing that while he has managed to control his environment, he has so far been unable to protect it. 5

Perhaps he simply is not far enough up the evolutionary ladder to survive on this planet for very much longer. To take only two of his inefficient physical 6 functions, he is so far unable to control either his body wastes or his population. Man is a natural polluter, and his invention of the bathroom and the incinerator has, it now becomes evident, only postponed the problem. On this island we burn our papers, bury our tin cans and dump our garbage in the bay. It is not very efficient and perhaps not even very civilized. Yet so long as there are only a few people here, it has no ill effects. But when the inevitable wave of population sweeps out from the mainland, the islanders will face the problem of their own pollution just as the New Yorker does today.

7   Man's sexual construction is perhaps the biggest accident of his physical makeup: it is only now becoming obvious—when it may well be too late—that it would have been better if he required artificial aid to *have* children, rather than to *avoid* having them.

8   Until the pollution of our deserted beach, it seemed simple to blame everything on the "population explosion." If the population of this island, for example, could be stabilized at a couple of hundred, there would be very little problem with the environment in this secluded area. There would be no pollution of the environment if there were not too many people using it. And so if we concentrate on winning the war against overpopulation, we can save the earth for mankind.

9   But the oil on the beach belies this too-easy assumption. Those tankers are not out there because too many Chinese and Indians are being born every minute. They are not even out there because there are too many Americans and Europeans. They are delivering their oil, and cleaning their tanks at sea and sending the residue up onto the beaches of the Atlantic and Pacific, in order to fuel the technology of mankind—and the factories and the power plants, the vehicles and the engines that have enabled mankind to survive on his planet are now spoiling the planet for life.

10   The fishermen on this island are perfectly right in preferring the outboard motor to the sail. Their livelihood is involved, and the motor, for all its fouling smell, has helped increase the fisherman's catch so that he can now afford to dispense with the far more obnoxious outdoor privy. But the danger of technology is in its escalation, and there has already been a small amount of escalation here. You can see the motor oil slicks around the town dock. Electric generators can be heard over the sound of the surf. And while there are only about two dozen automobiles for the ten miles of road, already there is a wrecked jeep rusting in the harbor waters where it was dumped and abandoned. The escalation of technological pollution is coming here just as surely as it came to the mainland cities that are now shrouded by fly ash.

11   If the oil is killing the life along the coral heads, what must it not be doing to the phytoplankton at sea which provide 70 percent of the oxygen we breathe? The lesson of our fouled beach is that we may not even have realized how late it is already. Mankind, because of his technology, may require far more space per person on this globe than we had ever thought, but it is more than a matter of a certain number of square yards per person. There is instead a delicate balance of nature in which many square miles of ocean and vegetation and clean air are needed to sustain only a relatively few human beings. We may find, as soon as the end of this century, that the final despoliation of our environment has been signaled

not by starvation but by people choking to death. The technology—the machine—will then indeed have had its ultimate, mindless, all-unintended triumph over man, by destroying the atmosphere he lives in just as surely as you can pinch off a diver's breathing tube.

Sitting on a lonely but spoiled beach, it is hard to imagine but possible to believe.   12

Vocabulary

congeal, despoiled, phytoplankton

Questions

1. What are the causal links leading from oil spills to people's choking to death? (Consider the role of phytoplankton.)
2. "There is no longer any escape" from what?
3. Is it fair for Whipple to say he is a *witness* to the beginning of the island's pollution? Or is *he*, as a visitor, the beginning?
4. What physical functions is man unable to control? Can other animals control theirs? What protects the environment from them?
5. The oil on the beach is a by-product of our modern need to sustain technology. Is technology the villain?

Topics for Writing

Technology: The Source of Our Trouble

Technology: A Necessary Evil

Save Our Beaches for Whom?

The Pigeon Shoot

JAMES FENIMORE COOPER (1789–1851) created a near-mythic character in Natty Bumppo, variously known as the Deerslayer, Hawkeye, Pathfinder, and Leather-Stocking, the hero of five novels. In this scene from *The Pioneers*, Natty is now old, but he still lives in tune with nature and at peace with himself. Just such scenes as this one, repeated over the years, led to the extinction of the passenger pigeon in America.

> Men, boys, and girls,
> Desert th' unpeopled village; and wild crowds
> Spread o'er the plain, by the sweet frenzy driven.
>
> SOMERVILLE

1   From this time to the close of April the weather continued to be a succession of great and rapid changes. One day, the soft airs of spring seemed to be stealing along the valley, and in unison with an invigorating sun, attempting covertly to rouse the dormant powers of the vegetable world; while on the next, the surly blasts from the north would sweep across the lake, and erase every impression left by their gentle adversaries. The snow, however, finally disappeared, and the green wheatfields were seen in every direction, spotted with the dark and charred stumps that had, the preceding season, supported some of the proudest trees of the forest. Ploughs were in motion, wherever those useful implements could be used, and the smokes of the sugar-camps were no longer seen issuing from the woods of maple. The lake had lost the beauty of a field of ice, but still a dark and gloomy covering concealed its waters, for the absence of currents left them yet hidden under a porous crust, which, saturated with the fluid, barely retained enough strength to preserve the contiguity of its parts. Large flocks of wild geese were seen passing over the country, which hovered, for a time, around the hidden sheet of water, apparently searching for a resting-place; and then, on finding themselves excluded by the chill covering, would soar away to the north, filling the air with discordant screams, as if venting their complaints at the tardy operations of nature.

2   For a week, the dark covering of the Otsego was left to the undisturbed possession of two eagles, who alighted on the center of its field, and sat eying their undisputed territory. During the presence of these monarchs of the air, the flocks of migrating birds avoided crossing the plain of ice, by turning into the hills, apparently seeking the protection of the forests, while the white and bald heads of the tenants of the lake were turned upwards, with a look of contempt. But the time had come, when even these kings of birds were to be dispossessed. An opening had been gradually increasing at the lower extremity of the lake, and around the dark spot where the current of the river prevented the formation of ice, during even the

coldest weather; and the fresh southerly winds, that now breathed freely upon the valley, made an impression on the waters. Mimic waves began to curl over the margin of the frozen field, which exhibited an outline of crystallizations that slowly receded towards the north. At each step the power of the winds and the waves increased, until, after a struggle of a few hours, the turbulent little billows succeeded in setting the whole field in motion, when it was driven beyond the reach of the eye, with a rapidity that was as magical as the change produced in the scene by this expulsion of the lingering remnant of winter. Just as the last sheet of agitated ice was disappearing in the distance, the eagles rose, and soared with a wide sweep above the clouds, while the waves tossed their little caps of snow into the air, as if rioting in their release from a thraldom of five months' duration.

The following morning Elizabeth was awakened by the exhilarating sounds of the martins, who were quarrelling and chattering around the little boxes suspended above her windows, and the cries of Richard, who was calling in tones animating as the signs of the season itself,— 3

"Awake! awake! my fair lady! the gulls are hovering over the lake already, and the heavens are alive with pigeons. You may look an hour before you can find a hole through which to get a peep at the sun. Awake! awake! lazy ones! Benjamin is overhauling the ammunition, and we only wait for our breakfasts, and away for the mountains and pigeon shooting." 4

There was no resisting this animated appeal, and in a few minutes Miss Temple and her friend descended to the parlor. The doors of the hall were thrown open, and the mild, balmy air of a clear spring morning was ventilating the apartment, where the vigilance of the ex-steward had been so long maintaining an artificial heat with such unremitted diligence. The gentlemen were impatiently waiting for their morning's repast, each equipped in the garb of a sportsman. Mr. Jones made many visits to the southern door, and would cry,— 5

"See, cousin Bess! see, 'Duke, the pigeon-roosts of the south have broken up! They are growing more thick every instant. Here is a flock that the eye cannot see the end of. There is food enough in it to keep the army of Xerxes for a month, and feathers enough to make beds for the whole country. Xerxes, Mr. Edwards, was a Grecian king, who—no, he was a Turk, or a Persian, who wanted to conquer Greece, just the same as these rascals will overrun our wheat-fields, when they come back in the fall. Away! away! Bess; I long to pepper them." 6

In this wish both Marmaduke and young Edwards seemed equally to participate, for the sight was exhilarating to a sportsman; and the ladies soon dismissed the party after a hasty breakfast. 7

If the heavens were alive with pigeons, the whole village seemed equally in motion, with men, women, and children. Every species of fire-arms, from the French ducking-gun with a barrel near six feet in length, to the common horseman's pistol, was to be seen in the hands of the men and boys; while bows and arrows, some made of the simple stick of a walnut sapling, and others in a rude imitation of the ancient cross-bows, were carried by many of the latter. 8

The houses and the signs of life apparent in the village, drove the alarmed birds 9 from the direct line of their flight toward the mountains, along the sides and near the bases of which they were glancing in dense masses, equally wonderful by the rapidity of their motion, and their incredible numbers.

10   We have already said, that across the inclined plane which fell from the steep ascent of the mountain to the banks of the Susquehanna, ran the highway, on either side of which a clearing of many acres had been made at a very early day. Over those clearings, and up the eastern mountain, and along the dangerous path that was cut into its side, the different individuals posted themselves, and in a few moments the attack commenced.

11   Among the sportsmen was the tall, gaunt form of Leather-Stocking walking over the field, with his rifle hanging on his arm, his dogs at his heels; the latter now scenting the dead or wounded birds, that were beginning to tumble from the flocks, and then crouching under the legs of their master, as if they participated in his feelings at this wasteful and unsportsmanlike execution.

12   The reports of the fire-arms became rapid, whole volleys rising from the plain, as flocks of more than ordinary numbers darted over the opening, shadowing the field like a cloud; and then the light smoke of a single piece would issue from among the leafless bushes on the mountain, as death was hurled on the retreat of the affrighted birds, who were rising from a volley, in a vain effort to escape. Arrows, and missiles of every kind were in the midst of the flocks; and so numerous were the birds, and so low did they take their flight, that even long poles, in the hands of those on the sides of the mountain, were used to strike them to the earth.

13   During all this time, Mr. Jones, who disdained the humble and ordinary means of destruction used by his companions, was busily occupied, aided by Benjamin, in making arrangements for an assault of more than ordinarily fatal character. Among the relics of the old military excursions, that occasionally are discovered throughout the different districts of the western part of New York, there had been found in Templeton, at its settlement, a small swivel, which would carry a ball of a pound weight. It was thought to have been deserted by a war party of the whites, in one of their inroads into the Indian settlements, when, perhaps, convenience or their necessity induced them to leave such an incumbrance behind them in the woods. This miniature cannon had been released from the rust, and being mounted on little wheels, was now in a state for actual service. For several years, it was the sole organ for extraordinary rejoicings used in those mountains. On the mornings of the Fourths of July, it would be heard ringing among the hills; and even Captain Hollister, who was the highest authority in that part of the country on all such occasions, affirmed that, considering its dimensions, it was no despicable gun for a salute. It was somewhat the worse for the service it had performed, it is true, there being but a trifling difference in size between the touch-hole and the muzzle. Still, the grand conceptions of Richard had suggested the importance of such an instrument in hurling death at his nimble enemies. The swivel was dragged by a horse into a part of the open space that the Sheriff thought most eligible for planting a battery of the kind, and Mr. Pump proceeded to load it. Several handfuls of duck-shot were placed on top of the powder, and the major-domo announced that his piece was ready for service.

The sight of such an implement collected all the idle spectators to the spot, 14
who, being mostly boys, filled the air with cries of exultation and delight. The gun
was pointed high, and Richard, holding a coal of fire in a pair of tongs, patiently
took his seat on a stump, awaiting the appearance of a flock worthy of his notice.

So prodigious was the number of the birds, that the scattering fire of the guns, 15
with the hurling of missiles, and the cries of the boys, had no other effect than to
break off small flocks from the immense masses that continued to dart along the
valley, as if the whole of the feathered tribe were pouring through that one pass.
None pretended to collect the game, which lay scattered over the fields in such
profusion as to cover the very ground with the fluttering victims.

Leather-Stocking was a silent, but uneasy spectator of all these proceedings, 16
but was able to keep his sentiments to himself, until he saw the introduction of the
swivel into the sports.

"This comes of settling a country!" he said; "here have I known the pigeons to 17
fly for forty long years, and, till you made your clearings, there was nobody to skear
or to hurt them. I loved to see them in the woods, for they were company to a body;
hurting nothing; being, as it was, as harmless as a garter-snake. But now it gives me
sore thoughts when I hear the frighty things whizzing through the air, for I know it's
only a motion to bring out all the brats in the village. Well! the Lord won't see the
waste of his creatures for nothing, and right will be done to the pigeons, as well as
others, by and by. There's Mr. Oliver, as bad as the rest of them, firing into the
flocks, as if he was shooting down nothing but Mingo warriors."

Among the sportsmen was Billy Kirby, who, armed with an old musket, was 18
loading, and without even looking into the air, was firing and shouting as his
victims fell even on his own person. He heard the speech of Natty, and took upon
himself to reply:—

"What! old Leather-Stocking," he cried, "grumbling at the loss of a few pi- 19
geons! If you had to sow your wheat twice, and three times, as I have done, you
wouldn't be so massyfully feeling towards the divils. Hurrah, boys! scatter the
feathers! This is better than shooting at a turkey's head and neck, old fellow."

"It's better for you, maybe, Billy Kirby," replied the indignant old hunter, 20
"and all them that don't know how to put a ball down a rifle barrel, or how to bring
it up again with a true aim; but it's wicked to be shooting into flocks in this wasty
manner; and none do it, who know how to knock over a single bird. If a body has a
craving for pigeon's flesh, why, it's made the same as all other creatur's, for man's
eating; but not to kill twenty and eat one. When I want such a thing I go into the
woods till I find one to my liking, and then I shoot him off the branches, without
touching the feather of another, though there might be a hundred on the same tree.
You couldn't do such a thing, Billy Kirby—you couldn't do it, if you tried."

"What's that, old corn-stalk! you sapless stub!" cried the wood-chopper. "You 21
have grown wordy, since the affair of the turkey; but if you are for a single shot, here
goes at that bird which comes on by himself."

The fire from the distant part of the field had driven a single pigeon below the 22
flock to which it belonged, and, frightened with the constant reports of the muskets,
it was approaching the spot where the disputants stood, darting first to one side, and

then to the other, cutting the air with the swiftness of lightning and making a noise with its wings, not unlike the rushing of a bullet. Unfortunately for the wood-chopper, notwithstanding his vaunt, he did not see this bird until it was too late to fire as it approached, and he pulled his trigger at the unlucky moment when it was darting immediately over his head. The bird continued its course with the usual velocity.

23   Natty lowered the rifle from his arm when the challenge was made, and waiting a moment, until the terrified victim had got in a line with his eye, and had dropped near the bank of the lake, he raised it again with uncommon rapidity, and fired. It might have been chance, or it might have been skill, that produced the result; it was probably a union of both; but the pigeon whirled over in the air, and fell into the lake, with a broken wing. At the sound of his rifle, both his dogs started from his feet, and in a few minutes the "slut" brought out the bird, still alive.

24   The wonderful exploit of Leather-Stocking was noised through the field with great rapidity, and the sportsmen gathered in, to learn the truth of the report.

25   "What!" said young Edwards, "have you really killed a pigeon on the wing, Natty, with a single ball?"

26   "Haven't I killed loons before now, lad, that dive at the flash?" returned the hunter. "It's much better to kill only such as you want, without wasting your powder and lead, than to be firing into God's creatures in this wicked manner. But I came out for a bird, and you know the reason why I like small game, Mr. Oliver, and now I have got one I will go home, for I don't relish to see these wasty ways that you are all practysing, as if the least thing wasn't made for use, and not to destroy."

27   "Thou sayest well, Leather-Stocking," cried Marmaduke, "and I begin to think it time to put an end to this work of destruction."

28   "Put an ind, Judge, to your clearings. Ain't the woods His work as well as the pigeons? Use, but don't waste. Wasn't the woods made for the beasts and birds to harbor in? and when man wanted their flesh, their skins, or their feathers, there's the place to seek them. But I'll go to the hut with my own game, for I wouldn't touch one of the harmless things that cover the ground here, looking up with their eyes on me, as if they only wanted tongues to say their thoughts."

29   With this sentiment in his mouth, Leather-Stocking threw his rifle over his arm, and followed by his dogs stepped across the clearing with great caution, taking care not to tread on one of the wounded birds in his path. He soon entered the bushes on the margin of the lake, and was hid from view.

30   Whatever impression the morality of Natty made on the Judge, it was utterly lost on Richard. He availed himself of the gathering of the sportsmen, to lay a plan for one "fell swoop" of destruction. The musket-men were drawn up in battle array, in a line extending on each side of his artillery, with orders to await the signal of firing from himself.

31   "Stand by, my lads," said Benjamin, who acted as an aide-de-camp on this occasion, "stand by, my hearties, and when Squire Dickens heaves out the signal to begin firing, d' ye see, you may open upon them in a broadside. Take care and fire low, boys, and you'll be sure to hull the flock."

32   "Fire low!" shouted Kirby: "hear the old fool! If we fire low, we may hit the stumps, but not ruffle a pigeon."

"How should you know, you lubber?" cried Benjamin, with a very unbecom-   33
ing heat for an officer on the eve of battle; "how should you know, you grampus?
Haven't I sailed aboard of the Boadishey for five years? and wasn't it a standing order
to fire low, and to hull your enemy? Keep silence at your guns, boys, and mind the
order that is passed."

The loud laughs of the musket-men were silenced by the more authoritative   34
voice of Richard, who called for attention and obedience to his signals.

Some millions of pigeons were supposed to have already passed, that morning,   35
over the valley of Templeton; but nothing like the flock that was now approaching
had been seen before. It extended from mountain to mountain in one solid blue
mass, and the eye looked in vain, over the southern hills, to find its termination.
The front of this living column was distinctly marked by a line but very slightly
indented, so regular and even was the flight. Even Marmaduke forgot the morality
of Leather-Stocking as it approached, and, in common with the rest, brought his
musket to a poise.

"Fire!" cried the Sheriff, clapping a coal to the priming of the cannon. As half   36
of Benjamin's charge escaped through the touch-hole, the whole volley of the
musketry preceded the report of the swivel. On receiving this united discharge of
small-arms, the front of the flock darted upwards, while at the same instant, myriads
of those in the rear rushed with amazing rapidity into their places, so that when the
column of white smoke gushed from the mouth of the little cannon, an accumulated mass of objects was gliding over its point of direction. The roar of the
gun echoed along the mountains, and died away to the north, like distant thunder,
while the whole flock of alarmed birds seemed, for a moment, thrown into one
disorderly and agitated mass. The air was filled with their irregular flight, layer
rising above layer, far above the tops of the highest pines, none daring to advance
beyond the dangerous pass; when, suddenly, some of the leaders of the feathered
tribe shot across the valley, taking their flight directly over the village, and hundreds
of thousands in their rear followed the example, deserting the eastern side of the
plain to their persecutors and the slain.

"Victory!" shouted Richard, "victory! we have driven the enemy from the   37
field."

"Not so, Dickon," said Marmaduke: "the field is covered with them; and, like   38
the Leather-Stocking, I see nothing but eyes, in every direction, as the innocent
sufferers turn their heads in terror. Full one half of those that have fallen are yet
alive; and I think it is time to end the sport, if sport it be."

"Sport!" cried the Sheriff; "it is princely sport! There are some thousands of the   39
blue-coated boys on the ground, so that every old woman in the village may have a
pot-pie for the asking."

"Well, we have happily frightened the birds from this side of the valley," said   40
Marmaduke, "and the carnage must of necessity end, for the present. Boys, I will
give you sixpence a hundred for the pigeons' heads only: so go to work, and bring
them into the village."

This expedient produced the desired effect, for every urchin on the ground   41
went industriously to work to wring the necks of the wounded birds. Judge Temple
retired towards his dwelling with that kind of feeling that many a man has experi-

enced before him, who discovers, after the excitement of the moment has passed, that he has purchased pleasure at the price of misery to others. Horses were loaded with the dead; and, after this first burst of sporting, the shooting of pigeons became a business, with a few idlers, for the remainder of the season. Richard, however, boasted for many a year, of his shot with the "cricket"; and Benjamin gravely asserted, that he thought they killed nearly as many pigeons on that day, as there were Frenchmen destroyed on the memorable occasion of Rodney's victory.

Vocabulary

covertly, discordant, thraldom, incumbrance, major-domo, prodigious, expedient

Questions

1. Does civilization inevitably destroy something in nature?
2. What effect did the presence of the eagles have on the migrating birds?
3. What was the ordinary use of the small cannon?
4. Upon what does Leather-Stocking blame the indiscriminate killing?
5. Is Leather-Stocking a mere sentimentalist? What evidence supports your opinion?
6. Do you find the size of the flock of pigeons hard to believe?
7. What can the pigeon-shooters say in their own defense?
8. Why does Marmaduke offer to pay for pigeon heads? Is this an effect of Leather-Stocking's speech?

Topics for Writing

Leather-Stocking: Conservationist or Sentimentalist?

A Defense of Hunting as a Sport

Civilization: The Enemy?

What Are Flowers For?

JOSEPH WOOD KRUTCH (1893–1970), literary and social critic, was also an amateur naturalist. Here he brings together the observational powers of the scientist with the aesthetic sense of the humanist.

There are those who are indifferent to the sea or oppressed by the mountains, who find forests gloomy and animals repulsive. There are even those who say that they hate the country. But no one ever hated flowers, and no other beauty—not even woman—has been more often celebrated.

There is nothing to which poets have referred more frequently, and the poetry of everyday speech pays its own tribute in a score of familiar phrases: the flower of youth; the flower of chivalry; the flower of civilization. Nothing else, either natural or man-made, seems to embody so completely or to symbolize so adequately that perfect beauty which, if the expression be permissible, flowers in the flower.

Grass and leaves are grateful to the eye. No other color is so restful as green. But how monotonous the earth would be if this green were not shattered again and again by the joyous exclamation of the flower! It seems to add just that touch of something more than the merely utilitarian which human beings need if they are to find life fully satisfactory. Flowers seem like a luxury that nature has grown prosperous enough to afford.

The stern scientist will, of course, dismiss this last statement as an absurd fantasy. Flowers, he will insist, are strictly utilitarian—except, of course, in the case of those which man himself has perverted in cultivation. Flowers are the plants' organs of generation and their purpose is not to be beautiful, but to produce seeds with a maximum of efficiency. Yet even the stern scientist will admit that nature invented many remarkable devices before she hit upon anything at once so useful and so pleasing to the human eye.

It was—so he will tell us—a mere hundred million or so years ago that the very first flower opened its petals to the sun. And though that was a long time ago as we measure time, though ninety-nine million of those years were to pass before the first member of our own species was there to see a flower and to begin, no one knows how soon, his long love affair with it, still it was not long ago in the history of living things. Primitive green plants had already been thriving in the water for perhaps a billion years or even more. They had come out upon dry land many millions of years later, and the great forests that laid down the coal beds flourished at a time which antedates the first flowers by a longer stretch than that which separates the first flowers from us. Then, quite suddenly as such things go (so suddenly indeed that evolutionists are still puzzled by the phenomenon), the earth burst into bloom. Moreover, some of the earliest blossoms of which a record has been preserved in stone were already quite spectacular, and the late dinosaurs may have looked with dull eyes on the dogwood and the magnolia that their sluggish brains were no doubt incapable of admiring.

6   Having granted that much and instructed us thus far, the scientist will go on to say that the poets have, as usual, preferred their own silly fantasies to the truth and preferred them so persistently that it was not until about the time of the American Revolution, when mankind was already half a million years old at the very least, that he cared enough about facts to discover that the flower, like everything else in nature, is merely part of the struggle for survival. Thomas Gray could just possibly be forgiven for babbling about the flower that "wastes its fragrance on the desert air," because most of his contemporaries did not know that this fragrance was not wasted if it enticed the insects it was secreted to attract. But Wordsworth was only deceiving himself when he found in the meanest flower that blows "a thought too deep for tears," and as for Tennyson, who lived in one of the great ages of science, he ought to have been ashamed of himself to write anything so foolish as his apostrophe to the "Flower in the Crannied Wall":

> . . . if I could understand
> What you are, root and all, and all and all,
> I should know what God and man is.

7   The flower, the scientist will go on, was not invented (or rather did not mechanically invent itself) to please us. It flaunted its petals and spread its perfumes because the pollen wasted when distributed at random by the winds could be conserved if an insect could be tricked into carrying it directly from flower to flower. What we call a flower's beauty is merely, so he would conclude, a by-product and a human invention. The perfume isn't there to please us; it pleases us because it is there and we have been conditioned to it. A few flowers pollinated by flesh-eating flies have the odor of rotten meat. If that were usual, rather than unusual, we would by now love the stink.

8   In some of these contentions the scientist is right, or at least partly right, if you grant him his premise that man is a mere accident in nature, a freak to whose desires and needs nature is serenely indifferent. But there are other ways of looking at the matter. Nature did create man and did create his unique qualities, among which is the ability to believe that beauty, even if useful, is also its own excuse for being. That conviction is, therefore, as natural as anything else—as natural, for instance, as the struggle for survival. Man is quite properly proud of the fact that he sometimes succeeds in transforming the sex impulse into something beautiful, and he finds some of what the anatomists call "secondary sex characteristics" very appealing in themselves. But the plants were millions of years ahead of him, and if flowers are merely the organs of reproduction, they are the most attractive of such in all animate nature.

9   In fact, it was in this light that the eighteenth century tended to see its new realization that plants also could "love." Aristotle, the master of those who knew, had proved by logic absolute and to his own satisfaction that the vegetable kingdom was sexless; in spite of the fact that the people of the Near East had known since Babylonian times that their female date palms would bear no fruit unless they were married to the male blossoms from another tree. But even Linnaeus, the prince of

botanists, saw this as a reason for, not an argument against, the poetic interpretation of the flowers he so much loved. And he described them in quaintly rapturous terms: "The petals of the flower contribute nothing to generation but serve only as bridal beds, gloriously arranged by the great Creator, who has adorned with such noble bed curtains and perfumed them with so many sweet perfumes that the bridegroom may celebrate his nuptials with all the greater solemnity." The grandfather of Charles Darwin wrote an enormously popular poem called "The Love of the Flowers" in which he included such lines as these (which, incidentally, seemed very embarrassing to his famous descendant):

> With honey'd lips the enamoured woodbines meet,
> Clasped with fond arms, and mix their kisses sweet.

If that is extravagant, it is hardly more so than the sternly scientific view which sees nothing but mechanics in the evolution of the flower.

Is it wholly fantastic to admit the possibility that nature herself strove toward what we call beauty? Face to face with any one of the elaborate flowers which man's cultivation has had nothing to do with, it does not seem fantastic to me. We put survival first. But when we have a margin of safety left over, we expend it in the search for the beautiful. Who can say that nature does not do the same?   10

To that botanist who said that "the purpose of a flower is to produce seeds" John Ruskin replied in high indignation that it was the other way around. The purpose of the seed is to produce a flower. To be able to see the way in which Ruskin was as right as the botanist is itself one of the flowers of human sensibility and perhaps man's greatest creative act. If nature once interested herself in nothing but survival (and who knows that she did not care for anything else?) she at least created in time a creature who cared for many other things. There may still be something to learn from one of the first English naturalists who defended his science by insisting on man's duty to admire what he called The Works of God because "no creature in this sublunary world is capable of doing so, save man." Even if nature was blind until man made his appearance, it is surely his duty not to blind himself in the interest of what he calls "sober fact." It will be a great pity if science in its search for one kind of knowledge should forget to exercise a peculiarly human capacity. Gardeners who believe the purpose of seed is to produce the flower should keep that capacity alive.   11

Vocabulary

utilitarian, evolutionists, rapturous, sublunary

Questions

1. Does Krutch agree with the scientist that man is a "freak," "a mere accident of nature"?

2. What are secondary sex characteristics?
3. Is nature the cause of beauty?
4. Do the poet and the scientist see beauty differently?

Topics for Writing

The Flower: Cause or Effect?

Beauty: Its Own Excuse for Being

Three Cheers for the Snail Darter

JAMES L. BUCKLEY (1923–) was a one-term senator from New York. Like other members of his family, he has often espoused conservative causes. His defense of the snail darter is based, however, upon philosophical grounds that one associates with no single political category.

Few laws in recent years have caused such apoplexy among so-called practical men of affairs as the Endangered Species Act of 1973. It first burst upon the public consciousness two years ago, when it was invoked twice to scuttle projected dams in Tennessee and Maine; the first time, to save a nondescript little fish called the snail darter, and the other, an inconspicuous flower called the furbish lousewort.

It is idiotic, cry the practical men of affairs, to allow sentimentality over a few hundred weeds or minnows to stand in the way of progress. It is irresponsible, reply the conservationists, to destroy forever a unique pool of genetic material; and the conservationists can marshal a host of nonsentimental arguments in support of what many consider to be the most important environmental legislation of this decade.

Having said this, I can hear the p.m.o.a.s swallow in disbelief as they ask, "Of what possible dollars-and-cents value is the snail darter?" To which conservationists will have to reply, "Other than having inadvertently saved us from a costly mistake,[1] none that we *know* of." And that, paradoxically, is one of the major scientific justifications for the Endangered Species Act.

Our biological knowledge is still so pitifully small that it is less than likely that science can identify the immediate worth of any given species. The roster of species directly useful to man, however, is far greater than most of us would suspect; and we know just enough about the extent of our ignorance to understand how huge our untapped biological resources must be. It is therefore imprudent to allow an estimate of immediate worth, as perceived by men trained to think in terms only of near-term goals, to be the basis for deciding whether a given species is to be preserved.

What good is a snail darter? As practical men measure "good," probably none; but we simply don't know. What value would they have placed on the cowpox virus before Jenner; or on penicillium molds (other than those inhabiting blue cheese) before Fleming; or on wild rubber trees before Goodyear learned to vulcanize their sap? Yet the life of almost every American is profoundly different because of these

---

[1] A re-examination of the economics of the Tellico Dam demonstrates that it is yet another public works boondoggle. It would add only about 0.01 percent to the TVA's electric generating capacity while flooding 16,000 acres of prime farmland having a productive potential of more than $50 million a year; and in order to add yet another to the chain of lakes created by TVA, it would have destroyed the last stretch of free-flowing river in Tennessee.

143

species. The list goes on. As we squash the fruit fly on our kitchen counter, are we aware of its importance to medical research? And who would have thought the armadillo would prove of critical importance in the study of leprosy?

6   Fully 40 per cent of modern drugs have been derived from nature. Most of the food man eats comes from only about twenty out of the thousands of plants known to be edible. And even those currently being cultivated require the preservation of large pools of genetic material on which plant scientists can draw in order to produce more useful strains or to restore the vigor of the highly inbred varieties that have revolutionized agriculture in recent years.

7   Just a few months ago a front-page story in the *New York Times* announced: "In a remote mountain region in Mexico, a perennial plant that cross-breeds with corn has been discovered, awakening hopes for producing a perennial variety of that food crop with revolutionary implications for agriculture." This wild grass offers the prospect of a dramatic reduction in the cost of producing one of the world's most important foods. Had practical men of affairs been in charge of building dams in the Mexican sierras, however, it might have been lost—forever.

8   I say "forever," because extinction is one of the few processes that man cannot reverse. In the course of time the dams in question will have silted up and outlived their usefulness; but it will be too late then to decide that we would like to have the snail darter and the furbish lousewort back. If man cannot restore a species, though, he is fully capable of destroying it; which he is now doing at an astonishing rate. This century has witnessed over half the extinctions of animal species known to have occurred during recorded history; and, largely because of the vast scale on which tropical rain forests are now being cut around the world, it is estimated that by the year 2000 upwards of a million additional species—about 20 per cent of those now in existence—may become extinct.

9   The Endangered Species Act was passed in order to slow down this accelerating rate of man-caused extinctions. Its purpose is not only to help save species that might prove of direct value to man, but to help preserve the biological diversity that, in America and on the rest of our planet, provides the fundamental support system for man and other living things.

10   As living creatures, the more we understand of biological processes, the more wisely we will be able to manage ourselves. Thus the deliberate extermination of a species can be an act of recklessness. By permitting high rates of extinction to continue, we are limiting the potential growth of biological knowledge. In essence, the process is tantamount to book-burning; but it is even worse, in that it involves books yet to be deciphered and read.

11   As originally enacted, the legislation was defective, but not for the reasons given by those for whom the snail darter has become the symbol of environmental extremism. As correctly interpreted by the Supreme Court, the Act prohibits *any* federally financed activity that might lead to the extermination of *any* species. Critics were quick to point out that the legislation rendered unlawful America's contribution to the successful effort to exterminate smallpox. Man cannot escape the need to make difficult choices, and such choices will necessarily be made in the context of man's perception of his own best interests. All one can hope for, there-

fore, is to establish safeguards that will tend to assure that those unavoidable choices will reflect a truly enlightened view of where those best interests lie.

This need to provide for some exceptions to the operation of the Act was the focus of a sometimes bitter debate leading to the adoption of a series of amendments on the last day of the Ninety-fifth Congress. These amendments have been damned with equal vehemence by total protectionists and by the bulldozer set—which suggests that the Congress may, on the whole, have worked out as reasonable a compromise as can be expected in any area giving rise to such strong emotion. Conservationists, for example, are concerned that the criteria for exemptions are too loosely drawn, but they can take heart from the fact that in the first two tests under the amended Act, the Cabinet-level committee appointed under its terms unanimously voted to forbid the completion of the Tellico Dam in Tennessee, and to require the safeguarding of vital whooping-crane feeding grounds as a condition for approving the completion of the Greylocks Dam in Wyoming. The Greylocks decision suggests that progress and protection are not mutually exclusive objectives.   12

One might contend, of course, that our country's biological diversity is still so great and the land is so developed—so criss-crossed with the works of man—that it will soon be hard to locate a dam anywhere without endangering some species. But as we develop a national inventory of endangered species, we certainly can plan our *necessary* developments so as to exterminate the smallest number possible, if not to preclude man-caused extinction altogether. This, of course, is what the legislation, as amended, aims to accomplish.   13

This objective represents a quantum jump in man's acknowledgment of his *moral* responsibility for the integrity of the natural world he passes on to future generations.   14

It is this which lends the Endangered Species Act its special significance. It recognizes values, be they ethical or aesthetic, that transcend the purely practical and admit to awe in the face of the diversity of creation. Not everyone will be moved by them, and they no more lend themselves to a cost-effective calculus than does a Bach chorale. But surely it is an act of unseemly arrogance to decree the extinction of a unique form of life without compelling justification. Such an act is irreversible, and it diminishes by however small a fraction the biological diversity that has come down to us from eons past.   15

Edmund Burke reminds us that the men and women of any generation are but "temporary possessors and life-rentors" who "should not think it among their rights to cut off the entail, or commit waste on the inheritance," lest they "leave to those who come after them a ruin instead of a habitation."   16

That, in sum, is the purpose of the Endangered Species Act and its ultimate justification: to protect our natural inheritance against the awesome waste that this generation of temporary possessors has proven itself so prone to commit.   17

Vocabulary

scuttle, nondescript, vulcanize, quantum, entail (noun)

Questions

1. Who are the "p.m.o.a.s"?
2. How is human-caused extinction like bookburning?
3. How was the Endangered Species Act originally defective?
4. The snail darter was saved when the Tellico Dam project was halted. What other effects may have been caused by the halt? Are all the effects good?
5. Can we halt all human-caused extinction?
6. Human beings probably had nothing to do with the extinction of the dinosaurs. Should we try to prevent Nature from exterminating a species?

Topics for Writing

We Saved the Snail Darter—at What Cost?

Man, the Destroyer

Man, the Preserver

Overpopulated America

WAYNE H. DAVIS (1930–) is a professor of biological science at the University of Kentucky. He has long been concerned with the way we Americans use and abuse our natural resources.

I define as most seriously overpopulated that nation whose people by virtue of their numbers and activities are most rapidly decreasing the ability of the land to support human life. With our large population, our affluence and our technological monstrosities the United States wins first place by a substantial margin.   1

Let's compare the United States to India, for example. We have 203 million people, whereas she has 540 million on much less land. But look at the impact of people on the land.   2

The average Indian eats his daily few cups of rice (or perhaps wheat, whose production on American farms contributed to our one percent per year drain in quality of our active farmland), draws his bucket of water from the communal well and sleeps in a mud hut. In his daily rounds to gather cow dung to burn to cook his rice and warm his feet, his footsteps, along with those millions of his countrymen, help bring about a slow deterioration of the ability of the land to support people. His contribution to the destruction of the land is minimal.   3

An American, on the other hand, can be expected to destroy a piece of land on which he builds a home, garage and driveway. He will contribute his share to the 142 million tons of smoke and fumes, 7 million junked cars, 20 million tons of paper, 48 billion cans, and 26 billion bottles the overburdened environment must absorb each year. To run his air conditioner we will strip-mine a Kentucky hillside, push the dirt and slate down into the stream, and burn coal in a power generator, whose smokestack contributes to a plume of smoke massive enough to cause cloud seeding and premature precipitation from Gulf winds which should be irrigating the wheat farms of Minnesota.   4

In his lifetime he will personally pollute three million gallons of water, and industry and agriculture will use ten times this much water in his behalf. To provide these needs the U.S. Army Corps of Engineers will build dams and flood farmland. He will also use 21,000 gallons of leaded gasoline containing boron, drink 28,000 pounds of milk and eat 10,000 pounds of meat. The latter is produced and squandered in a life pattern unknown to Asians. A steer on a Western range eats plants containing minerals necessary for plant life. Some of these are incorporated into the body of the steer which is later shipped for slaughter. After being eaten by man these nutrients are flushed down the toilet into the ocean or buried in the cemetery, the surface of which is cluttered with boulders called tombstones and has been removed from productivity. The result is a continual drain on the productivity of range land. Add to this the erosion of overgrazed lands, and the effects of the falling water table   5 as we mine Pleistocene deposits of groundwater to irrigate to produce food for more people, and we can see why our land is dying far more rapidly than did the great civilization of the Middle East, which experienced the same cycle. The average Indian citizen, whose fecal material goes back to the land, has but a minute fraction of the destructive effect on the land that the affluent American does.

6   Thus I want to introduce a new term, which I suggest be used in future discussions of human population and ecology. We should speak of our numbers in "Indian equivalents." An Indian equivalent I define as the average number of Indian citizens required to have the same detrimental effect on the land's ability to support human life as would the average American. This value is difficult to determine, but let's take an extremely conservative working figure of 25. To see how conservative this is, imagine the addition of 1,000 citizens to your town and 25,000 to an Indian village. Not only would the Americans destroy much more land for homes, highways and a shopping center, but they would contribute far more to environmental deterioration in hundreds of other ways as well. For example, their demand for steel for new autos might increase the daily pollution equivalent of 130,000 junk autos which *Life* tells us that U.S. Steel Corporation dumps into Lake Michigan. Their demand for textiles would help the cotton industry destroy the life in the Black Warrior River in Alabama with endrin. And they would contribute to the massive industrial pollution of our oceans (we provide one-third to one-half the world's share) which has caused the precipitous downward trend in our commercial fisheries landings during the past seven years.

7   The per capita gross national product of the United States is thirty-eight times that of India. Most of our goods and services contribute to the decline in the ability of the environment to support life. Thus it is clear that a figure of 25 for an Indian equivalent is conservative. It has been suggested to me that a more realistic figure would be 500.

8   In Indian equivalents, therefore, the population of the United States is at least four billion. And the rate of growth is even more alarming. We are growing at one percent per year, a rate which would double our numbers in seventy years. India is growing at 2.5 percent. Using the Indian equivalent of 25, our population growth becomes ten times as serious as that of India. According to the Rienows in their recent book *Moment in the Sun,* just one year's crop of American babies can be expected to use up 25 billion pounds of beef, 200 million pounds of steel and 9.1 billion gallons of gasoline during their collective lifetime. And the demands on water and land for our growing population are expected to be far greater than the supply available in the year 2000. We are destroying our land at a rate of over a million acres a year. We now have only 2.6 agricultural acres per person. By 1975 this will be cut to 2.2, the critical point for the maintenance of what we consider a decent diet, and by the year 2000 we might expect to have 1.2.

9   You might object that I am playing with statistics in using the Indian equivalent on the rate of growth. I am making the assumption that today's child will live thirty-five years (the average Indian life span) at today's level of affluence. If he lives an American seventy years, our rate of population growth would be twenty times as serious as India's.

But the assumption of continued affluence at today's level is unfounded. If our   10
numbers continue to rise, our standard of living will fall so sharply that by the year
2000 any surviving Americans might consider today's average Asian to be well off.
Our children's destructive effects on their environment will decline as they sink ever
lower into poverty.

The United States is in serious economic trouble now. Nothing could be more   11
misleading than today's affluence, which rests precariously on a crumbling foundation. Our productivity, which had been increasing steadily at about 3.2 percent a
year since World War II, has been falling during 1969. Our export over import
balance has been shrinking steadily from $7.1 billion in 1964 to $0.15 billion in the
first half of 1969. Our balance of payments deficit for the second quarter was $3.7
billion, the largest in history. We are now importing iron ore, steel, oil, beef,
textiles, cameras, radios and hundreds of other things.

Our economy is based upon the Keynesian concept of a continued growth in   12
population and productivity. It worked in an underpopulated nation with excess
resources. It could continue to work only if the earth and its resources were expanding at an annual rate of 4 to 5 percent. Yet neither the number of cars, the
economy, the human population, nor anything else can expand indefinitely at an
exponential rate in a finite world. We must face this fact *now*. The crisis is here.
When Walter Heller says that our economy will expand by 4 percent annually
through the latter 1970s he is dreaming. He is in a theoretical world totally unaware
of the realities of human ecology. If the economists do not wake up and devise a
new system for us now somebody else will have to do it for them.

A civilization is comparable to a living organism. Its longevity is a function of   13
its metabolism. The higher the metabolism (affluence), the shorter the life. Keynesian economics has allowed us an affluent but shortened life span. We have now run
our course.

The tragedy facing the United States is even greater and more imminent than   14
that descending upon the hungry nations. The Paddock brothers in their book,
Famine 1975!, say that India "cannot be saved" no matter how much food we ship
her. But India will be here after the United States is gone. Many millions will die in
the most colossal famines India has ever known, but the land will survive and she
will come back as she always has before. The United States, on the other hand, will
be a desolate tangle of concrete and ticky-tacky, of strip-mined moonscape and silt-
choked reservoirs. The land and water will be so contaminated with pesticides,
herbicides, mercury fungicides, lead, boron, nickel, arsenic and hundreds of other
toxic substances, which have been approaching critical levels of concentration in
our environment as a result of our numbers and affluence, that it may be unable to
sustain human life.

Thus as the curtain gets ready to fall on man's civilization let it come as no   15
surprise that it shall first fall on the United States. And let no one make the mistake
of thinking we can save ourselves by "cleaning up the environment." Banning DDT
is the equivalent of the physician's treating syphilis by putting a bandaid over the
first chancre to appear. In either case you can be sure that more serious and
widespread trouble will soon appear unless the disease itself is treated. We cannot

survive by planning to treat the symptoms such as air pollution, water pollution, soil erosion, etc.

16   What can we do to slow the rate of destruction of the United States as a land capable of supporting human life? There are two approaches. First, we must reverse the population growth. We have far more people now than we can continue to support at anything near today's level of affluence. American women average slightly over three children each. According to the *Population Bulletin* if we reduced this number to 2.5 there would still be 330 million people in the nation at the end of the century. And even if we reduced this to 1.5 we would have 57 million more people in the year 2000 than we have now. With our present longevity patterns it would take more than thirty years for the population to peak even when reproducing at this rate, which would eventually give us a net decrease in numbers.

17   Do not make the mistake of thinking that technology will solve our population problem by producing a better contraceptive. Our problem now is that people want too many children. Surveys show the average number of children wanted by the American family is 3.3. There is little difference between the poor and the wealthy, black and white, Catholic and Protestant. Production of children at this rate during the next thirty years would be so catastrophic in effect on our resources and the viability of the nation as to be beyond my ability to contemplate. To prevent this trend we must not only make contraceptives and abortion readily available to everyone, but we must establish a system to put severe economic pressure on those who produce children and reward those who do not. This can be done within our system of taxes and welfare.

18   The other thing we must do is to pare down our Indian equivalents. Individuals in American society vary tremendously in Indian equivalents. If we plot Indian equivalents versus their reciprocal, the percentage of land surviving a generation, we obtain a linear regression. We can then place individuals and occupation types on this graph. At one end would be the starving blacks of Mississippi; they would approach unity in Indian equivalents, and would have the least destructive effect on the land. At the other end of the graph would be the politicians slicing pork for the barrel, the highway contractors, strip-mine operators, real estate developers, and public enemy number one—the U.S. Army Corps of Engineers.

19   We must halt land destruction. We must abandon the view of land and minerals as private property to be exploited in any way economically feasible for private financial gain. Land and minerals are resources upon which the very survival of the nation depends, and their use must be planned in the best interests of the people.

20   Rising expectations for the poor is a cruel joke foisted upon them by the Establishment. As our new economy of use-it-once-and-throw-it-away produces more and more products for the affluent, the share of our resources available for the poor declines. Blessed be the starving blacks of Mississippi with their outdoor privies, for they are ecologically sound, and they shall inherit a nation. Although I hope that we will help these unfortunate people attain a decent standard of living by

diverting war efforts to fertility control and job training, our most urgent task to assure this nation's survival during the next decade is to stop the affluent destroyers.

Vocabulary

communal, premature, Pleistocene, fecal, endrin, precipitous

Questions

1. Do you accept Davis's definition of "most seriously overpopulated"?
2. What are "Indian equivalents"? What is the population of America in Indian equivalents?
3. When he argues that "India will be here after the United States is gone," is Davis talking about people or land?
4. We are now some years beyond 1975, "the critical point for the maintenance of what we consider a decent diet," according to the author. Does "a decent diet" seem to have become a problem? Cite examples to support your opinion.
5. Look up the rate of America's economic growth during the 1970s. Was it greater or less than 4 percent?
6. Is it fair to call affluence the metabolism of a civilization? Why not some other characteristic—say, industry or education?
7. What does Davis recommend we do "to slow the rate of destruction"?
8. What means would he use to slow population growth? Do you agree with these means? Would you suggest others?
9. Why does he call the Army Corps of Engineers "public enemy number one"?
10. The "starving blacks" are "ecologically sound." Comment on this.
11. If you had to choose, would you prefer a nearly endless existence at today's Indian level or a relatively short one at today's American level?

Topics for Writing

Dead Men Are Ecologically Sound

A Plan for Reducing Population

It's a Free Country, Isn't It?

7

Analyzing Processes / The World of Science and Technology

When we analyze something, we take it apart mentally to see how it is made or what makes it work. (The opposite, the mental reconstruction of the object, we call *synthesis*). To write a process analysis, therefore, is to give a written account of the steps or stages that lead to a specific result. How-to-do-it articles ("How to Tune Your Volkswagen" or "How to Make Chili con Carne") and how-it-was-done articles ("The Road to Emancipation" or "The Writing of *The Declaration of Independence*") are examples. In the first instance, the writer is, like Benjamin Franklin on the subject of lightning rods, an expert giving directions. In the second, the writer explains, as Annie Dillard does, how a thing (the snakeskin "knot") came to be.

This is a two-part matter. The writer must first analyze the subject. That is, he must think systematically about it, asking what went into its making and by what steps it came to be what it is. Once the process has been analyzed, the writer must describe it in terms that others can understand and in a sequence that they can follow.

More often than not, the sequence will be chronological: "First, stand A on its base; then attach B to A, using two half-inch wood screws; next . . ." and so on until the task is completed. Sometimes, however, a strictly chronological development is impossible, as when several stages of a complex process take place simultaneously. In such cases, the writer will organize the stages in some logical way, treating each one in order, but reminding the reader of other stages happening at the same time. For example, a subject like "A Successful Football Practice" might call for division into "Defensive Line Practice," "Passing Drill," and so forth, each division demanding separate treatment. But the skillful writer will guide the reader with transitional aids: "While the backfield coaches are working with the running backs, the defensive unit will be . . . ." The aim is to help the reader see the process as clearly as possible.

Students of science and technology have always had ample opportunities to use the techniques of process analysis. As any scientist will agree, no experiment is complete until it has been written up. And those who know how things are done or how matters came to be are usually glad to share their knowledge with others.

Benjamin Franklin's "how-to-do-it" piece can be followed by a child; Rachel Carson, James Jeans, and Thomas Henry Huxley are as lucid with the slightly more difficult questions, How does it happen? How is it done? J. B. S. Haldane deflates some unscientific notions about "What would happen if . . .?" Two scientists of an older generation use process analysis only as part of a larger effort—Samuel Scudder to describe his first step on the road to learning, Charles Darwin to summarize the results of long observation. Whether analyzing the simple or the very complex, all show one characteristic of great teachers: a desire to share what they have learned. They make it easy for us to be learners, and they demonstrate a method of writing that has practical applications in every field of work.

How to Make a Lightning Rod

BENJAMIN FRANKLIN (see Chapter 1) wrote the following directions to David Hume, the Scottish philosopher, in a letter dated 24 January 1762.

1   Prepare a steel rod about five or six feet long, about half an inch thick at its largest end, and tapering to a sharp point. This point should be gilded to prevent its rusting. Secure to the big end of the rod a strong eye or a ring half an inch in diameter. Fix the rod upright to the chimney or the highest part of a house. It should be fixed with some sort of staples or special nails to keep it steady. The pointed end should extend upward, and should rise three or four feet above the chimney or building to which the rod is fixed. Drive into the ground an iron rod about one inch in diameter, and ten or twelve feet long. This rod should also have an eye or ring fixed to its upper end. It is best to place the iron rod some distance from the foundation of the house. Ten feet away is a good distance, if the size of the property permits. Then take as much length of iron rod of a smaller diameter as will be necessary to reach from the eye on the rod above to the eye of the rod below. Fasten this securely to the fixed rods by passing it through the eyes and bending the ends to form rings too. Then close all the joints with lead. This is easily done by making a small bag of strong paper around the joints, tying it tight below, and then pouring in the molten lead. It is useful to have these joints treated in this way so that there will be a considerable area of contact between each piece. To prevent the wind from shaking this long rod, it may be fastened to the building by several staples. If the building is especially large or long, extending more than one hundred feet for example, it is wise to erect a rod at each end. If there is a well sufficiently near to the building to permit placing the iron rod in the water, this is even better than the use of the iron rod in the ground. It may also be wise to paint the iron to prevent it from rusting. A building so protected will not be damaged by lightning.

Vocabulary

gilded, diameter

Questions

1. To analyze a process is to break it down into its parts and then to reconstruct it logically, step-by-step. Could you make a lightning rod by following Franklin's directions? Are any steps in the process left unclear?
2. Why doesn't Franklin begin, "Go to your ironmonger and get a rod about five or six feet long . . . ."?

3. Why doesn't Franklin explain how the lightning rod works?

Topics for Writing

How to Bathe a Dog
How to Shave
How to —————

Why the Sky Looks Blue

JAMES JEANS (1877–1946) was a British scientist and a mathematician. His books (*Through Space and Time* and *The Mysterious Universe* are two) and articles helped to explain the mysteries of astronomy and astrophysics to the general public.

1   Imagine that we stand on an ordinary seaside pier, and watch the waves rolling in and striking against the iron columns of the pier. Large waves pay very little attention to the columns—they divide right and left and reunite after passing each column, much as a regiment of soldiers would if a tree stood in their road; it is almost as though the columns had not been there. But the short waves and ripples find the columns of the pier a much more formidable obstacle. When the short waves impinge on the columns, they are reflected back and spread as new ripples in all directions. To use the technical term, they are "scattered." The obstacle provided by the iron columns hardly affects the long waves at all, but scatters the short ripples.

2   We have been watching a sort of working model of the way in which sunlight struggles through the earth's atmosphere. Between us on earth and outer space the atmosphere interposes innumerable obstacles in the form of molecules of air, tiny droplets of water, and small particles of dust. These are represented by the columns of the pier.

3   The waves of the sea represent the sunlight. We know that sunlight is a blend of many colors—as we can prove for ourselves by passing it through a prism, or even through a jug of water, or as nature demonstrates to us when she passes it through the raindrops of a summer shower and produces a rainbow. We also know that light consists of waves, and that the different colors of light are produced by waves of different lengths, red light by long waves and blue light by short waves. The mixture of waves which constitutes sunlight has to struggle past the columns of the pier. And these obstacles treat the light waves much as the columns of the pier treat the sea-waves. The long waves which constitute red light are hardly affected but the short waves which constitute blue light are scattered in all directions.

4   Thus the different constituents of sunlight are treated in different ways as they struggle through the earth's atmosphere. A wave of blue light may be scattered by a dust particle, and turned out of its course. After a time a second dust particle again turns it out of its course, and so on, until finally it enters our eyes by a path as zigzag as that of a flash of lightning. Consequently the blue waves of the sunlight enter our eyes from all directions. And that is why the sky looks blue.

Vocabulary

impinge, constituents

Questions

1. Jeans explains a natural phenomenon as though it were a simple process. In the first paragraph, he describes the way a model of the process works. This model is analogous to the action of light waves coming through the atmosphere. Why is the analogy helpful?
2. Is the correspondence between sea waves and light waves exact?
3. How do short waves act differently from long ones when they meet obstacles?

Topics for Writing

Jeans: Oversimplifier or Expert Teacher?

A Process I Would Like Explained

In the Laboratory with Agassiz

SAMUEL H. SCUDDER (1837–1911) was himself a scientist and university professor. This article first appeared in *Every Saturday* in 1874. Louis Agassiz was one of America's first great scientists, internationally famed in geology and zoology.

1   It was more than fifteen years ago that I entered the laboratory of Professor Agassiz, and told him I had enrolled my name in the Scientific School as a student of natural history. He asked me a few questions about my object in coming, my antecedents generally, the mode in which I afterwards proposed to use the knowledge I might acquire, and, finally, whether I wished to study any special branch. To the latter I replied that, while I wished to be well grounded in all departments of zoology, I purposed to devote myself specially to insects.

2   "When do you wish to begin?" he asked.

3   "Now," I replied.

4   This seemed to please him, and with an energetic "Very well!" he reached from a shelf a huge jar of specimens in yellow alcohol.

5   "Take this fish," said he, "and look at it; we call it a haemulon; by and by I will ask what you have seen."

6   With that he left me, but in a moment returned with explicit instructions as to the care of the object entrusted to me.

7   "No man is fit to be a naturalist," said he, "who does not know how to take care of specimens."

8   I was to keep the fish before me in a tin tray, and occasionally moisten the surface with alcohol from the jar, always taking care to replace the stopper tightly. Those were not the days of ground-glass stoppers and elegantly shaped exhibition jars; all the old students will recall the huge neckless glass bottles with their leaky, wax-besmeared corks, half eaten by insects, and begrimed with cellar dust. Entomology was a cleaner science than ichthyology, but the example of the Professor, who had unhesitatingly plunged to the bottom of the jar to produce the fish, was infectious; and though this alcohol had a "very ancient and fishlike smell," I really dared not show any aversion within these sacred precincts, and treated the alcohol as though it were pure water. Still I was conscious of a passing feeling of disappointment, for gazing at a fish did not commend itself to an ardent entomologist. My friends at home, too, were annoyed when they discovered that no amount of eau-de-Cologne would drown the perfume which haunted me like a shadow.

9   In ten minutes I had seen all that could be seen in that fish, and started in search of the Professor—who had, however, left the Museum; and when I returned, after lingering over some of the odd animals stored in the upper apartment, my

specimen was dry all over. I dashed the fluid over the fish as if to resuscitate the beast from a fainting-fit, and looked with anxiety for a return of the normal sloppy appearance. This little excitement over, nothing was to be done but to return to a steadfast gaze at my mute companion. Half an hour passed—an hour—another hour; the fish began to look loathsome. I turned it over and around; looked it in the face—ghastly; from behind, beneath, above, sideways, at a three-quarters' view— just as ghastly. I was in despair; at an early hour I concluded that lunch was necessary; so, with infinite relief, the fish was carefully replaced in the jar, and for an hour I was free.

On my return, I learned that Professor Agassiz had been at the Museum, but   10
had gone, and would not return for several hours. My fellow-students were too busy to be disturbed by continued conversation. Slowly I drew forth that hideous fish, and with a feeling of desperation again looked at it. I might not use a magnifying-glass; instruments of all kinds were interdicted. My two hands, my two eyes, and the fish; it seemed a most limited field. I pushed my finger down its throat to feel how sharp the teeth were. I began to count the scales in the different rows, until I was convinced that that was nonsense. At last a happy thought struck me—I would draw the fish; and now with surprise I began to discover new features in the creature. Just then the Professor returned.

"That is right," said he; "a pencil is one of the best of eyes. I am glad to notice,   11
too, that you keep your specimen wet, and your bottle corked."

With these encouraging words, he added: 12

"Well, what is it like?"   13

He listened attentively to my brief rehearsal of the structure of parts whose   14
names were still unknown to me: the fringed gill-arches and movable operculum; the pores of the head, fleshy lips and lidless eyes; the lateral line, the spinous fins and forked tail; the compressed and arched body. When I had finished, he waited as if expecting more, and then, with an air of disappointment:

"You have not looked very carefully; why," he continued more earnestly, "you   15
haven't even seen one of the most conspicuous features of the animal, which is as plainly before your eyes as the fish itself; look again, look again!" and he left me to my misery.

I was piqued; I was mortified. Still more of that wretched fish! But now I set   16
myself to my task with a will, and discovered one new thing after another, until I saw how just the Professor's criticism had been. The afternoon passed quickly; and when, toward its close, the Professor inquired:

"Do you see it yet?"   17

"No," I replied, "I am certain I do not, but I see how little I saw before."   18

"That is next best," said he, earnestly, "but I won't hear you now; put away   19
your fish and go home; perhaps you will be ready with a better answer in the morning. I will examine you before you look at the fish."

This was disconcerting. Not only must I think of my fish all night, studying,   20
without the object before me, what this unknown but most visible feature might be; but also, without reviewing my discoveries, I must give an exact account of them

the next day. I had a bad memory; so I walked home by Charles River in a distracted state, with my two perplexities.

21   The cordial greeting from the Professor the next morning was reassuring; here was a man who seemed to be quite as anxious as I that I should see for myself what he saw.

22   "Do you perhaps mean," I asked, "that the fish has symmetrical sides with paired organs?"

23   His thoroughly pleased "Of course! of course!" repaid the wakeful hours of the previous night. After he had discoursed most happily and enthusiastically—as he always did—upon the importance of this point, I ventured to ask what I should do next.

24   "Oh, look at your fish!" he said, and left me again to my own devices. In a little more than an hour he returned, and heard my new catalogue.

25   "That is good, that is good!" he repeated; "but that is not all; go on"; and so for three long days he placed that fish before my eyes, forbidding me to look at anything else, or to use any artificial aid. "Look, look, look," was his repeated injunction.

26   This was the best entomological lesson I ever had—a lesson whose influence has extended to the details of every subsequent study; a legacy the Professor has left to me, as he has left it to many others, of inestimable value, which we could not buy, with which we cannot part.

27   A year afterward, some of us were amusing ourselves with chalking outlandish beasts on the Museum blackboard. We drew prancing starfishes; frogs in mortal combat; hydra-headed worms; stately crawfishes, standing on their tails, bearing aloft umbrellas; and grotesque fishes with gaping mouths and staring eyes. The Professor came in shortly after, and was as amused as any at our experiments. He looked at the fishes.

28   "Haemulons, every one of them," he said; "Mr. —— drew them."

29   True; and to this day, if I attempt a fish, I can draw nothing but haemulons.

30   The fourth day, a second fish of the same group was placed beside the first, and I was bidden to point out the resemblances and differences between the two; another and another followed, until the entire family lay before me, and a whole legion of jars covered the table and surrounding shelves; the odor had become a pleasant perfume; and even now, the sight of an old, six-inch, worm-eaten cork brings fragrant memories.

31   The whole group of haemulons was thus brought in review; and, whether engaged upon the dissection of the internal organs, the preparation and examination of the bony framework, or the description of the various parts, Agassiz's training in the method of observing facts and their orderly arrangement was ever accompanied by the urgent exhortation not to be content with them.

32   "Facts are stupid things," he would say, "until brought into connection with some general law."

33   At the end of eight months, it was almost with reluctance that I left these friends and turned to insects; but what I had gained by this outside experience has been of greater value than years of later investigation in my favorite groups.

Vocabulary

antecedents, entomology, ichthyology, infectious, resuscitate, interdicted, operculum, piqued, perplexities, injunction, legacy

Questions

1. What words and turns of phrase communicate Scudder's fondness for this memory?
2. Is there any sentence that expresses Scudder's definition of education? Is one necessary?
3. Does the alternation of narrative and dialogue disrupt the flow of this essay?
4. Was it curiosity or boredom that led Scudder to examine the fish closely?
5. At what point did Scudder begin to grow fond of that "loathsome" fish?
6. Couldn't Scudder have learned more rapidly with a textbook on haemulons at hand?
7. Why is "a pencil one of the best of eyes"?

Topics for Writing

Facts Are Stupid Things

My Best Lesson

A Complete Description of My Left Hand

The Birth and Death of Islands

RACHEL L. CARSON (1907–1964), scientist and writer, has done much to make us conscious of the physical world. This process analysis comes from her most popular book, *The Sea Around Us*.

1   Millions of years ago, a volcano built a mountain on the floor of the Atlantic. In eruption after eruption, it pushed up a great pile of volcanic rock, until it had accumulated a mass a hundred miles across at its base, reaching upward toward the surface of the sea. Finally its cone emerged as an island with an area of about two hundred square miles. Thousands of years passed, and thousands of thousands. Eventually the waves of the Atlantic cut down the cone and reduced it to a shoal— all of it, that is, but a small fragment which remained above water. This fragment we know as Bermuda.

2   With variations, the life story of Bermuda has been repeated by almost every one of the islands that interrupt the watery expanses of the oceans far from land. For these isolated islands in the sea are fundamentally different from the continents. The major land masses and the ocean basins are today much as they have been throughout the greater part of geologic time. But islands are ephemeral, created today, destroyed tomorrow. With few exceptions, they are the result of the violent, explosive, earth-shaking eruptions of submarine volcanoes, working perhaps for millions of years to achieve their end. It is one of the paradoxes in the ways of earth and sea that a process seemingly so destructive, so catastrophic in nature, can result in an act of creation.

3   Islands have always fascinated the human mind. Perhaps it is the instinctive response of man, the land animal, welcoming a brief intrusion of earth in the vast, overwhelming expanse of sea. Here in a great oceanic basin, a thousand miles from the nearest continent, with miles of water under our vessel, we come upon an island. Our imaginations can follow its slopes down through darkening waters to where it rests on the sea floor. We wonder why and how it arose here in the midst of the ocean.

4   The birth of a volcanic island is an event marked by prolonged and violent travail: the forces of the earth striving to create, and all the forces of the sea opposing. The sea floor, where an island begins, is probably nowhere more than about fifty miles thick—a thin covering over the vast bulk of the earth. In it are deep cracks and fissures, the result of unequal cooling and shrinkage in past ages. Along such lines of weakness the molten lava from the earth's interior presses up and finally bursts forth into the sea. But a submarine volcano is different from a terrestrial eruption, where the lava, molten rocks, gases, and other ejecta are hurled into

the air through an open crater. Here on the bottom of the ocean the volcano has resisting it all the weight of the ocean water above it. Despite the immense pressure of, it may be, two or three miles of sea water, the new volcanic cone builds upward toward the surface, in flow after flow of lava. Once within reach of the waves, its soft ash and tuff are violently attacked, and for a long period the potential island may remain a shoal, unable to emerge. But, eventually, in new eruptions, the cone is pushed up into the air and a rampart against the attacks of the waves is built of hardened lava.

Navigators' charts are marked with numerous recently discovered submarine   5
mountains. Many of these are the submerged remnants of the islands of a geologic yesterday. The same charts show islands that emerged from the sea at least fifty million years ago, and others that arose within our own memory. Among the undersea mountains marked on the charts may be the islands of tomorrow, which at this moment are forming, unseen, on the floor of the ocean and are growing upward toward its surface.

For the sea is by no means done with submarine eruptions; they occur fairly   6
commonly, sometimes detected only by instruments, sometimes obvious to the most casual observer. Ships in volcanic zones may suddenly find themselves in violently disturbed water. There are heavy discharges of steam. The sea appears to bubble or boil in a furious turbulence. Fountains spring from its surface. Floating up from the deep, hidden places of the actual eruption come the bodies of fishes and other deep-sea creatures, and quantities of volcanic ash and pumice.

One of the youngest of the large volcanic islands of the world is Ascension in   7
the South Atlantic. During the Second World War the American airmen sang

> If we don't find Ascension
> Our wives will get a pension

this island being the only piece of dry land between the hump of Brazil and the bulge of Africa. It is a forbidding mass of cinders, in which the vents of no less than forty extinct volcanoes can be counted. It has not always been so barren, for its slopes have yielded the fossil remains of trees. What happened to the forests no one knows: the first men to explore the island, about the year 1500, found it tree-less, and today it has no natural greenness except on its highest peak, known as Green Mountain.

In modern times we have never seen the birth of an island as large as Ascen-   8
sion. But now and then there is a report of a small island appearing where none was before. Perhaps a month, a year, five years later, the island has disappeared into the sea again. These are the little, stillborn islands, doomed to only a brief emergence above the sea.

About 1830 such an island suddenly appeared in the Mediterranean between   9
Sicily and the coast of Africa, rising from one hundred-fathom depths after there had been signs of volcanic activity in the area. It was little more than a black cinder pile, perhaps two hundred feet high. Waves, wind, and rain attacked it. Its soft and

porous materials were easily eroded; its substance was rapidly eaten away and it sank beneath the sea. Now it is a shoal, marked on the charts as Graham's Reef.

10   Falcon Island, the tip of a volcano projecting above the Pacific nearly two thousand miles east of Australia, suddenly disappeared in 1913. Thirteen years later, after violent eruptions in the vicinity, it as suddenly rose again above the surface and remained as a physical bit of the British Empire until 1949. Then it was reported by the Colonial Under Secretary to be missing again.

11   Almost from the moment of its creation, a volcanic island is foredoomed to destruction. It has in itself the seeds of its own dissolution, for new explosions, or landslides of the soft soil, may violently accelerate its disintegration. Whether the destruction of an island comes quickly or only after long ages of geologic time may also depend on external forces: the rains that wear away the loftiest of land mountains, the sea, and even man himself.

12   South Trinidad, or in the Portuguese spelling, "Ilha Trinidade," is an example of an island that has been sculptured into bizarre forms through centuries of weathering—an island in which the signs of dissolution are clearly apparent. This group of volcanic peaks lies in the open Atlantic, about a thousand miles north-east of Rio de Janeiro. E. F. Knight wrote in 1907 that Trinidad "is rotten throughout, its substance has been disintegrated by volcanic fires and by the action of water, so that it is everywhere tumbling to pieces." During an interval of nine years between Knight's visits, a whole mountainside had collapsed in a great landslide of broken rocks and volcanic debris.

13   Sometimes the disintegration takes abrupt and violent form. The greatest explosion of historic time was the literal evisceration of the island of Krakatoa. In 1680 there had been a premonitory eruption on this small island in Sunda Strait, between Java and Sumatra in the Netherlands Indies. Two hundred years later there had been a series of earthquakes. In the spring of 1883, smoke and steam began to ascend from fissures in the volcanic cone. The ground became noticeably warm, and warning rumblings and hissings came from the volcano. Then, on 27 August, Krakatoa literally exploded. In an appalling series of eruptions, that lasted two days, the whole northern half of the cone was carried away. The sudden inrush of ocean water added the fury of superheated steam to the cauldron. When the inferno of white-hot lava, molten rock, steam, and smoke had finally subsided, the island that had stood 1,400 feet above the sea had become a cavity a thousand feet below sea level. Only along one edge of the former crater did a remnant of the island remain.

14   Krakatoa, in its destruction, became known to the entire world. The eruption gave rise to a hundred-foot wave that wiped out villages along the Strait and killed people by tens of thousands. The wave was felt on the shores of the Indian Ocean and at Cape Horn; rounding the Cape into the Atlantic, it sped northward and retained its identity even as far as the English Channel. The sound of the explosions was heard in the Philippine Islands, in Australia, and on the Island of Madagascar, nearly 3,000 miles away. And clouds of volcanic dust, the pulverized rock that had been torn from the heart of Krakatoa, ascended into the stratosphere and were carried around the globe to give rise to a series of spectacular sunsets in every country of the world for nearly a year.

Vocabulary

shoal, geologic, ephemeral, paradoxes, catastrophic, travail, fissures, terrestrial, rampart, pumice, fathom, dissolution, bizarre, literal, evisceration, premonitory, appalling, cauldron, pulverized, stratosphere

Questions

1. How are volcanic islands fundamentally different from the continents?
2. Why are volcanic islands "foredoomed to destruction"?
3. Outline the process which led to the spectacular sunsets of 1883.
4. Consider some natural object nearby—a tree, say, a stream, or a hill. How did it get to be where it is, the size or shape it is? Starting with the object as you see it now, and working backwards step by step, write down the process you think led to the object's present existence.

Topics for Writing

The Analysis of a Natural Process

A Tree Grows in ——

Thinking Scientifically

THOMAS HENRY HUXLEY (1825–1895) Although Thomas Henry Huxley is always remembered as an associate of Darwin and a defender of evolutionary theory, he was a scientist in his own right and wanted to educate ordinary people to appreciate modern science. The Royal Society rewarded him with its presidency in 1883.

1   There is a well-known incident in one of Molière's plays, where the author makes the hero express unbounded delight on being told that he had been talking prose during the whole of his life. In the same way, I trust that you will take comfort, and be delighted with yourselves, on the discovery that you have been acting on the principles of inductive and deductive philosophy during the same period. Probably there is not one here who has not in the course of the day had occasion to set in motion a complex train of reasoning, of the very same kind, though differing of course in degree, as that which a scientific man goes through in tracing the causes of natural phenomena.

2   A very trivial circumstance will serve to exemplify this. Suppose you go into a fruiterer's shop, wanting an apple,—you take up one, and, on biting it, you find it sour; you look at it, and see that it is hard and green. You take up another one, and that too is hard, green, and sour. The shopman offers you a third; but, before biting it, you examine it, and find that it is hard and green, and you immediately say that you will not have it, as it must be sour, like those that you have already tried.

3   Nothing can be more simple than that, you think; but if you will take the trouble to analyse and trace out into its logical elements what has been done by the mind, you will be greatly surprised. In the first place you have performed the operation of induction. You found that, in two experiences, hardness and greenness in apples went together with sourness. It was so in the first case, and it was confirmed by the second. True, it is a very small basis, but still it is enough to make an induction from; you generalise the facts, and you expect to find sourness in apples where you get hardness and greenness. You found upon that a general law, that all hard and green apples are sour; and that, so far as it goes, is a perfect induction. Well, having got your natural law in this way, when you are offered another apple which you find is hard and green, you say, "All hard and green apples are sour; this apple is hard and green, therefore this apple is sour." That train of reasoning is what logicians call a syllogism, and has all its various parts and terms,—its major premise, its minor premise, and its conclusion. And, by the help of further reasoning, which if drawn out, would have to be exhibited in two or three other syllogisms, you arrive at your final determination, "I will not have that apple." So that, you see, you have, in the first place, established a law by induction, and upon that you have founded a deduction, and reasoned out the special conclusion of the particular case. Well now, suppose, having got your law, that at some time

afterwards, you are discussing the qualities of apples with a friend: you will say to him, "It is a very curious thing,—but I find that all hard and green apples are sour!" Your friend says to you, "But how do you know that?" You at once reply, "Oh, because I have tried them over and over again, and have always found them to be so." Well, if we were talking science instead of common sense, we should call that an experimental verification. And if still opposed, you go further, and say, "I have heard from the people in Somersetshire and Devonshire, where a large number of apples are grown, that they have observed the same thing. It is also found to be the case in Normandy, and in North America. In short, I find it to be the universal experience of mankind wherever attention has been directed to the subject." Whereupon, your friend, unless he is a very unreasonable man, agrees with you, and is convinced that you are quite right in the conclusion you have drawn. He believes, although perhaps he does not know he believes it, that the more extensive verifications are,—that the more frequently experiments have been made, and results of the same kind arrived at,—that the more varied the conditions under which the same results are attained, the more certain is the ultimate conclusion, and he disputes the question no further. He sees that the experiment has been tried under all sorts of conditions, as to time, place and people, with the same result; and he says with you, therefore, that the law you have laid down must be a good one, and he must believe it.

In science we do the same thing;—the philosopher exercises precisely the same   4
faculties, though in a much more delicate manner. In scientific inquiry it becomes a matter of duty to expose a supposed law to every possible kind of verification, and to take care, moreover, that this is done intentionally, and not left to a mere accident, as in the case of the apples. And in science, as in common life, our confidence in a law is in exact proportion to the absence of variation in the result of our experimental verifications. For instance, if you let go your grasp of an article you may have in your hand, it will immediately fall to the ground. That is a very common verification of one of the best established laws of nature—that of gravitation. The method by which men of science establish the existence of that law is exactly the same as that by which we have established the trivial proposition about the sourness of hard and green apples. But we believe it in such an extensive, thorough, and unhesitating manner because the universal experience of mankind verifies it, and we can verify it ourselves at any time; and that is the strongest possible foundation on which any natural law can rest.

Vocabulary

inductive, deductive, syllogism, premise, proposition

Questions

1. Why does Huxley begin with the anecdote from Molière? Why not begin, as Franklin did, with the first step in the process of thinking?

2. List the steps which led to the conclusion that the apple must be sour. Must it?
3. Induction leads from specific experiences to a general law; deduction is the reverse process. Which is the scientific method?
4. Huxley calls his proposition about the sourness of hard, green apples "trivial." Does he mean "unimportant"?
5. What is the strongest foundation upon which a natural law can be based?
6. Suppose you found a strain of hard, green apples that were sweet. Would this fact destroy Huxley's general law? Would it force you to rephrase the law? How would you rephrase it?

Topics for Writing

Huxley, a Model Teacher

The Limitations of Inductive Thinking

The Case of the Sweet, Green Apple

The Struggle for Existence

CHARLES DARWIN (1809–1882), English natural scientist, became the father of evolutionary science when in 1859 he published *The Origin of Species.* In this passage he explains what he means by "the survival of the fittest."

Nothing is easier than to admit in words the truth of the universal struggle for life, or more difficult—at least I have found it so—than constantly to bear this conclusion in mind. Yet unless it be thoroughly engrained in the mind, I am convinced that the whole economy of nature, with every fact on distribution, rarity, abundance, extinction, and variation, will be dimly seen or quite misunderstood. We behold the face of nature bright with gladness, we often see superabundance of food; we do not see, or we forget, that the birds which are idly singing round us mostly live on insects or seeds, and are thus constantly destroying life; or we forget how largely these songsters, or their eggs, or their nestlings, are destroyed by birds and beasts of prey; we do not always bear in mind, that though food may be now superabundant, it is not so at all seasons of each recurring year. 1

I should premise that I use the term Struggle for Existence in a large and metaphorical sense, including dependence of one being on another, and including (which is more important) not only the life of the individual, but success in leaving progeny. Two canine animals in a time of dearth, may be truly said to struggle with each other which shall get food and live. But a plant on the edge of a desert is said to struggle for life against the drought, though more properly it should be said to be dependent on the moisture. A plant which annually produces a thousand seeds, of which on an average only one comes to maturity, may be more truly said to struggle with the plants of the same and other kinds which already clothe the ground. . . . In these several senses, which pass into each other, I use for convenience sake the general term of struggle for existence. 2

A struggle for existence inevitably follows from the high rate at which all organic beings tend to increase. Every being, which during its natural lifetime produces several eggs or seeds, must suffer destruction during some period of its life, and during some season or occasional year, otherwise, on the principle of geometrical increase, its numbers would quickly become so inordinately great that no country could support the product. Hence, as more individuals are produced than can possibly survive, there must in every case be a struggle for existence, either one individual with another of the same species, or with the individuals of distinct species, or with the physical conditions of life. It is the doctrine of Malthus applied with manifold force to the whole animal and vegetable kingdoms; for in this case there can be no artificial increase of food, and no prudential restraint from marriage. Although some species may be now increasing, more or less rapidly, in numbers, all cannot do so, for the world would not hold them. 3

4   There is no exception to the rule that every organic being naturally increases at so high a rate, that if not destroyed, the earth would soon be covered by the progeny of a single pair. Even slow-breeding man has doubled in twenty-five years, and at this rate, in a few thousand years, there would literally not be standing room for his progeny. Linnæus has calculated that if an annual plant produced only two seeds— and there is no plant so unproductive as this—and their seedlings next year produced two, and so on, then in twenty years there would be a million plants. The elephant is reckoned to be the slowest breeder of all known animals, and I have taken some pains to estimate its probable minimum rate of natural increase: it will be under the mark to assume that it breeds when thirty years old, and goes on breeding till ninety years old, bringing forth three pair of young in this interval; if this be so, at the end of the fifth century there would be alive fifteen million elephants, descended from the first pair.

5   But we have better evidence on this subject than mere theoretical calculations, namely, the numerous recorded cases of the astonishingly rapid increase of various animals in a state of nature, when circumstances have been favourable to them during two or three following seasons. Still more striking is the evidence from our domestic animals of many kinds which have run wild in several parts of the world: if the statements of the rate of increase of slow breeding cattle and horses in South-America, and latterly in Australia, had not been well authenticated, they would have been quite incredible. So it is with plants: cases could be given of introduced plants which have become common throughout whole islands in a period of less than ten years. . . . The obvious explanation is that the conditions of life have been very favourable, and that there has consequently been less destruction of the old and young, and that nearly all the young have been enabled to breed. In such cases the geometrical ratio of increase, the result of which never fails to be surprising, simply explains the extraordinarily rapid increase and wide diffusion of naturalised productions in their new homes. . . .

6   Many cases are on record showing how complex and unexpected are the checks and relations between organic beings, which have to struggle together in the same country. I will give only a single instance, which, though a simple one, has interested me. In Staffordshire, on the estate of a relation where I had ample means of investigation, there was a large and extremely barren heath, which had never been touched by the hand of man; but several hundred acres of exactly the same nature had been enclosed twenty-five years previously and planted with Scotch fir. The change in the native vegetation of the planted part of the heath was most remarkable, more than is generally seen in passing from one quite different soil to another: not only the proportional numbers of the heath-plants were wholly changed, but twelve species of plants (not counting grasses and carices) flourished in the plantations, which could not be found on the heath. The effect on the insects must have been still greater, for six insectivorous birds were very common in the plantations, which were not to be seen on the heath; and the heath was frequented by two or three distinct insectivorous birds. Here we see how potent has been the effect of the introduction of a single tree, nothing whatever else having been done, with the exception that the land had been enclosed, so that cattle could not enter.

But how important an element enclosure is, I plainly saw near Farnham, in Surrey. Here there are extensive heaths, with a few clumps of old Scotch firs on the distant hill-tops: within the last ten years large spaces have been enclosed, and self-sown firs are now springing up in multitudes, so close together that all cannot live. When I ascertained that these young trees had not been sown or planted, I was so much surprised at their numbers that I went to several points of view, whence I could examine hundreds of acres of the unenclosed heath, and literally I could not see a single Scotch fir, except the old planted clumps. But on looking closely between the stems of the heath, I found a multitude of seedlings and little trees, which had been perpetually browsed down by the cattle. In one square yard, at a point some hundred yards distant from one of the old clumps, I counted thirty-two little trees; and one of them, judging from the rings of growth, had during twenty-six years tried to raise its head above the stems of the heath, and had failed. No wonder that, as soon as the land was enclosed, it became thickly clothed with vigorously growing young firs. Yet the heath was so extremely barren and so extensive that no one would ever have imagined that cattle would have so closely and effectually searched it for food.

Here we see that cattle absolutely determine the existence of the Scotch fir; but in several parts of the world insects determine the existence of cattle. Perhaps Paraguay offers the most curious instance of this; for here neither cattle nor horses nor dogs have ever run wild, though they swarm southward and northward in a feral state; and Azara and Rengger have shown that this is caused by the greater number in Paraguay of a certain fly, which lays its eggs in the navels of these animals when first born. The increase of these flies, numerous as they are, must be habitually checked by some means, probably by birds. Hence if certain insectivorous birds (whose numbers are probably regulated by hawks or beasts of prey) were to increase in Paraguay, the flies would decrease—then cattle and horses would become feral, and this would certainly greatly alter (as indeed I have observed in parts of South America) the vegetation: this again would largely affect the insects; and this, as we just have seen in Staffordshire, the insectivorous birds, and so onwards in ever-increasing circles of complexity. We began this series by insectivorous birds, and we have ended with them. Not that in nature the relations can ever be as simple as this. Battle within battle must ever be recurring with varying success; and yet in the long-run the forces are so nicely balanced, that the face of nature remains uniform for long periods of time, though assuredly the merest trifle would often give the victory to one organic being over another. Nevertheless so profound is our ignorance and so high our presumption, that we marvel when we hear of the extinction of an organic being; and as we do not see the cause, we invoke cataclysms to desolate the world, or invent laws on the duration of the forms of life!

7

Vocabulary

engraved, metaphorical, progeny, geometrical, theoretical, latterly, diffusion, naturalised (naturalized), carices, insectivorous, feral, organic, cataclysms

Questions

1. In what sense can it be said that plant life "struggles" for existence?
2. What would happen if there were no struggle for existence?
3. What were the effects of enclosing pieces of land in Staffordshire and Surrey?
4. What is the connection Darwin found between cattle and the Scotch fir?
5. Is the balance of nature maintained by members of one species killing those of another?
6. Does the extinction of a species seem unnatural to Darwin?
7. If Darwin is right, can we plan the preservation of every species? Why or why not?

Topics for Writing

If There Were No Struggle

No Death, No Balance

Natural Extinction vs. Unnatural

On Being the Right Size

J.B.S. HALDANE (1892–1964), a Scottish scientist, wrote popular essays (some collected in *Keeping Cool and Other Essays,* 1940) as well as serious works on human biology and genetics. This well-known piece comes from *Possible Worlds.*

The most obvious differences between different animals are differences of size, but for some reason the zoologists have paid singularly little attention to them. In a large textbook of zoology before me I find no indication that the eagle is larger than the sparrow, or the hippopotamus bigger than the hare, though some grudging admissions are made in the case of the mouse and the whale. But yet it is easy to show that a hare could not be as large as a hippopotamus, or a whale as small as a herring. For every type of animal there is a most convenient size, and a large change in size inevitably carries with it a change of form.

Let us take the most obvious of possible cases, and consider a giant man sixty feet high—about the height of Giant Pope and Giant Pagan in the illustrated *Pilgrim's Progress* of my childhood. These monsters were not only ten times as high as Christian, but ten times as wide and ten times as thick, so that their total weight was a thousand times his, or about eighty to ninety tons. Unfortunately the cross sections of their bones were only a hundred times those of Christian, so that every square inch of giant bone had to support ten times the weight borne by a square inch of human bone. As the human thigh-bone breaks under about ten times the human weight, Pope and Pagan would have broken their thighs every time they took a step. This was doubtless why they were sitting down in the picture I remember. But it lessens one's respect for Christian and Jack the Giant Killer.

To turn to zoology, suppose that a gazelle, a graceful little creature with long thin legs, is to become large, it will break its bones unless it does one of two things. It may make its legs short and thick, like the rhinoceros, so that every pound of weight has still about the same area of bone to support it. Or it can compress its body and stretch out its legs obliquely to gain stability, like the giraffe. I mention these two beasts because they happen to belong to the same order as the gazelle, and both are quite successful mechanically, being remarkably fast runners.

Gravity, a mere nuisance to Christian, was a terror to Pope, Pagan, and Despair. To the mouse and any smaller animal it presents practically no dangers. You can drop a mouse down a thousand-yard mine shaft; and, on arriving at the bottom, it gets a slight shock and walks away. A rat would probably be killed, though it can fall safely from the eleventh story of a building; a man is killed, a horse splashes. For the resistance presented to movement by the air is proportional to the surface of the moving object. Divide an animal's length, breadth, and height each by ten; its weight is reduced to a thousandth, but its surface only to a hundredth. So the resistance to falling in the case of a small animal is relatively ten times greater than the driving force.

5   An insect, therefore, is not afraid of gravity; it can fall without danger, and can cling to the ceiling with remarkably little trouble. It can go in for elegant and fantastic forms of support like that of the daddy-long-legs. But there is a force which is as formidable to an insect as gravitation to a mammal. This is surface tension. A man coming out of a bath carries with him a film of water of about one-fiftieth of an inch in thickness. This weighs roughly a pound. A wet mouse has to carry about its own weight of water. A wet fly has to lift many times its own weight and, as every one knows, a fly once wetted by water or any other liquid is in a very serious position indeed. An insect going for a drink is in as great danger as a man leaning out over a precipice in search of food. If it once falls into the grip of the surface tension of the water—that is to say, gets wet—it is likely to remain so until it drowns. A few insects, such as water-beetles, contrive to be unwettable, the majority keep well away from their drink by means of a long proboscis.

6   Of course tall land animals have other difficulties. They have to pump their blood to greater heights than a man and, therefore, require a larger blood pressure and tougher blood-vessels. A great many men die from burst arteries, especially in the brain, and this danger is presumably still greater for an elephant or a giraffe. But animals of all kinds find difficulties in size for the following reason. A typical small animal, say a microscopic worm or rotifer, has a smooth skin through which all the oxygen it requires can soak in, a straight gut with sufficient surface to absorb its food, and a simple kidney. Increase its dimensions tenfold in every direction, and its weight is increased a thousand times, so that if it is to use its muscles as efficiently as its miniature counterpart, it will need a thousand times as much food and oxygen per day and will excrete a thousand times as much of waste products.

7   Now if its shape is unaltered its surface will be increased only a hundredfold, and ten times as much oxygen must enter per minute through each square millimetre of skin, ten times as much food through each square millimetre of intestine. When a limit is reached to their absorptive powers their surface has to be increased by some special device. For example, a part of the skin may be drawn out into tufts to make gills or pushed in to make lungs, thus increasing the oxygen-absorbing surface in proportion to the animal's bulk. A man, for example, has a hundred square yards of lung. Similarly, the gut, instead of being smooth and straight, becomes coiled and develops a velvety surface, and other organs increase in complication. The higher animals are not larger than the lower because they are more complicated. They are more complicated because they are larger. Just the same is true of plants. The simplest plants, such as the green algae growing in stagnant water or on the bark of trees, are mere round cells. The higher plants increase their surface by putting out leaves and roots. Comparative anatomy is largely the story of the struggle to increase surface in proportion to volume.

8   Some of the methods of increasing the surface are useful up to a point, but not capable of a very wide adaptation. For example, while vertebrates carry the oxygen from the gills or lungs all over the body in the blood, insects take air directly to every part of their body by tiny blind tubes called tracheae which open to the surface at

many different points. Now, although by their breathing movements they can renew the air in the outer part of the tracheal system, the oxygen has to penetrate the finer branches by means of diffusion. Gases can diffuse easily through very small distances, not many times larger than the average length travelled by a gas molecule between collisions with other molecules. But when such vast journeys— from the point of view of a molecule—as a quarter of an inch have to be made, the process becomes slow. So the portions of an insect's body more than a quarter of an inch from the air would always be short of oxygen. In consequence hardly any insects are much more than half an inch thick. Land crabs are built on the same general plan as insects, but are much clumsier. Yet like ourselves they carry oxygen around in their blood, and are therefore able to grow far larger than any insects. If the insects had hit on a plan for driving air through their tissues instead of letting it soak in, they might well have become as large as lobsters, though other considerations would have prevented them from becoming as large as man.

Exactly the same difficulties attach to flying. It is an elementary principle of aeronautics that the minimum speed needed to keep an aeroplane of a given shape in the air varies as the square root of its length. If its linear dimensions are increased four times, it must fly twice as fast. Now the power needed for the minimum speed increases more rapidly than the weight of the machine. So the larger aeroplane, which weighs sixty-four times as much as the smaller, needs one hundred and twenty-eight times its horsepower to keep up. Applying the same principles to the birds, we find that the limit to their size is soon reached. An angel whose muscles developed no more power weight for weight than those of an eagle or a pigeon would require a breast projecting for about four feet to house the muscles engaged in working its wings, while to economize in weight, its legs would have to be reduced to mere stilts. Actually a large bird such as an eagle or kite does not keep in the air mainly by moving its wings. It is generally to be seen soaring, that is to say balanced on a rising column of air. And even soaring becomes more and more difficult with increasing size. Were this not the case eagles might be as large as tigers and as formidable to man as hostile aeroplanes.

But it is time that we passed to some of the advantages of size. One of the most obvious is that it enables one to keep warm. All warm-blooded animals at rest lose the same amount of heat from a unit area of skin, for which purpose they need a food-supply proportional to their surface and not to their weight. Five thousand mice weigh as much as a man. Their combined surface and food or oxygen consumption are about seventeen times a man's. In fact a mouse eats about one quarter its own weight of food every day, which is mainly used in keeping it warm. For the same reason small animals cannot live in cold countries. In the arctic regions there are no reptiles or amphibians, and no small mammals. The smallest mammal in Spitzbergen is the fox. The small birds fly away in the winter, while the insects die, though their eggs can survive six months or more of frost. The most successful mammals are bears, seals, and walruses.

Similarly, the eye is a rather inefficient organ until it reaches a large size. The back of the human eye on which an image of the outside world is thrown, and which corresponds to the film of a camera, is composed of a mosaic of "rods and cones" whose diameter is little more than a length of an average light wave. Each eye has about half a million, and for two objects to be distinguishable their images must fall on separate rods or cones. It is obvious that with fewer but larger rods and cones we should see less distinctly. If they were twice as broad two points would have to be twice as far apart before we could distinguish them at a given distance. But if their size were diminished and their number increased we should see no better. For it is impossible to form a definite image smaller than a wave-length of light. Hence a mouse's eye is not a small-scale model of a human eye. Its rods and cones are not much smaller than ours, and therefore there are far fewer of them. A mouse could not distinguish one human face from another six feet away. In order that they should be of any use at all the eyes of small animals have to be much larger in proportion to their bodies than our own. Large animals on the other hand only require relatively small eyes, and those of the whale and elephant are little larger than our own.

12   For rather more recondite reasons the same general principle holds true of the brain. If we compare the brain-weights of a set of very similar animals such as the cat, cheetah, leopard, and tiger, we find that as we quadruple the body-weight the brain-weight is only doubled. The larger animal with proportionately larger bones can economize on brain, eyes, and certain other organs.

13   Such are a very few of the considerations which show that for every type of animal there is an optimum size. Yet although Galileo demonstrated the contrary more than three hundred years ago, people still believe that if a flea were as large as a man it could jump a thousand feet into the air. As a matter of fact the height to which an animal can jump is more nearly independent of its size than proportional to it. A flea can jump about two feet, a man about five. To jump a given height, if we neglect the resistance of the air, requires an expenditure of energy proportional to the jumper's weight. But if the jumping muscles form a constant fraction of the animal's body, the energy developed per ounce of muscle is independent of the size, provided it can be developed quickly enough in the small animal. As a matter of fact an insect's muscles, although they can contract more quickly than our own, appear to be less efficient; as otherwise a flea or grasshopper could rise six feet into the air.

14   And just as there is a best size for every animal, so the same is true for every human institution. In the Greek type of democracy all the citizens could listen to a series of orators and vote directly on questions of legislation. Hence their philosophers held that a small city was the largest possible democratic state. The English invention of representative government made a democractic nation possible, and the possibility was first realized in the United States, and later elsewhere. With the development of broadcasting it has once more become possible for every citizen to listen to the political views of representative orators, and the future may perhaps see the return of the national state to the Greek form of democracy. Even the referendum has been made possible only by the institution of daily newspapers.

15   To the biologist the problem of socialism appears largely as a problem of size. The extreme socialists desire to run every nation as a single business concern. I do not suppose that Henry Ford would find much difficulty in running Andorra or

Luxembourg on a socialistic basis. He has already more men on his pay-roll than their populations. It is conceivable that a syndicate of Fords, if we could find them, would make Belgium Ltd. or Denmark Inc. pay their way. But while nationalization of certain industries is an obvious possibility in the largest of states, I find it no easier to picture a completely socialized British Empire or United States than an elephant turning somersaults or a hippopotamus jumping a hedge.

Vocabulary

rotifer, vertebrates, formidable, recondite, socialism, nationalization

Questions

1. Do we tend to overlook the obvious?
2. Try to state Haldane's thesis (at the end of his first paragraph) in your own words.
3. Why does gravity pose no danger to an insect?
4. What misconceptions does Haldane clear up for you about size?
5. Were you surprised to learn that the higher animals "are more complicated because they are larger" instead of the other way around?
6. Why must smaller animals eat more, proportionately, than large ones?
7. As a scientist, Haldane convinces us that there is a right size for animals and plants. But does he convince you that there is a right size for human institutions?

Topics for Writing

The Right Size for Government

The Biological Argument Against Socialism

The Fallacy in Haldane's Argument

Untying the Knot

ANNIE DILLARD (1945–) is a poet, editor, and amateur naturalist—a kind of contemporary Thoreau. "Untying the Knot" is from her first prose book, *Pilgrim at Tinker's Creek.*

1   Yesterday I set out to catch the new season, and instead I found an old snakeskin. I was in the sunny February woods by the quarry; the snakeskin was lying in a heap of leaves right next to an aquarium someone had thrown away. I don't know why that someone hauled the aquarium deep into the woods to get rid of it; it had only one broken glass side. The snake found it handy, I imagine; snakes like to rub against something rigid to help them out of their skins, and the broken aquarium looked like the nearest likely object. Together the snakeskin and the aquarium made an interesting scene on the forest floor. It looked like an exhibit at a trial—circumstantial evidence—of a wild scene, as though a snake had burst through the broken side of the aquarium, burst through his ugly old skin, and disappeared, perhaps straight up in the air, in a rush of freedom and beauty.

2   The snakeskin had unkeeled scales, so it belonged to a nonpoisonous snake. It was roughly five feet long by the yardstick, but I'm not sure because it was very wrinkled and dry, and every time I tried to stretch it flat it broke. I ended up with seven or eight pieces of it all over the kitchen table in a fine film of forest dust.

3   The point I want to make about the snakeskin is that, when I found it, it was whole and tied in a knot. Now there have been stories told, even by reputable scientists, of snakes that have deliberately tied themselves in a knot to prevent larger snakes from trying to swallow them—but I couldn't imagine any way that throwing itself into a half hitch would help a snake trying to escape its skin. Still, ever cautious, I figured that one of the neighborhood boys could possibly have tied it in a knot in the fall, for some whimsical boyish reason, and left it there, where it dried and gathered dust. So I carried the skin along thoughtlessly as I walked, snagging it sure enough on a low branch and ripping it in two for the first of many times. I saw that thick ice still lay on the quarry pond and that the skunk cabbage was already out in the clearings, and then I came home and looked at the skin and its knot.

4   The knot had no beginning. Idly I turned it around in my hand, searching for a place to untie; I came to with a start when I realized I must have turned the thing around fully ten times. Intently, then, I traced the knot's lump around with a finger: it was continuous. I couldn't untie it any more than I could untie a doughnut; it was a loop without beginning or end. These snakes *are* magic, I thought for a second, and then of course I reasoned what must have happened. The skin had been pulled inside-out like a peeled sock for several inches; then an inch or so of the inside-out part—a piece whose length was coincidentally equal to the diameter of the skin—had somehow been turned right-side out again, making a thick lump whose edges were lost in wrinkles, looking exactly like a knot.

So I have been thinking about the change of seasons. I don't want to miss 5
spring this year. I want to distinguish the last winter frost from the out-of-season
one, the frost of spring. I want to be there on the spot the moment the grass turns
green. I always miss this radical revolution; I see it the next day from a window, the
yard so suddenly green and lush I could envy Nebuchadnezzar down on all fours
eating grass. This year I want to stick a net into time and say "now," as men plant
flags on the ice and snow and say, "here." But it occurred to me that I could no
more catch spring by the tip of the tail than I could untie the apparent knot in the
snakeskin; there are no edges to grasp. Both are continuous loops.

Vocabulary

circumstantial, unkeeled, half-hitch, whimsical, skunk cabbage, radical

Questions

1. Why does the author call the skin-aquarium evidence "circumstantial"?
2. Is the analogy between untying the knot and catching the new season enlightening?
3. Where in this brief essay is process analysis used?
4. Accounting for all of the circumstances described below, can you work out a plausible solution to "The Mystery of Apartment 13"? Mr. X, the resident of Apartment 13, has four pets—a goldfish, a parakeet, a Persian cat, and a poodle—that have always gotten along well together. Returning from work one day, he unlocks his apartment door and comes upon the following scene: the goldfish is swimming frantically around his bowl, the poodle is hiding under the bed, the cat is curled next to the radiator, and the bird is in his usual place, but his cage door is open and a small pool of water lies below his perch. What happened while Mr. X was out?

Topic for Writing

The Mystery of Apartment 13: A Solution

PART II

Description

Description means word painting; in fact, the Latin word from which it comes means "to copy or to draw." The writer who wants us to "see" an object, whether it be physical (a person, a city square, or a bird in flight) or abstract (the loneliness of an old man, a sense of trouble ahead) must draw a picture for us.

The key to effective description is the choice of significant details. And this means, as always, that the writer must have a good eye and a stock of words. To tell readers that a tomb is built of "odd beat-up damp stone that looks kind of dilapidated" doesn't help them visualize it. But tell them, as one of Browning's characters does, that the material is "Gritstone, a-crumble! Clammy squares which sweat / As if the corpse they keep were oozing through," and you have given them something to see and feel.

Description tests the writer's sense of language, too, his or her feeling for words. *Clammy* has an emotional impact in Browning's description that *wet* or *damp* lacks. Again, the writer can tell us that a *fire* started in the wastebasket because someone was careless with a cigarette, but if he or she wants us to share in the surprise, the writer might prefer the word *blaze*. On the other hand, synonyms like *conflagration* or *holocaust*, whose connotations are inappropriate in this instance, would be avoided.

Advice to the descriptive writer is not complicated: look for significant details in the subject you are describing; keep the reader in mind; use exact language to set the details before the reader. In the next three chapters, persons, places, and events are described by writers who have mastered the art. The result, as you will see, is a series of vivid pictures that may startle you with the possibilities inherent in descriptive writing.

8

Describing Persons/Eccentric Lives

What you have read in the introduction to Part II requires very little adaptation to the method of describing persons, but certain reminders may be useful. First of all and most obviously, people are not mere physical objects. They have personalities, and these differ widely and sometimes wildly from one to another. To describe a person effectively, therefore, writers must show us more than size, shape, age, and occupation. They must help us to hear the sound of a voice, feel the texture of a thought, catch some sight of a subject's essential being. This requires knowledge of the person, either through first-hand acquaintance or through systematic research. The writers in this chapter demonstrate both kinds of knowledge.

As you will see from the collection of eccentrics in the following pages, there are many ways of bringing life to characters, whether real or fictional. None of the writers neglect the subject's physical appearance, but none limit themselves to the physical. Examples of characteristic speech tell us more about Gertrude Stein and Uncle Jimbilly than do their physical appearances. John Mytton, Wagner, and Sherlock Holmes (who, though fictional, is more real in the minds of Conan Doyle devotees than some of their personal acquaintances!) are vividly portrayed by eccentric, some would say egocentric, behavior. Lewis Carroll's dialogue in verse indicates that the distance between individuality and eccentricity is largely in the eye of the beholder.

Although they all seem a bit larger and sharper than life, these odd and memorable folk may only be exaggerated examples of tendencies that exist less prominently in the circle of our own friends and family. Indeed, we may find, if we look dispassionately, that some of them exist even closer to home than that.

Tea with Gertrude Stein

WAMBLY BALD (1902–) American writer and sometime editor of the Paris *Herald-Tribune*, helped to create the idea of the Left Bank with his accounts of the artists, writers, and other birds-of-passage who haunted Paris in the 1920s.

1   We drank tea with Gertrude Stein a few days ago. She lives quietly with another woman in the Rue de Fleurus, about ten jumps from the Dôme. For the past twenty-five years, Gertrude Stein has been saving the English language from that studio.

2   The walls are covered with Picasso. One of them is a portrait of Gertrude herself, for which she sat ninety-one times. That portrait and the actual Gertrude immediately put the visitor in his place. But John, who was with me, said:

3   "Your prose, I think, is obscure."

4   "My prose," said she who looks like Caesar, "is obscure only to the lazy-minded. It is like a deep well."

5   "Some people," said John, "are inclined to believe that it is a bottomless well or one with a false bottom."

6   John was a bit cruel. After all, Gertrude had been a star pupil of William James. She had graduated with high honors from Johns Hopkins. She has mastered the run of the sciences and her knowledge of literature is oceanic.

7   "I'll give you," said the writer, "a lesson in American history." Her eye is clear and her voice is incisive. Gertrude does not stutter when she talks. Here is what she said:

8   "America made the twentieth century just as England made the nineteenth. We have given Europe everything. The natural line of descent is the big four: Poe to Whitman to James to myself. I am the last."

9   "You are the last?" said John.

10   "Of course. My reputation is international and is spreading all the time."

11   "There is James Joyce," said John.

12   Gertrude smiled. "You would, of course, Joyce is *good*. He is a *good* writer. Let's not say anything about that. But who started the whole thing? My first great book, *The Making of Americans*, was published in 1905. That was long before the birth of *Ulysses*. But Joyce has done something even if his influence is local. John Synge, another Irish writer, has had his day. Have some more tea."

13   This fellow John is implacable. He followed with:

14   "I understand that Wyndham Lewis drops you into the Anita Loos category. The naive approach. . . ."

15   "Wyndham wrote that, of course. But all that is British propaganda against great American writers." John almost dropped his spoon. Gertrude went on: "You

might learn that American writing is signalized by the consistent tendency towards abstraction without mysticism. There is no mysticism in my work."

John had nothing more to say. We went back to the Dôme.   16

Vocabulary

implacable

Questions

1. How much of a physical picture of Miss Stein can you put together?
2. What does "she who looks like Caesar" imply? Is her physical image part of her eccentricity?
3. One gets the impression of a strong, almost dominating personality. How does Bald create that impression?
4. Why does John turn silent at the end?
5. Do you get the impression that Miss Stein is joking about her place in literature?

The Witness

KATHERINE ANNE PORTER (1890–1980) set most of her carefully crafted short stories in the American South. Her novel *Ship of Fools* (1962) became a best seller and was made into a motion picture.

1   Uncle Jimbilly was so old and had spent so many years bowed over things, putting them together and taking them apart, making them over and making them do, he was bent almost double. His hands were closed and stiff from gripping objects tightly, while he worked at them, and they could not open altogether even if a child took the thick black fingers and tried to turn them back. He hobbled on a stick; his purplish skull showed through patches in his wool, which had turned greenish gray and looked as if the moths had got at it.

2   He mended harness and put half soles on the other Negroes' shoes; he built fences and chicken coops and barn doors; he stretched wires and put in new window panes and fixed sagging hinges and patched up roofs; he repaired carriage tops and cranky plows. Also he had a gift for carving miniature tombstones out of blocks of wood; give him almost any kind of piece of wood and he could turn out a tombstone, shaped very like the real ones, with carving, and a name and date on it if they were needed. They were often needed, for some small beast or bird was always dying and having to be buried with proper ceremonies: the cart draped as a hearse, a shoe-box coffin with a pall over it, a profuse floral outlay, and, of course, a tombstone. As he worked, turning the long blade of his bowie knife deftly in circles to cut a flower, whittling and smoothing the back and sides, stopping now and then to hold it at arm's length and examine it with one eye closed, Uncle Jimbilly would talk in a low, broken, abstracted murmur, as if to himself; but he was really saying something he meant one to hear. Sometimes it would be an incomprehensible ghost story; listen ever so carefully, at the end it was impossible to decide whether Uncle Jimbilly himself had seen the ghost, whether it was a real ghost at all, or only another man dressed like one; and he dwelt much on the horrors of slave times.

3   "Dey used to take 'em out and tie 'em down and whup 'em," he muttered, "wid gret big leather strops inch thick long as yo' ahm, wid round holes bored in 'em so's evey time dey hit 'em de hide and de meat done come off dey bones in little round chunks. And when dey had whupped 'em wid de strop till dey backs was all raw and bloody, dey spread dry cawnshucks on dey backs and set 'em afire and pahched 'em, and den dey poured vinega all ovah 'em . . . Yassuh. And den, the ve'y nex day dey'd got to git back to work in de fiels or dey'd do the same thing right ovah agin. Yassah. Dat was it. If dey didn't git back to work dey got it all right ovah agin."

4   The children—three of them: a serious, prissy older girl of ten, a thoughtful sad looking boy of eight, and a quick flighty little girl of six—sat disposed around

Uncle Jimbilly and listened with faint tinglings of embarrassment. They knew, of course, that once upon a time Negroes had been slaves; but they had all been freed long ago and were now only servants. It was hard to realize that Uncle Jimbilly had been born in slavery, as the Negroes were always saying. The children thought that Uncle Jimbilly had got over his slavery very well. Since they had known him, he had never done a single thing that anyone told him to do. He did his work just as he pleased and when he pleased. If you wanted a tombstone, you had to be very careful about the way you asked for it. Nothing could have been more impersonal and faraway than his tone and manner of talking about slavery, but they wriggled a little and felt guilty. Paul would have changed the subject, but Miranda, the little quick one, wanted to know the worst. "Did they act like that to you, Uncle Jimbilly?" she asked.

"No, *mam*," said Uncle Jimbilly. "Now whut name you want on dis one? Dey   5
nevah did. Dey done 'em dat way in the rice swamps. I always worked right here close to the house or in town with Miss Sophia. Down in the swamps . . ."

"Didn't they ever die, Uncle Jimbilly?" asked Paul.   6

"Cose dey died," said Uncle Jimbilly, "cose dey died—dey died," he went on,   7
pursing his mouth gloomily, "by de thousands and tens upon thousands."

"Can you carve 'Safe in Heaven' on that, Uncle Jimbilly?" asked Maria in her   8
pleasant, mincing voice.

"To put over a tame jackrabbit, Missy?" asked Uncle Jimbilly indignantly. He   9
was very religious. "A heathen like dat? No, *mam*. In de swamps dey used to stake 'em out all day and all night, and all day and all night and all day wid de hans and feet tied so dey couldn't scretch and let de muskeeters eat 'em alive. De muskeeters 'ud bite 'em tell dey was all swole up like a balloon all over, and you could heah em howlin and prayin all ovah the swamp. Yassuh. Dat was it. And nary a drop of watah noh a moufful of braid . . . Yassah, dat's it. Lawd, dey done it. Hosanna! Now take dis yere tombstone and don' bother me no more . . . or I'll . . ."

Uncle Jimbilly was apt to be suddenly annoyed and you never knew why. He   10
was easily put out about things, but his threats were always so exorbitant that not even the most credulous child could be terrified by them. He was always going to do something quite horrible to somebody and then he was going to dispose of the remains in a revolting manner. He was going to skin somebody alive and nail the hide on the barn door, or he was just getting ready to cut off somebody's ears with a hatchet and pin them on Bongo, the crop-eared brindle dog. He was often all prepared in his mind to pull somebody's teeth and make a set of false teeth for Ole Man Ronk . . . Ole Man Ronk was a tramp who had been living all summer in the little cabin behind the smokehouse. He got his rations along with the Negroes and sat all day mumbling his naked gums. He had skimpy black whiskers which appeared to be set in wax, and angry red eyelids. He took morphine, it was said; but what morphine might be, or how he took it, or why, no one seemed to know . . . Nothing could have been more unpleasant than the notion that one's teeth might be given to Ole Man Ronk.

The reason why Uncle Jimbilly never did any of these things he threatened   11
was, he said, because he never could get round to them. He always had so much

other work on hand he never seemed to get caught up on it. But some day, somebody was going to get a mighty big surprise, and meanwhile everybody had better look out.

Vocabulary

abstracted (adjective), prissy, flighty, heathen, exorbitant, credulous, brindle

Questions

1. Do the children respect Uncle Jimbilly?
2. Does he show his resentment of slavery? Why doesn't he talk about it?
3. Why won't Uncle Jimbilly write an epitaph on the rabbit's tombstone?
4. Do the children learn anything from Uncle Jimbilly?
5. Who is the witness of the title?

Topics for Writing

How Children Learn from the Old

"The Witness": My Interpretation

John Mytton

EDITH SITWELL (1887–1964) was a major modern English poet with a flair for the dramatic in style and dress as well as in her experimental verse. "John Mytton" is a chapter in her delightful *English Eccentrics*.

Here he comes, that poor driven drunken ghost, blown by a turbulent hurricane weather. His life seemed to be spent in running like an ostrich—he walked as fast and as strongly as that bird—racing, jumping, driving, hunting, chased always by a high mad black wind.

He meant, always, to cheat that wind. Let it blow through him and eat him to the bone. He would show it how little he cared.

This half-mad hunting hunted creature never wore any but the thinnest of silk stockings, with very thin boots or shoes, so that in winter his feet were nearly always wet. His hunting breeches were unlined, he wore only one small waistcoat, and that was nearly always open. He rarely wore a hat, and in winter went shooting in white linen trousers without either a lining or drawers and, with this, a light jacket. No matter how black the frost, no matter how high and mad was the black turbulent wind in which he lived, he would wade through any water, break down the ice of any pond and trample through it, such was his impatience to have his way. He might often be seen stripped to the shirt and following wild-fowl in the snowiest weather, and once lay down in his shirt to await their arrival at dusk. And once the keepers at Woodhouse, an estate belonging to his uncle, were surprised, to say the least of it, to see Squire Mytton, stark naked, pursuing some ducks over the ice in a most determined manner.

It is a matter for wonder, indeed, that Squire Mytton reached his thirty-eighth year, for no man in a peaceful countryside ever ran more risks or had more accidents. "How often," enquired his friend Nimrod, admiring but regretful, "has he been run away with by gigs, how often struggling in deep water without being able to swim? How was it that he did not get torn to pieces in the countless street brawls in which he was engaged?" On one occasion he nearly was torn into two pieces, at a race-meeting in Lancashire, for one gang of thieves took it into their heads to pull Squire Mytton into a house at the very moment when a rival gang of thieves took it into *their* heads to pull him out of it. In this encounter, neither side won, because the Squire's enormous physical strength kept him stationary and, in the end, one of the gentlemen engaged in the struggle was transported to the Colonies as a reward for his violence and the attempted robbery.

The Squire was constantly riding at dangerous fences, falling off his horse when drunk, driving his tandem at a frantic speed, and paying no more attention to crossroads and corners than he did to creditors. "There goes Squire Mytton," the country people would say, when they saw a crazily driven tandem, rushing along alike the north wind; and they would raise a cheer, for the Squire was warm-hearted and beloved. Once he galloped at full speed over a rabbit-warren, to find out if his horse would fall. He found out. Rolling over and over, after a time both horse and Squire rose to their feet unhurt.

6   John Mytton was as dangerous to others as to himself; it was not only that he did not mind accidents, he positively *liked* them; and when one unhappy gentleman was rash enough to venture into the Squire's gig, and, when having done so and had some slight experience of the resultant steeplechasing, he begged the Squire to consider their necks, the latter enquired: "Were you ever much hurt then, by being upset in a gig?" "No, thank God," was the reply, "for I never was upset in one." The next moment, all was confusion. For the Squire, much shocked by this omission on the part of Providence, ejaculated: "What, never upset in a gig? What a damned slow fellow you must have been all your life," and running the near wheel up the bank, he rectified the omission. Fortunately, according to Nimrod, neither gentleman was injured seriously.

7   Indeed, carriage accidents were Squire Mytton's strongest point. Having bought some carriage horses from a horse-dealer named Clarke, he put one of them into a gig, tandem, to see if it would make a good leader. "Do you think he is a good timber-jumper?" he enquired of the alarmed Mr. Clarke, who sat beside him. Not waiting for that unhappy gentleman's reply, the Squire exclaimed: "We'll try him." And a closed turnpike being before him, he gave the horse his head. The horse did himself credit, leaving Squire Mytton, the other horse, Mr. Clarke, and the gig at the other side of the gate in grand style and almost inextricable confusion. But once again, nobody was hurt. The Squire had, too, a horse that would rear up in his gig at the word of command, "until the hinder part of it absolutely touched the ground." But in spite of this talented animal's frequently repeated achievement, the Squire remained alive.

8   Master and horses were so friendly with the country people that they would help themselves to anything that took their fancy on their way home from hunting, and Squire Mytton, if his coat was wet, would think nothing of taking a country woman's red flannel petticoat from a hedge, slipping it over his head, and leaving his coat drying in its place. It was, too, not in the least unusual for Squire Mytton, if he felt cold when out hunting, to go into the house of a cottager, accompanied by his favourite horse Baronet, and ask her to light a good fire to warm Baronet and himself, for he did not believe in a heaven from which animals were excluded. Baronet and he would then lounge by the fire, side by side, until they were warm again, and then they would start for home. But alas, there was one moment when disaster came from the master's habit of sharing all good things with the subject beast, for a horse named Sportsman dropped dead because John Mytton, out of kindness of heart, had given him a bottle of mulled port. There was a day, too, when disaster came because Squire Mytton deserted the horse as a steed and rode into the dining-room on a large brown bear. Dinner was waiting, and all went well until the Squire, who was dressed in full hunting costume, applied his spurs to the bear, whereupon that injured pet bit him through the calf of his leg, inflicting a

severe wound. Nimrod produces, in his life of Mytton, a striking picture of the bear, who was of the gentler sex, with flames spouting from her nose and mouth, and Squire Mytton straddled across her back, in very much the attitude of Arion astride the Dolphin.

There was a heronry at Halston, containing from fifty to eighty nests, and   9
Squire Mytton wished to have some herons taken, so that it might be proven if heron pie is more delicious than rook pie. The nests were on the tops of such high trees that neither keepers nor grooms dared to climb them. "Here goes then," said the Squire, and swarmed to the highest of the trees. Often he would be seen, with the temperature at zero, walking to his stables before breakfast, dressed only in a shirt, dressing-gown, and slippers.

Throughout his career, money fell like rain, dripped and melted like rain. In   10
the last fifteen years of his life, indeed, more than half a million pounds drifted through his fingers. Some of this, it is true, went on the upkeep of his foxhounds or his racing establishment, in which he had, as a rule, at least fifteen or twenty horses in training at the same time. Some of the money, again, was spent on those thin shoes which were worn out after two of his mad, storklike races over the stony countryside, through or over anything which came in his way, for this man's daily walks were a kind of symbol of his life and his half-crazy, driven mind.

He had a hundred and fifty-two pairs of trousers and breeches, and the same   11
amount of coats and waistcoats, while, in his cellars, "hogsheads of ale stood like soldiers in close formation." So careless was he of money, that several thousand pounds were one night blown, by that high wind in which always he seems to have lived, out of his carriage, as he was returning from Doncaster Races—blown along the road and far away. For he had been counting the notes on the seat of the carriage, in which he was alone, and he had fallen asleep, and up sprang that cold night wind of fortune, and swept the notes away. Often, again, when going on a journey, he would take handfuls of bank-notes; and, without counting them, would roll them into a lump and throw them to his servant, as if they had been wastepaper. On one occasion, Nimrod picked up one of these lumps, containing £37, in the plantation at Halston, where, to judge from its wet appearance, it must have lain for many days.

The strangest exploit, perhaps, in which Mytton was concerned, was the   12
episode of the Nightshirt and the Hiccup. It is better to relate this story in the stately terms of his biographer Nimrod. "You have read that somebody set fire to Troy, Alexander to Persepolis, Nero to Rome, a baker to London, a rascally caliph to the treasures of Alexandria, and the brave Mucius Scaevola to his own hand and arm to frighten the proud Lars Porsena into a peace; but did you ever hear of a man setting fire to his own nightshirt to frighten away the hiccup? Such, however, is the climax I have alluded to, and this was the manner in which it was performed. 'Damn this hiccup,' said Mytton, as he stood undressed on the floor, apparently in the act of getting into his bed; 'but I'll frighten it away'; so, seizing a lighted candle he applied it to the tab of his shirt and, it being a cotton one, he was instantly enveloped in flames."

13   In the subsequent mêlée, during which two intrepid gentlemen knocked down and rolled upon the Squire in their attempt to put out the flames, and the flames did their worst against both nightshirt and hiccup, the two gentlemen won, for they tore his shirt from his body piecemeal. As for the hiccup, it was frightened away. "The hiccup is gone, by G——," said the Squire, as, appallingly burnt, he reeled into bed.

14   The next morning, he greeted his friends with a loud "view-halloo" to show them how he could bear pain.

15   This took place in Calais, whither he had fled in order to avoid his creditors; but as soon as he had recovered from his terrible burns, he returned to Halston in, I suppose, some mad fit of bravado, for he knew that every bailiff in England was on his track, and that his return must mean that he would be seized and put in a debtor's prison. It is better not to think of his sufferings in that chilled, deserted, and wretched place in which he had spent his childhood; but he was not to remain there for long. He was imprisoned in the King's Bench Prison, then in other prisons both in England and France, until, after the utmost misery of mind and body that such a man could know—his wife, whom he loved, had been forced to leave him—he died, at the age of thirty-eight, worn out by too much foolishness, too much wretchedness, and too much brandy.

16   Nimrod, who was his friend, says of him: "As to his dying in peace with all mankind, how could he do otherwise who never attempted to revenge himself on any human being, but who, though his communication was not 'yea, yea, or nay, nay,' so far from demanding the eye for the eye, and the tooth for the tooth, would have actually given his cloak to him who stole his coat; whose heart was as warm as those of most of the world are cold; and whose warmth of heart had brought him into the prison in which he died."

17   I hope that this pitiful creature has found a warm, country heaven of horses and hounds, an old and kindly heaven of country habits and country sweetness, with heavenly mansions where he and Baronet can sit by the fire together once more, horse and man, and where the master can forget the dirt and wretchedness of the debtor's prison, and the eight bottles of port a day, and all the ancient foolishness.

Vocabulary

waistcoat, gig, tandem, warren, turnpike, inextricable, mulled, Arion, rook, hogshead, mêlée, bailiff

Questions

1. Mytton's race with the wind is the dominating image in this characterization. Why does it seem appropriate? What other images of weather does Edith Sitwell use to bring him to life before our eyes?

2. "Black wind"—what makes this different from any other wind? How can the wind be black?
3. Mytton was never dressed warmly. Why?
4. Was Mytton cruel to animals?
5. Mytton seemed unconcerned about money. Does Sitwell imply that he was stupid about its value?
6. Does Sitwell mock her foolish subject? What is the strongest evidence to support your view?

Topics for Writing

Was Mytton Mad?

Mytton's Motives: An Interpretation

The Monster

DEEMS TAYLOR (1885–1966), a composer, critic, and popularizer of classical music and opera, published this essay in 1937 in *Of Men and Music*.

1   He was an undersized little man, with a head too big for his body—a sickly little man. His nerves were bad. He had skin trouble. It was agony for him to wear anything next to his skin coarser than silk. And he had delusions of grandeur.

2   He was a monster of conceit. Never for one minute did he look at the world or at people, except in relation to himself. He was not only the most important person in the world, to himself; in his own eyes he was the only person who existed. He believed himself to be one of the greatest dramatists in the world, one of the greatest thinkers, and one of the greatest composers. To hear him talk, he was Shakespeare, and Beethoven, and Plato, rolled into one. And you would have had no difficulty in hearing him talk. He was one of the most exhausting conversationalists that ever lived. An evening with him was an evening spent in listening to a monologue. Sometimes he was brilliant; sometimes he was maddeningly tiresome. But whether he was being brilliant or dull, he had one sole topic of conversation: himself. What *he* thought and what *he* did.

3   He had a mania for being in the right. The slightest hint of disagreement, from anyone, on the most trivial point, was enough to set him off on a harangue that might last for hours, in which he proved himself right in so many ways, and with such exhausting volubility, that in the end his hearer, stunned and deafened, would agree with him, for the sake of peace.

4   It never occurred to him that he and his doing were not of the most intense and fascinating interest to anyone with whom he came in contact. He had theories about almost any subject under the sun, including vegetarianism, the drama, politics, and music; and in support of these theories he wrote pamphlets, letters, books . . . thousands upon thousands of words, hundreds and hundreds of pages. He not only wrote these things, and published them—usually at somebody else's expense—but he would sit and read them aloud, for hours, to his friends and his family.

5   He wrote operas; and no sooner did he have the synopsis of a story, but he would invite—or rather summon—a crowd of his friends to his house and read it aloud to them. Not for criticism. For applause. When the complete poem was written, the friends had to come again, and hear *that* read aloud. Then he would publish the poem, sometimes years before the music that went with it was written. He played the piano like a composer, in the worst sense of what that implies, and he would sit down at the piano before parties that included some of the finest pianists of his time, and play for them, by the hour, his own music, needless to say. He had a composer's voice. And he would invite eminent vocalists to his house, and sing them his operas, taking all the parts.

He had the emotional stability of a six-year-old child. When he felt out of sorts, he would rave and stamp, or sink into suicidal gloom and talk darkly of going to the East to end his days as a Buddhist monk. Ten minutes later, when something pleased him, he would rush out of doors and run around the garden, or jump up and down on the softa or stand on his head. He could be grief-stricken over the death of a pet dog, and he could be callous and heartless to a degree that would have made a Roman emperor shudder.

He was almost innocent of any sense of responsibility. Not only did he seem incapable of supporting himself, but it never occurred to him that he was under any obligation to do so. He was convinced that the world owed him a living. In support of this belief, he borrowed money from everybody who was good for a loan—men, women, friends, or strangers. He wrote begging letters by the score, sometimes groveling without shame, at others loftily offering his intended benefactor the privilege of contributing to his support, and being mortally offended if the recipient declined the honor. I have found no record of his ever paying or repaying money to anyone who did not have a legal claim upon it.

What money he could lay his hands on he spent like an Indian rajah. The mere prospect of a performance of one of his operas was enough to set him to running up bills amounting to ten times the amount of his prospective royalties. On an income that would reduce a more scrupulous man to doing his own laundry, he would keep two servants. Without enough money in his pocket to pay his rent, he would have the walls and ceilings of his study lined with pink silk. No one will ever know—certainly he never knew—how much money he owed. We do know that his greatest benefactor gave him $6,000 to pay the most pressing of his debts in one city, and a year later had to give him $16,000 to enable him to live in another city without being thrown into jail for debt.

He was equally unscrupulous in other ways. An endless procession of women marches through his life. His first wife spent twenty years enduring and forgiving his infidelities. His second wife had been the wife of his most devoted friend and admirer, from whom he stole her. And even while he was trying to persuade her to leave her first husband he was writing to a friend to inquire whether he could suggest some wealthy woman—*any* wealthy woman—whom he could marry for her money.

He was completely selfish in his other personal relationships. His liking for his friends was measured solely by the completeness of their devotion to him, or by their usefulness to him, whether financial or artistic. The minute they failed him— even by so much as refusing a dinner invitation—or began to lessen in usefulness, he cast them off without a second thought. At the end of his life he had exactly one friend left whom he had known even in middle age.

He had a genius for making enemies. He would insult a man who disagreed with him about the weather. He would pull endless wires in order to meet some man who admired his work, and was able and anxious to be of use to him—and would proceed to make a mortal enemy of him with some idiotic and wholly uncalled-for exhibition of arrogance and bad manners. A character in one of his operas was a caricature of one of the most powerful music critics of his day. Not content with burlesquing him, he invited the critic to his house and read him the libretto aloud in front of his friends.

12   The name of this monster was Richard Wagner. Everything that I have said about him you can find on record—in newspapers, in police reports, in the testimony of people who knew him, in his own letters, between the lines of his autobiography. And the curious thing about this record is that it doesn't matter in the least.

13   Because this undersized, sickly, disagreeable, fascinating little man was right all the time. The joke was on us. He *was* one of the world's great dramatists; he *was* a great thinker; he *was* one of the most stupendous musical geniuses that, up to now, the world has ever seen. The world did owe him a living. People couldn't know those things at the time, I suppose; and yet to us, who know his music, it does seem as though they should have known. What if he did talk about himself all the time? If he had talked about himself for twenty-four hours every day for the span of his life he would not have uttered half the number of words that other men have spoken and written about him since his death.

14   When you consider what he wrote—thirteen operas and music dramas, eleven of them still holding the stage, eight of them unquestionably worth ranking among the world's great musico-dramatic masterpieces—when you listen to what he wrote, the debts and heartaches that people had to endure from him don't seem much of a price. Eduard Hanslick, the critic whom he caricatured in *Die Meistersinger* and who hated him ever after, now lives only because he was caricatured in *Die Meistersinger*. The women whose hearts he broke are long since dead; and the man who could never love anyone but himself has made them deathless atonement, I think, with *Tristan und Isolde*. Think of the luxury with which for a time, at least, fate rewarded Napoleon, the man who ruined France and looted Europe; and then perhaps you will agree that a few thousand dollars' worth of debts were not too heavy a price to pay for the *Ring* trilogy.

15   What if he was faithless to his friends and to his wives? He had one mistress to whom he was faithful to the day of his death: Music. Not for a single moment did he ever compromise with what he believed, with what he dreamed. There is not a line of his music that could have been conceived by a little mind. Even when he is dull, or downright bad, he is dull in the grand manner. There is greatness about his worst mistakes. Listening to his music, one does not forgive him for what he may or may not have been. It is not a matter of forgiveness. It is a matter of being dumb with wonder that his poor brain and body didn't burst under the torment of the demon of creative energy that lived inside him, struggling, clawing, scratching to be released; tearing, shrieking at him to write the music that was in him. The miracle is that what he did in the little space of seventy years could have been done at all, even by a great genius. Is it any wonder that he had no time to be a man?

Vocabulary

harangue, volubility, synopsis, callous, rajah, scrupulous

Questions

1. Would you call Wagner a manic-depressive?
2. Do you agree that Wagner's work reduces his faults?
3. Taylor was a music critic who loved Wagnerian music. How might he have reacted had he been in Eduard Hanslick's place?
4. What allowances do you demand from your friends?
5. What is the limit of your tolerance with difficult friends? Where do you draw the line?

Topics for Writing

Genius Is No Excuse

A Monster I Know

Sherlock Holmes

ARTHUR CONAN DOYLE (1859–1930), physician and author, created in Sherlock Holmes and Dr. Watson two lasting characters of popular litera- ture. Here, in the opening pages of *A Study in Scarlet,* you see Holmes and his companion-biographer as the British public first met them in 1887. For the pair in action, see "A Scandal in Bohemia" in Chapter 13.

1   In the year 1878 I took my degree of Doctor of Medicine of the University of London, and proceeded to Netley to go through the course prescribed for surgeons in the Army. Having completed my studies there, I was duly attached to the Fifth Northumberland Fusiliers as assistant surgeon. The regiment was stationed in India at the time, and before I could join it, the second Afghan war had broken out. On landing at Bombay, I learned that my corps had advanced through the passes, and was already deep in the enemy's country. I followed, however, with many other officers who were in the same situation as myself, and succeeded in reaching Candahar in safety, where I found my regiment, and at once entered upon my new duties.

2   The campaign brought honours and promotion to many, but for me it had nothing but misfortune and disaster. I was removed from my brigade and attached to the Berkshires, with whom I served at the fatal battle of Maiwand. There I was struck on the shoulder by a Jezail bullet, which shattered the bone and grazed the subclavian artery. I should have fallen into the hands of the murderous Ghazis had it not been for the devotion and courage shown by Murray, my orderly, who threw me across a pack-horse, and succeeded in bringing me safely to the British lines.

3   Worn with pain, and weak from the prolonged hardships which I had under- gone, I was removed, with a great train of wounded sufferers, to the base hospital at Peshawar. Here I rallied, and had already improved so far as to be able to walk about the wards, and even to bask a little upon the veranda, when I was struck down by enteric fever, that curse of our Indian possessions. For months my life was despaired of, and when at last I came to myself and became convalescent, I was so weak and emaciated that a medical board determined that not a day should be lost in sending me back to England. I was despatched, accordingly, in the troopship *Orontes,* and landed a month later on Portsmouth jetty, with my health irretrievably ruined, but with permission from a paternal government to spend the next nine months in attempting to improve it.

4   I had neither kith nor kin in England, and was therefore as free as air—or as free as an income of eleven shillings and sixpence a day will permit a man to be. Under such circumstances I naturally gravitated to London, that great cesspool into which all the loungers and idlers of the Empire are irresistibly drained. There I stayed for some time at a private hotel in the Strand, leading a comfortless, meaningless existence, and spending such money as I had, considerably more freely

than I ought. So alarming did the state of my finances become, that I soon realized that I must either leave the metropolis and rusticate somewhere in the country, or that I must make a complete alteration in my style of living. Choosing the latter alternative, I began by making up my mind to leave the hotel, and take up my quarters in some less pretentious and less expensive domicile.

On the very day that I had come to this conclusion, I was standing at the 5
Criterion Bar, when someone tapped me on the shoulder, and turning round I recognized young Stamford, who had been a dresser under me at Bart's. The sight of a friendly face in the great wilderness of London is a pleasant thing indeed to a lonely man. In old days Stamford had never been a particular crony of mine, but now I hailed him with enthusiasm, and he, in his turn, appeared to be delighted to see me. In the exuberance of my joy, I asked him to lunch with me at the Holborn, and we started off together in a hansom.

"Whatever have you been doing with yourself, Watson?" he asked in undis- 6
guised wonder, as we rattled through the crowded London streets. "You are as thin as a lath and as brown as a nut."

I gave him a short sketch of my adventures, and had hardly concluded it by the 7
time that we reached our destination.

"Poor devil!" he said, commiseratingly, after he had listened to my misfor- 8
tunes. "What are you up to now?"

"Looking for lodgings," I answered. "Trying to solve the problem as to whether 9
it is possible to get comfortable rooms at a reasonable price."

"That's a strange thing," remarked my companion; "you are the second man 10
to-day that has used that expression to me."

"And who was the first?" I asked. 11

"A fellow who is working at the chemical laboratory up at the hospital. He was 12
bemoaning himself this morning because he could not get someone to go halves with him in some nice rooms which he had found, and which were too much for his purse."

"By Jove!" I cried; "if he really wants someone to share the rooms and the 13
expense, I am the very man for him. I should prefer having a partner to being alone."

Young Stamford looked rather strangely at me over his wineglass. "You don't 14
know Sherlock Holmes yet," he said; "perhaps you would not care for him as a constant companion."

"Why, what is there against him?" 15

"Oh, I didn't say there was anything against him. He is a little queer in his 16
ideas—an enthusiast in some branches of science. As far as I know he is a decent fellow enough."

"A medical student, I suppose?" said I. 17

"No—I have no idea what he intends to go in for. I believe he is well up in 18
anatomy, and he is a first-class chemist; but, as far as I know, he has never taken out any systematic medical classes. His studies are very desultory and eccentric, but he has amassed a lot of out-of-the-way knowledge which would astonish his profes-sors."

19   "Did you never ask him what he was going in for?" I asked.

20   "No; he is not a man that it is easy to draw out, though he can be communicative enough when the fancy seizes him."

21   "I should like to meet him," I said. "If I am to lodge with anyone, I should prefer a man of studious and quiet habits. I am not strong enough yet to stand much noise or excitement. I had enough of both in Afghanistan to last me for the remainder of my natural existence. How could I meet this friend of yours?"

22   "He is sure to be at the laboratory," returned my companion. "He either avoids the place for weeks, or else he works there from morning till night. If you like, we will drive round together after luncheon."

23   "Certainly," I answered, and the conversation drifted away into other channels.

24   As we made our way to the hospital after leaving the Holborn, Stamford gave me a few more particulars about the gentleman whom I proposed to take as a fellow-lodger.

25   "You mustn't blame me if you don't get on with him," he said; "I know nothing more of him than I have learned from meeting him occasionally in the laboratory. You proposed this arrangement, so you must not hold me responsible."

26   "If we don't get on it will be easy to part company," I answered. "It seems to me, Stamford," I added, looking hard at my companion, "that you have some reason for washing your hands of the matter. Is this fellow's temper so formidable, or what is it? Don't be mealymouthed about it."

27   "It is not easy to express the inexpressible," he answered with a laugh. "Holmes is a little too scientific for my tastes—it approaches to cold-bloodedness. I could imagine his giving a friend a little pinch of the latest vegetable alkaloid, not out of malevolence, you understand, but simply out of a spirit of inquiry in order to have an accurate idea of the effects. To do him justice, I think that he would take it himself with the same readiness. He appears to have a passion for definite and exact knowledge."

28   "Very right too."

29   "Yes, but it may be pushed to excess. When it comes to beating the subjects in the dissecting-rooms with a stick, it is certainly taking rather a bizarre shape."

30   "Beating the subjects!"

31   "Yes, to verify how far bruises may be produced after death. I saw him at it with my own eyes."

32   "And yet you say he is not a medical student?"

33   "No. Heaven knows what the objects of his studies are. But here we are, and you must form your own impressions about him." As he spoke, we turned down a narrow lane and passed through a small side-door, which opened into a wing of the great hospital. It was familiar ground to me, and I needed no guiding as we ascended the bleak stone staircase and made our way down the long corridor with its vista of whitewashed wall and dun-coloured doors. Near the farther end a low arched passage branched away from it and led to the chemical laboratory.

34   This was a lofty chamber, lined and littered with countless bottles. Broad, low tables were scattered about, which bristled with retorts, test-tubes, and little Bunsen

lamps, with their blue flickering flames. There was only one student in the room, who was bending over a distant table absorbed in his work. At the sound of our steps he glanced round and sprang to his feet with a cry of pleasure. "I've found it! I've found it," he shouted to my companion, running towards us with a test-tube in his hand. "I have found a re-agent which is precipitated by haemoglobin, and by nothing else." Had he discovered a gold mine, greater delight could not have shone upon his features.

"Dr. Watson, Mr. Sherlock Holmes," said Stamford, introducing us.   35

"How are you?" he said cordially, gripping my hand with a strength for which I   36
should hardly have given him credit. "You have been in Afghanistan, I perceive."

"How on earth did you know that?" I asked in astonishment.   37

"Never mind," said he, chuckling to himself. "The question now is about   38
haemoglobin. No doubt you see the significance of this discovery of mine?"

"It is interesting, chemically, no doubt," I answered, "but practically—"   39

"Why, man, it is the most practical medico-legal discovery for years. Don't   40
you see that it gives us an infallible test for blood stains? Come over here now!" He seized me by the coat-sleeve in his eagerness, and drew me over to the table at which he had been working. "Let us have some fresh blood," he said, digging a long bodkin into his finger, and drawing off the resulting drop of blood in a chemical pipette. "Now, I add this small quantity of blood to a litre of water. You perceive that the resulting mixture has the appearance of pure water. The proportion of blood cannot be more than one in a million. I have no doubt, however, that we shall be able to obtain the characteristic reaction." As he spoke, he threw into the vessel a few white crystals, and then added some drops of a transparent fluid. In an instant the contents assumed a dull mahogany colour, and a brownish dust was precipitated to the bottom of the glass jar.

"Ha! ha!" he cried, clapping his hands, and looking as delighted as a child with   41
a new toy. "What do you think of that?"

"It seems to be a very delicate test," I remarked.   42

"Beautiful! beautiful! The old guaiacum test was very clumsy and uncertain.   43
So is the microscopic examination for blood corpuscles. The latter is valueless if the stains are a few hours old. Now, this appears to act as well whether the blood is old or new. Had this test been invented, there are hundreds of men now walking the earth who would long ago have paid the penalty of their crimes."

"Indeed!" I murmured.   44

"Criminal cases are continually hinging upon that one point. A man is sus-   45
pected of a crime months perhaps after it has been committed. His linen or clothes are examined and brownish stains discovered upon them. Are they blood stains, or mud stains, or rust stains, or fruit stains, or what are they? That is a question which has puzzled many an expert, and why? Because there was no reliable test. Now we have the Sherlock Holmes's test, and there will no longer be any difficulty."

His eyes fairly glittered as he spoke, and he put his hand over his heart and   46
bowed as if to some applauding crowd conjured up by his imagination.

"You are to be congratulated," I remarked, considerably surprised at his en-   47
thusiasm.

48   "There was the case of Von Bischoff at Frankfort last year. He would certainly have been hung had this test been in existence. Then there was Mason of Bradford, and the notorious Muller, and Lefevre of Montpellier, and Samson of New Orleans. I could name a score of cases in which it would have been decisive."

49   "You seem to be a walking calendar of crime," said Stamford with a laugh. "You might start a paper on those lines. Call it the 'Police News of the Past.'"

50   "Very interesting reading it might be made, too," remarked Sherlock Holmes, sticking a small piece of plaster over the prick on his finger. "I have to be careful," he continued, turning to me with a smile, "for I dabble with poisons a good deal." He held out his hand as he spoke, and I noticed that it was all mottled over with similar pieces of plaster, and discoloured with strong acids.

51   "We came here on business," said Stamford, sitting down on a high three-legged stool, and pushing another one in my direction with his foot. "My friend here wants to take diggings; and as you were complaining that you could get no one to go halves with you, I thought that I had better bring you together."

52   Sherlock Holmes seemed delighted at the idea of sharing his rooms with me. "I have my eye on a suite in Baker Street," he said, "which would suit us down to the ground. You don't mind the smell of strong tobacco, I hope?"

53   "I always smoke 'ship's' myself," I answered.

54   "That's good enough. I generally have chemicals about, and occasionally do experiments. Would that annoy you?"

55   "By no means."

56   "Let me see—what are my other shortcomings? I get in the dumps at times, and don't open my mouth for days on end. You must not think I am sulky when I do that. Just let me alone, and I'll soon be right. What have you to confess now? It's just as well for two fellows to know the worst of one another before they begin to live together."

57   I laughed at this cross-examination. "I keep a bull pup," I said, "and I object to rows because my nerves are shaken, and I get up at all sorts of ungodly hours, and I am extremely lazy. I have another set of vices when I'm well, but those are the principal ones at present."

58   "Do you include violin playing in your category of rows?" he asked, anxiously.

59   "It depends on the player," I answered. "A well-played violin is a treat for the gods—a badly played one—"

60   "Oh, that's all right," he cried, with a merry laugh. "I think we may consider the thing as settled—that is, if the rooms are agreeable to you."

61   "When shall we see them?"

62   "Call for me here at noon to-morrow, and we'll go together and settle everything," he answered.

63   "All right—noon exactly," said I, shaking his hand.

64   We left him working among his chemicals, and we walked together towards my hotel.

65   "By the way," I asked suddenly, stopping and turning upon Stamford, "how the deuce did he know that I had come from Afghanistan?"

My companion smiled an enigmatical smile. "That's just his little peculiarity," he said. "A good many people have wanted to know how he finds things out."   66

"Oh! a mystery is it?" I cried, rubbing my hands. "This is very piquant. I am much obliged to you for bringing us together. 'The proper study of mankind is man,' you know."   67

"You must study him, then," Stamford said, as he bade me good-bye. "You'll find him a knotty problem, though. I'll wager he learns more about you than you about him. Good-bye."   68

"Good-bye," I answered, and strolled on to my hotel, considerably interested in my new acquaintance.   69

We met next day as he had arranged, and inspected the rooms at No. 221B, Baker Street, of which he had spoken at our meeting. They consisted of a couple of comfortable bedrooms and a single large airy sitting-room, cheerfully furnished, and illuminated by two broad windows. So desirable in every way were the apartments, and so moderate did the terms seem when divided between us, that the bargain was concluded upon the spot, and we at once entered into possession. That very evening I moved my things round from the hotel, and on the following morning Sherlock Holmes followed me with several boxes and portmanteaus. For a day or two we were busily employed in unpacking and laying out our property to the best advantage. That done, we gradually began to settle down and to accommodate ourselves to our new surroundings.   70

Holmes was certainly not a difficult man to live with. He was quiet in his ways, and his habits were regular. It was rare for him to be up after ten at night, and he had invariably breakfasted and gone out before I rose in the morning. Sometimes he spent his day at the chemical laboratory, sometimes in the dissecting-rooms, and occasionally in long walks, which appeared to take him into the lowest portions of the city. Nothing could exceed his energy when the working fit was upon him; but now and again a reaction would seize him, and for days on end he would lie upon the sofa in the sitting-room, hardly uttering a word or moving a muscle from morning to night. On these occasions I have noticed such a dreamy, vacant expression in his eyes, that I might have suspected him of being addicted to the use of some narcotic, had not the temperance and cleanliness of his whole life forbidden such a notion.   71

As the weeks went by, my interest in him and my curiosity as to his aims in life gradually deepened and increased. His very person and appearance were such as to strike the attention of the most casual observer. In height he was rather over six feet, and so excessively lean that he seemed to be considerably taller. His eyes were sharp and piercing, save during those intervals of torpor to which I have alluded; and his thin, hawk-like nose gave his whole expression an air of alertness and decision. His chin, too, had the prominence and squareness which mark the man of determination. His hands were invariably blotted with ink and stained with chemicals, yet he was possessed of extraordinary delicacy of touch, as I frequently had occasion to observe when I watched him manipulating his fragile philosophical instruments.   72

73   The reader may set me down as a hopeless busybody, when I confess how much this man stimulated my curiosity, and how often I endeavoured to break through the reticence which he showed on all that concerned himself. Before pronouncing judgment, however, be it remembered how objectless was my life, and how little there was to engage my attention. My health forbade me from venturing out unless the weather was exceptionally genial, and I had no friends who would call upon me and break the monotony of my daily existence. Under these circumstances, I eagerly hailed the little mystery which hung around my companion, and spent much of my time in endeavouring to unravel it.

74   He was not studying medicine. He had himself, in reply to a question, confirmed Stamford's opinion upon that point. Neither did he appear to have pursued any course of reading which might fit him for a degree in science or any other recognized portal which would give him an entrance into the learned world. Yet his zeal for certain studies was remarkable, and within eccentric limits his knowledge was so extraordinarily ample and minute that his observations have fairly astounded me. Surely no man would work so hard or attain such precise information unless he had some definite end in view. Desultory readers are seldom remarkable for the exactness of their learning. No man burdens his mind with small matters unless he has some very good reason for doing so.

75   His ignorance was as remarkable as his knowledge. Of contemporary literature, philosophy and politics he appeared to know next to nothing. Upon my quoting Thomas Carlyle, he inquired in the naïvest way who he might be and what he had done. My surprise reached a climax, however, when I found incidentally that he was ignorant of the Copernican Theory and of the composition of the Solar System. That any civilized human being in this nineteenth century should not be aware that the earth travelled round the sun appeared to me to be such an extraordinary fact that I could hardly realize it.

76   "You appear to be astonished," he said, smiling at my expression of surprise. "Now that I do know it I shall do my best to forget it."

77   "To forget it!"

78   "You see," he explained, "I consider that a man's brain originally is like a little empty attic, and you have to stock it with such furniture as you choose. A fool takes in all the lumber of every sort that he comes across, so that the knowledge which might be useful to him gets crowded out, or at best is jumbled up with a lot of other things, so that he has a difficulty in laying his hands upon it. Now the skilful workman is very careful indeed as to what he takes into his brain-attic. He will have nothing but the tools which may help him in doing his work, but of these he has a large assortment, and all in the most perfect order. It is a mistake to think that that little room has elastic walls and can distend to any extent. Depend upon it there comes a time when for every addition of knowledge you forget something that you knew before. It is of the highest importance, therefore, not to have useless facts elbowing out the useful ones."

79   "But the Solar System!" I protested.

80   "What the deuce is it to me?" he interrupted impatiently: "you say that we go

round the sun. If we went round the moon it would not make a pennyworth of difference to me or to my work."

I was on the point of asking him what that work might be, but something in his manner showed me that the question would be an unwelcome one. I pondered over our short conversation, however, and endeavoured to draw my deductions from it. He said that he would acquire no knowledge which did not bear upon his object. Therefore all the knowledge which he possessed was such as would be useful to him. I enumerated in my own mind all the various points upon which he had shown me that he was exceptionally well informed. I even took a pencil and jotted them down. I could not help smiling at the document when I had completed it. It ran in this way:

Sherlock Holmes—his limits

1. Knowledge of Literature.—Nil.
2. "   " Philosophy.—Nil.
3. "   " Astronomy.—Nil.
4. "   " Politics.—Feeble.
5. "   " Botany.—Variable.
      Well up in belladonna, opium, and poisons generally. Knows nothing of practical gardening.
6. Knowledge of Geology.—Practical, but limited.
      Tells at a glance different soils from each other. After walks has shown me splashes upon his trousers, and told me by their colour and consistence in what part of London he had received them.
7. Knowledge of Chemistry.—Profound.
8. "   " Anatomy.—Accurate, but unsystematic.
9. "   " Sensational Literature.—Immense.
      He appears to know every detail of every horror perpetrated in the century.
10. Plays the violin well.
11. Is an expert singlestick player, boxer, and swordsman.
12. Has a good practical knowledge of British law.

When I had got so far in my list I threw it into the fire in despair. "If I can only find what the fellow is driving at by reconciling all these accomplishments, and discovering a calling which needs them all," I said to myself, "I may as well give up the attempt at once."

I see that I have alluded above to his powers upon the violin. These were very remarkable, but as eccentric as all his other accomplishments. That he could play pieces, and difficult pieces, I knew well, because at my request he has played me some of Mendelssohn's *Lieder,* and other favourites. When left to himself, however, he would seldom produce any music or attempt any recognized air. Leaning back in his armchair of an evening, he would close his eyes and scrape carelessly at the fiddle which was thrown across his knee. Sometimes the chords were sonorous and melancholy. Occasionally they were fantastic and cheerful. Clearly they reflected the thoughts which possessed him, but whether the music aided those thoughts, or whether the playing was simply the result of a whim or fancy, was more than I could determine. I might have rebelled against these exasperating solos had it not been that he usually terminated them by playing in quick succession a whole series of my favourite airs as a slight compensation for the trial upon my patience.

84   During the first week or so we had no callers, and I had begun to think that my companion was as friendless a man as I was myself. Presently, however, I found that he had many acquaintances, and those in the most different classes of society. There was one little sallow, rat-faced, dark-eyed fellow, who was introduced to me as Mr. Lestrade, and who came three or four times in a single week. One morning a young girl called, fashionably dressed, and stayed for half an hour or more. The same afternoon brought a gray-headed, seedy visitor, looking like a Jew peddler, who appeared to me to be much excited, and who was closely followed by a slipshod elderly woman. On another occasion an old white-haired gentleman had an interview with my companion; and on another, a railway porter in his velveteen uniform. When any of these nondescript individuals put in an appearance, Sherlock Holmes used to beg for the use of the sitting-room, and I would retire to my bedroom. He always apologized to me for putting me to this inconvenience. "I have to use this room as a place of business," he said, "and these people are my clients." Again I had an opportunity of asking him a point-blank question, and again my delicacy prevented me from forcing another man to confide in me. I imagined at the time that he had some strong reason for not alluding to it, but he soon dispelled the idea by coming round to the subject of his own accord.

85   It was upon the fourth of March, as I have good reason to remember, that I rose somewhat earlier than usual, and found that Sherlock Holmes had not yet finished his breakfast. The landlady had become so accustomed to my late habits that my place had not been laid nor my coffee prepared. With the unreasonable petulance of mankind I rang the bell and gave a curt intimation that I was ready. Then I picked up a magazine from the table and attempted to while away the time with it, while my companion munched silently at his toast. One of the articles had a pencil mark at the heading, and I naturally began to run my eye through it.

86   Its somewhat ambitious title was "The Book of Life," and it attempted to show how much an observant man might learn by an accurate and systematic examination of all that came in his way. It struck me as being a remarkable mixture of shrewdness and of absurdity. The reasoning was close and intense, but the deductions appeared to me to be far fetched and exaggerated. The writer claimed by a momentary expression, a twitch of a muscle or a glance of an eye, to fathom a man's inmost thoughts. Deceit, according to him, was an impossibility in the case of one trained to observation and analysis. His conclusions were as infallible as so many propositions of Euclid. So startling would his results appear to the uninitiated that until they learned the processes by which he had arrived at them they might well consider him as a necromancer.

87   "From a drop of water," said the writer, "a logician could infer the possibility of an Atlantic or a Niagara without having seen or heard of one or the other. So all life is a great chain, the nature of which is known whenever we are shown a single link of it. Like all other arts, the Science of Deduction and Analysis is one which can only be acquired by long and patient study, nor is life long enough to allow any

mortal to attain the highest possible perfection in it. Before turning to those moral and mental aspects of the matter which present the greatest difficulties, let the inquirer begin by mastering more elementary problems. Let him, on meeting a fellow-mortal, learn at a glance to distinguish the history of the man, and the trade or profession to which he belongs. Puerile as such an exercise may seem, it sharpens the faculties of observation, and teaches one where to look and what to look for. By a man's finger-nails, by his coat-sleeve, by his boots, by his trouser-knees, by the callosities of his forefinger and thumb, by his expression, by his shirt-cuffs—by each of these things a man's calling is plainly revealed. That all united should fail to enlighten the competent inquirer in any case is almost inconceivable."

"What ineffable twaddle!" I cried, slapping the magazine down on the table; "I never read such rubbish in my life." 88

"What is it?" asked Sherlock Holmes. 89

"Why, this article," I said, pointing at it with my eggspoon as I sat down to my breakfast. "I see that you have read it since you have marked it. I don't deny that it is smartly written. It irritates me, though. It is evidently the theory of some armchair lounger who evolves all these neat little paradoxes in the seclusion of his own study. It is not practical. I should like to see him clapped down in a third-class carriage on the Underground, and asked to give the trades of all his fellow-travellers. I would lay a thousand to one against him." 90

"You would lose your money," Holmes remarked calmly. "As for the article, I wrote it myself." 91

"You!" 92

"Yes; I have a turn both for observation and for deduction. The theories which I have expressed there, and which appear to you to be so chimerical, are really extremely practical—so practical that I depend upon them for my bread and cheese." 93

"And how?" I asked involuntarily. 94

"Well, I have a trade of my own. I suppose I am the only one in the world. I'm a consulting detective, if you can understand what that is. Here in London we have lots of government detectives and lots of private ones. When these fellows are at fault, they come to me, and I manage to put them on the right scent. They lay all the evidence before me, and I am generally able, by the help of my knowledge of the history of crime, to set them straight. There is a strong family resemblance about misdeeds, and if you have all the details of a thousand at your finger ends, it is odd if you can't unravel the thousand and first. Lestrade is a well-known detective. He got himself into a fog recently over a forgery case, and that was what brought him here." 95

"And these other people?" 96

"They are mostly sent on by private inquiry agencies. They are all people who are in trouble about something and want a little enlightening. I listen to their story, they listen to my comments, and then I pocket my fee." 97

"But do you mean to say," I said, "that without leaving your room you can unravel some knot which other men can make nothing of, although they have seen every detail for themselves?" 98

99   "Quite so. I have a kind of intuition that way. Now and again a case turns up which is a little more complex. Then I have to bustle about and see things with my own eyes. You see I have a lot of special knowledge which I apply to the problem, and which facilitates matters wonderfully. Those rules of deduction laid down in that article which aroused your scorn are invaluable to me in practical work. Observation with me is second nature. You appeared to be surprised when I told you, on our first meeting, that you had come from Afghanistan."

100   "You were told, no doubt."

101   "Nothing of the sort. I *knew* you came from Afghanistan. From long habit the train of thoughts ran so swiftly through my mind that I arrived at the conclusion without being conscious of intermediate steps. There were such steps, however. The train of reasoning ran, 'Here is a gentleman of a medical type, but with the air of a military man. Clearly an army doctor, then. He has just come from the tropics, for his face is dark, and that is not the natural tint of his skin, for his wrists are fair. He has undergone hardship and sickness, as his haggard face says clearly. His left arm has been injured. He holds it in a stiff and unnatural manner. Where in the tropics could an English army doctor have seen much hardship and got his arm wounded? Clearly in Afghanistan.' The whole train of thought did not occupy a second. I then remarked that you came from Afghanistan, and you were astonished."

102   "It is simple enough as you explain it," I said, smiling. "You remind me of Edgar Allan Poe's Dupin. I had no idea that such individuals did exist outside of stories."

103   Sherlock Holmes rose and lit his pipe. "No doubt you think that you are complimenting me in comparing me to Dupin," he observed. "Now, in my opinion, Dupin was a very inferior fellow. That trick of his of breaking in on his friends' thoughts with an apropos remark after a quarter of an hour's silence is really very showy and superficial. He had some analytical genius, no doubt; but he was by no means such a phenomenon as Poe appeared to imagine."

104   "Have you read Gaboriau's works?" I asked. "Does Lecoq come up to your idea of a detective?"

105   Sherlock Holmes sniffed sardonically. "Lecoq was a miserable bungler," he said, in an angry voice; "he had only one thing to recommend him, and that was his energy. That book made me positively ill. The question was how to identify an unknown prisoner. I could have done it in twenty-four hours. Lecoq took six months or so. It might be made a textbook for detectives to teach them what to avoid."

106   I felt rather indignant at having two characters whom I had admired treated in this cavalier style. I walked over to the window and stood looking out into the busy street. "This fellow may be very clever," I said to myself, "but he is certainly very conceited."

107   "There are no crimes and no criminals in these days," he said, querulously. "What is the use of having brains in our profession? I know well that I have it in me to make my name famous. No man lives or has ever lived who has brought the same

amount of study and of natural talent to the detection of crime which I have done. And what is the result? There is no crime to detect, or, at most, some bungling villainy with a motive so transparent that even a Scotland Yard official can see through it."

I was still annoyed at his bumptious style of conversation. I thought it best to change the topic.   108

"I wonder what that fellow is looking for?" I asked, pointing to a stalwart, plainly dressed individual who was walking slowly down the other side of the street, looking anxiously at the numbers. He had a large blue envelope in his hand, and was evidently the bearer of a message.   109

"You mean the retired sergeant of Marines," said Sherlock Holmes.   110

"Brag and bounce!" thought I to myself. "He knows that I cannot verify his guess."   111

The thought had hardly passed through my mind when the man whom we were watching caught sight of the number on our door, and ran rapidly across the roadway. We heard a loud knock, a deep voice below, and heavy steps ascending the stair.   112

"For Mr. Sherlock Holmes," he said, stepping into the room and handing my friend the letter.   113

Here was an opportunity of taking the conceit out of him. He little thought of this when he made that random shot. "May I ask, my lad," I said, in the blandest voice, "what your trade may be?"   114

"Commissionaire, sir," he said, gruffly. "Uniform away for repairs."   115

"And you were?" I asked, with a slightly malicious glance at my companion.   116

"A sergeant, sir, Royal Marine Light Infantry, sir. No answer? Right, sir."   117

He clicked his heels together, raised his hand in salute, and was gone.   118

Vocabulary

subclavian, enteric fever, rusticate, pretentious, hansom, commiseratingly, desultory, formidable, mealymouthed, alkaloid, malevolence, precipitated, haemo(hemo)globin, bodkin, guaiacum, mottled, diggings (slang), piquant, portmanteaus, Copernican Theory, belladonna, necromancer, ineffable, chimerical

Questions

1. What is the effect of Doyle's making Watson a medical doctor and wounded veteran?
2. List several ways by which Doyle tries to arouse our curiosity about Holmes.
3. If you have seen Nigel Bruce play Dr. Watson opposite Basil Rathbone's Holmes, you might conclude that Watson was stupid. Does Doyle make him appear so?
4. What rescues Watson from the charge of idle curiosity?

5. Are you impressed by Holmes's deductive powers?

Topic for Writing

Holmes as a Potential Roommate

You Are Old, Father William

LEWIS CARROLL (1832–1898)—actually, Charles Lutwidge Dodgson—
was an Oxford mathematician most of his life. Like most of the poems in the
Alice books, this poem is a parody that achieved a life independent of its
original.

"You are old, Father William," the young man said
   "And your hair has become very white;
And yet you incessantly stand on your head—
   Do you think, at your age, it is right?"

"In my youth," Father William replied to his son,   5
   "I feared it might injure the brain;
But, now that I'm perfectly sure I have none,
   Why, I do it again and again."

"You are old," said the youth, "as I mentioned before.
   And have grown most uncommonly fat;   10
Yet you turned a back-somersault in at the door—
   Pray, what is the reason of that?"

"In my youth," said the sage, as he shook his grey locks,
   "I kept all my limbs very supple
By the use of this ointment—one shilling the box—   15
   Allow me to sell you a couple?"

"You are old," said the youth, "and your jaws are too weak
   For anything tougher than suet;
Yet you finished the goose, with the bones and the beak—
   Pray, how did you manage to do it?"   20

"In my youth," said his father, "I took to the law,
   And argued each case with my wife;
And the muscular strength, which it gave to my jaw
   Has lasted the rest of my life."

"You are old," said the youth, "one would hardly suppose   25
   That your eye was as steady as ever;
Yet you balanced an eel on the end of your nose—
   What made you so awfully clever?"

30

"I have answered three questions, and that is enough,"
Said his father. "Don't give yourself airs!
Do you think I can listen all day to such stuff?
Be off, or I'll kick you down-stairs!"

Questions

1. The son thinks Father William eccentric. Is he right?
2. What single adjective would you suggest to describe Father William? To describe the son?

Topic for Writing

"You Are Old, Father William"—A Case of the Generation Gap

9

Describing Places/Where Are You Going; Where Have You Been?

A conversation with a new acquaintance will come very quickly to the ritual question, "Where are you from?" At bottom, it is part of the more fundamental one: "Who are you?"

We live in time and space. Our experiences (and our memories of them) are colored, often formed, by the places in which we have lived. Seeing those places in your mind's eye—describing them, in short, to yourself—is a part of the process of self-knowledge. Describing them to others can be an exercise in self-revelation.

As you have already learned, description demands a two-fold effort. First, you must see the thing clearly, noticing all the details that matter. Second, you must help your reader to see what you have seen. And this requires skills basic to every kind of writing: selecting and arranging details; using vivid images; choosing an appropriate tone and diction. In describing places, writers are often also concerned with controlling our distance, and therefore our breadth of sight, by the use of "long" and "short" scenes. This is a technique used commonly in motion pictures. A scene may open with a "pan" shot—a panoramic view of a large farm, say—and be followed by a close-up showing the expression of a farmer as he examines an ear of corn. We are given details as well as sweep. The results of effective description are as varied as life itself.

Robert Graves, for example, describes a quiet scene of rural beauty that is especially touching because it occurs in the middle of his account of trench warfare in France. Herman Melville, on the other hand, gives us a foretaste of danger and adventure by describing the ominous and exotic decor of the Spouter Inn, where Ishmael will spend his last night on land before joining the *Pequod*'s fatal pursuit of Moby Dick. With his dramatic contrast between the glittering gin-mill and the grim slums surrounding it, Charles Dickens makes it clear that those who grew up in the "Rookery" will have memories very different from those Grace King recovers from her childhood in the deep South.

The humorist Mark Twain, the poet William Butler Yeats, the essayists Joan Didion and N. Scott Momaday picture for us their various worlds and, inevitably, allow us glimpses into their lives and personalities. Such diversity reminds us of life's richness, encourages us to recreate in memory and words the places in which we have our roots, and in the process helps us to understand who we are by describing where we have been.

No-Man's Land

ROBERT GRAVES (1895–), an English poet, novelist, and translator, wrote *I, Claudius,* which was dramatized on television's *Masterpiece Theatre.* He came to sudden maturity, like many of his generation, as a young infantry officer in the trenches of World War I. This paragraph is from his autobiography *Goodbye to All That.*

1   At stand-to, rum and tea were served out. I looked at the German trenches through a periscope—a distant streak of sandbags. Some of these were made of coloured cloth, whether for camouflage or from a shortage of plain sacking, I do not know. The enemy gave no sign, except for a wisp or two of wood-smoke where they, too, were boiling up a hot drink. Between us and them lay a flat meadow with cornflowers, marguerites and poppies growing in the long grass, a few shell-holes, the bushes I had seen the night before, the wreck of an aeroplane, our barbed wire and theirs. Three-quarters of a mile away stood a big ruined house; a quarter of a mile behind that, a red-brick village—Auchy—poplars and haystacks, a tall chimney, and another village—Haisnes. Half-right, pit-head and smaller slag-heaps. La Bassée lay half-left; the sun caught the weathervane of the church and made it twinkle.

Vocabulary

camouflage, marguerites

Questions

1. Notice that Graves observes no-man's land through a periscope. What effect does this fact have on the description?
2. Do the details associated with war—the wrecked plane, for instance—disturb the peaceful effect of this passage? Explain your answer.
3. Does it seem to you that Graves has sequenced these details for a purpose? Try the effect of reversing the order of the last three sentences in his paragraph.
4. Describe some familiar place as though you were observing it from a fixed spot and were able to use only your sense of sight. Describe the same place, but without these limitations. Which version do you find more effective? Why?

Topics for Writing

A Visual Description

An Unlimited Description

The Spouter-Inn

HERMAN MELVILLE (1819–1891), American novelist and poet, went to sea as a young man, first on a merchant vessel and later on a whaler. *Moby Dick,* his masterpiece and the source of this description, was published in 1851.

Entering that gable-ended Spouter-Inn, you found yourself in a wide, low, straggling entry with old-fashioned wainscots, reminding one of the bulwarks of some condemned old craft. On one side hung a very large oil-painting so thoroughly besmoked, and every way defaced, that in the unequal cross-lights by which you viewed it, it was only by diligent study and a series of systematic visits to it, and careful inquiry of the neighbors, that you could any way arrive at an understanding of its purpose. Such unaccountable masses of shades and shadows, that at first you almost thought some ambitious young artist, in the time of the New England hags, had endeavored to delineate chaos bewitched. But by dint of much and earnest contemplation, and oft repeated ponderings, and especially by throwing open the little window towards the back of the entry, you at last come to the conclusion that such an idea, however wild, might not be altogether unwarranted.

But what most puzzled and confounded you was a long, limber, portentous, black mass of something hovering in the centre of the picture over three blue, dim, perpendicular lines floating in a nameless yeast. A boggy, soggy, squitchy picture truly, enough to drive a nervous man distracted. Yet was there a sort of indefinite, half-attained, unimaginable sublimity about it that fairly froze you to it, till you involuntarily took an oath with yourself to find out what that marvellous painting meant. Ever and anon a bright, but, alas, deceptive idea would dart you through.—It's the Black Sea in a midnight gale.—It's the unnatural combat of the four primal elements.—It's a blasted heath.—It's a Hyperborean winter scene.—It's the breaking-up of the ice-bound stream of Time. But at last all these fancies yielded to that one portentous something in the picture's midst. *That* once found out, and all the rest were plain. But stop; does it not bear a faint resemblance to a gigantic fish? even the great leviathan himself?

In fact, the artist's design seemed this: a final theory of my own, partly based upon the aggregated opinions of many aged persons with whom I conversed upon the subject. The picture represents a Cape-Horner in a great hurricane; the half-foundered ship weltering there with its three dismantled masts alone visible; and an exasperated whale, purposing to spring clean over the craft, is in the enormous act of impaling himself upon the three mast-heads.

The opposite wall of this entry was hung all over with a heathenish array of monstrous clubs and spears. Some were thickly set with glittering teeth resembling ivory saws; others were tufted with knots of human hair; and one was sickle-shaped, with a vast handle sweeping round like the segment made in the new-mown grass by a long-armed mower. You shuddered as you gazed, and wondered what monstrous cannibal and savage could ever have gone a death-harvesting with such a hacking, horrifying implement. Mixed with these were rusty old whaling lances and harpoons all broken and deformed. Some were storied weapons. With this once long lance, now wildly elbowed, fifty years ago did Nathan Swain kill fifteen whales between a sunrise and a sunset. And that harpoon—so like a corkscrew now—was flung in Javan seas, and run away with by a whale, years afterwards slain off the Cape of Blanco. The original iron entered nigh the tail, and, like a restless needle sojourning in the body of a man, travelled full forty feet, and at last was found imbedded in the hump.

5   Crossing this dusky entry, and on through yon low-arched way—cut through what in old times must have been a great central chimney with fire-places all round—you enter the public room. A still duskier place is this, with such low ponderous beams above, and such old wrinkled planks beneath, that you would almost fancy you trod some old craft's cockpits, especially of such a howling night, when this corner-anchored old ark rocked so furiously. On one side stood a long, low, shelf-like table covered with cracked glass cases, filled with dusty rarities gathered from this wide world's remotest nooks. Projecting from the further angle of the room stands a dark-looking den—the bar—a rude attempt at a right whale's head. Be that how it may, there stands the vast arched bone of the whale's jaw, so wide, a coach might almost drive beneath it. Within are shabby shelves, ranged round with old decanters, bottles, flasks; and in those jaws of swift destruction, like another cursed Jonah (by which name indeed they called him), bustles a little withered old man, who, for their money, dearly sells the sailors deliriums and death.

Vocabulary

wainscots, bulwarks, portentous, Hyperborean, leviathan, Jonah

Questions

1. Note the images of darkness and violence in this selection. Do you find the effect depressing or exhilarating?
2. Why does Melville open with the description of a painting instead, say, of the people who patronize the inn?
3. Does Melville gain anything by giving the bartender a biblical name? Does calling him "Jonah" force you to supply details from your memory of the biblical story?
4. Melville mentions only one whaler, Nathan Swain, by name. Would "a harpooneer" have served as well? Are "Nathan Swain" and "Jonah" used for the same purpose?

5. Among other things, *Moby Dick* is an account of man's struggle against age-old forces. What details in Melville's description of the Spouter-Inn prepare us for it?

6. Study the progression of ideas through the first three paragraphs. Notice in particular the steps by which the narrator comes to understand the subject of the oil painting. He moves from a vague first impression to confused speculation ("It's the Black Sea in a midnight gale.—It's the unnatural combat of the four primal elements.—It's a blasted heath . . . . ") to final recognition. What does Melville gain by this delay?

7. How would you describe a moment of suspended action—a diver leaving the springboard, a tennis player in mid-serve, a ballet dancer on point. Where would you start, with the scene or the actor? How would you suggest the stillness of the instant?

Topics for Writing

Action Suspended: A Description

Is "Jonah" an Appropriate Name?

A Gin-Shop

CHARLES DICKENS (see Chapter 3) was a court stenographer and a lively journalist before his novels brought him fame and wealth. He knew the slums of London from personal observation, and his interest in easing the harsh life of the poor endured.

1　We will endeavour to sketch the bar of a large gin-shop, and its ordinary customers, for the edification of such of our readers as may not have had opportunities of observing such scenes; and on the chance of finding one well suited to our purpose, we will make for Drury-lane, through the narrow streets and dirty courts which divide it from Oxford-street, and that classical spot adjoining the brewery at the bottom of Tottenham-court-road, best known to the initiated as the "Rookery."

2　The filthy and miserable appearance of this part of London can hardly be imagined by those (and there are many such) who have not witnessed it. Wretched houses with broken windows patched with rags and paper: every room let out to a different family, and in many instances to two or even three—fruit and "sweet-stuff" manufacturers in the cellars, barbers and red-herring vendors in the front parlours, cobblers in the back; a bird-fancier in the first floor, three families on the second, starvation in the attics, Irishmen in the passage, a "musician" in the front kitchen, and a charwoman and five hungry children in the back one—filth everywhere—a gutter before the houses and a drain behind—clothes drying and slops emptying, from the windows; girls of fourteen or fifteen, with matted hair, walking about barefoot, and in white great-coats, almost their only covering; boys of all ages, in coats of all sizes and no coats at all; men and women, in every variety of scanty and dirty apparel, lounging, scolding, drinking, smoking, squabbling, fighting, and swearing.

3　You turn the corner. What a change! All is light and brilliancy. The hum of many voices issues from that splendid gin-shop which forms the commencement of the two streets opposite; and the gay building with the fantastically ornamented parapet, the illuminated clock, the plate-glass windows surrounded by stucco rosettes, and its profusion of gas-lights in richly gilt burners, is perfectly dazzling when contrasted with the darkness and dirt we have just left. The interior is even gayer than the exterior. A bar of French-polished mahogany, elegantly carved, extends the whole width of the place; and there are two side-aisles of great casks, painted green and gold, enclosed within a light brass rail, and bearing such inscriptions, as "Old Tom, 549"; "Young Tom, 360"; "Samson, 1421"—the figures agreeing, we presume, with "gallons," understood. Beyond the bar is a lofty and spacious saloon, full of the same enticing vessels, with a gallery running round it, equally well furnished. On the counter, in addition to the usual spirit apparatus, are two or three little baskets of cakes and biscuits, which are carefully secured at top with wicker-work, to prevent their contents being unlawfully abstracted. Behind it, are two showily dressed damsels with large necklaces, dispensing the spirits and "compounds." They are assisted by the ostensible proprietor of the concern, a stout, coarse fellow in a fur cap, put on very much on one side to give him a knowing air, and to display his sandy whiskers to the best advantage.

The two old washerwomen, who are seated on the little bench to the left of the   4
bar, are rather overcome by the headdresses and haughty demeanour of the young ladies who officiate. They receive their half-quartern of gin and peppermint, with considerable deference, prefacing a request for "one of them soft biscuits," with a "Jist be good enough, ma'am." They are quite astonished at the impudent air of the young fellow in a brown coat and bright buttons, who, ushering in his two compan-ions, and walking up to the bar in as careless a manner as if he had been used to green and gold ornaments all his life, winks at one of the young ladies with singular coolness, and calls for a "kervorten and a three-out-glass," just as if the place were his own. "Gin for you, sir?" says the young lady when she has drawn it: carefully looking every way but the right one, to show that the wink had no effect upon her. "For me, Mary, my dear," replies the gentleman in brown. "My name an't Mary as it happens," says the young girl, rather relaxing as she delivers the change. "Well, if it an't, it ought to be," responds the irresistible one; "all the Marys as ever I see, was handsome gals." Here the young lady, not precisely remembering how blushes are managed in such cases, abruptly ends the flirtation by addressing the female in the faded feathers who has just entered, and who, after stating explicitly, to prevent any subsequent misunderstanding, that "this gentleman pays," calls for "a glass of port wine and a bit of sugar."

Those two old men who came in "just to have a drain," finished their third   5
quartern a few seconds ago; they have made themselves crying drunk; and the fat comfortable-looking elderly women, who had "a glass of rum-shrub" each, having chimed in with their complaints on the hardness of the times, one of the women has agreed to stand a glass round, jocularly observing that "grief never mended no broken bones, and as good people's wery scarce, what I says is, make the most on 'em, and that's all about it!" a sentiment which appears to afford unlimited satisfac-tion to those who have nothing to pay.

It is growing late, and the throng of men, women, and children, who have   6
been constantly going in and out, dwindles down to two or three occasional strag-glers—cold, wretched-looking creatures, in the last stage of emaciation and disease. The knot of Irish labourers at the lower end of the place, who have been alternately shaking hands with, and threatening the life of each other, for the last hour, become furious in their disputes, and finding it impossible to silence one man, who is particularly anxious to adjust the difference, they resort to the expedient of knocking him down and jumping on him afterwards. The man in the fur cap, and the potboy rush out; a scene of riot and confusion ensues; half the Irishmen get shut out, and the other half get shut in; the potboy is knocked among the tubs in no time; the landlord hits everybody, and everybody hits the landlord; the barmaids scream; the police come in; the rest is a confused mixture of arms, legs, staves, torn coats, shouting, and struggling. Some of the party are borne off to the station-house, and

the remainder slink home to beat their wives for complaining, and kick the children for daring to be hungry.

7   We have sketched this subject very slightly, not only because our limits compel us to do so, but because, if it were pursued farther, it would be painful and repulsive. Well-disposed gentlemen, and charitable ladies, would alike turn with coldness and disgust from a description of the drunken besotted men, and wretched broken-down miserable women, who form no inconsiderable portion of the fre-quenters of these haunts; forgetting, in the pleasant consciousness of their own rectitude, the poverty of the one, and the temptation of the other. Gin-drinking is a great vice in England, but wretchedness and dirt are a greater; and until you improve the homes of the poor, or persuade a half-famished wretch not to seek relief in the temporary oblivion of his own misery, with the pittance which, divided among his family, would furnish a morsel of bread for each, gin-shops will increase in number and splendour. If Temperance Societies would suggest an antidote against hunger, filth, and foul air, or could establish dispensaries for the gratuitous distribution of bottles of Lethe-water, gin-palaces would be numbered among the things that were.

Vocabulary

edification, charwoman, ostensible, quartern, deference, rectitude, pittance, Lethe

Questions

1. Note where Dickens's sketch of the gin-shop begins—in the Rookery, an area notorious for its low-life vigor. Why does he do so?
2. Most of the second paragraph is a single, long sentence. But the third opens with three very short ones. What connection do you see between this sudden change of style and the content of the third paragraph?
3. Is Dickens a cool observer or a social reformer?
4. Where do temperance societies fail? What could eliminate the need for gin-palaces?
5. What message does Dickens leave the reader?

Topics for Writing

Drunkenness: Cause or Effect?

Why People Drink

A Stagecoach Station on the Overland Trail

MARK TWAIN Twain (see Chapter 3) published this description in *Roughing It* (1871) to startle and amuse the greenhorns back East.

The station buildings were long, low huts, made of sun-dried, mud-colored   1
bricks, laid up without mortar (*adobes*, the Spaniards call these bricks, and Americans shorten it to "'*dobies*"). The roofs, which had no slant to them worth speaking of, were thatched and then sodded or covered with a thick layer of earth, and from this sprang a pretty rank growth of weeds and grass. It was the first time we had ever seen a man's front yard on top of his house. The buildings consisted of barns, stable room for twelve or fifteen horses, and a hut for an eating room for passengers. This latter had bunks in it for the station keeper and a hostler or two. You could rest your elbow on its eaves, and you had to bend in order to get in at the door. In place of a window there was a square hole about large enough for a man to crawl through, but this had no glass in it. There was no flooring, but the ground was packed hard. There was no stove, but the fireplace served all needful purposes. There were no shelves, no cupboards, no closets. In a corner stood an open sack of flour, and nestling against its base were a couple of black and venerable tin coffeepots, a tin teapot, a little bag of salt, and a side of bacon.

By the door of the station keeper's den, outside, was a tin washbasin, on the   2
ground. Near it was a pail of water and a piece of yellow bar soap, and from the eaves hung a hoary blue woolen shirt, significantly—but this latter was the station keeper's private towel, and only two persons in all the party might venture to use it—the stage driver and the conductor. The latter would not, from a sense of decency; the former would not, because he did not choose to encourage the advances of a station keeper. We had towels—in the valise; they might as well have been in Sodom and Gomorrah. We (and the conductor) used our handkerchiefs, and the driver his pantaloons and sleeves. By the door, inside, was fastened a small, old-fashioned, looking-glass frame, with two little fragments of the original mirror lodged down in one corner of it. This arrangement afforded a pleasant double-barreled portrait of you when you looked into it, with one half of your head set up a couple of inches above the other half. From the glass frame hung the half of a comb by a string—but if I had to describe that patriarch or die, I believe I would order some sample coffins. It had come down from Esau and Samson, and had been accumulating hair ever since—along with certain impurities. In one corner of the room stood three or four rifles and muskets, together with horns and pouches of ammunition. The station men wore pantaloons of course, country-woven stuff, and into the seat and the inside of the legs were sewed ample additions of buckskin, to do duty in place of leggings, when the man rode horseback—so the pants were half

dull blue and half yellow, and unspeakably picturesque. The pants were stuffed into the tops of high boots, the heels whereof were armed with great Spanish spurs, whose little iron clogs and chains jingled with every step. The man wore a huge beard and mustachios, an old slouch hat, a blue woolen shirt, no suspenders, no vest, no coat—in a leathern sheath in his belt, a great long "navy" revolver (slung on right side, hammer to the front), and projecting from his boot a horn-handled bowie knife. The furniture of the hut was neither gorgeous nor much in the way. The rocking chairs and sofas were not present, and never had been, but they were represented by two three-legged stools, a pineboard bench four feet long, and two empty candle boxes. The table was a greasy board on stilts, and the tablecloth and napkins had not come—and they were not looking for them, either. A battered tin platter, a knife and fork, and a tin pint cup were at each man's place, and the driver had a queensware saucer that had seen better days. Of course this duke sat at the head of the table. There was one isolated piece of table furniture that bore about it a touching air of grandeur in misfortune. This was the caster. It was German silver, and crippled and rusty, but it was so preposterously out of place there that it was suggestive of a tattered exiled king among barbarians, and the majesty of its native position compelled respect even in its degradation. There was only one cruet left, and that was a stopperless, fly-specked, broken-necked thing, with two inches of vinegar in it, and a dozen preserved flies with their heels up and looking sorry they had invested there.

Vocabulary

hostler, hoary, caster, cruet

Questions

1. Does Twain's description of the station strike you as visually accurate? How does his third sentence affect your judgment on this point?
2. He says that certain pieces of furniture "were not present." Do such negatives serve to describe? Can you describe a thing or place using only negatives?
3. What is a caster? Do the "kingly" images help you to visualize it?
4. Frontier humor is often marked by exaggeration and unexpected juxtapositions. Pick out examples of each.
5. Twain's observation of the flies is not literally accurate. Does the inaccuracy detract from his description?
6. Twain's station-house is more primitive than the Spouter-Inn, but in which place would you rather spend a night? Why?

Topics for Writing

The Most Uncomfortable Motel of All

How Twain Would Describe Our Dormitory

The Santa Ana

JOAN DIDION (1934–), former magazine editor, is the author of novels as well as sensitive essays on contemporary life. "The Santa Ana" is from her collection *Slouching Towards Bethlehem*, the title of which is taken from Yeats's apocalyptic "The Second Coming."

There is something uneasy in the Los Angeles air this afternoon, some unnatural stillness, some tension. What it means is that tonight a Santa Ana will begin to blow, a hot wind from the northeast whining down through the Cajon and San Gorgonio Passes, blowing up sandstorms out along Route 66, drying the hills and the nerves to the flash point. For a few days now we will see smoke back in the canyons, and hear sirens in the night. I have neither heard nor read that a Santa Ana is due, but I know it, and almost everyone I have seen today knows it too. We know it because we feel it. The baby frets. The maid sulks. I rekindle a waning argument with the telephone company, then cut my losses and lie down, given over to whatever it is in the air. To live with the Santa Ana is to accept, consciously or unconsciously, a deeply mechanistic view of human behavior.

I recall being told, when I first moved to Los Angeles and was living on an isolated beach, that the Indians would throw themselves into the sea when the bad wind blew. I could see why. The Pacific turned ominously glossy during a Santa Ana period, and one woke in the night troubled not only by the peacocks screaming in the olive trees but by the eerie absence of surf. The heat was surreal. The sky had a yellow cast, the kind of light sometimes called "earthquake weather." My only neighbor would not come out of her house for days, and there were no lights at night, and her husband roamed the place with a machete. One day he would tell me that he had heard a trespasser, the next a rattlesnake.

"On nights like that," Raymond Chandler once wrote about the Santa Ana, "every booze party ends in a fight. Meek little wives feel the edge of the carving knife and study their husbands' necks. Anything can happen." That was the kind of wind it was. I did not know then that there was any basis for the effect it had on all of us, but it turns out to be another of those cases in which science bears out folk wisdom. The Santa Ana, which is named for one of the canyons it rushes through, is a *foehn* wind, like the *foehn* of Austria and Switzerland and the *hamsin* of Israel. There are a number of persistent malevolent winds, perhaps the best known of which are the mistral of France and the Mediterranean sirocco, but a *foehn* wind has distinct characteristics: it occurs on the leeward slope of a mountain range and, although the air begins as a cold mass, it is warmed as it comes down the mountain and appears finally as a hot dry wind. Whenever and wherever a *foehn* blows, doctors hear about headaches and nausea and allergies, about "nervousness," about "depression." In Los Angeles some teachers do not attempt to conduct formal classes during a Santa Ana, because the children become unmanageable. In Swit-zerland the suicide rate goes up during the *foehn*, and in the courts of some Swiss cantons the wind is considered a mitigating circumstance for crime. Surgeons are said to watch the wind, because blood does not clot normally during a *foehn*. A few years ago an Israeli physicist discovered that not only during such winds, but for the ten or twelve hours which precede them, the air carries an unusually high ratio of positive to negative ions. No one seems to know exactly why that should be; some talk about friction and others suggest solar disturbances. In any case the positive ions are there, and what an excess of positive ions does, in the simplest terms, is make people unhappy. One cannot get much more mechanistic than that.

4   Easterns commonly complain that there is no "weather" at all in Southern California, that the days and the seasons slip by relentlessly, numbingly bland. That is quite misleading. In fact the climate is characterized by infrequent but violent extremes: two periods of torrential subtropical rains which continue for weeks and wash out the hills and send subdivisions sliding toward the sea; about twenty scattered days a year of the Santa Ana, which, with its incendiary dryness, invari-ably means fire. At the first prediction of a Santa Ana, the Forest Service flies men and equipment from northern California into the southern forests, and the Los Angeles Fire Department cancels its ordinary nonfirefighting routines. The Santa Ana caused Malibu to burn the way it did in 1956, and Bel Air in 1961, and Santa Barbara in 1964. In the winter of 1966–67 eleven men were killed fighting a Santa Ana fire that spread through the San Gabriel Mountains.

5   Just to watch the front-page news out of Los Angeles during a Santa Ana is to get very close to what it is about the place. The longest single Santa Ana period in recent years was in 1957, and it lasted not the usual three or four days but fourteen days, from November 21 until December 4. On the first day 25,000 acres of the San Gabriel Mountains were burning, with gusts reaching 100 miles an hour. In town, the wind reached Force 12, or hurricane force, on the Beaufort Scale; oil derricks were toppled and people ordered off the downtown streets to avoid injury from flying objects. On November 22 the fire in the San Gabriels was out of control. On November 24 six people were killed in automobile accidents, and by the end of the week the Los Angeles *Times* was keeping a box score of traffic deaths. On November 26 a prominent Pasadena attorney, depressed about money, shot and killed his wife, their two sons, and himself. On November 27 a South Gate divorcee, twenty-two, was murdered and thrown from a moving car. On November 30 the San Gabriel fire was still out of control, and the wind in town was blowing eighty miles an hour. On the first day of December four people died violently, and on the third the wind began to break.

6   It is hard for people who have not lived in Los Angeles to realize how radically the Santa Ana figures in the local imagination. The city burning is Los Angeles's deepest image of itself: Nathanael West perceived that, in *The Day of the Locust*; and at the time of the 1965 Watts riots what struck the imagination most indelibly were the fires. For days one could drive the Harbor Freeway and see the city on fire, just as we had always known it would be in the end. Los Angeles weather is the weather of catastrophe, of apocalypse, and, just as the reliably long and bitter

winters of New England determine the way life is lived there, so the violence and the unpredictability of the Santa Ana affect the entire quality of life in Los Angeles, accentuate its impermanence, its unreliability. The wind shows us how close to the edge we are.

Vocabulary

mechanistic, malevolent, mitigating, ions, radically, apocalypse

Questions

1. The word *some* occurs three times in the first sentence. To what effect?
2. What details forewarn that a Santa Ana is coming? Can you detail your sensations when a storm is coming on?
3. Does the Santa Ana suffer by comparison with the foreign winds listed in the third paragraph? Does their inclusion help our understanding?
4. Who is Raymond Chandler? Would a statement by a meteorologist be as effective in this context?
5. Note the pattern of sentence openings in the fifth paragraph. Does this repetition help or hurt?
6. Because wind can't be seen, Didion cannot rely entirely on visual imagery. Which of her images most helps you to "see" the wind?
7. At the close, Didion makes an assertion. Has she convinced you that "the wind shows us how close to the edge we are"? Which details did you find most convincing? Least convincing?

Topics for Writing

The Weather I Love
The Weather I Hate

The Way to Rainy Mountain

N. SCOTT MOMADAY (1934–) is an American Indian author who has written both poetry and prose. His best-known book, *The Way to Rainy Mountain,* was published in 1969; this essay appeared in *The Reporter* two years earlier.

1   A single knoll rises out of the plain in Oklahoma, north and west of the Wichita Range. For my people, the Kiowas, it is an old landmark, and they gave it the name Rainy Mountain. The hardest weather in the world is there. Winter brings blizzards, hot tornadic winds arise in the spring, and in summer the prairie is an anvil's edge. The grass turns brittle and brown, and it cracks beneath your feet. There are green belts along the rivers and creeks, linear groves of hickory and pecan, willow and witch hazel. At a distance in July or August the steaming foliage seems almost to writhe in fire. Great green and yellow grasshoppers are everywhere in the tall grass, popping up like corn to sting the flesh, and tortoises crawl about on the red earth, going nowhere in the plenty of time. Loneliness is an aspect of the land. All things in the plain are isolate; there is no confusion of objects in the eye, but *one* hill or *one* tree or *one* man. To look upon that landscape in the early morning, with the sun at your back, is to lose the sense of proportion. Your imagination comes to life, and this, you think, is where Creation was begun.

2   I returned to Rainy Mountain in July. My grandmother had died in the spring, and I wanted to be at her grave. She had lived to be very old and at last infirm. Her only living daughter was with her when she died, and I was told that in death her face was that of a child.

3   I like to think of her as a child. When she was born, the Kiowas were living the last great moment of their history. For more than a hundred years they had controlled the open range from the Smoky Hill River to the Red, from the headwaters of the Canadian to the fork of the Arkansas and Cimarron. In alliance with the Comanches, they had ruled the whole of the southern Plains. War was their sacred business, and they were among the finest horsemen the world has ever known. But warfare for the Kiowas was preeminently a matter of disposition rather than of survival, and they never understood the grim, unrelenting advance of the U.S. Cavalry. When at last, divided and ill-provisioned, they were driven onto the Staked Plains in the cold rains of autumn, they fell into panic. In Palo Duro Canyon they abandoned their crucial stores to pillage and had nothing then but their lives. In order to save themselves, they surrendered to the soldiers at Fort Sill and were imprisoned in the old stone corral that now stands as a military museum. My grandmother was spared the humiliation of those high gray walls by eight or ten years, but she must have known from birth the affliction of defeat, the dark brooding of old warriors.

Her name was Aho, and she belonged to the last culture to evolve in North   4
America. Her forebears came down from the high country in western Montana
nearly three centuries ago. They were a mountain people, a mysterious tribe of
hunters whose language has never been positively classified in any major group. In
the late seventeenth century they began a long migration to the south and east. It
was a journey toward the dawn, and it led to a golden age. Along the way the
Kiowas were befriended by the Crows, who gave them the culture and religion of
the Plains. They acquired horses, and their ancient nomadic spirit was suddenly
free of the ground. They acquired Tai-me, the sacred Sun Dance doll, from that
moment the object and symbol of their worship, and so shared in the divinity of the
sun. Not least, they acquired the sense of destiny, therefore courage and pride.
When they entered upon the southern Plains they had been transformed. No longer
were they slaves to the simple necessity of survival; they were a lordly and dangerous
society of fighters and thieves, hunters and priests of the sun. According to their
origin myth, they entered the world through a hollow log. From one point of view,
their migration was the fruit of an old prophecy, for indeed they emerged from a
sunless world.

Although my grandmother lived out her long life in the shadow of Rainy   5
Mountain, the immense landscape of the continental interior lay like memory in
her blood. She could tell of the Crows, whom she had never seen, and of the Black
Hills, where she had never been. I wanted to see in reality what she had seen more
perfectly in the mind's eye, and traveled fifteen hundred miles to begin my pilgrimage.

Yellowstone, it seemed to me, was the top of the world, a region of deep lakes   6
and dark timber, canyons and waterfalls. But, beautiful as it is, one might have the
sense of confinement there. The skyline in all directions is close at hand, the high
wall of the woods and deep cleavages of shade. There is a perfect freedom in the
mountains, but it belongs to the eagle and the elk, the badger and the bear. The
Kiowas reckoned their stature by the distance they could see, and they were bent
and blind in the wilderness.

Descending eastward, the highland meadows are a stairway to the plain. In   7
July the inland slope of the Rockies is luxuriant with flax and buckwheat, stonecrop
and larkspur. The earth unfolds and the limit of the land recedes. Clusters of trees,
and animals grazing far in the distance, cause the vision to reach away and wonder
to build upon the mind. The sun follows a longer course in the day, and the sky is
immense beyond all comparison. The great billowing clouds that sail upon it are
shadows that move upon the grain like water, dividing light. Farther down, in the
land of the Crows and Blackfeet, the plain is yellow. Sweet clover takes hold of the
hills and bends upon itself to cover and seal the soil. There the Kiowas paused on
their way; they had come to the place where they must change their lives. The sun
is at home on the plains. Precisely there does it have the certain character of a god.
When the Kiowas came to the land of the Crows, they could see the dark lees of the
hills at dawn across the Bighorn River, the profusion of light on the grain shelves,
the oldest deity ranging after the solstices. Not yet would they veer southward to the
caldron of the land that lay below; they must wean their blood from the northern

winter and hold the mountains a while longer in their view. They bore Tai-me in procession to the east.

8   A dark mist lay over the Black Hills, and the land was like iron. At the top of a ridge I caught sight of Devil's Tower upthrust against the gray sky as if in the birth of time the core of the earth had broken through its crust and the motion of the world was begun. There are things in nature that engender an awful quiet in the heart of man; Devil's Tower is one of them. Two centuries ago, because they could not do otherwise, the Kiowas made a legend at the base of the rock. My grandmother said:

> Eight children were there at play, seven sisters and their brother. Suddenly the boy was struck dumb; he trembled and began to run upon his hands and feet. His fingers became claws, and his body was covered with fur. Directly there was a bear where the boy had been. The sisters were terrified; they ran, and the bear after them. They came to the stump of a great tree, and the tree spoke to them. It bade them climb upon it, and as they did so it began to rise into the air. The bear came to kill them, but they were just beyond its reach. It reared against the tree and scored the bark all around with its claws. The seven sisters were borne into the sky, and they became the stars of the Big Dipper.

From that moment, and so long as the legend lives, the Kiowas have kinsmen in the night sky. Whatever they were in the mountains, they could be no more. However tenuous their well-being, however much they had suffered and would suffer again, they had found a way out of the wilderness.

9   My grandmother had a reverence for the sun, a holy regard that now is all but gone out of mankind. There was a wariness in her, and an ancient awe. She was a Christian in her later years, but she had come a long way about, and she never forgot her birthright. As a child she had been to the Sun Dances; she had taken part in those annual rites, and by them she had learned the restoration of her people in the presence of Tai-me. She was about seven when the last Kiowa Sun Dance was held in 1887 on the Washita River above Rainy Mountain Creek. The buffalo were gone. In order to consummate the ancient sacrifice—to impale the head of a buffalo bull upon the medicine tree—a delegation of old men journeyed into Texas, there to beg and barter for an animal from the Goodnight herd. She was ten when the Kiowas came together for the last time as a living Sun Dance culture. They could find no buffalo; they had to hang an old hide from the sacred tree. Before the dance could begin, a company of soldiers rode out from Fort Sill under orders to disperse the tribe. Forbidden without cause the essential act of their faith, having seen the wild herds slaughtered and left to rot upon the ground, the Kiowas backed away forever from the medicine tree. That was July 20, 1890, at the great bend of the Washita. My grandmother was there. Without bitterness, and for as long as she lived, she bore a vision of deicide.

10   Now that I can have her only in memory, I see my grandmother in the several postures that were peculiar to her: standing at the wood stove on a winter morning and turning meat in a great iron skillet; sitting at the south window, bent above her beadwork, and afterwards, when her vision failed, looking down for a long time into the fold of her hands; going out upon a cane, very slowly as she did when the weight of age came upon her; praying. I remember her most often at prayer. She made

long, rambling prayers out of suffering and hope, having seen many things. I was never sure that I had the right to hear, so exclusive were they of all mere custom and company. The last time I saw her she prayed standing by the side of her bed at night, naked to the waist, the light of a kerosene lamp moving upon her dark skin. Her long, black hair, always drawn and braided in the day, lay upon her shoulders and against her breasts like a shawl. I do not speak Kiowa, and I never understood her prayers, but there was something inherently sad in the sound, some merest hesitation upon the syllables of sorrow. She began in a high and descending pitch, exhausting her breath to silence; then again and again—and always the same intensity of effort, of something that is, and is not, like urgency in the human voice. Transported so in the dancing light among the shadows of her room, she seemed beyond the reach of time. But that was illusion; I think I knew then that I should not see her again.

Houses are like sentinels in the plain, old keepers of the weather watch. There, in a very little while, wood takes on the appearance of great age. All colors wear soon away in the wind and rain, and then the wood is burned gray and the grain appears and the nails turn red with rust. The windowpanes are black and opaque; you imagine there is nothing within, and indeed there are many ghosts, bones given up to the land. They stand here and there against the sky, and you approach them for a longer time than you expect. They belong in the distance; it is their domain.   11

Once there was a lot of sound in my grandmother's house, a lot of coming and going, feasting and talk. The summers there were full of excitement and reunion. The Kiowas are a summer people; they abide the cold and keep to themselves, but when the season turns and the land becomes warm and vital they cannot hold still; an old love of going returns upon them. The aged visitors who came to my grand-mother's house when I was a child were made of lean and leather, and they bore themselves upright. They wore great black hats and bright ample shirts that shook in the wind. They rubbed fat upon their hair and wound their braids with strips of colored cloth. Some of them painted their faces and carried the scars of old and cherished enmities. They were an old council of warlords, come to remind and be reminded of who they were. Their wives and daughters served them well. The women might indulge themselves; gossip was at once the mark and compensation of their servitude. They made loud and elaborate talk among themselves, full of jest and gesture, fright and false alarm. They went abroad in fringed and flowered shawls, bright beadwork and German silver. They were at home in the kitchen, and they prepared meals that were banquets.   12

There were frequent prayer meetings, and great nocturnal feasts. When I was a child I played with my cousins outside, where the lamplight fell upon the ground and the singing of the old people rose up around us and carried away into the darkness. There were a lot of good things to eat, a lot of laughter and surprise. And afterwards, when the quiet returned, I lay down with my grandmother and could hear the frogs away by the river and feel the motion of the air.   13

Now there is a funeral silence in the rooms, the endless wake of some final word. The walls have closed in upon my grandmother's house. When I returned to it in mourning, I saw for the first time in my life how small it was. It was late at night, and there was a white moon, nearly full. I sat for a long time on the stone   14 steps by the kitchen door. From there I could see out across the land; I could see the long row of trees by the creek, the low light upon the rolling plains, and the stars of the Big Dipper. Once I looked at the moon and caught sight of a strange thing. A cricket had perched upon the handrail, only a few inches away from me. My line of vision was such that the creature filled the moon like a fossil. It had gone there, I thought, to live and die, for there, of all places, was its small definition made whole and eternal. A warm wind rose up and purled like the longing within me.

15   The next morning I awoke at dawn and went out on the dirt road to Rainy Mountain. It was already hot, and the grasshoppers began to fill the air. Still, it was early in the morning, and the birds sang out of the shadows. The long yellow grass on the mountain shone in the bright light, and a scissortail hied above the land. There, where it ought to be, at the end of a long and legendary way, was my grandmother's grave. Here and there on the dark stones were ancestral names. Looking back once, I saw the mountain and came away.

Vocabulary

preeminently, nomadic, lees, solstices, caldron, tenuous, deicide

Questions

1. Momaday draws connections between Rainy Mountain and his grandmother. Which of the two is the primary object of his essay?
2. In the sixth paragraph, Momaday mentions "the eagle and the elk, the badger and the bear." The parallels make for vivid, memorable writing. Many parallels—like alliteration and rhyme—act like burrs that stick to the memory. As an experiment, judge which of the following is easier to memorize:
   a. And so no force, however great,
        Can draw a cord, however fine,
        Into a horizontal line,
      Which shall be absolutely straight.
   b. It is impossible, regardless of the amount of force applied, to pull even the finest of cords into an absolutely straight, horizontal line.
3. Momaday mentions a number of growing things in his seventh paragraph. Is *naming* an essential element of *describing*?
4. What growing things did you actually *notice* on your way to class? Are you hampered by your inability to name the plants and trees you see? What does the answer tell you about the reader's needs?
5. Contrast Twain's stop on the Overland Trail with Momaday's return to Rainy Mountain. How do we sense that one man is a visitor, the other a native returning home?

Topics for Writing

On My Way to Class

Hometown: A Stranger's Impressions

from Memories of a Southern Woman of Letters

GRACE KING (1852–1932) Fascinated by the culture and customs of her native New Orleans, Grace King mined the historical vein in fiction (*La Dame de Sainte Hermine*) as well as in more plainly factual works (like *Creole Families of Louisiana* and *New Orleans: The Place and the People*).

The past is our only real possession in life. It is the one piece of property of which time cannot deprive us; it is our own in a way that nothing else in life is. It never leaves our consciousness. In a word, we are our past; we do not cling to it, it clings to us.

Innumerable filaments of memory fasten it to us, and we go through life with them dangling behind us. The memories do not date merely from our childhood. They go back far beyond our experience, out of sight of it, to fasten upon parents and grandparents. Blessed are the children who have parents and grandparents who can relate the stories of their own pasts and so connect the younger with the older memories, lighting a taper in the imagination that never goes out, no matter what extinguishes the great lights of acquired memories, but that, on the contrary, flickers away persistently until, as by a miracle, with time these filaments increase in brilliance and color, so that at the end of a long life we see them shining through the vista of years like beacons.

Many a grandmother and grandfather are still carrying such tapers set alight by their grandmothers and grandfathers, and will live in their illumination to the end of their lives.

I was particularly blessed in this regard. My mother, a charming raconteuse, witty and inexhaustible in speech, never displayed these qualities so well as when talking to her children. We were never beyond or above that entertainment. "Tell us about when you were a little girl," was our prayer to her, and she loved to do so, dropping into our minds the never-forgettable picture of a pale little girl with white hair and eyes ever reddened by sties, always sickly but always full of fun, and quick to see the funny side of her little life; the only Protestant in the school where she was a day boarder, picking up French as she went along, conforming in everything to her Creole and Catholic mates, even to allowing herself to be prepared for her first communion, when at last she felt forced to acknowledge the truth. "But, *mon père,* I am a Protestant!"

"What a pity," said the good priest placidly, and dropped her from the class.

She drank wine for breakfast and practised her piano on Sunday as though she too were a good little Creole. Her handsome, good-natured father, who did not mind breaking rules, would have it that she must go to the theater with him every night, his wife not being fond of the theater. Of course nothing pleased her more.

231

She saw all the famous actors of the day who came to New Orleans: the elder Booth, Macready, McCullough, the beautiful Alice Placide; and she met the famous impresario, Caldwell, who knew all the plays and all the actors and actresses and impersonated their rôles delightfully. And of all this she told her children. Everything happened to her so beautifully. She never forgot anything funny or pleasant that had come to her; and her children never found anything that happened to them worth while, so tame and listless their lives seemed in contrast.

7   The grandmother's stories were quite different. Huguenot by descent, she came from Georgia, of an austere family. Her memories and stories were never amusing; but they were interesting. All about the Revolutionary War, and General Marion, who was related to her mother; and of Continental soldiers, and jay-hawkers, and the sinfulness of New Orleans when she came to the city as a bride, fresh from the piety and civilization of Georgia, which she represented—for so she remembered it—as an earthly paradise.

8   The home in which memory began to make these first gatherings was a plain dwelling of the usual prosperous American lawyer. It seemed ordinary in comparison with the rich houses of the neighborhood, set in the midst of great gardens. But it had a distinct personality in memory. It was three stories high, with broad galleries in front. There were a good garden and grass plot with a backyard, provided with the usual dependencies of the time, servants' quarters of course, outhouses, a gigantic cistern, and a great cellar of plastered brick.

9   The first story of the house was devoted to a large drawing-room, called "the parlor," whose folding doors opened into the dining room, with its huge sideboard, and its long table in the center. The walls were plentifully supplied with pictures in gilt frames. A majestic-looking bookcase packed with books stood opposite the sideboard.

10   The upper stories held the bedrooms of the family and of the French governess, who was made one of us. The rooms of the father and mother, the front rooms of the second floor, were always held in awe by the children, and we avoided them as much as possible.

11   The third story dwells in a bright light always—the grandmother's apartment—her realm and the children's. The rooms, large and commodious, seem in memory plain and bare. The room used as the nursery had none of the prettiness of the modern nursery. Two plain little beds, some chairs, and a table furnished all that at that time was deemed necessary—for boys. The little girls were kept in the room of the grandmother. They slept in what was then known as a "trundle-bed," that was by day rolled, or trundled, under the great mahogany bed of the grandmother.

12   The furniture of this room all came from the grandmother's home in Georgia—the square-looking bureau, with its small mirror and glass handles to the drawers; a cavernous-looking *armoire*, a treasure cave of precious relics. On the walls hung the portraits of the dead-and-gone grandfather, a handsome man of about forty, with the pleasant face of a father who would take his little girl every night to the theater with him, and who loved the good things to eat and drink that played a part in the spirited stories about him.

Far away in a dark corner, on the floor, was a taper floating in its bowl of oil.   13
Its wick flaring up and down during the dreadful black nights used to frighten the
little girls in their trundle-beds, who imagined it was the eye of God watching them!

After we were waked in the morning and dressed, the good grandmother would   14
range us on our knees alongside her bed and make us say our prayers in unison,
standing behind us to correct at the first mistake. How she managed it I cannot say,
but she made us feel that God was listening to us, and that He could and would
make us the good children we petitioned to be, and bless our long list of relatives
carefully recited, winding up with the general petition for "all our kind friends."
After our prayers we would read a verse in the Bible, standing beside a low table,
each spelling out the words of the Great Book. On Sundays a little catechism was
added to these rites, and the verse of a hymn; and then we were sent to Sunday
school.

The light filaments that hold this memory seem to break here, and evening   15
comes dangling down to us. We go to bed; the lights are put out; and we are left to
ourselves. The heavy tread of the father sounds downstairs, and his sonorous voice.
He and the mother go to the upper gallery for their after-dinner talk; and black night
hides all the rest.

Vocabulary

filaments, raconteuse, Creole, Huguenot, austere, jayhawkers, dependencies,
cistern, sideboard, commodious, *armoire*, catechism, sonorous

Questions

1. Descriptions are often aimed at one or the other of our senses. Some authors
   want us to experience the sounds, others the smells, still others the sights of a
   place. At which of our senses does Grace King aim?
2. Have the experiences of your parents and grandparents gotten mixed in with
   your own memories? Can you give a couple of examples?
3. What distinctions are made between the Catholic Creoles and the Protestant
   Huguenots?
4. Do you find a pattern in the author's frequent references to light and light
   images?

Topic for Writing

The Sounds of Childhood

The Lake Isle of Innisfree

WILLIAM BUTLER YEATS   (1865–1939), the Irish poet, playwright, and statesman, did much to forward the Irish literary and dramatic renaissance. His poetry ranges from the complex and mystical, difficult of interpretation, to peasantlike simplicity, of which "The Lake Isle of Innisfree," published in 1890, is a shining example.

I will arise and go now, and go to Innisfree,
And a small cabin build there, of clay and wattles made;
Nine bean rows will I have there, a hive for the honey bee,
And live alone in the bee-loud glade.

5   And I shall have some peace there, for peace comes dropping slow,
Dropping from the veils of the morning to where the cricket sings;
There midnight's all a glimmer, and noon a purple glow,
And evening full of the linnet's wings.

I will arise and go now, for always night and day
10 I hear lake water lapping with low sounds by the shore;
While I stand on the roadway, or on the pavements gray,
I hear it in the deep heart's core.

Vocabulary

wattles, glade, linnet

Questions

1. Does Yeats bring his anticipated rest in Innisfree to life for you?
2. Innisfree is, of course, a real place. Need it be?
3. Would Yeats be happy in a four-story house? Why not?
4. What is a "bee-loud glade"?
5. What do you picture when you read "on the pavements gray"?
6. Why doesn't he hear the sounds of Innisfree in his "mind's ear" instead of his "heart's core"? Surely the latter is no more logical than the former, is it?

Topics for Writing

The Most Peaceful Place I Know

Hearing with the Heart

10

Describing Events/Breakthrough!

In describing events, the writer combines the arts of description with those of analysis and storytelling (narration), but the emphasis is on the event. "How did it happen?" the writer asks. To answer the question, the steps which led to the result are analyzed; those steps are organized in a way that focuses our attention on the result; significant details are singled out to help us share the sense of a goal achieved or an end reached.

The descriptions in this chapter are, with one possible exception, accounts of human triumphs: over the elements, over adversity, over darkness. Not all events end in success—Edmund Hillary succeeded only where many others failed—and the description of failure can be poignant. But the techniques and principles are the same.

This chapter opens with three factual descriptions regarding the atom—the building of the first atomic pile, lunar exploration, and the role Einstein played in moving the United States towards the development of the atomic bomb. They are reportorial accounts, with little emphasis on emotion. But ordinarily, as we see in the remaining selections, authors are very much concerned to add the emotional dimension to the description of a breakthrough. Anne Sullivan and John Keats are elated by their triumphs. Howard Carter and Hillary want to share the suspense and the difficulties they experienced. And Victor Hugo spares no emotional trick when he describes Cambronne's defiant act as an ultimate triumph.

The events marking the moments of triumph in our own lives may seem, at first glance, trivial compared to these events of glory. What Everests, after all, have we climbed? Still, there is Keats, entering a novel country by the act of reading—and accounting himself a dazzled explorer as a consequence. Perhaps the drama of an event lies as much in the challenge it presents to us as in its "size" relative to other events?

Zip Out

TIME MAGAZINE The national news magazines, *Time* prominently among them, report regularly on science and national concerns. Atomic energy and the development of the atomic bomb were secret matters during World War II, and only after it was over could the public learn such details as "Zip Out" includes. This article appeared in the issue of December 9, 1946.

1   By U.S. Army chronology, the Atomic Age was born on December 2, 1942, a good thirty-two months before Hiroshima. Now the Army, beaming proudly, has released a detailed description of the birth.

2   In a squash court under the stands of the University of Chicago's football stadium, a curious structure had grown, watched by the hopeful, nervous eyes of some of the world's best physicists. It was built of dead-black graphite bricks with small cubes of uranium or uranium oxide imbedded in some of their corners.

3   This was the world's first uranium pile. Within it, if all went well, would rage the first nuclear chain reaction. Physicist Enrico Fermi, Italian-born Nobel Prize-winner, was sure that all would go well. He had figured every smallest detail, advancing through theory and mathematics far into the unknown.

4   On December 2, a small group of physicists gathered in the squash court for the final test. Partly shrouded in balloon cloth, the pile squatted black and menacing. Within it, all knew or hoped, a monstrous giant sat chained. Control rods plated with cadmium (which readily absorbs neutrons) had been thrust into holes in the graphite. When the control rods were removed, Fermi had calculated, the chain reaction would start spontaneously, and the giant would be free.

5   One of the rods was automatic, controlled by a motor which could shoot it back into the pile when instruments warned that neutrons were getting too thick. Another (called "Zip") was attached to a heavy weight by a rope running over a pulley. When in the "withdrawn" position, it was tethered by another rope; a man with an ax stood ready to cut it free, send it zipping into the pile if anything went wrong. The last rod, marked in feet and inches, was to be worked by hand.

6   But all the physicists knew that they were in dangerous, unknown territory. So above the pile was stationed a "liquid-control squad" to douse mutinous neutrons with cadmium-salt solution.

7   Fermi ran the test. At 9:54 A.M. he gave an order. A whining motor withdrew the automatic control rod. The Geiger counters on the instrument panel clicked a little faster; a pen drew a slightly higher curve on a strip of paper.

8   "Zip out!" ordered Fermi a few minutes later. Physicist Walter H. Zinn pulled out the Zip rod and tied it carefully. The counters clicked still faster. The graph pen moved up again.

9   "Pull it to thirteen feet, George," commanded Fermi. Physicist George Weil

drew the final control rod part way out of the pile. Faster clicked the counters. He
drew it out another foot; then another six inches.

At 11:35, the counters were clicking furiously. The physicists watched fas-   10
cinated as the curve climbed steadily upward. Then, Wham! With a clang, the
automatic control rod (which had been set for too low a neutron count) slammed
back into the pile. "I'm hungry," said Fermi calmly. "Let's go to lunch." The other
rods were inserted, the pile quieted down.

At two o'clock the physicists gathered again in the squash court. One by one,   11
on Fermi's orders, the control rods were withdrawn, the counters clicked faster. The
pile was alive with neutrons now; the giant was straining his bonds. But it was not
quite a chain reaction. The neutron curve moved up, leveled off.

At 3:25 Fermi ordered the control rod out another foot. "This is going to do   12
it," he said. "The curve will . . . not level off." Now the counters were roaring, not
clicking, the graph curve was climbing upward. Fermi studied the instruments,
grinned broadly: "The reaction is self-sustaining."

For twenty-eight minutes the physicists watched as the curve climbed sharply   13
upward. The giant was flexing his muscles.

"O.K." said Fermi. "Zip in." The Zip rod shot into the pile. The counters   14
slowed their clicking. The graph curve sagged. But the world outside the squash
court would not be the same again.

Vocabulary

uranium pile, neutrons, mutinous

Questions

1. This news report proceeds chronologically. Do you find the technique effective? Does it help describe the event?
2. Is the title of the piece appropriate?
3. What phrases convey the sense of danger and uncertainty?
4. What is the function of the cadmium rods?
5. How could neutrons become "mutinous"?
6. What does the last sentence mean? Do you think it true?

Topics for Writing

Nuclear Power, Hope of the Future
Nuclear Power, a Constant Threat

Observation and Exploration

JAMES D. BURKE (1937–) This essay, written by a space scientist for nonscientists, appears in the *Encyclopedia Americana*.

1   The dawn of lunar science can be seen in such ancient monuments as Stonehenge and in the early lunar calendars and eclipse records and predictions of Chinese, Babylonian, Egyptian, and Mayan astronomers. By the time of the flowering of Greek civilization and the Alexandrian school of Aristarchus, Hipparchus, Eratosthenes, and Ptolemy between the third century B.C. and the first century A.D., the lunar phases and eclipses were correctly understood, the distance to the moon was approximately known, and the spherical shape and size of the earth were determined by observing its shadow on the moon during lunar eclipses. During the long hegemony of Islam, astronomy and mathematics progressed through careful observation and calculation, and it became possible to predict the moon's complicated motions among the stars closely enough for timekeeping. In the sixteenth century, Nicholas Copernicus, Tycho Brahe, and Johannes Kepler founded the modern science of planetary astronomy. Kepler wrote a remarkable work of fiction, the *Somnium (Dream)*, published posthumously in 1634. In it, he correctly described many aspects of the moon, including the long, scorching days and frigid nights and the ever-present earth overhead.

2   In 1609, Thomas Harriot in England and, in 1610, Galileo Galilei in Padua first observed the moon through telescopes, beginning four centuries of detailed investigation of the moon's earthward face. By the mid-seventeenth century, Johannes Hevelius and Giovanni Riccioli had produced accurate maps of the moon. Between 1670 and 1700, Robert Hooke, Isaac Newton, and Giovanni Cassini applied the new understandings of mathematics, physics, and astronomy to explain the motions, shape, and surface features of the moon. As the age of enlightenment progressed, the study of the moon was advanced rapidly through the work of Johann Tobias Mayer, Joseph Louis Lagrange, Immanuel Kant, Pierre Simon de Laplace, Sir William Herschel, and others.

3   As the great age of ocean voyaging began in the seventeenth century, uses of the moon for navigation stimulated an effort to understand and predict its complicated motions among the stars. An important goal was to develop a reliable and simple method for determining longitude at sea. In principle, this could be done by using the moon as a clock. Work was done by Mayer and by astronomers of the Royal Greenwich Observatory, beginning with John Flamsteed, the first astronomer royal, to reduce the principle to practice. Their method is feasible and can be used today, but it has been rendered obsolete by the development of seagoing chronometers and radio time signals.

4   In the early Victorian age, William Parsons, third earl of Rosse, built an

238

immense reflecting telescope with a mirror 6 feet (1.8 meters) in diameter. He used it at his Parsonstown estate in Ireland. Despite the cloudy Irish skies, Rosse made several important discoveries. He measured the approximate photometric properties and the temperature of the moon, and he drew the first portrait of the spiral structure of a galaxy.

In 1850 the great age of telescopic observation by eye began to wane with the advent of photography. Lunar photography from the earth reached its highest stage with the publication of Gerard P. Kuiper's great photographic lunar atlas in 1960.

As the space age dawned, interest in lunar problems revived. A rich literature was produced by Harold C. Urey, Kuiper, Ralph B. Baldwin, Eugene M. Shoemaker, Barbara M. Middlehurst, and other scientists. They summarized and added to all the lunar knowledge gained by observation from the earth. Thus, on the eve of the first lunar missions, much was known about the moon as a satellite, though there were still enormous gaps. Nothing was known of lunar chemistry, magnetism, or small-scale topography. Although relative geologic ages were partly deciphered, no absolute time scale was available. The old argument about impact versus vulcanism as the source of lunar craters remained unresolved. And nothing was known of the moon's unseen far side.

In January 1959 a Soviet spacecraft called Mechta (Russian for "dream," perhaps recalling Kepler's *Somnium*) became the first man-made machine to escape the earth's gravity. It flew by the moon and into interplanetary space. In September 1959, Luna 2 crashed into the moon, having determined on its approach that the moon's magnetic field, if any, was very weak. In October 1959, Luna 3 looped beyond the moon and fulfilled an age-old human desire by sending back the first photos of the moon's far side. These photos revealed the relative absence of maria there.

There followed a decade-long outburst of lunar discovery as the earth's two great adversaries engaged in a contest to explore the moon. In its scope, quality, and spirit, this peaceful competitive effort was unprecedented. Year after year, it engaged the highest technical skills of both the United States and the Soviet Union on a scale known previously only in war. Huge organizations were formed in both countries, immense facilities were built, giant rockets and spacecraft were prepared, and brave astronauts and cosmonauts flew mission after mission in earth orbit to get ready for the leap to the moon. In 1967 pilots were killed by accidents in both countries, but the drive continued. In 1968, U. S. astronauts orbited the moon. On July 20, 1969, the contest ended with the Apollo 11 mission when two U. S. astronauts, Neil Armstrong and Edward Aldrin, stepped onto the moon while a third astronaut, Michael Collins, circled overhead.

Vocabulary

lunar phases, hegemony, longitude, photometric, magnetism, topography, vulcanism, maria (see mare)

Questions

1. Why is the tone of this article so much different from the tone of "Zip Out"?
2. Why doesn't Burke attempt to dramatize these important space discoveries?
3. What are some of the virtues of the "encyclopedia style"?

Einstein

C. P. SNOW (1905–1980) bridged the gap between "the two cultures"—a phrase he invented—of science and the humanities. A scientist by training and a government official of great skill in England, Snow wrote an eleven-volume sequence of novels, *Strangers and Brothers,* which illuminates the corridors of power and the varieties of men who walk them. This factual account was meant to clarify Einstein's minor role in America's development of the atomic bomb, a role no doubt overestimated in the popular mind. It is part of a longer essay on Einstein reprinted in *A Variety of Men.*

Let me try to clear the ground. First, Einstein's work had nothing to do either with the discovery or the potential use of nuclear fission. From the moment of the Meitner-Frisch paper in January 1939 (as Niels Bohr said at the time, everyone ought to have seen the meaning of Hahn's 1938 experiments much earlier—"we were all fools"), nuclear fission was a known fact to all physicists in the field. Second, the possible use of nuclear energy had been speculated about long before Einstein produced the equation $E = mc^2$. After the fission experiments, it would have been empirically apparent if there had been no theory at all. Every nuclear physicist in the world—and a good many non-nuclear physicists—were talking about the conceivability of a nuclear bomb from early 1939 onwards. Third, all responsible nuclear physicists wanted to bring this news to their governments as effectively as they could. It happened in England months *before* the Einstein letter was signed. Fourth, a group of refugee scientists in America (Szilard, Wigner, Teller, Fermi) had no direct channels of communication with the White House. Very sensibly, they explained the position to Einstein. It was easy for him to understand. A letter drafted by them, signed by him, handed on by Sachs (an economist with an entrée to the President), would get straight to Roosevelt. "I served as a pillar box," said Einstein. It was signed on Long Island on July 2: it did not reach Roosevelt until October 11. Fifth, if this letter had not been sent, similar messages would have been forced on Roosevelt. For some time *after* the letter, the Americans were much slower off the mark than the English. Peierls's calculations, which showed that the bomb was a possibility, were ready by mid-1940. These had, in historical fact, a major effect upon the *American* scientists. Sixth, in July 1939, there was—unless one was an unqualified pacifist—no moral dilemma. Everyone was afraid that the Nazis would get the bomb first. If so, they would rule the world. It was as simple as that. It was as simple to Einstein as to the crudest of men.

Vocabulary

fission, empirically, entrée, pillar box, dilemma

Questions

1. Snow wants to separate fact from fiction—in this case, the popular belief that the development of the atomic bomb can be traced to Einstein's letter to Roosevelt in 1939. Why is it necessary for Snow to "clear the ground"?
2. Where does the positive description of the event begin?
3. Does Snow imply that Einstein's role in this matter was not important?
4. Why didn't Einstein see a moral dilemma in telling the president that an atomic bomb was a possibility? Do you agree that there was no dilemma?

Topics for Writing

An Event of Importance

Einstein's Choice: The Lesser of Two Evils?

Helen Keller's Lesson

ANNE SULLIVAN (1866–1936), a teacher of the handicapped, will always be associated with Helen Keller, the deaf and blind child who went on to a fruitful life, a life that began with this dramatic episode. (See Chapter 12 for Miss Keller's account of the same incident).

Tuscumbia, Alabama, March 11, 1887. Since I wrote you, Helen and I have gone to live all by ourselves in a little garden-house about a quarter of a mile from her home, only a short distance from Ivy Green, the Keller homestead. I very soon made up my mind that I could do nothing with Helen in the midst of the family, who have always allowed her to do exactly as she pleased. She has tyrannized over everybody, her mother, her father, the servants, the little darkies who play with her, and nobody had ever seriously disputed her will, except occasionally her brother James, until I came; and like all tyrants she holds tenaciously to her divine right to do as she pleases. If she ever failed to get what she wanted, it was because of her inability to make the vassals of her household understand what it was. Every thwarted desire was the signal for a passionate outburst, and as she grew older and stronger, these tempests became more violent. As I began to teach her, I was beset by many difficulties. She wouldn't yield a point without contesting it to the bitter end. I couldn't coax her or compromise with her. To get her to do the simplest thing, such as combing her hair or washing her hands or buttoning her boots, it was necessary to use force, and, of course, a distressing scene followed. The family naturally felt inclined to interfere, especially her father, who cannot bear to see her cry. So they were all willing to give in for the sake of peace. Besides, her past experiences and associations were all against me. I saw clearly that it was useless to try to teach her language or anything else until she learned to obey me. I have thought about it a great deal, and the more I think, the more certain I am that obedience is the gateway through which knowledge, yes, and love, too, enter the mind of the child. As I wrote you, I meant to go slowly at first. I had an idea that I could win the love and confidence of my little pupil by the same means that I should use if she could see and hear. But I soon found that I was cut off from all the usual approaches to the child's heart. She accepted everything I did for her as a matter of course, and refused to be caressed, and there was no way of appealing to her affection or sympathy or childish love of approbation. She would or she wouldn't, and there was an end of it. Thus it is, we study, plan and prepare ourselves for a task, and when the hour for action arrives, we find that the system we have followed with such labour and pride does not fit the occasion; and then there's nothing for us to do but rely on something within us, some innate capacity for knowing and doing, which we did not know we possessed until the hour of our great need brought it to light.

2   I had a good, frank talk with Mrs. Keller, and explained to her how difficult it was going to be to do anything with Helen under the existing circumstances. I told her that in my opinion the child ought to be separated from the family for a few weeks at least—that she must learn to depend on and obey me before I could make any headway. After a long time Mrs. Keller said that she would think the matter over and see what Captain Keller thought of sending Helen away with me. Captain Keller fell in with the scheme most readily and suggested that the little garden-house at the "old place" be got ready for us. He said that Helen might recognize the place, as she had often been there; but she would have no idea of her surroundings, and they could come every day to see that all was going well, with the understanding, of course, that she was to know nothing of their visits. I hurried the preparations for our departure as much as possible, and here we are.

3   The little house is a genuine bit of paradise. It consists of one large square room with a great fireplace, a spacious bay-window, and a small room where our servant, a little negro boy, sleeps. There is a piazza in front, covered with vines that grow so luxuriantly that you have to part them to see the garden beyond. Our meals are brought from the house, and we usually eat on the piazza. The little negro boy takes care of the fire when we need one; so I can give my whole attention to Helen.

4   She was greatly excited at first, and kicked and screamed herself into a sort of stupor; but when supper was brought she ate heartily and seemed brighter, although she refused to let me touch her. She devoted herself to her dolls the first evening, and when it was bedtime she undressed very quietly; but when she felt me get into bed with her, she jumped out on the other side, and nothing that I could do would induce her to get in again. But I was afraid she would take cold, and I insisted that she must go to bed. We had a terrific tussle, I can tell you. The struggle lasted for nearly two hours. I never saw such strength and endurance in a child. But fortunately for us both, I am a little stronger, and quite as obstinate when I set out. I finally succeeded in getting her on the bed and covered her up, and she lay curled up as near the edge of the bed as possible.

5   The next morning she was very docile, but evidently homesick. She kept going to the door, as if she expected some one, and every now and then she would touch her cheek, which is her sign for her mother, and shake her head sadly. She played with her dolls more than usual, and would have nothing to do with me. It is amusing and pathetic to see Helen with her dolls. I don't think she has any special tenderness for them—I have never seen her caress them; but she dresses and undresses them many times during the day and handles them exactly as she has seen her mother and the nurse handle her baby sister.

6   This morning Nancy, her favourite doll, seemed to have some difficulty about swallowing the milk that was being administered to her in large spoonfuls; for Helen suddenly put down the cup and began to slap her on the back and turn her over on her knees, trotting her gently and patting her softly all the time. This lasted for several minutes; then this mood passed, and Nancy was thrown ruthlessly on the floor and pushed to one side, while a large, pink-cheeked, fuzzy-haired member of the family received the little mother's undivided attention.

7   Helen knows several words now, but has no idea how to use them, or that

everything has a name. I think, however, she will learn quickly enough by and by. As I have said before, she is wonderfully bright and active and as quick as lightning in her movements.

March 20, 1887. My heart is singing for joy this morning. A miracle has 8 happened! The light of understanding has shone upon my little pupil's mind, and behold, all things are changed!

The wild little creature of two weeks ago has been transformed into a gentle 9 child. She is sitting by me as I write, her face serene and happy, crocheting a long red chain of Scotch wool. She learned the stitch this week, and is very proud of the achievement. When she succeeded in making a chain that would reach across the room, she patted herself on the arm and put the first work of her hands lovingly against her cheek. She lets me kiss her now, and when she is in a particularly gentle mood, she will sit in my lap for a minute or two; but she does not return my caresses. The great step—the step that counts—has been taken. The little savage has learned her first lesson in obedience, and finds the yoke easy. It now remains my pleasant task to direct and mould the beautiful intelligence that is beginning to stir in the child-soul. Already people remark the change in Helen. Her father looks in at us morning and evening as he goes to and from his office, and sees her contentedly stringing her beads or making horizontal lines on her sewing-card, and exclaims, "How quiet she is!" When I came, her movements were so insistent that one always felt there was something unnatural and almost weird about her. I have noticed also that she eats much less, a fact which troubles her father so much that he is anxious to get her home. He says she is homesick. I don't agree with him; but I suppose we shall have to leave our little bower very soon.

Helen has learned several nouns this week. "M-u-g" and "m-i-l-k," have given 10 her more trouble than other words. When she spells "milk," she points to the mug, and when she spells "mug," she makes the sign for pouring or drinking, which shows that she has confused the words. She has no idea yet that everything has a name.

Yesterday I had the little negro boy come in when Helen was having her 11 lesson, and learn the letters, too. This pleased her very much and stimulated her ambition to excel Percy. She was delighted if he made a mistake, and made him form the letter over several times. When he succeeded in forming it to suit her, she patted him on his woolly head so vigorously that I thought some of his slips were intentional.

One day this week Captain Keller brought Belle, a setter of which he is very 12 proud, to see us. He wondered if Helen would recognize her old playmate. Helen was giving Nancy a bath, and didn't notice the dog at first. She usually feels the softest step and throws out her arms to ascertain if any one is near her. Belle didn't seem very anxious to attract her attention. I imagine she has been rather roughly handled sometimes by her little mistress. The dog hadn't been in the room more than half a minute, however, before Helen began to sniff, and dumped the doll into the wash-bowl and felt about the room. She stumbled upon Belle, who was crouching near the window where Captain Keller was standing. It was evident that she recognized the dog; for she put her arms round her neck and squeezed her. Then Helen sat down by her and began to manipulate her claws. We couldn't think for a second what she was doing; but when we saw her make the letters "d-o-l-l" on her own fingers, we knew that she was trying to teach Belle to spell.

Vocabulary

tenaciously, vassals, approbation, innate, stupor, bower

Questions

1. Do you think Anne Sullivan's decision to separate Helen from the family represented an unnatural interference in the child's life?
2. Is it cruel to call Helen "a little savage"?
3. Must obedience precede learning? Doesn't this method sound like one you might use to train a young dog?
4. What is the "light of understanding" which Anne calls a miracle?
5. There is still a link missing at this stage of Helen's education. Can you find it?

Topics for Writing

Obedience: The First Step?
The Harm That Parents Do

The Last Square and Cambronne

VICTOR HUGO (1802–1885), the French writer, includes many items of history and philosophic observation in his massive novel *Les Miserables*. Here he describes a touching and noble incident that occurred as the Duke of Wellington's assembled forces were destroying the last of Napoleon's Grand Army at the Battle of Waterloo. Cambronne's defiant cry is, for Hugo, a sign of man's unconquerable will—a major theme of *Les Miserables*. The names of places and generals sprinkled through this narrative are real, of course, but they are also part of the mythic scene Hugo creates. To footnote them would be pedantic.

A few squares of the guard, standing motionless in the swash of the rout, like rocks in running water, held out till night. They awaited the double shadow of night and death, and let them surround them. Each regiment, isolated from the others, and no longer connected with the army which was broken on all sides, died where it stood. In order to perform this last exploit, they had taken up a position, some on the heights of Rossomme, others on the plain of Mont St. Jean. The gloomy squares, deserted, conquered, and terrible, struggled formidably with death, for Ulm, Wagram, Jena, and Friedland were dying in it.

When twilight set in at nine in the evening, one square still remained at the foot of the plateau of Mont St. Jean. In this mournful valley, at the foot of the slope scaled by the cuirassiers, now inundated by the English masses, beneath the converging fire of the hostile and victorious artillery, under fearful hailstorm of projectiles, this square still resisted. It was commanded by an obscure officer of the name of Cambronne. At each volley the square diminished, but continued to reply to the canister with musketry fire, and each moment contracted its four walls. Fugitives in the distance, stopping at moments to draw breath, listened in the darkness to this gloomy diminishing thunder.

When this legion had become only a handful, when their colors were but a rag, when their ammunition was exhausted and muskets were clubbed, and when the pile of corpses was greater than the living group, the victors felt a species of sacred awe, and the English artillery ceased firing. It was a sort of respite; these combatants had around them an army of specters, outlines of mounted men, the black profile of guns, and the white sky visible through the wheels; the colossal death's-head, which heroes ever glimpse in the smoke of a battle, advanced and looked at them. They could hear in the twilight gloom that the guns were being loaded; the lighted matches, resembling the eyes of a tiger in the night, formed a circle round their heads. The linstocks of the English batteries approached the guns, and at this moment an English general, Colville according to some, Maitland according to others, holding the supreme moment suspended over the heads of these men, shouted to them, "Brave Frenchmen, surrender!"

4   Cambronne answered: "*Merde.*"

5   As the French reader desires to be respected, the most sublime word ever uttered by any Frenchman cannot be repeated. "Post no sublimity on history."

6   At our own risk and peril we will defy this notice.

7   Among these giants, then, there was a Titan, Cambronne.

8   To utter this word and then die, what could be more grand! To die is to be willing to die, and it is not the fault of this man, if, mowed down by grape-shot, he survived.

9   The man who gained the battle of Waterloo was not Napoleon with his routed army; it was not Wellington, giving way at four o'clock, and desperate at five; it was not Blücher, for he had not fought,—the man who won the battle of Waterloo is Cambronne.

10   To smite with the lightning of such a word the thunderbolt which kills you is to be victorious.

11   To make such a reply to disaster, to say this to destiny, to lay such a base for the future lion, to hurl this answer to the rain of the night, to the treacherous wall of Hougomont, to the Hollow Road of Ohain, to the delay of Grouchy, to the arrival of Blücher, to be irony in the tomb, to stand erect, as it were, after one shall have fallen to submerge in two syllables the European coalition, to present to kings the latrines already known by the Caesars, to make the last words the first, by imparting to it the brilliancy of France, to insultingly close Waterloo by Shrove Tuesday repartee, to complete Leonidas by Rabelais, to sum up this victory in one supreme word, impossible to pronounce, to lose ground and preserve history, after such a carnage to have the laughers on your side,—this is immense.

12   It is to defy the lightning with Aeschylean grandeur.

13   The utterance of Cambronne has the effect of a breakage. It is the breaking of the bosom by disdain, it is the excess of the agony which makes the explosion. Who conquered? Wellington? No. Without Blücher he had been lost. Is it Blücher? No. If Wellington had not begun, Blücher could not have finished. This Cambronne, this passer-by at the last hour, this unknown soldier, this infinitely little bit of the war, feels that there is a lie beneath the catastrophe doubly bitter; and at the instant when he is bursting with rage they offer him that absurdity—life! How could he refrain from breaking out? There they are, all the kings of Europe, the lucky generals, the thundering Joves; they have one hundred thousand victorious soldiers; behind them, a hundred thousand, a million; their cannon, with matches lighted, are gaping; they have under their heels the Imperial guard and the Grand army; they have crushed Napoleon, Cambronne only remains,—only this earth-worm is left to protest, and he will protest. He looked for a word as he would for a sword. Foam is on his lips, and this foam is the word. In presence of this victory, prodigious yet commonplace, of this victory without victors, the desperate man erects himself; he submits to its magnitude, but he demonstrates its nothingness; he does more than spit on it, and under the crushing load of numbers, force, and material he finds for his soul one sole term—*excrement*. We repeat it, to say this, to do this, to invent this, is to be the victor.

At this fated moment the spirit of the great days entered this unknown man.   14
Cambronne found the word of Waterloo as Rouget de l'Isle found the *Marseillaise*
by an inspiration from on high. A breath of the divine hurricane passed over these
men, and they shuddered; one sings the supreme song, the other utters the fearful
cry. This word, full of Titanic scorn, was hurled by Cambronne not only at Europe
in the name of the Empire,—that would have been little,—but at the past in the
name of the Revolution. We hear and see in Cambronne the old soul of the giants;
it seems as if Danton were speaking or Kleber roaring.

To Cambronne's exclamation, an English voice replied, "Fire!" The batteries   15
flashed, the hillside trembled, from all these throats of brass came a last eruption of
grape, a vast cloud of smoke vaguely whitened by the rising moon rolled up, and
when the smoke had been dissipated there was nothing. The dreaded remnant was
annihilated, the guard was dead. The four walls of the living redoubt lay low, with
here and there a scarcely perceptible quiver among the corpses. Thus the French
legions, grander than those of Rome, expired at Mont St. Jean, on the earth sodden
with rain and blood, in the gloomy corn-fields at the spot where now at four o'clock
in the morning Joseph, the driver of the mail-cart from Nivelles, passes, whistling
and gayly whipping up his horse.

Vocabulary

cuirassiers, inundated, canister, respite, linstocks, grape-shot, Titan, Shrove
Tuesday, repartee, Aeschylean, redoubt

Questions

1. Hugo writes several one-sentence paragraphs. Are they effective?
2. This passage is full of high-flown rhetoric, of exaggeration and bombast. Is this
   tone too overwhelming for Cambronne's single word?
3. In what sense can a vulgarism be called "the most sublime word ever uttered
   by any Frenchman"?
4. Do you approve Hugo's definition of *victorious*?
5. What is "Shrove Tuesday repartee"?
6. Is it inappropriate for Hugo to close this chapter with Joseph, the mailman,
   passing the historic spot so gaily?

Topics for Writing

A Definition of *Victory*

The Brave Never Lose

The Lesson of Cambronne

Everest Conquered

EDMUND HILLARY (1919–), the New Zealand mountain climber, published this account of his famous ascent of Mt. Everest in *High Adventure* (1955). Although only he and Tenzing Norgay, his Nepalese companion, made the final assault on the peak, the efforts of a team of many men brought them to the point at which the narrative is picked up here.

1   I was greatly encouraged to find how, even at 28,700 feet and with no oxygen, I could work out slowly but clearly the problems of mental arithmetic that the oxygen supply demanded. A correct answer was imperative—any mistake could well mean a trip with no return. But we had no time to waste. I stood up and took a series of photographs in every direction, then thrust my camera back to its warm home inside my clothing. I heaved my now pleasantly light oxygen load on to my back and connected up my tubes. I did the same for Tenzing, and we were ready to go. I asked Tenzing to belay me and then, with a growing air of excitement, I cut a broad and safe line of steps down to the snow saddle below the South Summit. I wanted an easy route when we came back up here weak and tired. Tenzing came down the steps and joined me, and then belayed once again.

2   I moved along on to the steep snow slope on the left side of the ridge. With the first blow of my ice-axe my excitement increased. The snow—to my astonishment—was crystalline and hard. A couple of rhythmical blows of the ice-axe produced a step that was big enough even for our oversize high-altitude boots. But best of all the steps were strong and safe. A little conscious of the great drops beneath me, I chipped a line of steps for the full length of the rope—forty feet—and then forced the shaft of my ice-axe firmly into the snow. It made a fine belay and I looped the rope around it. I waved to Tenzing to join me, and as he moved slowly and carefully along the steps I took in the rope. When he reached me, he thrust his ice-axe into the snow and protected me with a good tight rope as I went on cutting steps. It was exhilarating work—the summit ridge of Everest, the crisp snow and the smooth easy blows of the ice-axe all combined to make me feel a greater sense of power than I had ever felt at great altitudes before. I went on cutting for rope length after rope length.

3   We were now approaching a point where one of the great cornices was encroaching on to our slope. We'd have to go down to the rocks to avoid it. I cut a line of steps steeply down the slope to a small ledge on top of the rocks. There wasn't much room, but it made a reasonably safe stance. I waved to Tenzing to join me. As he came down to me I realised there was something wrong with him. I had been so absorbed in the technical problems of the ridge that I hadn't thought much about Tenzing, except for a vague feeling that he seemed to move along the steps with unnecessary slowness. But now it was quite obvious that he was not only moving extremely slowly, but he was breathing quickly and with difficulty and was in

considerable distress. I immediately suspected his oxygen set and helped him down on to the ledge so that I could examine it. The first thing I noticed was that from the outlet of his face-mask there were hanging some long icicles. I looked at it more closely and found that the outlet tube—about two inches in diameter—was almost completely blocked up with ice. This was preventing Tenzing from exhaling freely and must have made it extremely unpleasant for him. Fortunately the outlet tube was made of rubber and by manipulating this with my hand I was able to release all the ice and let it fall out. The valves started operating and Tenzing was given immediate relief. Just as a check I examined my own set and found that it, too, had partly frozen up in the outlet tube, but not sufficiently to have affected me a great deal. I removed the ice out of it without a great deal of trouble. Automatically I looked at our pressure gauges—just over 2,900 pounds (2,900 pounds was just over 700 litres; 180 into 700 was about 4)—we had nearly four hours' endurance left. That meant we weren't going badly.

I looked at the route ahead. This next piece wasn't going to be easy. Our rock ledge was perched right on top of the enormous bluff running down into the Western Cwm. In fact, almost under my feet, I could see the dirty patch on the floor of the Cwm which I knew was Camp IV. In a sudden urge to escape our isolation I waved and shouted, and then as suddenly stopped as I realised my foolishness. Against the vast expanse of Everest, 8,000 feet above them, we'd be quite invisible to the best binoculars. I turned back to the problem ahead. The rock was far too steep to attempt to drop down and go around this pitch. The only thing to do was to try to shuffle along the ledge and cut handholds in the bulging ice that was trying to push me off it. Held on a tight rope by Tenzing, I cut a few handholds and then thrust my ice-axe as hard as I could into the solid snow and ice. Using this to take my weight I moved quickly along the ledge. It proved easier than I had anticipated. A few more handholds, another quick swing across them, and I was able to cut a line of steps up on to a safe slope and chop out a roomy terrace from which to belay Tenzing as he climbed up to me.

We were now fast approaching the most formidable obstacle on the ridge—a great rock step. This step had always been visible in aerial photographs, and in 1951 on the Everest Reconnaissance we had seen it quite clearly with glasses from Thyangboche. We had always thought of it as the obstacle on the ridge which could well spell defeat. I cut a line of steps across the last snow slope, and then commenced traversing over a steep rock slab that led to the foot of the great step. The holds were small and hard to see, and I brushed my snow-glasses away from my eyes. Immediately I was blinded by a bitter wind sweeping across the ridge and laden with particles of ice. I hastily replaced my glasses and blinked away the ice and tears until I could see again. But it made me realise how efficient was our clothing in protecting us from the rigours of even a fine day at 29,000 feet. Still half blinded, I climbed across the slab, and then dropped down into a tiny snow hollow at the foot of the step. And here Tenzing joined me.

I looked anxiously up at the rocks. Planted squarely across the ridge in a vertical bluff, they looked extremely difficult, and I knew that our strength and ability to climb steep rock at this altitude would be severely limited. I examined the route out to the left. By dropping fifty or a hundred feet over steep slabs, we might be able to get around the bottom of the bluff, but there was no indication that we'd be able to climb back on to the ridge again. And to lose any height now might be fatal. Search as I would, I was unable to see an easy route up to the step or, in fact, any route at all. Finally, in desperation I examined the right-hand end of the bluff. Attached to this and overhanging the precipitous East face was a large cornice. This cornice, in preparation for its inevitable crash down the mountainside, had started to lose its grip on the rock and a long narrow vertical crack had been formed between the rock and the ice. The crack was large enough to take the human frame, and though it offered little security, it was at least a route. I quickly made up my mind—Tenzing had an excellent belay and we must be near the top—it was worth a try.

7   Before attempting the pitch, I produced my camera once again. I had no confidence that I would be able to climb this crack, and with a surge of competitive pride which unfortunately afflicts even mountaineers, I determined to have proof that at least we had reached a good deal higher than the South Summit. I took a few photographs and then made another rapid check of the oxygen—2,550 pounds pressure. (2,550 from 3,300 leaves 750; 750 over 3,300 is about two-ninths. Two-ninths off 800 litres leaves about 600 litres; 600 divided by 180 is nearly $3\frac{1}{2}$.) Three and a half hours to go. I examined Tenzing's belay to make sure it was a good one and then slowly crawled inside the crack.

8   In front of me was the rock wall, vertical but with a few promising holds. Behind me was the ice-wall of the cornice, glittering and hard but cracked here and there. I took a hold on the rock in front and then jammed one of my crampons hard into the ice behind. Leaning back with my oxygen set on the ice, I slowly levered myself upwards. Searching feverishly with my spare boot, I found a tiny ledge on the rock and took some of the weight off my other leg. Leaning back on the cornice, I fought to regain my breath. Constantly at the back of my mind was the fear that the cornice might break off, and my nerves were taut with suspense. But slowly I forced my way up—wriggling and jambing and using every little hold. In one place I managed to force my ice-axe into a crack in the ice, and this gave me the necessary purchase to get over a holdless stretch. And then I found a solid foothold in a hollow in the ice, and next moment I was reaching over the top of the rock and pulling myself to safety. The rope came tight—its forty feet had been barely enough.

9   I lay on the little rock ledge panting furiously. Gradually it dawned on me that I was up the step, and I felt a glow of pride and determination that completely subdued my temporary feelings of weakness. For the first time on the whole expedition I really knew I was going to get to the top. "It will have to be pretty tough to stop us now" was my thought. But I couldn't entirely ignore the feeling of astonishment and wonder that I'd been able to get up such a difficulty at 29,000 feet even with oxygen.

10   When I was breathing more evenly I stood up and, leaning over the edge, waved to Tenzing to come up. He moved into the crack and I gathered in the rope and took some of his weight. Then he, in turn, commenced to struggle and jam and force his way up until I was able to pull him to safety—gasping for breath. We

rested for a moment. Above us the ridge continued on as before—enormous over-hanging cornices on the right and steep snow slopes on the left running down to the rock bluffs. But the angle of the snow slopes was easing off. I went on chipping a line of steps, but thought it safe enough for us to move together in order to save time. The ridge rose up in a great series of snakelike undulations which bore away to the right, each one concealing the next. I had no idea where the top was. I'd cut a line of steps around the side of one undulation and another would come into view. We were getting desperately tired now and Tenzing was going very slowly. I'd been cutting steps for almost two hours, and my back and arms were starting to tire. I tried cramponing along the slope without cutting steps, but my feet slipped uncomfortably down the slope. I went on cutting. We seemed to have been going for a very long time and my confidence was fast evaporating. Bump followed bump with maddening regularity. A patch of shingle barred our way, and I climbed dully up it and started cutting steps around another bump. And then I realised that this was the last bump, for ahead of me the ridge dropped steeply away in a great corniced curve, and out in the distance I could see the pastel shades and fleecy clouds of the highlands of Tibet.

To my right a slender snow ridge climbed up to a snowy dome about forty feet 11 above our heads. But all the way along the ridge the thought had haunted me that the summit might be the crest of a cornice. It was too late to take risks now. I asked Tenzing to belay me strongly, and I started cutting a cautious line of steps up the ridge. Peering from side to side and thrusting with my ice-axe, I tried to discover a possible cornice, but everything seemed solid and firm. I waved Tenzing up to me. A few more whacks of the ice-axe, a few very weary steps, and we were on the summit of Everest.

Vocabulary

belay, crystalline, cornices, Cwm., traversing, crampons, undulations, shingle

Questions

1. Hillary presents many details—"I heaved my . . . oxygen load on to my back," "I waved to Tenzing," "I looked at it more closely," and so on—in this step-by-step account. Yet few readers are bored. Why not?
2. At what point is Hillary sure he will succeed? Does Hillary treat Tenzing like a true partner or a reliable servant? (Look to the last sentence for a possible clue.)
3. Do you "feel" Hillary's triumphant weariness at the close?

Topics for Writing

Why Men Climb Mountains
Tenzing Norgay, Unsung Hero?

Finding the Tomb

HOWARD CARTER (1873–1939), English archeologist, led the search for Tutankhamen's tomb. His scientific planning, combined with a little luck, resulted in the triumph recorded here. But Lord Carnarvon, an amateur Egyptologist himself, financed the dig—which is why Carter, with proper British reserve, delayed opening the sealed door.

1   The history of the Valley, as I have endeavoured to show in former chapters, has never lacked the dramatic element, and in this, the latest episode, it has held to its traditions. For consider the circumstances. This was to be our final season in the Valley. Six full seasons we had excavated there, and season after season had drawn a blank; we had worked for months at a stretch and found nothing, and only an excavator knows how desperately depressing that can be; we had almost made up our minds that we were beaten, and were preparing to leave the Valley and try our luck elsewhere; and then—hardly had we set hoe to ground in our last despairing effort than we made a discovery that far exceeded our wildest dreams. Surely, never before in the whole history of excavation has a full digging season been compressed within the space of five days.

2   Let me try and tell the story of it all. It will not be easy, for the dramatic suddenness of the initial discovery left me in a dazed condition, and the months that have followed have been so crowded with incident that I have hardly had time to think. Setting it down on paper will perhaps give me a chance to realize what has happened and all that it means.

3   I arrived in Luxor on 28 October, and by 1 November I had enrolled my workmen and was ready to begin. Our former excavations had stopped short at the north-east corner of the tomb of Rameses VI, and from this point I started trenching southwards. It will be remembered that in this area there were a number of roughly constructed workmen's huts, used probably by the labourers in the tomb of Rameses. These huts, built about three feet above bed-rock, covered the whole area in front of the Ramesside tomb, and continued in a southerly direction to join up with a similar group of huts on the opposite side of the Valley, discovered by Davis in connexion with his work on the Akhenaten cache. By the evening of 3 November we had laid bare a sufficient number of these huts for experimental purposes, so, after we had planned and noted them, they were removed, and we were ready to clear away the three feet of soil that lay beneath them.

4   Hardly had I arrived on the work next morning (4 November) than the unusual silence, due to the stoppage of the work, made me realize that something out of the ordinary had happened, and I was greeted by the announcement that a step cut in the rock had been discovered underneath the very first hut to be attacked. This seemed too good to be true, but a short amount of extra clearing revealed the fact

that we were actually in the entrance of a steep cut in the rock, some thirteen feet below the entrance to the tomb of Rameses VI, and a similar depth from the present bed level of the Valley. The manner of cutting was that of the sunken stairway entrance so common in the Valley, and I almost dared to hope that we had found our tomb at last. Work continued feverishly throughout the whole of that day and the morning of the next, but it was not until the afternoon of 5 November that we succeeded in clearing away the masses of rubbish that overlay the cut, and were able to demarcate the upper edges of the stairway on all its four sides.

It was clear by now beyond any question that we actually had before us the entrance to a tomb, but doubts, born of previous disappointments, persisted in creeping in. There was always the horrible possibility, suggested by our experience in the Thothmes III Valley, that the tomb was an unfinished one, never completed and never used: if it had been finished there was the depressing probability that it had been completely plundered in ancient times. On the other hand, there was just the chance of an untouched or only partially plundered tomb, and it was with ill-suppressed excitement that I watched the descending steps of the staircase, as one by one they came to light. The cutting was excavated in the side of a small hillock, and, as the work progressed, its western edge receded under the slope of the rock until it was, first partially, and then completely, roofed in, and became a passage, ten feet high by six feet wide. Work progressed more rapidly now; step succeeded step, and at the level of the twelfth, towards sunset, there was disclosed the upper part of a doorway, blocked, plastered, and sealed.

A sealed doorway—it was actually true, then! Our years of patient labour were to be rewarded after all, and I think my first feeling was one of congratulation that my faith in the Valley had not been unjustified. With excitement growing to fever heat I searched the seal impressions on the door for evidence of the identity of the owner, but could find no name: the only decipherable ones were those of the well-known royal necropolis seal, the jackal and nine captives. Two facts, however, were clear: first, the employment of this royal seal was certain evidence that the tomb had been constructed for a person of very high standing; and second, that the sealed door was entirely screened from above by workmen's huts of the Twentieth Dynasty was sufficiently clear proof that at least from that date it had never been entered. With that for the moment I had to be content.

While examining the seals I noticed, at the top of the doorway, where some of the plaster had fallen away, a heavy wooden lintel. Under this, to assure myself of the method by which the doorway had been blocked, I made a small peephole, just large enough to insert an electric torch, and discovered that the passage beyond the door was filled completely from floor to ceiling with stones and rubble—additional proof this of the care with which the tomb had been protected.

It was a thrilling moment for an excavator. Alone, save for my native work-men, I found myself, after years of comparatively unproductive labour, on the threshold of what might prove to be a magnificent discovery. Anything, literally anything, might lie beyond that passage, and it needed all my self-control to keep from breaking down the doorway, and investigating then and there.

One thing puzzled me, and that was the smallness of the opening in comparison with the ordinary Valley tombs. The design was certainly of the Eighteenth Dynasty. Could it be the tomb of a noble buried here by royal consent? Was it a royal cache, a hiding-place to which a mummy and its equipment had been removed for safety? Or was it actually the tomb of the king for whom I had spent so many years in search?

10   Once more I examined the seal impressions for a clue, but on the part of the door so far laid bare only those of the royal necropolis seal already mentioned were clear enough to read. Had I but known that a few inches lower down there was a perfectly clear and distinct impression of the seal of Tutankhamen, the king I most desired to find, I would have cleared on, had a much better night's rest in consequence, and saved myself nearly three weeks of uncertainty. It was late, however, and darkness was already upon us. With some reluctance I re-closed the small hole that I had made, filled in our excavation for protection during the night, selected the most trustworthy of my workmen—themselves almost as excited as I was—to watch all night above the tomb, and so home by moonlight, riding down the Valley.

11   Naturally my wish was to go straight ahead with our clearing to find out the full extent of the discovery, but Lord Carnarvon was in England, and in fairness to him I had to delay matters until he could come. Accordingly, on the morning of 6 November I sent him the following cable: "At last have made wonderful discovery in Valley; a magnificent tomb with seals intact; re-covered same for your arrival; congratulations."

12   My next task was to secure the doorway against interference until such time as it could finally be reopened. This we did by filling our excavation up again to surface level, and rolling on top of it the large flint boulders of which the workmen's huts had been composed. By the evening of the same day, exactly forty-eight hours after we had discovered the first step of the staircase, this was accomplished. The tomb had vanished. So far as the appearance of the ground was concerned there never had been any tomb, and I found it hard to persuade myself at times that the whole episode had not been a dream.

13   I was soon to be reassured on this point. News travels fast in Egypt, and within two days of the discovery congratulations, inquiries, and offers of help descended upon me in a steady stream from all directions. It became clear, even at this early stage, that I was in for a job that could not be tackled single-handed, so I wired to Callender, who had helped me on various previous occasions, asking him if possible to join me without delay, and to my relief he arrived on the very next day. On the 8th I had received two messages from Lord Carnarvon in answer to my cable, the first of which read, "Possibly come soon," and the second, received a little later, "Propose arrive Alexandria 20th."

14   We had thus nearly a fortnight's grace, and we devoted it to making preparations of various kinds, so that when the time of reopening came, we should be able, with the least possible delay, to handle any situation that might arise. On the night of the 18th I went to Cairo for three days, to meet Lord Carnarvon and make a number of necessary purchases, returning to Luxor on the 21st. On the 23rd Lord Carnarvon arrived in Luxor with his daughter, Lady Evelyn Herbert, his devoted

companion in all his Egyptian work, and everything was in hand for the beginning of the second chapter of the discovery of the tomb. Callender had been busy all day clearing away the upper layer of rubbish, so that by morning we should be able to get into the staircase without any delay.

By the afternoon of the 24th the whole staircase was clear, sixteen steps in all, and we were able to make a proper examination of the sealed doorway. On the lower part the seal impressions were much clearer, and we were able without any difficulty to make out on several of them the name of Tutankhamen. This added enormously to the interest of the discovery. If we had found, as seemed almost certain, the tomb of that shadowy monarch, whose tenure of the throne coincided with one of the most interesting periods in the whole of Egyptian history, we should indeed have reason to congratulate ourselves.

With heightened interest, if that were possible, we renewed our investigation of the doorway. Here for the first time a disquieting element made its appearance. Now that the whole door was exposed to light it was possible to discern a fact that had hitherto escaped notice—that there had been two successive openings and re-closings of a part of its surface: furthermore, that the sealing originally discovered, the jackal and nine captives, had been applied to the re-closed portions, whereas the sealings of Tutankhamen covered the untouched part of the doorway, and were therefore those with which the tomb had been originally secured. The tomb then was not absolutely intact, as we had hoped. Plunderers had entered it, and entered it more than once—from the evidence of the huts above, plunderers of a date not later than the reign of Rameses VI—but that they had not rifled it completely was evident from the fact that it had been re-sealed.

Then came another puzzle. In the lower strata of rubbish that filled the staircase we found masses of broken potsherds and boxes, the latter bearing the names of Akhenaten, Smenkhkare and Tutankhamen, and, what was much more upsetting, a scarab of Thothmes III and a fragment with the name of Amenhetep III. Why this mixture of names? The balance of evidence so far would seem to indicate a cache rather than a tomb, and at this stage in the proceedings we inclined more and more to the opinion that we were about to find a miscellaneous collection of objects of the Eighteenth Dynasty kings, brought from Tell el Amarna by Tutankhamen and deposited here for safety.

So matters stood on the evening of the 24th. On the following day the sealed doorway was to be removed, so Callender set carpenters to work making a heavy wooden grille to be set up in its place. Mr. Engelbach, Chief Inspector of the Antiquities Department, paid us a visit during the afternoon, and witnessed part of the final clearing of rubbish from the doorway.

On the morning of the 25th the seal impressions on the doorway were carefully noted and photographed, and then we removed the actual blocking of the door, consisting of rough stones carefully built from floor to lintel, and heavily plastered on their outer faces to take the seal impressions.

This disclosed the beginning of a descending passage (not a staircase), the same width as the entrance stairway, and nearly seven feet high. As I had already discovered from my hole in the doorway, it was filled completely with stone and rubble, probably the chip from its own excavation. This filling, like the doorway, showed distinct signs of more than one opening and re-closing of the tomb, the untouched part consisting of clean white chip, mingled with dust, whereas the disturbed part was composed mainly of dark flint. It was clear that an irregular tunnel had been cut through the original filling at the upper corner on the left side, a tunnel corresponding in position with that of the hole in the doorway.

21   As we cleared the passage we found, mixed with the rubble of the lower levels, broken potsherds, jar sealings, alabaster jars, whole and broken, vases of painted pottery, numerous fragments of smaller articles, and water skins, these last having obviously been used to bring up the water needed for the plastering of the doorways. These were clear evidence of plundering, and we eyed them askance. By night we had cleared a considerable distance down the passage, but as yet saw no sign of second doorway or of chamber.

22   The day following (26 November) was the day of days, the most wonderful that I have ever lived through, and certainly one whose like I can never hope to see again. Throughout the morning the work of clearing continued, slowly perforce, on account of the delicate objects that were mixed with the filling. Then, in the middle of the afternoon, thirty feet down from the outer door, we came upon a second sealed doorway, almost an exact replica of the first. The seal impressions in this case were less distinct, but still recognizable as those of Tutankhamen and of the royal necropolis. Here again the signs of opening and re-closing were clearly marked upon the plaster. We were firmly convinced by this time that it was a cache that we were about to open, and not a tomb. The arrangement of stairway, entrance passage and doors reminded us very forcibly of the cache of Akhenaten and Tyi material found in the very near vicinity of the present excavation by Davis, and the fact that Tutankhamen's seals occurred there likewise seemed almost certain proof that we were right in our conjecture. We were soon to know. There lay the sealed doorway, and behind it was the answer to the question.

23   Slowly, desperately slowly it seemed to us as we watched, the remains of passage debris that encumbered the lower part of the doorway were removed, until at last we had the whole door clear before us. The decisive moment had arrived. With trembling hands I made a tiny breach in the upper left-hand corner. Darkness and blank space, as far as an iron testing-rod could reach, showed that whatever lay beyond was empty, and not filled like the passage we had just cleared. Candle tests were applied as a precaution against possible foul gases, and then, widening the hole a little, I inserted the candle and peered in, Lord Carnarvon, Lady Evelyn and Callender standing anxiously beside me to hear the verdict. At first I could see nothing, the hot air escaping from the chamber causing the candle flame to flicker, but presently, as my eyes grew accustomed to the light, details of the room within emerged slowly from the mist, strange animals, statues, and gold—everywhere the glint of gold. For the moment—an eternity it must have seemed to the others standing by—I was struck dumb with amazement, and when Lord Carnarvon, unable to stand the suspense any longer, inquired anxiously, "Can you see anything?" it was all I could do to get out the words, "Yes, wonderful things." Then, widening the hole a little further, so that we both could see, we inserted an electric torch.

Vocabulary

cache, necropolis, jackal, lintel, potsherds, askance

Questions

1. Carter was not a writer by profession, but he has an exciting story to tell, and he wants to share the excitement. Can you find any signs that he enjoys keeping his reader in suspense?
2. Are you able to picture the area in which Carter's work force began its trenching?
3. Is he able to give you the sense of archeological work? Which details help you to appreciate it?
4. Why didn't Carter open the sealed door at once? What does this tell you about his relationship with Lord Carnarvon?
5. Are you disappointed in his three-word answer to Lord Carnarvon's anxious question?

Topics for Writing

Carter's Delay: A Study in Good Manners

Carter's Delay: A Study in Will-Power

What Hillary and Carter Had in Common

On First Looking into Chapman's Homer

JOHN KEATS (1795–1821), the English poet, knew no Greek and so could not "enter" the world of Homer until his friend and former schoolmaster, Charles Cowden Clarke, introduced him to a translation of Homer made by George Chapman in Shakespeare's time. The discovery of this new "realm of gold" resulted in this famous sonnet, which Keats sent the next morning to his tutor.

> Much have I travell'd in the realms of gold,
> And many goodly states and kingdoms seen;
> Round many western islands have I been
> Which bards in fealty to Apollo hold.
5> Oft of one wide expanse had I been told
> That deep-brow'd Homer ruled as his demesne;
> Yet did I never breathe its pure serene
> Till I heard Chapman speak out loud and bold;
> Then felt I like some watcher of the skies
10> When a new planet swims into his ken;
> Or like stout Cortez when with eagle eyes
> He star'd at the Pacific—and all his men
> Look'd at each other with a wild surmise—
> Silent, upon a peak in Darien.

Vocabulary

bards, fealty, demesne, serene, ken

Questions

1. What does "deep-brow'd" suggest to you?
2. Are the analogies in lines 9–14 appropriate?
3. It is often noted that, in the last four lines, Keats had his discoverer and his geography wrong. Do his errors damage the poem?

Topics for Writing

Reading as an Adventure

Keats's Ignorance: Trivial or Important?

An Analysis of Keats's Analogies

PART III
Narration

All narration is by its nature storytelling, the telling of a sequence of events, each developing out of the last and all leading toward a concluding event. Some narratives are factual, some fictional, some mixed. In any case, the narrator is more intent on representation of the story than on explanation of it. In this essential respect, narration differs from exposition.

In most narratives, there are characters (sometimes the author among them) and causally connected incidents leading to a specific point. The writer works to see that we will be concerned with what happens to him or her or to the characters, that the chain of events will engage our curiosity to follow where they lead, and that the point to which they lead is worth the journey.

Many subsidiary skills are useful in narrative writing, especially narrative of the more complex sorts. Sequencing events and working out causal relationships call upon analytic skills. Creating a setting—fixing time, place, and ambiance—calls upon descriptive powers, as does the portrayal of the characters who act out the story. Dialogue—the faithful reporting or inventing of verbal exchanges—is often needed to forward the story line or to give reality to character. (It is better to put a witty sentence into the mouth of John Protagonist than to tell the readers, "John is a witty man"). And the author must decide on the point of view to be employed. Will it be the first-person method, i.e., telling the story as though it happened to the author ("There I was, at 30,000 feet, when the motor fell off . . .") or the third-person ("Flying at 30,000 feet, John Protagonist watched in dismay as his motor fell off . . .")? Both methods—and a good many variations of them—work when the writer makes an intelligent choice.

These skills come into play whether we are telling of things that have actually happened or of things that happen only in our imaginations. In the chapters that make up this section, authors will employ them all in an unconscious demonstration of a great truth: that learning can be a pleasant experience indeed.

11

Diaries, Journals, and Notebooks/ Private Reactions to Public Events

In theory, those who keep a diary, notebook, or journal do it for their own benefit. (Of course, we are sometimes justified in suspecting that some writers keep one eye on posterity as they make the daily entry.) Sometimes the diarist records little other than dull and recurring fact: "*Sept. 1.* Raining. *Sept. 4.* Still raining. *Sept. 5.* Rain stopped." Such diaries are not of much interest, except to a few specialists. But we are interested in the record of great people or of ordinary ones who have lived through great events and recorded them or reactions to them.

The diarist, simply by the act of writing, gives some shape to experience: he or she must choose a place to start ("Basic training began today"), must select and order the details, and stop at some point. With practice, most people who write their own records develop considerable interest and skill in what they are doing, and the journal becomes a meditation on the world or a continuing dialogue of the self.

For the reader, diaries, notebooks, and journals can be mother lodes of information and unfailing sources of interest. Two distinct pleasures are involved. In reading Pepys, for instance, we learn many details of daily life in seventeenth-century England (many of which find no place in conventional books of history), but as we read we also come to know a fascinating human being—not, perhaps, a great man, but an interesting one, a man whose recorded hopes, fears, faith, and foibles rescue him from the mists of time.

Victoria gives a very simple account of the fact that her uncle's death has made her queen of England. She was, after all, a young girl. Anne Frank, even younger, shows the enthusiasm of youth at unalloyed good news, the beginning of the end of Nazi power. John Quincy Adams records the day he reached our country's highest office, and Gideon Welles one of the darkest nights the nation suffered. Charles Greville and Tennyson react, the latter with passionate rhetoric, to a bloody and potentially scandalous error in the Crimean War, whereas nearly a century later Evelyn Waugh, displaying in his *Diaries* the ironic detachment that marks his novels, looks with apparent coolness on Britain's entrance into World War II. Natural disasters—a volcanic eruption and earthquake, an outbreak of the plague—occupy the pens of men who lived through them, giving us details and emotions that bring moments of the past briefly to life again.

Perhaps in an age of television commentary, "specials," and extended newspaper coverage of events, much of our reacting to public happenings is done for us. And yet, no one else can feel for us. As the examples of our diarists show, our personal responses are unique. To the keeping of diaries, therefore, there is no end.

I Become Queen

QUEEN VICTORIA (1819–1901) Victoria was barely eighteen years old when her uncle died and she became queen of England. At the time she wrote this entry in her journal she could hardly have foreseen that she would have a reign of sixty-four years, the longest in English history.

Tuesday, 20th June [1837].—I was awoke at 6 o'clock by Mamma, who told 1 me that the Archbishop of Canterbury and Lord Conyngham were here, and wished to see me. I got out of bed and went into my sitting-room (only in my dressing-gown), and *alone*, and saw them. Lord Conyngham (the Lord Chamberlain) then acquainted me that my poor Uncle, the King, was no more, and had expired at 12 minutes p. 2 this morning, and consequently that I am *Queen*. Lord Conyngham knelt down and kissed my hand, at the same time delivering to me the official announcement of the poor King's demise. The Archbishop then told me that the Queen was desirous that he should come and tell me the details of the last moments of my poor, good Uncle; he said that he had directed his mind to religion, and had died in a perfectly happy, quiet state of mind, and was quite prepared for his death. He added that the King's sufferings at the last were not very great but that there was a good deal of uneasiness. Lord Conyngham, whom I charged to express my feelings of condolence and sorrow to the poor Queen, returned directly to Windsor. I then went to my room and dressed.

Since it has pleased Providence to place me in this station, I shall do my 2 utmost to fulfil my duty towards my country; I am very young and perhaps in many, though not in all things, inexperienced, but I am sure, that very few have more real good will and more real desire to do what is fit and right than I have.

Vocabulary

Lord Chamberlain, demise, condolence, Providence

Questions

1. Why does Victoria underscore *alone?* Is this a sign of lack of confidence?
2. Does Victoria feel unfit to become queen? Do you see anything "queenly" in the behavior of this eighteen-year-old girl?

Inauguration Day

JOHN QUINCY ADAMS (1767–1848), was the sixth president of the United States, the son of the second president, and the grandfather of Henry Adams. This account of his inauguration makes an interesting contrast with our more elaborate modern ceremonies. The selection is from *The Diary of John Quincy Adams, 1794–1845.*

1   *Washington, March 4, 1825.*—After two successive sleepless nights, I entered upon this day with a supplication to Heaven, first, for my country; secondly, for myself and for those connected with my good name and fortunes, that the last results of its events may be auspicious and blessed. About half past eleven o'clock I left my house with an escort of several companies of militia and a cavalcade of citizens, accompanied in my carriage by Samuel L. Southard, Secretary of the Navy, and William Wirt, Attorney-General, and followed by James Monroe, late President of the United States, in his own carriage. We proceeded to the Capitol, and to the Senate-chamber. The Senate were in session, and John C. Calhoun presiding in the chair, having been previously sworn into office as Vice-President of the United States and President of the Senate. The Senate adjourned, and from the Senate-chamber, accompanied by the members of that body and by the judges of the Supreme Court, I repaired to the hall of the House of Representatives, and after delivering from the Speaker's chair my inaugural address to a crowded auditory, I pronounced from a volume of the laws held up to me by John Marshall, Chief Justice of the United States, the oath faithfully to execute the office of President of the United States, and, to the best of my ability, to preserve, protect, and defend the Constitution of the United States. After exchanging salutations from the late President, and many other persons present, I retired from the hall, passed in review the military companies drawn up in front of the Capitol, and returned to my house with the same procession which accompanied me from it. I found at my house a crowd of visitors, which continued about two hours, and received their felicitations. Before the throng had subsided, I went myself to the President's house, and joined with the multitude of visitors to Mr. Monroe there. I then returned home to dine, and in the evening attended the ball, which was also crowded, at Carusi's Hall. Immediately after supper I withdrew, and came home. I closed the day as it had begun, with thanksgiving to God for all His mercies and favors past, and with prayers for the continuance of them to my country, and to myself and mine.

Vocabulary

supplication, auspicious, cavalcade, repaired, auditory, salutations, felicitations

Questions

1. Does Adams's inauguration seem different from a modern president's? If so, is it a difference in kind or degree?
2. Are there any similarities between Victoria's reaction and Adams's? If so, what might account for them?
3. Unlike Victoria, John Quincy Adams had to seek election to his country's highest office. Does a sense of triumph come through in this account?

D-Day

ANNE FRANK (1929–1945) did not survive World War II, but died with other members of her family in a concentration camp at the hands of the Nazis. Her diary (which she personified as "Kitty") is a moving account of the hope and spirit that did survive one of the blackest moments in history.

Tuesday, 6 June, 1944

Dear Kitty,

1   "This is D-day," came the announcement over the English news and quite rightly, "this is *the* day." The invasion has begun!

2   The English gave the news at eight o'clock this morning: Calais, Boulogne, Le Havre, and Cherbourg, also the Pas de Calais (as usual), were heavily bombarded. Moreover, as a safety measure for all occupied territories, all people who live within a radius of thirty-five kilometers from the coast are warned to be prepared for bombardments. If possible, the English will drop pamphlets one hour beforehand.

3   According to German news, English parachute troops have landed on the French coast, English landing craft are in battle with the German Navy, says the B.B.C.

4   We discussed it over the "Annexe" [the secret attic in which the Frank family was hidden] breakfast at nine o'clock: Is this just a trial landing like Dieppe two years ago?

5   English broadcast in German, Dutch, French, and other languages at ten o'clock: "The invasion has begun!"—that means the "real" invasion. English broadcast in German at eleven o'clock, speech by the Supreme Commander, General Dwight Eisenhower.

6   The English news at twelve o'clock in English: "This is D-day." General Eisenhower said to the French people: "Stiff fighting will come now, but after this the victory. The year 1944 is the year of complete victory; good luck."

7   English news in English at one o'clock (translated): 11,000 planes stand ready, and are flying to and fro non-stop, landing troops and attacking behind the lines; 4,000 landing boats, plus small craft, are landing troops and matériel between Cherbourg and Le Havre incessantly. English and American troops are already engaged in hard fighting. Speeches by Gerbrandy, by the Prime Minister of Belgium, King Haakon of Norway, De Gaulle of France, the King of England, and last, but not least, Churchill.

8   Great commotion in the "Secret Annexe"! Would the long-awaited liberation that has been talked of so much, but which still seems *too* wonderful, *too* much like a fairy tale, every come true? Could we be granted victory this year, 1944? We don't know yet, but hope is revived within us; it gives us fresh courage, and makes us

strong again. Since we must put up bravely with all the fears, privations, and sufferings, the great thing now is to remain calm and steadfast. Now more than ever we must clench our teeth and not cry out. France, Russia, Italy, and Germany, too, can all cry out and give vent to their misery, but we haven't the right to do that yet!

Oh, Kitty, the best part of the invasion is that I have the feeling that friends are 9 approaching. We have been oppressed by those terrible Germans for so long, they have had their knives so at our throats, that the thought of friends and delivery fills us with confidence!

Now it doesn't concern the Jews any more; no, it concerns Holland and all 10 occupied Europe. Perhaps, Margot says, I may yet be able to go back to school in September or October.

Yours, Anne

P.S. I'll keep you up to date with all the latest news!

Vocabulary

matériel, privations

Questions

1. Anne Frank's diary takes on a special poignancy because we know that she died in a concentration camp. But if you did not have this knowledge, could you deduce from this diary entry anything special about her?
2. Anne has had to grow up rapidly during her two years of forced confinement in the "Annexe." Are there still some signs of the young teen-ager in this entry?

Topics for Writing

The Generosity of Youth
Joy Will Bloom in the Most Unlikely Places

Vesuvius Erupts

PLINY THE YOUNGER (ca. 62–113 A.D.), Gaius Plinius Caecilius Secundus, known as Pliny the Younger, wrote this account of the events surrounding the eruption of Vesuvius, in which his uncle died and Pompeii was destroyed, to the historian Tacitus. Although it is in the form of a letter rather than a diary entry, the chance to present a first-hand account of one of the ancient world's most famous upheavals is too tempting to ignore.

1   So the letter which you asked me to write on my uncle's death has made you eager to hear about the terrors and also the hazards I had to face when left at Misenum, for I broke off at the beginning of this part of my story. "Though my mind shrinks from remembering . . . I will begin."[1]

2   After my uncle's departure I spent the rest of the day with my books, as this was my reason for staying behind. Then I took a bath, dined, and then dozed fitfully for a while. For several days past there had been earth tremors which were not particularly alarming because they are frequent in Campania: but that night the shocks were so violent that everything felt as if it were not only shaken but overturned. My mother hurried into my room and found me already getting up to wake her if she were still asleep. We sat down in the forecourt of the house, between the buildings and the sea close by. I don't know whether I should call this courage or folly on my part (I was only seventeen at the time) but I called for a volume of Livy and went on reading as if I had nothing else to do. I even went on with the extracts I had been making. Up came a friend of my uncle's who had just come from Spain to join him. When he saw us sitting there and me actually reading, he scolded us both— me for my foolhardiness and my mother for allowing it. Nevertheless, I remained absorbed in my book.

3   By now it was dawn [25 August in the year 79], but the light was still dim and faint. The buildings round us were already tottering, and the open space we were in was too small for us not to be in real and imminent danger if the house collapsed. This finally decided us to leave the town. We were followed by a panic-stricken mob of people wanting to act on someone else's decision in preference to their own (a point in which fear looks like prudence), who hurried us on our way by pressing hard behind in a dense crowd. Once beyond the buildings we stopped, and there we had some extraordinary experiences which thoroughly alarmed us. The carriages we had ordered to be brought out began to run in different directions though the ground was quite level, and would not remain stationary even when wedged with stones. We also saw the sea sucked away and apparently forced back by the earthquake: at any rate it receded from the shore so that quantities of sea creatures were

---

[1]*Aeneid* II. 12.

left stranded on dry sand. On the landward side a fearful black cloud was rent by forked and quivering bursts of flame, and parted to reveal great tongues of fire, like flashes of lightning magnified in size.

At this point my uncle's friend from Spain spoke up still more urgently: "If your brother, if your uncle is still alive, he will want you both to be saved; if he is dead, he would want you to survive him—so why put off your escape?" We replied that we would not think of considering our own safety as long as we were uncertain of his. Without waiting any longer, our friend rushed off and hurried out of danger as fast as he could.

Soon afterwards the cloud sank down to earth and covered the sea; it had already blotted out Capri and hidden the promontory of Misenum from sight. Then my mother implored, entreated, and commanded me to escape as best I could—a young man might escape, whereas she was old and slow and could die in peace as long as she had not been the cause of my death too. I told her I refused to save myself without her, and grasping her hand forced her to quicken her pace. She gave in reluctantly, blaming herself for delaying me. Ashes were already falling, not as yet very thickly. I looked round: a dense black cloud was coming up behind us, spreading over the earth like a flood. "Let us leave the road while we can still see," I said, "or we shall be knocked down and trampled underfoot in the dark by the crowd behind." We had scarcely sat down to rest when darkness fell, not the dark of a moonless or cloudy night, but as if the lamp had been put out in a closed room. You could hear the shrieks of women, the wailing of infants, and the shouting of men; some were calling their parents, others their children or their wives, trying to recognize them by their voices. People bewailed their own fate or that of their relatives, and there were some who prayed for death in their terror of dying. Many besought the aid of the gods, but still more imagined there were no gods left, and that the universe was plunged into eternal darkness forevermore. There were people, too, who added to the real perils by inventing fictitious dangers: some reported that part of Misenum had collapsed or another part was on fire, and though their tales were false they found others to believe them. A gleam of light returned, but we took this to be a warning of the approaching flames rather than daylight. However, the flames remained some distance off; then darkness came on once more and ashes began to fall again, this time in heavy showers. We rose from time to time and shook them off, otherwise we should have been buried and crushed beneath their weight. I could boast that not a groan or cry of fear escaped me in these perils, had I not derived some poor consolation in my mortal lot from the belief that the whole world was dying with me and I with it.

At last the darkness thinned and dispersed into smoke or cloud; then there was genuine daylight, and the sun actually shone out, but yellowish as it is during an eclipse. We were terrified to see everything changed, buried deep in ashes like snowdrifts. We returned to Misenum where we attended to our physical needs as best we could, and then spent an anxious night alternating between hope and fear. Fear predominated, for the earthquakes went on, and several hysterical individuals made their own and other people's calamities seem ludicrous in comparison with their frightful predictions. But even then, in spite of the dangers we had been

4

5

6

through and were still expecting, my mother and I had still no intention of leaving until we had news of my uncle.

7   Of course these details are not important enough for history, and you will read them without any idea of recording them; if they seem scarcely worth even putting in a letter, you have only yourself to blame for asking for them.

Vocabulary

imminent, promontory, entreated, dispersed, predominated, ludicrous

Questions

1. This is a letter rather than a diary entry. What differences would you expect to result from that fact?
2. Why did they sit in the forecourt rather than in the house?
3. Was it courage or folly for Pliny to continue reading? Can you think of other possibilities?
4. Which details of the experience impress you most dramatically? Are they the same ones Pliny found most impressive?
5. Why can't Pliny boast about his fortitude that fateful night?
6. Is the mother-son exchange true to life as you know it?
7. If you have ever been in danger of serious injury or death, try to describe your reactions at the time. (Hint: Hemingway's advice to writers was to ignore the emotions but to describe the events that *caused* the emotion.)

Topics for Writing

Pliny Was Too Modest

A Moment of Danger

The Plague in London

SAMUEL PEPYS (1633–1703) kept one of the most voluminous, and most famous, diaries of all time. As a civil servant, he saw much of official life. His writing, which reveals him to be an appealing observer of London life in the seventeenth century, brings history to life. The plague, which swept periodically across Europe, was devastating. Because contemporary medicine did not know how it was spread (by rats), only its symptoms could be treated, and the people had to trust to luck and God's providence to spare them.

May 24th [1665]. To the Coffee-house, where all the newes is . . . of the plague growing upon us in this towne; and of remedies against it: some saying one thing, some another. 1

June 7th. This day, much against my will, I did in Drury Lane see two or three houses marked with a red cross upon the doors, and "Lord have mercy upon us" writ there; which was a sad sight to me, being the first of the kind that, to my remembrance, I ever saw. It put me into an ill conception of myself and my smell, so that I was forced to buy some roll-tobacco to smell to and chaw, which took away the apprehension. 2

10th. In the evening home to supper; and there, to my great trouble, hear that the plague is come into the City (though it hath these three or four weeks since its beginning been wholly out of the City); but where should it begin but in my good friend and neighbour's Dr. Burnett, in Fanchurch Street: which in both points troubles me mightily. To bed, being troubled at the sickness, and my head filled also with other business enough, and particularly how to put my things and estate in order, in case it should please God to call me away, which God dispose of to his glory. 3

15th. Up, and put on my new stuff suit with close knees, which becomes me most nobly, as my wife says. At the office all day. At noon, put on my first laced band, all lace. . . . At Woolwich, discoursed with Mr. Sheldon about my bringing my wife down for a month or two to his house, which he approves of, and, I think, will be convenient. . . . The towne grows very sickly, and people to be afeard of it; there dying this last week of the plague 112, from 43 the week before, whereof but one in Fanchurch-streete, and one in Broad-streete, by the Treasurer's office. 4

17th. It struck me very deep this afternoon going with a hackney coach from my Lord Treasurer's down Holborne, the coachman I found to drive easily and easily, at last stood still, and came down hardly able to stand, and told me that he was suddenly struck very sicke, and almost blind, he could not see; so I 'light and went into another coach, with a sad heart for the poor man and trouble for myself, lest he should have been struck with the plague, being at the end of the towne that I took him up; but God have mercy upon us all. 5

6   *20th.* This day I informed myself that there died four or five at Westminster of the plague in one alley in several houses upon Sunday last, Bell Alley, over against the Palace-gate; yet people do think that the number will be fewer in the towne than it was the last weeke.

7   *21st.* I find all the towne almost going out of towne, the coaches and waggons being all full of people going into the country.

8   *26th.* The plague encreases mightily, I this day seeing a house, at a bitt-maker's over against St. Clement's Church, in the open street, shut up; which is a sad sight.

9   *28th.* In my way to Westminster Hall, I observed several plague houses in King's Street and near the Palace. I was fearful of going to any house but I did to the Swan, and thence to White Hall, giving the waterman a shilling.

10   *29th.* By water to White Hall, where the Court full of waggons and people ready to go out of towne. This end of the towne every day grows very bad of the plague. The Mortality Bill is come to 267; which is about ninety more than the last: and of these but four in the City, which is a great blessing to us.

11   *30th.* To White Hall, to the Duke of Albemarle, who I find at Secretary Bennet's, there being now no other great Statesman, I think, but my Lord Chancellor, in towne. . . . In the afternoon I down to Woolwich and after me my wife and Mercer, whom I led to Mr. Sheldon's, to see his house, and I find it a very pretty place for them to be at.

12   *July 1st.* To Westminster, where I hear the sickness encreases greatly. Sad at the newes that seven or eight houses in Bazing Hall street, are shut up of the plague.

13   *3rd.* Late at the office and so home resolving from this night forwards to close all my letters, if possible, and end all my business at the office by daylight, and put all my affairs in the world in good order, the season growing so sickly, that it is much to be feared how a man can escape having a share with others in it, for which the good Lord God bless me, or to be fitted to receive it.

14   *5th.* Up, and advised about sending of my wife's bedding and things to Woolwich, in order to her removal thither. . . . By water to Woolwich, where I found my wife come, and her two mayds, and very prettily accommodated they will be; and I left them going to supper, grieved in my heart to part with my wife, being worse by much without her, though some trouble there is in having the care of a family at home in this plague time.

15   *6th.* To see my Lord Brouncker, who is not well. I could not see him, nor had much mind, one of the great houses within two doors of him being shut up: and Lord! the number of houses visited, which this day I observed through the town quite round in my way by Long Lane and London Wall.

16   *7th.* Up, and having set my neighbour, Mr. Hudson, wine coopers, at work drawing out a tierce of wine for the sending of some of it to my wife, I abroad, only taking notice to what a condition it has pleased God to bring me that at this time I have two tierces of Claret, two quarter casks of Canary, and a smaller vessel of Sack; a vessel of Tent, another of Malaga, and another of white wine, all in my wine cellar together; which, I believe, none of my friends of my name now alive ever had of his owne at one time. Home, taking some new books, *5l.* worth home to my great content.

10th. Away by water to the Duke of Albemarle's, where he tells me that I must   17
be at Hampton Court anon. . . . Here though I have not been in many years, yet I
lacke time to stay, besides that it is, I perceive, an unpleasing thing to be at Court,
everybody being fearful one of another, and all so sad, enquiring after the plague, so
that I stole away by my horse.

18th. To the 'Change, where a little business and a very thin Exchange; and so   18
walked through London to the Temple, where I took water for Westminster to the
Duke of Albemarle, to wait on him, and so to Westminster Hall, and there paid for
my newes-books, and did give Mrs. Michell, who is going out of towne because of
the sicknesse, and her husband, a pint of wine. I was much troubled this day to hear
at Westminster how the officers do bury the dead in the open Tuttle-field, pretend-
ing want of room elsewhere; whereas the new chappell church-yard was walled in at
the publick charge in the last plague-time, merely for want of room and now none,
but such as are able to pay dear for it, can be buried there.

20th. Walked to Redriffe, where I hear the sickness is, and indeed is scattered   19
almost every where, there dying 1,089 of the plague this week. My Lady Carteret
did this day give me a bottle of plague-water home with me. . . . Lord! to see how
the plague spreads. It being now all over King's Streete, at the Axe, and next door to
it, and in other places. . . .

22nd. I to Fox-hall, where to the Spring garden; but I do not see one guest   20
there, the town being so empty of anybody to come thither. Only, while I was there,
a poor woman came to scold with the master of the house that a kinswoman, I
think, of her's, that was newly dead of the plague, might be buried in the church-
yard; for, for her part, she should not be buried in the commons, as they said she
should. I by coach home, not meeting with but two coaches, and but two carts from
White Hall to my own house, that I could observe; and the streets mighty thin of
people. I met this noon with Dr. Burnett, who told me, and I find in the news-book
this week that he posted upon the 'Change, that whoever did spread the report that,
instead of dying of the plague, his servant was by him killed, it was forgery, and
shewed me the acknowledgment of the master of the pest-house, that his servant
died of a bubon on his right groine, and two spots on his right thigh, which is the
plague.

25th. At noon to the 'Change, which was very thin, but sad the story of the   21
plague in the City, it growing mightily. This day my Lord Brouncker did give me
Mr. Grant's book upon the Bills of Mortality, new printed and enlarged. Thence to
my office awhile, full of business, and thence by coach to the Duke of Albemarle's,
not meeting one coach going nor coming from my house thither and back again,
which is very strange.

26th. The sickness is got into our parish this week, and is got, indeed, every   22
where; so that I begin to think of setting things in order, which I pray God enable
me to put both as to soul and body.

27th. To Hampton Court, where I saw the King and Queene set out towards   23
Salisbury, and after them the Duke and Duchesse, whose hand I did kiss. . . . At
home met the weekly Bill, where above 1,000 encreased in the Bill, and of them, in
all about 1,700 of the plague, which hath made the officers this day resolve of sitting
at Deptford, which puts me to some consideration what to do.

24   *28th*. Up betimes, and down to Deptford. . . . To Dagenhams. . . . But Lord! to see in what fear all the people here do live. How they are afeard of us that come to them, insomuch that I am troubled at it, and wish myself away. But some cause they have; for the chaplin, with whom but a week or two ago we were here mighty high disputing, is since fallen into a fever and dead, being gone hence to a friend's a good way off.

25   *29th*. Up betimes, and after viewing some of my wife's pictures, which now she is come to do very finely to my great satisfaction beyond what I could ever look for, I by water to the office. At noon to dinner, where I hear that my Will is come in thither and laid down upon my bed, ill of the headake, which put me into extraordinary fear; and I studied all I could to get him out of the house and set my people to work to do it without discouraging him, and myself went forth to the Old Exchange to pay my fair Batelier for some linnen, and took leave of her, they breaking up shop for a while; and so by coach to Kate Joyce's, and there used all the vehemence and rhetorique I could to get her husband to let her go down to Brampton, but I could not prevail with him; he urging some simple reasons, but most that of profit, minding the house, and the distance, if either of them should be ill. However, I did my best, and more than I had a mind to do, but that I saw him so resolved against it, while she was mightily troubled at it. At last he yielded she should go to Windsor, to some friends there. So I took my leave of them, believing that it is great odds that we ever all see one another again; for I dare not go any more to that end of the towne. So home in some ease of mind that Will is gone to his lodging and that he is likely to do well, it being only the headake.

26   *30th (Lord's day)*. Will was with me to-day, and is very well again. It was a sad noise to hear our bell to toll and ring so often to-day, either for deaths or burials; I think five or six times.

27   *Aug. 2nd*. Up, it being a publique fast, as being the first Wednesday of the month, for the plague; I within doors all day.

28   *3rd*. Up, and betimes to Deptford. . . . Then mounted and rode very finely to Dagenhams; all the way people, citizens, walking to and again to enquire how the plague is in the City this week by the Bill; which by chance, at Greenwich, I had heard was 2,020 of the plague, and 3,000 and odd of all diseases; but methought it was a sad question to be so often asked me. . . . Mr. Marr telling me by the way how a mayde servant of Mr. John Wright's (who lives thereabouts) falling sick of the plague, she was removed to an out-house, and a nurse appointed to look to her; who, being once absent, the mayde got out of the house at the window, and ran away. The nurse coming and knocking, and having no answer, believed she was dead, and went and told Mr. Wright so; who and his lady were in great strait what to do to get her buried. At last resolved to go to Burntwood hard by, being in the parish, and there get people to do it. But they would not; so he went home full of trouble, and in the way met the wench walking over the common, which frighted him worse than before; and was forced to send people to take her, which he did; and they got one of the pest coaches and put her into it to carry her to a pest house. And passing in a narrow lane, Sir Anthony Browne, with his brother and some friends in the coach, met this coach with the curtains drawn close. The brother being a young

man, and believing there might be some lady in it that would not be seen, and the way being narrow, he thrust his head out of his own into her coach, and to look, and there saw somebody look very ill, and in a sick dress, and stunk mightily; which the coachman also cried out upon. And presently they come up to some people that stood looking after it, and told our gallants that it was a mayde of Mr. Wright's carried away sick of the plague; which put the young gentleman into a fright had almost cost him his life, but is now well again.

8th. To my office a little, and then to the Duke of Albemarle's about some 29 business. The streets mighty empty all the way, now even in London, which is a sad sight. And to Westminster Hall, where talking, hearing very sad stories from Mrs. Mumford; among others, of Mr. Michell's son's family. And poor Will, that used to sell us ale at the Hall-door, his wife and three children died, all, I think, in a day. So home through the City again, wishing I may have taken no ill in going; but I will go, I think, no more thither.

10th. By and by to the office, where we sat all the morning; in great trouble to 30 see the Bill this week rise so high, to above 4,000 in all, and of them about 3,000 of the plague. And an odd story of Alderman Bence's stumbling at night over a dead corps in the streete, and going home and telling his wife, she at the fright, being with child, fell sicke and died of the plague. We sat late, and then by invitation to Sir G. Smith's to dinner, where very good company and good cheer. Captain Cocke was there and Jack Fenn, but to our great wonder Alderman Bence, and tells us that not a word of all this is true, but by his owne story his wife has been ill and he fain to leave his house and comes not to her, which continued a trouble to me all the time I was there. Home, to draw over anew my will, which I had bound myself by oath to dispatch by to-morrow night; the towne growing so unhealthy, that a man cannot depend upon living two days.

11th. To the Exchequer . . . and I find the Exchequer, by proclamation, 31 removing to Nonsuch. Back again and at my papers, and putting up my books into chests and settling my house and all things in the best and speediest order I can, lest it should please God to take me away, or force me to leave my house. I find that so long as I keepe myself in company at meals and do there eat lustily (which I cannot do alone, having no love to eating, but my mind runs upon my business), I am as well as can be, but when I come to be alone, I do not eat in time, nor can not with any good heart, and I immediately begin to be full of wind, which brings my pain, till I come to fill my belly adays again, then am presently well.

12th. The people die so, that now it seems they are fain to carry the dead to be 32 buried by day-light, the nights not sufficing to do it in. And my Lord Mayor commands people to be within at nine at night all, as they say, that the sick may have liberty to go abroad for ayre. There is one also dead out of one of our ships at Deptford, which troubles us mightily; the Providence, fire-ship, which was just fitted to go to sea. But they tell me to-day no more sick on board. And this day W. Bodham tells me that one is dead at Woolwich, not far from the Rope-yard. I am told, too, that a wife of one of the groomes at Court is dead at Salisbury.

13th (Lord's day). It being very wet all day, clearing all matters in packing up 33 my papers and books, and giving instructions in writing to my executors, thereby perfecting the whole business of my will, to my very great joy; so that I shall be in much better state of soul, I hope, if it should please the Lord to call me away this sickly time. To bed with a mind as free as to the business of the world as if I were not worth 100*l.* in the whole world, every thing being evened under my hand in my books and papers. Upon the whole I find myself worth, besides Brampton estate, the sum of 2,164*l.*, for which the Lord be praised!

34 　　*15th.* By water to the Duke of Albemarle. . . . It was dark before I could get home, and so land at Church-yard stairs, where, to my great trouble, I met a dead corps of the plague, in the narrow ally just bringing down a little pair of stairs. But I thank God I was not much disturbed at it. However, I shall beware of being late abroad again.

35 　　*16th.* To the Exchange, where I have not been a great while. But, Lord! how sad a sight it is to see the streets empty of people, and very few upon the 'Change. Jealous of every door that one sees shut up, lest it should be the plague; and about us two shops in three, if not more, generally shut up.

36 　　*19th.* Slept till 8 o'clock, and then up and met with letters from the King and Lord Arlington, for the removal of our office to Greenwich.

37 　　*21st.* To my Lord Brouncker, at Greenwich, to looke after the lodgings appointed for us there for our office, which do by no means please me, they being in the heart of all the labourers and workmen there, which makes it as unsafe as to be, I think, at London. . . . Messengers went to get a boat for me, to carry me to Woolwich, but all to no purpose; so I was forced to walk it in the darke, at ten o'clock at night, with Sir J. Minnes's George with me, being mightily troubled for fear of the doggs at Coome farme, and more for fear of rogues by the way, and yet more because of the plague which is there, which is very strange, it being a single house, all alone from the towne, but it seems they use to admit beggars, for their owne safety, to lie in their barns and they brought it to them; but I bless God I got about eleven of the clock well to my wife, and giving 4*s.* in recompence to George I to my wife, and having first viewed her last piece of drawing since I saw her, which is seven or eight days, which pleases me beyond any thing in the world, to bed with great content but weary.

38 　　*22nd.* Walked to Greenwich, in my way seeing a coffin with a dead body therein, dead of the plague, lying in an open close belonging to the Coome farme, which was carried out last night, and the parish have not appointed any body to bury it; but only set a watch there day and night, that nobody should go thither or come thence: this disease making us more cruel to one another than if we are doggs. Walked to Redriffe, troubled to go through the little lane, where the plague is, but did and took water and home, where all well.

39 　　*25th.* This day I am told that Dr. Burnett, my physician, is this morning dead of the plague; which is strange, his man dying so long ago, and his house this month open again. Now himself dead. Poor unfortunate man!

40 　　*26th.* Down by water to Greenwich. . . . Thence I by water home, in my way seeing a man taken up dead, out of the hold of a small catch that lay at Deptford. I doubt it might be the plague, which with the thought of Dr. Burnett, did something disturb me, so that I did not what I intended and should have done, but home sooner than ordinary, and after supper, to read melancholy alone, and then to bed.

28th. To Mr. Colvill, the goldsmith's, having not for some days been in the   41
streets; but now how few people I see, and those looking like people that had taken
leave of the world. I there and made even all accounts in the world between him
and I, in a very good condition, and I would have done the like with Sir R. Viner,
but he is out of towne, the sicknesse being every where thereabouts. I to the
Exchange, and I think there was not fifty people upon it, and but few more like to
be as they told me. Thus I think to take adieu to-day of the London streets, unless it
be to go again to Viner's. I think I have 1,800*l*. and more in the house, and, blessed
be God! no money out but what I can very well command and that but very little,
which is much the best posture I ever was in in my life, both as to the quantity and
the certainty I have of the money I am worth; having most of it in my hand. But
then this is a trouble to me what to do with it, being myself this day going to be
wholly at Woolwich; but for the present I am resolved to venture it in an iron chest,
at least for a while.

29th. To Greenwich, and called at Sir Theophilus Biddulph's, a sober, dis-   42
creet man, to discourse of the preventing of the plague in Greenwich, and Woolwich, and Deptford, where in every place it begins to grow very great.

30th. Abroad, and met with Hadley, our clerke, who, upon my asking how the   43
plague goes, told me it encreases much, and much in our parish; for, says he, there
died nine this week, though I have returned but six: which is a very ill practice, and
makes me think it is so in other places; and therefore the plague much greater than
people take it to be. I went forth and walked towards Moorefields to see (God forbid
my presumption!) whether I could see any dead corps going to the grave; but, as
God would have it, did not. But, Lord! how every body's looks, and discourse in the
street is of death, and nothing else, and few people going up and down, that the
towne is like a place distressed and forsaken. After one turne there back again to
Viner's, and there found my business ready for me, and evened all reckonings with
them to this day to my great content.

31st. Up; and, after putting several things in order to my removal, to Wool-   44
wich; the plague having a great encrease this week, beyond all expectation of almost
2,000, making the general Bill 7,000, odd 100; and the plague above 6,000. Thus
this month ends with great sadness upon the publick, through the greatness of the
plague every where through the kingdom almost. Every day sadder and sadder news
of its encrease. In the City died this week 7,496, and of them 6,102 of the plague.
But it is feared that the true number of the dead this week is near 10,000; partly from
the poor that cannot be taken notice of, through the greatness of the number, and
partly from the Quakers and others that will not have any bell ring for them.

Sept. 3rd (Lord's day). Up; and put on my coloured silk suit very fine, and my   45
new periwigg, bought a good while since, but durst not wear, because the plague
was in Westminster when I bought it; and it is a wonder what will be the fashion
after the plague is done, as to periwiggs, for nobody will dare to buy any haire, for
fear of the infection, that it had been cut off the heads of people dead of the plague.
. . . By water to Greenwich, where much ado to be suffered to come into the towne
because of the sicknesse, for fear I should come from London, till I told them who I
was. . . . My Lord Brouncker, Sir J. Minnes, and I up to the Vestry at the desire of
the Justices of the Peace, in order to the doing something for the keeping of the

plague from growing; but Lord! to consider the madness of the people of the town, who will (because they are forbid) come in crowds along with the dead corpses to see them buried; but we agreed on some orders for the prevention thereof. Among other stories, one was very passionate, methought, of a complaint brought against a man in the towne for taking a child from London from an infected house. Alderman Hooker told us it was the child of a very able citizen in Gracious Street, a saddler, who had buried all the rest of his children of the plague, and himself and wife now being shut up and in despair of escaping, did desire only to save the life of this little child; and so prevailed to have it received stark-naked into the arms of a friend, who brought it (having put it into new fresh clothes) to Greenwich; whereupon hearing the story, we did agree it should be permitted to be received and kept in the towne. By water to Woolwich, in great apprehensions of an ague.

46   *4th.* Walked home, my Lord Brouncker giving me a very neat cane to walk with; but it troubled me to pass by Coome farme where about twenty-one people have died of the plague, and three or four days since I saw a dead corps in a coffin lie in the Close unburied, and a watch is constantly kept there night and day to keep the people in, the plague making us cruel, as doggs, one to another.

47   *6th.* To London, to pack up more things; and there I saw fires burning in the street, as it is through the whole City, by the Lord Mayor's order. Thence by water to the Duke of Albemarle's: all the way fires on each side of the Thames, and strange to see in broad daylight two or three burials upon the Bankeside, one at the very heels of another: doubtless all of the plague; and yet at least forty or fifty people going along with every one of them.

48   *10th (Lord's day).* Walked home; being forced thereto by one of my watermen falling sick yesterday, and it was God's great mercy I did not go by water with them yesterday, for he fell sick on Saturday night, and it is to be feared of the plague. So I sent him away to London with his fellow; but another boat came to me this morning. I walked to Woolwich, and there found Mr. Hill, and he and I all the morning at musique and a song he has set of three parts, methinks, very good. My wife before I came out telling me the ill news that she hears that her father is very ill, and then I told her I feared of the plague, for that the house is shut up. And so she much troubled did desire me to send them something; and I said I would, and will do so.

49   *14th.* To London, where I have not been now a pretty while. . . . I did wonder to see the 'Change so full, I believe 200 people; but not a man or merchant of any fashion, but plain men all. And Lord! to see how I did endeavour all I could to talk with as few as I could, there being now no observation of shutting up of houses infected, that to be sure we do converse and meet with people that have the plague upon them. . . . So home, and put up several things to carry to Woolwich, and upon serious thoughts I am advised by W. Griffin to let my money and plate rest there, as being as safe as any place, nobody imagining that people would leave money in their houses now, when all their families are gone. But, Lord! to see the trouble that it puts a man to, to keep safe what with pain a man has been getting together, and there is good reason for it. . . . My finding the Angel tavern, at the lower end of Tower-hill, shut up, and more than that, the ale-house at the Tower-

stairs, and more than that, the person was then dying of the plague when I was last there, a little while ago, at night, to write a short letter, and I overheard the mistresse of the house sadly saying to her husband somebody was very ill, but did not think it was of the plague. To hear that poor Payne, my waiter, hath buried a child, and is dying himself. To hear that a labourer I sent but the other day to Dagenhams, to know how they did there, is dead of the plague; and that one of my own watermen, that carried me daily, fell sick as soon as he had landed me on Friday morning last, when I had been all night upon the water (and I believe he did get his infection that day at Brainford), and is now dead of the plague. . . . And, lastly, that both my servants, W. Hewer and Tom Edwards, have lost their fathers, both in St. Sepulchre's parish, of the plague this week, do put me into great apprehensions of melancholy, and with good reason. But I put off the thoughts of sadness as much as I can, and the rather to keep my wife in good heart and family also.

Vocabulary

apprehension, bitt-(bit-)maker, coopers, tierce, anon, commons, betimes, strait, periwig(g)

Questions

1. What are some of the signs that this is a true diary rather than an account intended for publication?
2. Why do the people admire Dr. Burnett?
3. Pepys has mixed emotions about sending his wife out of town. Is this a purely personal reaction?
4. What is his attitude toward his wine cellar, his clothing, and his other possessions?
5. Why does the Lord Mayor establish a curfew for the healthy?
6. Is Pepys resigned to death? Give evidence for your answer.
7. Does the plague have a dehumanizing effect on people?
8. Pepys wrote, ". . . a man cannot depend upon living two days." How would you spend tomorrow morning if such an uncertainty hung over you? Could you describe that morning in an essay?

Topics for Writing

Sidelight on the Plague: The Future of Periwiggs

How I Might Spend Tomorrow If ——

Lincoln Is Assassinated

GIDEON WELLES (1802–1878) was appointed secretary of the navy by Abraham Lincoln in 1861, and he continued in that office under Lincoln's successor, Andrew Johnson, until 1869. His position as an officer of the government that John Wilkes Booth and his fellow conspirators aimed at destroying makes this account of the Lincoln assassination objectively as well as personally touching.

1   I had retired to bed about half past-ten on the evening of the 14th of April [1865], and was just getting asleep when Mrs. Welles, my wife, said some one was at our door. Sitting up in bed, I heard a voice twice call to John, my son, whose sleeping-room was on the second floor directly over the front entrance. I arose at once and raised a window, when my messenger, James Smith, called to me that Mr. Lincoln, the President, had been shot, and said Secretary Seward and his son, Assistant Secretary Frederick Seward, were assassinated. James was much alarmed and excited. I told him his story was very incoherent and improbable, that he was associating men who were not together and liable to attack at the same time. "Where," I inquired, "was the President when shot?" James said he was at Ford's Theatre on 10th Street. "Well," said I, "Secretary Seward is an invalid in bed in his house yonder on 15th Street." James said he had been there, stopped in at the house to make inquiry before alarming me.

2   I immediately dressed myself, and, against the earnest remonstrance and appeals of my wife, went directly to Mr. Seward's, whose residence was on the east side of the square, mine being on the north. James accompanied me. As we were crossing 15th Street, I saw four or five men in earnest consultation, standing under the lamp on the corner by St. John's Church. Before I had got half across the street, the lamp was suddenly extinguished and the knot of persons rapidly dispersed. For a moment and but a moment I was disconcerted to find myself in darkness, but, recollecting that it was late and about time for the moon to rise, I proceeded on, not having lost five steps, merely making a pause without stopping. Hurrying forward into 15th Street, I found it pretty full of people, especially so near the residence of Secretary Seward, where there were many soldiers as well as citizens already gathered.

3   Entering the house, I found the lower hall and office full of persons, and among them most of the foreign legations, all anxiously inquiring what truth there was in the horrible rumors afloat. I replied that my object was to ascertain the facts. Proceeding through the hall to the stairs, I found one, and I think two, of the servants there holding the crowd in check. The servants were frightened and appeared relieved to see me. I hastily asked what truth there was in the story that an assassin or assassins had entered the house and assaulted the Secretary. They said it was true, and that Mr. Frederick was also badly injured. They wished me to go up,

but no others. At the head of the first stairs I met the elder Mrs. Seward, who was scarcely able to speak but desired me to proceed up to Mr. Seward's room. I met Mrs. Frederick Seward on the third story, who, although in extreme distress, was, under the circumstances, exceedingly composed. I asked for the Secretary's room, which she pointed out,—the southwest room. As I entered, I met Miss Fanny Seward, with whom I exchanged a single word, and proceeded to the foot of the bed. Dr. Verdi and, I think, two others were there. The bed was saturated with blood. The Secretary was lying on his back, the upper part of his head covered by a cloth, which extended down over his eyes. His mouth was open, the lower jaw dropping down. I exchanged a few whispered words with Dr. V. Secretary Stanton, who came after but almost simultaneously with me, made inquiries in a louder tone till admonished by a word from one of the physicians. We almost immediately withdrew and went into the adjoining front room, where lay Frederick Seward. His eyes were open but he did not move them, nor a limb, nor did he speak. Doctor White, who was in attendance, told me he was unconscious and more dangerously injured than his father.

As we descended the stairs, I asked Stanton what he had heard in regard to the President that was reliable. He said the President was shot at Ford's Theatre, that he had seen a man who was present and witnessed the occurrence. I said I would go immediately to the White House. Stanton told me the President was not there but was at the theatre. "Then," said I, "let us go immediately there." He said that was his intention, and asked me, if I had not a carriage, to go with him. In the lower hall we met General Meigs, whom he requested to take charge of the house, and to clear out all who did not belong there. General Meigs begged Stanton not to go down to 10th Street; others also remonstrated against our going. Stanton, I thought, hesitated. Hurrying forward, I remarked that I should go immediately, and I thought it his duty also. He said he should certainly go, but the remonstrants increased and gathered round him. I said we were wasting time, and, pressing through the crowd, entered the carriage and urged Stanton, who was detained by others after he had placed his foot on the step. I was impatient. Stanton, as soon as he had seated himself, turned round, rose partly, and said the carriage was not his. I said that was no objection. He invited Meigs to go with us, and Judge Cartter of the Supreme Court mounted with the driver. At this moment Major Eckert rode up on horseback beside the carriage and protested vehemently against Stanton's going to 10th Steet; said he had just come from there, that there were thousands of people of all sorts there, and he considered it very unsafe for the Secretary of War to expose himself. I replied that I knew not where he would be more safe, and that the duty of both of us was to attend the President immediately. Stanton concurred. Meigs called to some soldiers to go with us, and there was one on each side of the carriage. The streets were full of people. Not only the sidewalk but the carriage-way was to some extent occupied, all or nearly all hurrying towards 10th Street. When we entered that street we found it pretty closely packed.

The President had been carried across the street from the theatre, to the house of a Mr. Peterson. We entered by ascending a flight of steps above the basement and passing through a long hall to the rear, where the President lay extended on a bed, breathing heavily. Several surgeons were present, at least six, I should think more. Among them I was glad to observe Dr. Hall, who, however, soon left. I inquired of Dr. H., as I entered, the true condition of the President. He replied the President was dead to all intents, although he might live three hours or perhaps longer.

6   The giant sufferer lay extended diagonally across the bed, which was not long enough for him. He had been stripped of his clothes. His large arms, which were occasionally exposed, were of a size which one would scarce have expected from his spare appearance. His slow, full respiration lifted the clothes with each breath that he took. His features were calm and striking. I had never seen them appear to better advantage than for the first hour, perhaps, that I was there. After that, his right eye began to swell and that part of his face became discolored.

7   Senator Sumner was there, I think, when I entered. If not he came in soon after, as did Speaker Colfax, Mr. Secretary McCulloch, and the other members of the Cabinet, with the exception of Mr. Seward. A double guard was stationed at the door and on the sidewalk, to repress the crowd, which was of course highly excited and anxious. The room was small and overcrowded. The surgeons and members of the Cabinet were as many as should have been in the room, but there were many more, and the hall and other rooms in the front or main house were full. One of these rooms was occupied by Mrs. Lincoln and her attendants, with Miss Harris. Mrs. Dixon and Mrs. Kinney came to her about twelve o'clock. About once an hour Mrs. Lincoln would repair to the bedside of her dying husband and with lamentation and tears remain until overcome by emotion.

8   [*April 15.*] A door which opened upon a porch or gallery, and also the windows, were kept open for fresh air. The night was dark, cloudy, and damp, and about six it began to rain. I remained in the room until then without sitting or leaving it, when, there being a vacant chair which some one left at the foot of the bed, I occupied it for nearly two hours, listening to the heavy groans, and witnessing the wasting life of the good and great man who was expiring before me.

9   About 6 A.M. I experienced a feeling of faintness and for the first time after entering the room, a little past eleven, I left it and the house, and took a short walk in the open air. It was a dark and gloomy morning, and rain set in before I returned to the house, some fifteen minutes [later]. Large groups of people were gathered every few rods, all anxious and solicitous. Some one or more from each group stepped forward as I passed, to inquire into the condition of the President, and to ask if there was no hope. Intense grief was on every countenance when I replied that the President could survive but a short time. The colored people especially—and there were at this time more of them, perhaps, than of whites—were overwhelmed with grief.

10   Returning to the house, I seated myself in the back parlor, where the Attorney-General and others had been engaged in taking evidence concerning the assassination. Stanton, and Speed, and Usher were there, the latter asleep on the bed. There were three or four others also in the room. While I did not feel inclined to sleep, as many did, I was somewhat indisposed. I had been so for several days. The excitement and bad atmosphere from the crowded rooms oppressed me physically.

11   A little before seven, I went into the room where the dying President was rapidly drawing near the closing moments. His wife soon after made her last visit to

him. The death-struggle had begun. Robert, his son, stood with several others at the head of the bed. He bore himself well, but on two occasions gave way to overpowering grief and sobbed aloud, turning his head and leaning on the shoulder of Senator Sumner. The respiration of the President became suspended at intervals, and at last entirely ceased at twenty-two minutes past seven.

A prayer followed from Dr. Gurley; and the Cabinet, with the exception of Mr. Seward and Mr. McCulloch, immediately thereafter assembled in the back parlor, from which all other persons were excluded, and there signed a letter which was prepared by Attorney-General Speed to the Vice-President, informing him of the event, and that the government devolved upon him. 12

Mr. Stanton proposed that Mr. Speed, as the law officer, should communicate the letter to Mr. Johnson with some other member of the Cabinet. Mr. Dennison named me. I saw that, though all assented, it disconcerted Stanton, who had expected and intended to be the man and to have Speed associated with him. I was disinclined personally to disturb an obvious arrangement, and therefore named Mr. McCulloch as the first in order after the Secretary of State. 13

I arranged with Speed, with whom I rode home, for a Cabinet-meeting at twelve meridian at the room of the Secretary of the Treasury, in order that the government should experience no detriment, and that prompt and necessary action might be taken to assist the new Chief Magistrate in preserving and promoting the public tranquillity. We accordingly met at noon. Mr. Speed reported that the President had taken the oath, which was administered by the Chief Justice, and had expressed a desire that the affairs of the government should proceed without interruption. Some discussion took place as to the propriety of an inaugural address, but the general impression was that it would be inexpedient. I was most decidedly of that opinion. 14

President Johnson, who was invited to be present, deported himself admirably, and on the subject of an inaugural said his acts would best disclose his policy. In all essentials it would, he said, be the same as that of the late President. He desired the members of the Cabinet to go forward with their duties without any change. Mr. Hunter, Chief Clerk of the State Department, was designated to act *ad interim* as Secretary of State. I suggested Mr. Speed, but I saw it was not acceptable in certain quarters. Stanton especially expressed a hope that Hunter should be assigned to the duty. 15

A room for the President as an office was proposed until he could occupy the Executive Mansion, and Mr. McCulloch offered the room adjoining his own in the Treasury Building. I named the State Department as appropriate and proper, at least until the Secretary of State recovered, or so long as the President wished, but objections arose at once. The papers of Mr. Seward would, Stanton said, be disturbed; it would be better he should be here, etc., etc. Stanton, I saw, had a purpose; among other things, feared papers would fall under Mr. Johnson's eye which he did not wish to be seen. 16

On returning to my house this morning, Saturday, I found Mrs. Welles, who had been ill and confined to the house from indisposition for a week, had been twice sent for by Mrs. Lincoln to come to her at Peterson's. The housekeeper, knowing the state of Mrs. W.'s health, had without consultation turned away the 17 messenger, Major French, but Mrs. Welles, on learning the facts when he came the second time, had yielded, and imprudently gone, although the weather was inclement. She remained at the Executive Mansion through the day. For myself, wearied, shocked, exhausted, but not inclined to sleep, the day, when not actually and officially engaged, passed off strangely.

18   I went after breakfast to the Executive Mansion. There was a cheerless cold rain and everything seemed gloomy. On the Avenue in front of the White House were several hundred colored people, mostly women and children, weeping and wailing their loss. This crowd did not appear to diminish through the whole of that cold, wet day; they seemed not to know what was to be their fate since their great benefactor was dead, and their hopeless grief affected me more than almost anything else, though strong and brave men wept when I met them.

19   At the White House all was silent and sad. Mrs. W. was with Mrs. L. and came to meet me in the library. Speed came in, and we soon left together. As we were descending the stairs, "Tad," who was looking from the window at the foot, turned and, seeing us, cried aloud in his tears, "Oh, Mr. Welles, who killed my father?" Neither Speed nor myself could restrain our tears, nor give the poor boy any satisfactory answer.

Vocabulary

incoherent, improbable, remonstrance, legations, admonished, respiration, lamentation, solicitous, disconcerted, meridian, detriment, propriety, insufficient, *ad interim,* inclement

Questions

1. Welles notes the size of Lincoln's arms. Isn't this a trivial detail?
2. Are there any indications that Welles and Stanton were not the best of friends?
3. Welles records some of the details of government with which he was concerned after Lincoln's death. Do these details lessen the shock of the tragedy?

Topic for Writing

Details: The Life-Blood of History

England Enters World War II

EVELYN WAUGH (1903–1966), English man of letters, was one of this century's most important novelists. Conservative in many ways, acerbic in all, Waugh found adjustment to the shifting values of a modern world difficult to accept. He did serve as an officer on active duty, conducting himself with great personal courage when occasion demanded. As the war ground toward its end and his services were less in need, he lost interest in military life and began the readjustment to the writer's world. *The Diaries of Evelyn Waugh* appeared in 1976.

Sunday, 27 August 1939. Went to luncheon with Christopher at Mells. Maidie seems solely concerned about the way war will affect her housekeeping. Communion. My inclinations are all to join the army as a private. Laura is better placed than most wives, and if I could let the house for the duration very well placed financially. I have to consider thirty years of novel-writing ahead of me. Nothing would be more likely than work in a government office to finish me as a writer; nothing more likely to stimulate me than a complete change of habit. There is a symbolic difference between fighting as a soldier and serving as a civilian, even if the civilian is more valuable.

Monday, 28 August 1939. To Bath where Laura visited the dentist, I a house agent. Lunched with my aunts and took away some books from my great-grandfather's library. Evans back at work here hanging the picture of George III in the library. I think of putting 'scribble, scribble' on a ribbon across the top. Miss Metcalfe the schoolmistress came to tell me I was a billet. My heart sank. But it is not for children but for five adults who are coming to arrange for the children's arrival and go in a week's time.

Friday, 1 September 1939. The week has gone very slowly. Household admirably calm. My offer of services rejected by MI [Military Intelligence]. Have written, to please Laura rather than with any hope of result, to Sir Robert Vansittart and Gerry Liddell. I have put the house into the hands of several agents. The stone Gothic balustrade arrived from Box. Evans at work adapting the panels in the library to the George III portrait. Evacuated children due here today; also the Nympsfield school treat. As we expected, rain. Yesterday Highnam garden was open to public. We went and I was delighted with it and found many ideas for Victorian planting here.

Immediately after writing this I went to the vicarage and fetched the chairs which were being lent for the orphanage tea. Mr Page had just heard the ten o'clock wireless news. Germany had begun bombing Poland. Borrowed chairs in two loads. On returning with the second, Ellwood told me the bus company had had the bus for the afternoon commandeered. Meanwhile Stokes, the Wotton confectioner, had left with tea. We decided to take it to Nympsfield. Loaded huge drum of ice cream, toys, cakes, etc., on car and took them to nuns. After luncheon I planted fritillary bulbs round the Spanish chestnut, then at six went to receive the evacuated children at the village hut. Most of the notables of the village were there; no children, and complaints that Mrs Barnett had changed all the reception arrangements. Meanwhile we listened to wireless in a Mrs Lister's motor car. It said the evacuation was working like clockwork. Still no children. Then some empty buses. Finally a police officer in a two-seater who said the children had come 400 short and there were none for Stinchcombe. Rain came on so we dispersed, dropping Page at vicarage.

5　　　Today Evans finished the new arrangements of panels in the library. The west wall is now symmetrical and, with the George III portrait, looks absolutely splendid.

Vocabulary

billet, balustrade, vicarage, commandeered, confectioner, fritillary, evacuated, notables, symmetrical

Questions

1. List the advantages Waugh sees in soldiering. To whom would the differences between that and serving as a civilian be symbolic? Are they absolutely selfish?
2. Waugh buries the bombing of Poland in the details of daily life. Does this argue a callousness on his part? How else can you explain it?

The Blunder of the Light Brigade

CHARLES FULKE GREVILLE (1794–1865) The Crimean War (1854–1856), in which England and France sided with Turkey against Russia, was Great Britain's Vietnam. A good many blunders, political as well as military, were made by British leaders. Sending light cavalry into the guns of a well-prepared enemy at Balaclava was such an error. One observer, the French general Pierre Bosquet, said, "It is magnificent, but it isn't war." Two further views are offered here. The first is from the diary of Charles Fulke Greville. As clerk of the Privy Council for more than thirty years, Greville had a long and intimate acquaintance with English politics. His diaries, published after his death as *The Greville Memoirs*, shook a number of reputations.

Nov. 14, 1854. Yesterday morning we received telegraphic news of another battle, from which we may expect a long list of killed and wounded. The affair of the 25th, in which our light cavalry was cut to pieces, seems to have been the result of mismanagement in some quarter, and the blame must attach either to Lucan, Cardigan, Captain Nolan who was killed, or to Raglan himself. Perhaps nobody is really to blame, but, if any one be, my own impression is that it is Raglan. He *wrote* the order, and it was his business to make it so clear that it could not be mistaken and to give it conditionally, or with such discretionary powers as should prevent its being vigorously enforced under circumstances which he could not foresee, or of which he might have no cognisance.

Vocabulary

conditionally, discretionary, cognizance

Questions

1. Greville isn't quite sure where to place the blame for the suicidal charge, but he tends to blame Lord Raglan. Are his reasons for doing so good ones?
2. Do you think that people in positions of trust should be free to publish anything they may learn during the course of their employment? Does it make a difference if the information is recorded in a private diary which is not intended for publication?

The Charge of the Light Brigade

ALFRED, LORD TENNYSON (1809–1892) had been made poet laureate of England only a few years before the incident that inspired this poem, written in 1854.

I

Half a league, half a league,
Half a league onward,
All in the valley of Death
   Rode the six hundred.
"Forward the Light Brigade!
Charge for the guns!" he said.
Into the valley of Death
   Rode the six hundred.

II

"Forward, the Light Brigade!"
Was there a man dismay'd?
Not tho' the soldier knew
   Some one had blunder'd.
Theirs not to make reply,
Theirs not to reason why,
Theirs but to do and die.
Into the valley of Death
   Rode the six hundred.

III

Cannon to right of them,
Cannon to left of them,
Cannon in front of them
   Volley'd and thunder'd;
Storm'd at with shot and shell,
Boldly they rode and well,
Into the jaws of Death,
Into the mouth of hell
   Rode the six hundred.

IV

Flash'd all their sabres bare,
Flash'd as they turn'd in air
Sabring the gunners there,

Charging an army, while 30
   All the world wonder'd.
Plunged in the battery-smoke
Right thro' the line they broke;
Cossack and Russian
Reel'd from the sabre-stroke 35
   Shatter'd and sunder'd.
Then they rode back, but not,
   Not the six hundred.

V

Cannon to right of them,
Cannon to left of them, 40
Cannon behind them
   Volley'd and thunder'd;
Storm'd at with shot and shell,
While horse and hero fell,
They that had fought so well 45
Came thro' the jaws of Death,
Back from the mouth of hell,
All that was left of them,
   Left of six hundred.

VI

When can their glory fade? 50
O the wild charge they made!
   All the world wonder'd.
Honor the charge they made!
Honor the Light Brigade,
   Noble six hundred! 55

Vocabulary

league (distance), Cossack

Questions

1. Tennyson names no names, saying only that "some one had blunder'd." Does this mean that the poet doesn't have an opinion?
2. Who is the "he" in line 6?
3. The rhythm of the opening lines is meant to suggest the insistent forward-rocking movement of horses at the gallop. Does it succeed?
4. In this poem, Tennyson transmutes an inglorious error into a glorious event—one in which the English people can take pride. How does he accomplish this?

12

Autobiography / Crossroads

Whereas diaries and the like are rarely intended for public view, autobiography—the writer's account of his or her own life—is usually aimed at a reading public. Autobiographers know that their lives are on display, and they can never forget that fact.

Does this mean that autobiographers are dishonest, that they deliberately deceive or that they twist things to their own credit? Not at all—even though Jean-Jacques Rousseau claimed in 1782 that his *Confessions* was the first honest autobiography because he intended to show himself "in all the integrity of nature." Most autobiographers intend to be absolutely frank, and some go to considerable effort not to excuse their failings. But each of us stands inescapably at the center of his or her own universe, and each of us sees things from a slightly different angle. For instance, Thomas Merton records an important moment he experienced, but his view of himself at St. Bonaventure University (College, in his time) is not shared entirely by everyone who knew him in those days.

The autobiographer is writing a narrative of life as it is remembered. Certain details stand out in memory; others are lost in the mist. Certain events and people among the many seem to have caused other events: these are singled out, and the narrative—through hundreds of such choices—takes on a direction, a shape, a "plot."

In this chapter, individuals of distinction in a variety of fields write about incidents that they believe marked turning points in their lives. Graham Greene describes an exhilarating event for a would-be novelist—the acceptance of his first book. For Booker T. Washington, the turning point was the fulfillment of a dream—a chance to be educated—and for Richard Wright, that same chance lay in the acquisition of a simple scrap of cardboard. Helen Keller's road to full humanity opened only after she was shown a connection almost no child has ever missed—unless that child was, like Helen, deaf and blind. Merton believed that God's will for him was made apparent through a suggestion repeated by three unrelated people.

The autobiographical impulse, we see, is strong. "I should not talk so much about myself," wrote Thoreau, "if there were any body else whom I knew as well." The assertion is a modest one, and we notice that he does not claim to know himself perfectly. But what Thoreau says is true of all of us, and attempting to write autobiographically may be a step toward knowing ourselves even better.

The First Acceptance

GRAHAM GREENE (1904–), the son of an English headmaster, has had a long and prolific career as an author. He has been successful both as a playwright (*The Potting Shed*) and a writer of thrillers (*Orient Express* and *The Third Man*, which he called "entertainments," are classics of the genre). But it is as a serious novelist, a student of tormented men in books like *The Power and the Glory* and *The Heart of the Matter*, that he will be remembered. This selection is from his autobiography, *A Sort of Life*.

1   I married, and I was happy. In the evenings I worked at *The Times*, in the mornings I worked on my third novel. Now when I write I put down on the page a mere skeleton of a novel—nearly all my revisions are in the nature of additions, of second thoughts to make the bare bones live—but in those days to revise was to prune and prune and prune. I was much tempted, perhaps because of my admiration for the Metaphysical poets, by exaggerated similes and my wife became an adept at shooting them down. There was one, I remember, comparing something or someone in the quiet landscape of Sussex to a leopard crouching in a tree, which gave a name to the whole species. Leopards would be marked daily on the manuscript, but it took a great many years for me to get the beasts under control, and they growl at me sometimes yet.

2   One day in the winter of 1928 I lay in bed with a bad attack of flu, listening to my wife in the kitchen washing up the breakfast things. I had posted copies of the typescript to Heinemann and The Bodley Head about ten days before, and I was now resigned to a long delay. Hadn't I waited last time nine months for a refusal? Anyway, uncertainty was more agreeable to live with than the confirmation of failure. The telephone rang in the sitting room and my wife came in and told me, "There's a Mr. Evans wants to speak to you."

3   "I don't know anyone called Evans," I said. "Tell him I'm in bed. Tell him I'm ill." Suddenly a memory came back to me: Evans was the chairman of Heinemann's, and I ran to snatch the telephone.

4   "I've read your novel," he said. "We'd like to publish it. Would it be possible for you to look in here at eleven?" My flu was gone in that moment and never returned.

5   Nothing in a novelist's life later can equal that moment—the acceptance of his first book. Triumph is unalloyed by any doubt of the future. Mounting the wide staircase in the elegant eighteenth-century house in Great Russell Street I could have no foreboding of the failures and frustrations of the next ten years.

6   Charles Evans was a remarkable publisher. With his bald head and skinny form he looked like a family solicitor lean with anxieties, but a solicitor who had taken an overdose of some invigorating vitamin. His hands and legs were never still. He did everything, from shaking hands to ringing a bell, in quick jerks. Perhaps

because the flu had not entirely departed, I expected at any moment the legendary figures of Heinemann authors to enter the room behind me, Mr. Galsworthy, Mr. John Masefield, Mr. Maugham, Mr. George Moore, Mr. Joseph Hergesheimer. I sat on the edge of the chair ready to leap up. The bearded ghost of Conrad rumbled on the rooftops with the rain.

7   I was quite prepared to hear what I had always understood to be the invariable formula—"Of course a first novel is a great risk, we shall have to begin with a small royalty"—but that was not Evans's way with a young author. Just as he had substituted the direct telephone call for the guarded letter, so now he brushed aside any ancient rite of initiation.

8   "No publisher," he said, "can ever guarantee success, but all the same we have hopes . . ." The royalty would begin at 12½ per cent, with a fifty-pound advance, he recommended me to take an agent, for in the future there might be subsidiary rights to deal with. I went out dazed into Great Russell Street. My daydream had never continued further than a promise of publication and now my publisher (proud phrase, "my publisher") was suggesting even the possibility of success.

9   He was as good as his word, selling more than 8000 copies of the novel, so that I was all the more unprepared for the failures which succeeded it. In the flush of that success I would have refused to believe that success is slow and not sudden and that ten years later, with my tenth novel, *The Power and the Glory*, the publisher could risk printing only 3500 copies, one thousand copies more than he had printed of my first novel.

Vocabulary

unalloyed, foreboding, solicitor, legendary, rite, subsidiary

Questions

1. What did the leopard come to symbolize for Greene? Is this why he can call it a species?
2. A novelist's first acceptance is a landmark. What might be the equivalent for someone else, say a doctor or an accountant?
3. Was Evans unwise not to warn Greene of future struggles?
4. Is uncertainty better than outright failure? Can you express this sentiment positively?
5. Is Greene saying that the success of this novel made it harder to accept the failures to come?
6. Do you sense that Greene might not have continued writing if this book had not sold?

Topics for Writing

Uncertainty Is Better Than Failure

My First Success

Everything Has a Name

HELEN KELLER (1880–1968), deaf and blind from infancy, went on from the poignant and triumphant moment she describes in *The Story of My Life* to become a writer, lecturer, and educator. Her aim was always to encourage others to rise above their own handicaps. (See Chapter 10 for Anne Sullivan's account of this incident).

The most important day I remember in all my life is the one on which my teacher, Anne Mansfield Sullivan, came to me. I am filled with wonder when I consider the immeasurable contrast between the two lives which it connects. It was the third of March, 1887, three months before I was seven years old. 1

On the afternoon of that eventful day, I stood on the porch, dumb, expectant. 2 I guessed vaguely from my mother's signs and from the hurrying to and fro in the house that something unusual was about to happen, so I went to the door and waited on the steps. The afternoon sun penetrated the mass of honeysuckle that covered the porch, and fell on my upturned face. My fingers lingered almost unconsciously on the familiar leaves and blossoms which had just come forth to greet the sweet southern spring. I did not know what the future held of marvel or surprise for me. Anger and bitterness had preyed upon me continually for weeks and a deep languor had succeeded this passionate struggle.

Have you ever been at sea in a dense fog, when it seemed as if a tangible white 3 darkness shut you in, and the great ship, tense and anxious, groped her way toward the shore with plummet and sounding-line, and you waited with beating heart for something to happen? I was like that ship before my education began, only I was without compass or sounding-line, and had no way of knowing how near the harbour was. "Light! give me light!" was the wordless cry of my soul, and the light of love shone on me in that very hour.

I felt approaching footsteps. I stretched out my hand as I supposed to my 4 mother. Some one took it, and I was caught up and held close in the arms of her who had come to reveal all things to me, and, more than all things else, to love me.

The morning after my teacher came she led me into her room and gave me a 5 doll. The little blind children at the Perkins Institution had sent it and Laura Bridgman [the first deaf and blind person to be educated in the United States] had dressed it; but I did not know this until afterward. When I had played with it a little while, Miss Sullivan slowly spelled into my hand the word "d-o-l-l." I was at once interested in this finger play and tried to imitate it. When I finally succeeded in making the letters correctly I was flushed with childish pleasure and pride. Running downstairs to my mother I held up my hand and made the letters for doll. I did not know that I was spelling a word or even that words existed; I was simply making my fingers go in monkey-like imitation. In the days that followed I learned to spell in this uncomprehending way a great many words, among them *pin, hat, cup,* and a few verbs like *sit, stand* and *walk.* But my teacher had been with me several weeks before I understood that everything has a name.

6   One day, while I was playing with my new doll, Miss Sullivan put my big rag doll into my lap also, spelled "d-o-l-l" and tried to make me understand that "d-o-l-l" applied to both. Earlier in the day we had had a tussle over the words "m-u-g" and "w-a-t-e-r." Miss Sullivan had tried to impress it upon me that "m-u-g" is *mug* and that "w-a-t-e-r" is *water,* but I persisted in confounding the two. In despair she had dropped the subject for the time, only to renew it at the first opportunity. I became impatient at her repeated attempts and, seizing the new doll, I dashed it upon the floor. I was keenly delighted when I felt the fragments of the broken doll at my feet. Neither sorrow nor regret followed my passionate outburst. I had not loved the doll. In the still, dark world in which I lived there was no strong sentiment or tenderness. I felt my teacher sweep the fragments to one side of the hearth, and I had a sense of satisfaction that the cause of my discomfort was removed. She brought me my hat, and I knew I was going out into the warm sunshine. This thought, if a wordless sensation may be called a thought, made me hop and skip with pleasure.

7   We walked down the path to the well-house, attracted by the fragrance of the honeysuckle with which it was covered. Some one was drawing water and my teacher placed my hand under the spout. As the cool stream gushed over one hand she spelled into the other the word *water,* first slowly, then rapidly. I stood still, my whole attention fixed upon the motions of her fingers. Suddenly I felt a misty consciousness as of something forgotten—a thrill of returning thought; and some-how the mystery of language was revealed to me. I knew then that "w-a-t-e-r" meant the wonderful cool something that was flowing over my hand. That living word awakened my soul, gave it light, hope, joy, set it free! There were barriers still, it is true, but barriers that could in time be swept away.

8   I left the well-house eager to learn. Everything had a name, and each name gave birth to a new thought. As we returned to the house every object which I touched seemed to quiver with life. That was because I saw everything with the strange, new sight that had come to me. On entering the door I remembered the doll I had broken. I felt my way to the hearth and picked up the pieces. I tried vainly to put them together. Then my eyes filled with tears; for I realized what I had done, and for the first time I felt repentance and sorrow.

9   I learned a great many new words that day. I do not remember what they all were; but I do know that *mother, father, sister, teacher* were among them—words that were to make the world blossom for me, "like Aaron's rod, with flowers." It would have been difficult to find a happier child than I was as I lay in my crib at the close of that eventful day and lived over the joys it had brought me, and for the first time longed for a new day to come.

Vocabulary

languor, tangible, plummet, sounding-line, uncomprehending

Questions

1. This selection ends on a note of anticipation, which you should contrast with the opening paragraphs. How does Helen Keller make you sense the contrast?
2. Is Helen Keller's comparison of herself with the fogbound ship appropriate?
3. Do you find it possible that a child so young could experience "anger and bitterness"?
4. Why is her soul's cry "wordless"?
5. What word was the key to the mystery of language? Can you imagine the mental process by which Anne Sullivan designed this lesson? Or do you think the association was only a lucky accident?
6. Are words the names of things?

Topics for Writing

Words: The Names of Things

Success, an Accident?

Matriculating at Hampton

BOOKER T. WASHINGTON (1856–1915), educator, writer, and lecturer, was born a slave but overcame every obstacle to educate himself. He then devoted his life to helping others follow his example. As this selection from his autobiography, *Up from Slavery,* shows, Washington believed that work was a key to black advancement, that pride and dignity as well as sustenance accompany it. When later he founded Tuskegee Institute, he was proud to model it on Hampton and offer trade and applied skills to help generations of young people cross economic and social barriers.

1   The distance from Malden to Hampton is about five hundred miles. I had not been away from home many hours before it began to grow painfully evident that I did not have enough money to pay my fare to Hampton. One experience I shall long remember. I had been travelling over the mountains most of the afternoon in an old-fashioned stage-coach, when, late in the evening, the coach stopped for the night at a common unpainted house called a hotel. All the other passengers except myself were whites. In my ignorance I supposed that the little hotel existed for the purpose of accommodating the passengers who travelled on the stage-coach. The difference that the colour of one's skin would make I had not thought anything about. After all the other passengers had been shown rooms and were getting ready for supper, I shyly presented myself before the man at the desk. It is true I had practically no money in my pocket with which to pay for bed or food, but I had hoped in some way to beg my way into the good graces of the landlord, for at that season in the mountains of Virginia the weather was cold, and I wanted to get indoors for the night. Without asking as to whether I had any money, the man at the desk firmly refused to even consider the matter of providing me with food or lodging. This was my first experience in finding out what the colour of my skin meant. In some way I managed to keep warm by walking about, and so got through the night. My whole soul was so bent upon reaching Hampton that I did not have time to cherish any bitterness toward the hotel-keeper.

2   By walking, begging rides both in wagons and in the cars, in some way, after a number of days, I reached the city of Richmond, Virginia, about eighty-two miles from Hampton. When I reached there, tired, hungry, and dirty, it was late in the night. I had never been in a large city, and this rather added to my misery. When I reached Richmond, I was completely out of money. I had not a single acquaintance in the place, and, being unused to city ways, I did not know where to go. I applied at several places for lodging, but they all wanted money, and that was what I did not have. Knowing nothing else better to do, I walked the streets. In doing this I passed by many foodstands where fried chicken and half-moon apple pies were piled high and made to present a most tempting appearance. At that time it seemed to me that I would have promised all that I expected to possess in the future to have gotten hold

of one of those chicken legs or one of those pies. But I could not get either of these, nor anything else to eat.

I must have walked the streets till after midnight. At last I became so exhausted 3 that I could walk no longer. I was tired, I was hungry, I was everything but discouraged. Just about the time when I reached extreme physical exhaustion, I came upon a portion of a street where the board sidewalk was considerably elevated. I waited for a few minutes, till I was sure that no passers-by could see me, and then crept under the sidewalk and lay for the night upon the ground, with my satchel of clothing for a pillow. Nearly all night I could hear the tramp of feet over my head. The next morning I found myself refreshed, but I was extremely hungry, because it had been a long time since I had had sufficient food. As soon as it became light enough for me to see my surroundings I noticed that I was near a large ship, and that this ship seemed to be unloading a cargo of pig iron. I went at once to the vessel and asked the captain to permit me to help unload the vessel in order to get money for food. The captain, a white man, who seemed to be kind-hearted, consented. I worked long enough to earn money for my breakfast, and it seems to me, as I remember it now, to have been about the best breakfast that I have ever eaten.

My work pleased the captain so well that he told me if I desired I could 4 continue working for a small amount per day. This I was very glad to do. I continued working on this vessel for a number of days. After buying food with the small wages I received there was not much left to add to the amount I must get to pay my way to Hampton. In order to economize in every way possible, so as to be sure to reach Hampton in a reasonable time, I continued to sleep under the same sidewalk that gave me shelter the first night I was in Richmond. Many years after that the coloured citizens of Richmond very kindly tendered me a reception at which there must have been two thousand people present. This reception was held not far from the spot where I slept the first night I spent in that city, and I must confess that my mind was more upon the sidewalk that first gave me shelter than upon the reception, agreeable and cordial as it was.

When I had saved what I considered enough money with which to reach 5 Hampton, I thanked the captain of the vessel for his kindness, and started again. Without any unusual occurrence I reached Hampton, with a surplus of exactly fifty cents with which to begin my education. To me it had been a long, eventful journey; but the first sight of the large, three-story, brick school building seemed to have rewarded me for all that I had undergone in order to reach the place. If the people who gave the money to provide that building could appreciate the influence the sight of it had upon me, as well as upon thousands of other youths, they would feel all the more encouraged to make such gifts. It seemed to me to be the largest and most beautiful building I had ever seen. The sight of it seemed to give me new life. I felt that a new kind of existence had now begun—that life would now have a new meaning. I felt that I had reached the promised land, and I resolved to let no obstacle prevent me from putting forth the highest effort to fit myself to accomplish the most good in the world.

As soon as possible after reaching the grounds of the Hampton Institute, I 6 presented myself before the head teacher for assignment to a class. Having been so long without proper food, a bath and change of clothing, I did not, of course, make a very favourable impression upon her, and I could see at once that there were doubts in her mind about the wisdom of admitting me as a student. I felt that I could hardly blame her if she got the idea that I was a worthless loafer or tramp. For some time she did not refuse to admit me, neither did she decide in my favour, and I continued to linger about her, and to impress her in all the ways I could with my worthiness. In the meantime I saw her admitting other students, and that added greatly to my discomfort, for I felt, deep down in my heart, that I could do as well as they, if I could only get a chance to show what was in me.

7   After some hours had passed, the head teacher said to me: "The adjoining recitation-room needs sweeping. Take the broom and sweep it."

8   It occurred to me at once that here was my chance. Never did I receive an order with more delight. I knew that I could sweep, for Mrs. Ruffner had thoroughly taught me how to do that when I lived with her.

9   I swept the recitation-room three times. Then I got a dusting-cloth and I dusted it four times. All the woodwork around the walls, every bench, table, and desk, I went over four times with my dusting-cloth. Besides, every piece of furniture had been moved and every closet and corner in the room had been thoroughly cleaned. I had the feeling that in a large measure my future depended upon the impression I made upon the teacher in the cleaning of that room. When I was through, I reported to the head teacher. She was a "Yankee" woman who knew just where to look for dirt. She went into the room and inspected the floor and closets; then she took her handkerchief and rubbed it on the woodwork about the walls, and over the table and benches. When she was unable to find one bit of dirt on the floor, or a particle of dust on any of the furniture, she quietly remarked, "I guess you will do to enter this institution."

10   I was one of the happiest souls on earth. The sweeping of that room was my college examination, and never did any youth pass an examination for entrance into Harvard or Yale that gave him more genuine satisfaction. I have passed several examinations since then, but I have always felt that this was the best one I ever passed.

11   I have spoken of my own experience in entering the Hampton Institute. Perhaps few, if any, had anything like the same experience that I had, but about that same period there were hundreds who found their way to Hampton and other institutions after experiencing something of the same difficulties that I went through. The young men and women were determined to secure an education at any cost.

12   The sweeping of the recitation-room in the manner that I did it seems to have paved the way for me to get through Hampton. Miss Mary F. Mackie, the head teacher, offered me a position as janitor. This, of course, I gladly accepted, because it was a place where I could work out nearly all the cost of my board. The work was hard and taxing, but I stuck to it. I had a large number of rooms to care for, and had to work late into the night, while at the same time I had to rise by four o'clock in the morning, in order to build the fires and have a little time in which to prepare my lessons. In all my career at Hampton, and ever since I have been out in the world,

Miss Mary F. Mackie, the head teacher to whom I have referred, proved one of my strongest and most helpful friends. Her advice and encouragement were always helpful and strengthening to me in the darkest hour.

Vocabulary

matriculating, pig iron, recitation-room

Questions

1. Washington's vocabulary is as simple as his style, and yet he was an accomplished and educated man. What inferences could you draw from his style?
2. Physically, the three-story building at Hampton was probably no different from many buildings that Washington saw in Richmond. Why, then, does he make such a fuss about its size and beauty?
3. Can "the promised land" be something as prosaic and commonplace as a brick building?
4. Is the teacher looking for an efficient janitor or for a promising student? What did she learn from his cleaning the recitation-room?

Topics for Writing

My "Promised Land"

Desire, the Measure of Value

Washington's Character

The Library Card

RICHARD WRIGHT (1908–1960) overcame the obstacles he describes here to become a successful and respected writer. "The Library Card" is a chapter from his powerful autobiography, *Black Boy* (1937).

1   One morning I arrived early at work and went into the bank lobby where the Negro porter was mopping. I stood at a counter and picked up the Memphis *Commercial Appeal* and began my free reading of the press. I came finally to the editorial page and saw an article dealing with one H.L. Mencken. I knew by hearsay that he was the editor of the *American Mercury*, but aside from that I knew nothing about him. The article was a furious denunciation of Mencken, concluding with one, hot, short sentence: Mencken is a fool.

2   I wondered what on earth this Mencken had done to call down upon him the scorn of the South. The only people I had ever heard denounced in the South were Negroes, and this man was not a Negro. Then what ideas did Mencken hold that made a newspaper like the *Commercial Appeal* castigate him publicly? Undoubtedly he must be advocating ideas that the South did not like. Were there, then, people other than Negroes who criticized the South? I knew that during the Civil War the South had hated northern whites, but I had not encountered such hate during my life. Knowing no more of Mencken than I did at that moment, I felt a vague sympathy for him. Had not the South, which had assigned me the role of a non-man, cast at him its hardest words?

3   Now, how could I find out about this Mencken? There was a huge library near the riverfront, but I knew that Negroes were not allowed to patronize its shelves any more than they were the parks and playgrounds of the city. I had gone into the library several times to get books for the white men on the job. Which of them would now help me to get books? And how could I read them without causing concern to the white men with whom I worked? I had so far been successful in hiding my thoughts and feelings from them, but I knew that I would create hostility if I went about this business of reading in a clumsy way.

4   I weighed the personalities of the men on the job. There was Don, a Jew; but I distrusted him. His position was not much better than mine and I knew that he was uneasy and insecure; he had always treated me in an offhand, bantering way that barely concealed his contempt. I was afraid to ask him to help me to get books; his frantic desire to demonstrate a racial solidarity with the whites against Negroes might make him betray me.

5   Then how about the boss? No, he was a Baptist and I had the suspicion that he would not be quite able to comprehend why a black boy would want to read Mencken. There were other white men on the job whose attitudes showed clearly that they were Kluxers or sympathizers, and they were out of the question.

There remained only one man whose attitude did not fit into an anti-Negro 6
category, for I had heard the white men refer to him as a "Pope lover." He was an
Irish Catholic and was hated by the white Southerners. I knew that he read books,
because I had got him volumes from the library several times. Since he, too, was an
object of hatred, I felt that he might refuse me but would hardly betray me. I
hesitated, weighing and balancing the imponderable realities.

One morning I paused before the Catholic fellow's desk. 7
"I want to ask you a favor," I whispered to him. 8
"What is it?" 9
"I want to read. I can't get books from the library. I wonder if you'd let me use 10
your card?"
He looked at me suspiciously. 11
"My card is full most of the time," he said. 12
"I see," I said and waited, posing my question silently. 13
"You're not trying to get me into trouble, are you, boy?" he asked, staring at 14
me.
"Oh, no, sir." 15
"What book do you want?" 16
"A book by H. L. Mencken." 17
"Which one?" 18
"I don't know. Has he written more than one?" 19
"He has written several." 20
"I didn't know that." 21
"What makes you want to read Mencken?" 22
"Oh, I just saw his name in the newspaper," I said. 23
"It's good of you to want to read," he said. "But you ought to read the right 24
things."
I said nothing. Would he want to supervise my reading? 25
"Let me think," he said. "I'll figure out something." 26
I turned from him and he called me back. He stared at me quizzically. 27
"Richard, don't mention this to the other white men," he said. 28
"I understand," I said. "I won't say a word." 29
A few days later he called me to him. 30
"I've got a card in my wife's name," he said. "Here's mine." 31
"Thank you, sir." 32
"Do you think you can manage it?" 33
"I'll manage fine," I said. 34
"If they suspect you, you'll get in trouble," he said. 35
"I'll write the same kind of notes to the library that you wrote when you sent 36
me for books," I told him. "I'll sign your name."
He laughed. 37
"Go ahead. Let me see what you get," he said. 38
That afternoon I addressed myself to forging a note. Now, what were the 39
names of books written by H. L. Mencken? I did not know any of them. I finally
wrote what I thought would be a foolproof note: *Dear Madam: Will you please let*

this nigger boy—I used the word "nigger" to make the librarian feel that I could not possibly be the author of the note—*have some books by H. L. Mencken?* I forged the white man's name.

40   I entered the library as I had always done when on errands for whites, but I felt that I would somehow slip up and betray myself. I doffed my hat, stood a respectful distance from the desk, looked as unbookish as possible, and waited for the white patrons to be taken care of. When the desk was clear of people, I still waited. The white librarian looked at me.

41   "What do you want, boy?"

42   As though I did not possess the power of speech, I stepped forward and simply handed her the forged note, not parting my lips.

43   "What books by Mencken does he want?" she asked.

44   "I don't know, ma'am," I said, avoiding her eyes.

45   "Who gave you this card?"

46   "Mr. Falk," I said.

47   "Where is he?"

48   "He's at work, at the M —— Optical Company," I said. "I've been in here for him before."

49   "I remember," the woman said. "But he never wrote notes like this."

50   Oh, God, she's suspicious. Perhaps she would not let me have the books? If she had turned her back at that moment, I would have ducked out the door and never gone back. Then I thought of a bold idea.

51   "You can call him up, ma'am," I said, my heart pounding.

52   "You're not using these books, are you?" she asked pointedly.

53   "Oh, no, ma'am. I can't read."

54   "I don't know what he wants by Mencken," she said under her breath.

55   I knew now that I had won; she was thinking of other things and the race question had gone out of her mind. She went to the shelves. Once or twice she looked over her shoulder at me, as though she was still doubtful. Finally she came forward with two books in her hand.

56   "I'm sending him two books," she said. "But tell Mr. Falk to come in next time, or send me the names of the books he wants. I don't know what he wants to read."

57   I said nothing. She stamped the card and handed me the books. Not daring to glance at them, I went out of the library, fearing that the woman could call me back for further questioning. A block away from the library I opened one of the books and read a title: *A Book of Prefaces.* I was nearing my nineteenth birthday and I did not know how to pronounce the word "preface." I thumbed the pages and saw strange words and strange names. I shook my head, disappointed. I looked at the other book; it was called *Prejudices.* I knew what that word meant; I had heard it all my life. And right off I was on guard against Mencken's books. Why would a man want to call a book *Prejudices?* The word was so stained with all my memories of racial hate that I could not conceive of anybody using it for a title. Perhaps I had made a mistake about Mencken? A man who had prejudices must be wrong.

58   When I showed the books to Mr. Falk, he looked at me and frowned.

"That librarian might telephone you," I warned him.   59

"That's all right," he said. "But when you're through reading those books, I   60
want you to tell me what you get out of them."

That night in my rented room, while letting the hot water run over my can of   61
pork and beans in the sink, I opened *A Book of Prefaces* and began to read. I was
jarred and shocked by the style, the clear, clean, sweeping sentences. Why did he
write like that? And how did one write like that? I pictured the man as a raging
demon, slashing with his pen, consumed with hate, denouncing everything American, extolling everything European or German, laughing at the weaknesses of
people, mocking God, authority. What was this? I stood up, trying to realize what
reality lay behind the meaning of the words . . . Yes, this man was fighting, fighting
with words. He was using words as a weapon, using them as one would use a club.
Could words be weapons? Well, yes, for here they were. Then, maybe, perhaps, I
could use them as a weapon? No. It frightened me. I read on and what amazed me
was not what he said, but how on earth anybody had the courage to say it.

Occasionally I glanced up to reassure myself that I was alone in the room.   62
Who were these men about whom Mencken was talking so passionately? Who was
Anatole France? Joseph Conrad? Sinclair Lewis, Sherwood Anderson, Dostoevski,
George Moore, Gustave Flaubert, Maupassant, Tolstoy, Frank Harris, Mark
Twain, Thomas Hardy, Arnold Bennett, Stephen Crane, Zola, Norris, Gorky,
Bergson, Ibsen, Balzac, Bernard Shaw, Dumas, Poe, Thomas Mann, O. Henry,
Dreiser, H. G. Wells, Gogol, T. S. Eliot, Gide, Baudelaire, Edgar Lee Masters,
Stendhal, Turgenev, Huneker, Nietzsche, and scores of others? Were these men
real? Did they exist or had they existed? And how did one pronounce their names?

I ran across many words whose meanings I did not know, and I either looked   63
them up in a dictionary or, before I had a chance to do that, encountered the word
in a context that made its meaning clear. But what strange world was this? I
concluded the book with the conviction that I had somehow overlooked something
terribly important in life.I had once tried to write, had once reveled in feeling, had
let my crude imagination roam, but the impulse to dream had been slowly beaten
out of me by experience. Now it surged up again and I hungered for books, new
ways of looking and seeing. It was not a matter of believing or disbelieving what I
read, but of feeling something new, of being affected by something that made the
look of the world different.

As dawn broke I ate my pork and beans, feeling dopey, sleepy. I went to work,   64
but the mood of the book would not die; it lingered, coloring everything I saw,
heard, did. I now felt that I knew what the white men were feeling. Merely because
I had read a book that had spoken of how they lived and thought, I identified myself
with that book. I felt vaguely guilty. Would I, filled with bookish notions, act in a
manner that would make the whites dislike me?

I forged more notes and my trips to the library became frequent. Reading grew   65
into a passion. My first serious novel was Sinclair Lewis's *Main Street*. It made me
see my boss, Mr. Gerald, and identify him as an American type. I would smile
when I saw him lugging his golf bags into the office. I had always felt a vast distance
separating me from the boss, and now I felt closer to him, though still distant. I felt

now that I knew him, that I could feel the very limits of his narrow life. And this had happened because I had read a novel about a mythical man called George F. Babbitt.

66   The plots and stories in the novels did not interest me so much as the point of view revealed. I gave myself over to each novel without reserve, without trying to criticize it; it was enough for me to see and feel something different. And for me, everything was something different. Reading was like a drug, a dope. The novels created moods in which I lived for days. But I could not conquer my sense of guilt, my feeling that the white men around me knew that I was changing, that I had begun to regard them differently.

67   Whenever I brought a book to the job, I wrapped it in newspaper—a habit that was to persist for years in other cities and under other circumstances. But some of the white men pried into my packages when I was absent and they questioned me.

68   "Boy, what are you reading those books for?"

69   "Oh, I don't know, sir."

70   "That's deep stuff you're reading, boy."

71   "I'm just killing time, sir."

72   "You'll addle your brains if you don't watch out."

73   I read Dreiser's *Jennie Gerhardt* and *Sister Carrie* and they revived in me a vivid sense of my mother's suffering; I was overwhelmed. I grew silent, wondering about the life around me. It would have been impossible for me to have told anyone what I derived from these novels, for it was nothing less than a sense of life itself. All my life had shaped me for the realism, the naturalism of the modern novel, and I could not read enough of them.

74   Steeped in new moods and ideas, I bought a ream of paper and tried to write; but nothing would come, or what did come was flat beyond telling. I discovered that more than desire and feeling were necessary to write and I dropped the idea. Yet I still wondered how it was possible to know people sufficiently to write about them? Could I ever learn about life and people? To me, with my vast ignorance, my Jim Crow station in life, it seemed a task impossible of achievement. I now knew what being a Negro meant. I could endure the hunger. I had learned to live with hate. But to feel that there were feelings denied me, that the very breath of life itself was beyond my reach, that more than anything else hurt, wounded me. I had a new hunger.

75   In buoying me up, reading also cast me down, made me see what was possible, what I had missed. My tension returned, new, terrible, bitter, surging, almost too great to be contained. I no longer *felt* that the world about me was hostile, killing; I *knew* it. A million times I asked myself what I could do to save myself, and there were no answers. I seemed forever condemned, ringed by walls.

76   I did not discuss my reading with Mr. Falk, who had lent me his library card; it would have meant talking about myself and that would have been too painful. I smiled each day, fighting desperately to maintain my old behavior, to keep my disposition seemingly sunny. But some of the white men discerned that I had begun to brood.

77   "Wake up there, boy!" Mr. Olin said one day.

"Sir!" I answered for the lack of a better word.   78

"You act like you've stolen something," he said.   79

I laughed in the way I knew he expected me to laugh, but I resolved to be more   80
conscious of myself, to watch my every act, to guard and hide the new knowledge
that was dawning within me.

If I went north, would it be possible for me to build a new life then? But how   81
could a man build a life upon vague, unformed yearnings? I wanted to write and I
did not even know the English language. I bought English grammars and found
them dull. I felt that I was getting a better sense of the language from novels than
from grammars. I read hard, discarding a writer as soon as I felt that I had grasped
his point of view. At night the printed page stood before my eyes in sleep.

Mrs. Moss, my landlady, asked me one Sunday morning: 82

"Son, what is this you keep on reading?"   83

"Oh, nothing. Just novels."   84

"What you get out of 'em?"   85

"I'm just killing time," I said.   86

"I hope you know your own mind," she said in a tone which implied that she   87
doubted if I had a mind.

I knew of no Negroes who read the books I liked and I wondered if any Negroes   88
ever thought of them. I knew that there were Negro doctors, lawyers, newspa-
permen, but I never saw any of them. When I read a Negro newspaper I never
caught the faintest echo of my preoccupation in its pages. I felt trapped and occasionally, for a few days, I would stop reading. But a vague hunger would come over
me for books, books that opened up new avenues of feeling and seeing, and again I
would forge another note to the white librarian. Again I would read and wonder as
only the naïve and unlettered can read and wonder, feeling that I carried a secret,
criminal burden about with me each day.

That winter my mother and brother came and we set up housekeeping, buying   89
furniture on the installment plan, being cheated and yet knowing no way to avoid
it. I began to eat warm food and to my surprise found that regular meals enabled me
to read faster. I may have lived through many illnesses and survived them, never
suspecting that I was ill. My brother obtained a job and we began to save toward the
trip north, plotting our time, setting tentative dates for departure. I told none of the
white men on the job that I was planning to go north; I knew that the moment they
felt I was thinking of the North they would change toward me. It would have made
them feel that I did not like the life I was living, and because my life was completely
conditioned by what they said or did, it would have been tantamount to challenging
them.

I could calculate my chances for life in the South as a Negro fairly clearly now.   90

I could fight the southern whites by organizing with other Negroes, as my   91
grandfather had done. But I knew that I could never win that way; there were many
whites and there were but few blacks. They were strong and we were weak. Outright
black rebellion could never win. If I fought openly I would die and I did not want to
die. News of lynchings was frequent.

I could submit and live the life of a genial slave, but that was impossible. All of   92 my life had shaped me to live by my own feelings, and thoughts. I could make up to Bess and marry her and inherit the house. But that, too, would be the life of a slave; if I did that, I would crush to death something within me, and I would hate myself as much as I knew the whites already hated those who had submitted. Neither could I ever willingly present myself to be kicked, as Shorty had done. I would rather have died than do that.

93   I could drain off my restlessness by fighting with Shorty and Harrison. I had seen many Negroes solve the problem of being black by transferring their hatred of themselves to others with a black skin and fighting them. I would have to be cold to do that, and I was not cold and I could never be.

94   I could, of course, forget what I had read, thrust the whites out of my mind, forget them; and find release from anxiety and longing in sex and alcohol. But the memory of how my father had conducted himself made that course repugnant. If I did not want others to violate my life, how could I voluntarily violate it myself?

95   I had no hope whatever of being a professional man. Not only had I been so conditioned that I did not desire it, but the fulfillment of such an ambition was beyond my capabilities. Well-to-do Negroes lived in a world that was almost as alien to me as the world inhabited by whites.

96   What, then, was there? I held my life in my mind, in my consciousness each day, feeling at times that I would stumble and drop it, spill it forever. My reading had created a vast sense of distance between me and the world in which I lived and tried to make a living, and that sense of distance was increasing each day. My days and nights were one long, quiet, continuously contained dream of terror, tension, and anxiety. I wondered how long I could bear it.

Vocabulary

denunciation, castigate, patronize, Kluxer (see Ku Klux Klan), imponderable, extolling, addle, naturalism, Jim Crow, discerned, unlettered, tantamount, lynchings, genial, repugnant

Questions

1. Why does Wright feel sympathy with H. L. Mencken? Do his suspicions of Don and the boss betray paranoia?
2. What does his forged note to the librarian tell you about Wright? About society at the time?
3. What other things was the librarian thinking of, and why did Wright know then he had won?
4. In what way did Wright feel closer to his boss after reading *Main Street?* Has any novel or short story given you a better understanding of someone or something?
5. Can reading "addle your brains"?
6. Why didn't Wright discuss his reading with Falk?

7. Why does his reading habit create the feeling of "a secret, criminal burden"? Is it because he regularly deceives the librarian?
8. Why might the men change towards him if they knew he was going north?
9. "You are what you eat," we hear. Might we also say, "You become what you read"? Is that a fair conclusion in this case?
10. What would you expect to come next for young Richard Wright?

Topics for Writing

Are We What We Read?
Is Reading Revolutionary?
The Step Beyond Reading

The Decision

THOMAS MERTON (1915–1968), Trappist monk and spiritual writer, studied English at Columbia University, where he was deeply influenced by one of his professors, the critic-poet Mark van Doren. His early life was restless and unfocused, but after his conversion to Catholicism the idea of becoming a priest grew upon him. This selection from his autobiography, *The Seven Storey Mountain*—Dante's image of Purgatory in *The Divine Comedy*—tells how this idea was reinforced during the short time he spent teaching English at St. Bonaventure College (now University) in southwestern New York. He decided to join the Trappist monastery in Gethsemani, Kentucky. Of the people he mentions, two require special comment: the "Baroness" was Catherine de Heuck, the founder of Friendship House, a refuge for the poor in Harlem; Thomas Plassmann, "Father Tom," was the brilliant scholar, holy Franciscan, and sometimes autocratic administrator who served St. Bonaventure for twenty-five years as its president.

1   The Baroness was sitting in the front seat, talking to everybody. But presently she turned to me and said:

2   "Well, Tom, when are you coming to Harlem for good?"

3   The simplicity of the question surprised me. Nevertheless, sudden as it was, the idea struck me that this was my answer. This was probably what I had been praying to find out.

4   However, it was sudden enough to catch me off my guard, and I did not quite know what to say. I began to talk about writing. I said that my coming to Harlem depended on how much writing I would be able to do when I got there.

5   Both the priests immediately joined in and told me to stop making conditions and opening a lot of loopholes.

6   "You let her decide about all that," said Father Hubert.

7   So it began to look as if I were going to Harlem, at least for a while.

8   The Baroness said: "Tom, are you thinking of becoming a priest? People who ask all the questions you asked me in those letters usually want to become priests. . . ."

9   Her words turned the knife in that old wound. But I said: "Oh, no, I have no vocation to the priesthood."

10   When the conversation shifted to something else, I more or less dropped out of it to think over what had been said, and it soon became clear that it was the most plausible thing for me to do. I had no special sense that this was my vocation, but on the other hand I could no longer doubt that St. Bonaventure's had outlived its usefulness in my spiritual life. I did not belong there any more. It was too tame, too safe, too sheltered. It demanded nothing of me. It had no particular cross. It left me to myself, belonging to myself, in full possession of my own will, in full command of all that God had given me that I might give it back to Him. As long as I remained

there, I still had given up nothing, or very little, no matter how poor I happened to be.

At least I could go to Harlem, and join these people in their tenement, and live 11 on what God gave us to eat from day to day, and share my life with the sick and the starving and the dying and those who had never had anything and never would have anything, the outcasts of the earth, a race despised. If that was where I belonged, God would let me know soon enough and definitely enough.

When we got to St. Bonaventure's, I saw the head of the English Department 12 standing in the dim light under the arched door to the monastery, and I said to the Baroness:

"There's my boss. I'll have to go and tell him to hire somebody else for next 13 term if I'm leaving for Harlem."

And the next day we made it definite. In January, after the semester was 14 finished, I would come down to live at Friendship House. The Baroness said I would have plenty of time to write in the mornings.

I went to Father Thomas, the President, in his room in the Library, and told 15 him I was going to leave.

His face became a labyrinth of wrinkles. 16

"Harlem," he said slowly. "Harlem." 17

Father Thomas was a man of big silences. There was a long pause before he 18 spoke again: "Perhaps you are being a bit of an enthusiast."

I told him that it seemed to be what I ought to do. 19

Another big silence. Then he said: "Haven't you ever thought about being a 20 priest?"

Father Thomas was a very wise man, and since he was the head of a seminary 21 and had taught theology to generations of priests, one of the things he might be presumed to know something about was who might or might not have a vocation to the priesthood.

But I thought: he doesn't know my case. And there was no desire in me to talk 22 about it, to bring up a discussion and get all mixed up now that I had made up my mind to do something definite. So I said:

"Oh, yes, I have thought about it, Father. But I don't believe I have that 23 vocation."

The words made me unhappy. But I forgot them immediately, when Father 24 Thomas said, with a sigh:

"All right, then. Go to Harlem if you must." 25

After that, things began to move fast. 26

On the day before Thanksgiving I abandoned my Freshman class in English 27 Composition to their own devices and started to hitch-hike south to New York. At first I was in doubt whether to make for New York or Washington. My uncle and aunt were at the capital, since his company was putting up a hotel there, and they would be glad to see me; they were rather lonely and isolated there.

However, the first ride I got took me on the way to New York rather than 28 Washington. It was a big Standard Oil truck, heading for Wellsville. We drove out into the wild, bright country, the late November country, full of the light of Indian summer. The red barns glared in the harvested fields, and the woods were bare, but all the world was full of color and the blue sky swam with fleets of white clouds. The truck devoured the road with high-singing tires, and I rode throned in the lofty, rocking cab, listening to the driver telling me stories about all the people who lived in places we passed, and what went on in the houses we saw.

29   It was material for two dozen of those novels I had once desired to write, but as far as I was now concerned it was all bad news.

30   While I was standing on the road at the edge of Wellsville, just beyond a corner where there was a gas station, near the Erie tracks, a big trailer full of steel rails went past me. It was a good thing it did not stop and pick me up. Five or six miles further on there was a long hill. It led down to a sharp turn, in the middle of a village called I forget what—Jasper, or Juniper, or something like that. By the time I got another ride, and we came down the hill, my driver pointed to the bottom and said:

31   "Man, look at that *wreck!*"

32   There was a whole crowd standing around. They were pulling the two men out of the cab of the truck. I never saw anything so flat as that cab. The whole thing, steel rails and all, had piled up in an empty yard between two small houses. The houses both had glass store windows. If the truck had gone into one of those stores the whole house would have come down on top of them.

33   And yet, the funny thing was, the two men were both alive. . . .

34   A mile further on the man who had given me a lift turned off the road, and I started once again to walk. It was a big, wide-open place, with a sweep of huge fields all down the valley, and quails flew up out of the brown grass, vanishing down the wind. I took the Breviary out of my pocket and said the *Te Deum* on account of those two men who were not killed.

35   Presently I got to another village. Maybe that one was called Jasper or Juniper too. The kids were just getting out of school, at lunch time. I sat on some concrete steps that led down to the road from one of those neat white houses and started to say Vespers while I had a chance. Presently a big old-fashioned car, old and worn-out but very much polished, came along and stopped, and picked me up. It was a polite old man and his wife. They had a son who was a freshman at Cornell and they were going to bring him home for Thanksgiving. Outside of Addison they slowed down to show me a beautiful old colonial house that they always admired when they passed that way. And it was indeed a beautiful old colonial house.

36   So they dropped me at Horseheads and I got something to eat, and I broke a tooth on some nickel candy, and went walking off down the road reciting in my head this rhyme:

> So I broke my tooth
> On a bar of Baby-Ruth.

It was not so much the tooth that I broke as something a dentist had put there. And then a business man in a shiny Oldsmobile gave me a ride as far as Owego.

37   At Owego I stood at the end of the long iron bridge and looked at the houses across the river, with all their shaky old balconies, and wondered what it was like to

live in such a place. Presently a car with a geyser of steam spouting over the radiator pulled up and the door opened.

It was a man who said he had been working on an all-night shift in some war industry in Dunkirk that was operating twenty-four hours a day. And he said: "This car is running on borrowed time." 38

However, he was going all the way down to Peekskill for Thanksgiving. 39

I think it was on the day after Thanksgiving, Friday, the Feast of the Presentation, that I saw Mark. I had lunch with him at the Columbia Faculty Club. The main reason why I wanted to talk to him was that he had just read the book I had written that summer, the *Journal of My Escape from the Nazis*, and he had an idea that somebody he knew might publish it. That was what I thought was important about that talk, that day. 40

But Providence had arranged it, I think, for another reason. 41

We were downstairs, standing among a lot of iron racks and shelves and things for keeping hats and brief cases, putting on our coats, and we had been talking about the Trappists. 42

Mark asked me: 43

"What about your idea of being a priest? Did you ever take that up again?" 44

I answered with a sort of an indefinite shrug. 45

"You know," he said, "I talked about that to someone who knows what it is all about, and he said that the fact you had let it all drop, when you were told you had no vocation, might really be a sign that you had none." 46

This was the third time that shaft had been fired at me, unexpectedly, in these last days, and this time it really struck deep. For the reasoning that went with this statement forced my thoughts to take an entirely new line. If that were true, then it prescribed a new kind of an attitude to the whole question of my vocation. 47

I had been content to tell everybody that I had no such vocation: but all the while, of course, I had been making a whole series of adjustments and reservations with which to surround that statement in my own mind. Now somebody was suddenly telling me: "If you keep on making all those reservations, maybe you will lose this gift which you know you have. . . ." 48

Which I knew I had? How did I know such a thing? 49

The spontaneous rebellion against the mere thought that I might definitely *not* be called to the monastic life: that it might certainly be out of the question, once and for all—the rebellion against such an idea was so strong in me that it told me all I needed to know. 50

And what struck me most forcibly was that this challenge had come from Mark, who was not a Catholic, and who would not be expected to possess such inside information about vocations. 51

I said to him: "I think God's Providence arranged things so that you would tell me that today." Mark saw the point of that, too, and he was pleased by it. 52

As I was taking leave of him, on the corner of 116th Street, by the Law School, I said: 53

"If I ever entered any monastery, it would be to become a Trappist." 54

It did not seem to me that this should have any effect on my decision to go to 55

Harlem. If it turned out that I did not belong there, then I would see about the monastery. Meanwhile, I had gone down to Friendship House, and discovered that on Sunday they were all going to make their monthly day of retreat in the Convent of the Holy Child, on Riverside Drive.

56   Bob Lax went up with me, that Sunday morning, and together we climbed the steps to the convent door, and a Sister let us in. We were about the first ones there, and had to wait some time before the others came, and Mass began, but I think Father Furfey, their spiritual director, who was teaching philosophy at the Catholic University and running something like Friendship House in the Negro quarter of Washington, spoke to us first at the beginning of Mass. Everything he said that day made a strong impression on both me and Lax.

57   However, when I came back from receiving Communion, I noticed that Lax had disappeared. Later, when we went to breakfast, I found him there.

58   After we had all gone to Communion, he said he began to get the feeling that the place was going to fall down on top of him, so he went out to get some air. A Sister who had noticed me passing the Missal back and forth to him and showing him the place, hurried out after him and found him sitting with his head between his knees—and offered him a cigarette.

59   That night when we left the convent, neither of us could talk. We just walked down Riverside Drive in the dusk, saying nothing. I got on the train in Jersey City and started back for Olean.

60   Three days went by without any kind of an event. It was the end of November. All the days were short and dark.

61   Finally, on the Thursday of that week, in the evening, I suddenly found myself filled with a vivid conviction:

62   "The time has come for me to go and be a Trappist."

63   Where had the thought come from? All I knew was that it was suddenly there. And it was something powerful, irresistible, clear.

64   I picked up a little book called *The Cistercian Life*, which I had bought at Gethsemani, and turned over the pages, as if they had something more to tell me. They seemed to me to be all written in words of flame and fire.

65   I went to supper, and came back and looked at the book again. My mind was literally full of this conviction. And yet, in the way, stood hesitation: that old business. But now there could be no delaying. I must finish with that, once and for all, and get an answer. I must talk to somebody who would settle it. It could be done in five minutes. And now was the time. Now.

66   Whom should I ask? Father Philotheus was probably in his room downstairs. I went downstairs, and out into the court. Yes, there was a light in Father Philotheus' room. All right. Go in and see what he has to say.

67   But instead of that, I bolted out into the darkness and made for the grove.

68   It was a Thursday night. The Alumni Hall was beginning to fill. They were going to have a movie. But I hardly noticed it: it did not occur to me that perhaps Father Philotheus might go to the movie with the rest. In the silence of the grove my feet were loud on the gravel. I walked and prayed. It was very, very dark by the shrine of the Little Flower. "For Heaven's sake, help me!" I said.

I started back towards the buildings, "All right. Now I am really going to go in   69
there and ask him. Here's the situation, Father. What do you think? Should I go
and be a Trappist?"

There was still a light in Father Philotheus' room. I walked bravely into the   70
hall, but when I got within about six feet of his door it was almost as if someone had
stopped me and held me where I was with physical hands. Something jammed in
my will. I couldn't walk a step further, even though I wanted to. I made a kind of a
push at the obstacle, which was perhaps a devil, and then turned around and ran
out of the place once more.

And again I headed for the grove. The Alumni Hall was nearly full. My feet   71
were loud on the gravel. I was in the silence of the grove, among wet trees.

I don't think there was ever a moment in my life when my soul felt so urgent   72
and so special an anguish. I had been praying all the time, so I cannot say that I
began to pray when I arrived there where the shrine was: but things became more
definite.

"Please help me. What am I going to do? I can't go on like this. You can see   73
that! Look at the state I am in. What ought I to do? Show me the way." As if I
needed more information or some kind of a sign!

But I said this time to the Little Flower: "You show me what to do." And I   74
added, "If I get into the monastery, I will be your monk. Now show me what to do."

It was getting to be precariously near the wrong way to pray—making   75
indefinite promises that I did not quite understand and asking for some sort of a
sign.

Suddenly, as soon as I had made that prayer, I became aware of the wood, the   76
trees, the dark hills, the wet night wind, and then, clearer than any of these obvious
realities, in my imagination, I started to hear the great bell of Gethsemani ringing in
the night—the bell in the big grey tower, ringing and ringing, as if it were just
behind the first hill. The impression made me breathless, and I had to think twice
to realize that it was only in my imagination that I was hearing the bell of the
Trappist Abbey ringing in the dark. Yet, as I afterwards calculated, it was just about
that time that the bell is rung every night for the *Salve Regina*, towards the end of
Compline.

The bell seemed to be telling me where I belonged—as if it were calling me   77
home.

This fancy put such determination into me that I immediately started back for   78
the monastery—going the long way 'round, past the shrine of Our Lady of Lourdes
and the far end of the football field. And with every step I took my mind became
more and more firmly made up that now I would have done with all these doubts
and hesitations and questions and all the rest, and get this thing settled, and go to
the Trappists where I belonged.

When I came into the courtyard, I saw that the light in Father Philotheus'   79
room was out. In fact, practically all the lights were out. Everybody had gone to the
movies. My heart sank.

Yet there was one hope. I went right on through the door and into the corridor,   80
and turned to the Friars' common room. I had never even gone near that door

before. I had never dared. But now I went up and knocked on the glass panel and opened the door and looked inside.

81   There was nobody there except one Friar alone, Father Philotheus.

82   I asked if I could speak with him and we went to his room.

83   That was the end of all my anxiety, all my hesitation.

84   As soon as I proposed all my hesitations and questions to him, Father Philotheus said that he could see no reason why I shouldn't want to enter a monastery and become a priest.

85   It may seem irrational, but at that moment, it was as if scales fell off my own eyes, and looking back on all my worries and questions, I could see clearly how empty and futile they had been. Yes, it was obvious that I was called to the monastic life: and all my doubts about it had been mostly shadows. Where had they gained such a deceptive appearance of substance and reality? Accident and circumstances had all contributed to exaggerate and distort things in my mind. But now everything was straight again. And already I was full of peace and assurance—the consciousness that everything was right, and that a straight road had opened out, clear and smooth, ahead of me.

Vocabulary

vocation, labyrinth, enthusiast, breviary, *Te Deum,* Vespers, Feast of the Presentation, Trappists, monastic, retreat, missal, the Little Flower (see St. Thérèse de Lisieux), *Salve Regina,* compline, irrational

Questions

1. Life at St. Bonaventure is "too tame, too safe" for Merton. Does he imply that teaching elsewhere, say at Ohio State or UCLA, would give him the excitement he needs?
2. Once he might have written novels about what the truck driver told him. Why, then, is it now "all bad news"?
3. Does Merton believe in devils?
4. Merton mentions the names of many people—most of them quite unknown. Does this trivialize his account? Shouldn't he have mentioned only the most important of them, perhaps the three who asked the key questions?
5. Gethsemani, Kentucky, is hundreds of miles south of St. Bonaventure. How could Merton hear its great bell?
6. Do you find his decision irrational?

Topics for Writing

The Heart Has Reasons Reason Cannot Know

The Hardest Decision I Ever Made

13

The Short Story/ The Best-Laid Plans

The short story is the only complete form of fictional prose narration we can sample in this book. The novel, and even the novella, take up more space than we can spare. But physical brevity is not the only characteristic of the short story. It has other qualities that distinguish it from longer fiction: the plot of a short story tends to follow a single line (although, as O. Henry taught us, the line can take surprising twists). Next, the short story involves fewer characters and scenes than are usually found in novels. Character tends to be suggested more by action than by description, and description is more likely to be a matter of quick stroke-lines than of leisurely portraiture.

The form has had great appeal both for writers and readers. The writer is working at a task whose end is not months or years ahead and has the pleasure and the challenge of a limited canvas. Readers anticipate a unified pleasure: they can expect to finish reading in a single sitting, and they can, therefore, surrender themselves confidently to an uninterrupted, if brief, sojourn in the land the author has created.

Short stories take us into strange countries of the imagination, places where the best-laid plans "gang aft a-gley." Few characters have laid as many such plans as did O. Henry's amiable tramp, and nothing worked out exactly the way Conan Doyle's or Eudora Welty's characters intended. Still, not much harm seems to have been done in any of these instances. As much cannot be said for Ambrose Bierce's Captain Madwell. Frank Stockton's young lovers engage in a plan whose outcome we cannot divulge (for good reason).

In fiction, authors control their materials, the characters and their environment, much as a clever programmer designs computer simulations and plays with permutations of a model. The short-story writer shares the pleasures experienced by all creative artists; and an attempt at writing a short story can prove an exhilarating challenge—for which the study of these stories is a good preparation.

The Cop and the Anthem

O. HENRY (1862–1910) was the pen name of William Sydney Porter, an American writer whose popular short stories nearly all end, as this one does, with a twist.

1   On this bench in Madison Square Soapy moved uneasily. When wild geese honk high of nights, and when women without sealskin coats grow kind to their husbands, and when Soapy moves uneasily on his bench in the park, you may know that winter is near at hand.

2   A dead leaf fell in Soapy's lap. That was Jack Frost's card. Jack is kind to the regular denizens of Madison Square, and gives fair warning of his annual call. At the corners of four streets he hands his pasteboard to the North Wind, footman of the mansion of All Outdoors, so that the inhabitants thereof may make ready.

3   Soapy's mind became cognisant of the fact that the time had come for him to resolve himself into a singular Committee of Ways and Means to provide against the coming rigour. And therefore he moved uneasily on his bench.

4   The hibernatorial ambitions of Soapy were not of the highest. In them there were no considerations of Mediterranean cruises, of soporific Southern skies or drifting in the Vesuvian Bay. Three months on the Island was what his soul craved. Three months of assured board and bed and congenial company, safe from Boreas and bluecoats, seemed to Soapy the essence of things desirable.

5   For years the hospitable Blackwell's had been his winter quarters. Just as his more fortunate fellow New Yorkers had bought their tickets to Palm Beach and the Riviera each winter, so Soapy had made his humbler arrangements for his annual hegira to the Island. And now the time was come. On the previous night three Sabbath newspapers, distributed beneath his coat, about his ankles and over his lap, had failed to repulse the cold as he slept on his bench near the spurting fountain in the ancient square. So the Island loomed big and timely in Soapy's mind. He scorned the provisions made in the name of charity for the city's dependents. In Soapy's opinion the Law was more benign than Philanthropy. There was an endless round of institutions, municipal and eleemosynary, on which he might set out and receive lodging and food accordant with the simple life. But to one of Soapy's proud spirit the gifts of charity are encumbered. If not in coin you must pay in humiliation of spirit for every benefit received at the hands of philanthropy. As Caesar had his Brutus, every bed of charity must have its toll of a bath, every loaf of bread its compensation of a private and personal inquisition. Wherefore it is better to be a guest of the law, which though conducted by rules, does not meddle unduly with a gentleman's private affairs.

6   Soapy, having decided to go to the Island, at once set about accomplishing his desire. There were many easy ways of doing this. The pleasantest was to dine luxuriously at some expensive restaurant; and then, after declaring insolvency, be

handed over quietly and without uproar to a policeman. An accommodating magistrate would do the rest.

Soapy left his bench and strolled out of the square and across the level sea of 7 asphalt, where Broadway and Fifth Avenue flow together. Up Broadway he turned, and halted at a glittering café, where are gathered together nightly the choicest products of the grape, the silkworm and the protoplasm.

Soapy had confidence in himself from the lowest button of his vest upward. He 8 was shaven, and his coat was decent and his neat black, ready-tied four-in-hand had been presented to him by a lady missionary on Thanksgiving Day. If he could reach a table in the restaurant unsuspected success would be his. The portion of him that would show above the table would raise no doubt in the waiter's mind. A roasted mallard duck, thought Soapy, would be about the thing—with a bottle of Chablis, and then Camembert, a demitasse and a cigar. One dollar for the cigar would be enough. The total would not be so high as to call forth any supreme manifestation of revenge from the café management; and yet the meat would leave him filled and happy for the journey to his winter refuge.

But as Soapy set foot inside the restaurant the head waiter's eye fell upon his 9 frayed trousers and decadent shoes. Strong and ready hands turned him about and conveyed him in silence and haste to the sidewalk and averted the ignoble fate of the menaced mallard.

Soapy turned off Broadway. It seemed that his route to the coveted island was 10 not to be an epicurean one. Some other way of entering limbo must be thought of.

At a corner of Sixth Avenue electric lights and cunningly displayed wares 11 behind plate-glass made a shop window conspicuous. Soapy took a cobble-stone and dashed it through the glass. People came running around the corner, a policeman in the lead. Soapy stood still, with his hands in his pockets, and smiled at the sight of brass buttons.

"Where's the man that done that?" inquired the officer excitedly. 12

"Don't you figure out that I might have had something to do with it?" said 13 Soapy, not without sarcasm, but friendly, as one greets good fortune.

The policeman's mind refused to accept Soapy even as a clue. Men who smash 14 windows do not remain to parley with the law's minions. They take to their heels. The policeman saw a man half way down the block running to catch a car. With drawn club he joined in the pursuit. Soapy, with disgust in his heart, loafed along, twice unsuccessful.

On the opposite side of the street was a restaurant of no great pretensions. It 15 catered to large appetites and modest purses. Its crockery and atmosphere were thick; its soup and napery thin. Into this place Soapy took his accusive shoes and telltale trousers without challenge. At a table he sat and consumed beefsteak, flapjacks, doughnuts and pie. And then to the waiter he betrayed the fact that the minutest coin and himself were strangers.

"Now, get busy and call a cop," said Soapy. "And don't keep a gentleman 16 waiting."

"No cop for youse," said the waiter, with a voice like butter cakes and an eye 17 like the cherry in a Manhattan cocktail. "Hey, Con!"

18   Neatly upon his left ear on the callous pavement two waiters pitched Soapy. He arose, joint by joint, as a carpenter's rule opens, and beat the dust from his clothes. Arrest seemed but a rosy dream. The Island seemed very far away. A policeman who stood before a drug store two doors away laughed and walked down the street.

19   Five blocks Soapy travelled before his courage permitted him to woo capture again. This time the opportunity presented what he fatuously termed to himself a "cinch." A young woman of a modest and pleasing guise was standing before a show window gazing with sprightly interest at its display of shaving mugs and inkstands, and two yards from the window a large policeman of severe demeanour leaned against a water plug.

20   It was Soapy's design to assume the rôle of the despicable and execrated "masher." The refined and elegant appearance of his victim and the contiguity of the conscientious cop encouraged him to believe that he would soon feel the pleasant official clutch upon his arm that would insure his winter quarters on the right little, tight little isle.

21   Soapy straightened the lady missionary's ready-made tie, dragged his shrinking cuffs into the open, set his hat at a killing cant and sidled toward the young woman. He made eyes at her, was taken with sudden coughs and "hems," smiled, smirked and went brazenly through the impudent and contemptible litany of the "masher." With half an eye Soapy saw that the policeman was watching him fixedly. The young woman moved away a few steps, and again bestowed her absorbed attention upon the shaving mugs. Soapy followed, boldly stepping to her side, raised his hat and said:

22   "Ah there, Bedelia! Don't you want to come and play in my yard?"

23   The policeman was still looking. The persecuted young woman had but to beckon a finger and Soapy would be practically en route for his insular haven. Already he imagined he could feel the cozy warmth of the station-house. The young woman faced him and, stretching out a hand, caught Soapy's coat sleeve.

24   "Sure, Mike," she said joyfully, "if you'll blow me to a pail of suds. I'd have spoke to you sooner, but the cop was watching."

25   With the young woman playing the clinging ivy to his oak Soapy walked past the policeman overcome with gloom. He seemed doomed to liberty.

26   At the next corner he shook off his companion and ran. He halted in the district where by night are found the lightest streets, hearts, vows and librettos. Women in furs and men in greatcoats moved gaily in the wintry air. A sudden fear seized Soapy that some dreadful enchantment had rendered him immune to arrest. The thought brought a little of panic upon him, and when he came upon another policeman lounging grandly in front of a transplendent theatre he caught at the immediate straw of "disorderly conduct."

27   On the sidewalk Soapy began to yell drunken gibberish at the top of his harsh voice. He danced, howled, raved and otherwise disturbed the welkin.

28   The policeman twirled his club, turned his back to Soapy and remarked to a citizen.

29   "'Tis one of them Yale lads celebratin' the goose egg they give to the Hartford

College. Noisy; but no harm. We've instructions to lave them be."

Disconsolate, Soapy ceased his unavailing racket. Would never a policeman 30
lay hands on him? In his fancy the Island seemed an unattainable Arcadia. He
buttoned his thin coat against the chilling wind.

In a cigar store he saw a well-dressed man lighting a cigar at a swinging light. 31
His silk umbrella he had set by the door on entering. Soapy stepped inside, secured
the umbrella and sauntered off with it slowly. The man at the cigar light followed
hastily.

"My umbrella," he said, sternly. 32

"Oh, is it?" sneered Soapy, adding insult to petit larceny. "Well, why don't 33
you call a policeman? I took it. Your umbrella! Why don't you call a cop? There
stands one on the corner."

The umbrella owner slowed his steps. Soapy did likewise, with a presentiment 34
that luck would again run against him. The policeman looked at the two curiously.

"Of course," said the umbrella man—"that is—well, you know how these 35
mistakes occur—I—if it's your umbrella I hope you'll excuse me—I picked it up
this morning in a restaurant—If you recognise it as yours, why—I hope you'll—"

"Of course it's mine," said Soapy, viciously. 36

The ex-umbrella man retreated. The policeman hurried to assist a tall blonde 37
in an opera cloak across the street in front of a street car that was approaching two
blocks away.

Soapy walked eastward through a street damaged by improvements. He hurled 38
the umbrella wrathfully into an excavation. He muttered against the men who wear
helmets and carry clubs. Because he wanted to fall into their clutches, they seemed
to regard him as a king who could do no wrong.

At length Soapy reached one of the avenues to the east where the glitter and 39
turmoil was but faint. He set his face down this toward Madison Square, for the
homing instinct survives even when the home is a park bench.

But on an unusually quiet corner Soapy came to a standstill. Here was an old 40
church, quaint and rambling and gabled. Through one violet-stained window a soft
light glowed, where, no doubt, the organist loitered over the keys, making sure of
his mastery of the coming Sabbath anthem. For there drifted out to Soapy's ears
sweet music that caught and held him transfixed against the convolutions of the
iron fence. 41

The moon was above, lustrous and serene; vehicles and pedestrians were few;
sparrows twittered sleepily in the eaves—for a little while the scene might have been
a country churchyard. And the anthem that the organist played cemented Soapy to
the iron fence, for he had known it well in the days when his life contained such
things as mothers and roses and ambitions and friends and immaculate thoughts
and collars.

The conjunction of Soapy's receptive state of mind and the influences about 42
the old church wrought a sudden and wonderful change in his soul. He viewed with
swift horror the pit into which he had tumbled, the degraded days, unworthy
desires, dead hopes, wrecked faculties and base motives that made up his existence.

And also in a moment his heart responded thrillingly to this novel mood. An 43 instantaneous and strong impulse moved him to battle with his desperate fate. He would pull himself out of the mire; he would make a man of himself again; he would conquer the evil that had taken possession of him. There was time; he was comparatively young yet; he would resurrect his old eager ambitions and pursue them without faltering. Those solemn but sweet organ notes had set up a revolution in him. Tomorrow he would go into the roaring downtown district and find work. A fur importer had once offered him a place as driver. He would find him to-morrow and ask for the position. He would be somebody in the world. He would——

44   Soapy felt a hand laid on his arm. He looked quickly around into the broad face of a policeman.

45   "What are you doin' here?" asked the officer.

46   "Nothin'," said Soapy.

47   "Then come along," said the policeman.

48   "Three months on the Island," said the Magistrate in the Police Court the next morning.

Vocabulary

anthem, denizens, cognisant, hibernatorial, soporific, Boreas, hegira, philanthropy, eleemosynary, inquisition, insolvency, Chablis, Camembert, demitasse, decadent, epicurean, limbo, parley, minions, napery, fatuously, demeanor, litany, "masher," insular, librettos, transplendent, gibberish, welkin, disconsolate, Arcadia, presentiment, lustrous, conjunction

Questions

1. What is the effect of O. Henry's sophisticated diction in this story? Why not say "the rich folks" instead of "the choicest products of . . . the protoplasm"? Does it suit characters like Soapy?
2. Are there any signs that Soapy's fortunes were once better than they are now? Should we be told more about his past?
3. Do you pity Soapy? After all, he is poor and faces a hard winter. If not, why not?
4. At what point does Soapy give up trying? Does O. Henry imply that Soapy just didn't try hard enough?
5. Do you think Soapy will change his ways? Shouldn't O. Henry tell us more about Soapy's future? Why not?
6. O. Henry was famous for his surprise endings. Did he catch you off guard? Could you see the ending twist coming?

Topics for Writing

Soapy's Future

The Biography of Soapy

The Lady, or the Tiger?

FRANK R. STOCKTON (1834–1902) was a widely read American novelist and short-story writer in his time, but today he is remembered chiefly as the author of "The Lady, or the Tiger?" Its popularity since it was first published in 1882 has proved perennial.

In the very olden time there lived a semi-barbaric king, whose ideas, though somewhat polished and sharpened by the progressiveness of distant Latin neighbors, were still large, florid, and untrammeled, as became the half of him which was barbaric. He was a man of exuberant fancy, and, withal, of an authority so irresistible that, at his will, he turned his varied fancies into facts. He was greatly given to self-communing; and, when he and himself agreed upon anything, the thing was done. When every member of his domestic and political systems moved smoothly in its appointed course, his nature was bland and genial; but whenever there was a little hitch, and some of his orbs got out of their orbits, he was blander and more genial still, for nothing pleased him so much as to make the crooked straight, and crush down uneven places. 1

Among the borrowed notions by which his barbarism had become semified was that of the public arena, in which, by exhibitions of manly and beastly valor, the minds of his subjects were refined and cultured. 2

But even here the exuberant and barbaric fancy asserted itself. The arena of the king was built, not to give the people an opportunity of hearing the rhapsodies of dying gladiators, nor to enable them to view the inevitable conclusion of a conflict between religious opinions and hungry jaws, but for purposes far better adapted to widen and develop the mental energies of the people. This vast amphitheater, with its encircling galleries, its mysterious vaults, and its unseen passages, was an agent of poetic justice, in which crime was punished, or virtue rewarded, by the decrees of an impartial and incorruptible chance. 3

When a subject was accused of a crime of sufficient importance to interest the king, public notice was given that on an appointed day the fate of the accused person would be decided in the king's arena—a structure which well deserved its name; for, although its form and plan were borrowed from afar, its purpose emanated solely from the brain of this man, who, every barleycorn a king, knew no tradition to which he owed more allegiance than pleased his fancy, and who ingrafted on every adopted form of human thought and action the rich growth of his barbaric idealism. 4

When all the people had assembled in the galleries, and the king, surrounded by his court, sat high up on his throne of royal state on one side of the arena, he gave a signal, a door beneath him opened, and the accused subject stepped out into the amphitheater. Directly opposite him, on the other side of the enclosed space, 5 were two doors, exactly alike and side by side. It was the duty and the privilege of the person on trial to walk directly to these doors and open one of them. He could open either door he pleased: he was subject to no guidance or influence but that of the aforementioned impartial and incorruptible chance. If he opened the one, there came out of it a hungry tiger, the fiercest and most cruel that could be procured, which immediately sprang upon him, and tore him to pieces, as a punishment for his guilt. The moment that the case of the criminal was thus decided, doleful iron bells were clanged, great wails went up from the hired mourners posted on the outer rim of the arena, and the vast audience, with bowed heads and downcast hearts, wended slowly their homeward way, mourning greatly that one so young and fair, or so old and respected, should have merited so dire a fate.

6   But, if the accused person opened the other door, there came from it a lady, the most suitable to his years and station that his majesty could select among his fair subjects; and to this lady he was immediately married, as a reward of his innocence. It mattered not that he might already possess a wife and family, or that his affections might be engaged upon an object of his own selection; the king allowed no such subordinate arrangements to interfere with his great scheme of retribution and reward. The exercises, as in the other instance, took place immediately, and in the arena. Another door opened beneath the king, and a priest, followed by a band of choristers, and dancing maidens blowing joyous airs on golden horns and treading an epithalamic measure, advanced to where the pair stood, side by side; and the wedding was promptly and cheerily solemnized. Then the gay brass bells rang forth their merry peals, the people shouted glad hurrahs, and the innocent man, preceded by children strewing flowers on his path, led his bride to his home.

7   This was the king's semi-barbaric method of administering justice. Its perfect fairness is obvious. The criminal could not know out of which door would come the lady: he opened either he pleased, without having the slightest idea whether, in the next instant, he was to be devoured or married. On some occasions the tiger came out of one door, and on some out of the other. The decisions of this tribunal were not only fair, they were positively determinate: the accused person was instantly punished if he found himself guilty; and, if innocent, he was rewarded on the spot, whether he liked it or not. There was no escape from the judgments of the king's arena.

8   The institution was a very popular one. When the people gathered together on one of the great trial days they never knew whether they were to witness a bloody slaughter or a hilarious wedding. This element of uncertainty lent an interest to the occasion which it could not otherwise have attained. Thus the masses were entertained and pleased, and the thinking part of the community could bring no charge of unfairness against this plan; for did not the accused person have the whole matter in his own hands?

9   This semi-barbaric king had a daughter as blooming as his most florid fancies, and with a soul as fervent and imperious as his own. As is usual in such cases, she was the apple of his eye, and was loved by him above all humanity. Among his courtiers was a young man of that fineness of blood and lowness of station common to the conventional heroes of romance who love royal maidens. This royal maiden was well satisfied with her lover, for he was handsome and brave to a degree

unsurpassed in all this kingdom; and she loved him with an ardor that had enough of barbarism in it to make it exceedingly warm and strong. This love affair moved on happily for many months, until one day the king happened to discover its existence. He did not hesitate nor waver in regard to his duty in the premises. The youth was immediately cast into prison, and a day was appointed for his trial in the king's arena. This, of course, was an especially important occasion; and his majesty, as well as all the people, was greatly interested in the workings and development of this trial. Never before had such a case occurred; never before had a subject dared to love the daughter of a king. In after-years such things became commonplace enough; but then they were, in no slight degree, novel and startling.

The tiger-cages of the kingdom were searched for the most savage and relent- 10 less beasts, from which the fiercest monster might be selected for the arena; and the ranks of maiden youth and beauty throughout the land were carefully surveyed by competent judges, in order that the young man might have a fitting bride in case fate did not determine for him a different destiny. Of course, everybody knew that the deed with which the accused was charged had been done. He had loved the princess, and neither he, she, nor any one else thought of denying the fact; but the king would not think of allowing any fact of this kind to interfere with the workings of the tribunal, in which he took such great delight and satisfaction. No matter how the affair turned out, the youth would be disposed of; and the king would take an aesthetic pleasure in watching the course of events, which would determine whether or not the young man had done wrong in allowing himself to love the princess.

The appointed day arrived. From far and near the people gathered, and 11 thronged the great galleries of the arena; and crowds, unable to gain admittance, massed themselves against its outside walls. The king and his court were in their places, opposite the twin doors—those fateful portals, so terrible in their similarity.

All was ready. The signal was given. A door beneath the royal party opened, 12 and the lover of the princess walked into the arena. Tall, beautiful, fair, his appearance was greeted with a low hum of admiration and anxiety. Half the audience had not known so grand a youth had lived among them. No wonder the princess loved him! What a terrible thing for him to be there!

As the youth advanced into the arena, he turned, as the custom was, to bow to 13 the king: but he did not think at all of that royal personage; his eyes were fixed upon the princess, who sat to the right of her father. Had it not been for the moiety of barbarism in her nature, it is probable that lady would not have been there; but her intense and fervid soul would not allow her to be absent on an occasion in which she was so terribly interested. From the moment that the decree had gone forth, that her lover should decide his fate in the king's arena, she had thought of nothing, night or day, but this great event and the various subjects connected with it. Possessed of more power, influence, and force of character than any one who had ever before been interested in such a case, she had done what no other person had done—she had possessed herself of the secret of the doors. She knew in which of the two rooms, that lay behind those doors, stood the cage of the tiger, with its open front, and in which waited the lady. Through these thick doors, heavily curtained with skins on the inside, it was impossible that any noise or suggestion should come from within to the person who should approach to raise the latch of one of them; but gold, and the power of a woman's will, had brought the secret to the princess.

14   And not only did she know in which room stood the lady ready to emerge, all blushing and radiant, should her door be opened, but she knew who the lady was. It was one of the fairest and loveliest of the damsels of the court who had been selected as the reward of the accused youth, should he be proved innocent of the crime of aspiring to one so far above him; and the princess hated her. Often had she seen, or imagined that she had seen, this fair creature throwing glances of admiration upon the person of her lover, and sometimes she thought these glances were perceived and even returned. Now and then she had seen them talking together; it was but for a moment or two, but much can be said in a brief space; it may have been on most unimportant topics, but how could she know that? The girl was lovely, but she had dared to raise her eyes to the loved one of the princess; and, with all the intensity of the savage blood transmitted to her through long lines of wholly barbaric ancestors, she hated the woman who blushed and trembled behind that silent door.

15   When her lover turned and looked at her, and his eye met hers as she sat there paler and whiter than any one in the vast ocean of anxious faces about her, he saw, by that power of quick perception which is given to those whose souls are one, that she knew behind which door crouched the tiger, and behind which stood the lady. He had expected her to know it. He understood her nature, and his soul was assured that she would never rest until she had made plain to herself this thing, hidden to all other lookers-on, even to the king. The only hope for the youth in which there was any element of certainty was based upon the success of the princess in discovering this mystery; and the moment he looked upon her, he saw she had succeeded, as in his soul he knew she would succeed.

16   Then it was that his quick and anxious glance asked the question: "Which?" It was as plain to her as if he shouted it from where he stood. There was not an instant to be lost. The question was asked in a flash; it must be answered in another.

17   Her right arm lay on the cushioned parapet before her. She raised her hand, and made a slight, quick movement toward the right. No one but her lover saw her. Every eye but his was fixed on the man in the arena.

18   He turned, and with a firm and rapid step he walked across the empty space. Every heart stopped beating. Every breath was held, every eye was fixed immovably upon that man. Without the slightest hesitation, he went to the door on the right, and opened it.

19   Now, the point of the story is this: Did the tiger come out of that door, or did the lady?

20   The more we reflect upon this question, the harder it is to answer. It involves a study of the human heart which leads us through devious mazes of passion, out of which it is difficult to find our way. Think of it, fair reader, not as if the decision of the question depended upon yourself, but upon that hot-blooded, semi-barbaric princess, her soul at a white heat beneath the combined fires of despair and jealousy. She had lost him, but who should have him?

21   How often, in her waking hours and in her dreams, had she started in wild horror, and covered her face with her hands as she thought of her lover opening the door on the other side of which waited the cruel fangs of the tiger!

But how much oftener had she seen him at the other door! How in her 22
grievous reveries had she gnashed her teeth, and torn her hair, when she saw his
start of rapturous delight as he opened the door of the lady! How her soul had
burned in agony when she had seen him rush to meet that woman, with her
flushing cheek and sparkling eye of triumph; when she had seen him lead her forth,
his whole frame kindled with the joy of recovered life; when she had heard the glad
shouts from the multitude, and the wild ringing of the happy bells; when she had
seen the priest, with his joyous followers, advance to the couple, and make them
man and wife before her very eyes; and when she had seen them walk away together
upon their path of flowers, followed by the tremendous shouts of the hilarious
multitude, in which her one despairing shriek was lost and drowned!

Would it not be better for him to die at once, and go to wait for her in the 23
blessed regions of semi-barbaric futurity?

And yet, that awful tiger, those shrieks, that blood! 24

Her decision had been indicated in an instant, but it had been made after days 25
and nights of anguished deliberation. She had known she would be asked, she had
decided what she would answer, and, without the slightest hesitation, she had
moved her hand to the right.

The question of her decision is one not to be lightly considered, and it is not 26
for me to presume to set myself up as the one person able to answer it. And so I
leave it with all of you: Which came out of the opened door—the lady, or the tiger?

Vocabulary

florid, untrammeled, barbarism, exuberant, emanated, retribution, epithalamic,
determinate, moiety, fervid

Questions

1. Is it necessary that we have all this background on the king and his style of
   rule?
2. This is complex and decorated prose, leisurely and artificial. Does it suit the
   subject matter? Doesn't it slow the narrative pace? Is that a deliberate aim?
3. Does uncertainty sometimes add to our pleasures?
4. Why does the threatened youth keep his eye on the princess? How did she
   come to know which door concealed which fate?
5. Why does Stockton emphasize barbarism and barbarity so much? Is it because a civilized princess would act differently from this one?
6. Do the last seven paragraphs heighten or lower the effect of the story on you?

Topic for Writing

My Choice of Endings

The Coup de Grâce

AMBROSE BIERCE   (1842–1914?), journalist and short-story writer, took a sardonic view of life, as his "definitions" in *The Devil's Dictionary* prove ("Labor: one of the processes by which A acquires property for B"). He fought in the Civil War with the Ninth Indiana Volunteers, and the bitter experience was not forgotten, as this story shows. His later life went badly, and he disappeared in Mexico where he is thought to have died in 1914.

1   The fighting had been hard and continuous; that was attested by all the senses. The very taste of battle was in the air. All was now over; it remained only to succor the wounded and bury the dead—to "tidy up a bit," as the humorist of a burial squad put it. A good deal of "tidying up" was required. As far as one could see through the forests, among the splintered trees, lay wrecks of men and horses. Among them moved the stretcher-bearers, gathering and carrying away the few who showed signs of life. Most of the wounded had died of neglect while the right to minister to their wants was in dispute. It is an army regulation that the wounded must wait; the best way to care for them is to win the battle. It must be confessed that victory is a distinct advantage to a man requiring attention, but many do not live to avail themselves of it.

2   The dead were collected in groups of a dozen or a score and laid side by side in rows while the trenches were dug to receive them. Some, found at too great a distance from these rallying points, were buried where they lay. There was little attempt at identification, though in most cases, the burial parties being detailed to glean the same ground which they had assisted to reap, the names of the victorious dead were known and listed. The enemy's fallen had to be content with counting. But of that they got enough: many of them were counted several times, and the total, as given afterward in the official report of the victorious commander, denoted rather a hope than a result.

3   At some little distance from the spot where one of the burial parties had established its "bivouac of the dead," a man in the uniform of a Federal officer stood leaning against a tree. From his feet upward to his neck his attitude was that of weariness reposing; but he turned his head uneasily from side to side; his mind was apparently not at rest. He was perhaps uncertain in which direction to go; he was not likely to remain long where he was, for already the level rays of the setting sun straggled redly through the open spaces of the wood and the weary soldiers were quitting their task for the day. He would hardly make a night of it alone there among the dead. Nine men in ten whom you meet after a battle inquire the way to some fraction of the army—as if any one could know. Doubtless this officer was lost. After resting himself a moment he would presumably follow one of the retiring burial squads.

When all were gone he walked straight away into the forest toward the red   4
west, its light staining his face like blood. The air of confidence with which he now
strode along showed that he was on familiar ground; he had recovered his bearings.
The dead on his right and on his left were unregarded as he passed. An occasional
low moan from some sorely stricken wretch whom the relief-parties had not
reached, and who would have to pass a comfortless night beneath the stars with his
thirst to keep him company, was equally unheeded. What, indeed, could the officer
have done, being no surgeon and having no water?

At the head of a shallow ravine, a mere depression of the ground, lay a small   5
group of bodies. He saw, and swerving suddenly from his course walked rapidly
toward them. Scanning each one sharply as he passed, he stopped at last above one
which lay at a slight remove from the others, near a clump of small trees. He looked
at it narrowly. It seemed to stir. He stooped and laid his hand upon its face. It
screamed.

The officer was Captain Downing Madwell, of a Massachusetts regiment of   6
infantry, a daring and intelligent soldier, an honorable man.

In the regiment were two brothers named Halcrow—Caffal and Creede Hal-   7
crow. Caffal Halcrow was a sergeant in Captain Madwell's company, and these two
men, the sergeant and the captain, were devoted friends. In so far as disparity of
rank, differences in duties and considerations of military discipline would permit
they were commonly together. They had, indeed, grown up together from childhood. A habit of the heart is not easily broken off. Caffal Halcrow had nothing
military in his taste nor disposition, but the thought of separation from his friend
was disagreeable; he enlisted in the company in which Madwell was second-
lieutenant. Each had taken two steps upward in rank, but between the highest non-
commissioned and the lowest commissioned officer the gulf is deep and wide and
the old relation was maintained with difficulty and a difference.

Creede Halcrow, the brother of Caffal, was the major of the regiment—a   8
cynical, saturnine man, between whom and Captain Madwell there was a natural
antipathy which circumstances had nourished and strengthened to an active
animosity. But for the restraining influence of their mutual relation to Caffal these
two patriots would doubtless have endeavored to deprive their country of each
other's services.

At the opening of the battle that morning the regiment was performing outpost   9
duty a mile away from the main army. It was attacked and nearly surrounded in the
forest, but stubbornly held its ground. During a lull in the fighting, Major Halcrow
came to Captain Madwell. The two exchanged formal salutes, and the major said:
"Captain, the colonel directs that you push your company to the head of this ravine
and hold your place there until recalled. I need hardly apprise you of the dangerous
character of the movement, but if you wish, you can, I suppose, turn over the
command to your first-lieutenant. I was not, however, directed to authorize the
substitution; it is merely a suggestion of my own, unofficially made."

To this deadly insult Captain Madwell coolly replied: 10

"Sir, I invite you to accompany the movement. A mounted officer would be a   11 conspicuous mark, and I have long held the opinion that it would be better if you were dead."

12   The art of repartee was cultivated in military circles as early as 1862.

13   A half-hour later Captain Madwell's company was driven from its position at the head of the ravine, with a loss of one-third its number. Among the fallen was Sergeant Halcrow. The regiment was soon afterward forced back to the main line, and at the close of the battle was miles away. The captain was now standing at the side of his subordinate and friend.

14   Sergeant Halcrow was mortally hurt. His clothing was deranged; it seemed to have been violently torn apart, exposing the abdomen. Some of the buttons of his jacket had been pulled off and lay on the ground beside him and fragments of his other garments were strewn about. His leather belt was parted and had apparently been dragged from beneath him as he lay. There had been no great effusion of blood. The only visible wound was a wide, ragged opening in the abdomen. It was defiled with earth and dead leaves. Protruding from it was a loop of small intestine. In all his experience Captain Madwell had not seen a wound like this. He could neither conjecture how it was made nor explain the attendant circumstances—the strangely torn clothing, the parted belt, the besmirching of the white skin. He knelt and made a closer examination. When he rose to his feet, he turned his eyes in different directions as if looking for an enemy. Fifty yards away, on the crest of a low, thinly wooded hill, he saw several dark objects moving about among the fallen men—a herd of swine. One stood with its back to him, its shoulders sharply elevated. Its forefeet were upon a human body, its head was depressed and invisible. The bristly ridge of its chine showed black against the red west. Captain Madwell drew away his eyes and fixed them again upon the thing which had been his friend.

15   The man who had suffered these monstrous mutilations was alive. At intervals he moved his limbs; he moaned at every breath. He stared blankly into the face of his friend and if touched screamed. In his giant agony he had torn up the ground on which he lay; his clenched hands were full of leaves and twigs and earth. Articulate speech was beyond his power; it was impossible to know if he were sensible to anything but pain. The expression of his face was an appeal; his eyes were full of prayer. For what?

16   There was no misreading that look; the captain had too frequently seen it in eyes of those whose lips had still the power to formulate it by an entreaty for death. Consciously or unconsciously, this writhing fragment of humanity, this type and example of acute sensation, this handiwork of man and beast, this humble, un-heroic Prometheus, was imploring everything, all, the whole non-ego, for the boon of oblivion. To the earth and the sky alike, to the trees, to the man, to whatever took form in sense or consciousness, this incarnate suffering addressed that silent plea.

17   For what, indeed? For that which we accord to even the meanest creature without sense to demand it, denying it only to the wretched of our own race: for the blessed release, the rite of uttermost compassion, the *coup de grâce*.

18   Captain Madwell spoke the name of his friend. He repeated it over and over without effect until emotion choked his utterance. His tears plashed upon the livid face beneath his own and blinded himself. He saw nothing but a blurred and

moving object, but the moans were more distinct than ever, interrupted at briefer intervals by sharper shrieks. He turned away, struck his hand upon his forehead, and strode from the spot. The swine, catching sight of him, threw up their crimson muzzles, regarding him suspiciously a second, and then with a gruff, concerted grunt, raced away out of sight. A horse, its foreleg splintered by a cannon-shot, lifted its head sidewise from the ground and neighed piteously. Madwell stepped forward, drew his revolver and shot the poor beast between the eyes, narrowly observing its death-struggle, which, contrary to his expectation, was violent and long; but at last it lay still. The tense muscles of its lips, which had uncovered the teeth in a horrible grin, relaxed; the sharp, clean-cut profile took on a look of profound peace and rest.

Along the distant, thinly wooded crest to westward the fringe of sunset fire had now nearly burned itself out. The light upon the trunks of the trees had faded to a tender gray; shadows were in their tops, like great dark birds aperch. Night was coming and there were miles of haunted forest between Captain Madwell and camp. Yet he stood there at the side of the dead animal, apparently lost to all sense of his surroundings. His eyes were bent upon the earth at his feet; his left hand hung loosely at his side, his right still held the pistol. Presently he lifted his face, turned it toward his dying friend and walked rapidly back to his side. He knelt upon one knee, cocked the weapon, placed the muzzle against the man's forehead, and turning away his eyes pulled the trigger. There was no report. He had used his last cartridge for the horse. 19

The sufferer moaned and his lips moved convulsively. The froth that ran from them had a tinge of blood. 20

Captain Madwell rose to his feet and drew his sword from the scabbard. He passed the fingers of his left hand along the edge from hilt to point. He held it out straight before him, as if to test his nerves. There was no visible tremor of the blade; the ray of bleak skylight that it reflected was steady and true. He stooped and with his left hand tore away the dying man's shirt, rose and placed the point of the sword just over the heart. This time he did not withdraw his eyes. Grasping the hilt with both hands, he thrust downward with all his strength and weight. The blade sank into the man' body—through his body into the earth; Captain Madwell came near falling forward upon his work. The dying man drew up his knees and at the same time threw his right arm across his breast and grasped the steel so tightly that the knuckles of the hand visibly whitened. By a violent but vain effort to withdraw the blade the wound was enlarged; a rill of blood escaped, running sinuously down into the deranged clothing. At that moment three men stepped silently forward from behind the clump of young trees which had concealed their approach. Two were hospital attendants and carried a stretcher. 21

The third was Major Creede Halcrow. 22

Vocabulary

coup de grâce, succor, bivouac, disparity, saturnine, antipathy, apprise, repartee, effusion, chine, Prometheus, incarnate, sinuously

Questions

1. Is winning the battle the best way to care for the wounded? Can you defend the answer?
2. What is the difference between the treatment of dead enemies and dead friends? How does that affect the official reports?
3. What is the effect of "It screamed"?
4. Does Bierce "load the dice" against Captain Madwell? How?
5. Killing the horse foreshadows the next act of mercy. Does it make the second killing easier? Why does Madwell watch the horse's death struggle "narrowly"?
6. Do you view the ending of the story as a judgment on Captain Madwell or as a comment on fate?

Topics for Writing

The Dice Were Loaded

Was Madwell Justified?

The Court-Martial of Captain Madwell

Why I Live at the P.O.

EUDORA WELTY (1909–), prize-winning short-story writer and novelist, sets many of her pieces in her native Mississippi. Hers is the heritage of the southern storyteller; her ear for the sound of authentic voices and her sense of the genuinely funny are particularly acute. "Why I Live at the P.O." was published in *A Curtain of Green and Other Stories* (1941).

I was getting along fine with Mama, Papa-Daddy and Uncle Rondo until my sister Stella-Rondo just separated from her husband and came back home again. Mr. Whitaker! Of course I went with Mr. Whitaker first, when he first appeared here in China Grove, taking "Pose Yourself" photos, and Stella-Rondo broke us up. Told him I was one-sided. Bigger on one side than the other, which is a deliberate, calculated falsehood: I'm the same. Stella-Rondo is exactly twelve months to the day younger than I am and for that reason she's spoiled. 1

She's always had anything in the world she wanted and then she'd throw it away. Papa-Daddy gave her this gorgeous Add-a-Pearl necklace when she was eight years old and she threw it away playing baseball when she was nine, with only two pearls. 2

So as soon as she got married and moved away from home the first thing she did was separate! From Mr. Whitaker! This photographer with the popeyes she said she trusted. Came home from one of those towns up in Illinois and to our complete surprise brought this child of two. 3

Mama said she like to made her drop dead for a second. "Here you had this marvelous blonde child and never so much as wrote your mother a word about it," says Mama. "I'm thoroughly ashamed of you." But of course she wasn't. 4

Stella-Rondo just calmly takes off this *hat*, I wish you could see it. She says, "Why, Mama, Shirley-T.'s adopted, I can prove it." 5

"How?" says Mama, but all I says was, "H'm!" There I was over the hot stove, trying to stretch two chickens over five people and a completely unexpected child into the bargain, without one moment's notice. 6

"What do you mean—'H'm!'?" says Stella-Rondo, and Mama says, "I heard that, Sister." 7

"I said that oh, I didn't mean a thing, only that whoever Shirley-T. was, she was the spit-image of Papa-Daddy if he'd cut off his beard, which of course he'd never do in the world. Papa-Daddy's Mama's papa and sulks. 8

Stella-Rondo got furious! She said, "Sister, I don't need to tell you you got a lot of nerve and always did have and I'll thank you to make no future reference to my adopted child whatsoever." 9

"Very well," I said. "Very well, very well. Of course I noticed at once she looks like Mr. Whitaker's side too. That frown. She looks like a cross between Mr. Whitaker and Papa-Daddy." 10

11   "Well, all I can say is she isn't."

12   "She looks exactly like Shirley Temple to me," says Mama, but Shirley-T. just ran away from her.

13   So the first thing Stella-Rondo did at the table was turn Papa-Daddy against me.

14   "Papa-Daddy," she says. He was trying to cut up his meat. "Papa-Daddy!" I was taken completely by surprise. Papa-Daddy is about a million years old and's got this long-long beard. "Papa-Daddy, Sister says she fails to understand why you don't cut off your beard."

15   So Papa-Daddy l-a-y-s down his knife and fork! He's real rich. Mama says he is, he says he isn't. So he says, "Have I heard correctly? You don't understand why I don't cut off my beard?"

16   "Why," I says, "Papa-Daddy, of course I understand, I did not say any such of a thing, the idea!"

17   He says, "Hussy!"

18   I says, "Papa-Daddy, you know I wouldn't any more want you to cut off your beard than the man in the moon. It was the farthest thing from my mind! Stella-Rondo sat there and made that up while she was eating breast of chicken."

19   But he says, "So the postmistress fails to understand why I don't cut off my beard. Which job I got you through my influence with the government. 'Bird's nest'—is that what you call it?"

20   Not that it isn't the next to smallest P.O. in the entire state of Mississippi.

21   I says, "Oh, Papa-Daddy," I says, "I didn't say any such of a thing, I never dreamed it was a bird's nest, I have always been grateful though this is the next to smallest P.O. in the state of Mississippi, and I do not enjoy being referred to as a hussy by my own grandfather."

22   But Stella-Rondo says, "Yes, you did say it too. Anybody in the world could of heard you, that had ears."

23   "Stop right there," says Mama, looking at *me*.

24   So I pulled my napkin straight back through the napkin ring and left the table.

25   As soon as I was out of the room Mama says, "Call her back, or she'll starve to death," but Papa-Daddy says, "This is the beard I started growing on the Coast when I was fifteen years old." He would of gone on till nightfall if Shirley-T. hadn't lost the Milky Way she ate in Cairo.

26   So Papa-Daddy says, "I am going out and lie in the hammock, and you can all sit here and remember my words: I'll never cut off my beard as long as I live, even one inch, and I don't appreciate it in you at all." Passed right by me in the hall and went straight out and got in the hammock.

27   It would be a holiday. It wasn't five minutes before Uncle Rondo suddenly appeared in the hall in one of Stella-Rondo's flesh-colored kimonos, all cut on the bias, like something Mr. Whitaker probably thought was gorgeous.

28   "Uncle Rondo!" I says. "I didn't know who that was! Where are you going?"

29   "Sister," he says, "get out of my way, I'm poisoned."

30   "If you're poisoned stay away from Papa-Daddy," I says. "Keep out of the hammock. Papa-Daddy will certainly beat you on the head if you come within forty

miles of him. He thinks I deliberately said he ought to cut off his beard after he got me the P.O., and I've told him and told him and told him, and he acts like he just don't hear me. Papa-Daddy must of gone stone deaf."

"He picked a fine day to do it then," says Uncle Rondo, and before you could say "Jack Robinson" flew out in the yard.   31

What he'd really done, he'd drunk another bottle of that prescription. He does it every single Fourth of July as sure as shooting, and it's horribly expensive. Then he falls over in the hammock and snores. So he insisted on zigzagging right on out to the hammock, looking like a half-wit.   32

Papa-Daddy woke up with this horrible yell and right there without moving an inch he tried to turn Uncle Rondo against me. I heard every word he said. Oh, he told Uncle Rondo I didn't learn to read till I was eight years old and he didn't see how in the world I ever got the mail put up at the P.O., much less read it all, and he said if Uncle Rondo could only fathom the lengths he had gone to to get me that job! And he said on the other hand he thought Stella-Rondo had a brilliant mind and deserved credit for getting out of town. All the time he was just lying there swinging as pretty as you please and looping out his beard, and poor Uncle Rondo was *pleading* with him to slow down the hammock, it was making him as dizzy as a witch to watch it. But that's what Papa-Daddy likes about a hammock. So Uncle Rondo was too dizzy to get turned against me for the time being. He's Mama's only brother and is a good case of a one-track mind. Ask anybody. A certified pharmacist.   33

Just then I heard Stella-Rondo raising the upstairs window. While she was married she got this peculiar idea that it's cooler with the windows shut and locked. So she has to raise the window before she can make a soul hear her outdoors.   34

So she raises the window and says, "*Oh!*" You would have thought she was mortally wounded.   35

Uncle Rondo and Papa-Daddy didn't even look up, but kept right on with what they were doing. I had to laugh.   36

I flew up the stairs and threw the door open! I says, "What in the wide world's the matter, Stella-Rondo? You mortally wounded?"   37

"No," she says, "I am not mortally wounded but I wish you would do me the favor of looking out that window there and telling me what you see."   38

So I shade my eyes and look out the window.   39

"I see the front yard," I says.   40

"Don't you see any human beings?" she says.   41

"I see Uncle Rondo trying to run Papa-Daddy out of the hammock," I says. "Nothing more. Naturally, it's so suffocating-hot in the house, with all the windows shut and locked, everybody who cares to stay in their right mind will have to go out and get in the hammock before the Fourth of July is over."   42

"Don't you notice anything different about Uncle Rondo?" asks Stella-Rondo.   43

"Why, no, except he's got on some terrible-looking flesh-colored contraption I wouldn't be found dead in, is all I can see," I says.   44

"Never mind, you won't be found dead in it, because it happens to be part of my trousseau, and Mr. Whitaker took several dozen photographs of me in it," says   45

Stella-Rondo. "What on earth could Uncle Rondo *mean* by wearing part of my trousseau out in the broad open daylight without saying so much as 'Kiss my foot,' *knowing* I only got home this morning after my separation and hung my negligee up on the bathroom door, just as nervous as I could be?"

46   "I'm sure I don't know, and what do you expect me to do about it?" I says. "Jump out the window?"

47   "No, I expect nothing of the kind. I simply declare that Uncle Rondo looks like a fool in it, that's all," she says. "It makes me sick to my stomach."

48   "Well, he looks as good as he can," I says. "As good as anybody in reason could." I stood up for Uncle Rondo, please remember. And I said to Stella-Rondo, "I think I would do well not to criticize so freely if I were you and came home with a two-year-old child I had never said a word about, and no explanation whatever about my separation."

49   "I asked you the instant I entered this house not to refer one more time to my adopted child, and you gave me your word of honor you would not," was all Stella-Rondo would say, and started pulling out every one of her eyebrows with some cheap Kress tweezers.

50   So I merely slammed the door behind me and went down and made some green-tomato pickle. Somebody had to do it. Of course Mama had turned both the niggers loose; she always said no earthly power could hold one anyway on the Fourth of July, so she wouldn't even try. It turned out that Jaypan fell in the lake and came within a very narrow limit of drowning.

51   So Mama trots in. Lifts up the lid and says, "H'm! Not very good for your Uncle Rondo in his precarious condition, I must say. Or poor little adopted Shirley-T. Shame on you!"

52   That made me tired. I says, "Well, Stella-Rondo had better thank her lucky stars it was her instead of me came trotting in with that very peculiar-looking child. Now if it had been me that trotted in from Illinois and brought a peculiar-looking child of two, I shudder to think of the reception I'd of got, much less controlled the diet of an entire family."

53   "But you must remember, Sister, that you were never married to Mr. Whitaker in the first place and didn't go up to Illinois to live," says Mama, shaking a spoon in my face. "If you had I would of been just as overjoyed to see you and your little adopted girl as I was to see Stella-Rondo, when you wound up with your separation and came on back home."

54   "You would not," I says.

55   "Don't contradict me, I would," says Mama.

56   But I said she couldn't convince me though she talked till she was blue in the face. Then I said, "Besides, you know as well as I do that that child is not adopted."

57   "She most certainly is adopted," says Mama, stiff as a poker.

58   I says, "Why, Mama, Stella-Rondo had her just as sure as anything in this world, and just too stuck up to admit it."

59   "Why, Sister," said Mama. "Here I thought we were going to have a pleasant Fourth of July, and you start right out not believing a word your own baby sister tells you!"

"Just like Cousin Annie Flo. Went to her grave denying the facts of life," I 60
remind Mama.

"I told you if you ever mentioned Annie Flo's name I'd slap your face," says 61
Mama, and slaps my face.

"All right, you wait and see," I says. 62

"I," says Mama, "I prefer to take my children's word for anything when it's 63
humanly possible." You ought to see Mama, she weighs two hundred pounds and
has real tiny feet.

Just then something perfectly horrible occurred to me. 64

"Mama," I says, "can that child talk?" I simply had to whisper! "Mama, I 65
wonder if that child can be—you know—in any way? Do you realize," I says, "that
she hasn't spoken one single, solitary word to a human being up to this minute?
This is the way she looks," I says, and I looked like this.

Well, Mama and I just stood there and stared at each other. It was horrible! 66

"I remember well that Joe Whitaker frequently drank like a fish," says Mama. 67
"I believed to my soul he drank *chemicals*." And without another word she marches
to the foot of the stairs and calls Stella-Rondo.

"Stella-Rondo? O-o-o-o-o! Stella-Rondo!" 68

"What?" says Stella-Rondo from upstairs. Not even the grace to get up off the 69
bed.

"Can that child of yours talk?" asks Mama. 70

Stella-Rondo says, "Can she what?" 71

"Talk! Talk!" says Mama. "Burdyburdyburdyburdy!" 72

So Stella-Rondo yells back, "Who says she can't talk?" 73

"Sister says so," says Mama. 74

"You didn't have to tell me, I know whose word of honor don't mean a thing in 75
this house," says Stella-Rondo.

And in a minute the loudest Yankee voice I ever heard in my life yells out, 76
"OE'm Pop-OE the Sailor-r-r-r Ma-a-an!" and then somebody jumps up and down
in the upstairs hall. In another second the house would of fallen down.

"Not only talks, she can tap-dance!" calls Stella-Rondo. "Which is more than 77
some people I won't name can do."

"Why, the little precious darling thing!" Mama says, so surprised. "Just as 78
smart as she can be!" Starts talking baby talk right there. Then she turns on me.
"Sister, you ought to be thoroughly ashamed! Run upstairs this instant and
apologize to Stella-Rondo and Shirley-T."

"Apologize for what?" I says. "I merely wondered if the child was normal, 79
that's all. Now that she's proved she is, why, I have nothing further to say."

But Mama just turned on her heel and flew out, furious. She ran right upstairs 80
and hugged the baby. She believed it was adopted. Stella-Rondo hadn't done a
thing but turn her against me from upstairs while I stood there helpless over the hot
stove. So that made Mama, Papa-Daddy and the baby all on Stella-Rondo's side.

Next, Uncle Rondo. 81

I must say that Uncle Rondo has been marvelous to me at various times in the 82
past and I was completely unprepared to be made to jump out of my skin, the way it

turned out. Once Stella-Rondo did something perfectly horrible to him—broke a chain letter from Flanders Field—and he took the radio back he had given her and gave it to me. Stella-Rondo was furious! For six months we all had to call her Stella instead of Stella-Rondo, or she wouldn't answer. I always thought Uncle Rondo had all the brains of the entire family. Another time he sent me to Mammoth Cave, with all expenses paid.

83   But this would be the day he was drinking that prescription, the Fourth of July.

84   So at supper Stella-Rondo speaks up and says she thinks Uncle Rondo ought to try to eat a little something. So finally Uncle Rondo said he would try a little cold biscuits and ketchup, but that was all. So *she* brought it to him.

85   "Do you think it wise to disport with ketchup in Stella-Rondo's flesh-colored kimono?" I says. Trying to be considerate! If Stella-Rondo couldn't watch out for her trousseau, somebody had to.

86   "Any objections?" asks Uncle Rondo, just about to pour out all the ketchup.

87   "Don't mind what she says, Uncle Rondo," says Stella-Rondo. "Sister has been devoting this solid afternoon to sneering out my bedroom window at the way you look."

88   "What's that?" says Uncle Rondo. Uncle Rondo has got the most terrible temper in the world. Anything is liable to make him tear the house down if it comes at the wrong time.

89   So Stella-Rondo says, "Sister says, 'Uncle Rondo certainly does look like a fool in that pink kimono!' "

90   Do you remember who it was really said that?

91   Uncle Rondo spills out all the ketchup and jumps out of his chair and tears off the kimono and throws it down on the dirty floor and puts his foot on it. It had to be sent all the way to Jackson to the cleaners and re-pleated.

92   "So that's your opinion of your Uncle Rondo, is it?" he says. "I look like a fool, do I? Well, that's the last straw. A whole day in this house with nothing to do, and then to hear you come out with a remark like that behind my back!"

93   "I didn't say any such of a thing, Uncle Rondo," I says, "and I'm not saying who did, either. Why, I think you look all right. Just try to take care of yourself and not talk and eat at the same time," I says. "I think you better go lie down."

94   "Lie down my foot," says Uncle Rondo. I ought to of known by that he was fixing to do something perfectly horrible.

95   So he didn't do anything that night in the precarious state he was in—just played Casino with Mama and Stella-Rondo and Shirley-T. and gave Shirley-T. a nickel with a head on both sides. It tickled her nearly to death, and she called him "Papa." But at 6:30 A.M. the next morning, he threw a whole five-cent package of some unsold one-inch firecrackers from the store as hard as he could into my bedroom and they every one went off. Not one bad one in the string. Anybody else, there'd be one that wouldn't go off.

96   Well, I'm just terribly susceptible to noise of any kind, the doctor has always told me I was the most sensitive person he had ever seen in his whole life, and I was simply prostrated. I couldn't eat! People tell me they heard it as far as the cemetery, and old Aunt Jep Patterson, that had been holding her own so good, thought it was

Judgment Day and she was going to meet her whole family. It's usually so quiet here.

And I'll tell you it didn't take me any longer than a minute to make up my   97
mind what to do. There I was with the whole entire house on Stella-Rondo's side and turned against me. If I have anything at all I have pride.

So I just decided I'd go straight down to the P.O. There's plenty of room there   98
in the back, I says to myself.

Well! I made no bones about letting the family catch on to what I was up to. I   99
didn't try to conceal it.

The first thing they knew, I marched in where they were all playing Old Maid   100
and pulled the electric oscillating fan out by the plug, and everything got real hot. Next I snatched the pillow I'd done the needlepoint on right off the davenport from behind Papa-Daddy. He went "Ugh!" I beat Stella-Rondo up the stairs and finally found my charm bracelet in her bureau drawer under a picture of Nelson Eddy.

"So that's the way the land lies," says Uncle Rondo. There he was, piecing on   101
the ham. "Well, Sister, I'll be glad to donate my army cot if you got any place to set it up, providing you'll leave right this minute and let me get some peace." Uncle Rondo was in France.

"Thank you kindly for the cot and 'peace' is hardly the word I would select if I   102
had to resort to firecrackers at 6:30 A.M. in a young girl's bedroom," I says back to him. "And as to where I intend to go, you seem to forget my position as postmistress of China Grove, Mississippi," I says. "I've always got the P.O."

Well, that made them all sit up and take notice.   103

I went out front and started digging up some four-o'clocks to plant around the   104
P.O.

"Ah-ah-ah!" says Mama, raising the window. "Those happen to be my four-   105
o'clocks. Everything planted in that star is mine. I've never known you to make anything grow in your life."

"Very well," I says. "But I take the fern. Even you, Mama, can't stand there   106
and deny that I'm the one watered that fern. And I happen to know where I can send in a box top and get a package of one thousand mixed seeds, no two the same kind, free."

"Oh, where?" Mama wants to know.   107

But I says, "Too late. You 'tend to your house, and I'll 'tend to mine. You hear   108
things like that all the time if you know how to listen to the radio. Perfectly marvelous offers. Get anything you want free."

So I hope to tell you I marched in and got that radio, and they could of all bit a   109
nail in two, especially Stella-Rondo, that it used to belong to, and she well knew she couldn't get it back, I'd sue for it like a shot. And I very politely took the sewing-machine motor I helped pay the most on to give Mama for Christmas back in 1929, and a good big calendar, with the first-aid remedies on it. The thermometer and the Hawaiian ukulele certainly were rightfully mine, and I stood on the step-ladder and got all my watermelon-rind preserves and every fruit and vegetable I'd put up, every jar. Then I began to pull the tacks out of the bluebird wall vases on the archway to the dining room.

110   "Who told you you could have those, Miss Priss?" says Mama, fanning as hard as she could.

111   "I bought 'em and I'll keep track of 'em," I says. "I'll tack 'em up one on each side of the post-office window, and you can see 'em when you come to ask me for your mail, if you're so dead to see 'em."

112   "Not I! I'll never darken the door to that post office again if I live to be a hundred," Mama says. "Ungrateful child! After all the money we spent on you at the Normal."

113   "Me either," says Stella-Rondo. "You can just let my mail lie there and *rot*, for all I care. I'll never come and relieve you of a single, solitary piece."

114   "I should worry," I says. "And who you think's going to sit down and write you all those big fat letters and postcards, by the way? Mr. Whitaker? Just because he was the only man ever dropped down in China Grove and you got him—unfairly—is he going to sit down and write you a lengthy correspondence after you come home giving no rhyme nor reason whatsoever for your separation and no explanation for the presence of that child? I may not have your brilliant mind, but I fail to see it."

115   So Mama says, "Sister, I've told you a thousand times that Stella-Rondo simply got homesick, and this child is far too big to be hers," and she says, "Now, why don't you all just sit down and play Casino?"

116   Then Shirley-T. sticks out her tongue at me in this perfectly horrible way. She has no more manners than the man in the moon. I told her she was going to cross her eyes like that some day and they'd stick.

117   "It's too late to stop me now," I says. "You should have tried that yesterday. I'm going to the P.O. and the only way you can possibly see me is to visit me there."

118   So Papa-Daddy says, "You'll never catch me setting foot in that post office, even if I should take a notion into my head to write a letter some place." He says, "I won't have you reachin' out of that little old window with a pair of shears and cuttin' off any beard of mine. I'm too smart for you!"

119   "We all are," says Stella-Rondo.

120   But I said, "If you're so smart, where's Mr. Whitaker?"

121   So then Uncle Rondo says, "I'll thank you from now on to stop reading all the orders I get on postcards and telling everybody in China Grove what you think is the matter with them," but I says, "I draw my own conclusions and will continue in the future to draw them." I says, "If people want to write their inmost secrets on penny postcards, there's nothing in the wide world you can do about it, Uncle Rondo."

122   "And if you think we'll ever *write* another postcard you're sadly mistaken," says Mama.

123   "Cutting off your nose to spite your face then," I says. "But if you're all determined to have no more to do with the U.S. mail, think of this: What will Stella-Rondo do now, if she wants to tell Mr. Whitaker to come after her?"

124   "Wha!" says Stella-Rondo. I knew she'd cry. She had a conniption fit right there in the kitchen.

125   "It will be interesting to see how long she holds out," I says. "And now—I am leaving."

126   "Good-bye," says Uncle Rondo.

127   "Oh, I declare," says Mama, "to think that a family of mine should quarrel on

the Fourth of July, or the day after, over Stella-Rondo leaving old Mr. Whitaker and having the sweetest little adopted child! It looks like we'd all be glad!"

"Wah!" says Stella-Rondo, and has a fresh conniption fit.   128

"*He* left *her*—you mark my words," I says. "That's Mr. Whitaker. I know Mr.   129
Whitaker. After all, I knew him first. I said from the beginning he'd up and leave her. I foretold every single thing that's happened."

"Where did he go?" asks Mama.   130

"Probably to the North Pole, if he knows what's good for him," I says.   131

But Stella-Rondo just bawled and wouldn't say another word. She flew to her   132
room and slammed the door.

"Now look what you've gone and done, Sister," says Mama. "You go   133
apologize."

"I haven't got time, I'm leaving," I says.   134

"Well, what are you waiting around for?" asks Uncle Rondo.   135

So I just picked up the kitchen clock and marched off, without saying "Kiss my   136
foot" or anything, and never did tell Stella-Rondo good-bye.

There was a nigger girl going along on a little wagon right in front.   137

"Nigger girl," I says, "come help me haul these things down the hill, I'm going   138
to live in the post office."

Took her nine trips in her express wagon. Uncle Rondo came out on the porch   139
and threw her a nickel.

And that's the last I've laid eyes on any of my family or my family laid eyes on   140
me for five solid days and nights. Stella-Rondo may be telling the most horrible tales in the world about Mr. Whitaker, but I haven't heard them. As I tell everybody, I draw my own conclusions.

But oh, I like it here. It's ideal, as I've been saying. You see, I've got everything   141
cater-cornered, the way I like it. Hear the radio? All the war news. Radio, sewing machine, book ends, ironing board and that great big piano lamp—peace, that's what I like. Butter-bean vines planted all along the front where the strings are.

Of course, there's not much mail. My family are naturally the main people in   142
China Grove, and if they prefer to vanish from the face of the earth, for all the mail they get or the mail they write, why, I'm not going to open my mouth. Some of the folks here in town are taking up for me and some turned against me. I know which is which. There are always people who will quit buying stamps just to get on the right side of Papa-Daddy.

But here I am, and here I'll stay. I want the world to know I'm happy.   143

And if Stella-Rondo should come to me this minute, on bended knees, and   144
attempt to explain the incidents of her life with Mr. Whitaker, I'd simply put my fingers in both my ears and refuse to listen.

Vocabulary

calculated, trousseau, precarious, disport, prostrated, oscillating, normal (college), conniption fit

Questions

1. Is the narrative as disorganized as the narrator seems to be when she adds information about her relatives almost haphazardly? Consider the paragraph ending with Mama's "real tiny feet" or the one ending, "Ask anybody. A certified pharmacist."
2. To whom is the story being told?
3. Are these small-town Mississippians naive?
4. How much of her trouble does the narrator bring upon herself?
5. The details of Eudora Welty's story are, one hopes, uncommon, but do you see any reflections of family life as you know it?
6. Do you think the narrator is happy living at the P.O.?

Topics for Writing

Is the Narrator an Innocent Victim?

Life at the P.O.: A Typical Day

A Scandal in Bohemia

ARTHUR CONAN DOYLE (see Chapter 8) began a series of short stories about Holmes after the success of two novels, *A Study in Scarlet* and *The Sign of the Four,* disclosed an enthusiastic public for the world's "first consulting detective." "A Scandal in Bohemia" appeared in 1891 and gives us everything the "Baker Street Irregular" wants: a rousing story, examples of Holmes's cleverness, and—as important to the fan—teasing references to the "real" lives (Watson's marriage and medical practice, Holmes's habits) we imagine for the great characters of fiction.

To Sherlock Holmes she is always *the* woman. I have seldom heard him 1 mention her under any other name. In his eyes she eclipses and predominates the whole of her sex. It was not that he felt any emotion akin to love for Irene Adler. All emotions, and that one particularly, were abhorrent to his cold, precise but admirably balanced mind. He was, I take it, the most perfect reasoning and observing machine that the world has seen, but as a lover he would have placed himself in a false position. He never spoke of the softer passions, save with a gibe and a sneer. They were admirable things for the observer—excellent for drawing the veil from men's motives and actions. But for the trained reasoner to admit such intrusions into his own delicate and finely adjusted temperament was to introduce a distracting factor which might throw a doubt upon all his mental results. Grit in a sensitive instrument, or a crack in one of his own high-power lenses, would not be more disturbing than a strong emotion in a nature such as his. And yet there was but one woman to him, and that woman was the late Irene Adler, of dubious and questionable memory.

I had seen little of Holmes lately. My marriage had drifted us away from each 2 other. My own complete happiness, and the home-centred interests which rise up around the man who first finds himself master of his own establishment, were sufficient to absorb all my attention, while Holmes, who loathed every form of society with his whole Bohemian soul, remained in our lodgings in Baker Street, buried among his old books, and alternating from week to week between cocaine and ambition, the drowsiness of the drug, and the fierce energy of his own keen nature. He was still, as ever, deeply attracted by the study of crime, and occupied his immense faculties and extraordinary powers of observation in following out those clues, and clearing up those mysteries which had been abandoned as hopeless by the official police. From time to time I heard some vague account of his doings: of his summons to Odessa in the case of the Trepoff murder, of his clearing up of the singular tragedy of the Atkinson brothers at Trincomalee, and finally of the mission which he had accomplished so delicately and successfully for the reigning family of Holland. Beyond these signs of his activity, however, which I merely shared with all the readers of the daily press, I knew little of my former friend and companion.

3   One night—it was on the twentieth of March, 1888—I was returning from a journey to a patient (for I had now returned to civil practice), when my way led me through Baker Street. As I passed the well-remembered door, which must always be associated in my mind with my wooing, and with the dark incidents of the *Study in Scarlet*, I was seized with a keen desire to see Holmes again, and to know how he was employing his extraordinary powers. His rooms were brilliantly lit, and, even as I looked up, I saw his tall, spare figure pass twice in a dark silhouette against the blind. He was pacing the room swiftly, eagerly, with his head sunk upon his chest and his hands clasped behind him. To me, who knew his every mood and habit, his attitude and manner told their own story. He was at work again. He had risen out of his drug-created dreams and was hot upon the scent of some new problem. I rang the bell and was shown up to the chamber which had formerly been in part my own.

4   His manner was not effusive. It seldom was; but he was glad, I think, to see me. With hardly a word spoken, but with a kindly eye, he waved me to an armchair, threw across his case of cigars, and indicated a spirit case and a gasogene in the corner. Then he stood before the fire and looked me over in his singular introspective fashion.

5   "Wedlock suits you," he remarked. "I think, Watson, that you have put on seven and a half pounds since I saw you."

6   "Seven!" I answered.

7   "Indeed, I should have thought a little more. Just a trifle more, I fancy, Watson. And in practice again, I observe. You did not tell me that you intended to go into harness."

8   "Then, how do you know?"

9   "I see it, I deduce it. How do I know that you have been getting youself very wet lately, and that you have a most clumsy and careless servant girl?"

10   "My dear Holmes," said I, "this is too much. You would certainly have been burned, had you lived a few centuries ago. It is true that I had a country walk on Thursday and came home in a dreadful mess, but as I have changed my clothes I can't imagine how you deduce it. As to Mary Jane, she is incorrigible, and my wife has given her notice; but there, again, I fail to see how you work it out."

11   He chuckled to himself and rubbed his long, nervous hands together.

12   "It is simplicity itself," said he; "my eyes tell me that on the inside of your left shoe, just where the firelight strikes it, the leather is scored by six almost parallel cuts. Obviously they have been caused by someone who has very carelessly scraped round the edges of the sole in order to remove crusted mud from it. Hence, you see, my double deduction that you had been out in vile weather, and that you had a particularly malignant boot-slitting specimen of the London slavey. As to your practice, if a gentleman walks into my room smelling of iodoform, with a black mark of nitrate of silver upon his right forefinger, and a bulge on the right side of his top-hat to show where he has secreted his stethoscope, I must be dull, indeed, if I do not pronounce him to be an active member of the medical profession."

I could not help laughing at the ease with which he explained his process of   13
deduction. "When I hear you give your reasons," I remarked, "the thing always
appears to me to be so ridiculously simple that I could easily do it myself, though at
each successive instance of your reasoning I am baffled until you explain your
process. And yet I believe that my eyes are as good as yours."

"Quite so," he answered, lighting a cigarette, and throwing himself down into   14
an armchair. "You see, but you do not observe. The distinction is clear. For
example, you have frequently seen the steps which lead up from the hall to this
room."

"Frequently."   15

"How often?"   16

"Well, some hundreds of times."   17

"Then how many are there?"   18

"How many? I don't know."   19

"Quite so! You have not observed. And yet you have seen. That is just my   20
point. Now, I know that there are seventeen steps because I have both seen and
observed. By the way, since you are interested in these little problems, and since
you are good enough to chronicle one or two of my trifling experiences, you may be
interested in this." He threw over a sheet of thick, pink-tinted note-paper which had
been lying open upon the table. "It came by the last post," said he. "Read it aloud."

The note was undated, and without either signature or address.   21

"There will call upon you to-night, at a quarter to eight o'clock [it said], a
gentleman who desires to consult you upon a matter of the very deepest moment. Your
recent services to one of the royal houses of Europe have shown that you are one who
may safely be trusted with matters which are of an importance which can hardly be
exaggerated. This account of you we have from all quarters received. Be in your
chamber then at that hour, and do not take it amiss if your visitor wear a mask.

"This is indeed a mystery," I remarked. "What do you imagine that it means?"   22

"I have no data yet. It is a capital mistake to theorize before one has data.   23
Insensibly one begins to twist facts to suit theories, instead of theories to suit facts.
But the note itself. What do you deduce from it?"

I carefully examined the writing, and the paper upon which it was written.   24

"The man who wrote it was presumably well to do," I remarked, endeavouring   25
to imitate my companion's processes. "Such paper could not be bought under half a
crown a packet. It is peculiarly strong and stiff."

"Peculiar—that is the very word," said Holmes. "It is not an English paper at   26
all. Hold it up to the light."

I did so, and saw a large "E" with a small "g," a "P," and a large "G" with a   27
small "t" woven into the texture of the paper.

"What do you make of that?" asked Holmes.   28

"The name of the maker, no doubt; or his monogram, rather."   29

"Not at all. The 'G' with the small 't' stands for 'Gesellschaft,' which is the   30
German for 'Company.' It is a customary contraction like our 'Co.' 'P,' of course,
stands for 'Papier.' Now for the 'Eg.' Let us glance at our Continental Gazetteer."

He took down a heavy brown volume from his shelves. "Eglow, Eglonitz—here we are, Egria. It is in a German-speaking country—in Bohemia, not far from Carlsbad. 'Remarkable as being the scene of the death of Wallenstein, and for its numerous glass-factories and paper-mills.' Ha, ha, my boy, what do you make of that?" His eyes sparkled, and he sent up a great blue triumphant cloud from his cigarette.

31   "The paper was made in Bohemia," I said.

32   "Precisely. And the man who wrote the note is a German. Do you note the peculiar construction of the sentence—'This account of you we have from all quarters received.' A Frenchman or Russian could not have written that. It is the German who is so uncourteous to his verbs. It only remains, therefore, to discover what is wanted by this German who writes upon Bohemian paper and prefers wearing a mask to showing his face. And here he comes, if I am not mistaken, to resolve all our doubts."

33   As he spoke there was the sharp sound of horses' hoofs and grating wheels against the curb, followed by a sharp pull at the bell. Holmes whistled.

34   "A pair, by the sound," said he. "Yes," he continued, glancing out of the window. "A nice little brougham and a pair of beauties. A hundred and fifty guineas apiece. There's money in this case, Watson, if there is nothing else."

35   "I think that I had better go, Holmes."

36   "Not a bit, Doctor. Stay where you are. I am lost without my Boswell. And this promises to be interesting. It would be a pity to miss it."

37   "But your client—"

38   "Never mind him. I may want your help, and so may he. Here he comes. Sit down in that armchair, Doctor, and give us your best attention."

39   A slow and heavy step, which had been heard upon the stairs and in the passage, paused immediately outside the door. Then there was a loud and authoritative tap.

40   "Come in!" said Holmes.

41   A man entered who could hardly have been less than six feet six inches in height, with the chest and limbs of a Hercules. His dress was rich with a richness which would, in England, be looked upon as akin to bad taste. Heavy bands of astrakhan were slashed across the sleeves and fronts of his double-breasted coat, while the deep blue cloak which was thrown over his shoulders was lined with flame-coloured silk and secured at the neck with a brooch which consisted of a single flaming beryl. Boots which extended halfway up his calves, and which were trimmed at the tops with rich brown fur, completed the impression of barbaric opulence which was suggested by his whole appearance. He carried a broad-brimmed hat in his hand, while he wore across the upper part of his face, extending down past the cheek-bones, a black vizard mask, which he had apparently adjusted that very moment, for his hand was still raised to it as he entered. From the lower part of the face he appeared to be a man of strong character, with a thick, hanging lip, and a long, straight chin suggestive of resolution pushed to the length of obstinacy.

"You had my note?" he asked with a deep harsh voice and a strongly marked   42
German accent. "I told you that I would call." He looked from one to the other of
us, as if uncertain which to address.

"Pray take a seat," said Holmes. "This is my friend and colleague, Dr. Wat-   43
son, who is occasionally good enough to help me in my cases. Whom have I the
honour to address?"

"You may address me as the Count Von Kramm, a Bohemian nobleman. I   44
understand that this gentleman, your friend, is a man of honour and discretion,
whom I may trust with a matter of the most extreme importance. If not, I should
much prefer to communicate with you alone."

I rose to go, but Holmes caught me by the wrist and pushed me back into my   45
chair. "It is both, or none," said he. "You may say before this gentleman anything
which you may say to me."

The Count shrugged his broad shoulders. "Then I must begin," said he, "by   46
binding you both to absolute secrecy for two years; at the end of that time the matter
will be of no importance. At present it is not too much to say that it is of such weight
it may have an influence upon European history."

"I promise," said Holmes.   47

"And I."   48

"You will excuse this mask," continued our strange visitor. "The august person   49
who employs me wishes his agent to be unknown to you, and I may confess at once
that the title by which I have just called myself is not exactly my own."

"I was aware of it," said Holmes drily.   50

"The circumstances are of great delicacy, and every precaution has to be taken   51
to quench what might grow to be an immense scandal and seriously compromise
one of the reigning families of Europe. To speak plainly, the matter implicates the
great House of Ormstein, hereditary kings of Bohemia."

"I was also aware of that," murmured Holmes, settling himself down in his   52
armchair and closing his eyes.

Our visitor glanced with some apparent surprise at the languid, lounging figure   53
of the man who had been no doubt depicted to him as the most incisive reasoner
and most energetic agent in Europe. Holmes slowly reopened his eyes and looked
impatiently at his gigantic client.

"If your Majesty would condescend to state your case," he remarked, "I should   54
be better able to advise you."

The man sprang from his chair and paced up and down the room in uncon-   55
trollable agitation. Then, with a gesture of desperation, he tore the mask from his
face and hurled it upon the ground. "You are right," he cried; "I am the King. Why
should I attempt to conceal it?"

"Why, indeed?" murmured Holmes. "Your Majesty had not spoken before I   56
was aware that I was addressing Wilhelm Gottsreich Sigismond von Ormstein,
Grand Duke of Cassel-Felstein, and hereditary King of Bohemia."

"But you can understand," said our strange visitor, sitting down once more and   57
passing his hand over his high white forehead, "you can understand that I am not

accustomed to doing such business in my own person. Yet the matter was so delicate that I could not confide it to an agent without putting myself in his power. I have come incognito from Prague for the purpose of consulting you."

58   "Then, pray consult," said Holmes, shutting his eyes once more.

59   "The facts are briefly these: Some five years ago, during a lengthy visit to Warsaw, I made the acquaintance of the well-known adventuress, Irene Adler. The name is no doubt familiar to you."

60   "Kindly look her up in my index, Doctor," murmured Holmes without opening his eyes. For many years he had adopted a system of docketing all paragraphs concerning men and things, so that it was difficult to name a subject or a person on which he could not at once furnish information. In this case I found her biography sandwiched in between that of a Hebrew rabbi and that of a staff-commander who had written a monograph upon the deep-sea fishes.

61   "Let me see!" said Holmes. "Hum! Born in New Jersey in the year 1858. Contralto—hum! La Scala, hum! Prima donna Imperial Opera of Warsaw—yes! Retired from operatic stage—ha! Living in London—quite so! Your Majesty, as I understand, became entangled with this young person, wrote her some compromising letters, and is now desirous of getting those letters back."

62   "Precisely so. But how—"

63   "Was there a secret marriage?"

64   "None."

65   "No legal papers or certificates?"

66   "None."

67   "Then I fail to follow your Majesty. If this young person should produce her letters for blackmailing or other purposes, how is she to prove their authenticity?"

68   "There is the writing."

69   "Pooh, pooh! Forgery."

70   "My private note-paper."

71   "Stolen."

72   "My own seal."

73   "Imitated."

74   "My photograph."

75   "Bought."

76   "We were both in the photograph."

77   "Oh, dear! That is very bad! Your Majesty has indeed committed an indiscretion."

78   "I was mad—insane."

79   "You have compromised yourself seriously."

80   "I was only Crown Prince then. I was young. I am but thirty now."

81   "It must be recovered."

82   "We have tried and failed."

83   "Your Majesty must pay. It must be bought."

84   "She will not sell."

85   "Stolen, then."

86   "Five attempts have been made. Twice burglars in my pay ransacked her

house. Once we diverted her luggage when she travelled. Twice she has been waylaid. There has been no result."

"No sign of it?"   87

"Absolutely none."   88

Holmes laughed. "It is quite a pretty little problem," said he.   89

"But a very serious one to me," returned the King reproachfully.   90

"Very, indeed. And what does she propose to do with the photograph?"   91

"To ruin me."   92

"But how?"   93

"I am about to be married."   94

"So I have heard."   95

"To Clotilde Lothman von Saxe-Meningen, second daughter of the King of   96
Scandinavia. You may know the strict principles of her family. She is herself the very soul of delicacy. A shadow of a doubt as to my conduct would bring the matter to an end."

"And Irene Adler?"   97

"Threatens to send them the photograph. And she will do it. I know that she   98
will do it. You do not know her, but she has a soul of steel. She has the face of the most beautiful of women, and the mind of the most resolute of men. Rather than I should marry another woman, there are no lengths to which she would not go—none."

"You are sure that she has not sent it yet?"   99

"I am sure."   100

"And why?"   101

"Because she has said that she would send it on the day when the betrothal was   102
publicly proclaimed. That will be next Monday."

"Oh, then we have three days yet," said Holmes with a yawn. "That is very   103
fortunate, as I have one or two matters of importance to look into just at present. You Majesty will, of course, stay in London for the present?"

"Certainly. You will find me at the Langham under the name of the Count   104
Von Kramm."

"Then I shall drop you a line to let you know how we progress."   105

"Pray do so. I shall be all anxiety."   106

"Then, as to money?"   107

"You have *carte blanche*."   108

"Absolutely?"   109

"I tell you that I would give one of the provinces of my kingdom to have that   110
photograph."

"And for present expenses?"   111

The King took a heavy chamois leather bag from under his cloak and laid it on   112
the table.

"There are three hundred pounds in gold and seven hundred in notes," he   113
said.

Holmes scribbled a receipt upon a sheet of his note-book and handed it to him.   114

"And Mademoiselle's address?" he asked.   115

116   "Is Briony Lodge, Serpentine Avenue, St. John's Wood."

117   Holmes took a note of it. "One other question," said he. "Was the photograph a cabinet?"

118   "It was."

119   "Then, good-night, your Majesty, and I trust that we shall soon have some good news for you. And good-night, Watson," he added, as the wheels of the royal brougham rolled down the street. "If you will be good enough to call to-morrow afternoon at three o'clock I should like to chat this little matter over with you."

2

120   At three o'clock precisely I was at Baker Street, but Holmes had not yet returned. The landlady informed me that he had left the house shortly after eight o'clock in the morning. I sat down beside the fire, however, with the intention of awaiting him, however long he might be. I was already deeply interested in his inquiry, for, though it was surrounded by none of the grim and strange features which were associated with the two crimes which I have already recorded, still, the nature of the case and the exalted station of his client gave it a character of its own. Indeed, apart from the nature of the investigation which my friend had on hand, there was something in his masterly grasp of a situation, and his keen, incisive reasoning, which made it a pleasure to me to study his system of work, and to follow the quick, subtle methods by which he disentangled the most inextricable mysteries. So accustomed was I to his invariable success that the very possibility of his failing had ceased to enter into my head.

121   It was close upon four before the door opened, and a drunken-looking groom, ill-kempt and side-whiskered, with an inflamed face and disreputable clothes, walked into the room. Accustomed as I was to my friend's amazing powers in the use of disguises, I had to look three times before I was certain that it was indeed he. With a nod he vanished into the bedroom, whence he emerged in five minutes tweed-suited and respectable, as of old. Putting his hands into his pockets, he stretched out his legs in front of the fire and laughed heartily for some minutes.

122   "Well, really!" he cried, and then he choked and laughed again until he was obliged to lie back, limp and helpless, in the chair.

123   "What is it?"

124   "It's quite too funny. I am sure you could never guess how I employed my morning, or what I ended by doing."

125   "I can't imagine. I suppose that you have been watching the habits, and perhaps the house, of Miss Irene Adler."

126   "Quite so; but the sequel was rather unusual. I will tell you, however. I left the house a little after eight o'clock this morning in the character of a groom out of work. There is a wonderful sympathy and freemasonry among horsy men. Be one of them, and you will know all that there is to know. I soon found Briony Lodge. It is a *bijou* villa, with a garden at the back, but built out in front right up to the road, two stories. Chubb lock to the door. Large sitting-room on the right side, well furnished, with long windows almost to the floor, and those preposterous English window fasteners which a child could open. Behind there was nothing remarkable,

save that the passage window could be reached from the top of the coach-house. I walked round it and examined it closely from every point of view, but without noting anything else of interest.

"I then lounged down the street and found, as I expected, that there was a mews in a lane which runs down by one wall of the garden. I lent the ostlers a hand in rubbing down their horses, and received in exchange twopence, a glass of half and half, two fills of shag tobacco, and as much information as I could desire about Miss Adler, to say nothing of half a dozen other people in the neighbourhood in whom I was not in the least interested, but whose biographies I was compelled to listen to." 127

"And what of Irene Adler?" I asked. 128

"Oh, she has turned all the men's heads down in that part. She is the daintiest 129 thing under a bonnet on this planet. So say the Serpentine-mews, to a man. She lives quietly, sings at concerts, drives out at five every day, and returns at seven sharp for dinner. Seldom goes out at other times, except when she sings. Has only one male visitor, but a good deal of him. He is dark, handsome, and dashing, never calls less than once a day, and often twice. He is a Mr. Godfrey Norton, of the Inner Temple. See the advantages of a cabman as a confidant. They had driven him home a dozen times from Serpentine-mews, and knew all about him. When I had listened to all they had to tell, I began to walk up and down near Briony Lodge once more, and to think over my plan of campaign.

"This Godfrey Norton was evidently an important factor in the matter. He was 130 a lawyer. That sounded ominous. What was the relation between them, and what the object of his repeated visits? Was she his client, his friend, or his mistress? If the former, she had probably transferred the photograph to his keeping. If the latter, it was less likely. On the issue of this question depended whether I should continue my work at Briony Lodge, or turn my attention to the gentleman's chambers in the Temple. It was a delicate point, and it widened the field of my inquiry. I fear that I bore you with these details, but I have to let you see my little difficulties, if you are to understand the situation."

"I am following you closely," I answered. 131

"I was still balancing the matter in my mind when a hansom cab drove up to 132 Briony Lodge, and a gentleman sprang out. He was a remarkably handsome man, dark, aquiline, and moustached—evidently the man of whom I had heard. He appeared to be in a great hurry, shouted to the cabman to wait, and brushed past the maid who opened the door with the air of a man who was thoroughly at home.

"He was in the house about half an hour, and I could catch glimpses of him in 133 the windows of the sitting-room, pacing up and down, talking excitedly, and waving his arms. Of her I could see nothing. Presently he emerged, looking even more flurried than before. As he stepped up to the cab, he pulled a gold watch from his pocket and looked at it earnestly, 'Drive like the devil,' he shouted, 'first to Gross & Hankey's in Regent Street, and then to the Church of St. Monica in the Edgeware Road. Half a guinea if you do it in twenty minutes!'

"Away they went, and I was just wondering whether I should not do well to 134 follow them when up the lane came a neat little landau, the coachman with his coat only half-buttoned, and his tie under his ear, while all the tags of his harness were sticking out of the buckles. It hadn't pulled up before she shot out of the hall door and into it. I only caught a glimpse of her at the moment, but she was a lovely woman, with a face that a man might die for.

135   "'The Church of St. Monica, John,' she cried, 'and half a sovereign if you reach it in twenty minutes.'

136   "This was quite too good to lose, Watson. I was just balancing whether I should run for it, or whether I should perch behind her landau when a cab came through the street. The driver looked twice at such a shabby fare, but I jumped in before he could object. 'The Church of St. Monica,' said I, 'and half a sovereign if you reach it in twenty minutes.' It was twenty-five minutes to twelve, and of course it was clear enough what was in the wind.

137   "My cabby drove fast. I don't think I ever drove faster, but the others were there before us. The cab and the landau with their steaming horses were in front of the door when I arrived. I paid the man and hurried into the church. There was not a soul there save the two whom I had followed and a surpliced clergyman, who seemed to be expostulating with them. They were all three standing in a knot in front of the altar. I lounged up the side aisle like any other idler who has dropped into a church. Suddenly, to my surprise, the three at the altar faced round to me, and Godfrey Norton came running as hard as he could towards me.

138   " 'Thank God,' he cried. 'You'll do. Come! Come!'

139   "'What then?' I asked.

140   "'Come, man, come, only three minutes, or it won't be legal.'

141   "I was half-dragged up to the altar, and before I knew where I was I found myself mumbling responses which were whispered in my ear, and vouching for things of which I knew nothing, and generally assisting in the secure tying up of Irene Adler, spinster, to Godfrey Norton, bachelor. It was all done in an instant, and there was the gentleman thanking me on the one side and the lady on the other, while the clergyman beamed on me in front. It was the most preposterous position in which I ever found myself in my life, and it was the thought of it that started me laughing just now. It seems that there had been some informality about their license, that the clergyman absolutely refused to marry them without a witness of some sort, and that my lucky appearance saved the bridegroom from having to sally out into the streets in search of a best man. The bride gave me a sovereign, and I mean to wear it on my watch-chain in memory of the occasion."

142   "This is a very unexpected turn of affairs," said I; "and what then?"

143   "Well, I found my plans very seriously menaced. It looked as if the pair might take an immediate departure, and so necessitate very prompt and energetic measures on my part. At the church door, however, they separated, he driving back to the Temple, and she to her own house. 'I shall drive out in the park at five as usual,' she said as she left him. I heard no more. They drove away in different directions, and I went off to make my own arrangements."

144   "Which are?"

145   "Some cold beef and a glass of beer," he answered, ringing the bell. "I have

been too busy to think of food, and I am likely to be busier still this evening. By the way, Doctor, I shall want your coöperation."

"I shall be delighted." 146

"You don't mind breaking the law?" 147

"Not in the least." 148

"Nor running a chance of arrest?" 149

"Not in a good cause." 150

"Oh, the cause is excellent!" 151

"Then I am your man." 152

"I was sure that I might rely on you." 153

"But what is it you wish?" 154

"When Mrs. Turner has brought in the tray I will make it clear to you. Now," 155 he said as he turned hungrily on the simple fare that our landlady had provided, "I must discuss it while I eat, for I have not much time. It is nearly five now. In two hours we must be on the scene of action. Miss Irene, or Madame, rather, returns from her drive at seven. We must be at Briony Lodge to meet her."

"And what then?" 156

"You must leave that to me. I have already arranged what is to occur. There is 157 only one point on which I must insist. You must not interfere, come what may. You understand?"

"I am to be neutral?" 158

"To do nothing whatever. There will probably be some small unpleasantness. 159 Do not join in it. It will end in my being conveyed into the house. Four or five minutes afterwards the sitting-room window will open. You are to station yourself close to that open window."

"Yes." 160

"You are to watch me, for I will be visible to you." 161

"Yes." 162

"And when I raise my hand—so—you will throw into the room what I give 163 you to throw, at the same time, raise the cry of fire. You quite follow me?"

"Entirely." 164

"It is nothing very formidable," he said, taking a long cigar-shaped roll from 165 his pocket. "It is an ordinary plumber's smoke-rocket, fitted with a cap at either end to make it self-lighting. Your task is confined to that. When you raise your cry of fire, it will be taken up by quite a number of people. You may then walk to the end of the street, and I will rejoin you in ten minutes. I hope that I have made myself clear?"

"I am to remain neutral, to get near the window, to watch you, and at the 166 signal to throw in this object, then to raise the cry of fire, and to wait you at the corner of the street."

"Precisely." 167

"Then you may entirely rely on me." 168

"That is excellent. I think, perhaps, it is almost time that I prepare for the new 169 rôle I have to play."

170   He disappeared into his bedroom and returned in a few minutes in the character of an amiable and simple-minded Nonconformist clergyman. His broad black hat, his baggy trousers, his white tie, his sympathetic smile, and general look of peering and benevolent curiosity were such as Mr. John Hare alone could have equalled. It was not merely that Holmes changed his costume. His expression, his manner, his very soul seemed to vary with every fresh part that he assumed. The stage lost a fine actor, even as science lost an acute reasoner, when he became a specialist in crime.

171   It was a quarter past six when we left Baker Street, and it still wanted ten minutes to the hour when we found ourselves in Serpentine Avenue. It was already dusk, and the lamps were just being lighted as we paced up and down in front of Briony Lodge, waiting for the coming of its occupant. The house was just such as I had pictured it from Sherlock Holmes's succinct description, but the locality appeared to be less private than I expected. On the contrary, for a small street in a quiet neighbourhood, it was remarkably animated. There was a group of shabbily dressed men smoking and laughing in a corner, a scissors-grinder with his wheel, two guardsmen who were flirting with a nurse-girl, and several well-dressed young men who were lounging up and down with cigars in their mouths.

172   "You see," remarked Holmes, as we paced to and fro in front of the house, "this marriage rather simplifies matters. The photograph becomes a double-edged weapon now. The chances are that she would be as averse to its being seen by Mr. Godfrey Norton, as our client is to its coming to the eyes of his princess. Now the question is, Where are we to find the photograph?"

173   "Where, indeed?"

174   "It is most unlikely that she carries it about with her. It is cabinet size. Too large for easy concealment about a woman's dress. She knows that the King is capable of having her waylaid and searched. Two attempts of the sort have already been made. We may take it, then, that she does not carry it about with her."

175   "Where, then?"

176   "Her banker or lawyer. There is that double possibility. But I am inclined to think neither. Women are naturally secretive, and they like to do their own secreting. Why should she hand it over to anyone else? She could trust her own guardianship, but she could not tell what indirect or political influence might be brought to bear upon a business man. Besides, remember that she had resolved to use it within a few days. It must be where she can lay her hands upon it. It must be in her own house."

177   "But it has twice been burgled."

178   "Pshaw! They did not know how to look."

179   "But how will you look?"

180   "I will not look."

181   "What then?"

182   "I will get her to show me."

183   "But she will refuse."

184   "She will not be able to. But I hear the rumble of wheels. It is her carriage. Now carry out my orders to the letter."

As he spoke the gleam of the side-lights of a carriage came round the curve of   185
the avenue. It was a smart little landau which rattled up to the door of Briony
Lodge. As it pulled up, one of the loafing men at the corner dashed forward to open
the door in the hope of earning a copper, but was elbowed away by another loafer,
who had rushed up with the same intention. A fierce quarrel broke out, which was
increased by the two guardsmen, who took sides with one of the loungers, and by
the scissors-grinder, who was equally hot upon the other side. A blow was struck,
and in an instant the lady, who had stepped from her carriage, was the centre of a
little knot of flushed and struggling men, who struck savagely at each other with
their fists and sticks. Holmes dashed into the crowd to protect the lady; but just as he
reached her he gave a cry and dropped to the ground, with the blood running freely
down his face. At his fall the guardsmen took to their heels in one direction and the
loungers in the other, while a number of better-dressed people, who had watched
the scuffle without taking part in it, crowded in to help the lady and to attend to the
injured man. Irene Adler, as I will still call her, had hurried up the steps; but she
stood at the top with her superb figure outlined against the lights of the hall, looking
back into the street.

"Is the poor gentleman much hurt?" she asked.   186

"He is dead," cried several voices.   187

"No, no, there's life in him!" shouted another. "But he'll be gone before you   188
can get him to hospital."

"He's a brave fellow," said a woman. "They would have had the lady's purse   189
and watch if it hadn't been for him. They were a gang, and a rough one, too. Ah,
he's breathing now."

"He can't lie in the street. May we bring him in, marm?"   190

"Surely. Bring him into the sitting-room. There is a comfortable sofa. This   191
way, please!"

Slowly and solemnly he was borne into Briony Lodge and laid out in the   192
principal room, while I still observed the proceedings from my post by the window.
The lamps had been lit, but the blinds had not been drawn, so that I could see
Holmes as he lay upon the couch. I do not know whether he was seized with
compunction at that moment for the part he was playing, but I know that I never
felt more heartily ashamed of myself in my life than when I saw the beautiful
creature against whom I was conspiring, or the grace and kindliness with which she
waited upon the injured man. And yet it would be the blackest treachery to Holmes
to draw back now from the part which he had intrusted to me. I hardened my heart,
and took the smoke-rocket from under my ulster. After all, I thought, we are not
injuring her. We are but preventing her from injuring another.

Holmes had sat up upon the couch, and I saw him motion like a man who is in   193
need of air. A maid rushed across and threw open the window. At the same instant I
saw him raise his hand, and at the signal I tossed my rocket into the room with a cry
of "Fire!" The word was no sooner out of my mouth than the whole crowd of
spectators, well dressed and ill—gentlemen, ostlers, and servant-maids—joined in
a general shriek of "Fire!" Thick clouds of smoke curled through the room and out
at the open window. I caught a glimpse of rushing figures, and a moment later the

voice of Holmes from within assuring them that the fire was a false alarm. Slipping through the shouting crowd I made my way to the corner of the street, and in ten minutes was rejoiced to find my friend's arm in mine, and to get away from the scene of uproar. He walked swiftly and in silence for some few minutes until we had turned down one of the quiet streets which lead towards the Edgeware Road.

194   "You did it very nicely, Doctor," he remarked. "Nothing could have been better. It is all right."

195   "You have the photograph?"

196   "I know where it is."

197   "And how did you find out?"

198   "She showed me, as I told you she would."

199   "I am still in the dark."

200   "I do not wish to make a mystery," said he, laughing. "The matter was perfectly simple. You, of course, saw that everyone in the street was an accomplice. They were all engaged for the evening."

201   "I guessed as much."

202   "Then, when the row broke out, I had a little moist red paint in the palm of my hand. I rushed forward, fell down, clapped my hand to my face, and became a piteous spectacle. It is an old trick."

203   "That also I could fathom."

204   "Then they carried me in. She was bound to have me in. What else could she do? And into her sitting-room, which was the very room which I suspected. It lay between that and her bedroom, and I was determined to see which. They laid me on a couch, I motioned for air, they were compelled to open the window, and you had your chance."

205   "How did that help you?"

206   "It was all-important. When a woman thinks that her house is on fire, her instinct is at once to rush to the thing which she values most. It is a perfectly overpowering impulse, and I have more than once taken advantage of it. In the case of the Darlington substitution scandal it was of use to me, and also in the Arnsworth Castle business. A married woman grabs at her baby; an unmarried one reaches for her jewel-box. Now it was clear to me that our lady of to-day had nothing in the house more precious to her than what we are in quest of. She would rush to secure it. The alarm of fire was admirably done. The smoke and shouting were enough to shake nerves of steel. She responded beautifully. The photograph is in a recess behind a sliding panel just above the right bell-pull. She was there in an instant, and I caught a glimpse of it as she half-drew it out. When I cried out that it was a false alarm, she replaced it, glanced at the rocket, rushed from the room, and I have not seen her since. I rose, and, making my excuses, escaped from the house. I hesitated whether to attempt to secure the photograph at once; but the coachman had come in, and as he was watching me narrowly it seemed safer to wait. A little over-precipitance may ruin all."

207   "And now?" I asked.

208   "Our quest is practically finished. I shall call with the King to-morrow, and with you, if you care to come with us. We will be shown into the sitting-room to

wait for the lady, but it is probable that when she comes she may find neither us nor the photograph. It might be a satisfaction to his Majesty to regain it with his own hands."

"And when will you call?"   209

"At eight in the morning. She will not be up, so that we shall have a clear   210
field. Besides, we must be prompt, for this marriage may mean a complete change in her life and habits. I must wire to the King without delay."

We had reached Baker Street and had stopped at the door. He was searching   211
his pockets for the key when someone passing said:

"Good-night, Mister Sherlock Holmes."   212

There were several people on the pavement at the time, but the greeting   213
appeared to come from a slim youth in an ulster who had hurried by.

"I've heard that voice before," said Holmes, staring down the dimly lit street.   214
"Now, I wonder who the deuce that could have been."

3

I slept at Baker Street that night, and we were engaged upon our toast and   215
coffee in the morning when the King of Bohemia rushed into the room.

"You have really got it!" he cried, grasping Sherlock Holmes by either shoul-   216
der and looking eagerly into his face.

"Not yet."   217

"But you have hopes?"   218

"I have hopes."   219

"Then, come. I am all impatience to be gone."   220

"We must have a cab."   221

"No, my brougham is waiting."   222

"Then that will simplify matters." We descended and started off once more for   223
Briony Lodge.

"Irene Adler is married," remarked Holmes.   224

"Married! When?"   225

"Yesterday."   226

"But to whom?"   227

"To an English lawyer named Norton."   228

"But she could not love him."   229

"I am in hopes that she does."   230

"And why in hopes?"   231

"Because it would spare your Majesty all fear of future annoyance. If the lady   232
loves her husband, she does not love your Majesty. If she does not love your Majesty, there is no reason why she should interfere with your Majesty's plan."

"It is true. And yet—Well! I wish she had been of my own station! What a   233
queen she would have made!" He relapsed into a moody silence, which was not broken until we drew up in Serpentine Avenue.

The door of Briony Lodge was open, and an elderly woman stood upon the   234
steps. She watched us with a sardonic eye as we stepped from the brougham.

"Mr. Sherlock Holmes, I believe?" said she.   235

236   "I am Mr. Holmes," answered my companion, looking at her with a questioning and rather startled gaze.

237   "Indeed! My mistress told me that you were likely to call. She left this morning with her husband by the 5:15 train from Charing Cross for the Continent."

238   "What!" Sherlock Holmes staggered back, white with chagrin and surprise. "Do you mean that she has left England?"

239   "Never to return."

240   "And the papers?" asked the King hoarsely. "All is lost."

241   "We shall see." He pushed past the servant and rushed into the drawing-room, followed by the King and myself. The furniture was scattered about in every direction, with dismantled shelves and open drawers, as if the lady had hurriedly ransacked them before her flight. Holmes rushed at the bell-pull, tore back a small sliding shutter, and, plunging in his hand, pulled out a photograph and a letter. The photograph was of Irene Adler herself in evening dress, the letter was superscribed to "Sherlock Holmes, Esq. To be left till called for." My friend tore it open, and we all three read it together. It was dated at midnight of the preceding night and ran in this way:

My dear Mr. Sherlock Holmes:
        You really did it very well. You took me in completely. Until after the alarm of fire, I had not a suspicion. But then, when I found how I had betrayed myself, I began to think. I had been warned against you months ago. I had been told that if the King employed an agent it would certainly be you. And your address had been given me. Yet, with all this, you made me reveal what you wanted to know. Even after I became suspicious, I found it hard to think evil of such a dear, kind old clergyman. But, you know, I have been trained as an actress myself. Male costume is nothing new to me. I often take advantage of the freedom which it gives. I sent John, the coachman, to watch you, ran upstairs, got into my walking-clothes, as I call them, and came down just as you departed.
        Well, I followed you to your door, and so made sure that I was really an object of interest to the celebrated Mr. Sherlock Holmes. Then I, rather imprudently, wished you good-night, and started for the Temple to see my husband.
        We both thought the best resource was flight, when pursued by so formidable an antagonist; so you will find the nest empty when you call to-morrow. As to the photograph, your client may rest in peace. I love and am loved by a better man than he. The King may do what he will without hindrance from one whom he has cruelly wronged. I keep it only to safeguard myself, and to preserve a weapon which will always secure me from any steps which he might take in the future. I leave a photograph which he might care to possess; and I remain, dear Mr. Sherlock Holmes,

                                                    Very truly yours,
                                                    Irene Norton, *née* Adler.

242   "What a woman—oh, what a woman!" cried the King of Bohemia, when we had all three read this epistle. "Did I not tell you how quick and resolute she was? Would she not have made an admirable queen? Is it not a pity that she was not on my level?"

"From what I have seen of the lady she seems indeed to be on a very different   243
level to your Majesty," said Holmes coldly. "I am sorry that I have not been able to
bring your Majesty's business to a more successful conclusion."

"On the contrary, my dear sir," cried the King; "nothing could be more   244
successful. I know that her word is inviolate. The photograph is now as safe as if it
were in the fire."

"I am glad to hear your Majesty say so."   245

"I am immensely indebted to you. Pray tell me in what way I can reward you.   246
This ring—" He slipped an emerald snake ring from his finger and held it out upon
the palm of his hand.

"Your Majesty has something which I should value even more highly," said   247
Holmes.

"You have but to name it."   248

"This photograph!"   249

The King stared at him in amazement.   250

"Irene's photograph!" he cried. "Certainly, if you wish it."   251

"I thank your Majesty. Then there is no more to be done in the matter. I have   252
the honour to wish you a very good-morning." He bowed, and, turning away
without observing the hand which the King had stretched out to him, he set off in
my company for his chambers.

And that was how a great scandal threatened to affect the kingdom of   253
Bohemia, and how the best plans of Mr. Sherlock Holmes were beaten by a
woman's wit. He used to make merry over the cleverness of women, but I have not
heard him do it of late. And when he speaks of Irene Adler, or when he refers to her
photograph, it is always under the honourable title of *the* woman.

Vocabulary

gibe, Bohemian, brougham, astrakhan, incognito, *carte blanche*, ostlers,
aquiline, surpliced, expostulating, compunction, ulster, sardonic

Questions

1. Does the opening line capture your interest?
2. This story is divided into three parts. Can you see a logic to this division, or is
   Conan Doyle simply trying to break up the sweep of a long story?
3. The condition of Watson's boots has nothing to do with the story of Irene
   Adler. Why, then, is it introduced?
4. Why does Conan Doyle have Watson give us a specific date in the third
   paragraph?
5. Compare the character of Holmes in the opening paragraph with Watson's
   description of him in Chapter 8. Is the picture consistent?

6. Does Holmes use sound psychology to discover Irene Adler's hiding place?
7. Did you know that Sherlock Holmes in the early part of his career resorted to cocaine when he was without interesting work? Or that later he gave up the habit? Why should Conan Doyle have introduced such facts in the first place?
8. Where does Sherlock Holmes pass judgment upon his client's character?
9. Do you find Holmes unpleasantly self-centered? Watson stupid? Defend your answers.
10. This story—like most of the Sherlock Holmes stories—is told by Dr. Watson. What advantages do you see in this device? Are there any disadvantages?

Topics for Writing

Why Holmes Seems Alive

Holmes the Egotist

Holmes: Logic Machine or Man of Feeling?

The Story of an Hour

KATE CHOPIN (1851–1904) spent most of her life in St. Louis, where she was born, and New Orleans, the setting for many of her short stories. The desire for liberation that is at the heart of this story was developed more explicitly in *The Awakening*, a novel published in 1899.

Knowing that Mrs. Mallard was afflicted with a heart trouble, great care was taken to break to her as gently as possible the news of her husband's death. 1

It was her sister Josephine who told her, in broken sentences; veiled hints that revealed in half concealing. Her husband's friend Richards was there, too, near her. It was he who had been in the newspaper office when intelligence of the railroad disaster was received, with Brently Mallard's name leading the list of "killed." He had only taken the time to assure himself of its truth by a second telegram, and had hastened to forestall any less careful, less tender friend in bearing the sad message. 2

She did not hear the story as many women have heard the same, with a paralyzed inability to accept its significance. She wept at once, with sudden, wild abandonment, in her sister's arms. When the storm of grief had spent itself she went away to her room alone. She would have no one follow her. 3

There stood, facing the open window, a comfortable, roomy armchair. Into this she sank, pressed down by a physical exhaustion that haunted her body and seemed to reach into her soul. 4

She could see in the open square before her house the tops of trees that were all aquiver with the new spring life. The delicious breath of rain was in the air. In the street below a peddler was crying his wares. The notes of a distant song which some one was singing reached her faintly, and countless sparrows were twittering in the eaves. 5

There were patches of blue sky showing here and there through the clouds that had met and piled one above the other in the west facing her window. 6

She sat with her head thrown back upon the cushion of the chair, quite motionless, except when a sob came up into her throat and shook her, as a child who has cried itself to sleep continues to sob in its dreams. 7

She was young, with a fair, calm face, whose lines bespoke repression and even a certain strength. But now there was a dull stare in her eyes, whose gaze was fixed away off yonder on one of those patches of blue sky. It was not a glance of reflection, but rather indicated a suspension of intelligent thought. 8

There was something coming to her and she was waiting for it, fearfully. What was it? She did not know; it was too subtle and elusive to name. But she felt it, creeping out of the sky, reaching toward her through the sounds, the scents, the color that filled the air. 9

Now her bosom rose and fell tumultuously. She was beginning to recognize 10 this thing that was approaching to possess her, and she was striving to beat it back with her will—as powerless as her two white slender hands would have been.

11   When she abandoned herself a little whispered word escaped her slightly parted lips. She said it over and over under her breath: "free, free, free!" The vacant stare and the look of terror that had followed it went from her eyes. They stayed keen and bright. Her pulses beat fast, and the coursing blood warmed and relaxed every inch of her body.

12   She did not stop to ask if it were or were not a monstrous joy that held her. A clear and exalted perception enabled her to dismiss the suggestion as trivial.

13   She knew that she would weep again when she saw the kind, tender hands folded in death; the face that had never looked save with love upon her, fixed and gray and dead. But she saw beyond that bitter moment a long procession of years to come that would belong to her absolutely. And she opened and spread her arms out to them in welcome.

14   There would be no one to live for her during those coming years; she would live for herself. There would be no powerful will bending hers in that blind persistence with which men and women believe they have a right to impose a private will upon a fellow-creature. A kind intention or a cruel intention made the act seem no less a crime as she looked upon it in that brief moment of illumination.

15   And yet she had loved him—sometimes. Often she had not. What did it matter! What could love, the unsolved mystery, count for in face of this possession of self-assertion which she suddenly recognized as the strongest impulse of her being!

16   "Free! Body and soul free!" she kept whispering.

17   Josephine was kneeling before the closed door with her lips to the keyhole, imploring for admission. "Louise, open the door! I beg; open the door—you will make yourself ill. What are you doing, Louise? For heaven's sake open the door."

18   "Go away. I am not making myself ill." No; she was drinking in a very elixir of life through that open window.

19   Her fancy was running riot along those days ahead of her. Spring days, and summer days, and all sorts of days that would be her own. She breathed a quick prayer that life might be long. It was only yesterday she had thought with a shudder that life might be long.

20   She arose at length and opened the door to her sister's importunities. There was a feverish triumph in her eyes, and she carried herself unwittingly like a goddess of Victory. She clasped her sister's waist, and together they descended the stairs. Richards stood waiting for them at the bottom.

21   Some one was opening the front door with a latchkey. It was Brently Mallard who entered, a little travel-stained, composedly carrying his grip-sack and umbrella. He had been far from the scene of accident, and did not even know there had been one. He stood amazed at Josephine's piercing cry; at Richards' quick motion to screen him from the view of his wife.

22   But Richards was too late.

23   When the doctors came they said she had died of heart disease—of joy that kills.

Vocabulary

afflicted, veiled, forestall, abandonment, bespoke, exalted, perception, trivial, persistence, impose, illumination, elixir, importunities, unwittingly

Questions

1. It is considered unfair for a writer to surprise us with an ending for which the groundwork has not been laid. What evidence can you muster to show that Kate Chopin has been fair with us?
2. Is the heroine of this story unfeeling or unloving? Do you feel sorry for her, or do you think she got what she deserved?

Topic for Writing

My Opinion of Mrs. Mallard

PART IV
Persuasion

Writers of persuasion have one aim: to bring others into agreement with them. Whether writing to a congressman to oppose stronger gun control laws, or to a bank for a loan, or to a son in college urging greater economy, the writer hopes to persuade. In great issues and in small, we like to believe that others are with us; and when it seems likely that some are not, we like to think that they would be with us if they could see the issue properly—that is, as we see it. In these cases, we try to persuade. Our means are many. A sharp word or a loud smack on the rump may convince Fido that he does not belong on the sofa, but something more reasonable is called for when we want the boss to change his mind about transferring us to the branch office in Patagonia. *Reasonable* is the first clue.

If men and women are rational creatures, then the appeal to reason will often be the most effective means of persuasion. The writer will establish a calm tone, one which reflects confidence in the natural strength of a particular position. "Let us sit down and reason together," a recent president was fond of repeating. The seated person we imagine as relaxed, calm, friendly—not given to the violent gesticulation or the raised voice that we associate with standing folk, red-faced and glowering at one another.

The appeal to reason often includes the devices and rules of logic, the testimony of authorities, or examples and statistics to flesh out the bare bones of argument. It requires clear, analytic thinking and careful, precise use of language—including definition of all terms that, through obscurity or ambiguity, might lead to misunderstanding. (Failure to define can lead to odd situations. A classic case of verbal misunderstanding occurred in the early days of the United Nations, when the American delegate found himself in sharp, and needless, disagreement with his British ally, who had moved to table a resolution. Once it was discovered that the British and American meanings of "to table" were opposite, the problem disappeared.) Chapter 14 demonstrates rational arguments in support of democracy.

We know, however, that not all attempts at persuasion are calm and rational. We all know writers who appeal to our emotions—our fear of rejection or failure, or our desire to be successful and wanted, for example—or whose arguments are based on mistaken notions or evidence that doesn't stand up under inspection. We know people who love to argue for the sake of argument or simply for the delight that they take from "winning" arguments. Some are simply so passionate about what they see as the truth or so desirous of bringing us over to their side that they employ some tricks and tools of debate that don't quite meet the standards of pure logic. Strong emotions are aroused and sharp differences are most often exposed when certain controversial topics come up. Chapter 15 samples "debates" on three such topics and concludes with a classic example of brilliant satire.

Chapter 16 illustrates a specialized kind of argument, a very polite sort of discourse that occurs when men and women discuss the meaning and significance of the work of creative artists. Interpreters intend to persuade, of course, but they usually intend as well to enrich our appreciation of the work or the author under discussion.

The principles and techniques illustrated in this section have broad applications in academic work and in daily life. To recognize them and to learn how they are best employed is to take a giant step toward becoming a writer of persuasive power.

14

The Use of Logic / Democratic Government

The way people are governed, or ought to be governed, has been a matter for serious discourse for at least two thousand years. The American colonists accepted the democratic ideal that the right to govern, to choose governments, and to change them resides with the people. They defended that ideal in the War of Independence, but they also defended it then—and it has been defended and debated ever since—in eloquent argument, often by means of exquisite logic.

Two modes of logical argument, *deductive* and *inductive* reasoning, are so frequently used in persuasive writing that they require our attention here.

Deduction proceeds from a general statement (called the major premise) which we believe to be true, to a second statement (the minor premise) which places the matter under debate into the class of things covered by the major premise, and, finally, to a third statement (the conclusion) which cannot logically be denied by anyone who has accepted both premises. Two examples will serve here:

Major premise: All men require oxygen to live.

Minor premise: John is a man.

Conclusion: John requires oxygen to live.

Since the major premise is undeniable and since in the minor premise John is shown to be a member of the group described in the major premise, then it follows that the conclusion is true. Another way of saying this is that the conclusion was implicit in the premises.

Of course, if either premise is faulty, then this scheme (called a *syllogism*) proves nothing. Consider a second example:

Major premise: All seven-foot college men play basketball.

Minor premise: Mark is a seven-foot college man.

Conclusion: Mark plays basketball.

Nothing "follows" or is proved because the major premise, as we know by experience, is not true. From this, you can see that to argue against a deductive argument, one must attack either the opponent's generalization or the specific case placed under that generalization.

If *deduction* is moving logically from the general to the specific, *induction* reverses the method and moves from verifiable evidence toward generalization. Sitting under an apple tree, we see one apple fall to the ground. That is a bit of evidence. Another falls. Then another and another. At last we conclude from re- peated experience, "All apples fall to the ground." This last step is "the inductive leap" to a conclusion. Induction is often called the *scientific* or *experimental* method because it describes the way empiric scientists move from observation to repeated observation to generalization. As you can see, however, inductive rea- soning leads not to iron-clad conclusions but to highly probable generalizations, and scientists are aware that they work with varying degrees of probability rather than with certainties. One must be a bit careful even here, though, for not every repeated observation leads to a highly probable conclusion. We may have read, for example, that Helen of Troy was a blonde—and that Venus and ten other desirable female characters were supposed to have been golden-haired. "Aha! Gentlemen prefer blondes!" one concludes too hastily. Some do, some don't. We must always examine inductive logic—and can therefore attack inductive reasoning—for flaws in observation, in the size of the sample or the consistency of the facts observed, and in the generalization the logician has formed.

This chapter samples a variety of approaches to the subject of democracy, but all of them depend largely upon deductive and/or inductive logic. Several are familiar in part and should probably be familiar in every detail. Surely The Declara- tion of Independence is such a document. *Civil Disobedience* is not far behind in an honored American tradition, and John F. Kennedy's inaugural address is a model of political exhortation. Hugh Henry Brackenridge uses fiction to demonstrate a human difference between the thing preached and the thing practiced, and Margaret Mead shows us that democracy does not imply what people sometimes think it does.

You are, as a result of reading these authors, sure to find much to admire, some ideas to reject calmly, and one or two with which to disagree violently. You will find that each of these writers has a fundamental idea of what the human race is and is capable of becoming. Perhaps they will force you to examine your own assumptions and to state (or restate) your beliefs.

The Declaration of Independence

THOMAS JEFFERSON (1743–1826), our third president, was founder of the University of Virginia as well as of the Democratic party. An inventor, a scientific farmer, and many other things, he was a man worthy of his times. He had help in writing the Declaration, notably from Benjamin Franklin, but the fine clear prose style is his own.

When in the Course of human events, it becomes necessary for one people to dissolve the political bands which have connected them with another, and to assume among the powers of the earth, the separate and equal station to which the Laws of Nature and of Nature's God entitle them, a decent respect to the opinions of mankind requires that they should declare the causes which impel them to the separation.

We hold these truths to be self-evident, that all men are created equal, that they are endowed by their Creator with certain unalienable Rights, that among these are Life, Liberty, and the pursuit of Happiness. That to secure these rights, Governments are instituted among Men, deriving their just powers from the consent of the governed, That whenever any Form of Government becomes destructive of these ends, it is the Right of the People to alter or to abolish it, and to institute new Government, laying its foundation on such principles and organizing its powers in such form, as to them shall seem most likely to effect their Safety and Happiness. Prudence, indeed, will dictate that Governments long established should not be changed for light and transient causes; and accordingly all experience hath shewn that mankind are more disposed to suffer, while evils are sufferable, than to right themselves by abolishing the forms to which they are accustomed. But when a long train of abuses and usurpations, pursuing invariably the same Object evinces a design to reduce them under absolute Despotism, it is their right, it is their duty, to throw off such Government, and to provide new Guards for their future security. Such has been the patient sufferance of these Colonies; and such is now the necessity which constrains them to alter their former Systems of Government. The history of the present King of Great Britain is a history of repeated injuries and usurpations, all having in direct object the establishment of an absolute Tyranny over these States. To prove this, let Facts be submitted to a candid world.

He has refused his Assent to Laws, the most wholesome and necessary for the public good.

He has forbidden his Governors to pass Laws of immediate and pressing importance, unless suspended in their operation till his Assent should be obtained; and when so suspended, he has utterly neglected to attend to them.

He has refused to pass other Laws for the accommodation of large districts of people, unless those people would relinquish the right of Representation in the Legislature, a right inestimable to them and formidable to tyrants only.

6   He has called together legislative bodies at places unusual, uncomfortable, and distant from the depository of their public Records, for the sole purpose of fatiguing them into compliance with his measures.

7   He has dissolved Representative Houses repeatedly, for opposing with manly firmness his invasions on the rights of the people.

8   He has refused for a long time, after such dissolutions, to cause others to be elected; whereby the Legislative powers, incapable of Annihilation, have returned to the People at large for their exercise; the State remaining in the mean time exposed to all the dangers of invasion from without, and convulsions within.

9   He has endeavoured to prevent the population of these States; for that purpose obstructing the Laws for Naturalization of Foreigners; refusing to pass others to encourage their migrations hither, and raising the conditions of new Appropriations of Lands.

10   He has obstructed the Administration of Justice, by refusing his Assent to Laws for establishing Judiciary powers.

11   He has made Judges dependent on his Will alone, for the tenure of their offices, and the amount and payment of their salaries.

12   He has erected a multitude of New Offices, and sent hither swarms of Officers to harass our people, and eat out their substance.

13   He has kept among us, in times of peace, Standing Armies without the Consent of our legislatures.

14   He has affected to render the Military independent of and superior to the Civil power.

15   He has combined with others to subject us to a jurisdiction foreign to our constitution, and unacknowledged by our laws; giving his Assent to their Acts of pretended Legislation:

16   For quartering large bodies of armed troops among us;

17   For protecting them, by a mock Trial, from punishment for any Murders which they should commit on the Inhabitants of these States;

18   For cutting off our Trade with all parts of the world;

19   For imposing Taxes on us without our Consent;

20   For depriving us in many cases, of the benefits of Trial by Jury;

21   For transporting us beyond Seas to be tried for pretended offences;

22   For abolishing the free System of English Laws in a neighbouring Province, establishing therein an Arbitrary government, and enlarging its Boundaries so as to render it at once an example and fit instrument for introducing the same absolute rule into these Colonies;

23   For taking away our Charters, abolishing our most valuable Laws, and altering fundamentally the Forms of our Governments;

24   For suspending our own Legislatures, and declaring themselves invested with power to legislate for us in all cases whatsoever.

25   He has abdicated Government here, by declaring us out of his Protection and waging War against us.

26   He has plundered our seas, ravaged our Coasts, burnt our towns, and destroyed the lives of our people.

He is at this time transporting large Armies of foreign Mercenaries to compleat the works of death, desolation and tyranny, already begun with circumstances of Cruelty & perfidy scarcely paralleled in the most barbarous ages, and totally unworthy the Head of a civilized nation.

He has constrained our fellow Citizens taken Captive on the high Seas to bear Arms against their Country, to become the executioners of their friends and Brethren, or to fall themselves by their Hands.

He has excited domestic insurrections amongst us, and has endeavoured to bring on the inhabitants of our frontiers, the merciless Indian Savages, whose known rule of warfare is an undistinguished destruction of all ages, sexes and conditions.

In every stage of these Oppressions We have Petitioned for Redress in the most humble terms: Our repeated Petitions have been answered only by repeated injury. A Prince, whose character is thus marked by every act which may define a Tyrant, is unfit to be the ruler of a free people.

Nor have We been wanting in attentions to our British Brethren. We have warned them from time to time of attempts by their legislature to extend an unwarrantable jurisdiction over us. We have reminded them of the circumstances of our emigration and settlement here. We have appealed to their native justice and magnanimity, and we have conjured them by the ties of our common kindred to disavow these usurpations, which would inevitably interrupt our connections and correspondence. They too have been deaf to the voice of justice and of consanguinity. We must, therefore, acquiesce in the necessity, which denounces our Separation, and hold them, as we hold the rest of mankind. Enemies in War, in Peace Friends.

We, therefore, the Representatives of the United States of America, in General Congress, Assembled, appealing to the Supreme Judge of the world for the rectitude of our intentions, do, in the Name, and by authority of the good People of these Colonies, solemnly publish and declare, That these United Colonies are, and of Right ought to be Free and Independent States; that they are Absolved from all Allegiance to the British Crown, and that all political connection between them and the State of Great Britain, is and ought to be totally dissolved; and that as Free and Independent States, they have full Power to levy War, conclude Peace, contract Alliances, establish Commerce, and to do all other Acts and Things which Independent States may of right do. And for the support of this Declaration, with a firm reliance on the protection of divine Providence, we mutually pledge to each other our Lives, our Fortunes and our sacred Honor.

Vocabulary

self-evident, unalienable, transient, usurpations, despotism, sufferance, candid, accommodation, inestimable, formidable, legislative, naturalization, arbitrary, abdicated, perfidy, redress, unwarrantable, magnanimity, conjured, consanguinity, acquiesce, rectitude, absolved

Questions

The Declaration was intended as an address to the civilized world, a defense of a truly revolutionary act. The language in which it is couched was, therefore, of the greatest importance—and it was chosen after careful deliberation by men who respected the power and meaning of words. It is important, then, that we look carefully at the words Jefferson used. Notice, in particular, certain terms which seem to admit of no argument: for instance *necessary, impel,* and *unalienable,* and most especially *self-evident.*

1. What does it mean to say that a truth is self-evident? Does it mean that no one in the entire world could disagree?
2. Is happiness an unalienable right? Is the right to the pursuit of happiness a license to "do your own thing"?
3. The eighteenth century has often been called the Age of Reason. Are the facts presented in the Declaration a list of reasons or merely a list of complaints?
4. Why cannot legislative powers be annihilated?
5. Note the use of parallel constructions, for example, "For cutting off . . . ; For imposing . . . ; For depriving . . . ." What is the effect of this repetition? Why doesn't Jefferson continue it?
6. Try rearranging the order of "our Lives, our Fortunes and our sacred Honor."
7. Isn't Jefferson simply saying, "The king is a bad man and shouldn't rule us"?
8. "There is no other choice," Jefferson seems to say. Why is that an important point?
9. Is this a declaration of war? Argue the point.

Topics for Writing

A Declaration of Independence or of War?

Can a Truth Be Self-Evident?

Is Happiness a Right?

The Election

HUGH HENRY BRACKENRIDGE (1748–1816), American novelist, served as a chaplain in the Colonial army and went on to a career in law, reaching the position of supreme court judge in Pennsylvania. His *Modern Chivalry* (1792) is a kind of *Don Quixote* of the new nation, with Captain Farrago in the knight's role, Teague Oregan in Sancho Panza's. In this hilarious scene, the pair have blundered upon a community in the process of exercising the privilege of democracy: the vote.

The Captain rising early next morning, and setting out on his way, had now arrived at a place where a number of people were convened, for the purpose of electing persons to represent them in the legislature of the state. There was a weaver who was a candidate for this appointment, and seemed to have a good deal of interest among the people. But another, who was a man of education, was his competitor. Relying on some talent of speaking which he thought he possessed, he addressed the multitude. 1

Said he, Fellow citizens, I pretend not to any great abilities; but am conscious to myself that I have the best good will to serve you. But it is very astonishing to me, that this weaver should conceive himself qualified for the trust. For though my acquirements are not great, yet his are still less. The mechanical business which he pursues, must necessarily take up so much of his time, that he cannot apply himself to political studies. I should therefore think it would be more answerable to your dignity, and conducive to your interest, to be represented by a man at least of some letters, than by an illiterate handicraftsman like this. It will be more honourable for himself, to remain at his loom and knot threads, than to come forward in a legislative capacity: because, in the one case, he is in the sphere where God and nature has placed him; in the other, he is like a fish out of water, and must struggle for breath in a new element. 2

Is it possible he can understand the affairs of government, whose mind has been concentered to the small object of weaving webs; to the price by the yard, the grist of the thread, and such like matters as concern a manufacturer of cloths? The feet of him who weaves, are more occupied than the head, or at least as much; and therefore the whole man must be, at least, but in half accustomed to exercise his mental powers. For these reasons, all other things set aside, the chance is in my favour, with respect to information. However, you will decide, and give your suffrages to him or to me, as you shall judge expedient. 3

The Captain hearing these observations, and looking at the weaver, could not help advancing, and undertaking to subjoin something in support of what had been just said. Said he, I have no prejudice against a weaver more than another man. Nor do I know any harm in the trade; save that from the sedentary life in a damp place, there is usually a paleness of the countenance: but this is a physical, not a 4 moral evil. Such usually occupy subterranean apartments; not for the purpose, like Demosthenes, of shaving their heads, and writing over eight times the history of Thucydides, and perfecting a stile of oratory; but rather to keep the thread moist; or because this is considered but as an inglorious sort of trade, and is frequently thrust away into cellars, and damp outhouses, which are not occupied for a better use.

5   But to rise from the cellar to the senate house, would be an unnatural hoist. To come from counting threads, and adjusting them to the splits of a reed, to regulate the finances of a government, would be preposterous; there being no congruity in the case. There is no analogy between knotting threads and framing laws. It would be a reversion of the order of things. Not that a manufacturer of linen or woolen, or other stuff, is an inferior character, but a different one, from that which ought to be employed in affairs of state. It is unnecessary to enlarge on this subject; for you must all be convinced of the truth and propriety of what I say. But if you will give me leave to take the manufacturer aside a little, I think I can explain to him my ideas on the subject; and very probably prevail with him to withdraw his pretensions. The people seeming to acquiesce, and beckoning to the weaver, they drew aside, and the Captain addressed him in the following words:

6   Mr. Traddle, said he, for that was the name of the manufacturer, I have not the smallest idea of wounding your sensibility; but it would seem to me, it would be more your interest to pursue your occupation, than to launch out into that of which you have no knowledge. When you go to the senate house, the application to you will not be to warp a web; but to make laws for the commonwealth. Now, suppose that the making of these laws requires a knowledge of commerce, or of the interests of agriculture, or those principles upon which the different manufactures depend, what service could you render. It is possible you might think justly enough; but could you speak? You are not in the habit of public speaking. You are not furnished with those common place ideas, with which even very ignorant men can pass for knowing something. There is nothing makes a man so ridiculous as to attempt what is above his sphere. You are no tumbler for instance; yet should you give out that you could vault upon a man's back; or turn head over heels, like the wheels of a cart; the stiffness of your joints would encumber you; and you would fall upon your backside to the ground. Such a squash as that would do you damage. The getting up to ride on the state is an unsafe thing to those who are not accustomed to such horsemanship. It is a disagreeable thing for a man to be laughed at, and there is no way of keeping ones self from it but by avoiding all affectation.

7   While they were thus discoursing, a bustle had taken place among the croud. Teague hearing so much about elections, and serving the government, took it into his head, that he could be a legislator himself. The thing was not displeasing to the people, who seemed to favour his pretensions; owing, in some degree, to there being several of his countrymen among the croud; but more especially to the fluctuation of the popular mind, and a disposition to what is new and ignoble. For though the weaver was not the most elevated object of choice, yet he was still preferable to this tatter-demalion, who was but a menial servant, and had so much of what is called the brogue on his tongue, as to fall far short of an elegant speaker.

8   The Captain coming up, and finding what was on the carpet, was greatly chagrined at not having been able to give the multitude a better idea of the impor-

tance of a legislative trust; alarmed also, from an apprehension of the loss of his servant. Under these impressions he resumed his address to the multitude. Said he, This is making the matter still worse, gentlemen: this servant of mine is but a bog-trotter; who can scarcely speak the dialect in which your laws ought to be written; but certainly has never read a single treatise on any political subject; for the truth is, he cannot read at all. The young people of the lower class, in Ireland, have seldom the advantage of a good education; especially the descendants of the ancient Irish, who have most of them a great assurance of countenance, but little information, or literature. This young man, whose family name is Oregan, has been my servant for several years. And, except a too great fondness for women, which now and then brings him into scrapes, he has demeaned himself in a manner tolerable enough. But he is totally ignorant of the great principles of legislation; and more especially, the particular interests of the government. A free government is a noble possession to a people: and this freedom consists in an equal right to make laws, and to have the benefit of the laws when made. Though doubtless, in such a government, the lowest citizen may become chief magistrate; yet it is sufficient to possess the right; not absolutely necessary to exercise it. Or even if you should think proper, now and then, to shew your privilege, and exert, in a signal manner, the democratic prerogative, yet is it not descending too low to filch away from me a hireling, which I cannot well spare, to serve your purpose. You are surely carrying the matter too far, in thinking to make a senator of this hostler; to take him away from an employment to which he has been bred, and put him to another, to which he has served no apprenticeship: to set those hands which have been lately employed in currying my horse, to the draughting of bills, and preparing business for the house.

The people were tenacious of their choice, and insisted on giving Teague their 9 suffrages; and by the frown upon their brows, seemed to indicate resentment at what has been said; as indirectly charging them with want of judgment; or calling in question their privilege to do what they thought proper. It is a very strange thing, said one of them, who was a speaker for the rest, that after having conquered Burgoyne and Cornwallis, and got a government of our own, we cannot put in it whom we please. This young man may be your servant, or another man's servant; but if we chuse to make him a delegate, what is that to you. He may not be yet skilled in the matter, but there is a good day a-coming. We will impower him; and it is better to trust a plain man like him, than one of your high flyers, that will make laws to suit their own purposes.

Said the Captain, I had much rather you would send the weaver, though I 10 thought that improper, than to invade my household, and thus detract from me the very person that I have about me to brush my boots, and clean my spurs. The prolocutor of the people gave him to understand that his surmises were useless, for the people had determined on the choice, and Teague they would have, for a representative.

Finding it answered no end to expostulate with the multitude, he requested to 11 speak a word with Teague by himself. Stepping aside, he said to him, composing his voice, and addressing him in a soft manner; Teague, you are quite wrong in this matter they have put into your head. Do you know what it is to be a member of a deliberate body? What qualifications are necessary? Do you understand anything of geography? If a question should be, to make a law to dig a canal in some part of the state, can you describe the bearing of the mountains, and the course of the rivers? Or if commerce is to be pushed to some new quarter, by the force of regulations, are you competent to decide in such a case? There will be questions of law, and astronomy on the carpet. How you must gape and stare like a fool, when you come to be asked your opinion on these subjects? Are you acquainted with the abstract principles of finance; with the funding of public securities; the ways and means of raising the revenue; providing for the discharge of the public debts, and all other things which respect the economy of the government? Even if you had knowledge, have you a facility of speaking. I would suppose you would have too much pride to go to the house just to say, Ay, or No. This is not the fault of your nature, but of your education; having been accustomed to dig turf in your early years, rather than instructing yourself in the classics, or common school books.

12   When a man becomes a member of a public body, he is like a raccoon, or other beast that climbs up the fork of a tree; the boys pushing at him with pitchforks, or throwing stones, or shooting at him with an arrow, the dogs barking in the mean time. One will find fault with your not speaking; another with your speaking, if you speak at all. They will have you in the newspapers, and ridicule you as a perfect beast. There is what they call the caricatura; that is, representing you with a dog's head, or a cat's claw. As you have a red head, they will very probably make a fox of you, or a sorrel horse, or a brindled cow. It is the devil in hell to be exposed to the squibs and crackers of the gazette wits and publications. You know no more about these matters than a goose; and yet you would undertake rashly, without advice, to enter on the office; nay, contrary to advice. For I would not for a thousand guineas, though I have not the half of it to spare, that the breed of the Oregans should come to this; bringing on them a worse stain than stealing sheep; to which they are addicted. You have nothing but your character, Teague, in a new country to depend upon. Let it never be said, that you quitted an honest livelihood, the taking care of my horse, to follow the new fangled whims of the times, and to be a statesman.

13   Teague was moved chiefly with the last part of the address, and consented to give up the object.

14   The Captain, glad of this, took him back to the people, and announced his disposition to decline the honour which they had intended him.

15   Teague acknowledged that he had changed his mind, and was willing to remain in a private station.

16   The people did not seem well pleased with the Captain; but as nothing more could be said about the matter, they turned their attention to the weaver, and gave him their suffrages.

Vocabulary

farrago, mechanical, answerable, conducive, grist, suffrages, expedient, subjoin, sedentary, subterranean, reversion, propriety, warp, encumber, affectation, tatterdemalion, menial, bog-trotter, demeaned, hostler, prolocutor, expostulation

Questions

1. Do you like the arguments against the weaver's candidacy as given by his opponent? Is the study of government a necessary qualification for office?
2. Why does the Captain put in his two cents? Are there signs that he is a witty man? Are his ideas about politics sound?
3. Is the popular mind disposed to "what is new and ignoble"? What, aside from ignorance, is Teague's chief weakness?
4. What anti-Irish prejudice does the Captain betray?
5. Which argument against Teague's candidacy is most persuasive in his opinion? In yours?
6. How is a public figure like a raccoon up a tree?
7. If everything the Captain says about Teague is true, would the Irishman have made a good politician?
8. Can you argue that the Captain is only a theoretical democrat? What is your evidence?
9. Is there a hint that the Captain is more interested in his own welfare than in the good of the commonwealth? Would you judge from this that Brackenridge was optimistic about the future of democratic government?

Topics for Writing

An Argument for the Weaver

Captain Farrago's Motives

Inaugural Address

JOHN F. KENNEDY (1917–1963), our thirty-fifth president, stirred the nation with this address. He was assassinated before his term was completed.

1   We observe today not a victory of party but a celebration of freedom—symbolizing an end as well as a beginning—signifying renewal as well as change. For I have sworn before you and Almighty God the same solemn oath our forebears prescribed nearly a century and three quarters ago.

2   The world is very different now. For man holds in his mortal hands the power to abolish all forms of human poverty and all forms of human life. And yet the same revolutionary beliefs for which our forebears fought are still at issue around the globe—the belief that the rights of man come not from the generosity of the state but from the hand of God.

3   We dare not forget today that we are the heirs of that first revolution. Let the word go forth from this time and place, to friend and foe alike, that the torch has been passed to a new generation of Americans—born in this century, tempered by war, disciplined by a hard and bitter peace, proud of our ancient heritage—and unwilling to witness or permit the slow undoing of those human rights to which this Nation has always been committed, and to which we are committed today at home and around the world.

4   Let every nation know, whether it wishes us well or ill, that we shall pay any price, bear any burden, meet any hardship, support any friend, oppose any foe to assure the survival and the success of liberty.

5   This much we pledge—and more.

6   To those old allies whose cultural and spiritual origins we share, we pledge the loyalty of faithful friends. United, there is little we cannot do in a host of cooperative ventures. Divided, there is little we can do—for we dare not meet a powerful challenge at odds and split asunder.

7   To those new states whom we welcome to the ranks of the free, we pledge our word that one form of colonial control shall not have passed away merely to be replaced by a far more iron tyranny. We shall not always expect to find them supporting our view. But we shall always hope to find them strongly supporting their own freedom—and to remember that, in the past, those who foolishly sought power by riding the back of the tiger ended up inside.

8   To those peoples in the huts and villages of half the globe struggling to break the bonds of mass misery, we pledge our best efforts to help them help themselves, for whatever period is required—not because the Communists may be doing it, not because we seek their votes, but because it is right. If a free society cannot help the many who are poor, it cannot save the few who are rich.

To our sister republics south of our border, we offer a special pledge—to 9
convert our good words into good deeds—in a new alliance for progress—to assist
free men and free governments in casting off the chains of poverty. But this peaceful
revolution of hope cannot become the prey of hostile powers. Let all our neighbors
know that we shall join with them to oppose aggression or subversion anywhere in
the Americas. And let every other power know that this hemisphere intends to
remain the master of its own house.

To that world assembly of sovereign states, the United Nations, our last best 10
hope in an age where the instruments of war have far outpaced the instruments of
peace, we renew our pledge of support—to prevent it from becoming merely a
forum for invective—to strengthen its shield of the new and the weak—and to
enlarge the area in which its writ may run.

Finally, to those nations who would make themselves our adversary, we offer 11
not a pledge but a request: that both sides begin anew the quest for peace, before the
dark powers of destruction unleashed by science engulf all humanity in planned or
accidental self-destruction.

We dare not tempt them with weakness. For only when our arms are sufficient 12
beyond doubt can we be certain beyond doubt that they will never be employed.

But neither can two great and powerful groups of nations take comfort from 13
our present course—both sides overburdened by the cost of modern weapons, both
rightly alarmed by the steady spread of the deadly atom, yet both racing to alter that
uncertain balance of terror that stays the hand of mankind's final war.

So let us begin anew—remembering on both sides that civility is not a sign of 14
weakness, and sincerity is always subject to proof. Let us never negotiate out of fear.
But let us never fear to negotiate.

Let both sides explore what problems unite us instead of belaboring those 15
problems which divide us.

Let both sides, for the first time, formulate serious and precise proposals for the 16
inspection and control of arms—and bring the absolute power to destroy other
nations under the absolute control of all nations.

Let both sides seek to invoke the wonders of science instead of its terrors. 17
Together let us explore the stars, conquer the deserts, eradicate disease, tap the
ocean depths, and encourage the arts and commerce.

Let both sides unite to heed in all corners of the earth the command of 18
Isaiah—to "undo the heavy burdens . . . [and] let the oppressed go free."

And if a beachhead of cooperation may push back the jungle of suspicion, let 19
both sides join in creating a new endeavor, not a new balance of power, but a new
world of law, where the strong are just and the weak secure and the peace preserved.

All this will not be finished in the first one hundred days. Nor will it be 20
finished in the first one thousand days, nor in the life of this Administration, nor
even perhaps in our lifetime on this planet. But let us begin.

In your hands, my fellow citizens, more than mine, will rest the final success 21
or failure of our course. Since this country was founded, each generation of Americans has been summoned to give testimony to its national loyalty. The graves of
young Americans who answered the call to service surround the globe.

22   Now the trumpet summons us again—not as a call to bear arms, though arms we need—not as a call to battle, though embattled we are—but a call to bear the burden of a long twilight struggle, year in and year out, "rejoicing in hope, patient in tribulation"—a struggle against the common enemies of man: tyranny, poverty, disease, and war itself.

23   Can we forge against these enemies a grand and global alliance, North and South, East and West, that can assure a more fruitful life for all mankind? Will you join in that historic effort?

24   In the long history of the world, only a few generations have been granted the role of defending freedom in its hour of maximum danger. I do not shrink from responsibility—I welcome it. I do not believe that any of us would exchange places with any other people or any other generation. The energy, the faith, the devotion which we bring to this endeavor will light our country and all who serve it—and the glow from that fire can truly light the world.

25   And so, my fellow Americans: ask not what your country can do for you—ask what you can do for your country.

26   My fellow citizens of the world: ask not what America will do for you, but what together we can do for the freedom of man.

27   Finally, whether you are citizens of America or citizens of the world, ask of us here the same high standards of strength and sacrifice which we ask of you. With a good conscience our only sure reward, with history the final judge of our deeds, let us go forth to lead the land we love, asking His blessing and His help, but knowing that here on earth God's work must truly be our own.

Vocabulary

tempered, sovereign, invective, civility, belaboring, beachhead

Questions

1. Does the "ride the tiger" image seem out of keeping with the overall tone of the address?
2. What is meant by "where its writ may run"?
3. An address of this kind usually ends with a plea for unity of purpose or for action. Whether the auditors are persuaded depends on whether the speaker has been convincing. Would Kennedy's speech have convinced you? What are its strongest points to you? Its weakest?
4. What connection do you see between this address and the Declaration of Independence?

Topics for Writing

Ask Not What Your Country Can Do for You

The Citizen's Relationship to His or Her Country

The Egalitarian Error

MARGARET MEAD (1901–1978) A distinguished scholar whose *Coming of Age in Samoa* and *Growing Up in New Guinea* helped popularize anthropology, Margaret Mead in later life spoke out on many issues of general interest. This essay is an example of her thoughtful approach to a contemporary problem.

Almost all Americans want to be democratic, but many Americans are confused about what, exactly, democracy means. How do you know when someone is acting in a democratic—or an undemocratic—way? Recently several groups have spoken out with particular bitterness against the kind of democracy that means equal opportunity for all, regardless of race or national origin. They act as if all human beings did not belong to one species, as if some races of mankind were inferior to others in their capacity to learn what members of other races know and have invented. Other extremists attack religious group—Jews or Catholics—or deny the right of an individual to be an agnostic. One reason that these extremists, who explicitly do not want to be democratic, can get a hearing even though their views run counter to the Constitution and our traditional values is that people who *do* want to be democratic are frequently so muddled. 1

For many Americans, democratic behavior necessitates an outright denial of any significant differences among human beings. In their eyes it is undemocratic for anyone to refer, in the presence of any other person, to differences in skin color, manners or religious beliefs. Whatever one's private thoughts may be, it is necessary always to act as if everyone were exactly alike. 2

Behavior of this kind developed partly as a reaction to those who discriminated against or actively abused members of other groups. But it is artificial, often hypocritical behavior, nonetheless, and it dulls and flattens human relationships. If two people can't talk easily and comfortably but must forever guard against some slip of the tongue, some admission of what is in both persons' minds, they are likely to talk as little as possible. This embarrassment about differences reaches a final absurdity when a Methodist feels that he cannot take a guest on a tour of his garden because he might have to identify a wild plant with a blue flower, called the wandering Jew, or when a white lecturer feels he ought not to mention the name of Conrad's beautiful story *The Nigger of the "Narcissus."* But it is no less absurd when well-meaning people, speaking of the physically handicapped, tell prospective employers: "They don't want special consideration. Ask as much of them as you do of everyone else, and fire them if they don't give satisfaction!" 3

Another version of false democracy is the need to deny the existence of personal advantages. Inherited wealth, famous parents, a first-class mind, a rare voice, a beautiful face, an exceptional physical skill—any advantage has to be minimized or denied. Continually watched and measured, the man or woman who is rich or 4 talented or well educated is likely to be called "undemocratic" whenever he does anything out of the ordinary—more or less of something than others do. If he wants acceptance, the person with a "superior" attribute, like the person with an "inferior" attribute, often feels obliged to take on a protective disguise, to act as if he were just like everybody else. One denies difference; the other minimizes it. And both believe, as they conform to these false standards, that they act in the name of democracy.

5   For many Americans, a related source of confusion is success. As a people we Americans greatly prize success. And in our eyes success all too often means simply outdoing other people by virtue of achievement judged by some single scale—income or honors or headlines or trophies—and coming out at "the top." Only one person, as we see it, can be the best—can get the highest grades, be voted the most attractive girl or the boy mostly likely to succeed. Though we often rejoice in the success of people far removed from ourselves—in another profession, another community, or endowed with a talent that we do not covet—we tend to regard the success of people close at hand, within our own small group, as a threat. We fail to realize that there are many kinds of success, including the kind of success that lies within a person. We do not realize, for example, that there could be in the same class one hundred boys and girls—each of them a "success" in a different kind of way. Individuality is again lost in a refusal to recognize and cherish the differences among people.

6   The attitude that measures success by a single yardstick and isolates the *one* winner and the kind of "democracy" that denies or minimizes differences among people are both deeply destructive. Imagine for a moment a family with two sons, one of whom is brilliant, attractive and athletic while the other is dull, unattractive and clumsy. Both boys attend the same high school. In the interest of the slower boy, the parents would want the school to set equally low standards for everyone. Lessons should be easy; no one should be forced to study dead languages or advanced mathematics in order to graduate. Athletics should be noncompetitive; every boy should have a chance to enjoy playing games. Everyone should be invited to all the parties. As for special attention to gifted children, this is not fair to the other children. An all-round education should be geared to the average, normal child.

7   But in the interest of the other boy, these same parents would have quite opposite goals. After all, we need highly trained people; the school should do the most it can for its best students. Funds should be made available for advanced classes and special teachers, for the best possible coach, the best athletic equipment. Young people should be allowed to choose friends on their own level. The aim of education should be to produce topflight students.

8   This is an extreme example, but it illustrates the completely incompatible aims that can arise in this kind of "democracy." Must our country shut its eyes to the needs of either its gifted or its less gifted sons? It would be a good deal more sensible to admit, as some schools do today, that children differ widely from one another, that all successes cannot be ranged on one single scale, that there is room in a real democracy to help each child find his own level and develop to his fullest potential.

9   Moving now to a wider scene, before World War I Americans thought of

themselves as occupying a unique place in the world—and there was no question in most minds that this country was a "success." True, Europeans might look down on us for our lack of culture, but with a few notable, local exceptions, we simply refused to compete on European terms. There was no country in the world remotely like the one we were building. But since World War II we have felt the impact of a country whose size and strength and emphasis on national achievement more closely parallel our own. Today we are ahead of Russia, or Russia is ahead of us. Nothing else matters. Instead of valuing and developing the extraordinary assets and potential of our country for their own sake, we are involved in a simple set of competitions for wealth and power and dominance.

These are expensive and dangerous attitudes. When democracy ceases to be a   10
cherished way of life and becomes instead the name of one team, we are using the word democracy to describe behavior that places us and all other men in jeopardy.

Individually, nationally and, today, internationally, the misreading of the   11
phrase "all men are created equal" exacts a heavy price. The attitudes that follow from our misconceptions may be compatible with life in a country where land and rank and prestige are severely limited and the roads to success are few. But they are inappropriate in a land as rich, as open, as filled with opportunities as our own. They are the price we pay for being *less* democratic than we claim to be.

"All men are created equal" does not mean that all men are the same. What it   12
does mean is that each should be accorded full respect and full rights as a unique human being—full respect for his humanity *and* for his differences from other people.

Vocabulary

agnostic, necessitates, artificial, hypocritical, absurd, conform, endowed, incompatible, jeopardy, misconceptions, compatible, inappropriate

Questions

1. Is Margaret Mead's logic inductive or deductive? (Read the entire essay before deciding.)
2. Why is it false democracy to act as though everyone were alike?
3. Why does the author call this the "egalitarian" rather than the "democratic" error?
4. What examples of absurd carefulness does she cite? Can you add to her list from your own experience?
5. Is Margaret Mead denying that all men are created equal?
6. What does "all men are created equal" mean to you?

Topics for Writing

Absurd Carefulness, an Unavoidable Habit

Life Is Unfair

The Sense in Which All Men Are Equal

Civil Disobedience

HENRY DAVID THOREAU (see Chapter 1) acted on his beliefs and once was jailed overnight for refusal to pay taxes in support of a war he believed unjust. "Civil Disobedience" (1849) had its influence later in such causes as Gandhi's resistance to British rule in India and in Black American opposition to segregation laws.

1   I heartily accept the motto,—"That government is best which governs least"; and I should like to see it acted up to more rapidly and systematically. Carried out, it finally amounts to this, which also I believe,—"That government is best which governs not at all"; and when men are prepared for it, that will be the kind of government which they will have. Government is at best but an expedient; but most governments are usually, and all governments are sometimes, inexpedient. The objections which have been brought against a standing army, and they are many and weighty, and deserve to prevail, may also at last be brought against a standing government. The standing army is only an arm of the standing government. The government itself, which is only the mode which the people have chosen to execute their will, is equally liable to be abused and perverted before the people can act through it. Witness the present Mexican war, the work of comparatively a few individuals using the standing government as their tool; for, in the outset, the people would not have consented to this measure.

2   This American government,—what is it but a tradition, though a recent one, endeavoring to transmit itself unimpaired to posterity, but each instant losing some of its integrity? It has not the vitality and force of a single living man; for a single man can bend it to his will. It is a sort of wooden gun to the people themselves. But it is not the less necessary for this; for the people must have some complicated machinery or other, and hear its din, to satisfy that idea of government which they have. Governments show thus how successfully men can be imposed on, even impose on themselves, for their own advantage. It is excellent, we must all allow. Yet this government never of itself furthered any enterprise, but by the alacrity with which it got out of its way. *It* does not keep the country free. *It* does not settle the West. *It* does not educate. The character inherent in the American people has done all that has been accomplished; and it would have done somewhat more, if the government had not sometimes got in its way. For government is an expedient by which men would fain succeed in letting one another alone; and, as has been said, when it is most expedient, the governed are most let alone by it. Trade and commerce, if they were not made of India-rubber, would never manage to bounce over the obstacles which legislators are continually putting in their way; and, if one were to judge these men wholly by the effects of their actions and not partly by their intentions, they would deserve to be classed and punished with those mischievous persons who put obstructions on the railroads.

But, to speak practically and as a citizen, unlike those who call themselves no-government men, I ask for, not at once no government, but *at once* a better government. Let every man make known what kind of government would command his respect, and that will be one step toward obtaining it.

After all, the practical reason why, when the power is once in the hands of the people, a majority are permitted, and for a long period continue, to rule is not because they are most likely to be in the right, nor because this seems fairest to the minority, but because they are physically the strongest. But a government in which the majority rule in all cases cannot be based on justice, even as far as men understand it. Can there not be a government in which majorities do not virtually decide right and wrong, but conscience?—in which majorities decide only those questions to which the rule of expediency is applicable? Must the citizen ever for a moment, or in the least degree, resign his conscience to the legislator? Why has every man a conscience, then? I think that we should be men first, and subjects afterward. It is not desirable to cultivate a respect for the law, so much as for the right. The only obligation which I have a right to assume is to do at any time what I think right. It is truly enough said, that a corporation has no conscience; but a corporation of conscientious men is a corporation *with* a conscience. Law never made men a whit more just; and, by means of their respect for it, even the well-disposed are daily made the agents of injustice. A common and natural result of an undue respect for law is, that you may see a file of soldiers, colonel, captain, corporal, privates, powder-monkeys, and all, marching in admirable order over hill and dale to the wars, against their wills, ay, against their common sense and consciences, which makes it very steep marching indeed, and produces a palpitation of the heart. They have no doubt that it is a damnable business in which they are concerned; they are all peaceably inclined. Now, what are they? Men at all? or small movable forts and magazines, at the service of some unscrupulous man in power? Visit the Navy-Yard, and behold a marine, such a man as an American government can make, or such as it can make a man with its black arts,—a mere shadow and reminiscence of humanity, a man laid out alive and standing, and already, as one may say, buried under arms with funeral accompaniments, though it may be,—

> "Not a drum was heard, not a funeral note,
>   As his corse to the rampart we hurried;
> Not a soldier discharged his farewell shot
>   O'er the grave where our hero we buried."

The mass of men serve the state thus, not as men mainly, but as machines, with their bodies. They are the standing army, and the militia, jailers, constables, *posse comitatus*, etc. In most cases there is no free exercise whatever of the judgment or of the moral sense; but they put themselves on a level with wood and earth and stones; and wooden men can perhaps be manufactured that will serve the purpose as well. Such command no more respect than men of straw or a lump of dirt. They have the same sort of worth only as horses and dogs. Yet such as these even are commonly esteemed good citizens. Others—as most legislators, politicians, lawyers, ministers, and office-holders—serve the state chiefly with their heads; and, as they rarely make any moral distinctions, they are as likely to serve the Devil, without *intending* it, as God. A very few, as heroes, patriots, martyrs, reformers in the great sense, and *men*, serve the state with their consciences also, and so necessarily resist it for the most part; and they are commonly treated as enemies by it. A wise man will only be useful as a man, and will not submit to be "clay," and "stop a hole to keep the wind away," but leave that office to his dust at least:—

> "I am too high-born to be propertied,
> To be a secondary at control,
> Or useful serving-man and instrument
> To any sovereign state throughout the world."

6   He who gives himself entirely to his fellow-men appears to them useless and selfish; but he who gives himself partially to them is pronounced a benefactor and philanthropist.

7   How does it become a man to behave toward this American government to-day? I answer, that he cannot without disgrace be associated with it. I cannot for an instant recognize that political organization as *my* government which is the *slave's* government also.

8   All men recognize the right of revolution; that is, the right to refuse allegiance to, and to resist, the government, when its tyranny or its inefficiency are great and unendurable. But almost all say that such is not the case now. But such was the case, they think, in the Revolution of '75. If one were to tell me that this was a bad government because it taxed certain foreign commodities brought to its ports, it is most probable that I should not make an ado about it, for I can do without them. All machines have their friction; and possibly this does enough good to counter-balance the evil. At any rate, it is a great evil to make a stir about it. But when the friction comes to have its machine, and oppression and robbery are organized, I say, let us not have such a machine any longer. In other words, when a sixth of the population of a nation which has undertaken to be the refuge of liberty are slaves, and a whole country is unjustly overrun and conquered by a foreign army, and subjected to military law, I think that it is not too soon for honest men to rebel and revolutionize. What makes this duty the more urgent is the fact that the country so overrun is not our own, but ours is the invading army.

9   Paley, a common authority with many on moral questions, in his chapter on the "Duty of Submission to Civil Government," resolves all civil obligation into expediency; and he proceeds to say, "that so long as the interest of the whole society requires it, that is, so long as the established government cannot be resisted or changed without public inconveniency, it is the will of God that the established government be obeyed, and no longer. . . . This principle being admitted, the justice of every particular case of resistance is reduced to a computation of the quantity of the danger and grievance on the one side, and of the probability and expense of redressing it on the other." Of this, he says, every man shall judge for himself. But Paley appears never to have contemplated those cases to which the rule of expediency does not apply, in which a people, as well as an individual, must do justice, cost what it may. If I have unjustly wrested a plank from a drowning man, I

must restore it to him though I drown myself. This, according to Paley, would be inconvenient. But he that would save his life, in such a case, shall lose it. This people must cease to hold slaves, and to make war on Mexico, though it cost them their existence as a people.

In their practice, nations agree with Paley; but does any one think that   10
Massachusetts does exactly what is right at the present crisis?

> "A drab of state, a cloth-o'-silver slut,
> To have her train borne up, and her soul trail in the dirt."

Practically speaking, the opponents to a reform in Massachusetts are not a hundred thousand politicians at the South, but a hundred thousand merchants and farmers here, who are more interested in commerce and agriculture than they are in humanity, and are not prepared to do justice to the slave and to Mexico, *cost what it may*. I quarrel not with far-off foes, but with those who, near at home, coöperate with, and do the bidding of, those far away, and without whom the latter would be harmless. We are accustomed to say, that the mass of men are unprepared; but improvement is slow, because the few are not materially wiser or better than the many. It is not so important that many should be as good as you, as that there be some absolute goodness somewhere; for that will leaven the whole lump. There are thousands who are *in opinion* opposed to slavery and to the war, who yet in effect do nothing to put an end to them; who, esteeming themselves children of Washington and Franklin, sit down with their hands in their pockets, and say that they know not what to do, and do nothing; who even postpone the question of freedom to the question of free-trade, and quietly read the prices-current along with the latest advices from Mexico, after dinner, and, it may be, fall asleep over them both. What is the price-current of an honest man and patriot to-day? They hesitate, and they regret, and sometimes they petition; but they do nothing in earnest and with effect. They will wait, well disposed, for others to remedy the evil, that they may no longer have it to regret. At most, they give only a cheap vote, and a feeble countenance and Godspeed, to the right, as it goes by them. There are nine hundred and ninety-nine patrons of virtue to one virtuous man. But it is easier to deal with the real possessor of a thing than with the temporary guardian of it.

All voting is a sort of gaming, like checkers or backgammon, with a slight   11
moral tinge to it, a playing with right and wrong, with moral questions; and betting naturally accompanies it. The character of the voters is not staked. I cast my vote, perchance, as I think right; but I am not vitally concerned that that right should prevail. I am willing to leave it to the majority. Its obligation, therefore, never exceeds that of expediency. Even voting *for the right* is *doing* nothing for it. It is only expressing to men feebly your desire that it should prevail. A wise man will not leave the right to the mercy of chance, nor wish it to prevail through the power of the majority. There is but little virtue in the action of masses of men. When the majority shall at length vote for the abolition of slavery, it will be because they are indifferent to slavery, or because there is but little slavery left to be abolished by their vote. *They* will then be the only slaves. Only *his* vote can hasten the abolition of slavery who asserts his own freedom by his vote.

I hear of a convention to be held at Baltimore, or elsewhere, for the selection   12 of a candidate for the Presidency, made up chiefly of editors, and men who are politicians by profession; but I think, what is it to any independent, intelligent, and respectable man what decision they may come to? Shall we not have the advantage of his wisdom and honesty, nevertheless? Can we not count upon some independent votes? Are there not many individuals in the country who do not attend conventions? But no: I find that the respectable man, so called, has immediately drifted from his position, and despairs of his country, when his country has more reason to despair of him. He forthwith adopts one of the candidates thus selected as the only *available* one, thus proving that he is himself *available* for any purposes of the demagogue. His vote is of no more worth than that of any unprincipled foreigner or hireling native, who may have been bought. O for a man who is a *man*, and, as my neighbor says, has a bone in his back which you cannot pass your hand through! Our statistics are at fault: the population has been returned too large. How many *men* are there to a square thousand miles in this country? Hardly one. Does not America offer any inducement for men to settle here? The American has dwindled into an Odd Fellow,—one who may be known by the development of his organ of gregariousness, and a manifest lack of intellect and cheerful self-reliance; whose first and chief concern, on coming into the world, is to see that the Almshouses are in good repair; and, before yet he has lawfully donned the virile garb, to collect a fund for the support of the widows and orphans that may be; who, in short, ventures to live only by the aid of the Mutual Insurance company, which has promised to bury him decently.

13   It is not a man's duty, as a matter of course, to devote himself to the eradication of any, even the most enormous wrong; he may still properly have other concerns to engage him; but it is his duty, at least, to wash his hands of it, and, if he gives it no thought longer, not to give it practically his support. If I devote myself to other pursuits and contemplations, I must first see, at least, that I do not pursue them sitting upon another man's shoulders. I must get off him first, that he may pursue his contemplations too. See what gross inconsistency is tolerated. I have heard some of my townsmen say, "I should like to have them order me out to help put down an insurrection of the slaves, or to march to Mexico;—see if I would go"; and yet these very men have each, directly by their allegiance, and so indirectly, at least, by their money, furnished a substitute. The soldier is applauded who refuses to serve in an unjust war by those who do not refuse to sustain the unjust government which makes the war; is applauded by those whose own act and authority he disregards and sets at naught; as if the state were penitent to that degree that it hired one to scourge it while it sinned, but not to that degree that it left off sinning for a moment. Thus, under the name of Order and Civil Government, we are all made at last to pay homage to and support our own meanness. After the first blush of sin comes its indifference; and from immoral it becomes, as it were, *un*moral, and not quite unnecessary to that life which we have made.

14   The broadest and most prevalent error requires the most disinterested virtue to sustain it. The slight reproach to which the virtue of patriotism is commonly liable, the noble are most likely to incur. Those who, while they disapprove of the character and measures of a government, yield to it their allegiance and support are

undoubtedly its most conscientious supporters, and so frequently the most serious obstacles to reform. Some are petitioning the state to dissolve the Union, to disregard the requisitions of the President. Why do they not dissolve it themselves,—the union between themselves and the state,—and refuse to pay their quota into its treasury? Do not they stand in the same relation to the state that the state does to the Union? And have not the same reasons prevented the state from resisting the Union which have prevented them from resisting the state?

How can a man be satisfied to entertain an opinion merely, and enjoy *it*? Is there any enjoyment in it, if his opinion is that he is aggrieved? If you are cheated out of a single dollar by your neighbor, you do not rest satisfied with knowing that you are cheated, or with saying that you are cheated, or even with petitioning him to pay you your due; but you take effectual steps at once to obtain the full amount, and see that you are never cheated again. Action from principle, the perception and the performance of right, changes things and relations; it is essentially revolutionary, and does not consist wholly with anything which was. It not only divides states and churches, it divides families; ay, it divides the *individual*, separating the diabolical in him from the divine. 15

Unjust laws exist: shall we be content to obey them, or shall we endeavor to amend them, and obey them until we have succeeded, or shall we transgress them at once? Men generally, under such a government as this, think that they ought to wait until they have persuaded the majority to alter them. They think that, if they should resist, the remedy would be worse than the evil. But it is the fault of the government itself that the remedy *is* worse than the evil. *It* makes it worse. Why is it not more apt to anticipate and provide for reform? Why does it not cherish its wise minority? Why does it cry and resist before it is hurt? Why does it not encourage its citizens to be on the alert to point out its faults, and *do* better than it would have them? Why does it always crucify Christ, and excommunicate Copernicus and Luther, and pronounce Washington and Franklin rebels? 16

One would think, that a deliberate and practical denial of its authority was the only offense never contemplated by government; else, why has it not assigned its definite, its suitable and proportionate penalty? If a man who has no property refuses but once to earn nine shillings for the state, he is put in prison for a period unlimited by any law that I know, and determined only by the discretion of those who placed him there; but if he should steal ninety times nine shilllings from the state, he is soon permitted to go at large again. 17

If the injustice is part of the necessary friction of the machine of government, let it go, let it go: perchance it will wear smooth,—certainly the machine will wear out. If the injustice has a spring, or a pulley, or a rope, or a crank, exclusively for itself, then perhaps you may consider whether the remedy will not be worse than the evil; but if it is of such a nature that it requires you to be the agent of injustice to another, then, I say, break the law. Let your life be a counter friction to stop the machine. What I have to do is to see, at any rate, that I do not lend myself to the wrong which I condemn. 18

As for adopting the ways which the state has provided for remedying the evil, I know not of such ways. They take too much time, and a man's life will be gone. I 19 have other affairs to attend to. I came into this world, not chiefly to make this a good place to live in, but to live in it, be it good or bad. A man has not everything to do, but something; and because he cannot do *everything*, it is not necessary that he should do *something* wrong. It is not my business to be petitioning the Governor or the Legislature any more than it is theirs to petition me; and if they should not hear my petition, what should I do then? But in this case the state has provided no way: its very Constitution is the evil. This may seem to be harsh and stubborn and unconciliatory; but it is to treat with the utmost kindness and consideration the only spirit that can appreciate or deserve it. So is all change for the better, like birth and death, which convulse the body.

20   I do not hesitate to say, that those who call themselves Abolitionists should at once effectually withdraw their support, both in person and property, from the government of Massachusetts, and not wait till they constitute a majority of one, before they suffer the right to prevail through them. I think that it is enough if they have God on their side, without waiting for that other one. Moreover, any man more right than his neighbors constitutes a majority of one already.

21   I meet this American government, or its representative, the state government, directly, and face to face, once a year—no more—in the person of its tax-gatherer; this is the only mode in which a man situated as I am necessarily meets it; and it then says distinctly, Recognize me; and the simplest, the most effectual, and, in the present posture of affairs, the indispensablest mode of treating with it on this head, of expressing your little satisfaction with and love for it, is to deny it then. My civil neighbor, the tax-gatherer, is the very man I have to deal with,—for it is, after all, with men and not with parchment that I quarrel,—and he has voluntarily chosen to be an agent of the government. How shall he ever know well what he is and does as an officer of the government, or as a man, until he is obliged to consider whether he shall treat me, his neighbor, for whom he has respect, as a neighbor and well-disposed man, or as a maniac and disturber of the peace, and see if he can get over this obstruction to his neighborliness without a ruder and more impetuous thought or speech corresponding with his action. I know this well, that if one thousand, if one hundred, if ten men whom I could name,—if ten *honest* men only,—ay, if *one* HONEST man, in this State of Massachusetts, *ceasing to hold slaves*, were actually to withdraw from this copartnership, and be locked up in the county jail therefor, it would be the abolition of slavery in America. For it matters not how small the beginning may seem to be: what is once well done is done forever. But we love better to talk about it: that we say is our mission. Reform keeps many scores of newspapers in its service, but not one man. If my esteemed neighbor, the State's ambassador, who will devote his days to the settlement of the question of human rights in the Council Chamber, instead of being threatened with the prisons of Carolina, were to sit down the prisoner of Massachusetts, that State which is so anxious to foist the sin of slavery upon her sister,—though at present she can discover only an act of inhospitality to be the ground of a quarrel with her,—the Legislature would not wholly waive the subject the following winter.

22   Under a government which imprisons any unjustly, the true place for a just man is also a prison. The proper place to-day, the only place which Massachusetts

has provided for her freer and less desponding spirits, is in her prisons, to be put out and locked out of the State by her own act, as they have already put themselves out by their principles. It is there that the fugitive slave, and the Mexican prisoner on parole, and the Indian come to plead the wrongs of his race should find them; on that separate, but more free and honorable ground, where the State places those who are not *with* her, but *against* her,—the only house in a slave State in which a free man can abide with honor. If any think that their influence would be lost there, and their voices no longer afflict the ear of the State, that they would not be as an enemy within its walls, they do not know by how much truth is stronger than error, nor how much more eloquently and effectively he can combat injustice who has experienced a little in his own person. Cast your whole vote, not a strip of paper merely, but your whole influence. A minority is powerless while it conforms to the majority; it is not even a minority then; but it is irresistible when it clogs by its whole weight. If the alternative is to keep all just men in prison, or give up war and slavery, the State will not hesitate which to choose. If a thousand men were not to pay their tax-bills this year, that would not be a violent and bloody measure, as it would be to pay them, and enable the State to commit violence and shed innocent blood. This is, in fact, the definition of a peaceable revolution, if any such is possible. If the tax-gatherer, or any other public officer, asks me, as one has done, "But what shall I do?" my answer is, "If you really wish to do anything, resign your office." When the subject has refused allegiance, and the officer has resigned his office, then the revolution is accomplished. But even suppose blood should flow. Is there not a sort of blood shed when the conscience is wounded? Through this wound a man's real manhood and immortality flow out, and he bleeds to an everlasting death. I see this blood flowing now.

I have contemplated the imprisonment of the offender, rather than the seizure of his goods,—though both will serve the same purpose,—because they who assert the purest right, and consequently are most dangerous to a corrupt State, commonly have not spent much time in accumulating property. To such the State renders comparatively small service, and a slight tax is wont to appear exorbitant, particularly if they are obliged to earn it by special labor with their hands. If there were one who lived wholly without the use of money, the State itself would hesitate to demand it of him. But the rich man—not to make any invidious comparison—is always sold to the institution which makes him rich. Absolutely speaking, the more money, the less virtue; for money comes between a man and his objects, and obtains them for him; and it was certainly no great virtue to obtain it. It puts to rest many questions which he would otherwise be taxed to answer; while the only new question which it puts is the hard but superfluous one, how to spend it. Thus his moral ground is taken from under his feet. The opportunities of living are diminished in proportion as what are called the "means" are increased. The best thing a man can do for his culture when he is rich is to endeavor to carry out those schemes which he entertained when he was poor. Christ answered the Herodians according to their condition. "Show me the tribute-money," said he;—and one took a penny out of his pocket;—if you use money which has the image of Caesar on it, which he has made current and valuable, that is, *if you are men of the State*, and gladly enjoy

23

the advantages of Caesar's government, then pay him back some of his own when he demands it. "Render therefore to Caesar that which is Caesar's, and to God those things which are God's,"—leaving them no wiser than before as to which was which; for they did not wish to know.

24   When I converse with the freest of my neighbors, I perceive that, whatever they may say about the magnitude and seriousness of the question, and their regard for the public tranquillity, the long and the short of the matter is, that they cannot spare the protection of the existing government, and they dread the consequences to their property and families of disobedience to it. For my own part, I should not like to think that I every rely on the protection of the State. But, if I deny the authority of the State when it presents its tax-bill, it will soon take and waste all my property, and so harass me and my children without end. This is hard. This makes it impossible for a man to live honestly, and at the same time comfortably, in outward respects. It will not be worth the while to accumulate property; that would be sure to go again. You must hire or squat somewhere, and raise but a small crop, and eat that soon. You must live within yourself, and depend upon yourself always tucked up and ready for a start, and not have many affairs. A man may grow rich in Turkey even, if he will be in all respects a good subject of the Turkish government. Confucius said: "If a state is governed by the principles of reason, poverty and misery are subjects of shame; if a state is not governed by the principles of reason, riches and honors are the subjects of shame." No: until I want the protection of Massachusetts to be extended to me in some distant Southern port, where my liberty is endangered, or until I am bent solely on building up an estate at home by peaceful enterprise, I can afford to refuse allegiance to Massachusetts, and her right to my property and life. It costs me less in every sense to incur the penalty of disobedience to the State than it would to obey. I should feel as if I were worth less in that case.

25   Some years ago, the State met me in behalf of the Church, and commanded me to pay a certain sum toward the support of a clergyman whose preaching my father attended, but never I myself. "Pay," it said, "or be locked up in jail." I declined to pay. But, unfortunately, another man saw fit to pay it. I did not see why the schoolmaster should be taxed to support the priest, and not the priest the schoolmaster; for I was not the State's schoolmaster, but I supported myself by voluntary subscription. I did not see why the lyceum should not present its tax-bill, and have the State to back its demand, as well as the Church. However, at the request of the selectmen, I condescended to make some such statement as this in writing:—"Know all men by these presents, that I, Henry Thoreau, do not wish to be regarded as a member of any incorporated society which I have not joined." This I gave to the town clerk; and he has it. The State, having thus learned that I did not wish to be regarded as a member of that church, has never made a like demand on me since; though it said that it must adhere to its original presumption that time. If I had known how to name them, I should then have signed off in detail from all the societies which I never signed on to; but I did not know where to find a complete list.

26   I have paid no poll-tax for six years. I was put into a jail once on this account, for one night; and, as I stood considering the walls of solid stone, two or three feet

thick, the door of wood and iron, a foot thick, and the iron grating which strained the light, I could not help being struck with the foolishness of that institution which treated me as if I were mere flesh and blood and bones, to be locked up. I wondered that it should have concluded at length that this was the best use it could put me to, and had never thought to avail itself of my services in some way. I saw that, if there was a wall of stone between me and my townsmen, there was a still more difficult one to climb or break through before they could get to be as free as I was. I did not for a moment feel confined, and the walls seemed a great waste of stone and mortar. I felt as if I alone of all my townsmen had paid my tax. They plainly did not know how to treat me, but behaved like persons who are underbred. In every threat and in every compliment there was a blunder; for they thought that my chief desire was to stand the other side of that stone wall. I could not but smile to see how industriously they locked the door on my meditations, which followed them out again without let or hindrance, and *they* were really all that was dangerous. As they could not reach me, they had resolved to punish my body; just as boys, if they cannot come at some person against whom they have a spite, will abuse his dog. I saw that the State was half-witted, that it was timid as a lone woman with her silver spoons, and that it did not know its friends from its foes, and I lost all my remaining respect for it, and pitied it.

Thus the State never intentionally confronts a man's sense, intellectual or moral, but only his body, his senses. It is not armed with superior wit or honesty, but with superior physical strength. I was not born to be forced. I will breathe after my own fashion. Let us see who is the strongest. What force has a multitude? They only can force me who obey a higher law than I. They force me to become like themselves. I do not hear of *men* being *forced* to live this way or that by masses of men. What sort of life were that to live? When I meet a government which says to me, "Your money or your life," why should I be in haste to give it my money? It may be in a great strait, and not know what to do: I cannot help that. It must help itself; do as I do. It is not worth the while to snivel about it. I am not responsible for the successful working of the machinery of society. I am not the son of the engineer. I perceive that, when an acorn and a chestnut fall side by side, the one does not remain inert to make way for the other, but both obey their own laws, and spring and grow and flourish as best they can, till one, perchance, overshadows and destroys the other. If a plant cannot live according to its nature, it dies; and so a man.   27

The night in prison was novel and interesting enough. The prisoners in their shirt-sleeves were enjoying a chat and the evening air in the doorway, when I entered. But the jailer said, "Come, boys, it is time lock up"; and so they dispersed, and I heard the sound of their steps returning into the hollow apartments. My room-mate was introduced to me by the jailer as "a first-rate fellow and a clever man." When the door was locked, he showed me where to hang my hat, and how he managed matters there. The rooms were whitewashed once a month; and this one, at least, was the whitest, most simply furnished, and probably the neatest apartment in the town. He naturally wanted to know where I came from, and what brought me there; and, when I had told him, I asked him in my turn how he came   28 there, presuming him to be an honest man, of course; and, as the world goes, I believe he was. "Why," said he, "they accuse me of burning a barn; but I never did it." As near as I could discover, he had probably gone to bed in a barn when drunk, and smoked his pipe there; and so a barn was burnt. He had the reputation of being a clever man, had been there some three months waiting for his trial to come on, and would have to wait as much longer; but he was quite domesticated and contented, since he got his board for nothing, and thought that he was well treated.

29   He occupied one window, and I the other; and I saw that if one stayed there long, his principal business would be to look out the window. I had soon read all the tracts that were left there, and examined where former prisoners had broken out, and where a grate had been sawed off, and heard the history of the various occupants of that room; for I found that even here there was a history and a gossip which never circulated beyond the walls of the jail. Probably this is the only house in the town where verses are composed, which are afterward printed in a circular form, but not published. I was shown quite a long list of verses which were composed by some young men who had been detected in an attempt to escape, who avenged themselves by singing them.

30   I pumped my fellow-prisoner as dry as I could, for fear I should never see him again; but at length he showed me which was my bed, and left me to blow out the lamp.

31   It was like traveling into a far country, such as I had never expected to behold, to lie there for one night. It seemed to me that I never had heard the town-clock strike before, nor the evening sounds of the village; for we slept with the windows open, which were inside the grating. It was to see my native village in the light of the Middle Ages, and our Concord was turned into a Rhine stream, and visions of knights and castles passed before me. They were the voices of old burghers that I heard in the streets. I was an involuntary spectator and auditor of whatever was done and said in the kitchen of the adjacent village-inn,—a wholly new and rare experience to me. It was a closer view of my native town. I was fairly inside of it. I never had seen its institutions before. This is one of its peculiar institutions; for it is a shire town. I began to comprehend what its inhabitants were about.

32   In the morning, our breakfasts were put through the hole in the door, in small oblong-square tin pans, made to fit, and holding a pint of chocolate, with brown bread, and an iron spoon. When they called for the vessels again, I was green enough to return what bread I had left; but my comrade seized it, and said that I should lay that up for lunch or dinner. Soon after he was let out to work at haying in a neighboring field, whither he went every day, and would not be back till noon; so he bade me good-day, saying that he doubted if he should see me again.

33   When I came out of prison,—for some one interfered, and paid that tax,—I did not perceive that great changes had taken place on the common, such as he observed who went in a youth and emerged a tottering and gray-headed man; and yet a change had to my eyes come over the scene,—the town, and State, and country,—greater than any that mere time could effect. I saw yet more distinctly the State in which I lived. I saw to what extent the people among whom I lived could be trusted as good neighbors and friends; that their friendship was for summer

weather only; that they did not greatly propose to do right; that they were a distinct race from me by their prejudices and superstitions, as the Chinamen and Malays are; that in their sacrifices to humanity they ran no risks, not even to their property; that after all they were not so noble but they treated the thief as he had treated them, and hoped, by a certain outward observance and a few prayers, and by walking in a particular straight though useless path from time to time, to save their souls. This may be to judge my neighbors harshly; for I believe that many of them are not aware that they have such an institution as the jail in their village.

It was formerly the custom of our village, when a poor debtor came out of jail, for his acquaintances to salute him, looking through their fingers, which were crossed to represent the grating of a jail window, "How do ye do?" My neighbors did not thus salute me, but first looked at me, and then at one another, as if I had returned from a long journey. I was put into jail as I was going to the shoemaker's to get a shoe which was mended. When I was let out the next morning, I proceeded to finish my errand, and, having put on my mended shoe, joined a huckleberry party, who were impatient to put themselves under my conduct; and in half an hour, —for the horse was soon tackled, —was in the midst of a huckleberry field, on one of our highest hills, two miles off, and then the State was nowhere to be seen. 34

This is the whole history of "My Prisons." 35

I have never declined paying the highway tax, because I am as desirous of being a good neighbor as I am of being a bad subject; and as for supporting schools, I am doing my part to educate my fellow-countrymen now. It is for no particular item in the tax-bill that I refuse to pay it. I simply wish to refuse allegiance to the State, to withdraw and stand aloof from it effectually. I do not care to trace the course of my dollar, if I could, till it buys a man or a musket to shoot one with, — the dollar is innocent, —but I am concerned to trace the effects of my allegiance. In fact, I quietly declare war with the State, after my fashion, though I will still make what use and get what advantage of her I can, as is usual in such cases. 36

If others pay the tax which is demanded of me, from a sympathy with the State, they do but what they have already done in their own case, or rather they abet injustice to a greater extent than the State requires. If they pay the tax from a mistaken interest in the individual taxed, to save his property, or prevent his going to jail, it is because they have not considered wisely how far they let their private feelings interfere with the public good. 37

This, then, is my position at present. But one cannot be too much on his guard in such a case, lest his action be biased by obstinacy or an undue regard for the opinions of men. Let him see that he does only what belongs to himself and to the hour. 38

I think sometimes, Why, this people mean well, they are only ignorant; they would do better if they knew how: why give your neighbors this pain to treat you as they are not inclined to? But I think again, This is no reason why I should do as they do, or permit others to suffer much greater pain of a different kind. Again, I sometimes say to myself, When many millions of men, without heat, without ill will, without personal feeling of any kind, demand of you a few shillings only, 39 without the possibility, such is their constitution, of retracting or altering their present demand, and without the possibility, on your side, of appeal to any other millions, why expose yourself to this overwhelming brute force? You do not resist cold and hunger, the winds and the waves, thus obstinately; you quietly submit to a thousand similar necessities. You do not put your head into the fire. But just in proportion as I regard this as not wholly a brute force, but partly a human force, and consider that I have relations to those millions as to so many millions of men, and not of mere brute or inanimate things, I see that appeal is possible, first and instantaneously, from them to the Maker of them, and, secondly, from them to themselves. But if I put my head deliberately into the fire, there is no appeal to fire or to the Maker of fire, and I have only myself to blame. If I could convince myself that I have any right to be satisfied with men as they are, and to treat them accordingly, and not according, in some respects, to my requisitions and expectations of what they and I ought to be, then, like a good Mussulman and fatalist, I should endeavor to be satisfied with things as they are, and say it is the will of God. And, above all, there is this difference between resisting this and a purely brute or natural force, that I can resist this with some effect; but I cannot expect, like Orpheus, to change the nature of the rocks and trees and beasts.

40   I do not wish to quarrel with any man or nation. I do not wish to split hairs, to make fine distinctions, or set myself up as better than my neighbors. I seek rather, I may say, even an excuse for conforming to the laws of the land. I am but too ready to conform to them. Indeed, I have reason to suspect myself on this head; and each year, as the tax-gatherer comes round, I find myself disposed to review the acts and position of the general and State governments, and the spirit of the people, to discover a pretext for conformity.

> "We must affect our country as our parents,
> And if at any time we alienate
> Our love or industry from doing it honor,
> We must respect effects and teach the soul
> Matter of conscience and religion,
> And not desire of rule or benefit."

I believe that the State will soon be able to take all my work of this sort out of my hands, and then I shall be no better a patriot than my fellow-countrymen. Seen from a lower point of view, the Constitution, with all its faults, is very good; the law and the courts are very respectable; even this State and this American government are, in many respects, very admirable, and rare things, to be thankful for, such as a great many have described them; but seen from a point of view a little higher, they are what I have described them; seen from a higher still, and the highest, who shall say what they are, or that they are worth looking at or thinking of at all?

41   However, the government does not concern me much, and I shall bestow the fewest possible thoughts on it. It is not many moments that I live under a government, even in this world. If a man is thought-free, fancy-free, imagination-free, that which *is not* never for a long time appearing *to be* to him, unwise rulers or reformers cannot fatally interrupt him.

I know that most men think differently from myself; but those whose lives are   42
by profession devoted to the study of these or kindred subjects content me as little as
any. Statesmen and legislators, standing so completely within the institution, never
distinctly and nakedly behold it. They speak of moving society, but have no resting-
place without it. They may be men of a certain experience and discrimination, and
have no doubt invented ingenious and even useful systems, for which we sincerely
thank them; but all their wit and usefulness lie within certain not very wide limits.
They are wont to forget that the world is not governed by policy and expediency.
Webster never goes behind government, and so cannot speak with authority about
it. His words are wisdom to those legislators who contemplate no essential reform in
the existing government; but for thinkers, and those who legislate for all time, he
never once glances at the subject. I know of those whose serene and wise speculations
on this theme would soon reveal the limits of his mind's range and hospitality. Yet,
compared with the cheap professions of most reformers, and the still cheaper
wisdom and eloquence of politicians in general, his are almost the only sensible and
valuable words, and we thank Heaven for him. Comparatively, he is always strong,
original, and, above all, practical. Still, his quality is not wisdom, but prudence.
The lawyer's truth is not Truth, but consistency or a consistent expediency. Truth is
always in harmony with herself, and is not concerned chiefly to reveal the justice
that may consist with wrong-doing. He well deserves to be called, as he has been
called, the Defender of the Constitution. There are really no blows to be given by
him but defensive ones. He is not a leader, but a follower. His leaders are the men
of '87. "I have never made an effort," he says, "and never propose to make an effort;
I have never countenanced an effort, and never mean to countenance an effort, to
disturb the arrangement as originally made, by which the various States came into
the Union." Still thinking of the sanction which the Constitution gives to slavery,
he says, "Because it was a part of the original compact,—let it stand." Notwithstanding his special acuteness and ability, he is unable to take a fact out of its merely
political relations, and behold it as it lies absolutely to be disposed of by the
intellect,—what, for instance, it behooves a man to do here in America to-day with
regard to slavery,—but ventures, or is driven, to make some such desperate answer
as the following, while professing to speak absolutely, and as a private man,—from
which what new and singular code of social duties might be inferred? "The manner," says he, "in which the governments of those States where slavery exists are to
regulate it is for their own consideration, under their responsibility to their constituents, to the general laws of propriety, humanity, and justice, and to God.
Associations formed elsewhere, springing from a feeling of humanity, or any other
cause, have nothing whatever to do with it. They have never received any encouragement from me, and they never will."

They who know of no purer sources of truth, who have traced up its stream no   43
higher, stand, and wisely stand, by the Bible and the Constitution, and drink at it
there with reverence and humility; but they who behold where it comes trickling
into this lake or that pool, gird up their loins once more, and continue their
pilgrimage toward its fountain-head.

No man with a genius for legislation has appeared in America. They are rare in   44 the history of the world. There are orators, politicians, and eloquent men, by the thousand; but the speaker has not yet opened his mouth to speak who is capable of settling the much-vexed questions of the day. We love eloquence for its own sake, and not for any truth which it may utter, or any heroism it may inspire. Our legislators have not yet learned the comparative value of free-trade and of freedom, of union, and of rectitude, to a nation. They have no genius or talent for comparatively humble questions of taxation and finance, commerce and manufactures and agriculture. If we were left solely to the wordy wit of legislators in Congress for our guidance, uncorrected by the seasonable experience and the effectual complaints of the people, America would not long retain her rank among the nations. For eighteen hundred years, though perchance I have no right to say it, the New Testament has been written; yet where is the legislator who has wisdom and practical talent enough to avail himself of the light which it sheds on the science of legislation?

45   The authority of government, even such as I am willing to submit to,—for I will cheerfully obey those who know and can do better than I, and in many things even those who neither know nor can do so well,—is still an impure one: to be strictly just, it must have the sanction and consent of the governed. It can have no pure right over my person and property but what I concede to it. The progress from an absolute to a limited monarchy, from a limited monarchy to a democracy, is a progress toward a true respect for the individual. Even the Chinese philosopher was wise enough to regard the individual as the basis of the empire. Is a democracy, such as we know it, the last improvement possible in government? Is it not possible to take a further step towards recognizing and organizing the rights of man? There will never be a really free and enlightened State until the State comes to recognize the individual as a higher and independent power, from which all its own power and authority are derived, and treats him accordingly. I please myself with imagining a State at last which can afford to be just to all men, and to treat the individual with respect as a neighbor; which even would not think it inconsistent with its own repose if a few were to live aloof from it, not meddling with it, nor embraced by it, who fulfilled all the duties of neighbors and fellow-men. A State which bore this kind of fruit, and suffered it to drop off as fast as it ripened, would prepare the way for a still more perfect and glorious State, which also I have imagined, but not yet anywhere seen.

Vocabulary

expedient, alacrity, *posse comitatus*, redressing, gregariousness, penitent, disinterested, Abolitionist, strait, requisitions, Mussulman, behooves, rectitude

Questions

1. Why, according to Thoreau, does the majority rule?
2. How does he think people should behave toward a government they disapprove of?

3. Does Thoreau advocate working to change unjust laws?
4. Thoreau claims that he meets the government once a year, in the person of the tax collector. How often have you met the government during the past year?
5. Why did Thoreau find himself still free though in jail?
6. For the sake of preserving the Union, Daniel Webster was willing to compromise on the issue of slavery. Thoreau was not. Most today would agree that Thoreau was right. Which of today's issues bring out similar disagreements among people of good will?

Topics for Writing

Tax Revolt: The Peaceable Revolution

Thoreau's Ideal Government: Formula for Disaster

Individual Conscience vs. Public Good: Room for Compromise?

15

The Tricks and Tools of Argument / Divided Opinions

This chapter introduces a variety of argumentative tactics, a few of them not quite acceptable to logicians but all of them used in everyday situations. Alleen Nilsen, for example, uses the inductive method to show that American English is sexist, but a linguist might differ with some of her examples, an anthropologist might say that certain "male" and "female" words derive from natural and ordinary activities of the sexes rather than from preconceived attitudes, and still a third objector might claim that she is oversensitive and sees evil where none exists.

A debater taking Professor Nilsen's position, on the other hand, might complain that Merrel D. Clubb, Jr., does not take the issue seriously enough, or that his *reductio ad absurdum* does not prove that attempts to make language nonsexist should be abandoned, or that ironic humor should not replace the calmer tools of discourse.

When it comes to argument, fairness is often in the eye of the beholder. David Hoekema might complain that William F. Buckley's orderly presentation is skewed by such debonair phrases as "ambushed . . . taking no prisoners" and "the clincher." Buckley could easily suggest that the opening paragraphs of "Capital Punishment: The Question of Justification" constitute an assault on our emotions and are meant to soften us up for the neatly ordered arguments that follow.

The pro- and anti-gun control debate is a most interesting example of argumentation in which all the stops have been pulled out. And deliberately so. Either reporter could easily have bound himself within the strictest limits of logic had he so desired; but this was not the editorial assignment. The assigned task was a personal view of a controversial issue, and it is not difficult to see that the writers are enjoying themselves as they go at it hammer and tongs. The reader gets the value of strongly expressed views, some insight into the use of debate weaponry, and a certain satisfaction in separating fair from unfair tactics. Here we find some of the same pleasure we might get from a rough-and-tumble game in which the fun comes more from the tussle than from being on the winning side.

Swift's "A Modest Proposal" is a model of satire used to persuade people to action. Where logic and good sense have not prevailed, a combination of the rapier and the club may succeed. The result is powerful and worth close attention.

You will recognize in this chapter many of the means by which persuaders attempt to move us—hints at rewards, subtle arousals of our fears, confidential asides to make us feel part of the in-group, or psychological "stroking" to keep us pacific when that suits the author's needs. Studying these systematically will not only help us to arm ourselves against surprise but also to recognize the need for moderation in our own excursions into argument.

Sexism in English

ALLEEN NILSEN (1936–) whose essay appeared in *Female Studies VI: Closer to the Ground,* has written frequently about sexist attitudes in literature, especially in that written for children.

1   Does culture shape language? Or does language shape culture? This is as difficult a question as the old puzzler of which came first, the chicken or the egg, because there's no clear separation between language and culture.

2   A well-accepted linguistic principle is that as culture changes so will the language. The reverse of this—as a language changes so will the culture—is not so readily accepted. This is why some linguists smile (or even scoff) at feminist attempts to replace *Mrs.* and *Miss* with *Ms.* and to find replacements for those all-inclusive words which specify masculinity, e.g., *chairman, mankind, brotherhood, freshman,* etc.

3   Perhaps they are amused for the same reason that it is the doctor at a cocktail party who laughs the loudest at the joke about the man who couldn't afford an operation so he offered the doctor a little something to touch up the X-ray. A person working constantly with language is likely to be more aware of how really deep-seated sexism is in our communication system.

4   Last winter I took a standard desk dictionary and gave it a place of honor on my night table. Every night that I didn't have anything more interesting to do, I read myself to sleep making a card for each entry that seemed to tell something about male and female. By spring I had a rather dog-eared dictionary, but I also had a collection of note cards filling two shoe boxes. The cards tell some rather interesting things about American English.

5   First, in our culture it is a woman's body which is considered important while it is a man's mind or his activities which are valued. A woman is sexy. A man is successful.

6   I made a card for all the words which came into modern English from somebody's name. I have a two-and-one-half-inch stack of cards which are men's names now used as everyday words. The women's stack is less than a half inch high and most of them came from Greek mythology. Words coming from the names of famous American men include *lynch, sousaphone, sideburns, Pullman, rickettsia, Shick test, Winchester rifle, Franklin stove, Bartlett pear, teddy bear,* and *boysenberry.* The only really common words coming from the names of American women are *bloomers* (after Amelia Jenks Bloomer) and *Mae West jacket.* Both of these words are related in some way to a woman's physical anatomy, while the male words (except for *sideburns* after General Burnsides) have nothing to do with the namesake's body.

7   This reminded me of an earlier observation that my husband and I made about geographical names. A few years ago we became interested in what we called

"Topless Topography" when we learned that the Grand Tetons used to be simply called *The Tetons* by French explorers and *The Teats* by American frontiersmen. We wrote letters to several map makers and found the following listings: *Nippletop* and *Little Nipple Top* near Mt. Marcy in the Adirondacks, *Nipple Mountain* in Archuleta County, Colorado, *Nipple Peak* in Coke County, Texas, *Nipple Butte* in Pennington, South Dakota, *Squaw Peak* in Placer County, California (and many other places), *Maiden's Peak* and *Squaw Tit* (they're the same mountain) in the Cascade Range in Oregon, *Jane Russell Peaks* near Stark, New Hampshire, and *Mary's Nipple* near Salt Lake City, Utah.

We might compare these names to Jackson Hole, Wyoming, or Pikes Peak, Colorado. I'm sure we would get all kinds of protests from the Jackson and Pike descendants if we tried to say that these topographical features were named because they in some way resembled the bodies of Jackson and Pike, respectively. **8**

This preoccupation with women's breasts is neither new nor strictly American. I was amused to read the derivation of the word *Amazon*. According to Greek folk etymology, the *a* means "without" as in *atypical* or *amoral* while *mazon* comes from *mazōs* meaning "breast." According to the legend, these women cut off one breast so that they could better shoot their bows. Perhaps the feeling was that the women had to trade in part of their femininity in exchange for their active or masculine role. **9**

There are certain pairs of words which illustrate the way in which sexual connotations are given to feminine words while the masculine words retain a serious, businesslike aura. For example, being a *callboy* is perfectly respectable. It simply refers to a person who calls actors when it is time for them to go on stage, but being a *call girl* is being a prostitute. **10**

Also we might compare *sir* and *madam*. *Sir* is a term of respect while *madam* has acquired the meaning of a brothel manager. The same thing has happened to the formerly cognate terms, *master* and *mistress*. Because of its acquired sexual connotations, *mistress* is now carefully avoided in certain contexts. For example, the Boy Scouts have *scoutmasters* but certainly not *scoutmistresses*. And in a dog show the female owner of a dog is never referred to as the *dog's mistress*, but rather as the *dog's master*. **11**

Master appears in such terms as *master plan, concert master, schoolmaster, mixmaster, master charge, master craftsman*, etc. But *mistress* appears in very few compounds. This is the way it is with dozens of words which have male and female counterparts. I found two hundred such terms, e.g., *usher–usherette, heir–heiress, hero–heroine*, etc. In nearly all cases it is the masculine word which is the base with a feminine suffix being added for the alternate version. The masculine word also travels into compounds while the feminine word is a dead end; e.g., from *king–queen* comes *kingdom* but not *queendom*, from *sportsman–sportslady* comes *sportsmanship* but not *sportsladyship*, etc. There is one—and only one—semantic area in which the masculine word is not the base or more powerful word. This is the area dealing with sex and marriage. Here it is the feminine word which is dominant. *Prostitute* is the base word with *male prostitute* being the derived term. *Bride* appears in *bridal shower, bridal gown, bridal attendant, bridesmaid*, and even in **12** *bridegroom,* while *groom* in the sense of *bridegroom* does not appear in any compounds, not even to name the groom's attendants or his prenuptial party.

13   At the end of a marriage, this same emphasis is on the female. If it ends in divorce, the woman gets the title of *divorcée* while the man is usually described with a statement, such as, "He's divorced." When the marriage ends in death, the woman is a *widow* and the -*er* suffix which seems to connote masculine (probably because it is an agentive or actor type suffix) is added to make *widower.* *Widower* doesn't appear in any compounds (except for *grass widower,* which is another companion term), but *widow* appears in several compounds and in addition has some acquired meanings, such as the extra hand dealt to the table in certain card games and an undesirable leftover line of type in printing.

14   If I were an anthropological linguist making observations about a strange and primitive tribe, I would duly note on my tape recorder that I had found linguistic evidence to show that in the area of sex and marriage the female appears to be more important than the male, but in all other areas of the culture, it seems that the reverse is true.

15   But since I am not an anthropological linguist, I will simply go on to my second observation, which is that women are expected to play a passive role while men play an active one.

16   One indication of women's passive role is the fact that they are often identified as something to eat. What's more passive than a plate of food? Last spring I saw an announcement advertising the Indiana University English Department picnic. It read "Good Food! Delicious Women!" The publicity committee was probably jumped on by local feminists, but it's nothing new to look on women as "delectable morsels." Even women compliment each other with "You look good enough to eat," or "You have a peaches and cream complexion." Modern slang constantly comes up with new terms, but some of the old standbys for women are: *cute tomato, dish, peach, sharp cookie, cheese cake, honey, sugar,* and *sweetie-pie.* A man may occasionally be addressed as *honey* or described as a *hunk of meat,* but certainly men are not laid out on a buffet and labeled as women are.

17   Women's passivity is also shown in the comparisons made to plants. For example, to *deflower* a woman is to take away her virginity. A girl can be described as a *clinging vine,* a *shrinking violet,* or a *wall flower.* On the other hand, men are too active to be thought of as plants. The only time we make the comparison is when insulting a man we say he is like a woman by calling him a *pansy.*

18   We also see the active-passive contrast in the animal terms used with males and females. Men are referred to as *studs, bucks,* and *wolves,* and they go *tomcat-ting around.* These are all aggressive roles, but women have such pet names as *kitten, bunny, beaver, bird, chick, lamb,* and *fox.* The idea of being a pet seems much more closely related to females than to males. For instance, little girls grow up wearing *pigtails* and *ponytails* and they dress in *halters* and *dog collars.*

19   The active-passive contrast is also seen in the proper names given to boy babies and girl babies. Girls are much more likely to be given names like *Ivy, Rose, Ruby, Jewel, Pearl, Flora, Joy,* etc., while boys are given names describing active roles such as *Martin* (warlike), *Leo* (lion), *William* (protector), *Ernest* (resolute fighter), and so on.

Another way that women play a passive role is that they are defined in   20
relationship to someone else. This is what feminists are protesting when they ask to
be identified as *Ms.* rather than as *Mrs.* or *Miss.* It is a constant source of irritation
to women's organizations that when they turn in items to newspapers under their
own names, that is, Susan Glascoe, Jeanette Jones, and so forth, the editors consis-
tently rewrite the item so that the names read Mrs. John Glascoe, Mrs. Robert E.
Jones.

In the dictionary I found what appears to be an attitude on the part of editors   21
that it is almost indecent to let a respectable woman's name march unaccompanied
across the pages of a dictionary. A woman's name must somehow be escorted by a
male's name regardless of whether or not the male contributed to the woman's
reason for being in the dictionary, or in his own right, was as famous as the woman.
For example, Charlotte Brontë is identified as Mrs. Arthur B. Nicholls, Amelia
Earhart is identified as Mrs. George Palmer Putnam, Helen Hayes is identified as
Mrs. Charles MacArthur, Zona Gale is identified as Mrs. William Llwelyn Breese,
and Jenny Lind is identified as Mme. Otto Goldschmidt.

Although most of the women are identified as Mrs. —— or as the wife of   22
——, other women are listed with brothers, fathers, or lovers. Cornelia Otis Skin-
ner is identified as the daughter of Otis, Harriet Beecher Stowe is identified as the
sister of Henry Ward Beecher, Edith Sitwell is identified as the sister of Osbert
and Sacheverell, Nell Gwyn is identified as the mistress of Charles II, and Madame Pompadour is identified as the mistress of Louis XV.

The women who did get into the dictionary without the benefit of a masculine   23
escort are a group sort of on the fringes of respectability. They are the rebels and the
crusaders: temperance leaders Frances Elizabeth Caroline Willard and Carry Nation, women's rights leaders Carrie Chapman Catt and Elizabeth Cady Stanton,
birth control educator Margaret Sanger, religious leader Mary Baker Eddy, and
slaves Harriet Tubman and Phillis Wheatley.

I would estimate that far more than fifty percent of the women listed in the   24
dictionary were identified as someone's wife. But of all the men—and there are
probably ten times as many men as women—only one was identified as "the
husband of . . . ." This was the unusual case of Frederic Joliot who took the last
name of Joliot-Curie and was identified as "husband of Irene." Apparently Irene,
the daughter of Pierre and Marie Curie, did not want to give up her maiden name
when she married and so the couple took the hyphenated last name.

There are several pairs of words which also illustrate the more powerful role of   25
the male and the relational role of the female. For example a *count* is a high
political officer with a *countess* being simply the wife of a count. The same is true
for a *duke* and a *duchess* and a *king* and a *queen.* The fact that a king is usually more
powerful than a queen might be the reason that Queen Elizabeth's husband is given
the title of *prince* rather than *king.* Since *king* is a stronger word than *queen,* it is
reserved for a true heir to the throne because if it were given to someone coming
into the royal family by marriage, then the subjects might forget where the true
power lies. With the weaker word of *queen,* this would not be a problem; so a
woman marrying a ruling monarch is given the title without question.

My third observation is that there are many positive connotations connected   26 with the concept of masculine, while there are either trivial or negative connotations connected with the corresponding feminine concept.

27   Conditioning toward the superiority of the masculine role starts very early in life. Child psychologists point out that the only area in which a girl has more freedom than a boy is in experimenting with an appropriate sex role. She is much freer to be a *tomboy* than is her brother to be a *sissy*. The proper names given to children reflect this same attitude. It's perfectly all right for a girl to have a boy's name, but not the other way around. As girls are given more and more of the boys' names, parents shy away from using boy names that might be mistaken for girl names, so the number of available masculine names is constantly shrinking. Fifty years ago *Hazel, Beverly, Marion, Frances,* and *Shirley* were all perfectly acceptable boys' names. Today few parents give these names to baby boys and adult men who are stuck with them self-consciously go by their initials or by abbreviated forms such as *Haze* or *Shirl*. But parents of little girls keep crowding the masculine set and currently popular girls' names include *Jo, Kelly, Teri, Cris, Pat, Shawn, Toni,* and *Sam*.

28   When the mother of one of these little girls tells her to *be a lady*, she means for her to sit with her knees together. But when the father of a little boy tells him to *be a man*, he means for him to be noble, strong, and virtuous. The whole concept of manliness has such positive connotations that it is a compliment to call a male a *he-man*, a *manly man*, or a *virile man* (*virile* comes from the Indo-European *vir*, meaning "man"). In each of these three terms, we are implying that someone is doubly good because he is doubly a man.

29   Compare *chef* with *cook*, *tailor* and *seamstress*, and *poet* with *poetess*. In each case, the masculine form carries with it an added degree of excellence. In comparing the masculine *governor* with the feminine *governess* and the masculine *major* with the feminine *majorette*, the added feature is power.

30   The difference between positive male and negative female connotations can be seen in several pairs of words which differ denotatively only in the matter of sex. For instance compare *bachelor* with the terms *spinster* and *old maid*. *Bachelor* has such positive connotations that modern girls have tried to borrow the feeling in the term *bachelor-girl*. *Bachelor* appears in glamorous terms such as *bachelor pad, bachelor party*, and *bachelor button*. But *old maid* has such strong negative feelings that it has been adopted into other areas, taking with it the feeling of undesirability. It has the metaphorical meaning of shriveled and unwanted kernels of pop corn, and it's the name of the last unwanted card in a popular game for children.

31   *Patron* and *matron* (Middle English for *father* and *mother*) are another set where women have tried to borrow the positive masculine connotations, this time through the word *patroness*, which literally means "female father." Such a peculiar term came about because of the high prestige attached to the word *patron* in such phrases as *"a patron of the arts"* or *"a patron saint."* *Matron* is more apt to be used in talking about a woman who is in charge of a jail or a public restroom.

32   Even *lord* and *lady* have different levels of connotation. *Our Lord* is used as a title for deity, while the corresponding *Our Lady* is a relational title for Mary, the mortal mother of Jesus. *Landlord* has more dignity than *landlady* probably because the landlord is more likely to be thought of as the owner while the landlady is the

person who collects the rent and enforces the rules. *Lady* is used in many insignificant places where the corresponding *lord* would never be used, for example, *ladies room, ladies sizes, ladies aid society, ladybug,* etc.

This overuse of *lady* might be compared to the overuse of *queen* which is   33
rapidly losing its prestige as compared to *king*. Hundreds of beauty queens are crowned each year and nearly every community in the United States has its *Dairy Queen* or its *Freezer Queen*, etc. Male homosexuals have adopted the terms to identify the "feminine" partner. And advertisers who are constantly on the lookout for euphemisms to make unpleasant sounding products salable have recently dealt what might be a death blow to the prestige of the word *queen*. They have begun to use it as an indication of size. For example, *queen-size* panty hose are panty hose for fat women. The meaning comes through a comparison with *king-size*, meaning big. However, there's a subtle difference in that our culture considers it desirable for males to be big because size is an indication of power, but we prefer that females be small and petite. So using *king-size* as a term to indicate bigness partially enhances the prestige of *king*, but using *queen-size* to indicate bigness brings unpleasant associations to the word *queen*.

Another set that might be compared are *brave* and *squaw*. The word *brave*   34
carries with it the connotations of youth, vigor, and courage, while *squaw* implies almost opposite characteristics. With the set *wizard* and *witch*, the main difference is that *wizard* implies skill and wisdom combined with magic, while *witch* implies evil intentions combined with magic. Part of the unattractiveness of both *squaw* and *witch* is that they suggest old age, which in women is particularly undesirable. When I lived in Afghanistan (1967–1969), I was horrified to hear a proverb stating that when you see an old man you should sit down and take a lesson, but when you see an old woman you should throw a stone. I was equally startled when I went to compare the connotations of our two phrases *grandfatherly advice* and *old wives' tales*. Certainly it isn't expressed with the same force as in the Afghan proverb, but the implication is similar.

In some of the animal terms used for women the extreme undesirability of   35
female old age is also seen. For instance consider the unattractiveness of *old nag* as compared to *filly*, of *old crow* or *old bat* as compared to *bird*, and of being *catty* as compared to being *kittenish*. The chicken metaphor tells the whole story of a girl's life. In her youth she is a *chick*, then she marries and begins feeling *cooped up*, so she goes to *hen parties* where she *cackles* with her friends. Then she has her *brood* and begins to *henpeck* her husband. Finally she turns into *an old biddy*.

Vocabulary

anthropological, linguist, etymology, euphemisms

Questions

1. Do you find Nilsen's dictionary research scientifically adequate? Roughly so?

2. Are all of her examples convincing? Do you think sexism is at the root of the word *kingdom*?
3. In the following pairs, which word seems most clearly to support the charge of sexism: *sideburns, Mae West; master, mistress; patron, matron; king, queen*?
4. Do you agree that *king-size* indicates power, *queen-size* undesirable size?
5. Is she right about what mothers mean by "be a lady"? Is that the fault of language or of mothers?
6. Can you add to her list of examples?
7. Look up the etymology of *lord* and *lady*. Is sexism at the root here?
8. Is it fair to identify a woman by her relationship to a man? Is it necessary?
9. Do you find signs of sexism in the language used by your acquaintances?
10. "If women had invented more things, more things would be named after them." Is this a fair response to Nilsen's findings?

Topics for Writing

Nilsen Is Oversensitive

Right On, Ms. Nilsen!

And God Created Person

MERREL D. CLUBB, JR. (1921–) is a professor of English with a special interest in linguistics. His letter was first published in the *MLA Newsletter*, March 1974.

To the Editor:

The women's liberation movement has, of course, given birth to many worth-while improvements, but it has also spawned at least one linguistic monstrosity. One can, with some ease, accept the new form *Ms* as filling an empty slot in our language; but is *chairperson*, or even *chairwoman* really necessary? *Chairperson* is fast infiltrating our newspapers and magazines, but when it begins to appear in the publications of our most august Modern Language Association of America, it is time for those concerned with the "purity" of our language to cry forth. If we go the route of *chairperson* we may just as well start talking about *clergyperson, churchperson, countryperson, journeyperson, kinsperson, longshoreperson, foreperson, postperson, brakeperson, milkperson, Redperson, Peking person, inner person,* and *freshperson; personhour, personhunt, personservant, personslaughter, personhole, personmade, personkind, personhood, personly,* and *personliness; person of the world, person in the street, person of God, person of straw, person of war,* and *person o'war bird.* We may even talk about *personing the ship* and *personing the production lines.* And finally, *Persons' Room.* Now surely, we would want to be able to tell what is behind the door labeled "Persons' Room," wouldn't we? So, we will have to start talking about *Persons' Room* in contrast to *Wopersons' Room.* This will lead to *flagperson* and *flagwoperson, policeperson* and *policewoperson, salesperson* and *saleswoperson, personish* and *wopersonish, person of the house* and *woperson of the house,* and—*chairperson* and *chairwoperson.* Most surely, wopersons—or fepersons—would wish to distinguish *woperson power* from *person power, woperson suffrage* from *person suffrage,* and most of all, *wopersons' lib* from *persons' lib!*

The insistence on such forms as *chairperson, cochairperson,* and *chairperson-ship* only goes to show how uninformed avid wopersons and their campfollowers can be. What does the form *man* mean in its various contexts? The modern *man* comes from Old English *man* (in various spellings, as early as 971 A.D.). The meaning of Old English *man* along with its cognates in all the Germanic languages was twofold: (1) "an adult male human being" and (2) "a human being of either sex." Moreover, the more common meaning of *man* in Old English was the latter—"human being or person" without reference to age or sex—and the distinctive sex terms were *wer,* "man, adult male" and *wif,* "woman, adult female." The forerunner of modern *woman,* Old English *wifman,* meant literally "female human being" or "female person." The dual meaning of *man* has continued in English down to the present day, although the meaning "human being" has become somewhat more constricted in that it occurs now only in general or indefinite applications. In many words such as *swordsman, penman, policeman, chairman,* etc., the unstressed form *man* is no longer even a word, but, in effect, a derivational suffix with meanings of, roughly, "one who is skilled in the use of something" (a sword, a pen) or "one who is connected with some act" (policing, chairing). In short, why bring in a relative Johnny-come-lately *person* (originally from Old French) to replace a perfectly good English form *man?* Do we really want to talk about Shakespeare's *Two Gentlepersons of Verona,* Pope's *An Essay on Person,* Shaw's *Person and Superperson,* O'Neill's *The Iceperson Cometh?* Must we open Milton's *Paradise Lost* and read: "Of Person's First Disobedience, and the Fruit / Of that Forbidden tree . . ."?

Vocabulary

linguistic, derivational, suffix

Questions

1. The technique employed in this letter is the time-honored *reductio ad absurdum* (refuting an argument by pushing it to an illogical extreme). Has Clubb succeeded?
2. Is this absurdity the only reason he can show for retaining *man* in its common uses?
3. Does the historical explanation of *man* satisfy the desire for nonsexist language?
4. To change the title of *Man and Superman* seems patently ridiculous, even to one who is sensitive about sexism. But do you feel differently about other examples of offensive words—say, anti-Jewish terms in *The Merchant of Venice* or the use of *nigger* in *Huckleberry Finn?* Would you consider changing these?

Topics for Writing

The Laugh: Fair or Unfair Debate Tactic?

Common Sense in the Debate over Sexism in Language

Capital Punishment

WILLIAM F. BUCKLEY, JR. (1925–) writer, controversialist, and television personality, keeps up a running commentary on national affairs. This essay was printed in *Execution Eve, and Other Contemporary Ballads* in 1975.

There is national suspense over whether capital punishment is about to be abolished, and the assumption is that when it comes it will come from the Supreme Court. Meanwhile, (a) the prestigious State Supreme Court of California has interrupted executions, giving constitutional reasons for doing so; (b) the death wings are overflowing with convicted prisoners; (c) executions are a remote memory; and—for the first time in years—(d) the opinion polls show that there is sentiment for what amounts to the restoration of capital punishment.   1

The case for abolition is popularly known. The other case less so, and (without wholeheartedly endorsing it) I give it as it was given recently to the Committee of the Judiciary of the House of Representatives by Professor Ernest van den Haag, under whose thinking cap groweth no moss. Mr. van den Haag, a professor of social philosophy at New York University, ambushed the most popular arguments of the abolitionists, taking no prisoners.   2

(1) The business about the poor and the black suffering excessively from capital punishment is no argument against capital punishment. It is an argument against the *administration* of justice, not against the penalty. Any punishment can be unfairly or unjustly applied. Go ahead and reform the processes by which capital punishment is inflicted, if you wish; but don't confuse maladministration with the merits of capital punishment.   3

(2) The argument that the death penalty is "unusual" is circular. Capital punishment continues on the books of a majority of states, the people continue to sanction the concept of capital punishment, and indeed capital sentences are routinely handed down. What has made capital punishment "unusual" is that the courts and, primarily, governors have intervened in the process so as to collaborate in the frustration of the execution of the law. To argue that capital punishment is unusual, when in fact it has been made unusual by extra-legislative authority, is an argument to expedite, not eliminate, executions.   4

(3) Capital punishment is cruel. That is a historical judgment. But the Constitution suggests that what must be proscribed as cruel is (a) a particularly painful way of inflicting death, or (b) a particularly undeserved death; and the death penalty, as such, offends neither of these criteria and cannot therefore be regarded as objectively "cruel."   5

Viewed the other way, the question is whether capital punishment can be regarded as useful, and the question of deterrence arises.   6

(4) Those who believe that the death penalty does not intensify the disinclination to commit certain crimes need to wrestle with statistics that, in fact, it can't be proved that *any* punishment does that to any particular crime. One would rationally   7

suppose that two years in jail would cut the commission of crime if not exactly by 100 percent more than a penalty of one year in jail, at least that it would further discourage crime to a certain extent. The proof is unavailing. On the other hand, the statistics, although ambiguous, do not show either (a) that capital punishment net discourages; or (b) that capital punishment fails net to discourage. "The absence of proof for the additional deterrent effect of the death penalty must not be confused with the presence of proof for the absence of this effect."

8   The argument that most capital crimes are crimes of passion committed by irrational persons is no argument against the death penalty, because it does not reveal how many crimes might, but for the death penalty, have been committed by rational persons who are now deterred.

9   And the clincher. (5) Since we do not know for certain whether or not the death penalty adds deterrence, we have in effect the choice of two risks.

10   Risk One: If we execute convicted murderers without thereby deterring prospective murderers beyond the deterrence that could have been achieved by life imprisonment, we may have vainly sacrificed the life of the convicted murderer.

11   Risk Two: If we fail to execute a convicted murderer whose execution might have deterred an indefinite number of prospective murderers, our failure sacrifices an indefinite number of victims of future murderers.

12   "If we had certainty, we would not have risks. We do not have certainty. If we have risks—and we do—better to risk the life of the convicted man than risk the life of an indefinite number of innocent victims who might survive if he were executed."

Vocabulary

sanction, extra-legislative, expedite, proscribe, disinclination, unavailing, net

Questions

1. Is the lettering and numbering of arguments in this essay necessary? Does it tend to obscure the difference between stronger and weaker arguments?
2. Is there a logical order to the arguments "ambushed" by Mr. van den Haag?
3. Buckley is pretty obviously on the side of those who support capital punishment. Does his parenthesis in the second paragraph weaken the arguments that follow?
4. Do you agree that (5) is the "clincher"? Can you add to the risks presented for our choice? Would the addition of a third risk unclinch the argument?

Topics for Writing

The Strongest Argument for Capital Punishment

Should Society Kill?

When Society Should Kill

Capital Punishment: The Question
of Justification

DAVID HOEKEMA was a philosophy instructor at St. Olaf College in Minnesota when this article was published in *The Christian Century* in 1979.

In 1810 a bill introduced in the British Parliament sought to abolish capital punishment for the offense of stealing five shillings or more from a shop. Judges and magistrates unanimously opposed the measure. In the House of Lords, the chief justice of the King's Bench, Lord Ellenborough, predicted that the next step would be abolition of the death penalty for stealing five shillings from a house; thereafter no one could "trust himself for an hour without the most alarming apprehension that, on his return, every vestige of his property [would] be swept away by the hardened robber" (quoted by Herbert B. Ehrmann in "The Death Penalty and the Administration of Justice," in *The Death Penalty in America*, edited by Hugo Adam Bedau [Anchor, 1967], p. 415).

During the same year Parliament abolished the death penalty for picking pockets, but more than 200 crimes remained punishable by death. Each year in Great Britain more than 2,000 persons were being sentenced to die, though only a small number of these sentences were actually carried out.

I

In this regard as in many others, the laws of the English colonies in North America were much less harsh than those of the mother country. At the time of the Revolution, statutes in most of the colonies prescribed hanging for about a dozen offenses—among them murder, treason, piracy, arson, rape, robbery, burglary, sodomy and (in some cases) counterfeiting, horse theft and slave rebellion. But by the early nineteenth century a movement to abolish the death penalty was gaining strength.

The idea was hardly new: czarist Russia had eliminated the death penalty on religious grounds in the eleventh century. In the United States the movement had been launched by Benjamin Rush in the eighteenth century, with the support of such other distinguished citizens of Philadelphia as Benjamin Franklin and Attorney General William Bradford. By the 1830s, bills calling for abolition of capital punishment were being regularly introduced, and defeated, in several state legislatures. In 1846 Michigan voted effectively to abolish the death penalty—the first English-speaking jurisdiction in the world to do so.

In the years since, twelve states have abolished capital punishment entirely. Although statutes still in effect in some states permit the death penalty to be imposed for a variety of offenses—ranging from statutory rape to desecration of a grave to causing death in a duel—murder is virtually the only crime for which it has been recently employed. There are about 400 persons in U.S. prisons under sentence of death, but only one execution (Gary Gilmore's) has been carried out in this country in the past eleven years.

6   However, the issue of whether capital punishment is justifiable is by no means settled. Since the Supreme Court, in the case of *Furman* v. *Georgia* in 1972, invalidated most existing laws permitting capital punishment, several states have enacted new legislation designed to meet the court's objections to the Georgia law. And recent public-opinion surveys indicate that a large number, possibly a majority, of Americans favor imposing the death penalty for some crimes. But let us ask the ethical question: Ought governments to put to death persons convicted of certain crimes?

II

7   First, let us look at grounds on which capital punishment is defended. Most prominent is the argument from *deterrence*. Capital punishment, it is asserted, is necessary to deter potential criminals. Murderers must be executed so that the lives of potential murder victims may be spared.

8   Two assertions are closely linked here. First, it is said that convicted murderers must be put to death in order to protect the rest of us against those individuals who might kill others if they were at large. This argument, based not strictly on deterrence but on incapacitation of known offenders, is inconclusive, since there are other effective means of protecting the innocent against convicted murderers—for example, imprisonment of murderers for life in high-security institutions.

9   Second, it is said that the example of capital punishment is needed to deter those who would otherwise commit murder. Knowledge that a crime is punishable by death will give the potential criminal pause. This second argument rests on the assumption that capital punishment does in fact reduce the incidence of capital crimes—a presupposition that must be tested against the evidence. Surprisingly, none of the available empirical data shows any significant correlation between the existence or use of the death penalty and the incidence of capital crimes.

10   When studies have compared the homicide rates for the past fifty years in states that employ the death penalty and in adjoining states that have abolished it, the numbers have in every case been quite similar; the death penalty has had no discernible effect on homicide rates. Further, the shorter-term effects of capital punishment have been studied by examining the daily number of homicides reported in California over a ten-year period to ascertain whether the execution of convicts reduced the number. Fewer homicides were reported on days immediately following an execution, but this reduction was matched by an increase in the number of homicides on the day of execution and the preceding day. Executions had no discernible effect on the weekly total of homicides. (Cf. "Death and Imprisonment as Deterrents to Murder," by Thorsten Sellin, in Bedau, op. cit., pp. 274–284, and "The Deterrent Effect of Capital Punishment in California," by William F. Graves, in Bedau, op. cit., pp. 322–332.)

11   The available evidence, then, fails to support the claim that capital punish-

ment deters capital crime. For this reason, I think, we may set aside the deterrence argument. But there is a stronger reason for rejecting the argument—one that has to do with the way in which supporters of that argument would have us treat persons.

Those who defend capital punishment on grounds of deterrence would have us   12
take the lives of some—persons convicted of certain crimes—because doing so will discourage crime and thus protect others. But it is a grave moral wrong to treat one person in a way justified solely by the needs of others. To inflict harm on one person in order to serve the purposes of others is to use that person in an immoral and inhumane way, treating him or her not as a person with rights and responsibilities but as a means to other ends. The most serious flaw in the deterrence argument, therefore, is that it is the wrong *kind* of argument. The execution of criminals cannot be justified by the good which their deaths may do the rest of us.

III

A second argument for the death penalty maintains that some crimes, chief   13
among them murder, *morally require* the punishment of death. In particular, Christians frequently support capital punishment by appeal to the Mosaic code, which required the death penalty for murder. "The law of capital punishment," one writer has concluded after reviewing relevant biblical passages, "must stand as a silent but powerful witness to the sacredness of God-given life" ("Christianity and the Death Penalty," by Jacob Vellenga, in Bedau, op. cit., pp. 123–130).

In the Mosaic code, it should be pointed out, there were many capital crimes   14
besides murder. In the book of Deuteronomy, death is prescribed as the penalty for false prophecy, worship of foreign gods, kidnapping, adultery, deception by a bride concerning her virginity, and disobedience to parents. To this list the laws of the book of Exodus add witchcraft, sodomy, and striking or cursing a parent.

I doubt that there is much sentiment in favor of restoring the death penalty in   15
the United States for such offenses. But if the laws of Old Testament Israel ought not to govern our treatment of, say, adultery, why should they govern the penalty for murder? To support capital punishment by an appeal to Old Testament law is to overlook the fact that the ancient theocratic state of Israel was in nearly every respect profoundly different from any modern secular state. For this reason, we cannot simply regard the Mosaic code as normative for the United States today.

But leaving aside reference to Mosaic law, let me state more strongly the   16
argument we are examining. The death penalty, it may be urged, is the only just penalty for a crime such as murder; it is the only fair *retribution*. Stated thus, the argument at hand seems to be the right *kind* of argument for capital punishment. If capital punishment can be justified at all, it must be on the basis of the *seriousness of the offense* for which it is imposed. Retributive considerations *should* govern the punishment of individuals who violate the law, and chief among these considerations are the principle of proportionality between punishment and offense and the requirement that persons be punished only for acts for which they are truly responsible. I am not persuaded that retributive considerations are sufficient to set a particular penalty for a given offense, but I believe they do require that in comparative terms we visit more serious offenses with more severe punishment.

17   Therefore, the retributive argument seems the strongest one in support of capital punishment. We ought to deal with convicted offenders not as we want to, but as they deserve. And I am not certain that it is wrong to argue that a person who has deliberately killed another person deserves to die.

18   But even if this principle is valid, should the judicial branch of our governments be empowered to determine whether individuals deserve to die? Are our procedures for making laws and for determining guilt sufficiently reliable that we may entrust our lives to them? I shall return to this important question presently. But consider the following fact: During the years from 1930 to 1962, 466 persons were put to death for the crime of rape. Of these, 399 were black. Can it seriously be maintained that our courts are administering the death penalty to all those and only to those who deserve to die?

IV

19   Two other arguments deserve brief mention. It has been argued that, even if the penalty of life imprisonment were acceptable on other grounds, our society could not reasonably be asked to pay the cost of maintaining convicted murderers in prisons for the remainder of their natural lives.

20   This argument overlooks the considerable costs of retaining the death penalty. Jury selection, conduct of the trial, and the appeals process become extremely time-consuming and elaborate when death is a possible penalty. On the other hand, prisons should not be as expensive as they are. At present those prisoners who work at all are working for absurdly low wages, frequently at menial and degrading tasks. Prisons should be reorganized to provide meaningful work for all able inmates; workers should be paid fair wages for their work and charged for their room and board. Such measures would sharply reduce the cost of prisons and make them more humane.

21   But these considerations—important as they are—have little relevance to the justification of capital punishment. We should not decide to kill convicted criminals only because it costs so much to keep them alive. The cost to society of imprisonment, large or small, cannot justify capital punishment.

22   Finally, defenders of capital punishment sometimes support their case by citing those convicted offenders—for example, Gary Gilmore—who have asked to be executed rather than imprisoned. But this argument, too, is of little relevance. If some prisoners would prefer to die rather than be imprisoned, perhaps we should oblige them by permitting them to take their own lives. But this consideration has nothing to do with the question of whether we ought to impose the punishment of death on certain offenders, most of whom would prefer to live.

V

23   Let us turn now to the case *against* the death penalty. It is sometimes argued that capital punishment is unjustified because those guilty of crimes cannot help acting as they do: the environment, possibly interacting with inherited characteristics, causes some people to commit crimes. It is not moral culpability or choice that divides law-abiding citizens from criminals—so Clarence Darrow argued eloquently—but the accident of birth or social circumstances.

If determinism of this sort were valid, not only the death penalty but all forms of punishment would be unjustified. No one who is compelled by circumstances to act deserves to be punished. But there is little reason to adopt this bleak view of human action. Occasionally coercive threats compel a person to violate the law; and in such cases the individual is rightly excused from legal guilt. Circumstances of deprivation, hardship and lack of education—unfortunately much more widely prevalent—break down the barriers, both moral and material, which deter many of us from breaking the law. They are grounds for exercising extreme caution and for showing mercy in the application of the law, but they are not the sole causes of crimes: they diminish but do not destroy the responsibility of the individual. The great majority of those who break the law do so deliberately, by choice and not as a result of causes beyond their control. 24

Second, the case against the death penalty is sometimes based on the view that the justification of punishment lies in the reform which it effects. Those who break the law, it is said, are ill, suffering either from psychological malfunction or from maladjustment to society. Our responsibility is to treat them, to cure them of their illness, so that they become able to function in socially acceptable ways. Death, obviously, cannot reform anyone. 25

Like the deterrence argument for capital punishment, this seems to be the wrong *kind* of argument. Punishment is punishment and treatment is treatment, and one must not be substituted for the other. Some persons who violate the law are, without doubt, mentally ill. It is unreasonable and inhumane to punish them for acts which they may not have realized they were doing; to put such a person to death would be an even more grievous wrong. In such cases treatment is called for. 26

But most persons who break the law are not mentally ill and do know what they are doing. We may not force them to undergo treatment in place of the legal penalty for their offenses. To confine them to mental institutions until those put in authority over them judge that they are cured of their criminal tendencies is far more cruel than to sentence them to a term of imprisonment. Voluntary programs of education or vocational training, which help prepare prisoners for noncriminal careers on release, should be made more widely available. But compulsory treatment for all offenders violates their integrity as persons; we need only look to the Soviet Union to see the abuses to which such a practice is liable. 27

VI

Let us examine a third and stronger argument, a straightforward moral assertion; the state ought not to take life unnecessarily. For many reasons—among them the example which capital punishment sets, its effect on those who must carry out death sentences and, above all, its violation of a basic moral principle—the state ought not to kill people. 28

The counterclaim made by defenders of capital punishment is that in certain circumstances killing people is permissible and even required, and that capital punishment is one of those cases. If a terrorist is about to throw a bomb into a crowded theater, and a police officer is certain that there is no way to stop him except to kill him, the officer should of course kill the terrorist. In some cases of grave and immediate danger, let us grant, killing is justified. 29

30   But execution bears little resemblance to such cases. It involves the planned, deliberate killing of someone in custody who is not a present threat to human life or safety. Execution is not necessary to save the lives of future victims, since there are other means to secure that end.

31   Is there some vitally important purpose of the state or some fundamental right of persons which cannot be secured without executing convicts? I do not believe there is. And in the absence of any such compelling reason, the moral principle that it is wrong to kill people constitutes a powerful argument against capital punishment.

VII

32   Of the arguments I have mentioned in favor of the death penalty, only one has considerable weight. That is the retributive argument that murder, as an extremely serious offense, requires a comparably severe punishment. Of the arguments so far examined against capital punishment, only one, the moral claim that killing is wrong, is, in my view, acceptable.

33   There is, however, another argument against the death penalty which I find compelling—that based on the imperfection of judicial procedure. In the case of *Furman* v. *Georgia*, the Supreme Court struck down existing legislation because of the arbitrariness with which some convicted offenders were executed and others spared. Laws enacted subsequently in several states have attempted to meet the court's objection, either by making death mandatory for certain offenses or by drawing up standards which the trial jury must follow in deciding, after guilt has been established, whether the death penalty will be imposed in a particular case. But these revisions of the law diminish only slightly the discretion of the jury. When death is made the mandatory sentence for first-degree murder, the question of death or imprisonment becomes the question of whether to find the accused guilty as charged or guilty of a lesser offense, such as second-degree murder.

34   When standards are spelled out, the impression of greater precision is often only superficial. A recent Texas statute, for example, instructs the jury to impose a sentence of death only if it is established "beyond a reasonable doubt" that "there is a probability that the defendant would commit criminal acts of violence that would constitute a continuing threat to society" (Texas Code of Criminal Procedure, Art. 37.071; quoted in *Capital Punishment: The Inevitability of Caprice and Mistake*, by Charles L. Black, Jr. [Norton, 1974], p. 58). Such a law does not remove discretion but only adds confusion.

35   At many other points in the judicial process, discretion rules, and arbitrary or incorrect decisions are possible. The prosecutor must decide whether to charge the accused with a capital crime, and whether to accept a plea of guilty to a lesser charge. (In most states it is impossible to plead guilty to a charge carrying a mandatory death sentence.) The jury must determine whether the facts of the case as established by testimony in court fit the legal definition of the offense with which the defendant is charged—a definition likely to be complicated at best, incomprehensible at worst. From a mass of confusing and possibly conflicting testimony the jury must choose the most reliable. But evident reliability can be deceptive:

persons have been wrongly convicted of murder on the positive identification of eyewitnesses.

Jurors must also determine whether at the time of the crime the accused satisfied the legal definition of insanity. The most widely used definition—the McNaghten Rules formulated by the judges of the House of Lords in 1843—states that a person is excused from criminal responsibility if at the time of his act he suffered from a defect of reason which arose from a disease of the mind and as a result of which he did not "know the nature and quality of his act," or "if he did know it . . . he did not know he was doing what was wrong" (quoted in *Punishment and Responsibility*, by H. L. A. Hart [Oxford University Press, 1968], p. 189). Every word of this formula has been subject to legal controversy in interpretation, and it is unreasonable to expect that juries untrained in law will be able to apply it consistently and fairly. Even after sentencing, some offenders escape the death penalty as a result of appeals, other technical legal challenges, or executive clemency. | 36

Because of all these opportunities for arbitrary decision, only a small number of those convicted of capital crimes are actually executed. It is hardly surprising that their selection has little to do with the character of their crimes but a great deal to do with the skill of their legal counsel. And the latter depends in large measure on how much money is available for the defense. Inevitably, the death penalty has been imposed most frequently on the poor, and in this country it has been imposed in disproportionate numbers on blacks. | 37

To cite two examples in this regard: All those executed in Delaware between 1902 and the (temporary) abolition of the state's death penalty in 1958 were unskilled workers with limited education. Of 3,860 persons executed in the United States between 1930 and the present, 2,066, or 54 percent, were black. Although for a variety of reasons the per capita rate of conviction for most types of crime has been higher among the poor and the black, that alone cannot explain why a tenth of the population should account for more than half of those executed. Doubtless prejudice played a part. But no amount of goodwill and fair-mindedness can compensate for the disadvantage to those who cannot afford the highly skilled legal counsel needed to discern every loophole in the judicial process. | 38

VIII

Even more worrisome than the discriminatory application of the death penalty is the possibility of mistaken conviction and its ghastly consequences. In a sense, any punishment wrongfully imposed is irrevocable, but none is so irrevocable as death. Although we cannot give back to a person mistakenly imprisoned the time spent or the self-respect lost, we can release and compensate him or her. But we cannot do anything for a person wrongfully executed. While we ought to minimize the opportunities for capricious or mistaken judgments throughout the legal system, we cannot hope for perfect success. There is no reason why our mistakes must be fatal. | 39

Numerous cases of erroneous convictions in capital cases have been documented; several of those convicted were put to death before the error was discov- | 40 ered. However small their number, it is too large. So long as the death penalty exists, there are certain to be others, for every judicial procedure—however meticulous, however compassed about with safeguards—must be carried out by fallible human beings.

41   One erroneous execution is too many, because even lawful executions of the indisputably guilty serve no purpose. They are not justified by the need to protect the rest of us, since there are other means of restraining persons dangerous to society, and there is no evidence that executions deter the commission of crime. A wrongful execution is a grievous injustice that cannot be remedied after the fact. Even a legal and proper execution is a needless taking of human life. Even if one is sympathetic—as I am—to the claim that a murderer deserves to die, there are compelling reasons not to entrust the power to decide who shall die to the persons and procedures that constitute our judicial system.

Vocabulary

vestige, statutory, deterrence, incapacitation, empirical, discernible, retribution, culpability, coercive, discretion, irrevocable, capricious

Questions

1. Is the historical approach to the abolition of capital punishment a good one? Do Hoekema's first six paragraphs predispose you against capital punishment in general?
2. When we want to persuade others on a controversial subject, we want them to know that we are reasonable and unprejudiced. Having established our fairness, we can proceed more confidently with our argument. Do you find evidence of this technique in Hoekema's essay?
3. Do you find the evidence against deterrence convincing? Are statistical findings effective? Why or why not?
4. Do you agree with Hoekema that retribution for crime is the right *kind* of argument for capital punishment? Why, then, does he undercut that argument in paragraph 18?
5. Has Hoekema given a fair and equal presentation of both sides of the argument?
6. Do you think most murderers are mentally ill?
7. Do you agree that the chance of error should prevent the use of capital punishment in any case?

Topics for Writing

The Rich Get Off, the Poor Get It

Mistakes Are Inevitable, So—

Mistakes Are Inevitable, But—

Despite Evidence and Reason, Pro-Gun Talk Won't Go Away

RICHARD J. ROTH   is a reporter for a newspaper in Buffalo, New York.

Logic, statistics, common sense and public opinion are on the side of gun control, but America's firearms fanatics are insufferably relentless. Now, for pete's sake, they want their own political party.   1

With their own blind, the gun lovers can offer us candidates promising not a chicken in every pot, but a pistol in every pocket. And carnage in every home. Someone else to vote against.   2

There are already too many guns and too many nuts in this country. They have increased the power of despots and diminished the security of cities: No American president has ever been stabbed or clubbed to death; every four minutes someone in the U.S. is killed or wounded by gunfire, but fortunately, according to FBI statistics, in 70 percent of the cases, the people who are killed are shot by relatives or acquaintances, or by themselves.   3

For every burglar stopped by a gun, four gun owners or members of their families are killed in firearm accidents, according to a 1968 report by the National Commission on the Causes and Prevention of Violence. The gun is essentially useless against burglars because more than 90 percent of the burglaries are committed when no one is home.   4

On top of that, hunters and their guns have devastated Mother Nature. They kill an estimated 200 million birds and 50 million other animals each year; they would have you believe that such carnage is good for nature, but that is pure twaddle.   5

Many animals—from the passenger pigeon to the Great Plains wolf—are extinct because of the gunners. Scores of other innocent animals are on the "endangered species" list. Farmers have to use increasing amounts of toxic pesticides to make up for all the insect-eating animals slaughtered by the shooters. And, because they are such reckless shots, annually leaving what experts say are some 6,000 *tons* of spent lead on the land and in the lakes, a million or more animals die each year from lead poisoning. Presumably, some of the animals that man eats have the poisoning in them.   6

Considering all this, it is beyond my ken that public opinion polls show *only* about 70 percent of Americans favoring gun registration and only a little more than 50 percent favoring an outright and absolute ban. Still, it's a clear majority in favor of gun control.   7

But the gun minority has a dozen reasons, most of them pishposh, for keeping guns available to everyone, no matter the toll.   8

Usually operating under the umbrella of the National Rifle Association, and   9 perhaps now under their own political party, the gun owners say it is only too bad when a young child kills himself or his parents with a gun carelessly left loaded in the bureau drawer, or when an angry motorist pulls a trigger instead of pushing a horn, or when some scamp shoots a Kennedy, John Lennon or Martin Luther King. Too bad, that's the price of democracy.

10   *Democracy*, for god's sake! They continue to insist, against all evidence, that the Second Amendment to the Constitution gives them a "right to bear arms." Clearly, it doesn't.

11   Article II of the Bill of Rights must be read in context. It says, if you don't remember, "A well regulated militia being necessary to the security of a free state, the right of the people to keep and bear arms shall not be infringed."

12   Neither the Supreme Court nor any reliable legal expert has ever claimed that the language supports an unlimited right to have a gun. The amendment is typically viewed by the courts in terms of maintaining a militia.

13   Militia is in the Second Amendment of the Constitution because, at the time it was written, the colonists wanted and the bureaucrats didn't object to having citizen-soldiers. The colonists had been badly treated by the British Army, and they didn't want their defenders beholden to any king or any general or anyone, other than themselves. And the government did not object because providing a standing army was expensive.

14   That has all changed in modern America, but the dogmatic gun fanatics still somehow see themselves as the nation's protectors. They claim with their guns they will protect us from communism and socialism and nazism; no dictator would dare take over here, because we are all armed. They have forgotten about the ballot box and the free and unfettered press.

15   The gunners will save us, because they are he-men. Macho men. Psychologists insist that guns are phallic symbols, that men put pistols in their pockets to compensate for their own sexual inadequacies and insecurities. It is an American puberty rite for a gun lover to give his son a rifle on his thirteenth birthday.

16   Guns, these people insist, are also for protection—from folks who have guns. You never know when some punk will rob or assault you with a gun. But the National Commission on the Causes and Prevention of Violence produced volumes of statistics showing that the people most likely to get themselves killed during a crime are pistol packers, those who try to defend themselves with a gun.

17   And there is also the "sport" of guns. Gun fanatics enjoy not just blowing away docile creatures of nature, but other fun things like shooting at clay birds and targets. As Robert Sherrill says in his fine book, *Saturday Night Special*, targetshooters "will go out weekend after weekend to engage in a pastime that is about as gripping as a fast game of mumblety-peg."

18   There are no good reasons for having a gun. The very purpose of a gun is to kill. It's no coincidence that target shooters typically have a target shaped like a man. And while gun nuts rally behind the slogan that "guns don't kill people, people kill people," psychiatrists who study such things say that after hours and years of shooting targets, *the finger doesn't pull the trigger, the trigger pulls the finger.*

All the evidence notwithstanding, in this society that has grown up with the   19
TV and movie macho of glamorized (Gary Cooper, Paul Newman, et al.) gun-
slingers and private eyes, and children getting toy guns, it is little wonder that
some think there is something basically un-American about gun control.

But gun control may be our only salvation. With almost 200 million guns   20
already in our country, and a new gun being sold every thirteen *seconds*, the annual
murder rate will climb dramatically beyond the already unspeakable carnage of
more than 20,000 annual gun murders.

An absolute ban is necessary. But, considering the politics of Washington, that   21
won't happen for a while. Let us begin with tough *national* gun controls.

Every gun—handgun, rifle, and shotgun should be registered, the purchaser   22
should be required to stand a waiting period for a criminal records and psychiatric
background review, and every gun should be test-fired so the spent shell and slug
can be kept in police ballistics files along with the name, photograph and finger
prints of the gun's purchaser. When crimes are committed, they can be more easily
solved—particularly if the government has done its related part in eliminating
underground gun running. However, most guns used in crimes—be it Lee Harvey
Oswald's, Arthur Bremer's, David Berkowitz's or Mark David Chapman's are le-
gally purchased. If we had such a ballistics file, we might have stopped the .22-
Calibre Killer after his first attack.

How could responsible and law-abiding gun owners object to that? The answer   23
is that the responsible ones couldn't.

Tighter Controls on Pistols Won't Deter Attacks, Murder

MARSHALL J. BROWN   Like Roth, Marshall J. Brown is a newspaper reporter in Buffalo, New York.

1   It's ironic that in the midst of an unprecedented diatribe against pistol ownership we have seen six black men, in Buffalo, New York City and Rochester, die by the cold steel of knife blades.

2   And we've also learned that the four .22-caliber killer victims were slain not by a handgun but by a rifle. Rifle and shotgun barrels can be sawed off with a 59-cent hacksaw blade, making weapons more lethal than most handguns.

3   But hardly a day has gone by since the handgun murders of Dr. Michael Halberstam in Washington and John Lennon in New York City that we haven't seen newspaper editorials, cartoons and columns advocating "tighter" handgun control or an outright ban on handgun ownership by private citizens.

4   This antihandgun hysteria was interrupted briefly by reports of a madman fatally stabbing four blacks in New York City, and less than a week later black men in Buffalo and Rochester met the same fate.

5   They learned, as did Julius Caesar and countless other men in history, that a blade midline in the chest is a most deadly weapon.

6   Yet we saw no columns, editorials or cartoons advocating more strict knife control laws or a ban on possession of knives (other than dull butter knives—if you have a permit).

7   Certain writers frequently mock the National Rifle Association (NRA) statement that, "Guns don't kill people, people kill people."

8   In the light of the recent, vicious knife slayings, the NRA statement is very much to the point. Ask the grieving relatives of the victims.

9   Ask them if they favor tighter handgun control laws.

10   The very week last September in whch Gov. Hugh L. Carey announced that New York State had the toughest gun law in the nation (mandatory year in jail for unlicensed handgun possession) I covered as a crime writer:

11   —a murder in which a burglary victim was stabbed to death by an umbrella in the throat.

12   —a murder in which a man had his head bashed in by a brick.

13   A year earlier, I covered a murder in which a citizen met his end via a hunting arrow in the chest.

14   Some of the most brutal murders I have covered did not involve guns. The city's worst mass murder on record this century was committed with a knife and a hatchet wielded against five elderly people whose remains were then burned in an arson fire.

Just a few years ago, an ex-con on a college campus here raped a coed and then   15
slowly strangled her with a piece of rawhide. He stabbed a young male student to
death.

The Bible tells us that David slew Goliath with a rock from a slingshot.   16

John F. Kennedy, former president of the United States and an NRA member   17
who strongly believed in the citizens' right to bear arms, was slain with a rifle. (It
could have been a bomb, or grenade, or handgun, or knife).

When Lincoln was fatally shot by John Wilkes Booth, who used a Saturday   18
Night Special (a Derringer), there was no national cry for handgun control. When
Teddy Roosevelt was shot and wounded in the chest with a pistol, he finished a
speech he was making and when he recovered from his wound said what a great
organization the NRA was. He joined the NRA and was an ardent hunter and gun
fancier.

When McKinley was assassinated in Buffalo with a pistol there was no shrill   19
cry for handgun control.

Americans back then were a much simpler people, possessed of a common   20
sense that seems to be absent among the species today.

Today, Americans are supposed to be much better educated, but some of   21
them, at least insofar as the gun issue is concerned, are incredibly simplistic.

"Ban the handgun and you ban violence," appears to be their cry.   22

Of course, the sickness today is not the handgun. The handgun is a tool of   23
man, which, if used safely and properly defends good people (merchants, home-
owners, police officers) against deadly, criminal attack by thugs who ignore gun
laws, as well as laws against murder, rape and robbery.

Criminals have always been armed to the teeth. Gun laws (we have 20,000 of   24
them already) disarm people who obey the law, leaving them helpless in the face of
deadly attack.

So let us not fool ourselves with the simplistic notion that banning handguns   25
(to good people) or tightening up gun laws will make even a dent in our horrible
crime rate.

The states of New York and Massachusetts in their collective "unwisdom"   26
have passed laws mandating a year in jail for persons convicted of carrying unlicensed handguns—regardless of intent. There are no mandatory penalties in
either state for murder, arson, rape, robbery or assault.

But for carrying a gun without a license, even if your only intent was self-   27
defense, it's off to the slammer. That's not an anticrime law, it's an antigun law.

With such laws, we'll continue to see crime and violence escalate.   28

Because our sickness is not one of guns, it's one of tolerated violence. We as a   29
society have allowed a small number of people (criminals) to wreak havoc and
homicide against the rest of the population.

Some of the very people who call for a ban on handguns also fight against   30
capital punishment, and even rail against jail for criminals. These people are for
work release, early parole, alternatives to prison. And most of the violent felons who
are released under these programs pull their vicious stunts again, and the list of
victims grows.

31   And certain columnists call for more gun control laws.

32   In fact, handguns are much more unavailable now than they were before 1968 when they could even be had by mail order. In the early 1960s, in the 1950s and in the 1940s the crime and homicide rates in this nation were much lower than they have been since 1968 when a federal gun control act and a spate of state laws cracked down on handgun ownership.

33   If you examine figures supplied by the antigun groups themselves, you find a low rate of handgun misuse for a nation the size of the United States (226 million persons).

34   The antigunners say there are about 250,000 crimes annually that involve handguns (including menacing, robbery, assault and some 20,000 homicides), and they complain there are 50 million handguns abroad in the nation. If you figure it out, that means that of every 1,000 handguns in the hands of the populace, a grand total of five are misused in criminal acts (including threats).

35   With so many gun laws already on the books, do such statistics indicate the need for more of a crackdown on the 995 handgun owners out of 1,000 who are safe, responsible, law-abiding citizens?

36   Are we prepared as taxpayers to pay the millions of dollars to further license, register, search, seize and punish people who haven't done their paperwork with the government (and walk around with an unlicensed pistol)?

37   Any government, local, state or federal, has a lot of gall telling law-abiding citizens that they can't protect themselves with guns when the criminal justice system has just about stopped functioning . . . when violent criminals are returned again and again to maim and kill, when courts don't convict, when prisons are so quick to release the dangerous.

38   And make no mistake about it, the pistol licensing system is designed to deny citizens the right to carry guns. If you have any doubt, try to get a carry permit around here or in New York City.

39   It's foolish for people to talk about "civil rights" when your first right—your right to life—can be taken away in the street by a punk armed with a club, a knife or a gun. So your rights to free speech, to a secure home, to liberty and the pursuit of happiness are meaningless unless you have the right to defend your life, because dead people don't have rights.

40   And police admit that their chance of interrupting a crime of violence in progress is virtually nil.

41   Law-abiding citizens, therefore, should have the choice as to whether to exercise their God-given and law-given rights to self-defense, with a gun if necessary. The state, the government, should have little to say about it except, "Don't misuse that right, don't harm a fellow human being without justification, or you will be charged under existing criminal law for your transgression."

Vocabulary

Roth: despots, twaddle, dogmatic, unfettered, mumblety-peg; Brown: simplistic, transgression

Questions

1. Which is Roth's most convincing argument for gun control? Brown's? Roth's least convincing? Brown's?
2. Point out examples of appeal to emotions and personal attacks on opponents. Do you find them effective?
3. Should emotional arguments be ignored when laws are being considered? Why or why not?
4. Unless you live in western New York, you probably do not recognize some of the specific references—for example, to the .22 caliber killings, a series of brutal murders that occurred in Buffalo in 1980. Does this fact weaken the arguments?
5. Reporters are taught to illustrate and dramatize with specific examples their readers will recognize immediately. Have these reporters succeeded?

Topics for Writing

I Want Stronger Gun-Control Laws

I Do Not Want Stronger Gun-Control Laws

A Modest Proposal

JONATHAN SWIFT (1667–1745), churchman, poet, and satirist, is the author of *Gulliver's Travels.* "A Modest Proposal" was published in 1729, during his tenure as dean of St. Patrick's Cathedral in Dublin.

1   It is a melancholy object to those who walk through this great town, or travel in the country, when they see the streets, the roads, and cabin-doors crowded with beggars of the female sex, followed by three, four, or six children, all in rags, and importuning every passenger for an alms. These mothers, instead of being able to work for their honest livelihood, are forced to employ all their time in strolling to beg sustenance for their helpless infants: who, as they grow up, either turn thieves for want of work, or leave their dear native country to fight for the Pretender in Spain, or sell themselves to the Barbadoes.

2   I think it is agreed by all parties, that this prodigious number of children in the arms, or on the backs, or at the heels of their mothers, and frequently of their fathers, is, in the present deplorable state of the kingdom, a very great additional grievance; and, therefore, whoever could find out a fair, cheap, and easy method of making these children sound and useful members of the commonwealth, would deserve so well of the public, as to have his statue set up for a preserver of the nation.

3   But my intention is very far from being confined to provide only for the children of professed beggars; it is of a much greater extent, and shall take in the whole number of infants at a certain age, who are born of parents in effect as little able to support them as those who demand our charity in the streets.

4   As to my own part, having turned my thoughts for many years upon this important subject, and maturely weighed the several schemes of other projectors, I have always found them grossly mistaken in their computation. It is true, a child, just dropped from its dam, may be supported by her milk for a solar year with little other nourishment; at most, not above the value of two shillings, which the mother may certainly get, or the value in scraps, by her lawful occupation of begging; and it is exactly at one year old that I propose to provide for them in such a manner, as, instead of being a charge upon their parents or the parish, or wanting food and raiment for the rest of their lives, they shall, on the contrary, contribute to the feeding, and partly to the clothing, of many thousands.

5   There is likewise another great advantage in my scheme, that it will prevent those voluntary abortions, and that horrid practice of women murdering their bastard children, alas, too frequent among us, sacrificing the poor innocent babes, I doubt more to avoid the expense than the shame, which would move tears and pity in the most savage and inhuman breast.

6   The number of souls in this kingdom being usually reckoned one million and a half, of these I calculate there may be about two hundred thousand couple whose

wives are breeders; from which number I subtract thirty thousand couple, who are able to maintain their own children (although I apprehend there cannot be so many, under the present distresses of the kingdom); but this being granted, there will remain an hundred and seventy thousand breeders. I again subtract fifty thousand for those women who miscarry, or whose children die by accident or disease within the year. There only remain a hundred and twenty thousand children of poor parents annually born. The question therefore is how this number shall be reared and provided for? which, as I have already said, under the present situation of affairs, is utterly impossible by all the methods hitherto proposed. For we can neither employ them in handicraft or agriculture; we neither build houses (I mean in the country) nor cultivate land: they can very seldom pick up a livelihood by stealing until they arrive at six years old, except where they are of towardly parts; although I confess they learn the rudiments much earlier; during which time they can, however, be properly looked upon only as probationers; as I have been informed by a principal gentleman in the county of Cavan, who protested to me, that he never knew above one or two instances under the age of six, even in a part of the kingdom so renowned for the quickest proficiency in that art.

I am assured by our merchants that a boy or a girl before twelve years old is no   7
salable commodity; and even when they come to this age they will not yield above three pounds or three pounds and half-a-crown at most, on the exchange; which cannot turn to account either to the parents or kingdom, the charge of nutriment and rags having been at least four times that value.

I shall now, therefore, humbly propose my own thoughts, which I hope will   8
not be liable to the least objection.

I have been assured by a very knowing American of my acquaintance in   9
London, that a young healthy child, well nursed, is, at a year old, a most delicious, nourishing, and wholesome food, whether stewed, roasted, baked, or boiled; and I make no doubt that it will equally serve in a fricassee or a ragout.

I do therefore humbly offer it to public consideration, that of the hundred and   10
twenty thousand children already computed, twenty thousand may be reserved for breed, whereof only one-fourth part to be males; which is more than we allow to sheep, black cattle, or swine; and my reason is, that these children are seldom the fruits of marriage, a circumstance not much regarded by our savages, therefore one male will be sufficient to serve four females. That the remaining hundred thousand may, at a year old, be offered in sale to the persons of quality and fortune through the kingdom; always advising the mother to let them suck plentifully in the last month, so as to render them plump and fat for a good table. A child will make two dishes at an entertainment for friends; and when the family dines alone, the fore or hind quarter will make a reasonable dish, and, seasoned with a little pepper or salt, will be very good boiled on the fourth day, especially in winter.

I have reckoned, upon a medium, that a child just born will weigh twelve   11
pounds, and in a solar year, if tolerably nursed, increaseth to twenty-eight pounds.

I grant this food will be somewhat dear, and therefore very proper for land-   12
lords, who, as they have already devoured most of the parents, seem to have the best title to the children.

13   Infants' flesh will be in season throughout the year, but more plentifully in March, and a little before and after: for we are told by a grave author, an eminent French physician, that fish being a prolific diet, there are more children born in Roman Catholic countries about nine months after Lent than at any other season; therefore, reckoning a year after Lent, the markets will be more glutted than usual, because the number of popish infants is at least three to one in this kingdom; and therefore it will have one other collateral advantage, by lessening the number of papists among us.

14   I have already computed the charge of nursing a beggar's child (in which list I reckon all cottagers, labourers, and four-fifths of the farmers) to be about two shillings per annum, rags included; and I believe no gentleman would repine to give ten shillings for the carcass of a good fat child, which, as I have said, will make four dishes of excellent nutritive meat, when he has only some particular friend, or his own family, to dine with him. Thus the squire will learn to be a good landlord, and grow popular among his tenants; the mother will have eight shillings net profit, and be fit for work till she produces another child.

15   Those who are more thrifty (as I must confess the times require) may flay the carcass; the skin of which, artificially dressed, will make admirable gloves for ladies, and summer-boots for fine gentlemen.

16   As to our city of Dublin, shambles may be appointed for this purpose in the most convenient parts of it, and butchers we may be assured will not be wanting; although I rather recommend buying the children alive, and dressing them hot from the knife, as we do roasting pigs.

17   A very worthy person, a true lover of his country, and whose virtues I highly esteem, was lately pleased, in discoursing on this matter, to offer a refinement upon my scheme. He said, that many gentlemen of this kingdom, having of late destroyed their deer, he conceived that the want of venison might be well supplied by the bodies of young lads and maidens, not exceeding fourteen years of age, nor under twelve; so great a number of both sexes in every country being now ready to starve for want of work and service; and these to be disposed of by their parents, if alive, or otherwise by their nearest relations. But, with due deference to so excellent a friend, and so deserving a patriot, I cannot be altogether in his sentiments; for as to the males, my American acquaintance assured me from frequent experience, that their flesh was generally tough and lean, like that of our schoolboys, by continual exercise, and their taste disagreeable; and to fatten them would not answer the charge. Then as to the females, it would, I think, with humble submission, be a loss to the public, because they soon would become breeders themselves: and besides, it is not improbable that some scrupulous people might be apt to censure such a practice (although indeed very unjustly) as a little bordering upon cruelty; which, I confess hath always been with me the strongest objection against any project, how well soever intended.

18   But in order to justify my friend, he confessed that this expedient was put into his head by the famous Psalmanazar, a native of the island Formosa, who came from thence to London above twenty years ago; and in conversation told my friend,

that in his country, when any young person happened to be put to death, the executioner sold the carcass to persons of quality as a prime dainty; and that in his time the body of a plump girl of fifteen, who was crucified for an attempt to poison the emperor, was sold to his Imperial Majesty's prime minister of state, and other great mandarins of the court, in joints from the gibbet, at four hundred crowns. Neither indeed can I deny, that if the same use were made of several plump young girls in this town, who, without one single groat to their fortunes, cannot stir abroad without a chair, and appear at playhouse and assemblies in foreign fineries which they never will pay for, the kingdom would not be the worse.

Some persons of a desponding spirit are in great concern about that vast number of poor people who are aged, diseased, or maimed; and I have been desired to employ my thoughts what course may be taken to ease the nation of so grievous an encumbrance. But I am not in the least pain upon that matter, because it is very well known, that they are every day dying, and rotting, by cold and famine, and filth and vermin, as fast as can be reasonably expected. And as to the younger labourers, they are now in almost as hopeful a condition: they cannot get work, and consequently pine away for want of nourishment, to a degree, that if at any time they are accidentally hired to common labour, they have not strength to perform it; and thus the country and themselves are happily delivered from the evils to come. 19

I have too long digressed, and therefore shall return to my subject. I think the advantages by the proposal which I have made are obvious and many, as well as of the highest importance. 20

For first, as I have already observed, it would greatly lessen the number of papists, with whom we are yearly overrun, being the principal breeders of the nation as well as our most dangerous enemies; and who stay at home on purpose with a design to deliver the kingdom to the Pretender, hoping to take their advantage by the absence of so many good Protestants, who have chosen rather to leave their country than stay at home and pay tithes against their conscience to an idolatrous Episcopal curate. 21

Secondly, the poorer tenants will have something valuable of their own, which by law may be made liable to distress, and help to pay their landlord's rent; their corn and cattle being already seized, and money a thing unknown. 22

Thirdly, whereas the maintenance of an hundred thousand children, from two years old and upwards, cannot be computed at less than ten shillings a piece per annum, the nation's stock will be thereby increased fifty thousand pounds per annum; besides the profit of a new dish introduced to the tables of all gentlemen of fortune in the kingdom who have any refinement in taste. And the money will circulate among ourselves, the goods being entirely of our own growth and manufacture. 23

Fourthly, the constant breeders, besides the gain of eight shillings sterling per annum by the sale of their children, will be rid of the charge of maintaining them after the first year. 24

Fifthly, this food would likewise bring great custom to taverns; where the vintners will certainly be so prudent as to procure the best receipts for dressing it to 25 perfection, and, consequently, have their houses frequented by all the fine gentlemen, who justly value themselves upon their knowledge in good eating: and a skilful cook, who understands how to oblige his guests, will contrive to make it as expensive as they please.

26   Sixthly, this would be a great inducement to marriage, which all wise nations have either encouraged by rewards, or enforced by laws and penalties. It would increase the care and tenderness of mothers towards their children, when they were sure of a settlement for life to the poor babes, provided in some sort by the public, to their annual profit instead of expense. We should soon see an honest emulation among the married women, which of them could bring the fattest child to the market. Men would become as fond of their wives during the time of their pregnancy, as they are now of their mares in foal, their cows in calf, or sows when they are ready to farrow; nor offer to beat or kick them (as is too frequent a practice) for fear of a miscarriage.

27   Many other advantages might be enumerated. For instance the addition of some thousand carcasses in our exportation of barrelled beef; the propagation of swine's flesh, and improvement in the art of making good bacon, so much wanted among us by the great destruction of pigs, too frequent at our tables, which are no way comparable in taste or magnificence to a well-grown, fat yearling child, which, roasted whole, will make a considerable figure at a Lord Mayor's feast, or any other public entertainment. But this, and many others, I omit, being studious of brevity.

28   Supposing that one thousand families in this city would be constant customers for infants' flesh, besides others who might have it at merry meetings, particularly weddings and christenings, I compute that Dublin would take off annually about twenty thousand carcasses; and the rest of the kingdom (where probably they will be sold somewhat cheaper) the remaining eighty thousand.

29   I can think of no one objection that will possibly be raised against this proposal, unless it should be urged, that the number of people will be thereby much lessened in the kingdom. This I freely own, and it was indeed one principal design in offering it to the world. I desire the reader will observe that I calculate my remedy for this one individual kingdom of Ireland, and for no other that ever was, is, or I think ever can be, upon earth. Therefore let no man talk to me of other expedients: of taxing our absentees at five shillings a pound: of using neither clothes nor household-furniture except what is of our own growth and manufacture: of utterly rejecting the materials and instruments that promote foreign luxury: of curing the expensiveness of pride, vanity, idleness, and gaming in our women; of introducing a vein of parsimony, prudence, and temperance: of learning to love our country, wherein we differ even from Laplanders, and the inhabitants of Topinamboo: of quitting our animosities and factions, nor act any longer like the Jews, who were murdering one another at the very moment their city was taken: of being a little cautious not to sell our country and consciences for nothing: of teaching landlords to have at least one degree of mercy towards their tenants: lastly, of putting a spirit of honesty, industry, and skill into our shopkeepers; who, if a resolution could now be taken to buy only our native goods, would immediately unite to cheat and exact

upon us in the price, the measure, and the goodness, nor could ever yet be brought to make one fair proposal of just dealing, though often and earnestly invited to it.

Therefore I repeat, let no man talk to me of these and the like expedients, till   30
he hath at least some glimpse of hope that there will ever be some hearty and sincere attempt to put them in practice.

But, as to myself, having been wearied out for many years with offering vain,   31
idle, visionary thoughts, and at length utterly despairing of success, I fortunately fell upon this proposal; which, as it is wholly new, so it hath something solid and real, of no expense and little trouble, full in our own power, and whereby we can incur no danger in disobliging England. For this kind of commodity will not bear exportation, the flesh being of too tender a consistence to admit a long continuance in salt, although perhaps I could name a country which would be glad to eat up our whole nation without it.

After all, I am not so violently bent upon my own opinion as to reject any offer   32
proposed by wise men which shall be found equally innocent, cheap, easy, and effectual. But before something of that kind shall be advanced in contradiction to my scheme, and offering a better, I desire the author, or authors, will be pleased maturely to consider two points. First, as things now stand, how they will be able to find food and raiment for a hundred thousand useless mouths and backs? And, secondly, there being a round million of creatures in human figure throughout this kingdom, whose whole subsistence put into a common stock would leave them in debt two millions of pounds sterling, adding those who are beggars by profession, to the bulk of farmers, cottagers, and labourers, with the wives and children who are beggars in effect; I desire those politicians who dislike my overture, and may perhaps be so bold as to attempt an answer, that they will first ask the parents of these mortals, whether they would not at this day think it a great happiness to have been sold for food at a year old, in the manner I prescribe, and thereby have avoided such a perpetual scene of misfortunes as they have since gone through, by the oppression of landlords, the impossibility of paying rent without money or trade, the want of common sustenance, with neither house nor clothes to cover them from the inclemencies of weather, and the most inevitable prospect of entailing the like, or greater miseries, upon their breed for ever.

I profess, in the sincerity of my heart, that I have not the least personal interest   33
in endeavouring to promote this necessary work, having no other motive than the public good of my country, by advancing our trade, providing for infants, relieving the poor, and giving some pleasure to the rich. I have no children by which I can propose to get a single penny; the youngest being nine years old, and my wife past child-bearing.

Vocabulary

sustenance, prodigious, raiment, fricassee, ragout, repine, shambles, gibbet, groat, tithes, curate, vintners

Questions

1. This satire depends for its effect upon shocking the reader. Notice how calmly, harmlessly, Swift leads up to his "modest" proposal. What is the effect of Swift's setting off the proposal in such a brief paragraph? Wouldn't it have been as effective as the opening sentence of his essay?
2. Are there signs that Swift is preparing you psychologically for his treatment of children as food?
3. Point out instances that show Swift's sympathy with the poor in Ireland. Does he exonerate the poor entirely?
4. Why do you suppose Swift says an American told him that infants were delicious?

Topics for Writing

A Modest Proposal for Curing Street Crime

Curing Poverty in America

A Modest Proposal Regarding the Postal Service

16

Interpretation / What Did They Mean?

"Have you felt so proud to get at the meaning of poems?" Walt Whitman asked in *Leaves of Grass*. He recognized a truth about ourselves: we are pleased when we understand the creation of an artist, whether poet or sculptor, painter or motion-picture director. In the case of a painting, a portrait, perhaps, we stand back to get an overall impression. Beautiful. Something haunting about it . . . or questioning . . . or what? We step closer, examine the details, perhaps the brushwork or the thickness of paint, the shadow across the cheek, the background, the flecks of contrasting pigment around the pupils. We analyze. Perhaps those eyes . . . . We step back for another broad view, but now with the knowledge of certain details that we have studied. We synthesize, reconstruct, and—"Ah, yes! I see now what Da Vinci intended," we say; and we proceed to our interpretation.

This is a much simplified version of what the interpreters in this chapter are trying to do. But they are interested in one essential thing more: they want to share their interpretations with us because (1) they believe they have correctly understood what the artist has done and (2) they believe their understanding will enrich our appreciation of the work of art. Analysis, synthesis, description, and persuasion are all involved.

This chapter presents three examples of disagreement in artistic interpretation: one example consists of some reviews of a popular movie; the other two, a sampling of contradictory interpretations of famous poems. Each interpreter cites chapter and verse to support the argument. The evidence is there before you in the texts of "My Last Duchess" and "Upon Julia's Clothes," and you probably have seen *Superman*. You are in a good position, therefore, not only to weigh the critics' arguments but also to make some judgments of your own of what you have seen or read.

" 'Tis with our judgments as our watches, none / Go just alike, yet each believes his own" (Alexander Pope, *An Essay on Criticism*). Is this true of interpretation, too? Can Herrick's poem, a case in point, bear both readings suggested in the following pages? Do his words admit of both interpretations, or do you find yourself rejecting one, the other, or both? Do you (of a later generation than the reviewers of *Superman*) attribute its success to the sources the critics claim? As the reader here, you have final say.

Upon Julia's Clothes

ROBERT HERRICK   (1591–1674) was a Cavalier poet, a writer of light, witty, complimentary verse. He strove to say "much in little," and this lyric about Julia's clothes says just enough to force the reader to use imagination to fill in the picture. As imaginations often differ, it is not surprising that Earl Daniels and Elisabeth Schneider read the gap between the two stanzas very differently.

Whenas in silks my Julia goes,
Then, then, methinks, how sweetly flows
That liquefaction of her clothes!

Next, when I cast mine eyes, and see
That brave vibration each way free,
O, how that glittering taketh me!

Upon Julia's Clothes

EARL DANIELS   For many years before his death in 1970, Earl Daniels was an English professor at Colgate University.

Superficially the poem is obvious to the point of seeming to deprecate analysis, not to be worth it. A pretty girl moves through six lines, for a moment only catches an observer's eye, passes, and is gone. So slight is the impact of the experience that he writes not about the girl but about her clothes. Costume is defined by silks, and each stanza is centered in a single quality of silk in movement, and in light ("liquefaction," line 3, and "glittering," line 6). The positions of these words in the last lines of each stanza should be noted and, more particularly, the increased sharpness lent to "glittering" by the necessity, here, of pronunciation in two syllables only: the vowel sound of an acute and pointed short "i" is closed tightly in by consonants, "g" and "t" in one syllable, "tr" and "ng" in the other. The stab of that word, a superb mine-eyes-dazzle effect, suggests the poem is not so simple as it seems: that Julia-in-clothes is more important than clothes, the apparent subject; that the observer is more deeply moved than he wants a careless reader to suppose, possibly than he himself knows.

Attention to sound and movement reveals the implications of the single word "glittering" to be a clue worth following. The poem is Julia and Julia's clothes. But each stanza contains lines (I, 2; II, 1, 3) which turn to the observer, and seem to hint in sound and movement at a central ironic contrast between the states of mind of the observer and the girl. The Julia lines flow, as easy and as liquid as the smooth silks which dress and conceal a lovely body. But the observer lines throb unevenly; they start and stop; they image the excitement and disturbance of the poet. It may not be too far-fetched to wonder if they are not a symbol for the quickened beating of a heart, the surprised catch of breath, in the presence of beauty, especially beauty of a woman. An attentive reader now begins to understand it is not Julia's clothes but Julia herself who is the subject of the poem; and the poem begins to grow and to take on new richness of meaning. To be especially noted is the contrast in stanza I between lines 1 and 2: in line 1, word ripples into word, sound into sound, the caesural pause is so slight as to be almost not noticeable; in line 2, the opening repetition of "then, then," where each word must be distinctly separated by pauses, where vowels are imbedded between inescapable consonants, announces a change, farther stressed by the parenthetical "methinks." (Even the parenthesis plays its part here.) Only as this line, toward the end, moves to Julia and her costume does it begin to glide, to be liquefied again. The point is Julia moves through the poem serene, untouched; she may not even know the poet has so much as seen her. But he is in a different situation, for though he is ostensibly doing nothing more than writing a pretty lyric about a pretty dress, yet he reveals, in the sound, the movement, the pace of his words, how deeply he has been stirred by what seems so unimportant.

3   This makes for a basic ironic contrast, central to the poem: the ironic contrast between the girl and the man. Is it the irony of man (male) set over against woman (female)—a contrast as old as the Garden of Eden itself—or is it the profounder suggestion of the situation of man (not *a man*) in the presence of beauty—beauty here, as so often, being symbolized by a woman? I am reasonably certain that by implication and suggestion, by the subtlest of overtones, both ideas are in their way present, contributing rich values for a poem too often looked upon as too slight for serious consideration. Herrick has too long suffered from that kind of treatment.

Vocabulary

deprecate, liquefaction, implications, ironic, caesural, ostensibly

Questions

1. Daniels describes the essential subject of the poem in his second and third sentences. Do you agree with his account of what the poem is about?
2. Do you accept the distinction Daniels makes between "Julia lines" and "observer lines"? He claims that the former move smoothly, but the latter "throb unevenly," mirroring "the excitement and disturbance of the poet." Do you agree? (Test this by reading the lines aloud.)
3. Do you agree with his conclusion? Is there an ironic contrast between men and women? Is it suggested in this poem?

Upon Julia's Clothes

ELISABETH SCHNEIDER (1897–), a distinguished critic, is professor emeritus at Temple University.

Recently I read with astonishment the interpretation by Earl Daniels of Herrick's "Upon Julia's Clothes" . . . . Both E. M. W. Tillyard and C. S. Lewis (in *Essays and Studies*, XX and XXI) and, I find, a great many other people take the poem in the same way as far as literal meaning goes. This must have surprised at least some readers; it can scarcely be what Herrick meant.

His subject, surely, is nothing more, or less, than in stanza 1, Julia dressed, in stanza 2, Julia undressed. The word *next* must introduce a distinct change if the whole line "Next, when I cast mine eyes, and see" is not to become a waste of words intolerable in so short a poem and if all the last three lines are not to fall into flat anticlimax. The change is from Julia's motion as she walks ("goes," in seventeenth-century English) in the liquid flowing movement of silk, to the rhythmical motion back and forth, "each way free," of her unencumbered naked limbs, the contrast being marked by the symmetrical "when" formula and the triplet rhymes.

Two words that may have thrown readers off the track, *vibration* and *glitter*, today may not seem entirely appropriate. *Vibration* in the seventeenth century, however, did not necessarily imply swift oscillation; it was commonly associated in that and the following century with the movement of a pendulum, even a long one that swings slowly; and Jeremy Bentham called his indoor walking for exercise "vibrating" (see *NED*) [the New English Dictionary, Oxford]. The word *glitter* now seems rather too metallic to describe flesh, but the *NED* quotes from the sixteenth and seventeenth centuries "power of the godhead to *glittre* and shewe foorth in him" and "Nature *glitters* most in her own plain homely garb," examples in which the shining is evidently not thought of as hard or artificial. In Herrick's closing line the glitter of flesh replaces that of silk, no doubt with the half-physical, half-emotional meaning often conveyed by *shine* or *shine forth*. Julia is no passing stranger; she is "my" Julia. Among other poems about her is one "Upon Julia Unlacing Herself"; and in "To Julia, in Her Dawn or Daybreak" the poet hopes to see her tomorrow morning as naked as Eve or clothed only in lawn transparent as brook water.

Any other interpretation of the poem seems flat as well as unnatural; if Julia is made to keep her silks on, obviously something like the ingenuity of Professor Daniels is required to bestow point upon the conclusion. But this means of finding some richness or irony that could justify the poet's continuing beyond his first tercet without saying anything distinctly new only blurs the real effect of the poem, which is, it seems to me, neat, pointed, graceful, extremely symmetrical, and not particularly subtle. The essence of the poem is this neatness and symmetry, with the word *liquefaction* as its high light. If we revive the old connotations of *vibration*, which is the not quite so attractive high light of the second tercet, the symmetry is increased, for both words carry overtones of the scientific thought of the period. By bringing *liquefaction* and *vibration* to bear upon the wholly unscientific, mildly erotic theme, Herrick gave to the poem an edge and detachment, the unromantic grit in the oboe, the ironic flavor for which we so often look today.

5   I may add the unpublished suggestion of Professor Irwin Griggs' that Herrick's title seems to weigh in favor of this interpretation, "because it makes the subject Julia's *clothes*, not just *silk* or how pretty she is in silk."

Vocabulary

anticlimax, unencumbered, oscillation, ingenuity, tercet, symmetry, connotations

Questions

1. Schneider's opening is classical in its form: she expresses her disagreement with a commonly expressed interpretation, using it as a foil for her own explication. Her version of what the poem is about is expressed plainly in the first sentence of her second paragraph. She has made a flat assertion, but now she will attempt to persuade us of its accuracy. Can you find any signs, even at this early point, that she is working to bring the reader over to her side?
2. What evidence can she adduce to show that Julia is without clothes in the second stanza?
3. Suppose the first stanza is describing a front view (Julia approaching) and the second, a rear one (Julia moving away from the observer). Would this explain "Next"?

Topics for Writing

I Agree with Daniels

I Agree with Schneider

A Third Reading: Mine

My Last Duchess

ROBERT BROWNING (1812–1889) was an English poet who delighted in the portrayal of odd, sometimes enigmatic, characters. He seldom tells us what to think about his characters, but allows us to form our own opinions. Browning's "My Last Duchess" is a dramatic monologue, a poem in the form of a speech delivered by one character (not the author) to another character whose presence we sense but whose responses, if any, are not given. We learn about the speaker only by paying close attention to what he says and the way he says it. As the essays by B. R. Jerman and Laurence Perrine show, the technique can lead to differences in interpretation.

When we read any poem, it is essential that we understand each word—thus the need for frequent reference to the dictionary. When we read a dramatic monologue, like "My Last Duchess," we must determine (1) who is speaking, (2) to whom he is speaking, (3) why he is speaking, (4) what he is speaking about, and (5) whether he is a truthful speaker. In this poem, the Duke of Ferrara is speaking to an envoy of a Count. They have been negotiating a possible marriage between the Duke and the Count's daughter, but as the poem opens the Duke seats his visitor before a portrait and begins to talk about "my last Duchess." The answers to (3) and (5), as Jerman and Perrine show, are debatable.

Here we have more complex arguments than those involving "Upon Julia's Clothes"—partly because this poem is longer, but also because these interpreters of Browning's poem are writing for a somewhat more specialized audience. The ordinary reader of critical essays on Victorian poetry is likely to have sufficient interest and background to follow and appreciate evidence drawn from sources other than the words of the poem themselves, for example, Browning's ambiguous comments on his own poetry, his treatment of a character in another poem, or Whistler's remarks on the subject of a painting's value.

That's my last Duchess painted on the wall,
Looking as if she were alive. I call
That piece a wonder, now: Frà Pandolf's hands
Worked busily a day, and there she stands.
Will't please you sit and look at her? I said   5
"Frà Pandolf" by design, for never read
Strangers like you that pictured countenance,
The depth and passion of its earnest glance,
But to myself they turned (since none puts by
The curtain I have drawn for you, but I)   10
And seemed as they would ask me, if they durst,
How such a glance came there; so, not the first

Are you to turn and ask thus. Sir, 'twas not
Her husband's presence only, called that spot

15 Of joy into the Duchess' cheek: perhaps
Frà Pandolf chanced to say, "Her mantle laps
Over my lady's wrist too much," or "Paint
Must never hope to reproduce the faint
Half-flush that dies along her throat:" such stuff

20 Was courtesy, she thought, and cause enough
For calling up that spot of joy. She had
A heart—how shall I say?—too soon made glad,
Too easily impressed; she liked whate'er
She looked on, and her looks went everywhere.

25 Sir, 'twas all one! My favor at her breast,
The dropping of the daylight in the West,
The bough of cherries some officious fool
Broke in the orchard for her, the white mule
She rode with round the terrace—all and each

30 Would draw from her alike the approving speech,
Or blush, at least. She thanked men,—good! but thanked
Somehow—I know not how—as if she ranked
My gift of a nine-hundred-years-old name
With anybody's gift. Who'd stoop to blame

35 This sort of trifling? Even had you skill
In speech—(which I have not)—to make your will
Quite clear to such an one, and say, "Just this
Or that in you disgusts me; here you miss,
Or there exceed the mark"—and if she let

40 Herself be lessoned so, nor plainly set
Her wits to yours, forsooth, and made excuse,
—E'en then would be some stooping; and I choose
Never to stoop. Oh sir, she smiled, no doubt,
Whene'er I passed her; but who passed without

45 Much the same smile? This grew; I gave commands;
Then all smiles stopped together. There she stands
As if alive. Will't please you rise? We'll meet
The company below, then. I repeat,
The Count your master's known munificence

50 Is ample warrant that no just pretense
Of mine for dowry will be disallowed;
Though his fair daughter's self, as I avowed
At starting, is my object. Nay, we'll go
Together down, sir. Notice Neptune, though,

55 Taming a sea-horse, thought a rarity,
Which Claus of Innsbruck cast in bronze for me!

Browning's Witless Duke

B. R. JERMAN (1921–1978) The late B. R. Jerman was a Victorian scholar who taught English at Kent State University.

A number of critics who have written on Browning believe that the Duke's little chat with the emissary of the Count in "My Last Duchess"[1] constitutes a clever man's instructions as to the sort of behavior he expects of his next wife. Mrs. Sutherland Orr, for example, says that the Duke's "comments on the countenance of his last Duchess plainly state what he will expect of her successor."[2] Others, like Edward Berdoe, S. S. Curry, Ethel C. Mayne, William Lyon Phelps, and Ina B. Sessions,[3] not to mention numerous editors and anthologists,[4] find a similar purpose in the Duke's monologue. Although Berdoe's reading of the poem (p. 282) is perhaps not typical, it summarizes what the other critics have in mind: "When the Duke said 'Frà Pandolf' by design, he desired to impress on the envoy, and his master the Count, the sort of behavior he expected from the woman he was about to marry. He intimated that he would tolerate no rivals for his next wife's smiles. When he begs his guest to 'Notice Neptune—taming a sea horse,' he further intimated how he had tamed and killed his last duchess. All this was to convey to the envoy, and through him to the lady, that he demanded in his new wife the concentration of her whole being on himself, and the utmost devotion to his will." Browning himself is often quoted in support of at least the first part of this argument. Asked what the Duke meant by the words "by design," the poet answered briefly but equivocally, "To have some occasion for telling the story, and illustrating part of it."[5]

---

[1]See William C. DeVane, *A Browning Handbook* (2nd ed.; New York, 1955), pp. 102–103, 107–109, for details of publication. First entitled "Italy," the poem is said to catch the temper of the Italian Renaissance. Edward Dowden, *The Life of Robert Browning* (London, 1915), p. 79, observes that "the Duke is Italian of Renaissance days; insensible in his egoistic pride to the beautiful humanity before him." Pearl Hogrefe, *Browning and Italian Art and Artists* (Lawrence, Kans., 1914), p. 19, says that the poem sums up "the entire decadent Renaissance attitude toward art so fully that no historical names could improve it."

[2]*A Handbook to the Works of Robert Browning* (London, 1939), p. 251.

[3]*The Browning Cyclopaedia* (London, 1892), p. 282; *Browning and the Dramatic Monologue* (Boston, 1908), p. 98; *Browning's Heroines* (London, 1913), pp. 173–74; *Robert Browning* (Indianapolis, 1932), p. 175; "The Dramatic Monologue," *PMLA*, LXII (1947), 510. It should be clear that I have not made a collection here of the variant interpretations of "My Last Duchess." I cite only a handful to illustrate what seems to be the prevailing interpretation of the poem, however.

[4]A representative few are Charlotte Porter and Helen A. Clarke, ed., *The Complete Works of Robert Browning* (New York, 1901), IV, 384; William H. Rogers, ed., *The Best of Browning* (New York, 1942), pp. 518–19; James Stephens, Edwin L. Beck, and Royall H. Snow, ed., *Victorian and Later English Poets* (New York, 1937), p. 1198; R. R. Kirk and R. P. McCutcheon, ed., *An Introduction to the Study of Poetry* (New York, 1934), p. 20; Cleanth Brooks, John P. Purser, and Robert Penn Warren, ed., *An Approach to Literature* (New York, 1952), p. 293.

[5]See A. Allen Brockington, "Robert Browning's Answers to Questions Concerning Some of his Poems,"

2   There is good reason to doubt, however, that the Duke is intentionally warning his intended bride, as these critics believe. In the first place, we know that Browning was uncomfortable with factual-minded people who persisted in asking him what he had meant by this or that line or poem.[6] We also know that he, like most good poets, felt that it was necessary to make ambiguous statements about his poetry.[7] Again like most good poets, Browning wanted his readers to do their own interpreting, once even going so far as to tell an acquaintance that poetry was not "a substitute for a cigar, or a game of dominoes, to an idle man."[8] In the second place, if we must use Browning's statement about his poem (which he made, incidentally, nearly fifty years after the poem was first published), we need not necessarily conclude from it that the Duke is moralizing—as I hope to show. In the third place, although we, the audience (and certainly the emissary), might very well be aware of what His Grace expects of his wives, I see little in the poem to support the notion that the Duke is consciously warning, demanding, taking precautions to inform, insinuating, hinting, implying, or intimating—or whatever other terms these critics employ—that he expects or wants the envoy to tell the Count's daughter how she must behave once she is his wife. Finally, if he is not issuing a warning to his intended bride, it follows that the Duke, in pointing out the statue of Neptune taming the sea horse, is not suggesting "That's the way I break them in!" (Phelps, p. 175) or "just so do I tame my wives" (Rogers, p. 519). A closer analysis of "My Last Duchess" should show that the Duke does not have this purpose in mind.

3   The Duke of Ferrara is an art collector, not a moralist.[9] He is, further, a

---

Cornhill Magazine, XXXVI (1914), 316–18. On 22 Feb. 1889 Browning answered in writing the queries put to him by a member of The Day's End Club of Exeter, a literary group studying contemporary writers. The queries dealt with not only "My Last Duchess," but also "In a Gondola," "Earth's Immortalities," and "Parting at Morning." Brockington reprints this information in his *Browning and the Twentieth Century* (Oxford, 1932), pp. 117–18.

[6]On his reticence, see Richard D. Altick, "The Private Life of Robert Browning," *Yale Review*, XLI (1951), 247–62.

[7]Such statements abound in Browning scholarship, perhaps reinforcing the often repeated idea that what a poet has to say about his work is frequently not the most revealing word on the subject. One of Browning's comments on "My Last Duchess" should illustrate the poet's point, however. An American professor once asked him if the Duke's commands were that the Duchess be killed. Browning "made no reply, for a moment, and then said, meditatively, 'Yes, I meant that the commands were that she should be put to death.' And then, after a pause, he added, with a characteristic dash of expression, and as if the thought had just started in his mind, 'Or he might have had her shut up in a convent.'" This interviewer wisely points out that when Browning wrote the poem he most likely had not thought out exactly what the commands were. His art purpose was satisfied, nevertheless, in having the smiles stopped, whatever the method. See Hiram Corson, *An Introduction to the Study of Robert Browning's Poetry* (Boston, 1886), pp. vii–viii.

[8]Letter to W. G. Kingsland, dated 27 Nov. 1868 in *Letters of Robert Browning*, ed. Thurman L. Hood (New Haven, 1933), pp. 128–29.

[9]Louis S. Friedland, "Ferrara and 'My Last Duchess,'" SP, XXXIII (1936), 656–84, convincingly establishes the Duke as Alfonso II, fifth Duke of Ferrara (1553–98); the Duchess as the daughter of Cosimo I de Medici, the Duke of Florence; the Count as the Count of Tyrol; the envoy as possibly one Nikolaus Madruz of Innsbruck, etc. It is useless to suppose that Browning had all of these people in mind as the actual personages in the poem. Nevertheless, since he located the poem in Ferrara, there is every reason to believe that he meant the speaker to be the Duke of Ferrara and not some other Italian grandee, as John D. Rea suggests in " 'My Last Duchess,' " SP, XXIX (1932), 120–22. If the envoy is not patterned after Madruz, Browning surely intended him to be an intelligent and respected commoner, say, a scholarly diplomatist, and not an ordinary servant, as some readers might believe him to be.

splendid dilettante who prides himself on his possessions.[10] As the poem opens, he
is in his sublime role of collector, pointing out his various acquisitions to his visitor.
I hardly think that he went to all the trouble to lead the emissary upstairs so he
could, by telling the tale of the Duchess' demise, warn the Count's daughter, even
by indirection. More probably the Duke has been taking the emissary on the rounds
of his art gallery, a common courtesy in great houses, after chatting briefly about his
bride-to-be ("as I avowed/At starting"). When they come to one particular picture,
the Duke flings back the curtain which covers it, and, after determining his guest's
reaction to the portrait, goes into his act. He is pleased, even inspired, to talk about
this work of art.

> That's my last Duchess painted on the wall,
> Looking as if she were alive. I call
> That piece a wonder, now: Frà Pandolf's hands
> Worked busily a day, and there she stands.

His first mention of the artist is, as it were, bait. The envoy may have exclaimed,
"What a beautiful portrait! Who on earth did it?" "Picasso, of course!" the Duke
replies. The bait is out, and the Duke knows, from having stalked other prey,
what questions such a man as the envoy would ask. He is suave and confident in
this matter:

>   I said
> "Frà Pandolf" by design, for never read
> Strangers like you that pictured countenance,
> The depth and passion of its earnest glance,
> But to myself they turned (since none puts by
> The curtain I have drawn for you, but I)
> And seemed as they would ask me, if they durst,
> How such a glance came there; . . .

Although the Duke might ask him to "sit and look at her," we can be certain that
the envoy's eyes are soon turned to the speaker, for the Duke quickly draws attention to himself. The focus is, as Browning intended it to be, on the Duke, who is
less concerned with this man's knowing how the artist managed to paint the
Duchess than he is in pointing up his own stature as an art collector. The name of
the famous artist, then, is designed to give the Duke a gambit, or as Browning
called it, an "occasion for telling the story" of what he had to go through to get
this so-called "wonder."

    The Duchess was no doubt a very attractive but not necessarily beautiful
woman, whose great asset, and paradoxically, liability, was her warm personality.
Although the Duke disparages her personality (and well he might),[11] he praises her

4

---

[10]Elizabeth Nitchie, "Browning's 'Duchess,'" *Essays in Criticism*, III (1953), 475–76, once again calls
attention to "my" in the title and the first line of the poem as being significantly in keeping with the
Duke's pride of possession. We may add that a reading of the poem aloud with increased emphasis on
the personal pronouns should reveal this important aspect of the Duke's character.

[11]One can hardly resist the temptation to agree that "It was the deadly monotony [of her smile] that got
on the man's nerves." See Margaret H. Bates, *Browning Critiques* (Chicago, 1921), p. 84, for this
spirited note. Browning told The Day's End Club that the Duke used her shallowness "As an excuse—

portrait as being a "wonder," and his explanation of how this artist managed to paint her "earnest glance" is all in a day's work to him as an elegant connoisseur. He describes the portrait's virtues, which were his Duchess' faults, in such phrases as the "depth and passion of its earnest glance," "such a glance," "spot of joy," "blush," and "smile," suggesting, to be sure, that the portrait is a revelation of the woman's "soul," possibly a masterpiece. However, in deflating the real-life Duchess, surely to inflate himself before this nameless messenger, the Duke reveals that all the artist had to do was to paint what was on the surface, for she was shallow, undiscriminating, common. She smiled at everyone and everything ("Sir, 't was all one!"). Even the artist could call up that "spot of joy" by using comonplace flattery, he says. Moreover, Frà Pandolf painted the portrait in "a day," surely a supreme achievement even for a master doing a perfunctory job, let alone painting a "wonder." What appears at first glance to be a masterpiece, then, is (on the basis of the Duke's own description of its history, it must be remembered) a mechanically reproduced, realistic picture of a photogenic woman, a dilettante's trophy. Frà Pandolf would be quick to agree that his patron's knowledge of art is more apparent than real.

5   The Duke, of course, plays down the annoyance the real-life Duchess caused him, saying:

> Sir, 't was not
> Her husband's presence only, called that spot
> Of joy into the Duchess' cheek:

and, later:

> Oh sir, she smiled, no doubt,
> Whene'er I passed her; but who passed without
> Much the same smile?

In other words, the Duke explains "how such a glance came there" not, I think, because he feels compelled to make an accounting of his motives for getting rid of his last Duchess, thereby drawing a moral, but to state the "price" he had to pay for the portrait. A man as proud as His Grace would not condescend to explain why he had her put away.

6   The most obvious point againt the notion that the Duke is warning his bride-to-be is in this very matter of pride, which can best be seen in his attitude towards instructing her. "I choose/Never to stoop," he declares coldly. Petty wrangling, even polite suggestion that she might not spread her personality so thin, would have been beneath his dignity, he insists—and we believe him. After all, she was a duchess—His Duchess—and she should have known better than to have degraded him and his "nine-hundred-years-old name" by being "too easily impressed." It seems unlikely, therefore, that he would consciously unbend to tell "strangers" like the emissary, directly or even subtly, what he expects of this new woman.

---

mainly to himself—for taking revenge on one who had unwittingly wounded his absurdly pretentious vanity, by failing to recognize his superiority in even the most trifling matters."

As I see it the Duke's "design" is to exhibit his possessions, to pose as a patron   7
of the arts, and to explain how he suffered to get the Duchess on canvas—all for the
single purpose of directing attention to himself. In person she was a nuisance
because he could not possess her. Framed, the object of inquiries which appeal to
his vanity and, therefore, the subject of what he believes is a great portrait, she was
kept in his art gallery along with other presumed "rarities" like the statue of Neptune
taming a sea horse, which another apparently well-known artist cast in bronze for
"me!" Now, he has no more feeling for the one than for the other. He could as
easily be talking about the statue. He moves, not callously but unwittingly, from
one to the other, never guessing that because of the proximity of the two *objets d'art*
to each other, his audience might see him as Neptune. He keeps the portrait of his
last Duchess covered because he, like a jealous and insecure child, wants to show
complete possession of her "smile." He can now turn that smile on or off at will,
simply by pulling a rope.

The Duke would, in all likelihood, adopt similar measures against a new,   8
smiling Duchess who refused to be possessed, but he does not draw a parallel
between the two women, possibly because he sees no parallel. He says he wants to
marry the Count's daughter because she is "fair" (that is, beautiful), certainly a
tactful statement, not because she has a personality equal to or better than that of his
last Duchess. In spite of his insistence that he is interested in the daughter's "self"
and not her dowry, money is probably important to him, but he is too proud to
bargain for it. If it is money that he wants, it would seem that he and the Count are
indulging in out-and-out horse trading: he is offering a position of dignity and an
old name in exchange for the Count's money. The Duke remembers to mention
the Count's "known munificence." Only a man who has money can afford to have
the reputation for being generous.

"My Last Duchess," then, is a clever character study of a Renaissance noble-   9
man who does not appear to be as clever after all as some critics would have him.
This monologue is done with the same extraordinary irony exhibited in "Soliloquy
of the Spanish Cloister," its usual companion piece, where the petty and lecherous
monk, too, unmasks himself unwittingly. Where jealousy blinds the monk, vanity
and pride blind the Duke. His Grace is so pleased with himself that he does not
realize that he has given himself away. Nor would it ever occur to so vain and
possessive a dilettante that this conducted tour of his art gallery had revealed his
"soul," as Browning would term it, just as it would never occur to him to utilize the
tale of his sinister treatment of his last Duchess and the statue of Neptune taming
the seahorse as warnings to the Count's daughter about her behavior. The excellence of the poem lies in the dramatic irony of the Duke's witlessness, for we can be
certain that the envoy, unless he sees and feels less than we do, will advise the
Count against a marriage which might have put money in the Duke's pocket. As
one discerning critic observes, some of Browning's "best effects are produced by a
kind of dramatic irony, by which the speaker reveals himself as infinitely better or
(more often) worse than he supposes himself to be."[12]

---

[12]H. V. Routh, *Towards the Twentieth Century* (Cambridge, 1937), p. 107.

Vocabulary

intimated, equivocally, ambiguous, insinuating, dilettante, gambit, *objets d'art*, munificence, Renaissance, discerning

Questions

1. Jerman's opening follows the same pattern as Schneider's did. Why, however, does he list so many earlier interpreters before he goes on to his own interpretation? Does it weaken his case to show that so many others have held a view different from his own?
2. Does Jerman call upon any authorities to lend weight to his interpretation?
3. How many duchesses has the Duke of Ferrara had?
4. Point out some lines that give you your clearest picture of the Duke's character.
5. Do you find the Duchess faultless? Was she dull?
6. Did the Duke have his last Duchess killed? What makes you think so?

Browning's Shrewd Duke

LAURENCE PERRINE (1915–), literary scholar and author of successful textbooks, teaches at Southern Methodist University.

B. R. Jerman's challenge to the traditional view of Browning's Duke of Fer-   1
rara . . . should not pass without a rebuttal. According to Jerman, the Duke is not
at all the clever man he has usually been thought, who utilizes a casual conversation on his last Duchess to insinuate what he expects of his next one; rather, he is a
"witless" man who, blinded by vanity and pride, "does not realize that he has given
himself away" to the Count's emissary, with whom he is speaking. "The excellence
of the poem lies in the dramatic irony of the Duke's witlessness, for we can be
certain that the envoy, unless he sees and feels less than we do, will advise the
Count against a marriage which might have put money in the Duke's pocket."

I shall contend, quite otherwise, that the Duke, vain and proud as he assuredly   2
is, is also a shrewd bargainer and master diplomat who, while exposing himself fully
to the reader, not improbably obtains high commendation from the emissary in his
report to the Count. Inordinate egotism and intellect frequently cohabit, as may be
seen in characters from history (e.g., Benvenuto Cellini) or from Browning's other
poems (e.g., Cleon); and vanity, though it puffs a man up, by no means necessarily
blinds him in matters of self-interest.

If it seems paradoxical that the Duke should expose himself to the reader   3
without giving himself away to the Count's envoy, we must remember that the
envoy (1) does not have the privilege of viewing him through the lens of literature,
as we have, and (2) has not been subjected, as we have been for over two hundred
years, to such sentiments as "a man's a man for a' that" and "Kind hearts are more
than coronets, / And simple faith than Norman blood." The reader is fully prepared
to dismiss the Duke's position and family name as hollow trumperies, and to be
scornful of their possessor; but the envoy, living in a day when the prerogatives of
birth were still unquestioned, standing in the very presence of the Duke, and
surrounded by all the appurtenances of his power, may well have been impressed
and even dazzled.

We cannot know, however, how the envoy responded; we can only know how   4
the Duke handled him.[1] And first, why has the Duke summoned him to an upper
room? I agree with Mr. Jerman that he hardly "went to all the trouble to lead the
emissary upstairs so he could, by telling the tale of the Duchess' demise, warn the

---

[1]However, if historical evidence counts for anything, the marriage did take place. In 1565 Alfonso II,
Duke of Ferrara, took for his second duchess the daughter of Ferdinand I, Count of Tyrol. That these
historical figures were the prototypes of Browning's characters is convincingly established by Louis S.
Friedland in "Ferrara and *My Last Duchess*," *SP*, XXXIII (1936), 656–84.

Count's daughter," without joining him in the speculation that he "has been taking the emissary on the rounds of his art gallery." The purpose of their interview seems clearly indicated in the poem:

> I repeat,
> The Count your master's known munificence
> Is ample warrant that no just pretence
> Of mine for dowry will be disallowed;

The Duke and the Count's envoy have been closeted for a business conference: they have been discussing terms for the Duke's alliance with the Count's daughter. The Duke is indeed "indulging in out-and-out horse-trading": it is his position and nine-hundred-years-old name for her money. Such arrangements were probably common enough in those days of marriages of convenience; nevertheless, the Duke is too polished and subtle to avow openly that the dowry is his principal interest, so he adds,

> Though his fair daughter's self, as I avowed
> At starting, is my object.

The words "I repeat" and "as I avowed / At starting" are important. The Duke has mentioned both of these matters before, in reverse order; he is now driving them home in order of their real importance, making sure he is clearly understood. Notice also that the Duke's claiming of the Count's "fair daughter's self" as his object in marriage, is not at all equivalent, as Jerman says it is, to saying that he wants to marry the Count's daughter "because she is 'fair'."

5   The prime argument for the Duke's shrewdness is his skill in speech. His disclaimer of such skill is part of the evidence for it, and should remind the reader of a similar disclaimer by Shakespeare's Mark Antony in his oration on Caesar, for it serves a similar purpose. It is a rhetorical trick, to throw the listener off his guard. The Duke's momentary groping for words a few lines above ("She had / A heart— how shall I say?—too soon made glad") by no means supports his disclaimer, for actually the words he finds when he finds them are just the right words and, moreover, the break in the sentence serves very subtly to throw emphasis on the words which follow the break, which otherwise might have followed too smoothly, as if rehearsed. But the real proof of the Duke's skill in speech is the beautifully modulated passage, above quoted, in which he couches his demand for dowry. These lines are a masterpiece of diplomatic circumlocution. The nature of the demand is made amply clear, yet it is gloved in a sentence softened by a double negative and by a skillfully tactful and euphemistic choice of diction: not "riches" but "munificence"; not "proves" but "is ample warrant"; not "my demand" but "no just pretence of mine"; not "refused" but "disallowed." The hard bargaining is thus enveloped in an atmosphere of perfect courtesy and good breeding.

6   The Duke's skill in diplomacy is to be seen not only in his speech, however, but also in his whole deportment toward the emissary, which is subtly designed to flatter. Having risen from their business conference, they pass in the hall the

portrait of the Duke's last Duchess. We need not assume that the Duke has planned it this way: he is simply quick to take advantage of the opportunity. To show the emissary a specimen of his art collection is indeed, as Jerman says, a courtesy, but it hardly has the manner of a "common" courtesy when the Duke tells him, "none puts by/The curtain I have drawn for you, but I"; it is rather a special courtesy. The envoy may well feel honored that the Duke should thus draw aside the curtain for him and chat in a friendly manner about personal affairs. This friendly courtesy, from the man who is accustomed to give commands and who objected to too much courtesy in his Duchess, is apparent throughout the interview: "Will't please you sit and look at her? . . . Will't please you rise?" And when the envoy, having risen, waits respectfully for the Duke to precede him downstairs, as befits his eminence, the Duke, perhaps taking him by the elbow, tells him, "Nay, we'll go/Together down, sir." And so the envoy walks side by side down the stairway with the possessor of a nine-hundred-years-old name who has just said, "I choose/Never to stoop." Why shouldn't the envoy be flattered?

Mr. Jerman's interpretation would seem to assume that *because* the Duke is   7
glorying in showing off his possessions, he is *not* using the occasion also to intimate his prescriptions for his next wife. But the poem does not present us with any such *either-or* proposition. The Duke is a complex, not a simple individual, and Browning's is a complex characterization. The Duke is compounded of egotism and astuteness, cruelty and politeness, pride of possession and love of art, all at once. In his interview with the emissary his motives are at least three. He wishes (1) to stipulate politely but clearly exactly what he expects for his share in this bargain, both as to dowry and as to daughter, (2) to impress the envoy with his position, his power, and his importance, and (3) to flatter the envoy so as to ensure a favorable report on the envoy's return to his master. He accomplishes all three purposes. When he has been so subtle in presenting his demands for dowry, we need not balk at imputing to him subtlety also in presenting stipulations for his next bride. Mr. Jerman may find the irony he requires in the fact that when the Duke says,

> Even had you skill
> In speech—which I have not—to make your will
> Quite clear to such an one,

he is at that very moment by indirection making his will most clear to the envoy as to what he expects of his next wife. The Duke is vain, but he is no fool.

To support his interpretation Mr. Jerman advances the "obvious" point that   8
the Duke who chooses "never to stoop" to correct his first wife, would find it beneath his dignity to stipulate, even indirectly, what he expects of his next wife. But surely there is a difference between making clear what is wanted in a purchase and wrangling over the goods after they are provided. The man who is very particular in ordering a custom-built piece of furniture may simply cancel the order, rather than haggle over details, if it doesn't meet specifications on delivery. Moreover, if the Duke can "stoop" to state plainly what he expects in dowry, why should he not state subtly what he expects of a wife?

9   Another point that Mr. Jerman advances for the Duke's "witlessness" is his regarding as a "wonder" a portrait that has been painted in a day. There are various ways of meeting this objection. One is to question whether a masterpiece may not be painted in a day. Whistler, when cross-examined about one of his paintings, said he asked two hundred guineas for it, not for the labor of two days but "for the knowledge of a lifetime." Another is to question how literally the phrase "a day" is to be interpreted: perhaps only the sitting lasted a day. But suppose we grant that the painting may not have been the masterpiece the Duke thought it? We may grant a shallowness in his art appreciation without impairing our claim for cleverness in matters that touch him more personally. The Duke is proud of being a collector and art patron at a time when such patronage was fashionable. Millionaire collectors today often have very faulty artistic taste without being any less shrewd in their personal transactions with people.[2]

10   One other suggestion made by Mr. Jerman requires contention. He apparently regards the Duchess as superficial and insipid, and quotes approvingly the opinion of Margaret H. Bates that it was "the deadly monotony" of the Duchess' smile that got on the Duke's nerves. The poem does not support this view of the Duchess. Our reactions to the Duchess are controlled by the warmth of her response to compliments, by her graciousness to inferiors, and especially by the things she takes delight in: the beauty of a sunset, the gift of a bough of cherries, a ride round the terrace on a white mule. Her response to these things indicates a genuine and sensitive nature, which takes joy in simple, natural things rather than in gauds and baubles or the pomp of position and power which attract the Duke. To the Duke, who seldom smiles, the Duchess may seem to smile excessively. The Duke thinks his Duchess should be proud and unbending, like himself; she should give commands to her inferiors, not stoop to thank them for small favors. The Duke's response to her, therefore, is to do away with her. But the response of others in the poem is to bring her a bough of cherries or to remark on "the faint/Half-flush that dies along her throat."

11   Mr. Jerman ends his article by quoting H. V. Routh's comment that some of Browning's "best effects are produced by a kind of dramatic irony, by which the speaker reveals himself as infinitely better or (more often) worse than he supposes himself to be." The excellence of "My Last Duchess" does indeed lie in this kind of dramatic irony, in fact, in a double use of it, for the Duke while revealing himself as infinitely worse than he supposes himself to be (in human worth, not wit), is at the same time revealing his last Duchess as infinitely better than he supposed her to be. The Duke is trying to build himself up and run his Duchess down. He is given all the words, and he uses them skillfully. But for the reader (not necessarily for the envoy), he accomplishes just the reverse.

---

[2]B. N. Pipes, Jr., in "The Portrait of 'My Last Duchess'," *Victorian Studies*, 3 (June 1960), 381–386, published after this article, argues convincingly (1) that the poem itself offers evidence of the Duke's artistic perception and good taste, and (2) that the portrait was a fresco, painted directly on the wall—a kind of painting which *must* be executed rapidly, before the plaster dries.

Vocabulary

rebuttal, insinuate, inordinate, paradoxical, trumperies, appurtenances, disclaimer, modulated, circumlocution, euphemistic, deportment, stipulate, insipid

Questions

1. Perrine promises a rebuttal. Is it a point-by-point rebuttal or a general one?
2. Why doesn't Perrine list as many earlier interpreters as Jerman did?
3. Does he state Jerman's position fairly?
4. He has a very different interpretation from Jerman's of why the duke and the envoy were upstairs to begin with. With whom do you side? Why?
5. Is the duke a skillful speaker or not? Can you give examples?
6. Is Perrine justified when he adds phrases like "perhaps taking him by the elbow"? Did Jerman make any similar assumptions?
7. Do you find the duke simple or complex?

Topics for Writing

The Duke's Intelligence: My View

The Lying Duke

The Envoy's Report to the Count

Advice to the Count's Daughter

Simply Super: A Review of *Superman*

RICHARD A. BLAKE The lavish motion picture *Superman*, replete with stars, special effects, and a massive advertising budget, was released in the Christmas season of 1978. This review, by Richard A. Blake, appeared in the weekly magazine *America*.

1 Jackie Hudson had a broken front tooth that was the envy of the neighborhood. He also had a copy of the Superman comic book that traced the origins of the man of steel from the destruction of the planet Krypton to his discovery of his role in the fight for law and order. In a long and heated trading session, at the cost of several Green Hornets and Batmans, the prized Superman finally came into my possession. Few stories held such hypnotic fascination over my childhood imagination.

2 *Superman* has now leapt with a single bound into my adulthood, not as a 10-cent comic book but as a $35-million movie from Warners, with a script begun by Mario Puzo, father of "The Godfather," and cameo performances by Marlon Brando, Susannah York, Glenn Ford, Gene Hackman, Valerie Perrine and Jackie Cooper. A record album of the score by John Williams is an enthusiastic combination of the best of *Star Wars* and Richard Strauss's *Death and Transfiguration*. A paperback thriller, *Superman, The Last Son of Krypton*, by Elliott S. Maggin is billed as "first in Warner's new serial of Superman novels." The Broadway revival of George Bernard Shaw's "Man and Superman" is apparently merely a coincidence, but it does add to a general paranoia that the nation has been taken over by the Superman industry.

3 Like most other big-budget movies intended to drag in record audiences, "Superman" is aimed at young adults, who were, of course, not even in sight when Superman first dropped in from Krypton in 1938. The current version opens with a small-screen image of an old comic book and, as the pages turn and lumps of nostalgia rise in the throats of the pre-Beatles generation, the screen grows wider and the sound rises for what must be the longest and loudest set of credits in motion picture history. The audience is whisked away from its old comic book memories through the galaxies in a journey comparable to *2001: A Space Odyssey*. It turns out to be a joy ride from start to finish.

4 Three stories, each with its own character, are folded in upon one another in this two-and-a-half-hour epic of good humor. The first and most dominant story begins on the planet Krypton, as the wise and white-haired Jor-El (Marlon Brando) has just finished his summation to the jury and must cast the deciding vote in the conviction of three traitors. The traitors are condemned, compressed into a two-dimensional playing card and whisked off to space in some kind of magical time warp. They have nothing to do with the film, but the publicity gremlins at Warners have let out the word that this troublesome trio will return to their villainous ways in *Superman II*, now in production.

After the distraction of this preview of things to come, the real story begins. Krypton is coming apart at the seams. This should be no surprise, even to the densest of Kryptonians, since the whole place looks like a chandelier designed by one of Queen Victoria's favorite artists gone mad. Jor-El fires his son to Smallville, U.S.A., just as Krypton blows up. (It is a terrible thing to do to a child, with Glenn Ford as a foster father, too!) 5

Aw, shucks, he can't even get to first base with the girls and is making a gosh-darned mess out of his life, until that magic day when he travels to the North Pole, and there, amid the caves of ice, Jor-El appears as bard among the bergs and tells young Mr. Kent of his law-and-order destiny. The plot may seem a bit, shall we say, thin, but it does provide an excuse for the marvelous science-fiction special effects, and that is really what this Krypton story is all about anyway. 6

The second plot is cops-and-robbers comedy in the style of the old Batman television series. Archvillain Lex Luthor steals a missile from the United States and plans to blast California into the Pacific by dropping a superbomb into the San Andreas fault. As a precaution, he uses a chunk of kryptonite from an old meteor to capture Superman and render him powerless in an apartment that is a replica of Grand Central Terminal in, not New York, but Metropolis. At the last possible minute . . . well, you know. 7

Superman's love life, the third plot, is centered on the bumbling but nice Clark Kent, who has to put on his red cape and blue longjohns to have the courage to woo Lois Lane, a tough-talking but basically nice-once-you-get-to-know-her reporter for *The Daily Planet*. 8

Even though the three stories form an impossible mixture of *Star Wars*, "Batman" and *The Front Page*, the combination works. Most of the credit must go to the engaging performances of the two principals, Christopher Reeve in the title role and Margot Kidder as Lois. They seem to be enjoying themselves so much that an audience is swept right along by their enthusiasm. The director, Richard Donner, has left them enough humanity to make them believable and enough comic-book heroics to provide the laughs. 9

Analyses of *Superman* and the Superman phenomenon are already rolling out of typewriters across the nation, much to my dread. Before long, there will no doubt be theological interpretations of the story: A father sends his son to earth to do good and save mankind from its evil ways, yet he is not to use his special powers to change the course of human history. Clark Kent must die, so that Superman may conquer evil. And so on and on and on. 10

The reason for this compulsion is obvious. This is a big, enjoyable movie that is beautifully executed and competently marketed during a holiday season. Not able to believe in the skill of Hollywood fantasy makers and New York publicity crafters, the critics and commentators will search the crevices of their own imaginations to explain the enthusiasm. 11

Jackie Hudson knew the secret. He knew that his comic book was a valuable piece of property and he made his customers pay for it. He did not have to speculate on America's search for a hero or the age of cynicism that trivializes the heroic. No, he knew a good comic book when he saw one. 12

Vocabulary

paranoia, bard, cynicism

Questions

1. How does the memory of Jackie Hudson give a shape to this review? Do you agree that *Superman* is aimed at young adults?
2. Notice the order in which Blake presents the three plots of the movie. Would the reverse order be as effective?
3. Blake likes the movie and says so in his next-to-last paragraph. Can you find earlier clues to his opinion?
4. Blake forecasts gloomily that the movie will inspire serious interpretations of a relatively simple story. Does he imply that these interpretations will be wrong?
5. Read the article by Brown. Is it an example of what Blake fears?

A Review of *Superman*

STANLEY KAUFFMANN's (1916–) review appeared in *The New Republic,* also a weekly publication.

Around 1945, when *Superman* was a fifteen-minute-daily radio serial, a friend   1
and I, late one night, concocted a two-week story outline for the show, which next
day we sold to the producer. I can't remember one scrap of our story, but I'll bet that
it was better than the plot of the new *Superman* film (Warner Bros.). According to
the newspapers, the first script was written by Mario Puzo (possibly the most appropriately named man since Wallace Beery); he is still first on the bill, but his script
was completely rewritten by David Newman and Robert Benton who—though the
producers didn't even know it!—had written the book of a Broadway musical about
Superman in 1966, a show I liked. Benton had to leave before the script was
accepted, and (Mrs.) Leslie Newman carried on with her husband for six or seven
rewrites. I hardly need to add that the result is blah. (I *wish* I could remember what
my friend and I cooked up at two a.m. that night in 1945.) Not only blah but
occasionally inexplicable even in the script's own terms. For instance, the entrance
to the villain's headquarters seems to be far under Grand Central Terminal in New
York, but the interior seems to be in the terminal itself.

I suppose the blame levels finally on the producers, Alexander and Ilya Sal-   2
kind, along with the blame for casting the prosy Gene Hackman as the grandiloquent villain and the raspy Margot Kidder, who plays Lois Lane like a reformed
hooker. But then the Salkinds must also get the credit for casting Christopher
Reeve, a mammoth box of Wheaties, as Superman, just humorlessly right, and for
the good special effects, done in England, by Colin Chilvers, Roy Field, Les Bowie,
and Denys Coop. The director, if it matters, was Richard Donner.

The best actors in the film, none of them exactly at the pinnacle of his career   3
here, are all in the prologue on Krypton: Marlon Brando, Terence Stamp, Trevor
Howard, and Harry Andrews. When we get to earth, things get slimmer, although
Phyllis Thaxter—a touching ingénue in the 1940s, now Ilya Salkind's mother-in-
law—is nice as Superman's earthly foster-mother. We're told that a whole sequel
was filmed while this picture was being made. Why not? Why need things ever
stop? Why shouldn't there be a Superman picture every two years?

We Superman writers know that the big trouble is that he *is* Superman. How   4
do you keep him from solving all the plot difficulties right at the beginning? You
have to divert the viewer from that logic with lots of *stuff*: the wrestling with a
missile in flight, the rescue of the president's plane, the repairing of earthquakes.
There's plenty of such stuff here and Reeve is likable, so it's probably irrelevant to
press the picture further. (But the Broadway musical had some wit and point.) Two
notes. The first time Clark Kent has to change, his glance at one of those new
telephone non-booths is funny. And nobody says, "It's a bird. . . ." etc.

Vocabulary

grandiloquent, ingénue

Questions

1. Kauffmann opens with a story about his interest in *Superman* back in 1945 and follows it with several other examples of *Superman* entertainments. Does this brief historical view prepare you to accept Kauffmann's judgment on the modern film?
2. In his comments on the casting, can you show that Kauffmann is interested in giving an objective view? Are there other parts of the review in which you can find similar evidence?
3. List some of Kauffmann's reasons for disliking the movie. Are they "mere opinion" or conclusions supported by evidence?

Topics for Writing

There Is No Arguing over Taste

One Man's Meat, Another Man's Poison

Superman: My Review

Superman on the Screen: Counterfeit Myth?

HAROLD O. J. BROWN's (1933–) view, published in the April 1979 issue of *Christianity Today,* is a leisurely comment on the theological and moral implications of the Superman myth.

If the 1960s and early 1970s became an age without heroes, an age of the anti-hero in literature and on the stage and the screen, the past few years have seen the emergence of a new and somewhat perplexing phenomenon, the superhero. Since "superheroes" are confined in large measure to the pages of children's comics, it may seem out of place to take them seriously enough to discuss them in *Christianity Today.* Yet what children are taught to a large extent determines how they will act as adults, and what adults teach children tells us a great deal about how adults think—or, as the case may be, fail to think. Of what significance is it that true heroes have disappeared, to be replaced by superheroes?

A hero is a human being who through discipline, bravery, determination, and perhaps divine assistance accomplishes seemingly incredible feats. Heroes generally must be good and serve a good cause, though sometimes brave and generous men in the service of an evil cause are deemed to be heroes—usually tragic but noble figures. Thus Robert E. Lee is honored by most of those who disapproved the cause of the South, and Field Marshall Erwin Rommel, the "Desert Fox," appears as one of the last heroes of modern times, though the cause he served was truly evil.

A superhero, by contrast, is not a real human being, but a fantasy creature—Superman, Batman, Captain Marvel, Wonder Woman, *et al.* Superheroes, unlike the heroes of Greek mythology, have no Achilles' heel. Superman himself is vulnerable to the mineral kryptonite, but of course he will never be killed by it—unlike the great Achilles. Unlike the more traditional heroes of folklore and of reality, modern superheroes have no moral context. They are generally in the service of "good" and against "evil," of course. But the good that they serve is undefined, undistinguished, unmotivated, and the evil they oppose is likewise.

It is no doubt significant that one of the most successful novelists today, Mario Puzo, whose massive tales (such as *The Godfather*) have no heroes, but only cynicism and anti-heroes, was engaged to write the screenplay for *Superman.* It is due to Puzo's ability that the details of an essentially trivial and incredible tale hang together in such a way as to make it all vaguely believable. But it is probably also due to Puzo's basically cynical orientation that the good in Superman—which is abundantly evident—is without origin, frame, reference, or goal. In this it resembles the good of another modern counterfeit, *Close Encounters*—it is alien good, good simply by being alien. And there is a serious moral problem here: if it is the alien power, the infant stranger from the planet Krypton, who is good by virtue of

459

his origin, then the implication is that we human beings, who do not share that origin, are under no obligation to be good, not to speak of being heroic.

5   There are many parallels—and they cannot all be accidental—between the infant who comes to earth from the heavens (outer space) and the One who came from heaven. Marlon Brando, the wise Kryptonian who sends his son to earth to escape the destruction of his planet, speaks of his hopes for mankind, and of "giving them my only son." But the parallels are defective, for there is nothing divine and good about being Kryptonian. The movie's first scene involves the "eternal" judgment—itself a literally blasphemous concept—of Kryptonians who are not good but criminal. This itself may be a kind of parallel to the fall and banishment of Satan before the creation. In any event, Kryptonians are not good by virtue of being Kryptonian. In fact, they do not seem to be good for any reason at all.

6   Superman happens to be good, was good even as Superboy. But he can afford to be good, for no one can harm him, no one can touch him. It takes no special effort of will or courage for him to do the right thing, as for a human hero. The fact that he is not tyrannical is, of course, in some way commendable—yet it seems to tie in with his deep naïveté that makes good seem rather foolish by comparison with evil. What the impact of Superman's good on small viewers will be is hard to predict. Perhaps the fact that he, with his superpowers, is unequivocally committed to the good will impress them and encourage them to imitate him in doing good. Will older viewers get the message that good is a luxury possible only for those with impossible superpowers?

7   The Superman phenomenon is a mystifying one, and I must confess to being perplexed by it. If *Star Wars* was an old-fashioned heroic tale not unlike Homer's *Iliad*, showing uncomplicated good in virtuous (manly) and successful combat with uncomplicated evil, and *Close Encounters* a drama of enlightenment through contact with alien good, it is not clear what *Superman* is. It would be convenient to say that it is a satire on true heroism and on the good; that may be true, but it seems unlikely that it is a deliberate satire. It is more likely to be a true reflection of the situation of modern man, in which man—with the image of God ineradicably planted within him—somehow longs for something and someone good, but has become so cynical that he can postulate good only in an impossible person and situation.

8   If the anti-hero was a denial of the claim that any human acts like a hero, *Superman* and the superheroes, which show heroic qualities only in superhumans, may be a denial that heroic qualities exist at all. If they can manifest only in unreal persons, then they can hardly exist.

9   Perhaps the fundamental difference between heroes and superheroes lies in this: the tales of heroes, from Homer to the present, have been told by bards who knew men they regarded as heroes and honored them for it, who believed in heroism, and who hoped that their hearers, young and not so young, might one day perform heroic deeds themselves. The superhero phenomenon seems to be a catering to the deep-rooted human desire to have heroes and heroic qualities to admire and emulate. The catering is done by those who are fundamentally cynical and who do not believe in what they are presenting. Søren Kierkegaard once wrote that the

way to destroy true gospel preaching was not to prohibit it, but to subsidize a thousand bad preachers in a thousand pulpits. Is it inconceivable that one way to destroy any stirrings of true heroism is to spread fundamentally unbelievable examples, impossible to imitate, on tens of thousands of movie screens and eventually on millions of television screens?

There is another aspect of unreality in the Superman story that is worthy of   10 some thought, particularly by those concerned for the deteriorating relationship between the sexes. In *Superman,* as in *Star Wars* and *Close Encounters,* there is a modern, liberated woman—essentially, a very sympathetic character. Yet, unlike Helen of Troy and Andromache in the *Iliad,* or even Princess Leia in *Star Wars,* Lois Lane's independent, individual life seems almost extinguished as she takes on the role of Superman's votary. Lois makes this quite explicit when, after her celestial piggy-back ride, she speaks of having been "with a god." Even Hercules was but a demigod, and Achilles a mortal man. Confronted with supermanliness, the tough, cynical, and liberated Lois Lane is speechless with a wonder that seems less like sexual love than reverential awe. Why has Lois's conduct and attitude not been mocked in the circles of women's liberation? Can it be that a large part of women's ire at men stems not from male prerogatives but from the pretense on which those prerogatives are based? In other words, that if there were some substance undergirding them—as there is in Superman's case—women would not refuse to admire admirable qualities? Lois Lane's reaction to Superman may be seen as the expression of the way men, even less than super-men, wish women would react to them. On the other hand, the lack of outcry at the figure of Lois Lane indicates that women can recognize genuine virtue and admire it.

Virtue, the reader may recall, is from the Latin *vir,* man, and corresponds   11 roughly to the English manliness; to be virtuous is to be what a real man should be. The fact that "virtue" and "virtuous" have come to be terms of disdain or ridicule in modern usage may merely express the fact that there are so few true men who are virtuous and possess virtues. Virtue nevertheless still has its admirers, even when exemplified in an unreal man, a Superman. The deep question that *Superman* poses is this: does it tell us, and will we believe, that virtue is to be admired and emulated—or that virtue is an impossible dream, to be found only in a man who can fly?

Although *Superman* is an unreal tale, told by those with a far less Christian   12 view of reality than the far more fantastic J. R. R. Tolkein, it does provide us with a real moral. Strength, exercised in a good cause, is not ridiculous but admirable; and virtue, if real, will be respected—perhaps even imitated. The early Christians challenged the idealized humanity of Greek statuary not with ideal pictures of saints, but with real lives of human beings who were not only "called saints," in Paul's language, but acted like them. They exhibited Christian virtues that were not only worthy of admiration, but found imitators. The fantastic, nostalgic response of Americans, and indeed of people all over the world, to the somewhat simple, even simple-minded virtues of Luke Skywalker, Obi-Wan Kenobe, and now of Superman should encourage us to try to exhibit not unreal virtues, but real ones. We may be greeted with derision—but inevitably also with imitation.

Vocabulary

myth, emulate, votary

Questions

1. This is a reflective essay, not simply a review of a movie. What are some of the expository techniques you recognize here?
2. Do you find Brown's distinction between heroes and superheroes valid? Are his examples vivid ones?
3. Do you find Brown's use of definitions helpful? Consider *virtue*, for example.
4. Do superheroes deny the possibility "that any human acts like a hero"? Could you prove your answer from *Superman*?
5. Brown uses *myth* in its classic sense, not as we sometimes hear it used to describe a falsehood or mistaken idea. In this sense, do you agree that the movie reflected a counterfeit myth?

Topics for Writing

A Defense of Superheroes

A Review of My Favorite Movie

Appendix

Writing the 500-Word Essay

Writing well is one of the marks of the educated person, and the only way to acquire the skill is to write—to write regularly and often. For this reason, nearly every college and university requires that students take a course in English composition. The heart of that course is the 500-word essay, assigned frequently and marked carefully by an instructor whose aim is to help you express your ideas effectively on paper.

At first, the inexperienced cannot imagine how they will be able to fill up the required number of pages; but before long they discover that the problem is condensing, cutting, and revising to keep within the prescribed limits. Writing, they learn, is like any other challenging activity: it becomes easier with repetition, the results better with purposeful practice. The next few pages are meant to help you develop your abilities as an essay writer.

Although practice varies, English instructors ordinarily suggest specific topics for the first student essay, often assigning subjects that will give some insight into the student's personality and background or that draw upon the student's likely experience. Venerable chestnuts include "My Favorite Relative," "My Summer Vacation," and "What I Hope to Get from College." Let us consider a typical instance. Your instructor may say, "On Monday, please submit a 500-word essay on a topic of your own choosing, perhaps one that tells about some problem your family faced recently or that describes some activity at which you are particularly well skilled." Where, exactly, should you begin?

Before You Write

The soul of the essay is *the idea*—a thought, an opinion, a conception formed in the mind. The idea will be the life of your essay, its starting point, guiding principle, and shaping influence. Your first job, then, is to choose from among the many possibilities the idea that best suits your purpose.

Are there in fact many possibilities? There are. First, you do have a store of ideas and experiences to draw on—many more, probably, than you realize—because life brings them to us in abundance. Sometimes, of course, a stimulus may be needed, like a key to unlock the storehouse. For example, many people say they cannot remember jokes, but let someone else tell a funny story or two, and those who "can't remember" pop in with, "That reminds me of the salesman who . . . ." The assignment of a theme (we will use *theme* and *essay* interchangeably) is the first stimulus, the spur to start you thinking. If the topic assigned had been more specific ("My New Roommate" or "Busing to Achieve Racial Balance: A Good Idea?"), the spur would have been stronger: you would have a subject to focus on. This assignment, "a topic of your own choosing," is more general, but there is a hint of two directions you might take: "some problem your family faced recently" or "some activity at which you are particularly well skilled." Since every family has its problems and every person does something a little better than another, you can be certain that you will have something to write about. The question is how to make a sensible choice.

Begin with a pencil and paper, which are useful aids to thinking systematically. You may want to start with two columns. Under "Family Problems" perhaps you will list "Arguments with My Sister," "Moving from Scarsdale," "Financial Difficulties with Two of Us in College," "Grandfather Kelly's Death," and so on. Your list of "Special Skills" may be more limited, but even here you will find a few possibilities, say "Acting in Little Theater Productions," "Swimming Instructor at YMCA," "Grooming Dogs," and "Watercolor Painting."

As you write things down, you will find your memory stimulated, and you may be able to add items you otherwise would have overlooked. To one list, you may add something about the first time you crumpled a fender on the family car, or the crisis when your parents were afraid your brother was going to drop out of college and get married; to the other, you may add that you also did a lot of set-building for the theater group and that you were a better-than-average organizer of fund-raising activities for your high school class. Before long, you will realize that there is no shortage of possible topics. The problem is to select one of many.

You should not agonize over the choice. There is no "right" or "wrong" topic as long as you keep the characteristics of a *good* topic in mind:

1. You are interested in it.
2. You know—or are willing to learn—something about it.
3. You can make what you know or learn clear and, you hope, interesting to your reader.

Many of the items in your two lists ought to have those characteristics, but, let us suppose, because you think you were the best instructor on the pool staff, you decide to write about teaching people to swim. Furthermore, because you found that teaching children was more fun than teaching adolescents or adults, you make matters easier by choosing for your subject "Teaching Children to Swim." You have a useful topic now and can move forward.

The next step is to gather information about the subject. For many subjects, of course, you might have to consult books and articles; but in this case, your own experience should provide enough information for the 500-word theme. Again, pencil and paper are your most useful tools, the list your primary strategy.

My recommendation is that, rather than try to organize information at this stage, you begin by making a random or free-association list—the subjects and ideas that come to mind when you think about teaching a child to swim and you ask yourself the basic questions, Who? What? Where? When? Why? How? Such a list might look like this:

> swimming pool—you need water!
> kick
> free-style stroke
> back stroke
> butterfly stroke
> breast stroke
> breathing techniques
> floating—"dead man's float"
> diving—racing dives, one-and-a-half, etc.
> safety
> fun in the sun
> overcoming fear, gaining confidence
> advanced techniques—flutter kick, scissors

This list is long enough to start with (it need not be exhaustive, as you will see) and should not take more than a couple of minutes to make.

The next step is to analyze the list, that is, to group the items according to a scheme. This grouping can be chronological (that is, arranging events according to a time sequence) or logical (that is, fitting related things into reasonable categories) or a combination of the two. If you consider the items in the list and the nature of the topic, which is essentially a process analysis (a how-to-do-it or how-it-is-done approach), you can see that a combination of the two is in order.

Certain groupings occur naturally. "Strokes" will include free style, back, butterfly, breast—and now you may remember to add that unorthodox beginner's stroke, the dog-paddle. "Dives" will include the one-and-a-half, racing start, swan, and even the belly-flop. Certain items in the list, like "safety" and "overcoming fear" are important but seem to be preconditions to teaching rather than a part of swimming technique. Perhaps you will call this category "Preliminaries." "Fun in the sun" may be a result of knowing how to swim well, but it can hardly be taught. Other elements, you find, are related in similar groupings.

Next, consider your groups chronologically. In what sequence do these follow when you teach a child to swim?

In fact, that decision was made when you noted that certain things were preliminary to teaching. "Safety first" is a good rule around water and must be taken care of before anything else. Overcoming the child's fear of the water and helping him or her to gain confidence also come, as you noticed earlier, before effective teaching begins. You have further realized that, although you may associate a variety of dives, strokes, and racing techniques with swimming, some of these are not important to the beginner. It is at this point, I think, that the organization of your paper begins to suggest itself. You begin to see an outline forming:

I. Preliminaries
II. Basic Instruction

Although this is a two-part division, keep in mind that it will not be an equal division: your topic demands that II be the central matter and that it be given the fullest treatment. In practical terms, given the limit of 500 words, this may mean that item I will be given only a short paragraph, whereas item II will require three or four longer ones.

As you arrange items under the outline headings, you will find yourself excluding certain things ("swimming pool" is so obvious that it need not be stated) and adding others that occur to you to flesh out the bare bones of your outline.

I. Preliminaries: teaching safety (obeying rules, avoiding panic, buddy system) and building confidence (ducking, bobbing, eye-opening games)
II. Basic Instruction
   A. Floating and Kicking—the kick-board
   B. The Free-Style Stroke
   C. Proper Breathing
   D. Coordinating A through C—drill games and practice

This is not, perhaps, an outline you would want to submit as a model of elegance, but it will serve. If you add a very brief introduction to lead the reader into your subject and an equally brief conclusion to give a last look at what you have accomplished, you will have a solid design for the essay you are now ready to write.

Writing the Essay

The Introduction

You should accomplish two things in your introduction: one, attract the reader's attention to your subject, and two, state the purpose of your essay in a straightforward declarative sentence, called a *thesis sentence*. The importance of the first is obvious. But the thesis sentence is even more important because, for the reader, it will highlight the purpose of your paper; for you, it will serve as a ready reminder not to stray from the subject. If any sentence in your essay does not flow from the logic of your thesis sentence, it probably does not belong in your paper and should be removed.

Since we agreed that you can afford only a brief paragraph to introduce a 500-word theme, you should make the first sentence as interest-catching as possible without straining for effect, then move promptly to your thesis sentence. Something like this would do:

> This year thousands of American children will lose a wonderful chance for healthy enjoyment, and some will even lose their lives, because no one taught them a simple skill [*interest-catcher*]. No one taught them to swim. And yet, teaching a child

to swim, as I know from experience, involves a four-step process nearly anyone can follow [*thesis*].

The Body of the Essay

You have caught the reader's attention and have focused it on your thesis. Now, you can proceed to the body of your essay, which includes I and II of your outline.

We agreed that you could spare only a single paragraph for "Preliminaries," but, because it must cover two points, safety and confidence, this paragraph will probably be somewhat longer than the introduction. Just as the entire essay must be guided by a thesis, so too should every paragraph be shaped by a *topic sentence*. The topic sentence usually stands first in the paragraph and is followed by several sentences that provide supporting evidence, details, and examples. The paragraph covering "Preliminaries" might read like this:

> Of course [*this links what follows to the first paragraph*], the instructor must provide for the children's safety and must make them feel comfortable in the water before serious teaching can begin. I have found that a firm insistence on safety regulations—no running in the pool area, no jumping or diving where others are swimming, never swimming or playing alone in the pool, always looking to the lifeguards for help and guidance—goes over well with young people and helps them to form good safety habits. Building confidence is also [*a link with the last sentence*] easy. By making a game of holding their breath under water, of fetching coins from the bottom of the pool (when the children have ducked under, I move the coin; they won't find it unless they open their eyes!) or of trying to run by "giant steps" across the shallow end, I overcome any fear they may have of the water and help them associate fun with it. Once this is achieved, they are ready to learn [*a link to the next stage*].

The writer is now prepared—and the reader is, too—to move on to the heart of the paper, the basic process of teaching children to swim. As your outline shows, there are four simple stages to be discussed—floating and kicking, the free-style stroke, breathing, and coordination.

Four paragraphs, one devoted to each of these steps and each linked to the one before it by transitional phrases that help move the reader from point to point, constitute the body of your essay. These paragraphs may vary in length, but each will develop a topic sentence by means of specific examples and illustrations. Keep your reader in mind as you write. You want to make each stage in this process perfectly clear. You cannot assume, for example, that every reader will know what a kickboard is. When in doubt, explain.

The Conclusion

Once you have covered the four steps of the teaching process, you can proceed to your conclusion. This should not, in a 500-word essay, be an elaborate matter, and it should not begin with "In conclusion, . . ." or some similarly trite phrase. In some essays, the conclusion can actually be the last sentence of your last and strongest paragraph. But in themes like this one, a process analysis in which each paragraph treats a single stage, a separate conclusion that reflects or echoes your thesis is appropriate. "No youngster," you might conclude, "need miss out on the joy and the security that come from knowing how to swim. Almost any child can learn from an instructor who uses the teaching method I have described."

Revising the Essay

You are not finished with your theme when you have written the conclusion: the last step is to revise what you have written. A revision may take an hour or only a few minutes, but failure to revise carefully is always a mistake. The finishing touches often make the difference between first- and third-rate work.

Ideally, you should let some time pass between your draft of the essay and the revision of it. An overnight break is sensible, but even a few hours' pause—while you have dinner or do the laundry or study for another course—will give you the distance you need to look afresh at your work.

As you reread with revision in mind, you must try to see the paper as your reader will see it. Here is a checklist of questions to ask yourself:

About the thesis: Is the thesis sentence plainly and unambiguously stated? Does it tell the reader exactly what I intend to show in the body of the paper?

About the body of the paper: Have I shown everything I promised in the thesis? Have I maintained the proper proportion between the main and the subordinate parts of the paper, the introductory and concluding paragraphs? Have I placed the stages of my process in the best possible order? Have I used linking devices to show how the paragraphs are logically connected and to lead the reader easily from one stage to the next? Is my conclusion brief and convincing?

About style and correctness: Have I written the best English at my command? Is each sentence complete and clear? Have I varied the length and structure of my sentences? Have I avoided careless errors in grammar and punctuation? Have I checked all doubtful spellings in the dictionary?

In answering these questions you must be honest with yourself, and you must avoid the bias that all of us have in favor of our own work. Having written the paper, you of course know what you *meant* to say. Rereading it, you must not assume that what you meant is automatically what, to an objective reader, you actually *said*.

Besides letting time pass between the first draft and the revision, you might try another technique that has helped me to revise objectively. When you go over the draft, try to imagine that it was written by someone other than yourself—perhaps by a friend whom you especially want to please (or by a critical acquaintance you would like to put in his place). You see, your purpose is to look critically and objectively at the paper so that you can revise it sensibly.

Once you have made necessary revisions and written out or typed the final copy, set it aside. You will want a breather before your last task: proofreading.

Every English instructor who ever lived can remember sad examples of students whose work had to be marked down sharply because typographical errors spoiled the paper and made the students look as though they had respect for neither the reader nor their own work. The time and effort you have invested in your essay must not be thrown away at the last minute. If you proofread with hawklike attention to every detail, correcting minor errors where you find them, you will have the assurance of knowing you have done your best. And every essay you write will be another step toward becoming an effective writer.

Summarizing the Process

The lists in this section summarize the process we have just discussed. They are designed to provide you with a short, handy guide to consult while you are writing.

The Process of Writing the Essay

1. Choosing the topic

Pick one you have an interest in, know, or can learn easily about, and can make clear to a reader.

2. Gathering and analyzing the information

Use the free-association method, putting ideas into your list without worrying about order or completeness. When you have half-a-dozen items in your list, link related ideas. Ask yourself, "What comes first?"

3. Making a practical outline

Arrange your related ideas in a logical or chronological order. Remember that the outline is the blueprint for an essay and that you need a beginning, a middle, and an end.

4. Writing and revising the essay

Remember the proportions of the essay (see below). Write an introductory paragraph that ends with a clear statement of your thesis. Develop the body of your paper in a series of well-constructed paragraphs that cover everything your thesis promised. Keep the conclusion short. Revise and proofread carefully.

The Proportions of a Typical 500-Word Essay

Introduction	One paragraph that ends with a declarative sentence stating your thesis.	50–75 words
Body	Three to five paragraphs that develop the thesis in an organized way. Each paragraph includes a link with the one preceding it, a topic sentence, and several sentences that provide the examples and other details needed to support this topic sentence. This sequence of paragraphs must complete the support of your thesis.	350–400 words
Conclusion	One paragraph that echoes your thesis and reinforces its significance.	50–75 words

As in all things, practice makes perfect. During the next four years, you will find plenty of opportunities to write: essay examinations in many courses, critical and research papers in others, letters to prospective employers, and so forth. If you form the habit of writing systematically now, you will be doing yourself a favor.

Further Applications

In the first part of this discussion, we applied this scheme to an exercise in process analysis (how to teach children to swim) meant to be written out of class. It can, however, be adjusted to suit in-class essays and writing assignments of other sorts. Nothing more is needed than common sense and attention to the instructor's requirements.

If, for example, the instructor whose words opened this section had assigned the same topic for a 50-minute, in-class theme, several results would follow:

1. The assignment would call for a shorter paper, perhaps 350 words.
2. You would not be required to turn in the spotless copy you could have made out of class, where recopying or careful typing would have been possible.
3. The proportions of the paper would be retained, but all the individual parts would be done on a smaller scale—like an eight-foot statue of Venus reproduced in a six-foot copy.
4. The four steps by which the longer essay was done would be retained, but Steps 1 through 3 would have to be completed in five minutes or so, the revision and proofreading in not much more than that, in order to leave you sufficient time in which to compose the essay.

Nevertheless, the fact that time is limited must not lead you to omit any of the steps. Your "free-list" may be shorter than you could make it with half an hour at your disposal; your analysis of the information on the list may be no more than a series of marginal loops connecting related items; your outline may consist of the numerals 1, 2, and 3 or arrows designating main points. But five minutes spent in planning the essay will save you the time and embarrassment of major structural changes after the essay is two-thirds done and may prevent you from overlooking some essential point until it is too late for remedy. Likewise, a few minutes saved for minor revisions and careful proofreading will be time well spent.

The steps involved in this scheme also apply to all *kinds* of essays—definition, persuasion, and narration, as well as the other types of exposition explained and exemplified in this book. The strategies involved in persuading the reader to vote for your candidate or needed to describe your Uncle Henry may vary in detail or emphasis, but the principles—choosing, gathering and analyzing, outlining, writing and revising—are always valid.

And this is true of the result of your work, the essay. It must have a beginning, a middle, and an end. The parts themselves—the introduction, body, and conclusion—and the approximate proportions of the parts apply to every kind of writing you will do.

A Last Word

"Writing," Francis Bacon claimed in his essay "Of Studies," makes "an exact man." He was in this, as in so many other things, right. When we commit our thoughts to writing, we are forced to ask ourselves some fundamental questions: What is it, exactly, that I want to say? How best can I say it? Asking those questions forces us to concentrate, to think clearly. Answering them forces us to express our ideas, first to ourselves and then to others, as exactly as we can.

The results lie stark on the page before us. Reading them critically, we can judge how well or ill we have succeeded. More often than not, we will have to admit that we can do better and we revise. This word is close, but not quite the one needed. The connection between A and B is not clearly expressed. This paragraph is flabby and far too wordy. A complex sentence would express this idea more effectively than does the compound one. The revision results in a tighter, more precise prose—and teaches a lesson that will make the next essay closer-knit and more exact.

The acquiring of any skill, whether it be painting in oils, negotiating the steepest headwalls at your favorite ski area, or running a four-speed stick shift smoothly through the gears, brings with it a sense of achievement and becomes a source of pleasure. Writing good prose does those things, and more. The ability to express your thoughts exactly distinguishes you as an educated person. Handling the assignment of the 500-word essay systematically and with growing competence and confidence is an important step toward acquiring that distinction.

Glossary

abstract language   language that expresses general qualities, characteristics, or ideas. *Honor, love,* and *strength* are examples. See **concrete language.**

allusion   an incidental or indirect reference to a subject. When we say, "A mother with an active teenager needs the patience of Job," we are referring to a famous biblical story, but only to highlight the mother's situation.

analogy   a specialized form of comparison in which the writer explains one thing by showing its similarity to a different class of things. See the Introduction to Chapter 5.

analysis   discovering the divisions or parts of an entity, their relationship to each other and to the whole. See **process analysis.**

argument   in the narrow sense, a statement for or against an intellectual position. For example, we may argue for or against capital punishment. An argument may be *logical,* that is, appealing to reason ("Society has the right and the duty to defend itself against those who wantonly kill its members") or *emotional* ("How would you like your mother to be murdered by some bum who got out on parole after serving only six years on a murder rap?") See **persuasion.**

audience   the person or persons whom one is addressing or for whom one is writing.

autobiography   an account of a person's life written by himself.

biography   an account of one person's life written by another.

causal analysis   a study of the relationships between cause and effect. See the Introduction to Chapter 6.

cause   that which produces an effect. See the Introduction to Chapter 6.

chronological order   an arrangement of events beginning with the earliest and ending with the latest in time.

classification   imposing a logical order on a group of facts, ideas, events, or people. See the Introduction to Chapter 4.

472

comparison   discovering the similarities between things. See the Introduction to Chapter 3.

concrete language   language that names or describes things that we can perceive through our senses. *Chair, red,* and *oak leaf* are examples. See **abstract language.**

connotation   the implied, underlying, emotional meaning of a word, as opposed to its literal meaning. For instance, *flame* and *conflagration* bear very different connotations although both can be defined literally as *fire.* See **denotation.**

contrast   discovering the differences between two things. See the Introduction to Chapter 3.

deduction   a form of argument in which we move from an undeniable generalization through an intermediate premise to a logical conclusion. See the Introduction to Chapter 14.

definition   an explanation of the essential meaning or nature of a word, an idea, or a thing. See the Introduction to Chapter 2.

denotation   the exact, literal meaning of a word or phrase; sometimes (but mistakenly) called the "dictionary meaning." See **connotation.**

description   a word-picture of an object, event, person, or place. See the Introduction to Part II.

diary   a daily, often intimate, record of personal thoughts, observations, and experiences, intended usually for the writer's eyes only.

distinguishing   discovering the individual differences or characteristics among a group of persons, ideas, or objects. See the Introduction to Chapter 4.

effect   the result of a cause. See the Introduction to Chapter 6.

essay   a non-fiction prose composition, usually short, in which the writer expresses thoughts or feelings on a single subject. See the Appendix, "Writing the 500-Word Essay."

example   an instance or specific illustration given to show or to make clearer the nature of something more general. See the Introduction to Chapter 1.

exposition   a form of writing that explains or sets forth. See the Introduction to Part I.

generalization   inferring a principle or forming a conclusion from a few specifics. Of course, the more specifics one takes into consideration, the sounder the generalization is likely to be, but generalizations are frequently based upon insufficient evidence and ought not to be accepted lightly.

illustration   an example or instance meant to help the reader visualize a concept, sensation, or idea.

imagery   the use of words, phrases, and figures of speech that help a reader picture or imagine sensations and ideas.

induction   a form of argument in which we move from specific facts and instances to a generalized conclusion. See the Introduction to Chapter 14.

interpretation   an explanation or explication meant to help another grasp the meaning of something—a work of art, for instance, a poem, or a play.

journal   a daily written record of one's experiences and observations, usually less confidential in nature than a diary.

metaphor   a figure of speech indirectly comparing unlike things, without using such words as *like* or *as*. When we say, "The Amazon leader was a lion in the fight," we are employing metaphor. See **simile.**

narrative   in its simplest sense, story-telling—relating a series of events in a coherent way. See the Introduction to Part III.

obscurity   verbal unclearness, one of the cardinal sins writers try to avoid.

paradox   a statement that seems to contradict itself but, on closer examination, proves to be true or to contain an element of truth. "Enough is too much!" is a paradox used by Benjamin Franklin as a caution against overeating or overindulgence of any sort.

persuasion   attempting to bring another to the writer's way of thinking, or to prevail upon another to act. See the Introduction to Part IV.

premise   a proposition supporting or leading to a conclusion. See the Introduction to Chapter 14.

process analysis   discovering the logical or physical steps by which a result has been achieved or a complex process has taken place. See the Introduction to Chapter 7.

short story   a brief work of prose fiction, generally centering upon a small number of characters and developing a single line of plot. See the Introduction to Chapter 13 and the short stories presented there.

simile   a figure of speech directly comparing dissimilar things through the use of words like *like* or *as*. "My luv is like a red, red rose" is a simile Robert Burns made famous.

style   in composition, the expression of the writer's personality and individuality through the choice of words, sentence structure, idea arrangement, tone, attitude, and so forth. The pattern of these choices often becomes so distinctive that the experienced reader can recognize certain writers by even brief excerpts from their work. The beginning writer should not strain after a style, but should try to write clearly, concisely, and exactly. Style, after all, is—like happiness—a by-product, not an end in itself.

syllogism a formal argument consisting of a major premise, a minor premise, and a conclusion. See **premise** and the Introduction to Chapter 14.

symbol an image or object that represents something other, often broader and more important, than itself. A dove, for example, can symbolize peace; the ring, marriage or unity; a cross, Christianity.

synthesis combining separate, constituent parts into a coherent whole. See Chapter 7.

thesis a proposition, usually stated early in an essay, that the writer intends to develop and to prove. See the Appendix, "Writing the 500-Word Essay".

transition the means by which a writer guides the reader smoothly from one idea to the next, showing the relationship of the ideas to each other and linking the parts of a composition to form a coherent whole. See the Appendix, "Writing the 500-Word Essay".

1 2 3 4 5 6 7 8 9 0